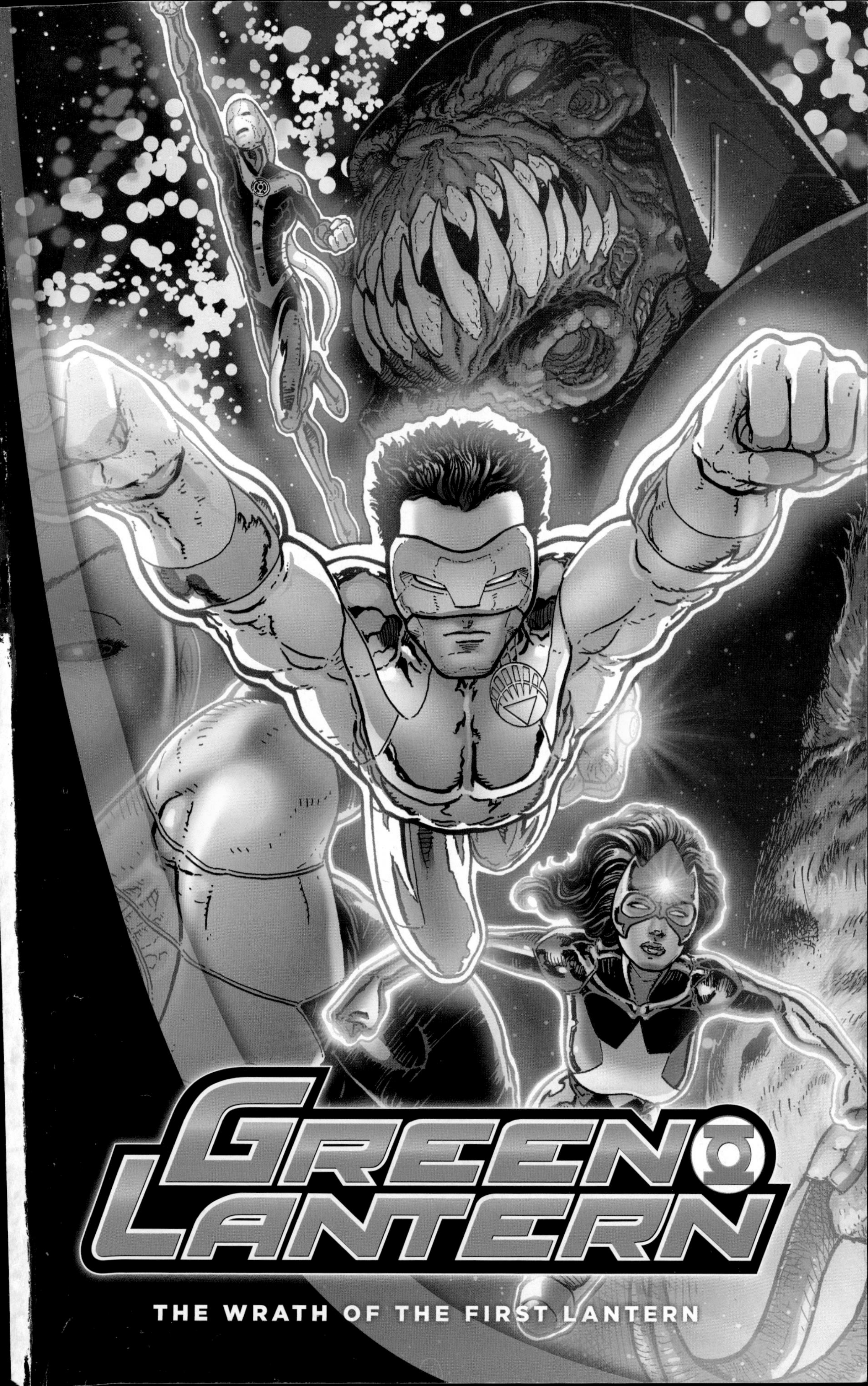
GREEN LANTERN
THE WRATH OF THE FIRST LANTERN

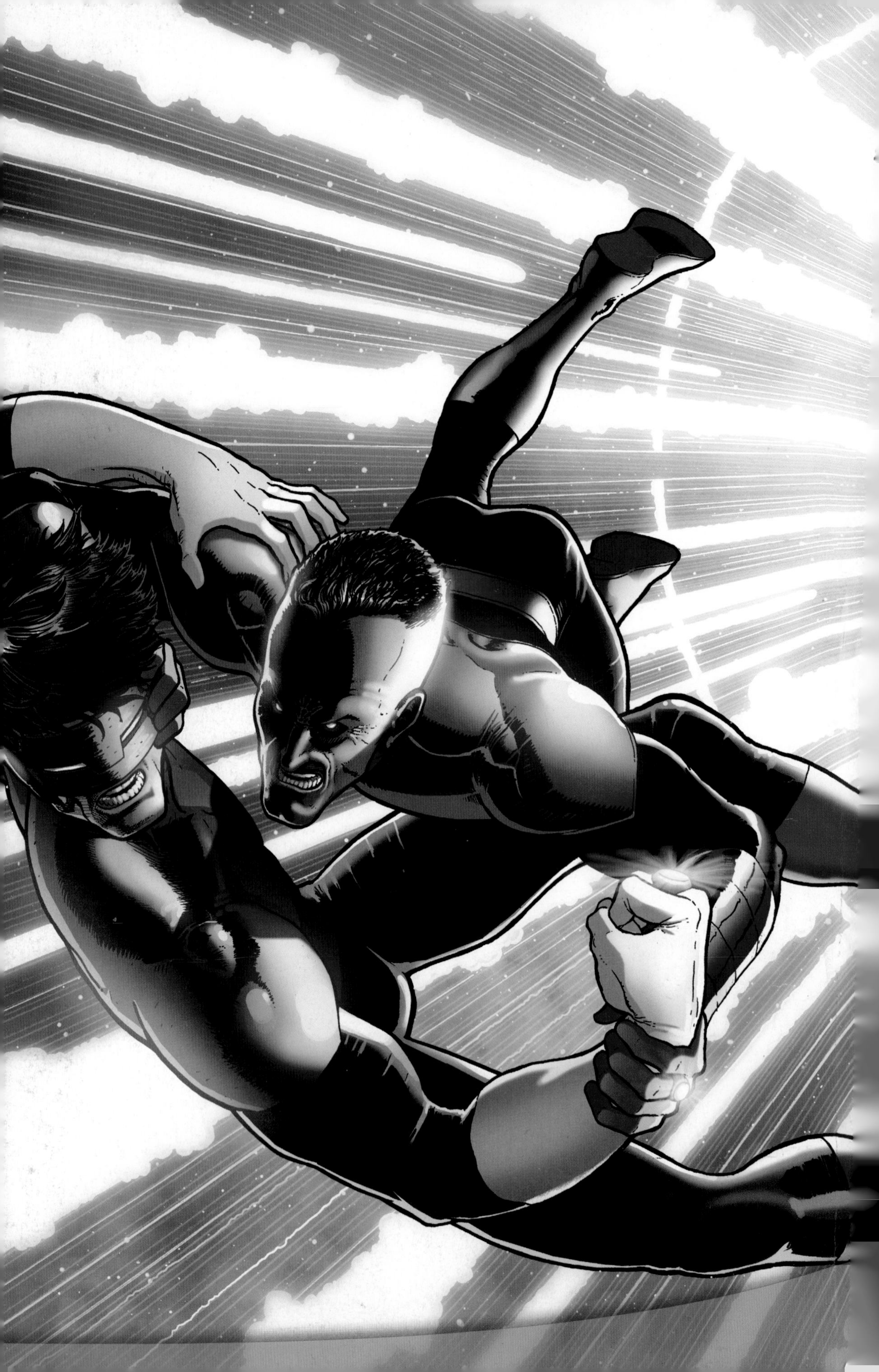

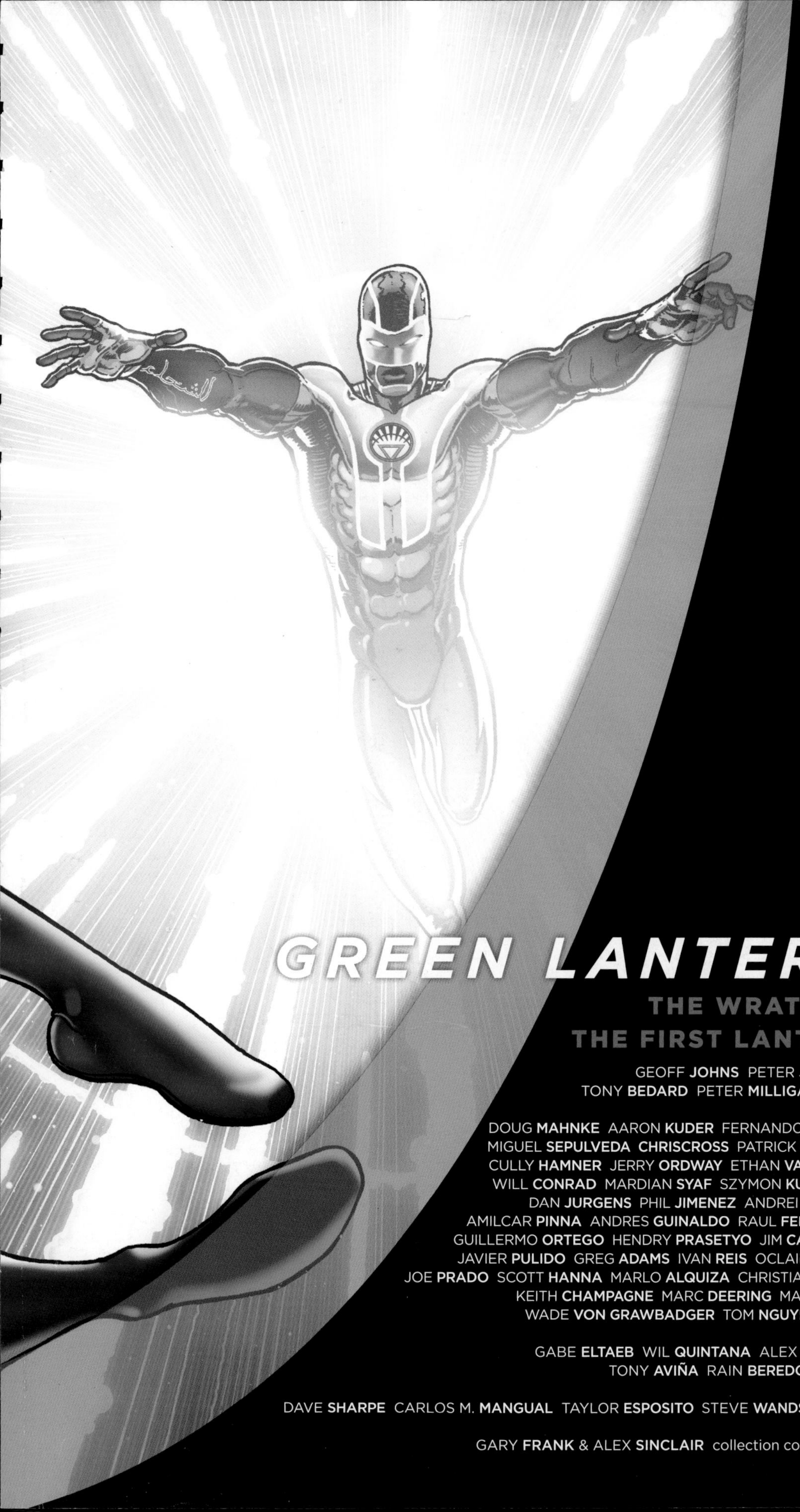

GREEN LANTERN

THE WRATH OF THE FIRST LANTERN

GEOFF **JOHNS** PETER J. **TOMASI**
TONY **BEDARD** PETER **MILLIGAN** writers

DOUG **MAHNKE** AARON **KUDER** FERNANDO **PASARIN**
MIGUEL **SEPULVEDA** **CHRISCROSS** PATRICK **GLEASON**
CULLY **HAMNER** JERRY **ORDWAY** ETHAN **VAN SCIVER**
WILL **CONRAD** MARDIAN **SYAF** SZYMON **KUDRANSKI**
DAN **JURGENS** PHIL **JIMENEZ** ANDREI **BRESSAN**
AMILCAR **PINNA** ANDRES **GUINALDO** RAUL **FERNANDEZ**
GUILLERMO **ORTEGO** HENDRY **PRASETYO** JIM **CALAFIORE**
JAVIER **PULIDO** GREG **ADAMS** IVAN **REIS** OCLAIR **ALBERT**
JOE **PRADO** SCOTT **HANNA** MARLO **ALQUIZA** CHRISTIAN **ALAMY**
KEITH **CHAMPAGNE** MARC **DEERING** MARK **IRWIN**
WADE **VON GRAWBADGER** TOM **NGUYEN** artists

GABE **ELTAEB** WIL **QUINTANA** ALEX **SINCLAIR**
TONY **AVIÑA** RAIN **BEREDO** colorists

DAVE **SHARPE** CARLOS M. **MANGUAL** TAYLOR **ESPOSITO** STEVE **WANDS** letterers

GARY **FRANK** & ALEX **SINCLAIR** collection cover artists

WIL MOSS CHRIS CONROY MATT IDELSON Editors – Original Series
KATE STEWART KYLE ANDRUKIEWICZ Assistant Editors – Original Series RACHEL PINNELAS Editor
ROBBIN BROSTERMAN Design Director – Books ROBBIE BIEDERMAN Publication Design

BOB HARRAS Senior VP – Editor-in-Chief, DC Comics

DIANE NELSON President DAN DIDIO and JIM LEE Co-Publishers
GEOFF JOHNS Chief Creative Officer
JOHN ROOD Executive VP – Sales, Marketing and Business Development
AMY GENKINS Senior VP – Business and Legal Affairs NAIRI GARDINER Senior VP – Finance
JEFF BOISON VP – Publishing Planning MARK CHIARELLO VP – Art Direction and Design
JOHN CUNNINGHAM VP – Marketing TERRI CUNNINGHAM VP – Editorial Administration
ALISON GILL Senior VP – Manufacturing and Operations HANK KANALZ Senior VP – Vertigo and Integrated Publishing
JAY KOGAN VP – Business and Legal Affairs, Publishing JACK MAHAN VP – Business Affairs, Talent
NICK NAPOLITANO VP – Manufacturing Administration SUE POHJA VP – Book Sales
COURTNEY SIMMONS Senior VP – Publicity BOB WAYNE Senior VP – Sales

DC Comics, 1700 Broadway, New York, NY 10019
A Warner Bros. Entertainment Company.
Printed by RR Donnelley, Salem, VA, USA. 1/17/14. First Printing.
HC ISBN: 978-1-4012-4409-5
SC ISBN: 978-1-4012-4693-8

SUSTAINABLE
FORESTRY
INITIATIVE

Certified Chain of Custody
At Least 20% Certified Forest Content
www.sfiprogram.org
SFI-01042
APPLIES TO TEXT STOCK ONLY

Library of Congress Cataloging-in-Publication Data

Green Lantern : Wrath of the First Lantern.
pages cm
"Originally published in single magazine form as GREEN LANTERN 17-20, GREEN LANTERN CORPS 17-20,
RED LANTERNS 17-20, GREEN LANTERN: NEW GUARDIANS 17-20."
ISBN 978-1-4012-4409-5
1. Graphic novels.
PN6728.G74G86 2014
741.5'973-dc23
                   2013039606

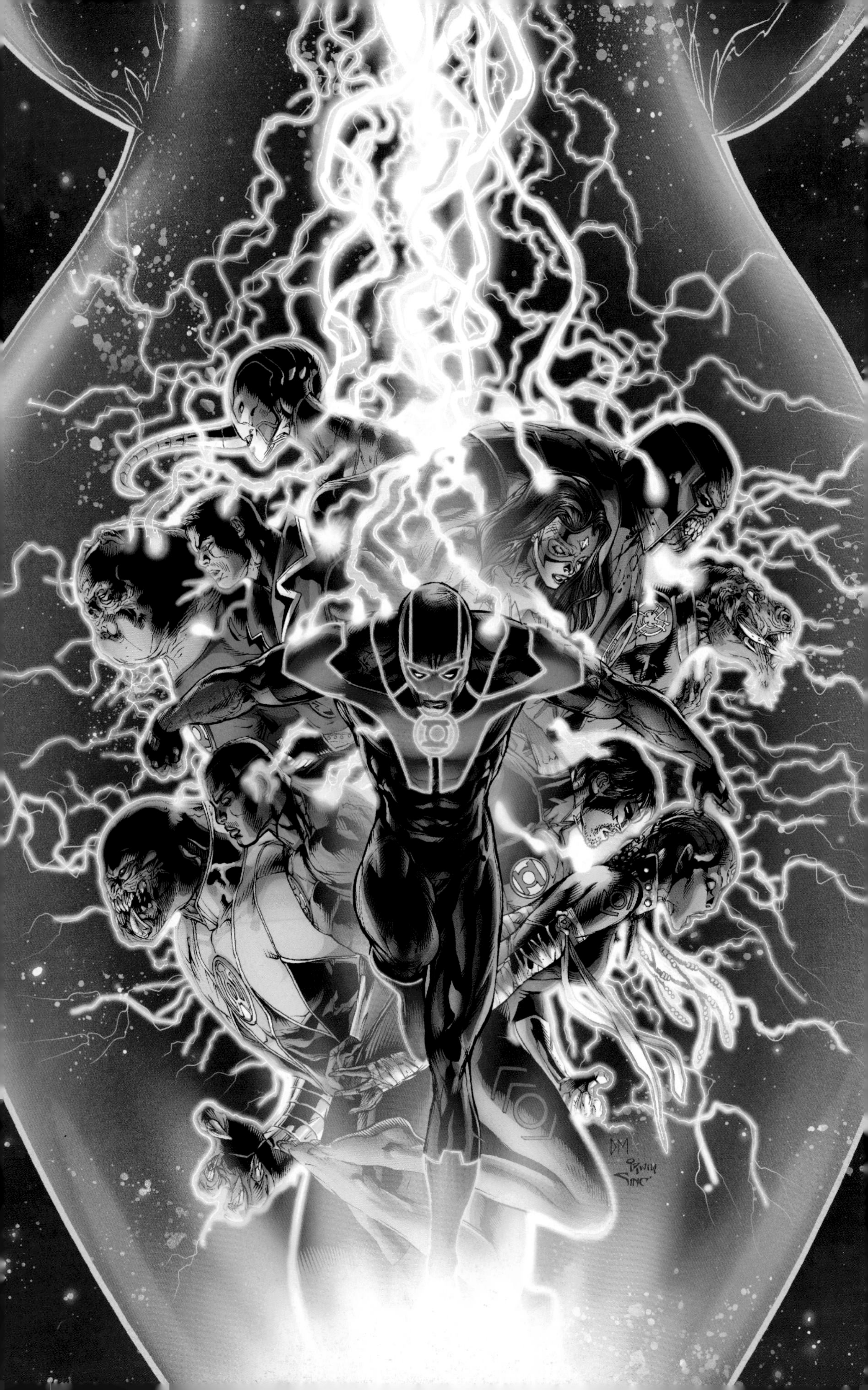

PART ONE: THE PUPPETEER

GEOFF JOHNS writer **DAN JURGENS** layouts – prolouge **PHIL JIMENEZ** finishes – prologue **DOUG MAHNKE** penciller
TOM NGUYEN, KEITH CHAMPAGNE, MARK IRWIN, CHRISTIAN ALAMY & DOUG MAHNKE inkers cover art by **DOUG MAHNKE, MARK IRWIN & ALEX SINCLAIR**

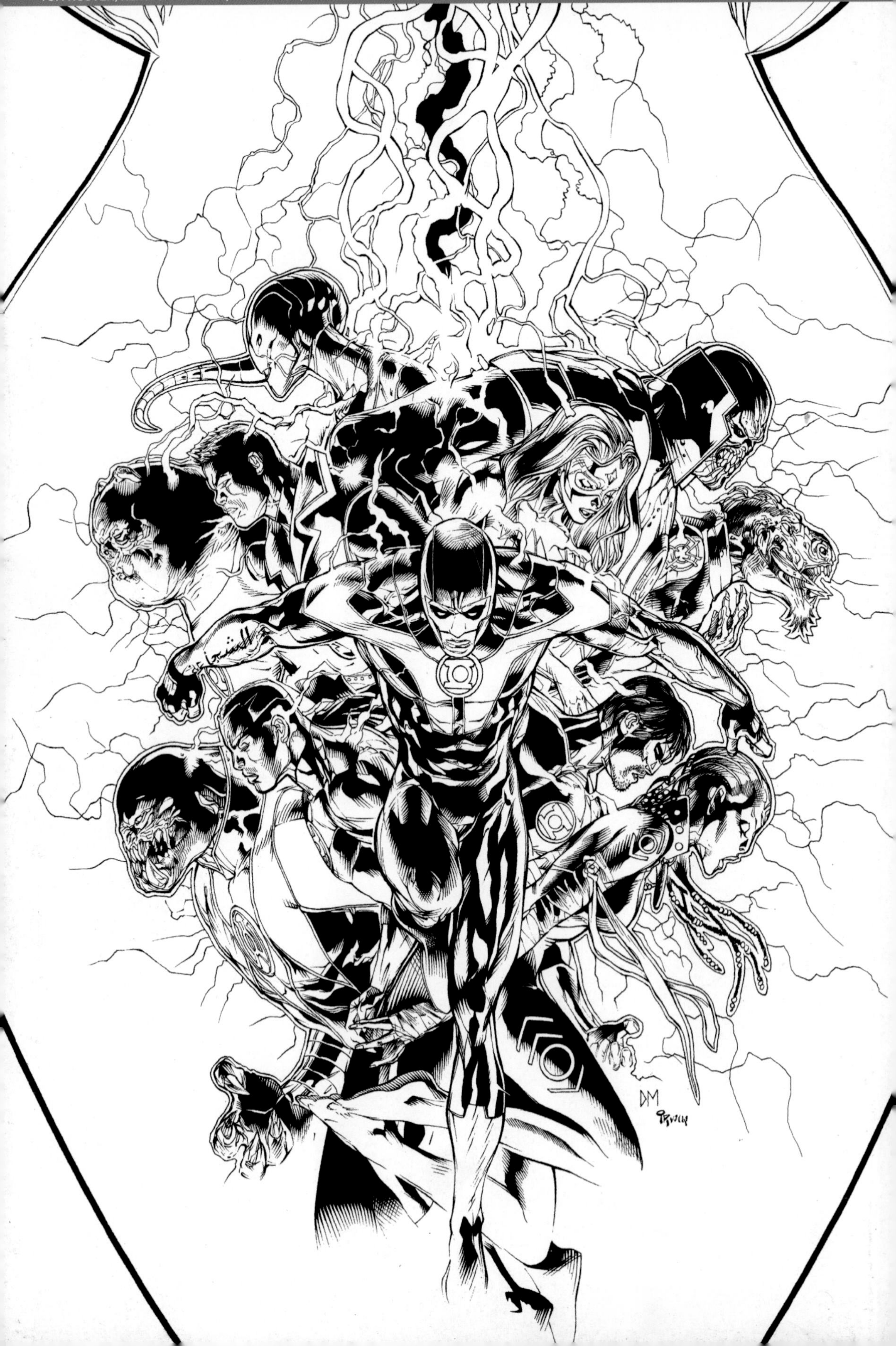

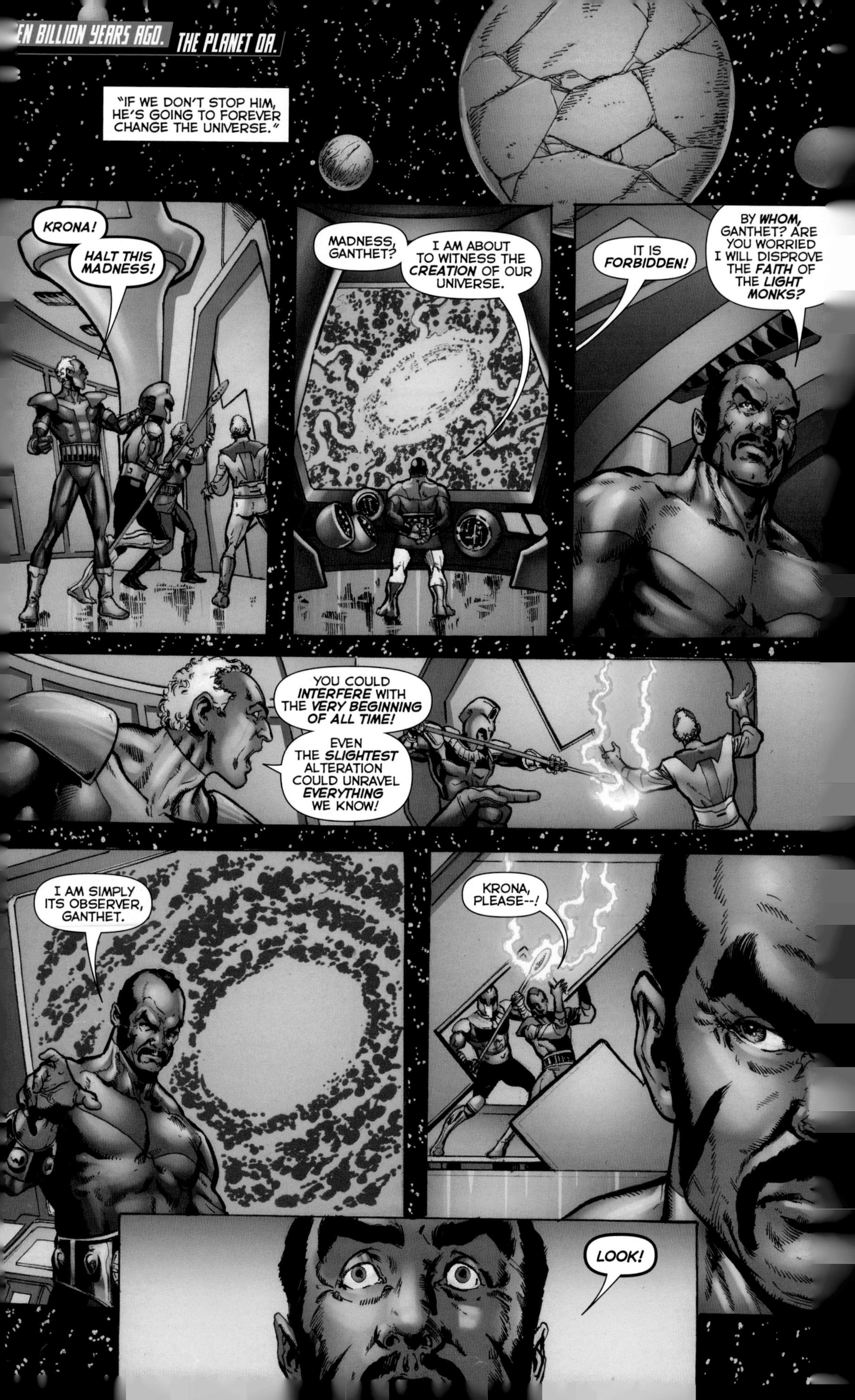
EN BILLION YEARS AGO.
THE PLANET OA.
"IF WE DON'T STOP HIM, HE'S GOING TO FOREVER CHANGE THE UNIVERSE."
KRONA!
HALT THIS MADNESS!
MADNESS, GANTHET?
I AM ABOUT TO WITNESS THE CREATION OF OUR UNIVERSE.
IT IS FORBIDDEN!
BY WHOM, GANTHET? ARE YOU WORRIED I WILL DISPROVE THE FAITH OF THE LIGHT MONKS?
YOU COULD INTERFERE WITH THE VERY BEGINNING OF ALL TIME!
EVEN THE SLIGHTEST ALTERATION COULD UNRAVEL EVERYTHING WE KNOW!
I AM SIMPLY ITS OBSERVER, GANTHET.
KRONA, PLEASE--!
LOOK!

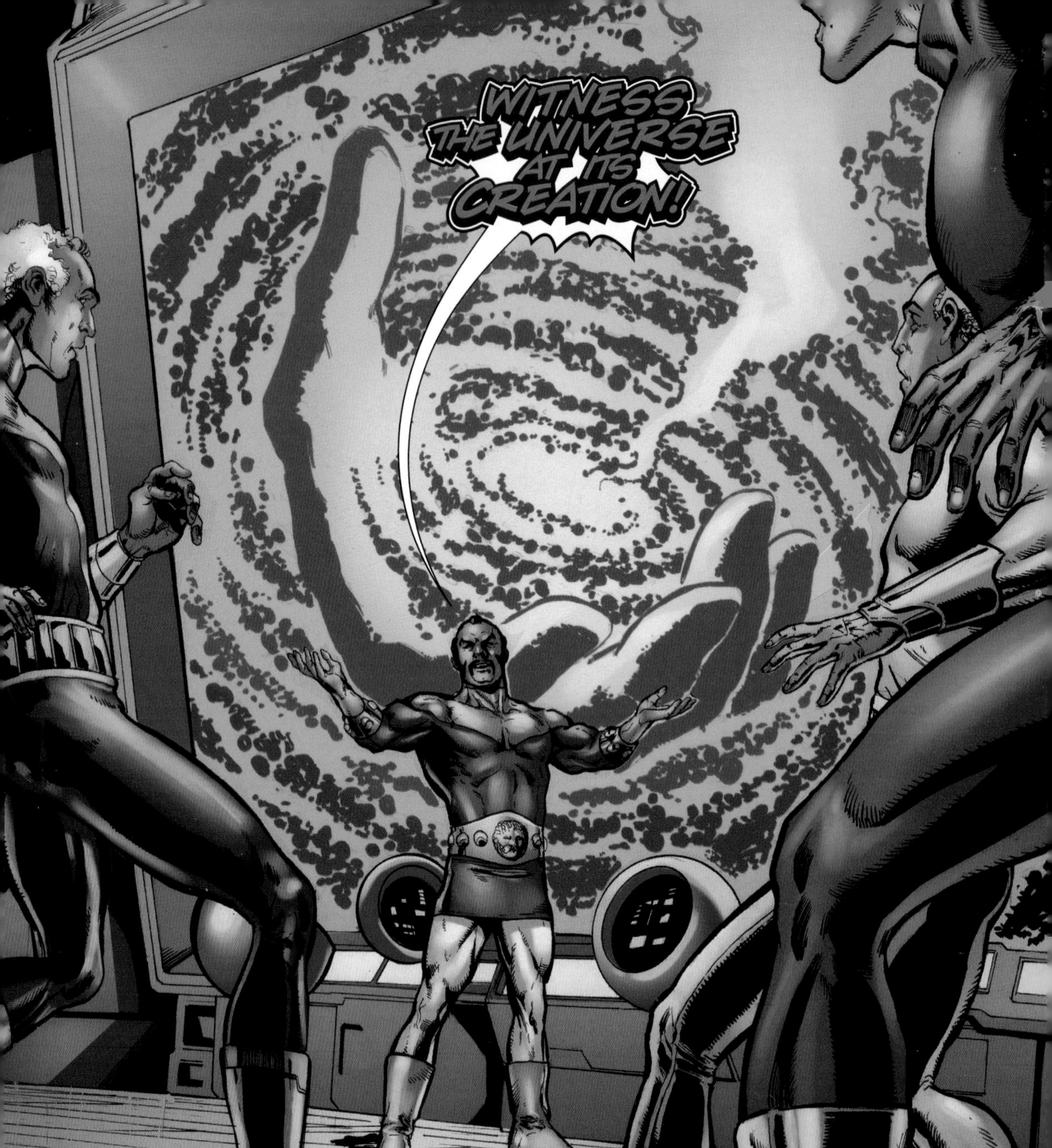
WITNESS THE UNIVERSE AT ITS CREATION!
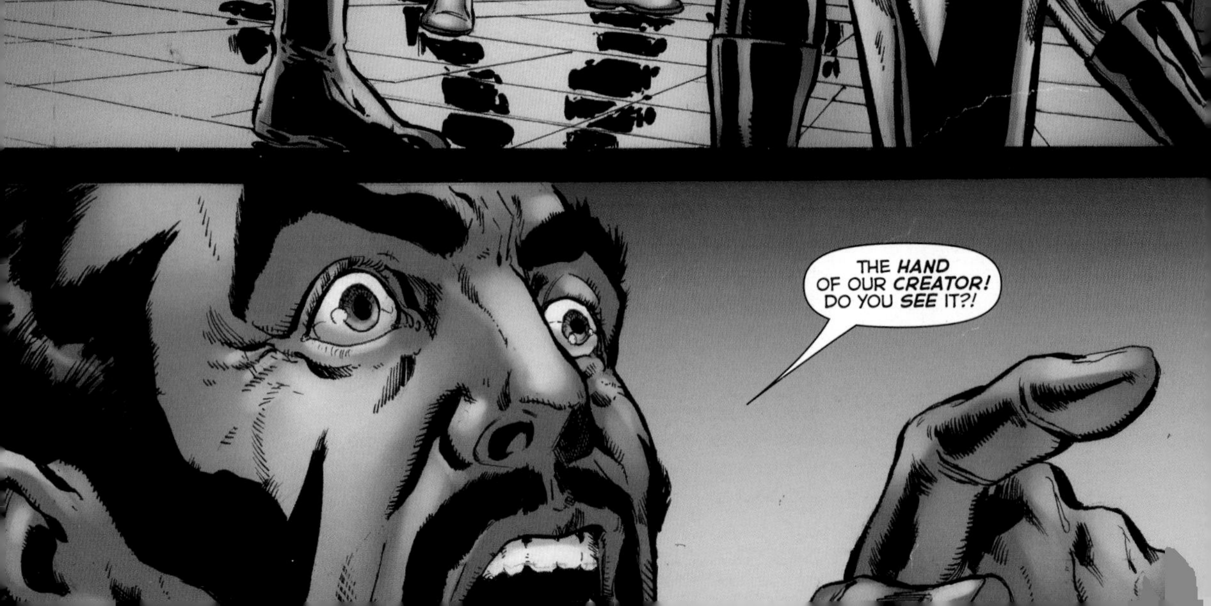
THE HAND OF OUR CREATOR! DO YOU SEE IT?!

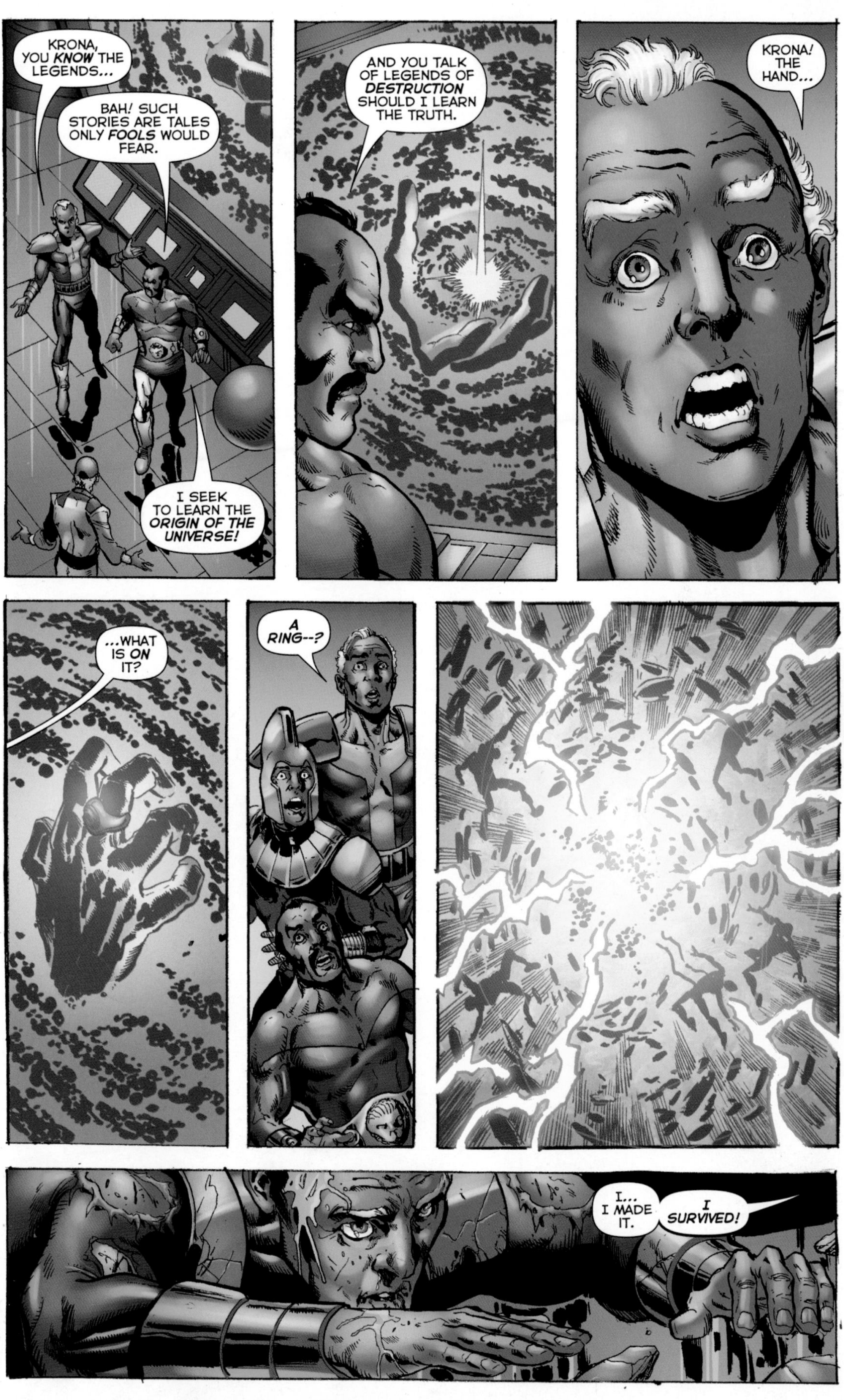
KRONA, YOU *KNOW* THE LEGENDS...
BAH! SUCH STORIES ARE TALES ONLY *FOOLS* WOULD FEAR.
I SEEK TO LEARN THE *ORIGIN OF THE UNIVERSE!*
AND YOU TALK OF LEGENDS OF *DESTRUCTION* SHOULD I LEARN THE TRUTH.
KRONA! THE HAND...
...WHAT IS *ON* IT?
A RING--?
I... I MADE IT.
I SURVIVED!

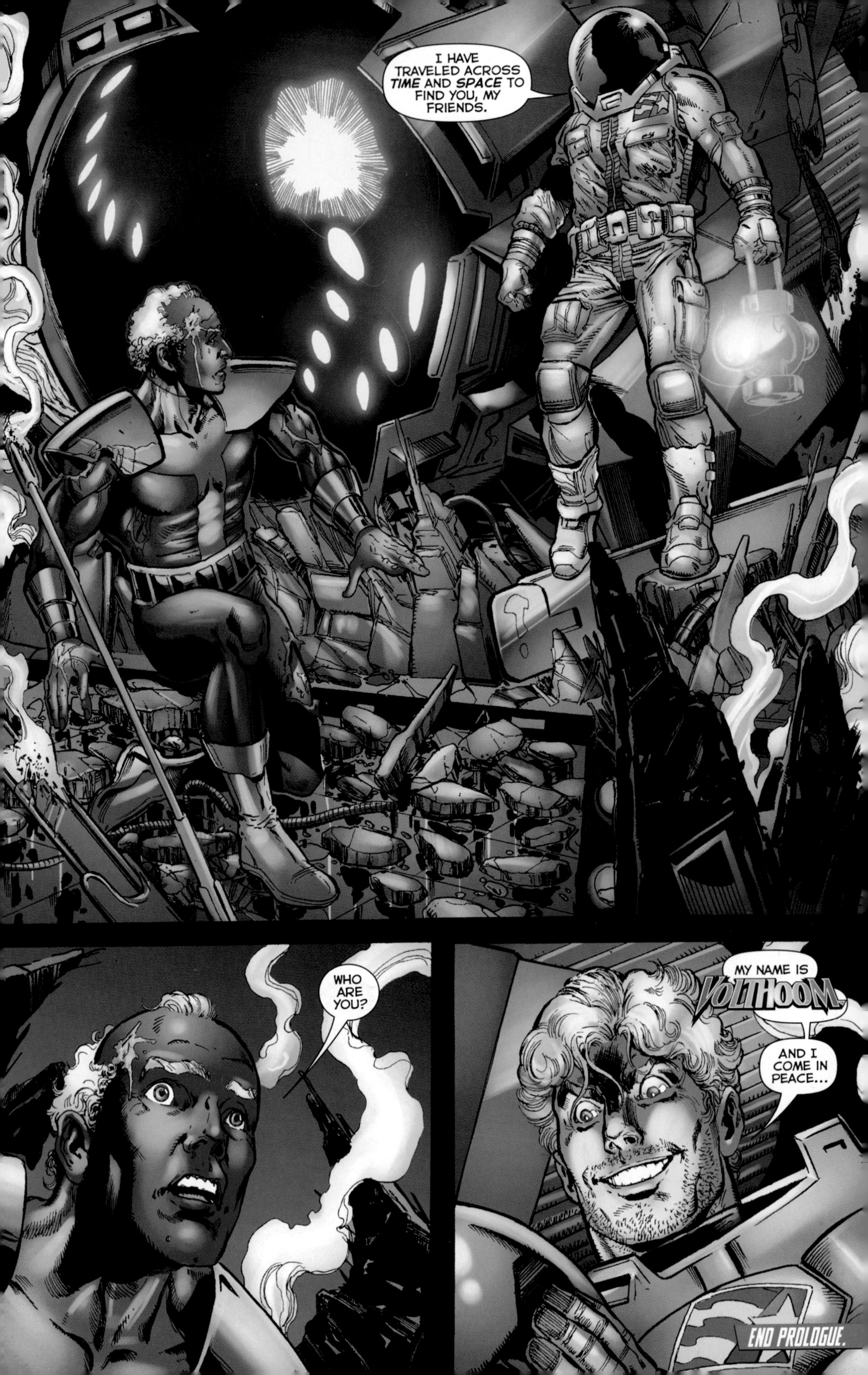
I HAVE TRAVELED ACROSS *TIME* AND *SPACE* TO FIND YOU, MY FRIENDS.
WHO ARE YOU?
MY NAME IS VOLTHOOM.
AND I COME IN PEACE...
END PROLOGUE.

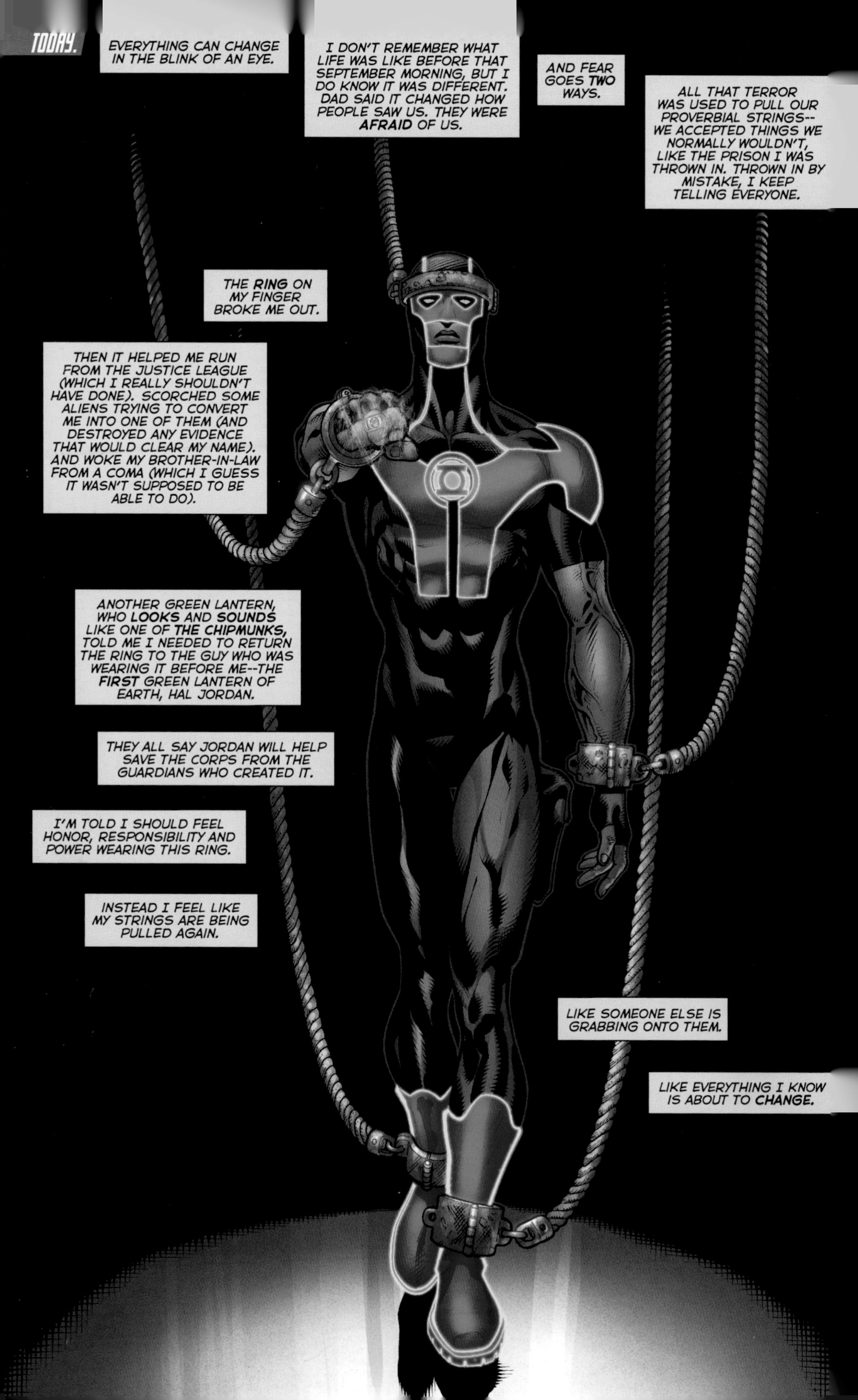
TODAY.
EVERYTHING CAN CHANGE IN THE BLINK OF AN EYE.
I DON'T REMEMBER WHAT LIFE WAS LIKE BEFORE THAT SEPTEMBER MORNING, BUT I DO KNOW IT WAS DIFFERENT. DAD SAID IT CHANGED HOW PEOPLE SAW US. THEY WERE AFRAID OF US.
AND FEAR GOES TWO WAYS.
ALL THAT TERROR WAS USED TO PULL OUR PROVERBIAL STRINGS-- WE ACCEPTED THINGS WE NORMALLY WOULDN'T, LIKE THE PRISON I WAS THROWN IN. THROWN IN BY MISTAKE, I KEEP TELLING EVERYONE.
THE RING ON MY FINGER BROKE ME OUT.
THEN IT HELPED ME RUN FROM THE JUSTICE LEAGUE (WHICH I REALLY SHOULDN'T HAVE DONE). SCORCHED SOME ALIENS TRYING TO CONVERT ME INTO ONE OF THEM (AND DESTROYED ANY EVIDENCE THAT WOULD CLEAR MY NAME). AND WOKE MY BROTHER-IN-LAW FROM A COMA (WHICH I GUESS IT WASN'T SUPPOSED TO BE ABLE TO DO).
ANOTHER GREEN LANTERN, WHO LOOKS AND SOUNDS LIKE ONE OF THE CHIPMUNKS, TOLD ME I NEEDED TO RETURN THE RING TO THE GUY WHO WAS WEARING IT BEFORE ME--THE FIRST GREEN LANTERN OF EARTH, HAL JORDAN.
THEY ALL SAY JORDAN WILL HELP SAVE THE CORPS FROM THE GUARDIANS WHO CREATED IT.
I'M TOLD I SHOULD FEEL HONOR, RESPONSIBILITY AND POWER WEARING THIS RING.
INSTEAD I FEEL LIKE MY STRINGS ARE BEING PULLED AGAIN.
LIKE SOMEONE ELSE IS GRABBING ONTO THEM.
LIKE EVERYTHING I KNOW IS ABOUT TO CHANGE.

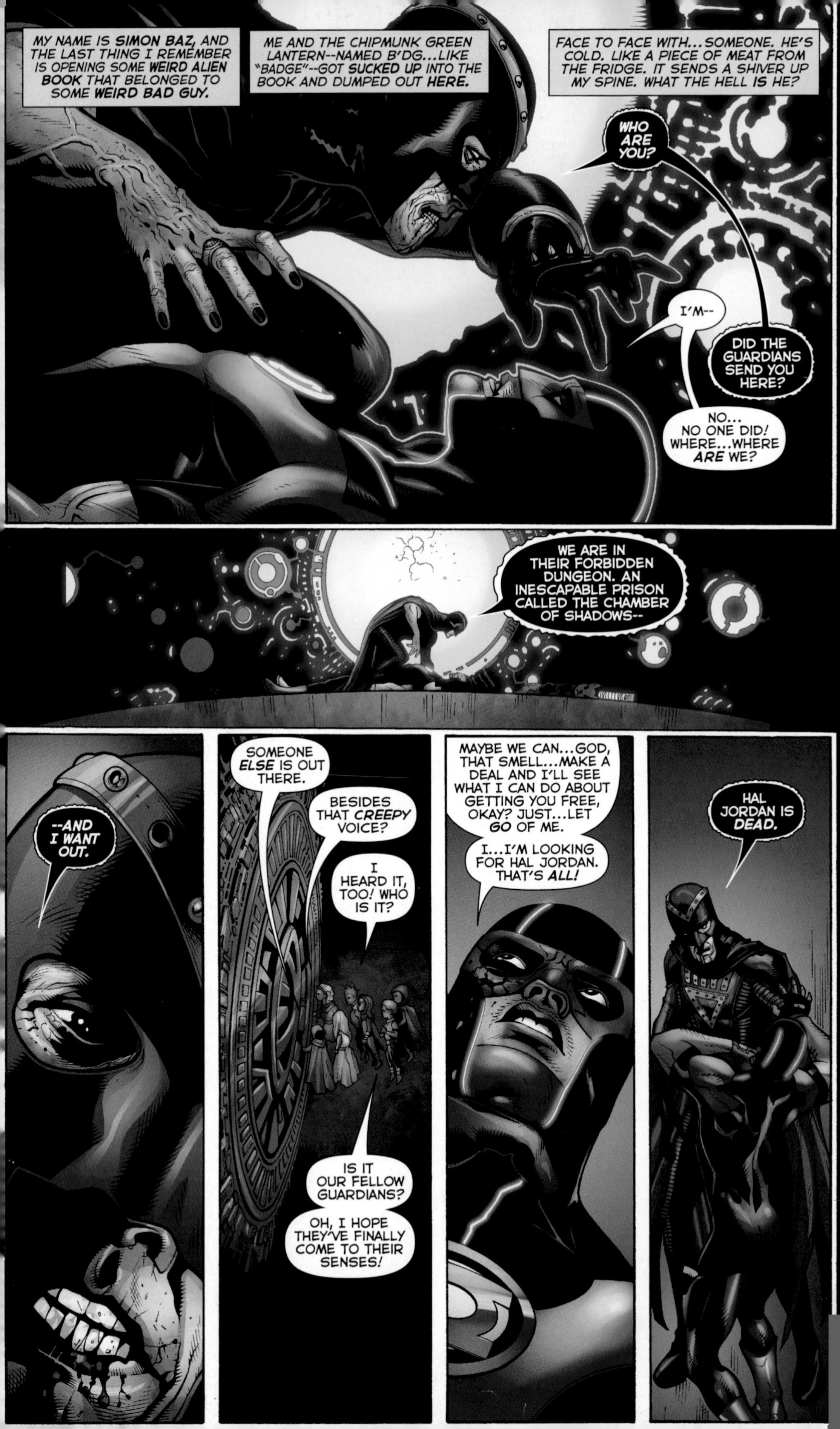
MY NAME IS SIMON BAZ, AND THE LAST THING I REMEMBER IS OPENING SOME WEIRD ALIEN BOOK THAT BELONGED TO SOME WEIRD BAD GUY.
ME AND THE CHIPMUNK GREEN LANTERN--NAMED B'DG...LIKE "BADGE"--GOT SUCKED UP INTO THE BOOK AND DUMPED OUT HERE.
FACE TO FACE WITH...SOMEONE. HE'S COLD. LIKE A PIECE OF MEAT FROM THE FRIDGE. IT SENDS A SHIVER UP MY SPINE. WHAT THE HELL IS HE?
WHO ARE YOU?
I'M--
DID THE GUARDIANS SEND YOU HERE?
NO... NO ONE DID! WHERE...WHERE ARE WE?
WE ARE IN THEIR FORBIDDEN DUNGEON. AN INESCAPABLE PRISON CALLED THE CHAMBER OF SHADOWS--
--AND I WANT OUT.
SOMEONE ELSE IS OUT THERE.
BESIDES THAT CREEPY VOICE?
I HEARD IT, TOO! WHO IS IT?
IS IT OUR FELLOW GUARDIANS?
OH, I HOPE THEY'VE FINALLY COME TO THEIR SENSES!
MAYBE WE CAN...GOD, THAT SMELL...MAKE A DEAL AND I'LL SEE WHAT I CAN DO ABOUT GETTING YOU FREE, OKAY? JUST...LET GO OF ME.
I...I'M LOOKING FOR HAL JORDAN. THAT'S ALL!
HAL JORDAN IS DEAD.

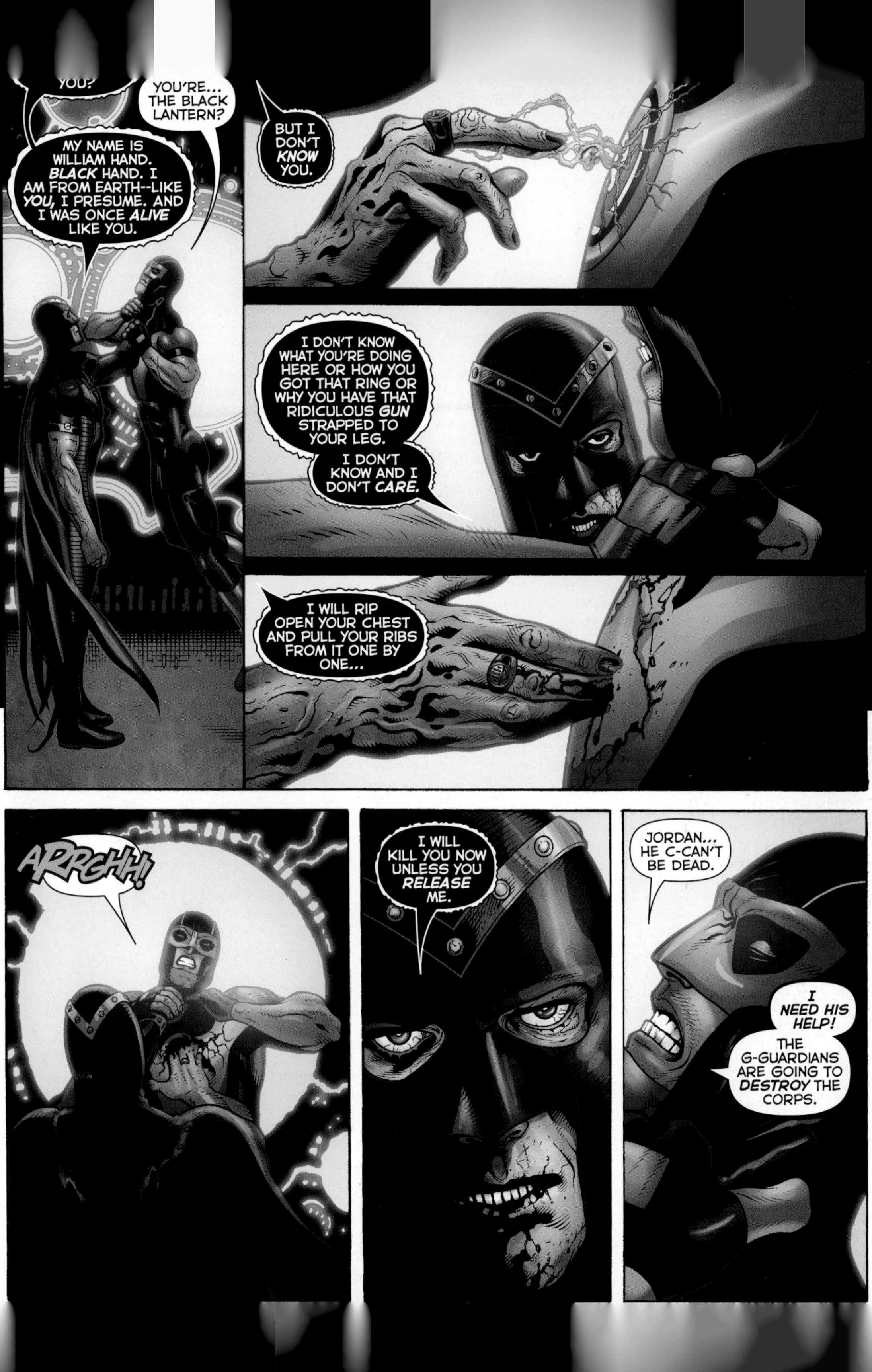
YOU?
YOU'RE... THE BLACK LANTERN?
MY NAME IS WILLIAM HAND. BLACK HAND. I AM FROM EARTH--LIKE YOU, I PRESUME. AND I WAS ONCE ALIVE LIKE YOU.
BUT I DON'T KNOW YOU.
I DON'T KNOW WHAT YOU'RE DOING HERE OR HOW YOU GOT THAT RING OR WHY YOU HAVE THAT RIDICULOUS GUN STRAPPED TO YOUR LEG.
I DON'T KNOW AND I DON'T CARE.
I WILL RIP OPEN YOUR CHEST AND PULL YOUR RIBS FROM IT ONE BY ONE...
ARRRGHH!
I WILL KILL YOU NOW UNLESS YOU RELEASE ME.
JORDAN... HE C-CAN'T BE DEAD.
I NEED HIS HELP!
THE G-GUARDIANS ARE GOING TO DESTROY THE CORPS.

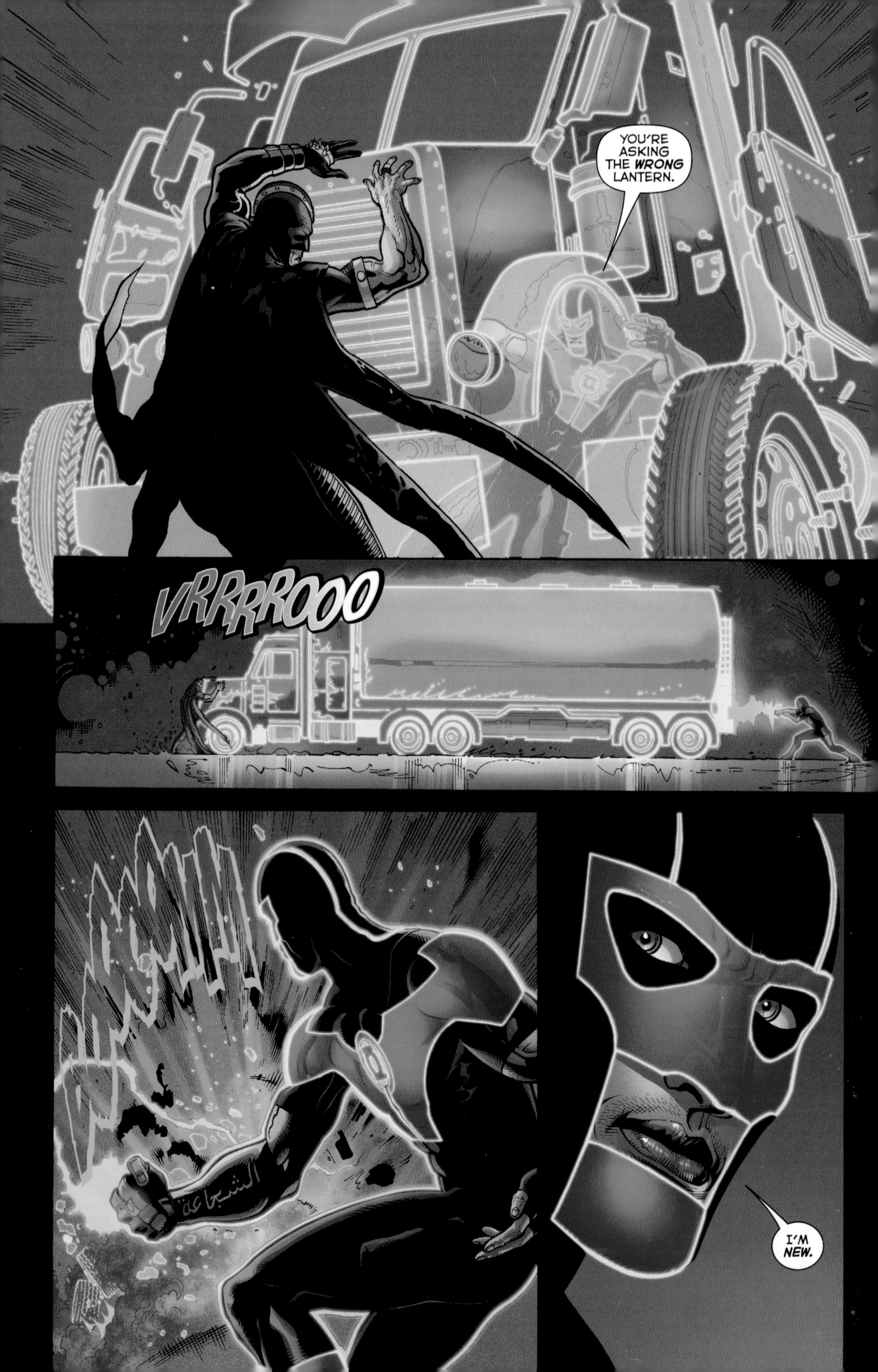

YOU'RE ASKING THE WRONG LANTERN.
VRRRROOO
الشجاعة
I'M NEW.

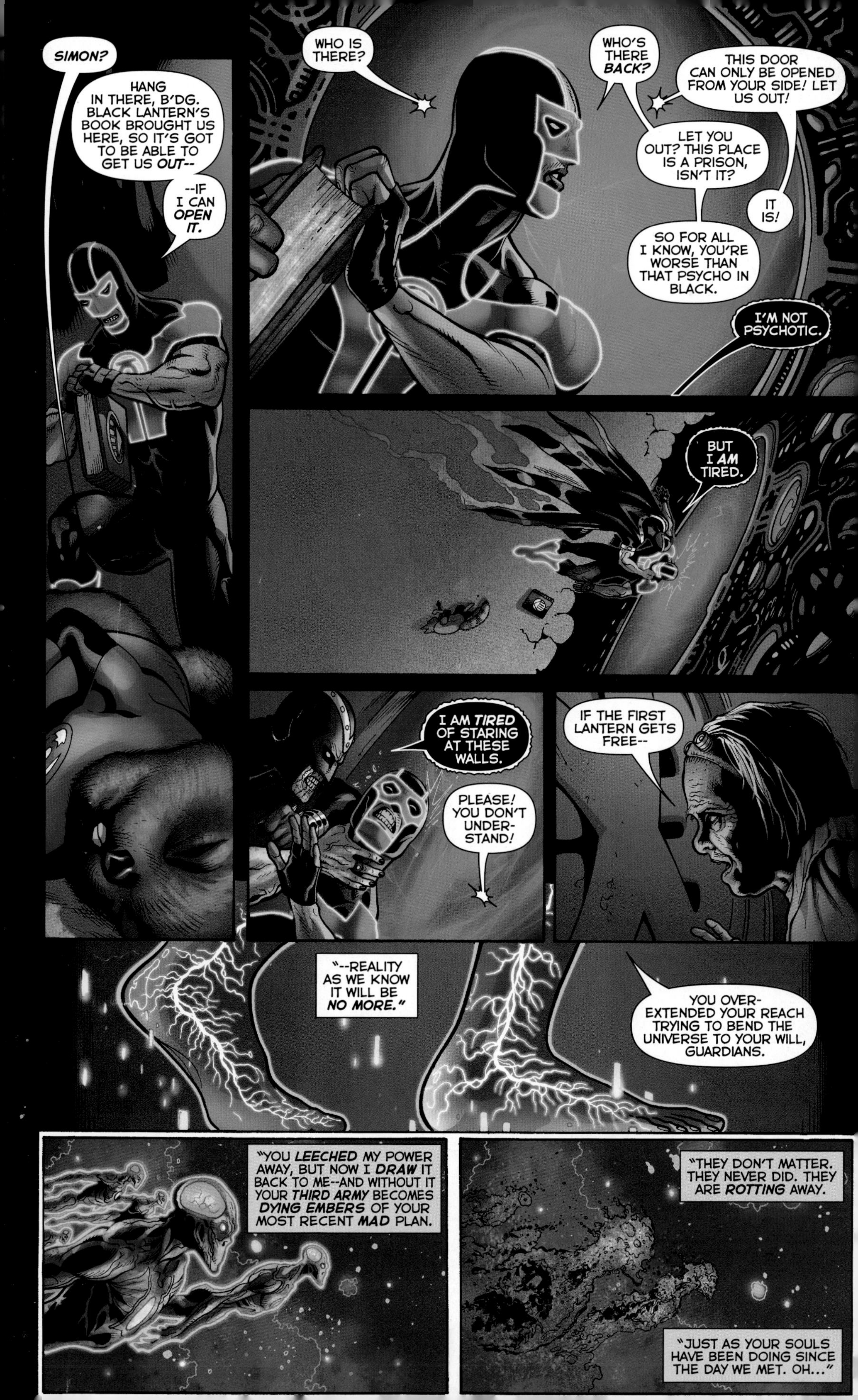
SIMON?
HANG IN THERE, B'DG. BLACK LANTERN'S BOOK BROUGHT US HERE, SO IT'S GOT TO BE ABLE TO GET US OUT--
--IF I CAN OPEN IT.
WHO IS THERE?
WHO'S THERE BACK?
THIS DOOR CAN ONLY BE OPENED FROM YOUR SIDE! LET US OUT!
LET YOU OUT? THIS PLACE IS A PRISON, ISN'T IT?
IT IS!
SO FOR ALL I KNOW, YOU'RE WORSE THAN THAT PSYCHO IN BLACK.
I'M NOT PSYCHOTIC.
BUT I AM TIRED.
I AM TIRED OF STARING AT THESE WALLS.
PLEASE! YOU DON'T UNDER-STAND!
IF THE FIRST LANTERN GETS FREE--
"--REALITY AS WE KNOW IT WILL BE NO MORE."
YOU OVER-EXTENDED YOUR REACH TRYING TO BEND THE UNIVERSE TO YOUR WILL, GUARDIANS.
"YOU LEECHED MY POWER AWAY, BUT NOW I DRAW IT BACK TO ME--AND WITHOUT IT YOUR THIRD ARMY BECOMES DYING EMBERS OF YOUR MOST RECENT MAD PLAN.
"THEY DON'T MATTER. THEY NEVER DID. THEY ARE ROTTING AWAY.
"JUST AS YOUR SOULS HAVE BEEN DOING SINCE THE DAY WE MET. OH..."

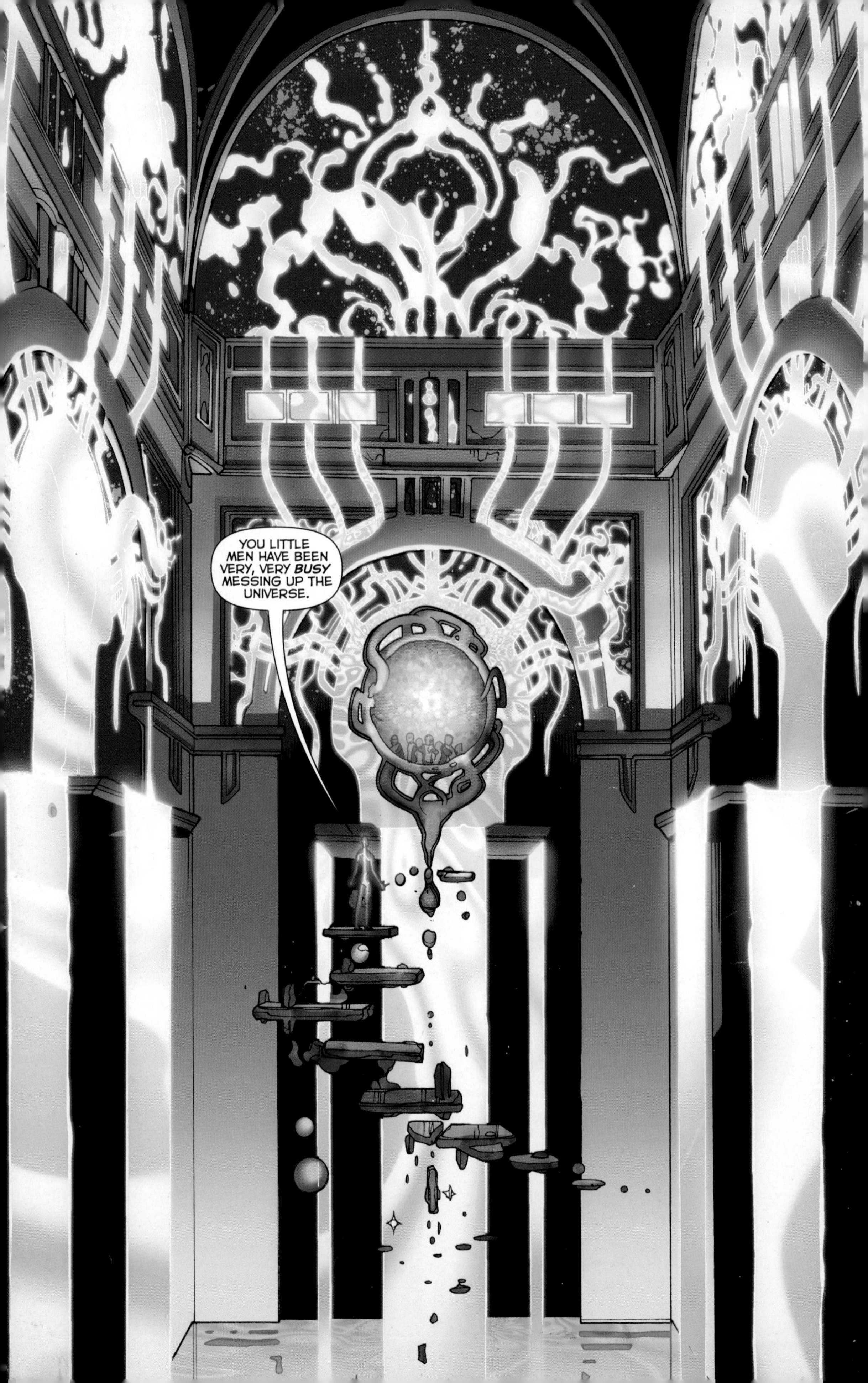
YOU LITTLE MEN HAVE BEEN VERY, VERY BUSY MESSING UP THE UNIVERSE.

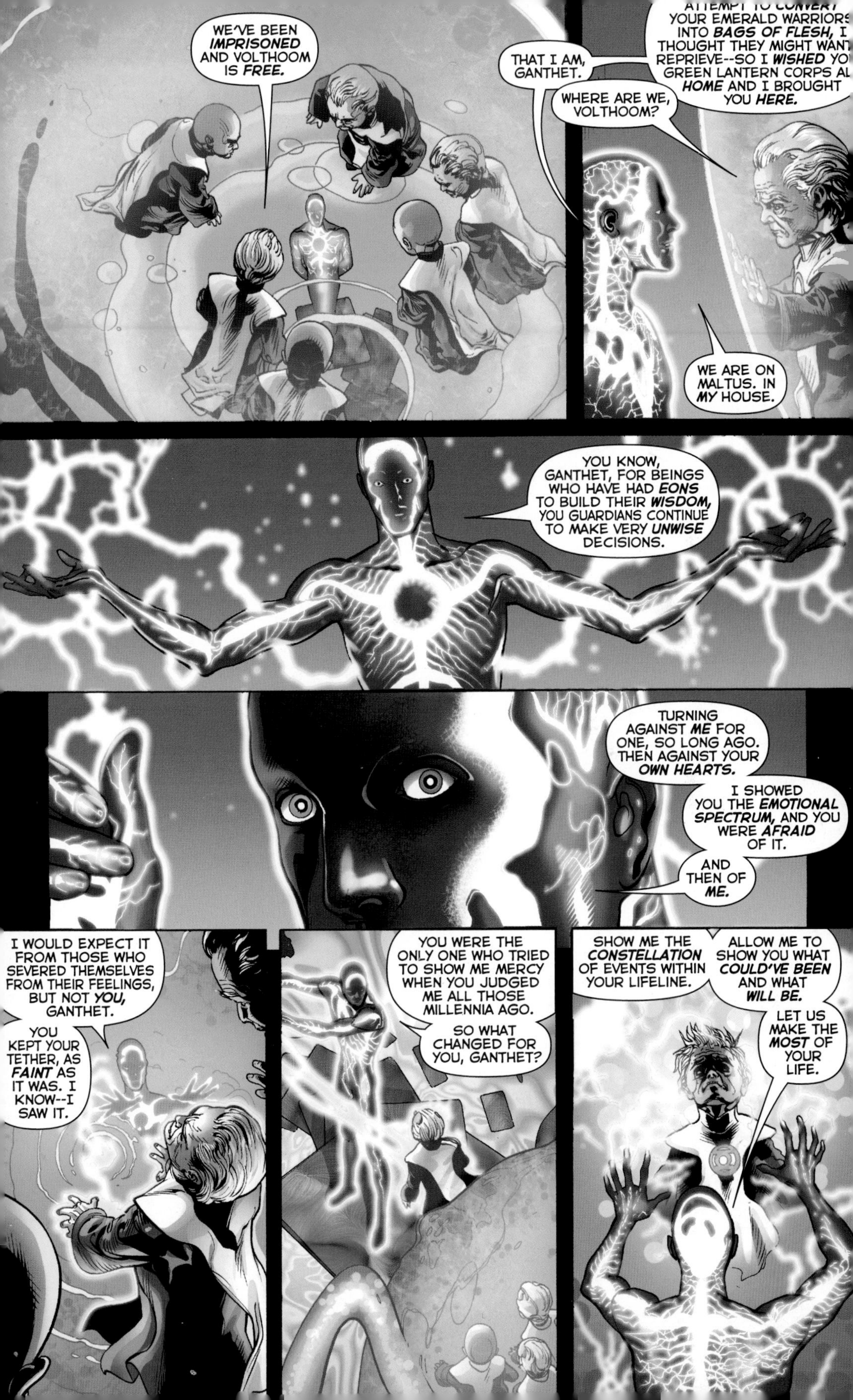
WE'VE BEEN IMPRISONED AND VOLTHOOM IS FREE.
THAT I AM, GANTHET.
WHERE ARE WE, VOLTHOOM?
ATTEMPT TO CONVERT YOUR EMERALD WARRIORS INTO BAGS OF FLESH, I THOUGHT THEY MIGHT WANT REPRIEVE--SO I WISHED YO GREEN LANTERN CORPS AL HOME AND I BROUGHT YOU HERE.
WE ARE ON MALTUS. IN MY HOUSE.
YOU KNOW, GANTHET, FOR BEINGS WHO HAVE HAD EONS TO BUILD THEIR WISDOM, YOU GUARDIANS CONTINUE TO MAKE VERY UNWISE DECISIONS.
TURNING AGAINST ME FOR ONE, SO LONG AGO. THEN AGAINST YOUR OWN HEARTS.
I SHOWED YOU THE EMOTIONAL SPECTRUM, AND YOU WERE AFRAID OF IT.
AND THEN OF ME.
I WOULD EXPECT IT FROM THOSE WHO SEVERED THEMSELVES FROM THEIR FEELINGS, BUT NOT YOU, GANTHET.
YOU KEPT YOUR TETHER, AS FAINT AS IT WAS. I KNOW--I SAW IT.
YOU WERE THE ONLY ONE WHO TRIED TO SHOW ME MERCY WHEN YOU JUDGED ME ALL THOSE MILLENNIA AGO.
SO WHAT CHANGED FOR YOU, GANTHET?
SHOW ME THE CONSTELLATION OF EVENTS WITHIN YOUR LIFELINE.
ALLOW ME TO SHOW YOU WHAT COULD'VE BEEN AND WHAT WILL BE.
LET US MAKE THE MOST OF YOUR LIFE.

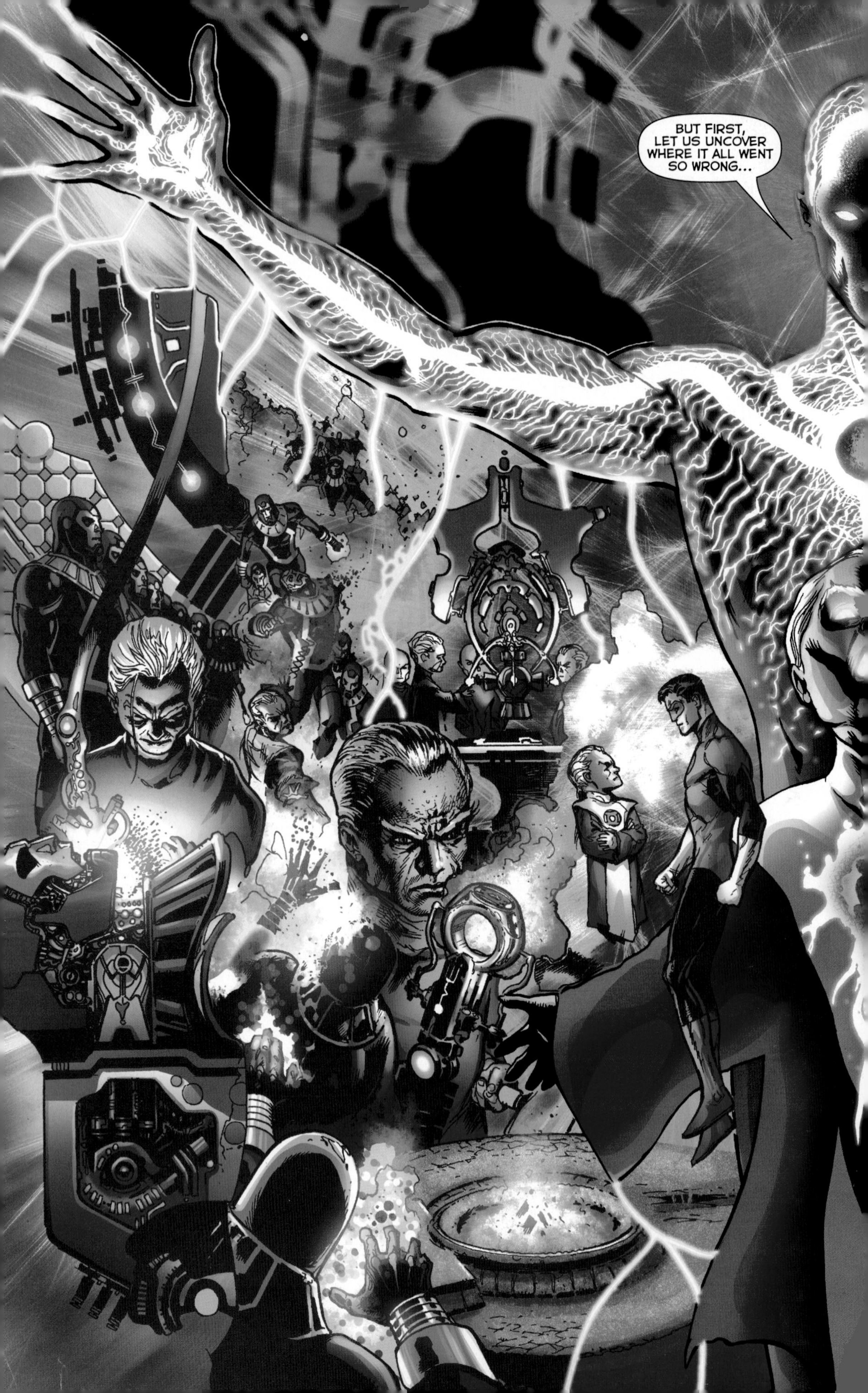
BUT FIRST, LET US UNCOVER WHERE IT ALL WENT SO WRONG...

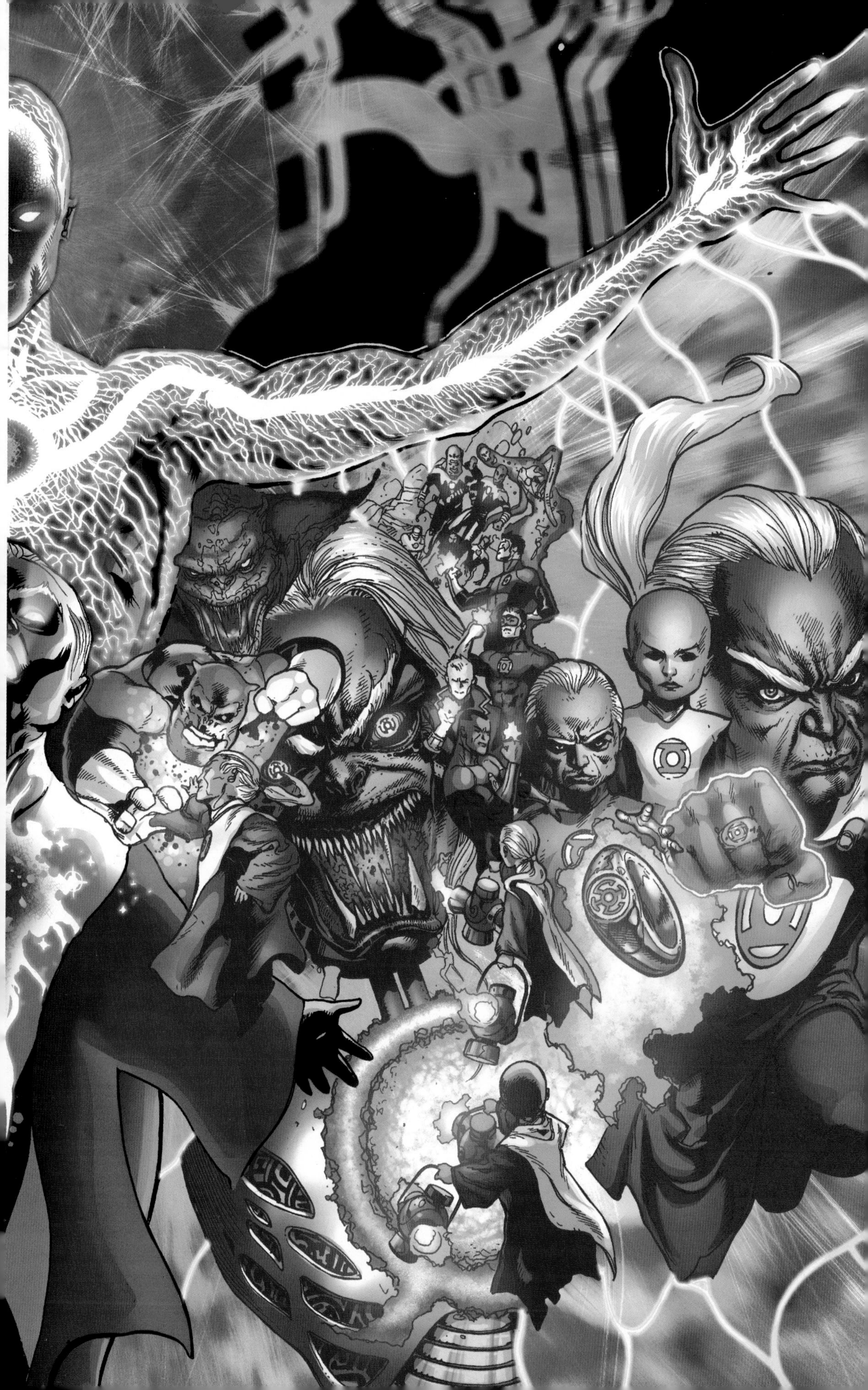

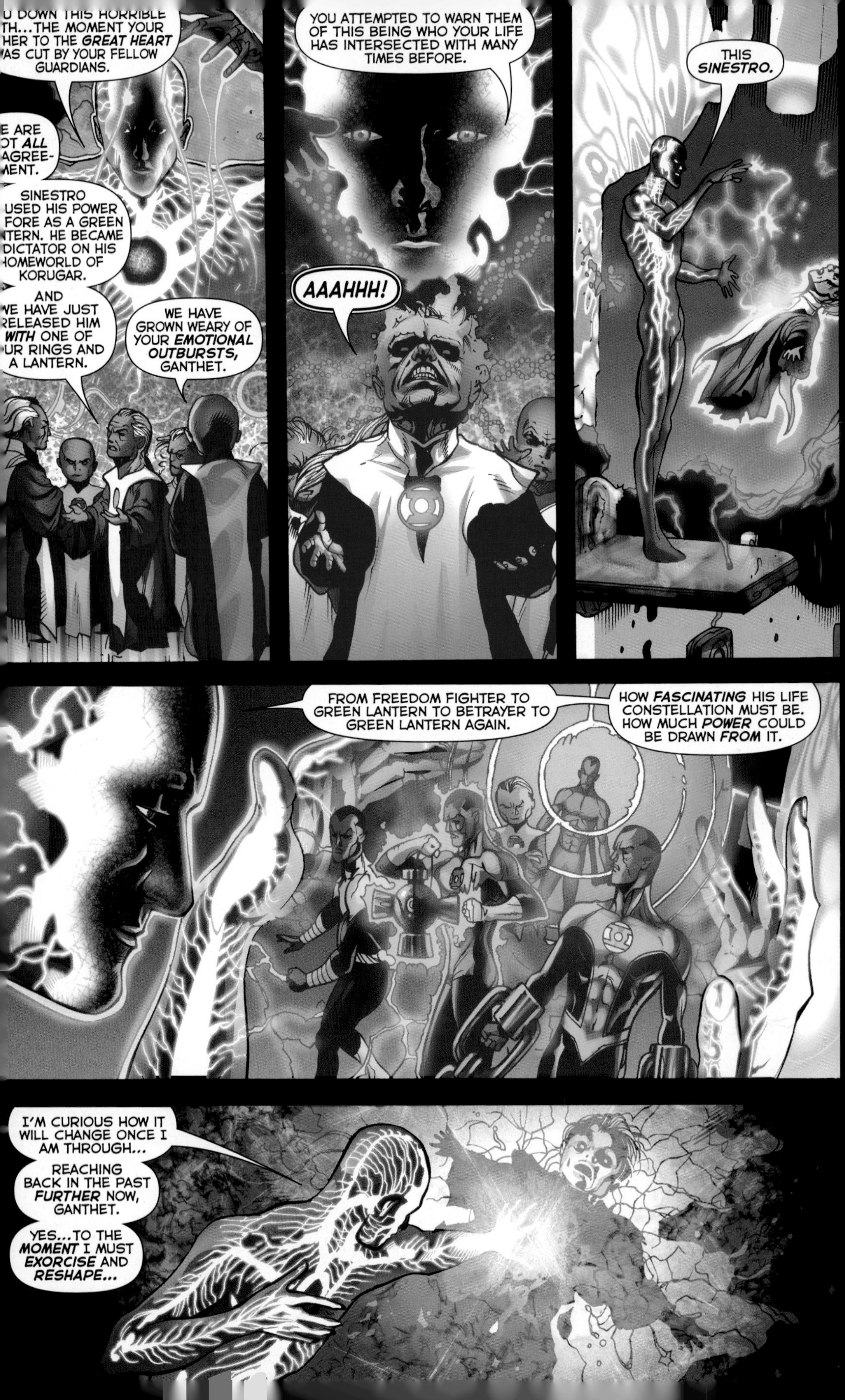

U DOWN THIS HORRIBLE TH...THE MOMENT YOUR HER TO THE GREAT HEART VAS CUT BY YOUR FELLOW GUARDIANS.
E ARE OT ALL AGREE- MENT.
SINESTRO USED HIS POWER FORE AS A GREEN NTERN. HE BECAME DICTATOR ON HIS HOMEWORLD OF KORUGAR.
AND VE HAVE JUST RELEASED HIM WITH ONE OF UR RINGS AND A LANTERN.
WE HAVE GROWN WEARY OF YOUR EMOTIONAL OUTBURSTS, GANTHET.
YOU ATTEMPTED TO WARN THEM OF THIS BEING WHO YOUR LIFE HAS INTERSECTED WITH MANY TIMES BEFORE.
AAAHHH!
THIS SINESTRO.
FROM FREEDOM FIGHTER TO GREEN LANTERN TO BETRAYER TO GREEN LANTERN AGAIN.
HOW FASCINATING HIS LIFE CONSTELLATION MUST BE. HOW MUCH POWER COULD BE DRAWN FROM IT.
I'M CURIOUS HOW IT WILL CHANGE ONCE I AM THROUGH...
REACHING BACK IN THE PAST FURTHER NOW, GANTHET.
YES...TO THE MOMENT I MUST EXORCISE AND RESHAPE...

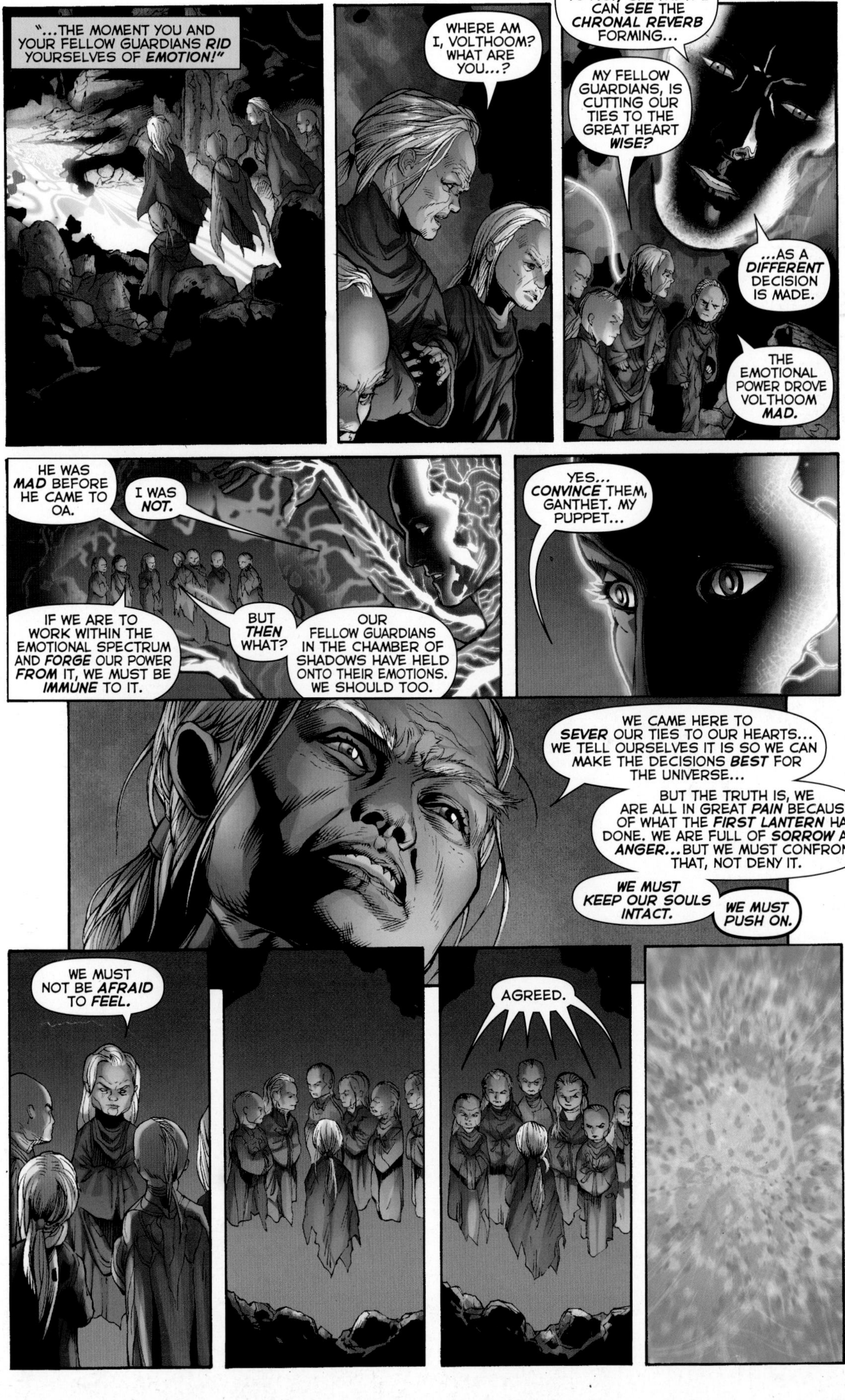
"...THE MOMENT YOU AND YOUR FELLOW GUARDIANS RID YOURSELVES OF EMOTION!"
WHERE AM I, VOLTHOOM? WHAT ARE YOU...?
YOU WILL ACT THE WAY I WILL YOU TO ACT, GANTHET. I CAN SEE THE CHRONAL REVERB FORMING...
MY FELLOW GUARDIANS, IS CUTTING OUR TIES TO THE GREAT HEART WISE?
...AS A DIFFERENT DECISION IS MADE.
THE EMOTIONAL POWER DROVE VOLTHOOM MAD.
HE WAS MAD BEFORE HE CAME TO OA.
I WAS NOT.
IF WE ARE TO WORK WITHIN THE EMOTIONAL SPECTRUM AND FORGE OUR POWER FROM IT, WE MUST BE IMMUNE TO IT.
BUT THEN WHAT?
OUR FELLOW GUARDIANS IN THE CHAMBER OF SHADOWS HAVE HELD ONTO THEIR EMOTIONS. WE SHOULD TOO.
YES... CONVINCE THEM, GANTHET. MY PUPPET...
WE CAME HERE TO SEVER OUR TIES TO OUR HEARTS... WE TELL OURSELVES IT IS SO WE CAN MAKE THE DECISIONS BEST FOR THE UNIVERSE...
BUT THE TRUTH IS, WE ARE ALL IN GREAT PAIN BECAUSE OF WHAT THE FIRST LANTERN HAS DONE. WE ARE FULL OF SORROW AND ANGER...BUT WE MUST CONFRONT THAT, NOT DENY IT.
WE MUST KEEP OUR SOULS INTACT.
WE MUST PUSH ON.
WE MUST NOT BE AFRAID TO FEEL.
AGREED.

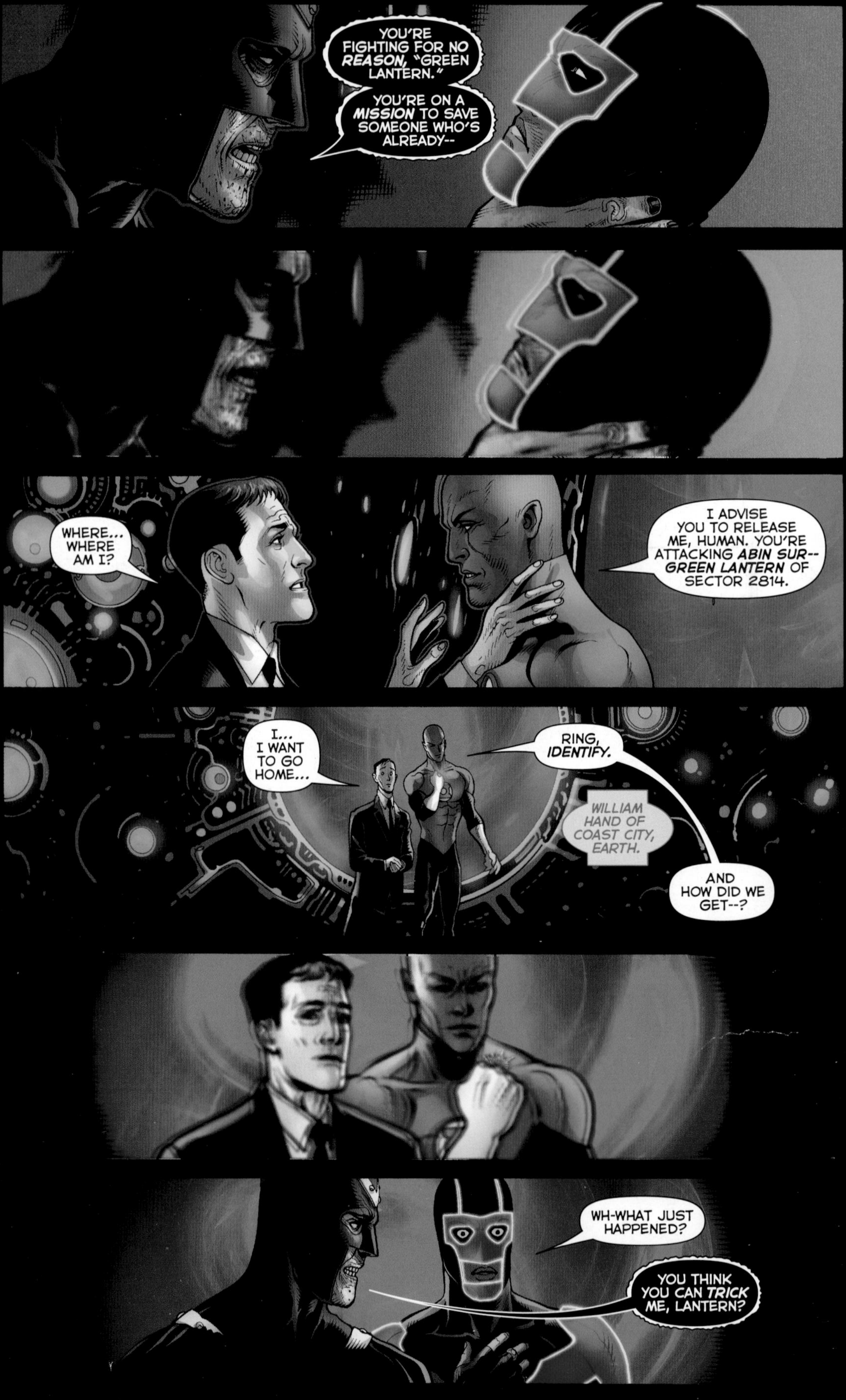
YOU'RE FIGHTING FOR NO REASON, "GREEN LANTERN."
YOU'RE ON A MISSION TO SAVE SOMEONE WHO'S ALREADY--
WHERE... WHERE AM I?
I ADVISE YOU TO RELEASE ME, HUMAN. YOU'RE ATTACKING ABIN SUR--GREEN LANTERN OF SECTOR 2814.
I... I WANT TO GO HOME...
RING, IDENTIFY.
WILLIAM HAND OF COAST CITY, EARTH.
AND HOW DID WE GET--?
WH-WHAT JUST HAPPENED?
YOU THINK YOU CAN TRICK ME, LANTERN?

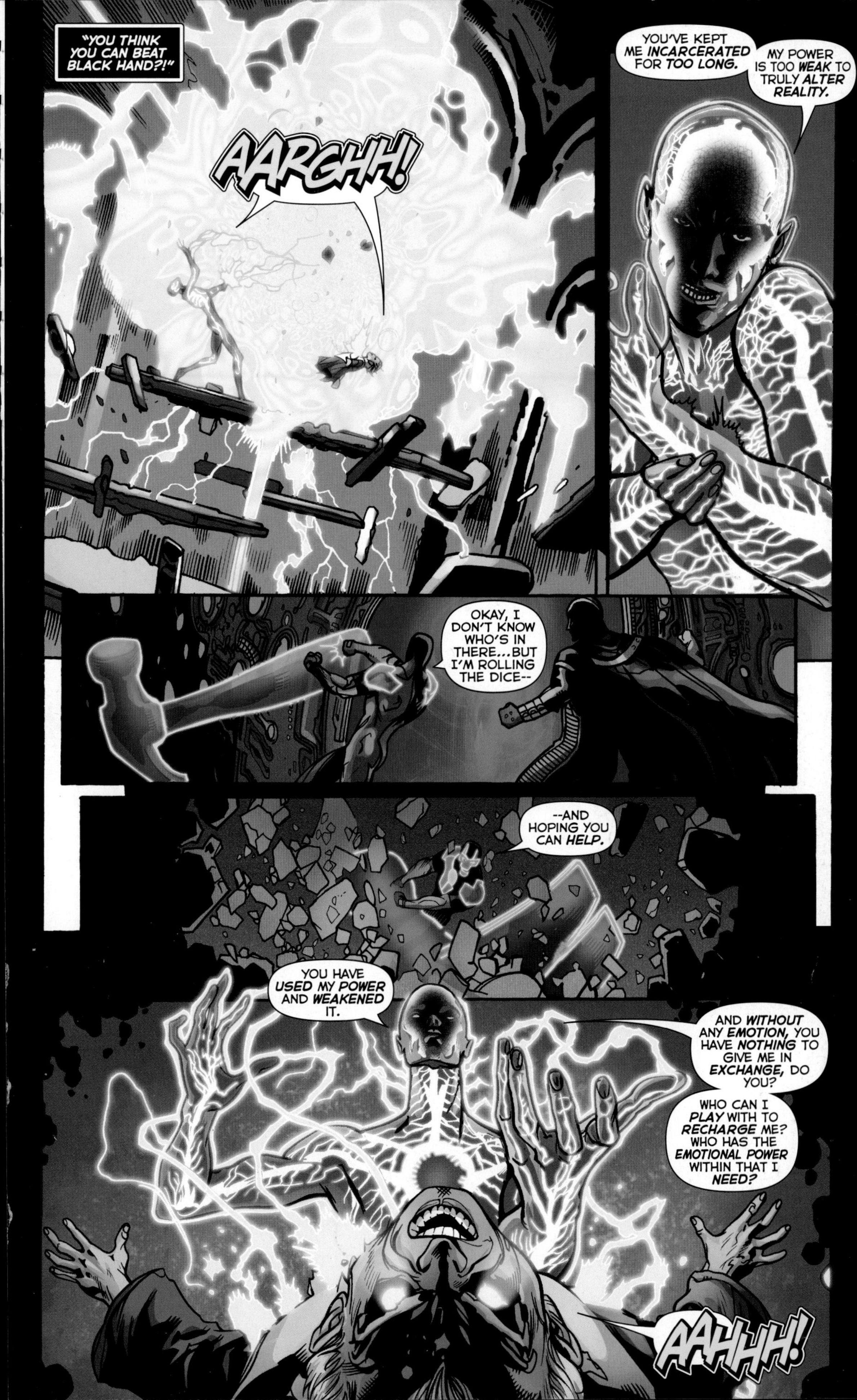
"YOU THINK YOU CAN BEAT BLACK HAND?!"
AARGHH!
YOU'VE KEPT ME INCARCERATED FOR TOO LONG.
MY POWER IS TOO WEAK TO TRULY ALTER REALITY.
OKAY, I DON'T KNOW WHO'S IN THERE...BUT I'M ROLLING THE DICE--
--AND HOPING YOU CAN HELP.
YOU HAVE USED MY POWER AND WEAKENED IT.
AND WITHOUT ANY EMOTION, YOU HAVE NOTHING TO GIVE ME IN EXCHANGE, DO YOU?
WHO CAN I PLAY WITH TO RECHARGE ME? WHO HAS THE EMOTIONAL POWER WITHIN THAT I NEED?
AAHHH!

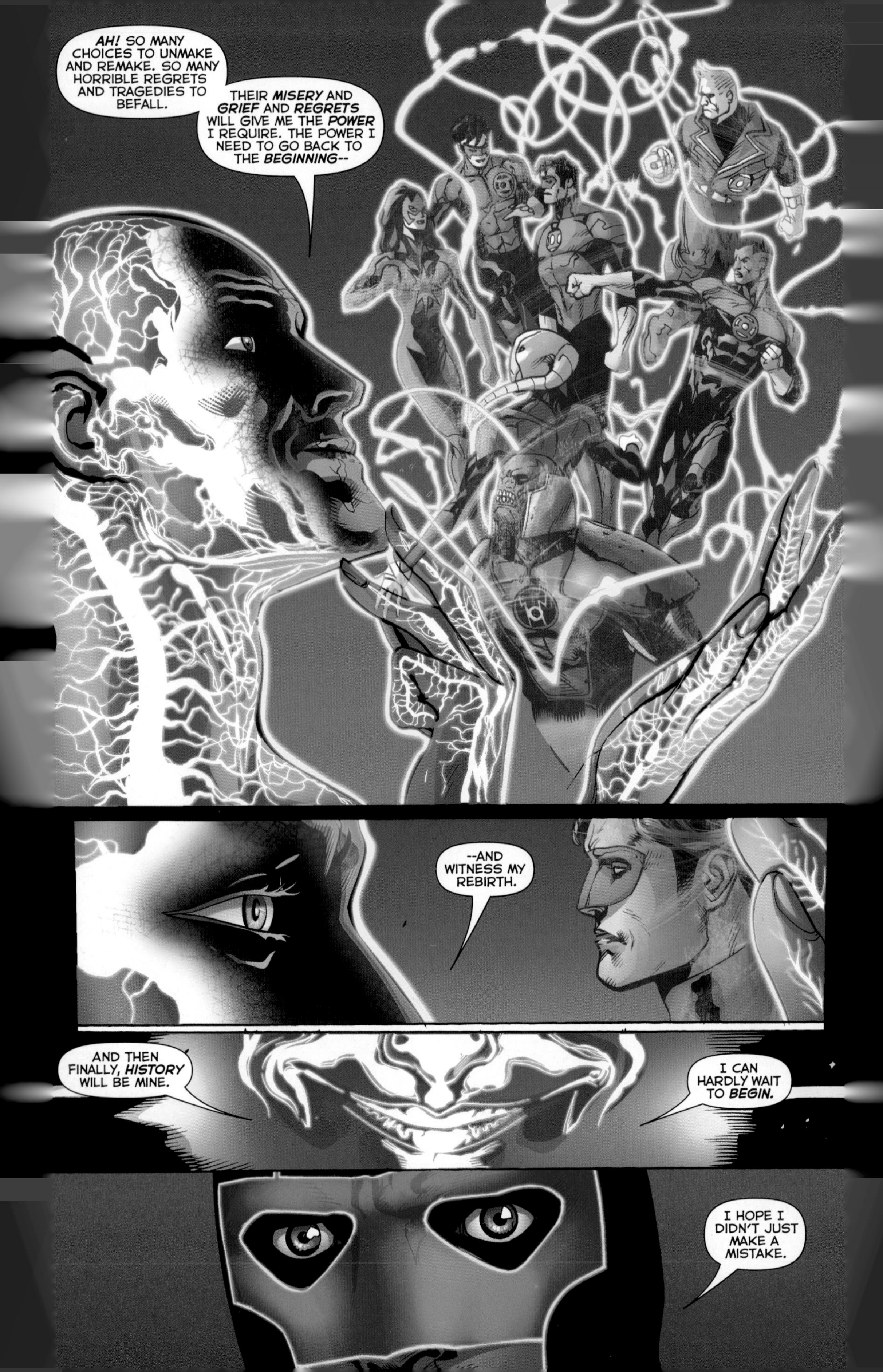
AH! SO MANY CHOICES TO UNMAKE AND REMAKE. SO MANY HORRIBLE REGRETS AND TRAGEDIES TO BEFALL.
THEIR MISERY AND GRIEF AND REGRETS WILL GIVE ME THE POWER I REQUIRE. THE POWER I NEED TO GO BACK TO THE BEGINNING--
--AND WITNESS MY REBIRTH.
AND THEN FINALLY, HISTORY WILL BE MINE.
I CAN HARDLY WAIT TO BEGIN.
I HOPE I DIDN'T JUST MAKE A MISTAKE.

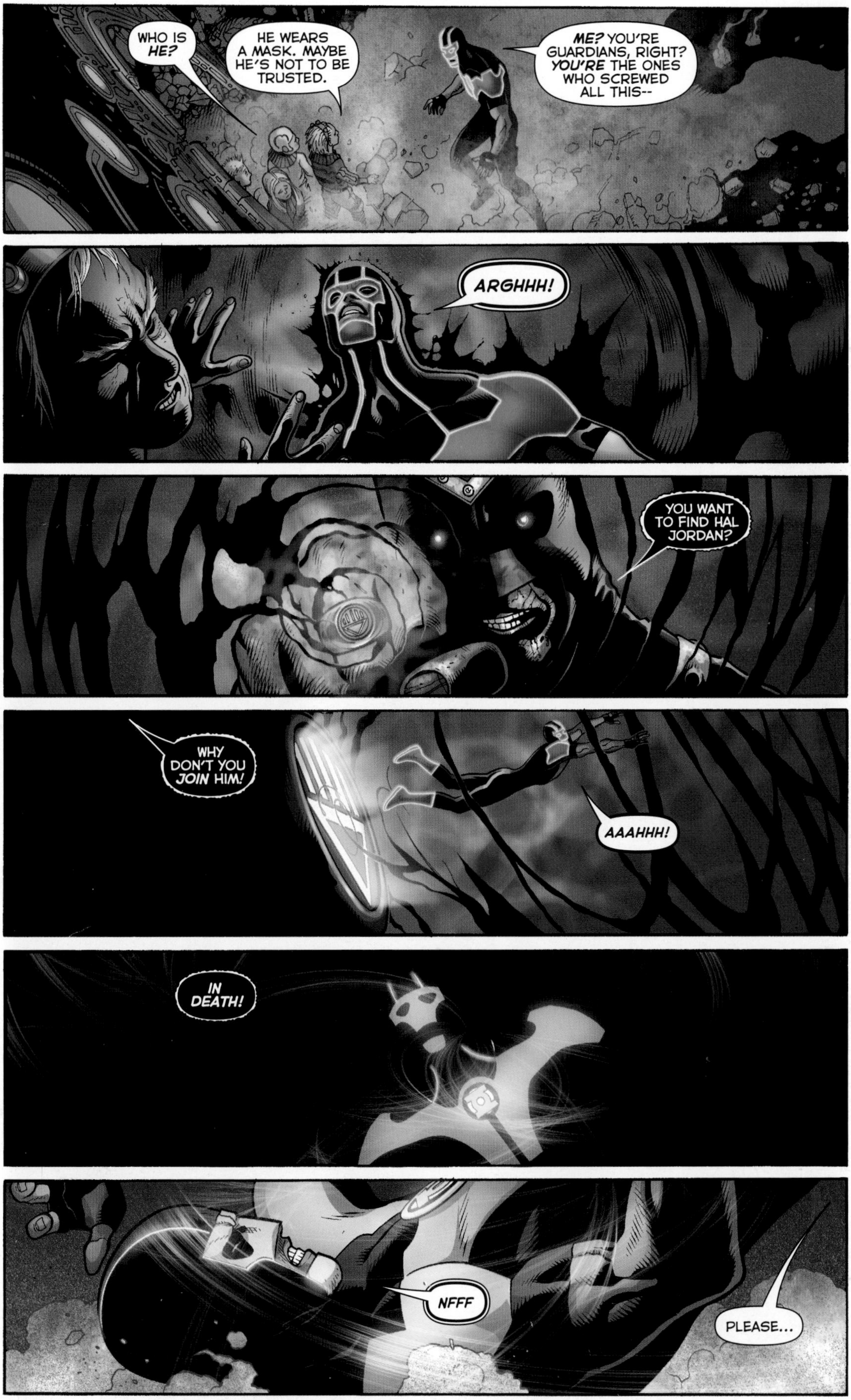
WHO IS HE?
HE WEARS A MASK. MAYBE HE'S NOT TO BE TRUSTED.
ME? YOU'RE GUARDIANS, RIGHT? YOU'RE THE ONES WHO SCREWED ALL THIS--
ARGHHH!
YOU WANT TO FIND HAL JORDAN?
WHY DON'T YOU JOIN HIM!
AAAHHH!
IN DEATH!
NFFF
PLEASE...

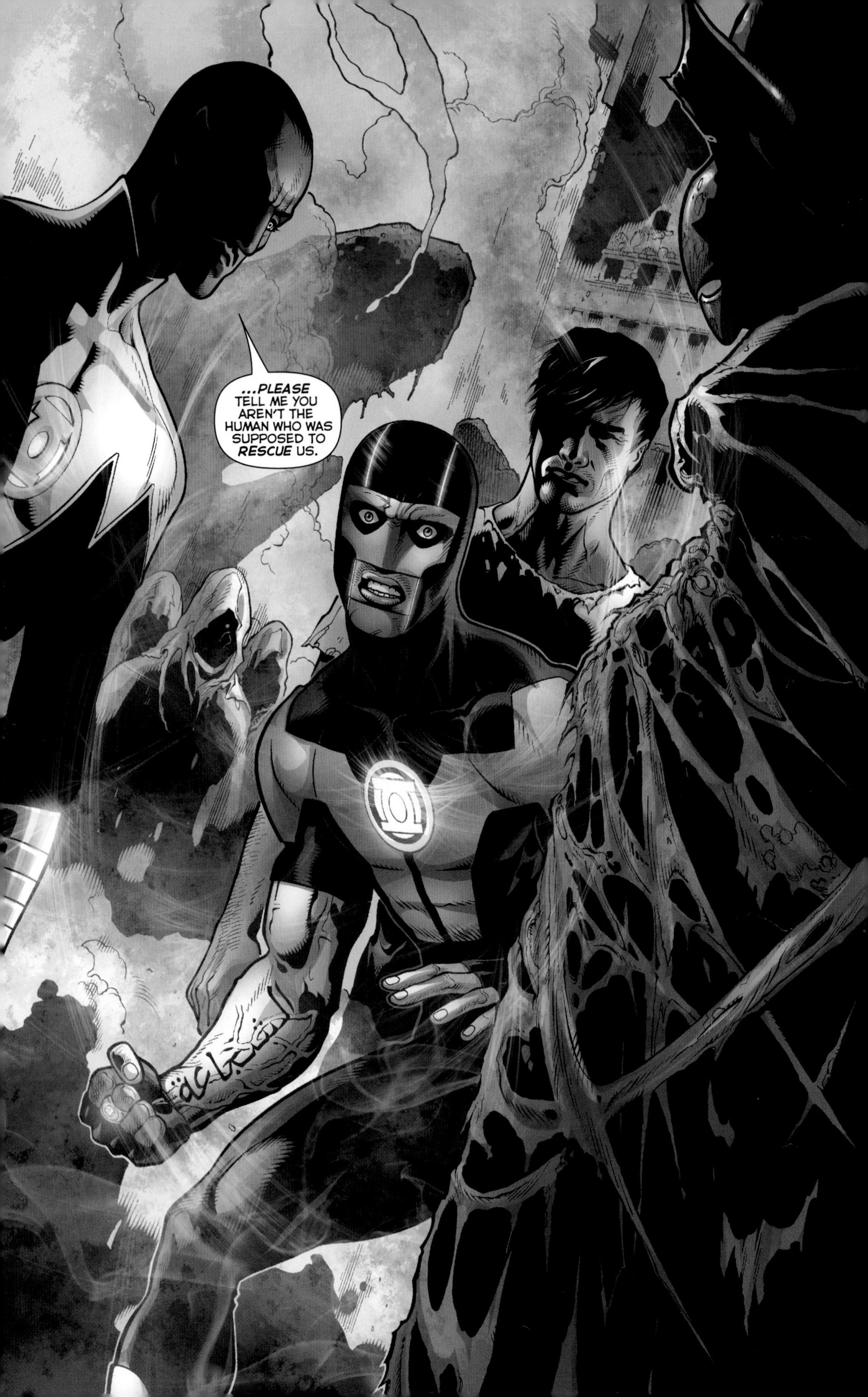
...PLEASE TELL ME YOU AREN'T THE HUMAN WHO WAS SUPPOSED TO RESCUE US.

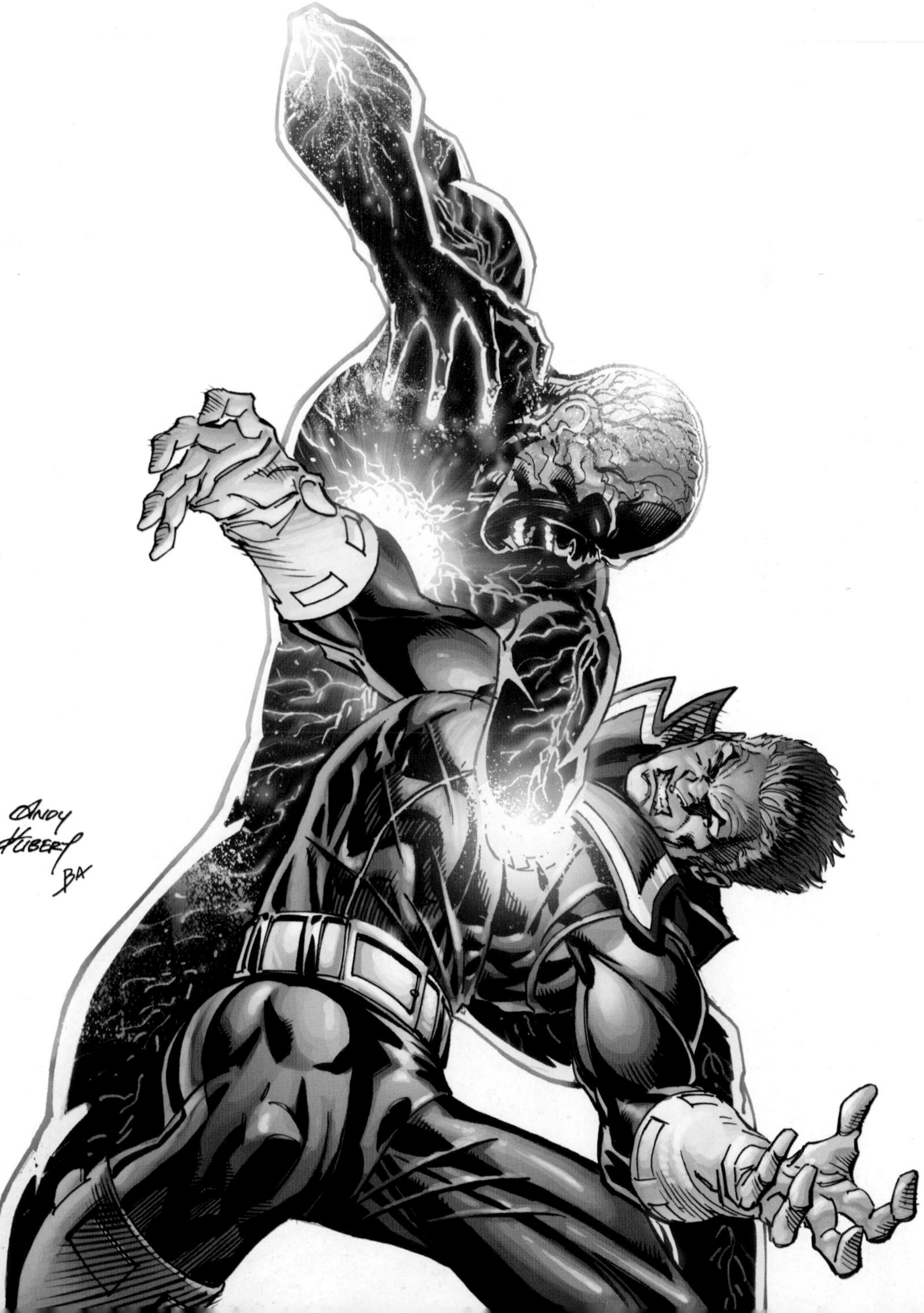
ANDY KUBERT
BA

PART TWO: DECIMATED

PETER J. TOMASI writer FERNANDO PASARIN penciller SCOTT HANNA inker
cover art by ANDY KUBERT & BRAD ANDERSON

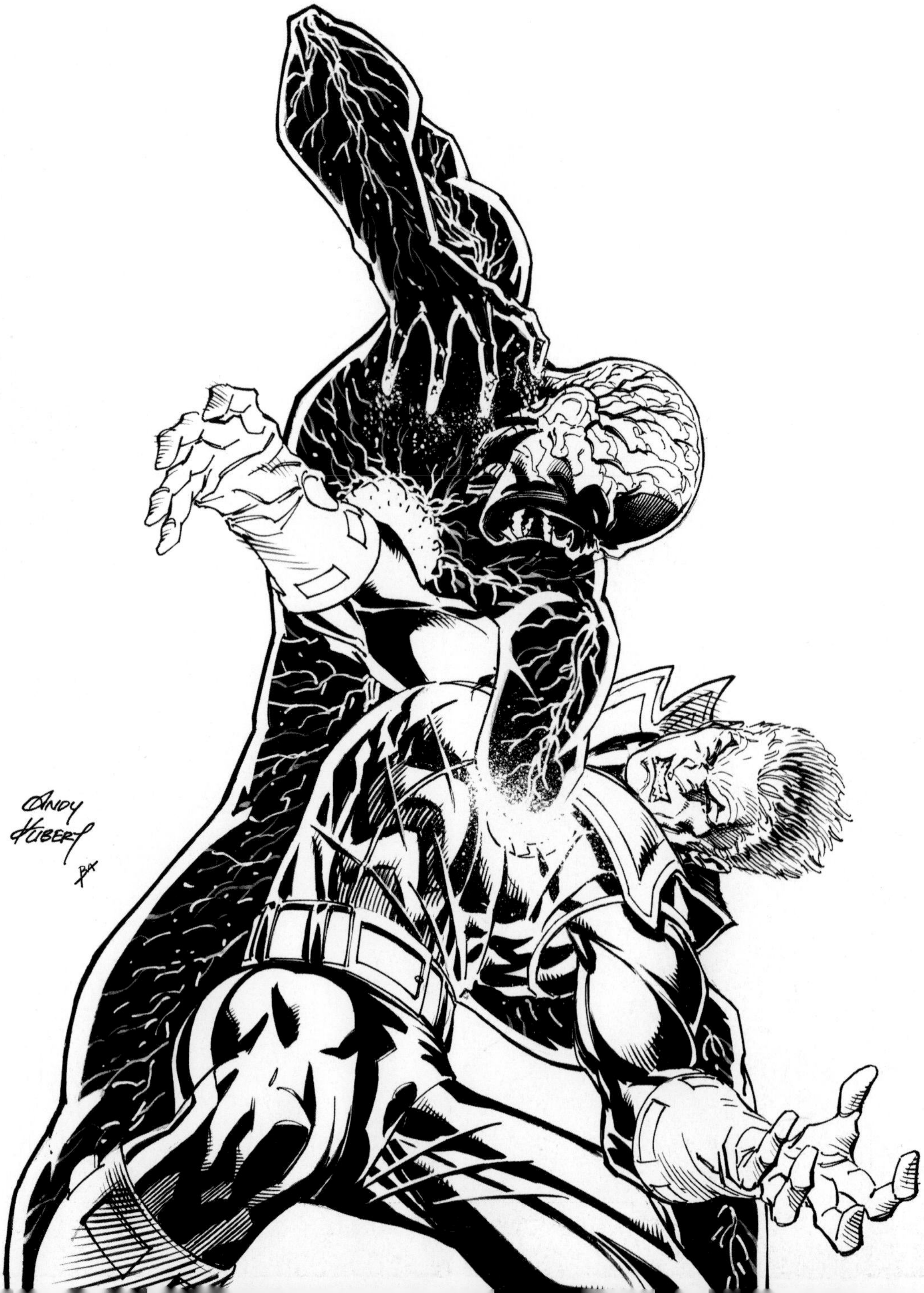

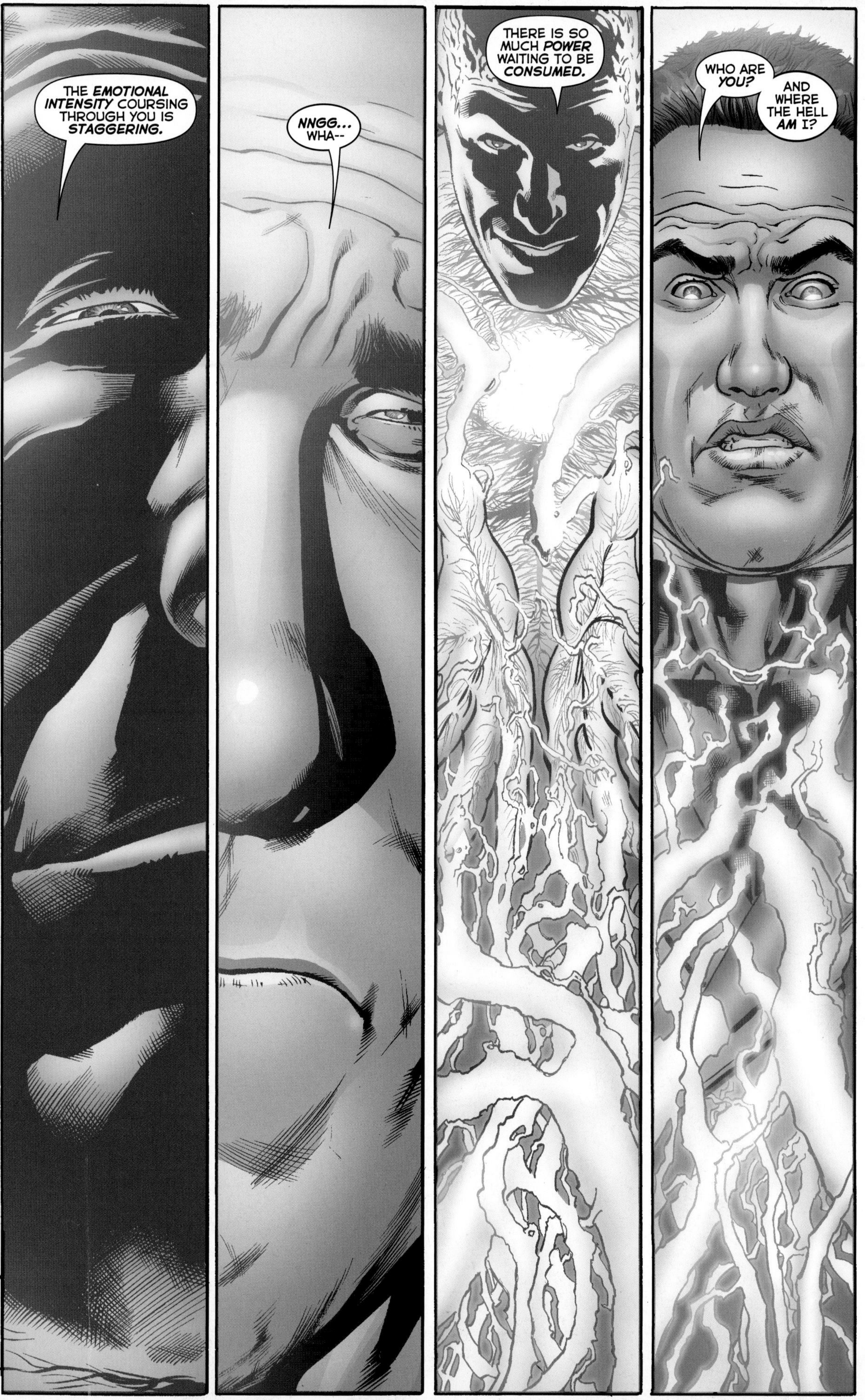

THE EMOTIONAL INTENSITY COURSING THROUGH YOU IS STAGGERING.
NNGG... WHA--
THERE IS SO MUCH POWER WAITING TO BE CONSUMED.
WHO ARE YOU?
AND WHERE THE HELL AM I?

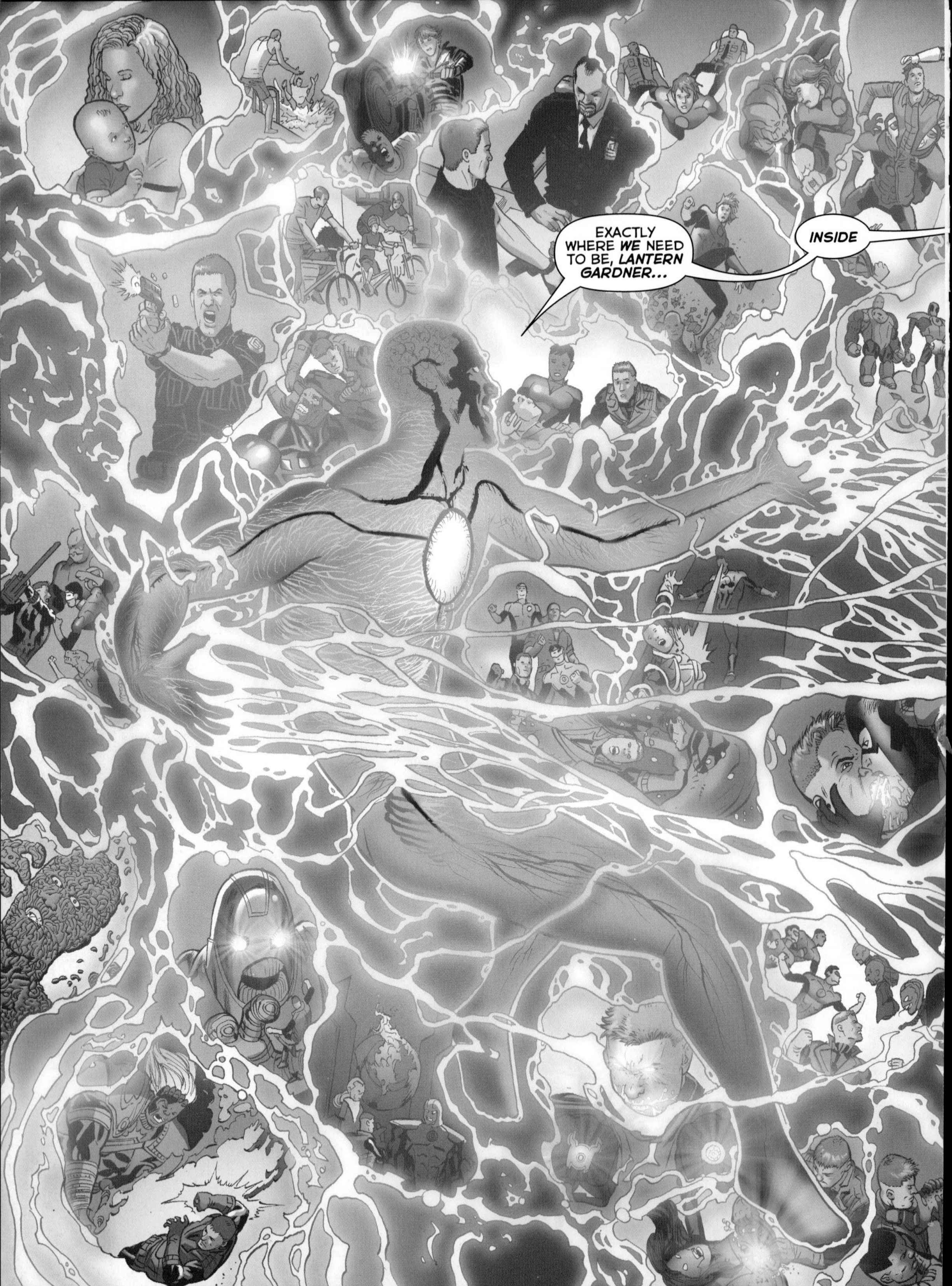
EXACTLY WHERE WE NEED TO BE, LANTERN GARDNER...
INSIDE

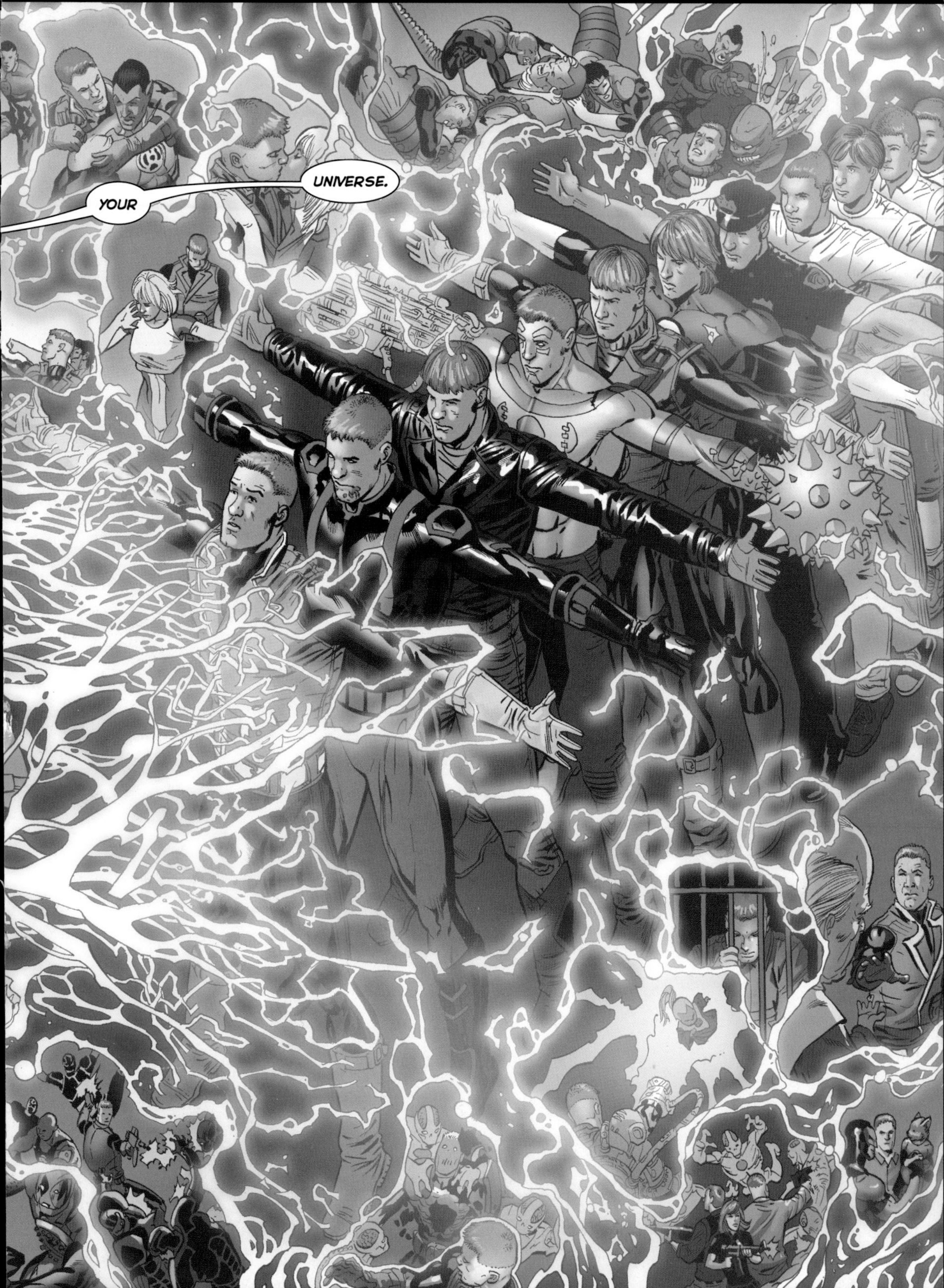
YOUR
UNIVERSE.

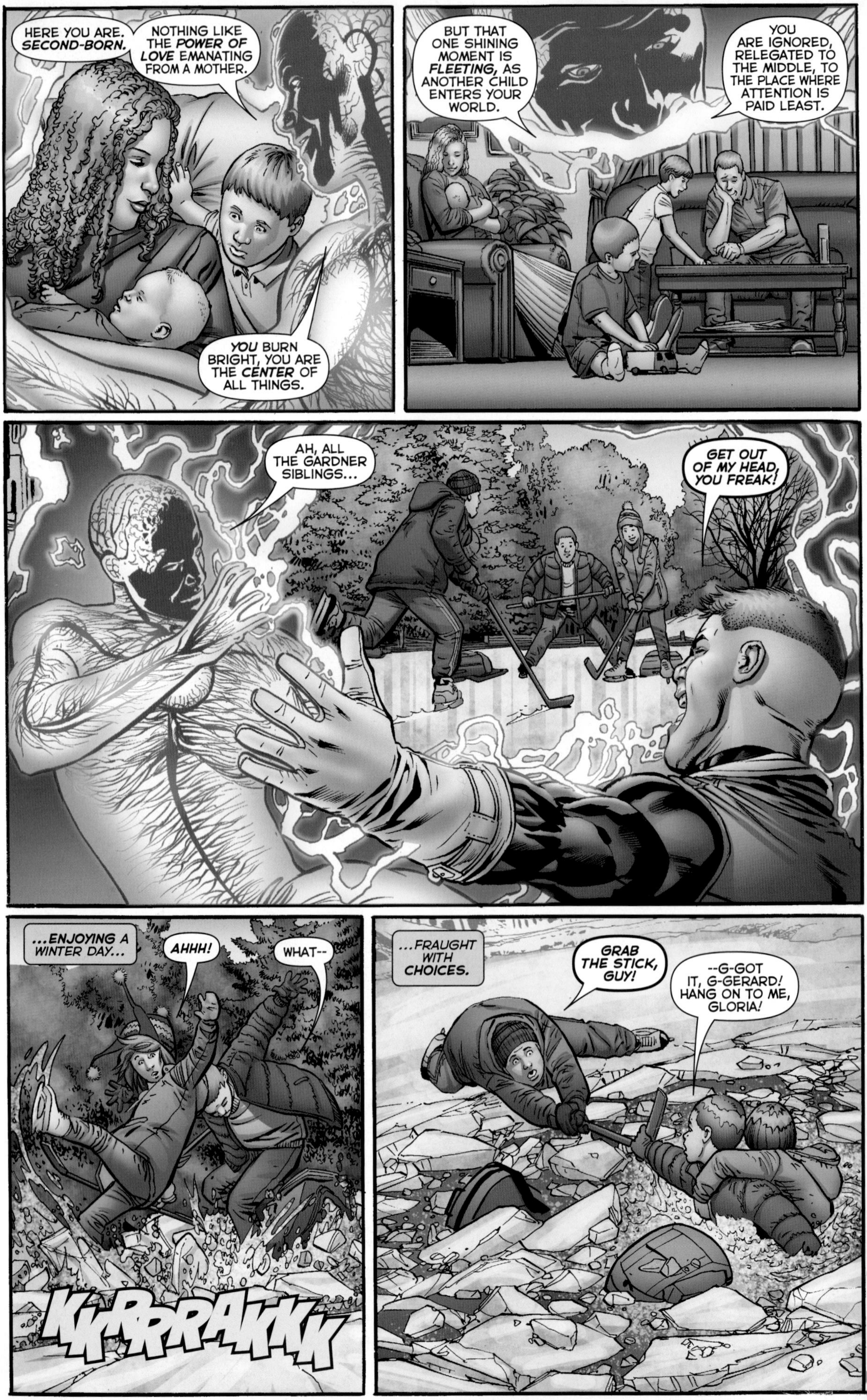
HERE YOU ARE. SECOND-BORN.
NOTHING LIKE THE POWER OF LOVE EMANATING FROM A MOTHER.
YOU BURN BRIGHT, YOU ARE THE CENTER OF ALL THINGS.
BUT THAT ONE SHINING MOMENT IS FLEETING, AS ANOTHER CHILD ENTERS YOUR WORLD.
YOU ARE IGNORED, RELEGATED TO THE MIDDLE, TO THE PLACE WHERE ATTENTION IS PAID LEAST.
AH, ALL THE GARDNER SIBLINGS...
GET OUT OF MY HEAD, YOU FREAK!
...ENJOYING A WINTER DAY...
AHHH!
WHAT--
KKRRRAKKKK
...FRAUGHT WITH CHOICES.
GRAB THE STICK, GUY!
--G-GOT IT, G-GERARD! HANG ON TO ME, GLORIA!

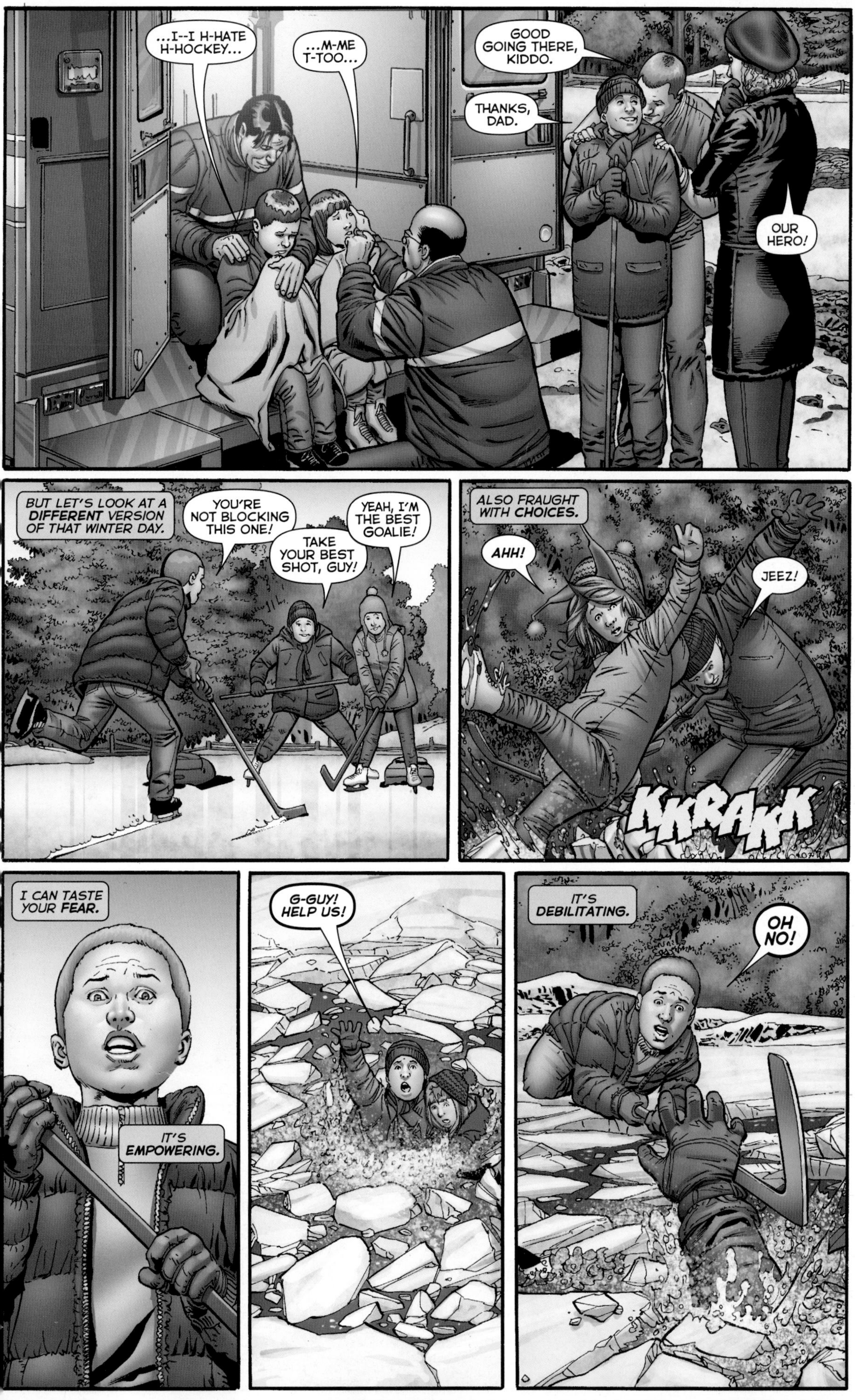
...I--I H-HATE H-HOCKEY...
...M-ME T-TOO...
GOOD GOING THERE, KIDDO.
THANKS, DAD.
OUR HERO!
BUT LET'S LOOK AT A DIFFERENT VERSION OF THAT WINTER DAY.
YOU'RE NOT BLOCKING THIS ONE!
TAKE YOUR BEST SHOT, GUY!
YEAH, I'M THE BEST GOALIE!
ALSO FRAUGHT WITH CHOICES.
AHH!
JEEZ!
KKRAKK
I CAN TASTE YOUR FEAR.
IT'S EMPOWERING.
G-GUY! HELP US!
IT'S DEBILITATING.
OH NO!

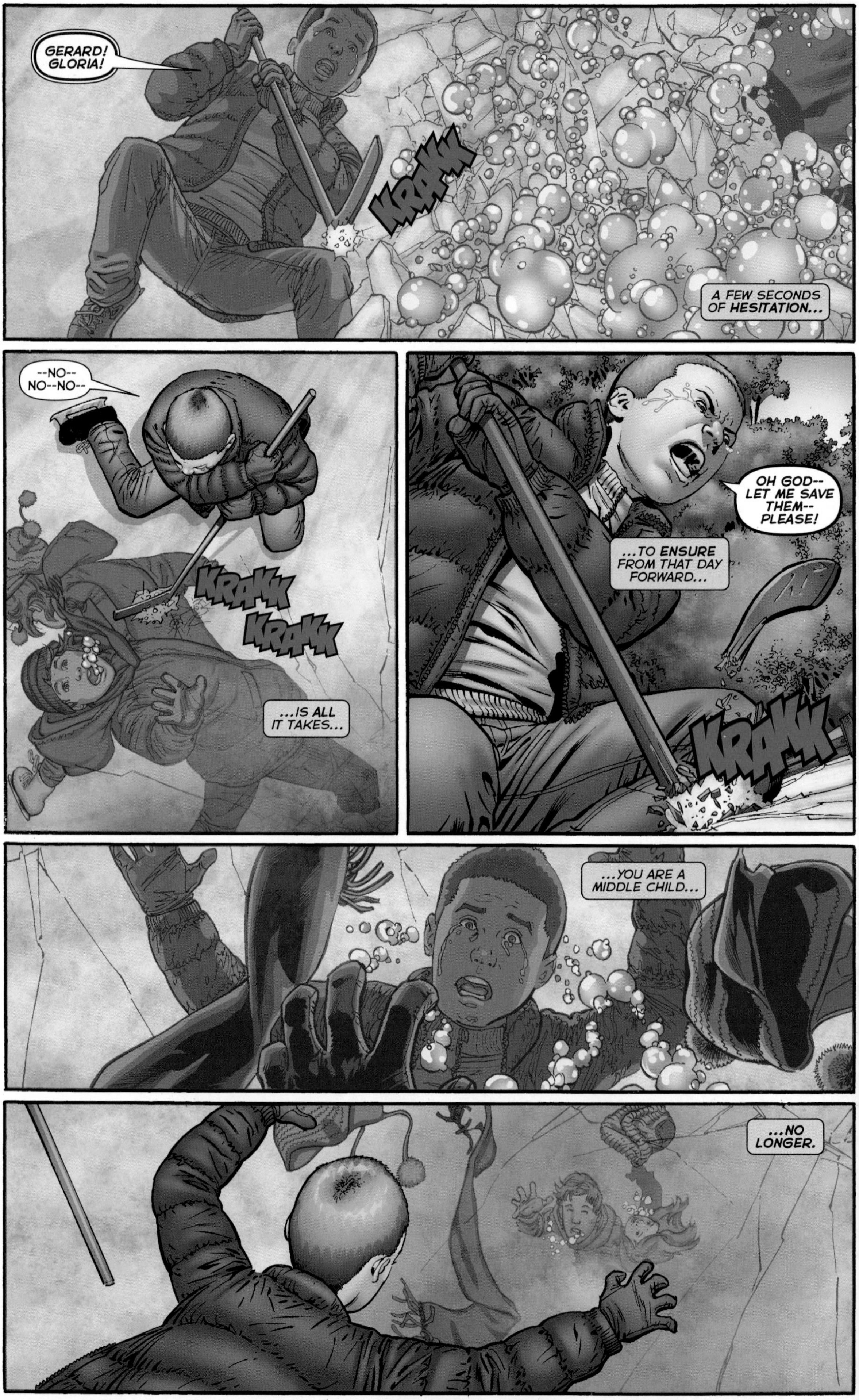
GERARD! GLORIA!
KRAKK
A FEW SECONDS OF HESITATION...
--NO-- NO--NO--
KRAKK
KRAKK
...IS ALL IT TAKES...
OH GOD-- LET ME SAVE THEM-- PLEASE!
...TO ENSURE FROM THAT DAY FORWARD...
KRAKK
...YOU ARE A MIDDLE CHILD...
...NO LONGER.

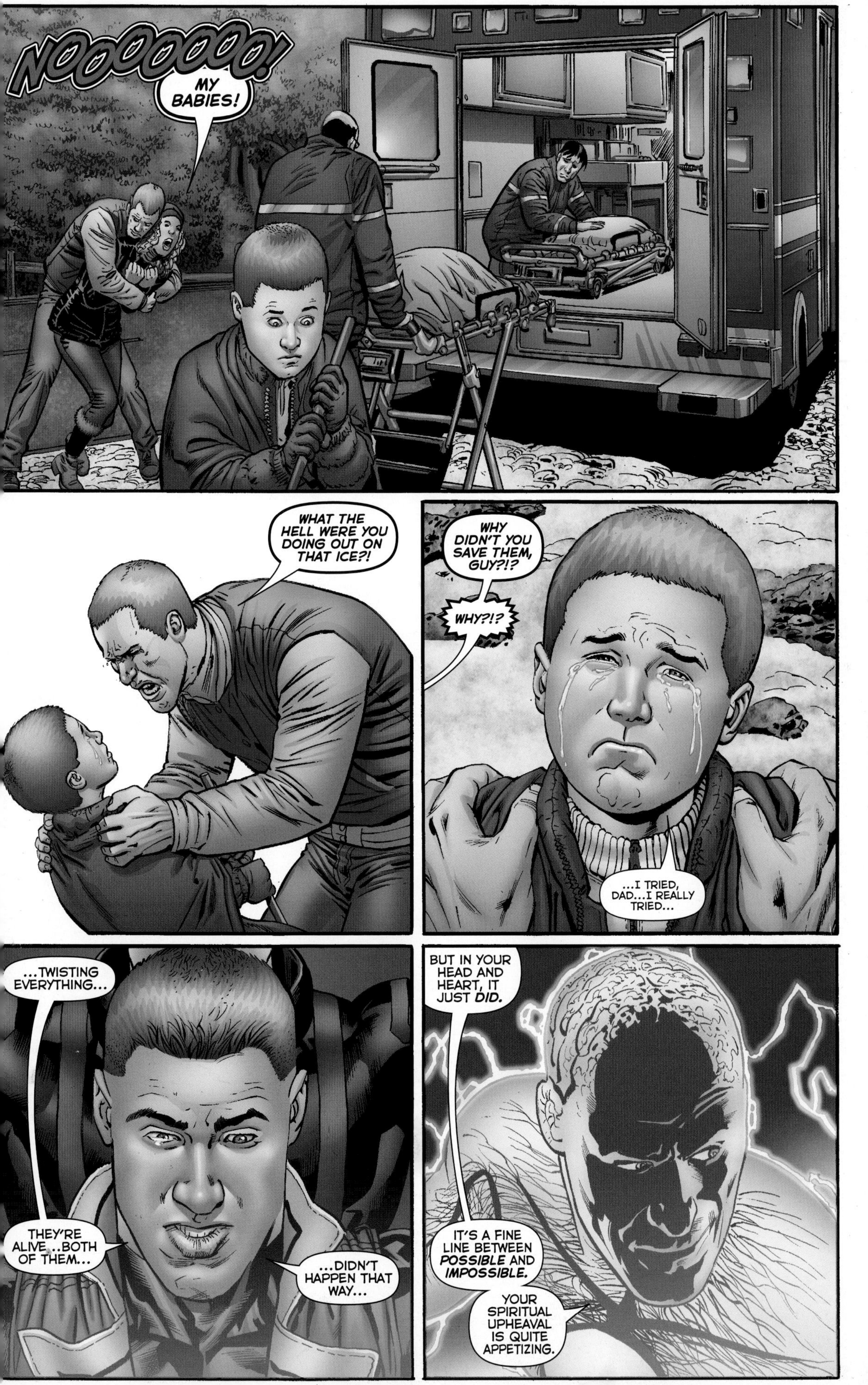
NOOOOOOO!
MY BABIES!
WHAT THE HELL WERE YOU DOING OUT ON THAT ICE?!
WHY DIDN'T YOU SAVE THEM, GUY?!?
WHY?!?
...I TRIED, DAD...I REALLY TRIED...
...TWISTING EVERYTHING...
THEY'RE ALIVE...BOTH OF THEM...
...DIDN'T HAPPEN THAT WAY...
BUT IN YOUR HEAD AND HEART, IT JUST DID.
IT'S A FINE LINE BETWEEN POSSIBLE AND IMPOSSIBLE.
YOUR SPIRITUAL UPHEAVAL IS QUITE APPETIZING.

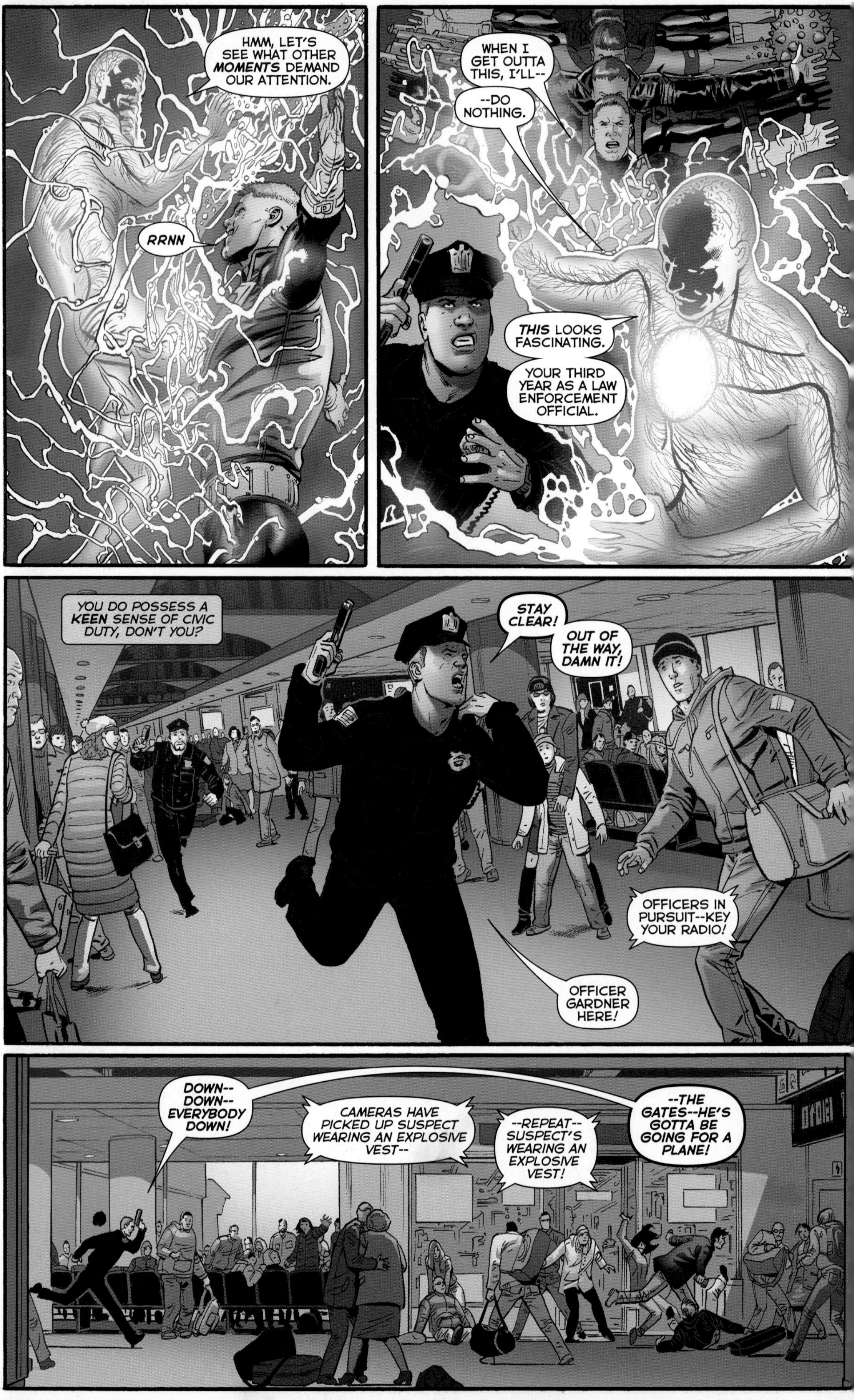
HMM, LET'S SEE WHAT OTHER MOMENTS DEMAND OUR ATTENTION.
RRNN
WHEN I GET OUTTA THIS, I'LL--
--DO NOTHING.
THIS LOOKS FASCINATING.
YOUR THIRD YEAR AS A LAW ENFORCEMENT OFFICIAL.
YOU DO POSSESS A KEEN SENSE OF CIVIC DUTY, DON'T YOU?
STAY CLEAR!
OUT OF THE WAY, DAMN IT!
OFFICERS IN PURSUIT--KEY YOUR RADIO!
OFFICER GARDNER HERE!
DOWN-- DOWN-- EVERYBODY DOWN!
CAMERAS HAVE PICKED UP SUSPECT WEARING AN EXPLOSIVE VEST--
--REPEAT-- SUSPECT'S WEARING AN EXPLOSIVE VEST!
--THE GATES--HE'S GOTTA BE GOING FOR A PLANE!

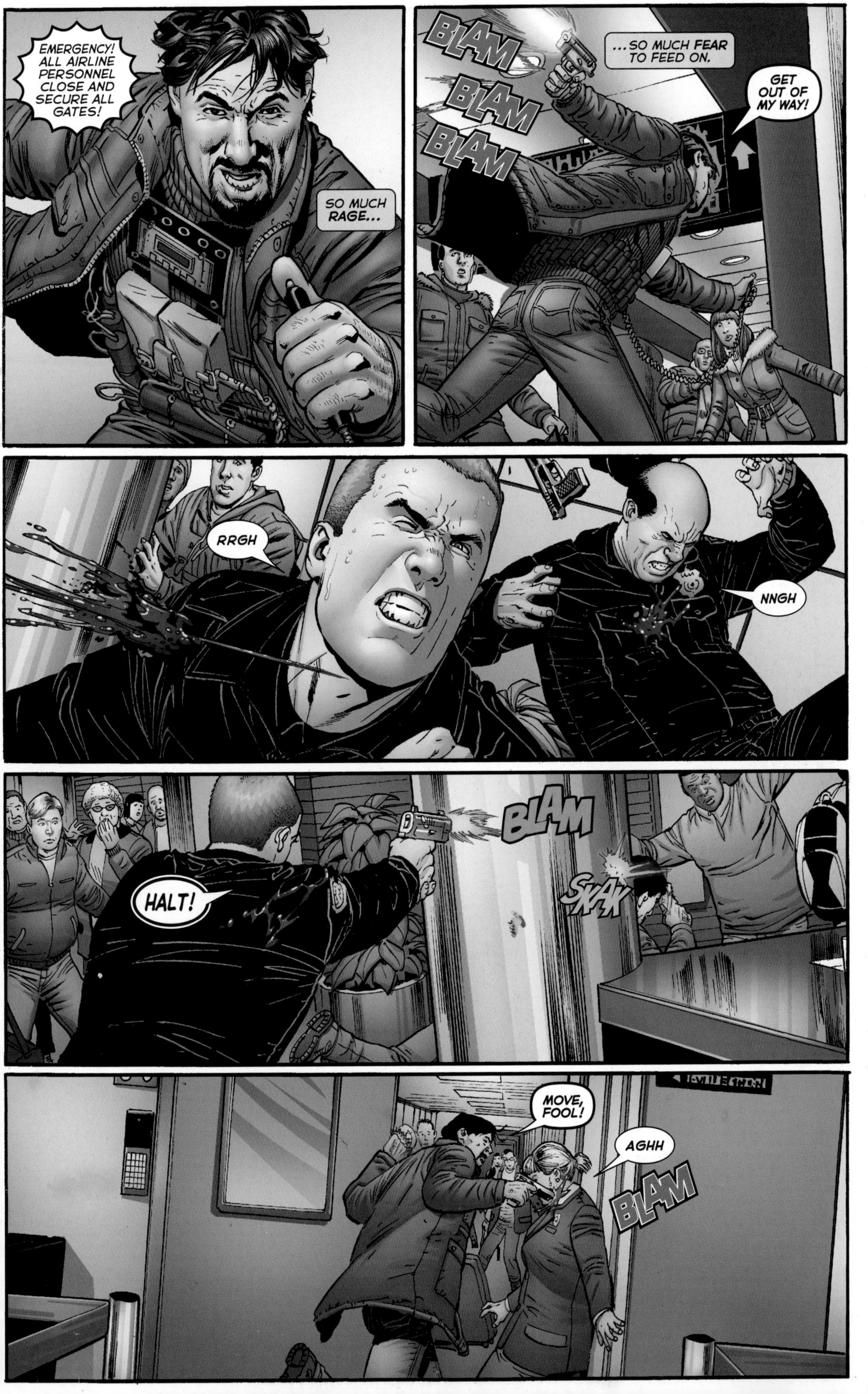
EMERGENCY! ALL AIRLINE PERSONNEL CLOSE AND SECURE ALL GATES!
SO MUCH RAGE...
BLAM
BLAM
BLAM
...SO MUCH FEAR TO FEED ON.
GET OUT OF MY WAY!
RRGH
NNGH
HALT!
BLAM
SKAK
MOVE, FOOL!
AGHH
BLAM

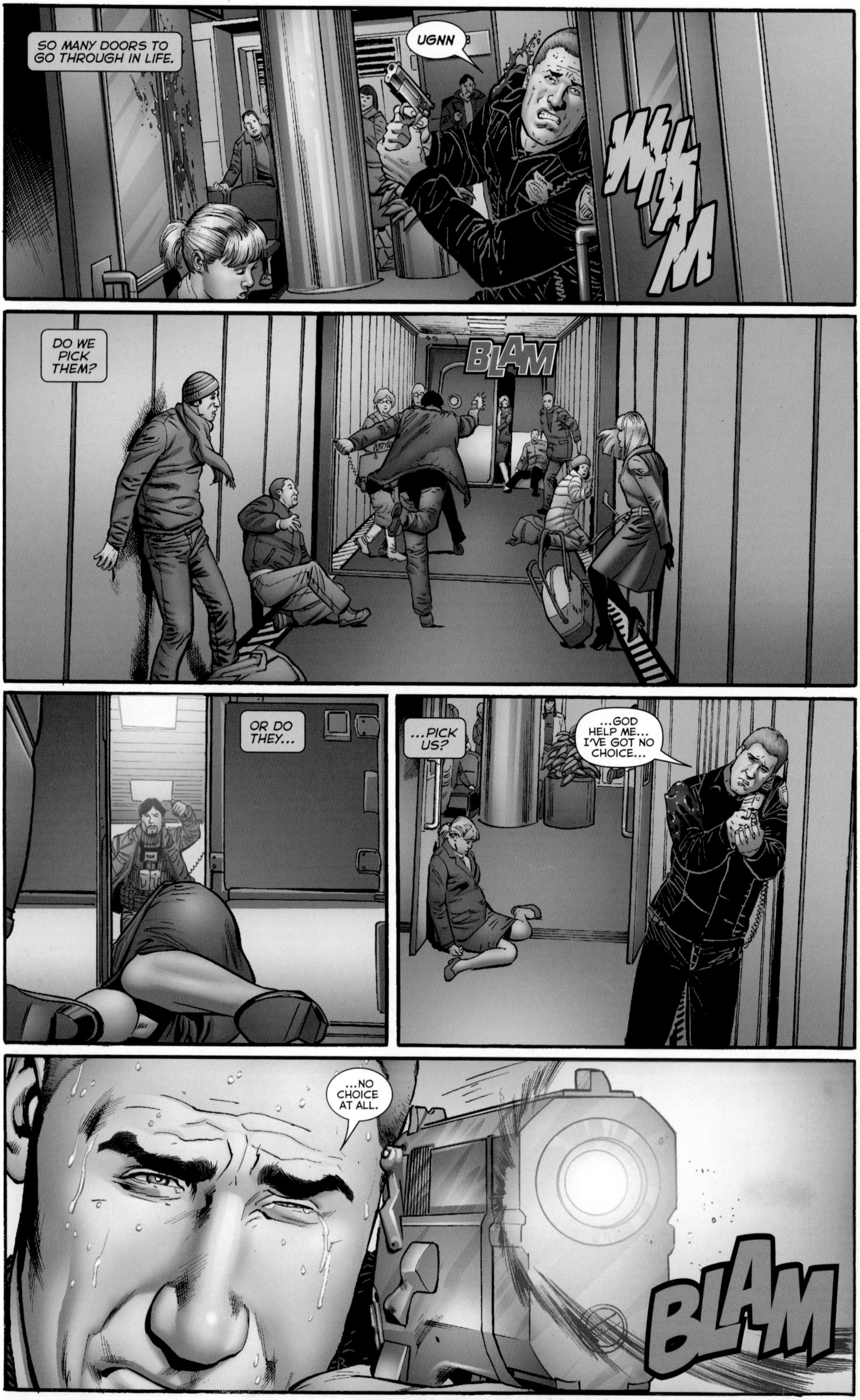
SO MANY DOORS TO GO THROUGH IN LIFE.
UGNN
WHAM
DO WE PICK THEM?
BLAM
OR DO THEY...
...PICK US?
...GOD HELP ME... I'VE GOT NO CHOICE...
...NO CHOICE AT ALL.
BLAM

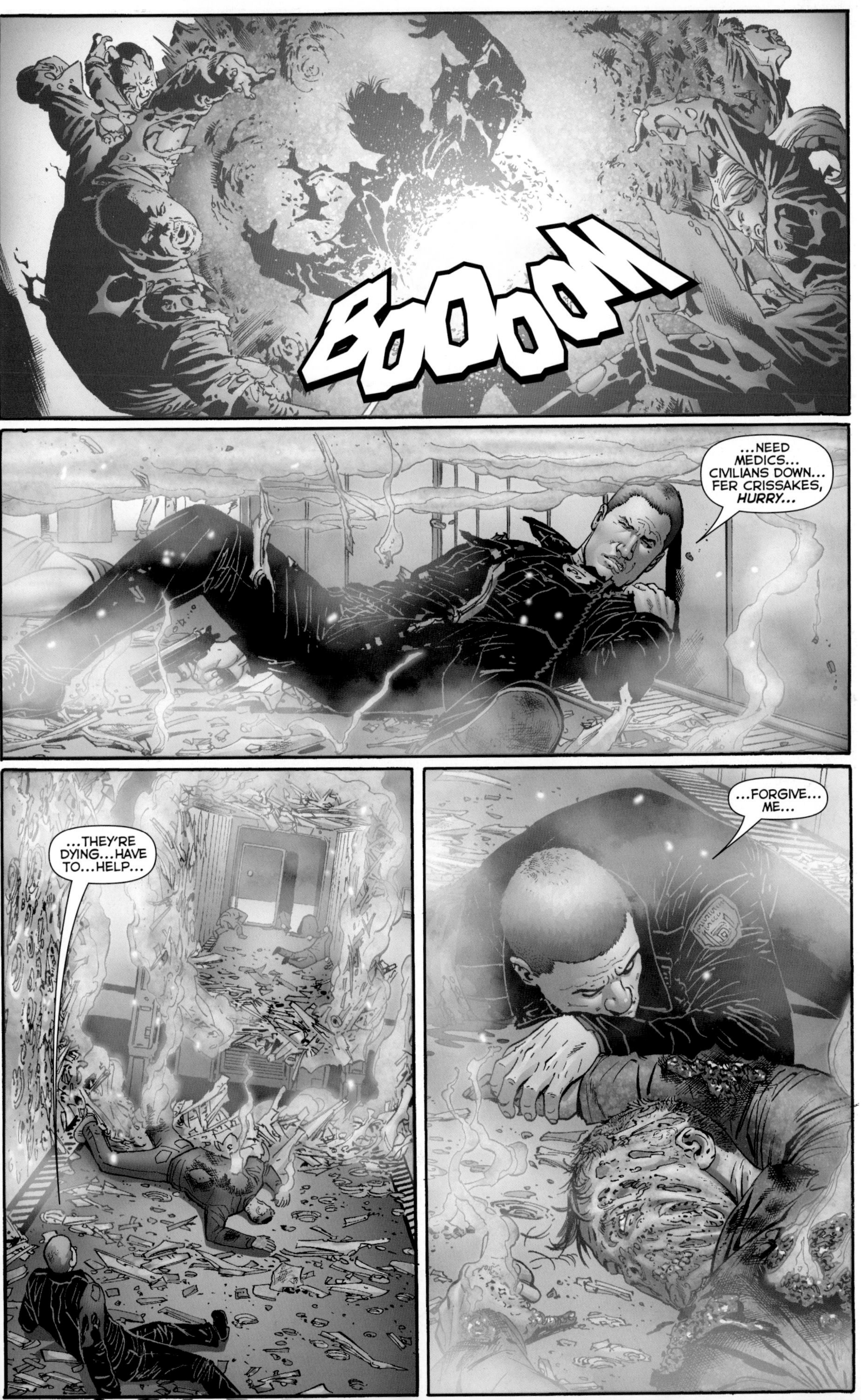
BOOOOOM
...NEED MEDICS... CIVILIANS DOWN... FER CRISSAKES, HURRY...
...THEY'RE DYING...HAVE TO...HELP...
...FORGIVE... ME...

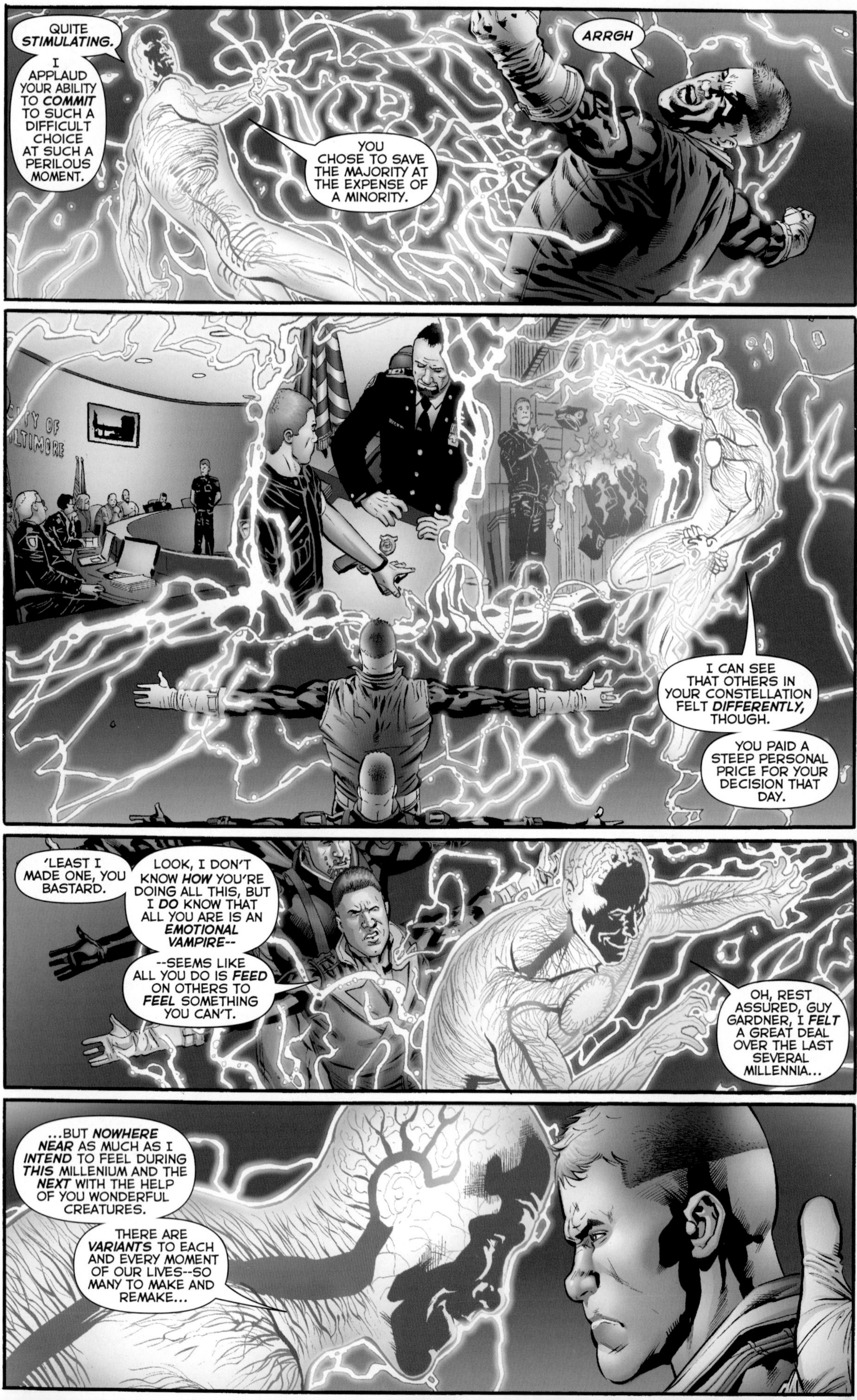
QUITE STIMULATING.
I APPLAUD YOUR ABILITY TO COMMIT TO SUCH A DIFFICULT CHOICE AT SUCH A PERILOUS MOMENT.
YOU CHOSE TO SAVE THE MAJORITY AT THE EXPENSE OF A MINORITY.
ARRGH
CITY OF BALTIMORE
I CAN SEE THAT OTHERS IN YOUR CONSTELLATION FELT DIFFERENTLY, THOUGH.
YOU PAID A STEEP PERSONAL PRICE FOR YOUR DECISION THAT DAY.
'LEAST I MADE ONE, YOU BASTARD.
LOOK, I DON'T KNOW HOW YOU'RE DOING ALL THIS, BUT I DO KNOW THAT ALL YOU ARE IS AN EMOTIONAL VAMPIRE--
--SEEMS LIKE ALL YOU DO IS FEED ON OTHERS TO FEEL SOMETHING YOU CAN'T.
OH, REST ASSURED, GUY GARDNER, I FELT A GREAT DEAL OVER THE LAST SEVERAL MILLENNIA...
...BUT NOWHERE NEAR AS MUCH AS I INTEND TO FEEL DURING THIS MILLENIUM AND THE NEXT WITH THE HELP OF YOU WONDERFUL CREATURES.
THERE ARE VARIANTS TO EACH AND EVERY MOMENT OF OUR LIVES--SO MANY TO MAKE AND REMAKE...

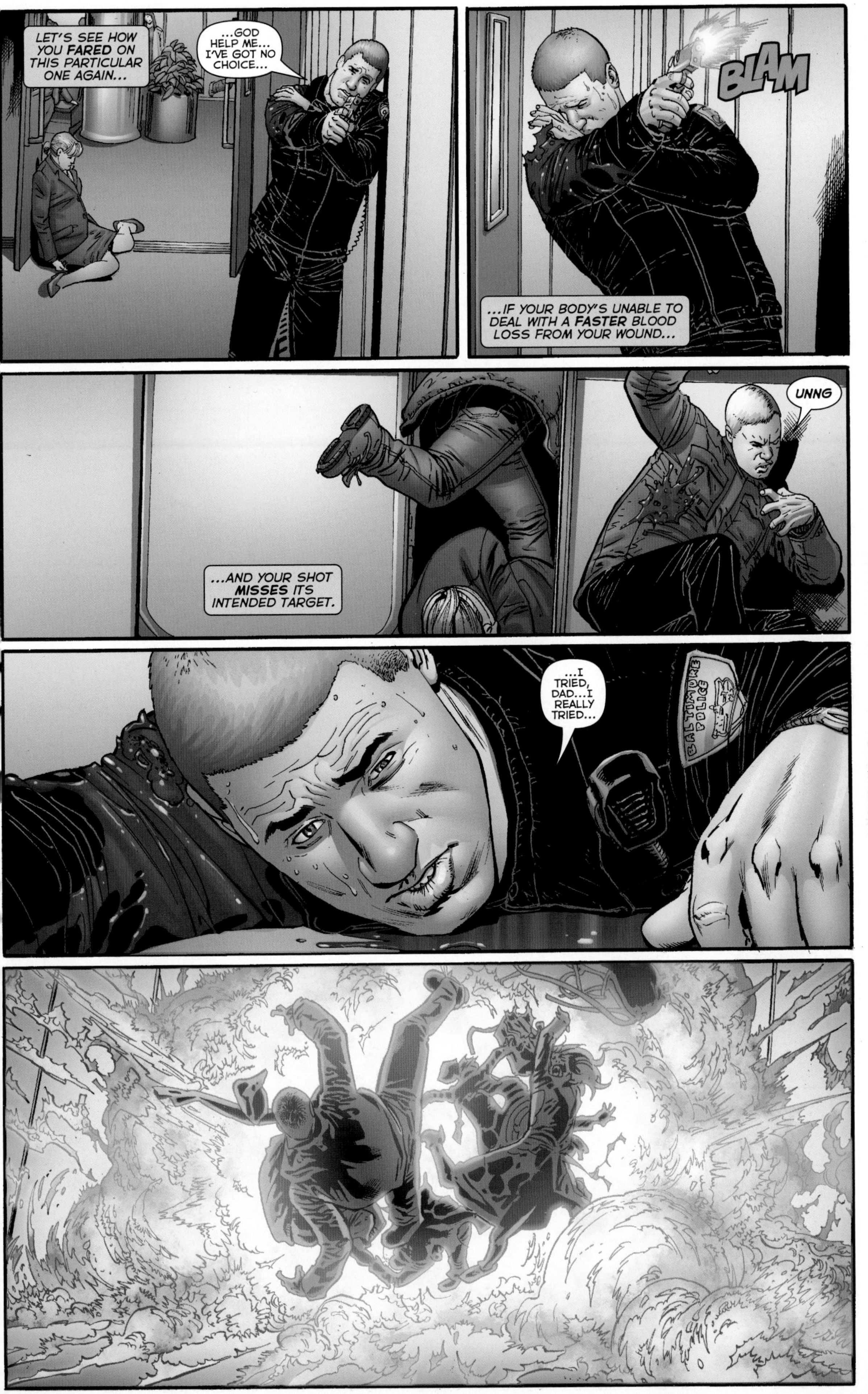
LET'S SEE HOW YOU FARED ON THIS PARTICULAR ONE AGAIN...
...GOD HELP ME... I'VE GOT NO CHOICE...
BLAM
...IF YOUR BODY'S UNABLE TO DEAL WITH A FASTER BLOOD LOSS FROM YOUR WOUND...
UNNG
...AND YOUR SHOT MISSES ITS INTENDED TARGET.
...I TRIED, DAD...I REALLY TRIED...
BALTIMORE POLICE

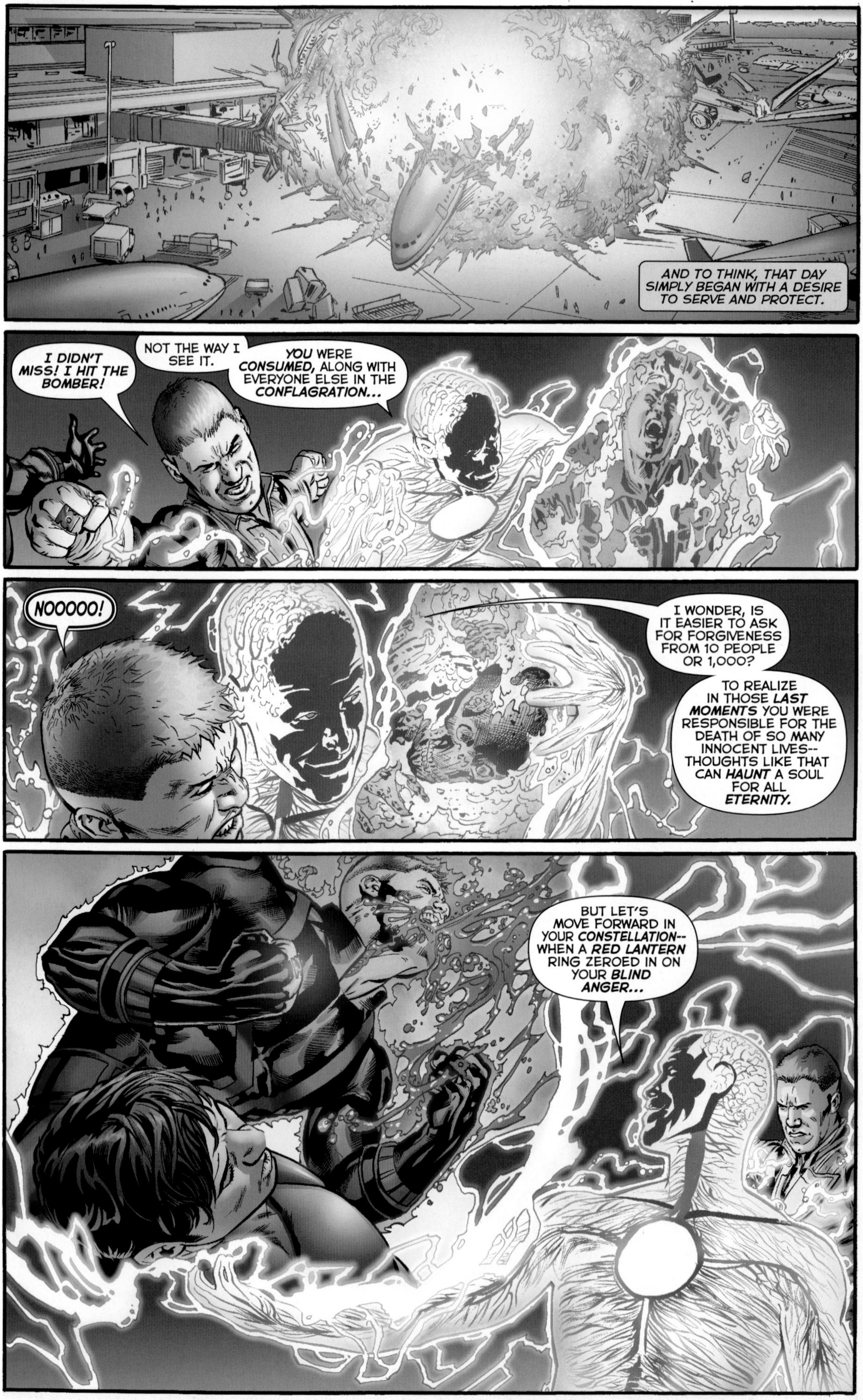
AND TO THINK, THAT DAY SIMPLY BEGAN WITH A DESIRE TO SERVE AND PROTECT.
I DIDN'T MISS! I HIT THE BOMBER!
NOT THE WAY I SEE IT.
YOU WERE CONSUMED, ALONG WITH EVERYONE ELSE IN THE CONFLAGRATION...
NOOOOO!
I WONDER, IS IT EASIER TO ASK FOR FORGIVENESS FROM 10 PEOPLE OR 1,000?
TO REALIZE IN THOSE LAST MOMENTS YOU WERE RESPONSIBLE FOR THE DEATH OF SO MANY INNOCENT LIVES-- THOUGHTS LIKE THAT CAN HAUNT A SOUL FOR ALL ETERNITY.
BUT LET'S MOVE FORWARD IN YOUR CONSTELLATION-- WHEN A RED LANTERN RING ZEROED IN ON YOUR BLIND ANGER...

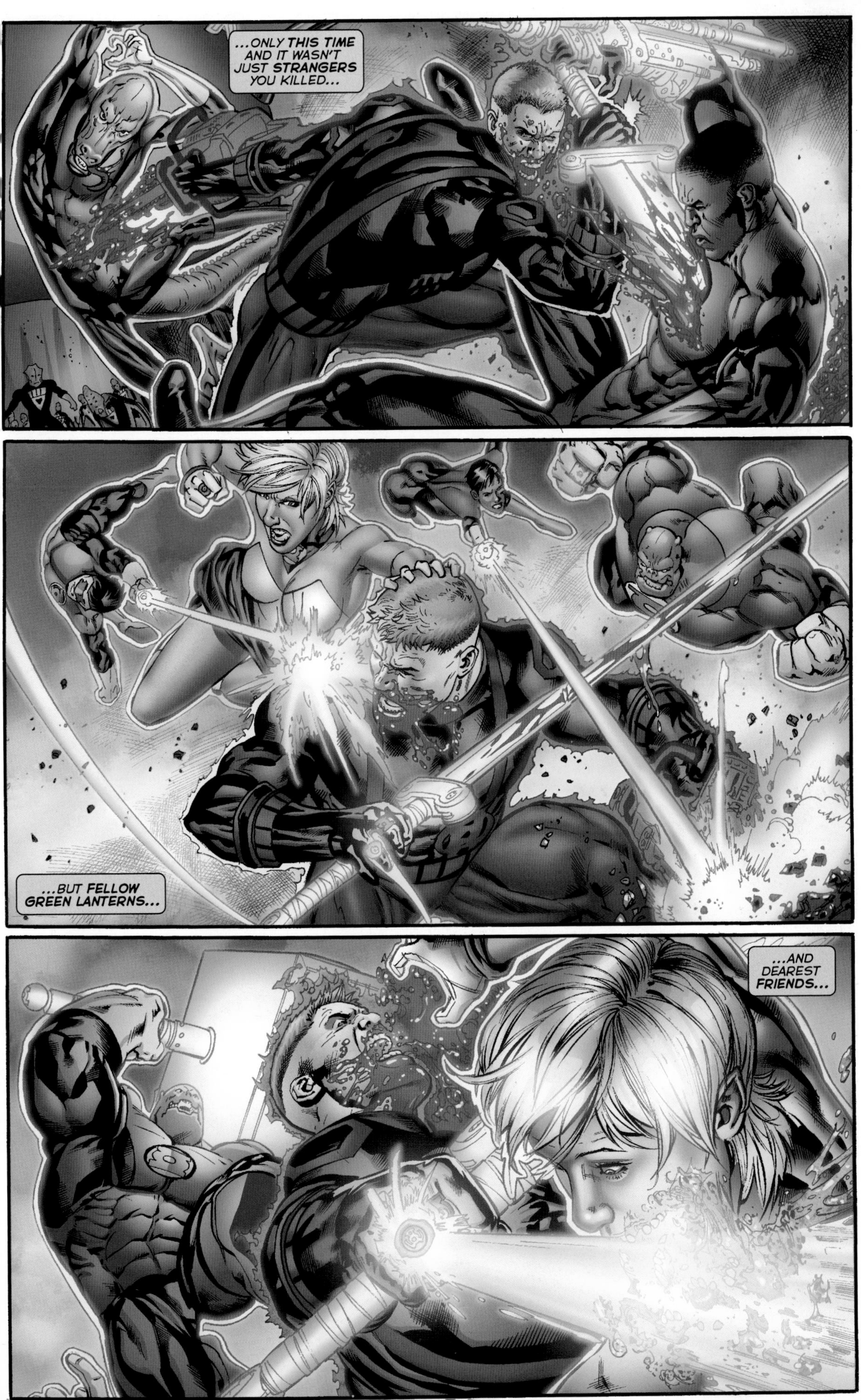
...ONLY THIS TIME AND IT WASN'T JUST STRANGERS YOU KILLED...
...BUT FELLOW GREEN LANTERNS...
...AND DEAREST FRIENDS...

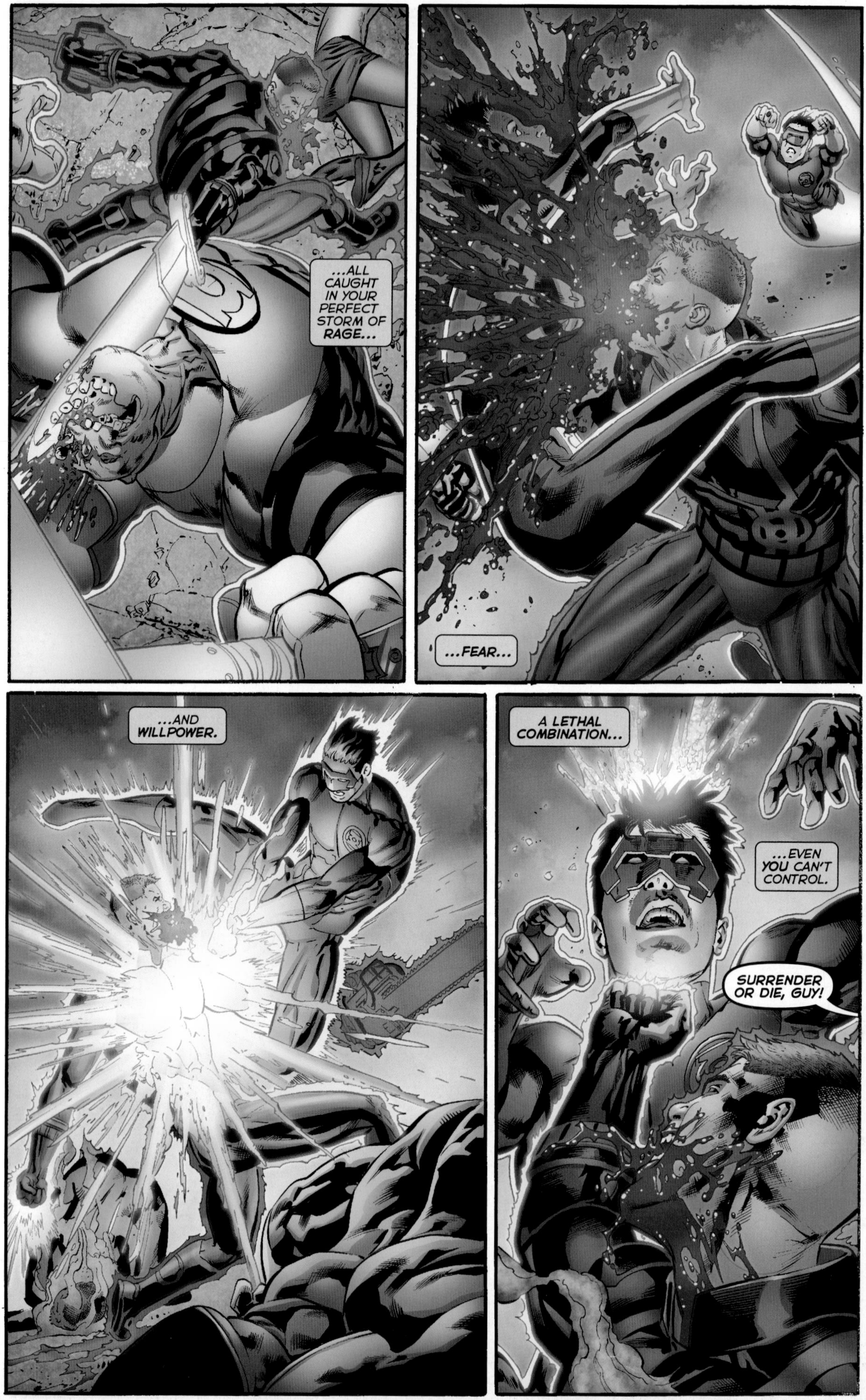
...ALL CAUGHT IN YOUR PERFECT STORM OF RAGE...
...FEAR...
...AND WILLPOWER.
A LETHAL COMBINATION...
...EVEN YOU CAN'T CONTROL.
SURRENDER OR DIE, GUY!

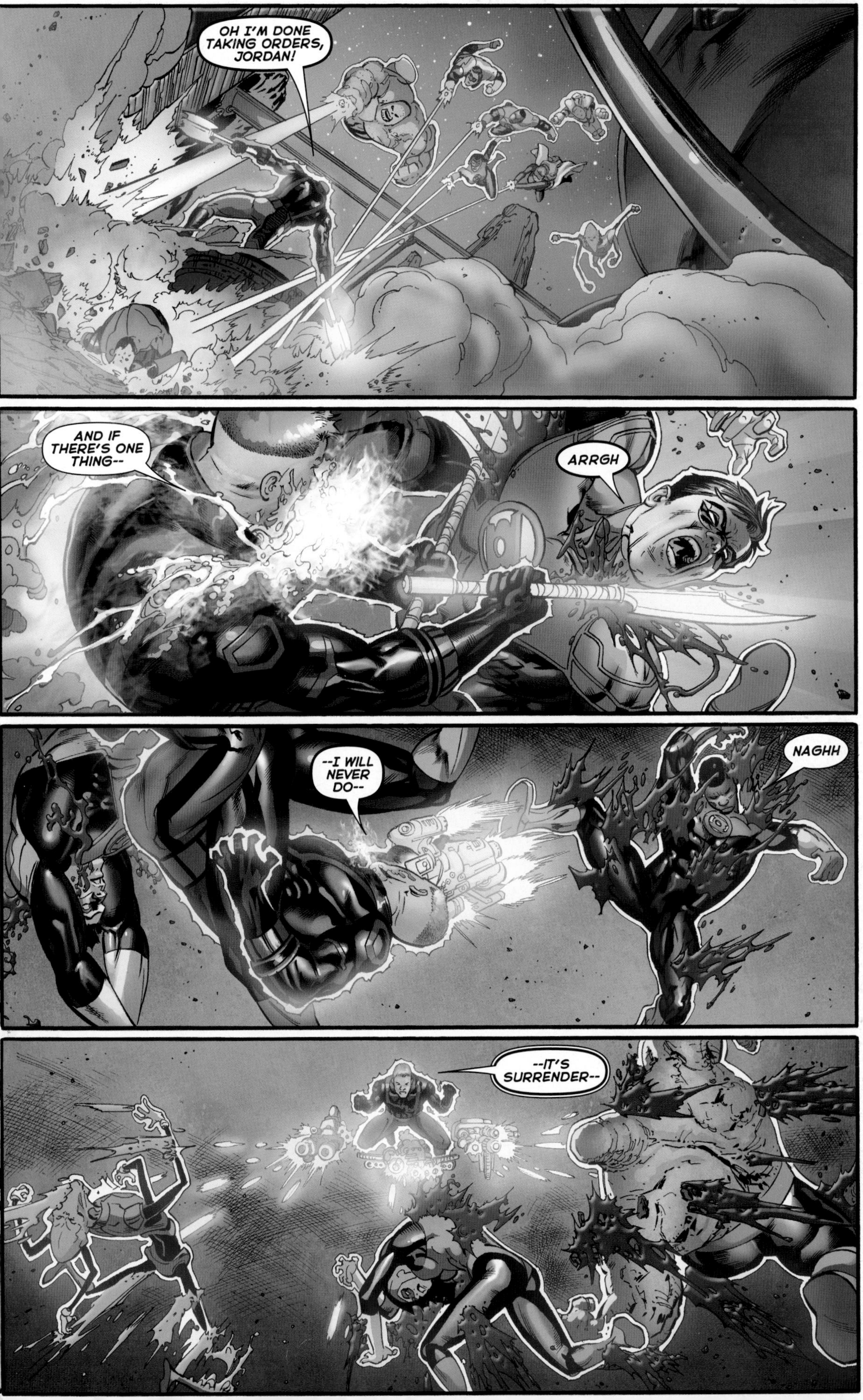
OH I'M DONE TAKING ORDERS, JORDAN!
AND IF THERE'S ONE THING--
ARRGH
--I WILL NEVER DO--
NAGHH
--IT'S SURRENDER--

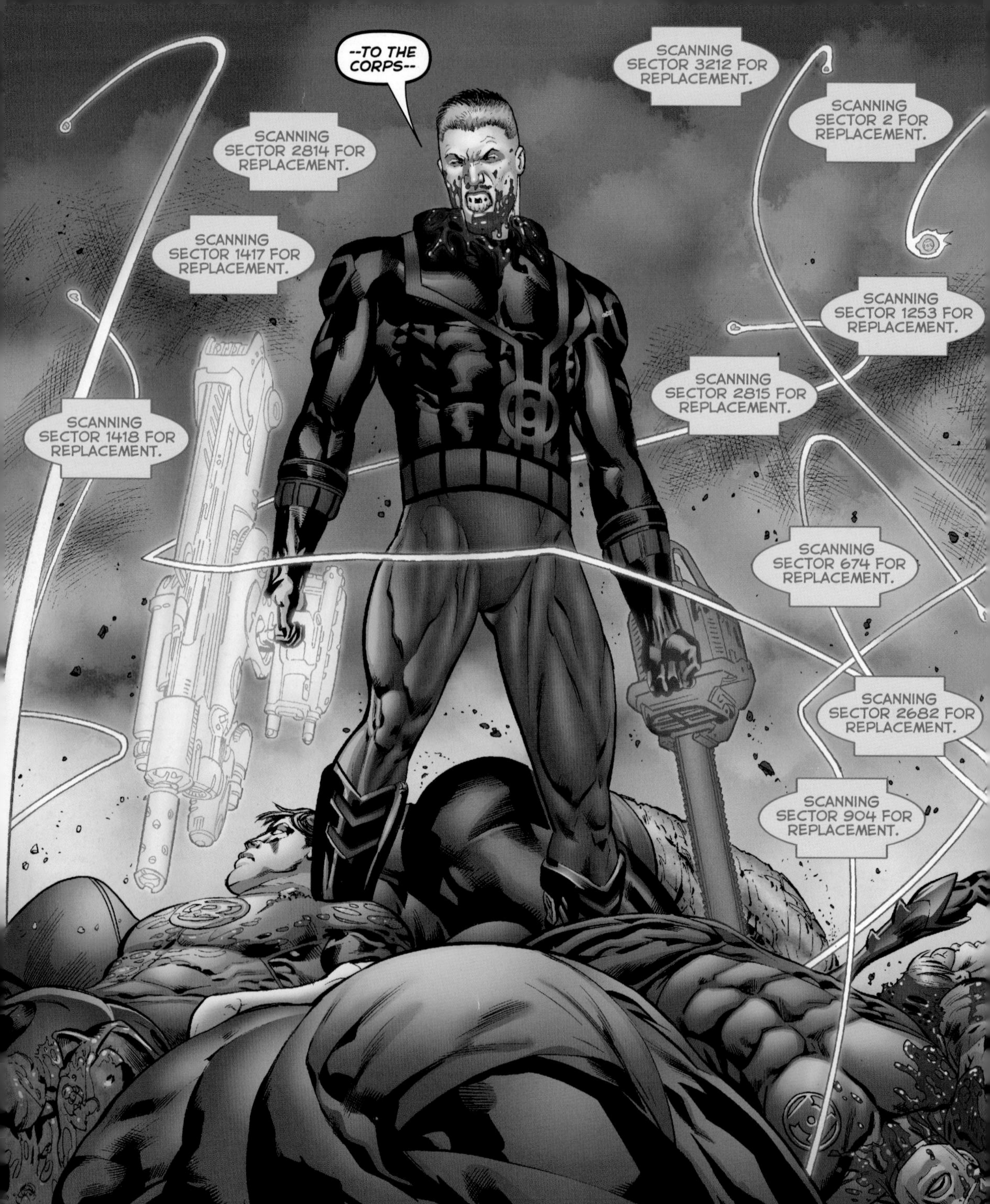
--TO THE CORPS--
SCANNING SECTOR 3212 FOR REPLACEMENT.
SCANNING SECTOR 2 FOR REPLACEMENT.
SCANNING SECTOR 2814 FOR REPLACEMENT.
SCANNING SECTOR 1417 FOR REPLACEMENT.
SCANNING SECTOR 1253 FOR REPLACEMENT.
SCANNING SECTOR 2815 FOR REPLACEMENT.
SCANNING SECTOR 1418 FOR REPLACEMENT.
SCANNING SECTOR 674 FOR REPLACEMENT.
SCANNING SECTOR 2682 FOR REPLACEMENT.
SCANNING SECTOR 904 FOR REPLACEMENT.

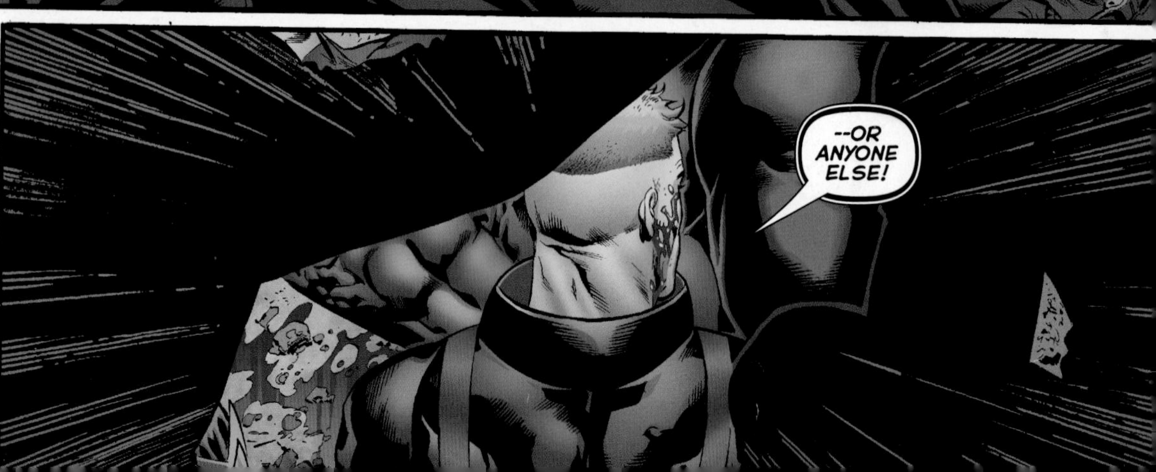
--OR ANYONE ELSE!

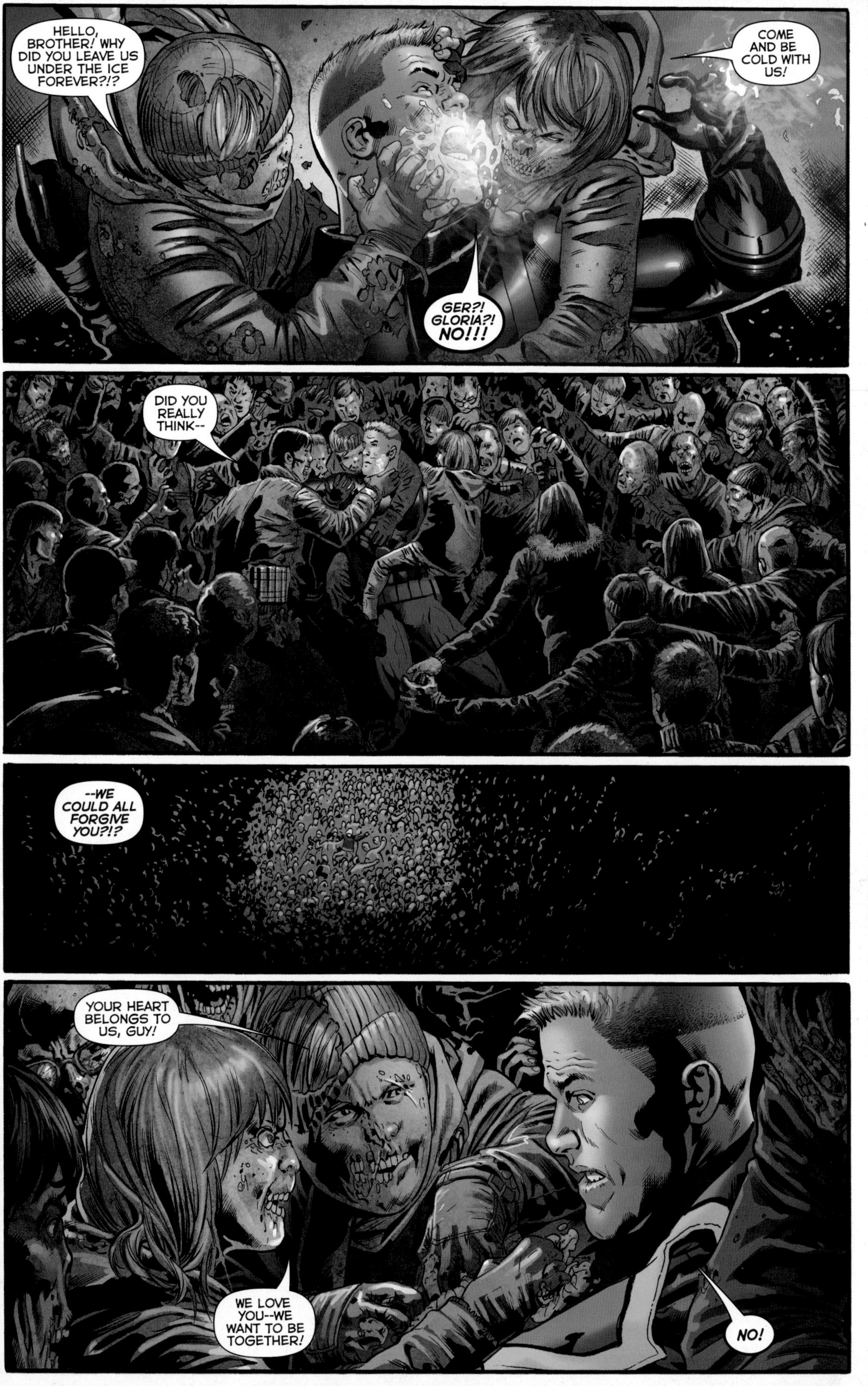
HELLO, BROTHER! WHY DID YOU LEAVE US UNDER THE ICE FOREVER?!?
COME AND BE COLD WITH US!
GER?! GLORIA?! NO!!!
DID YOU REALLY THINK--
--WE COULD ALL FORGIVE YOU?!?
YOUR HEART BELONGS TO US, GUY!
WE LOVE YOU--WE WANT TO BE TOGETHER!
NO!

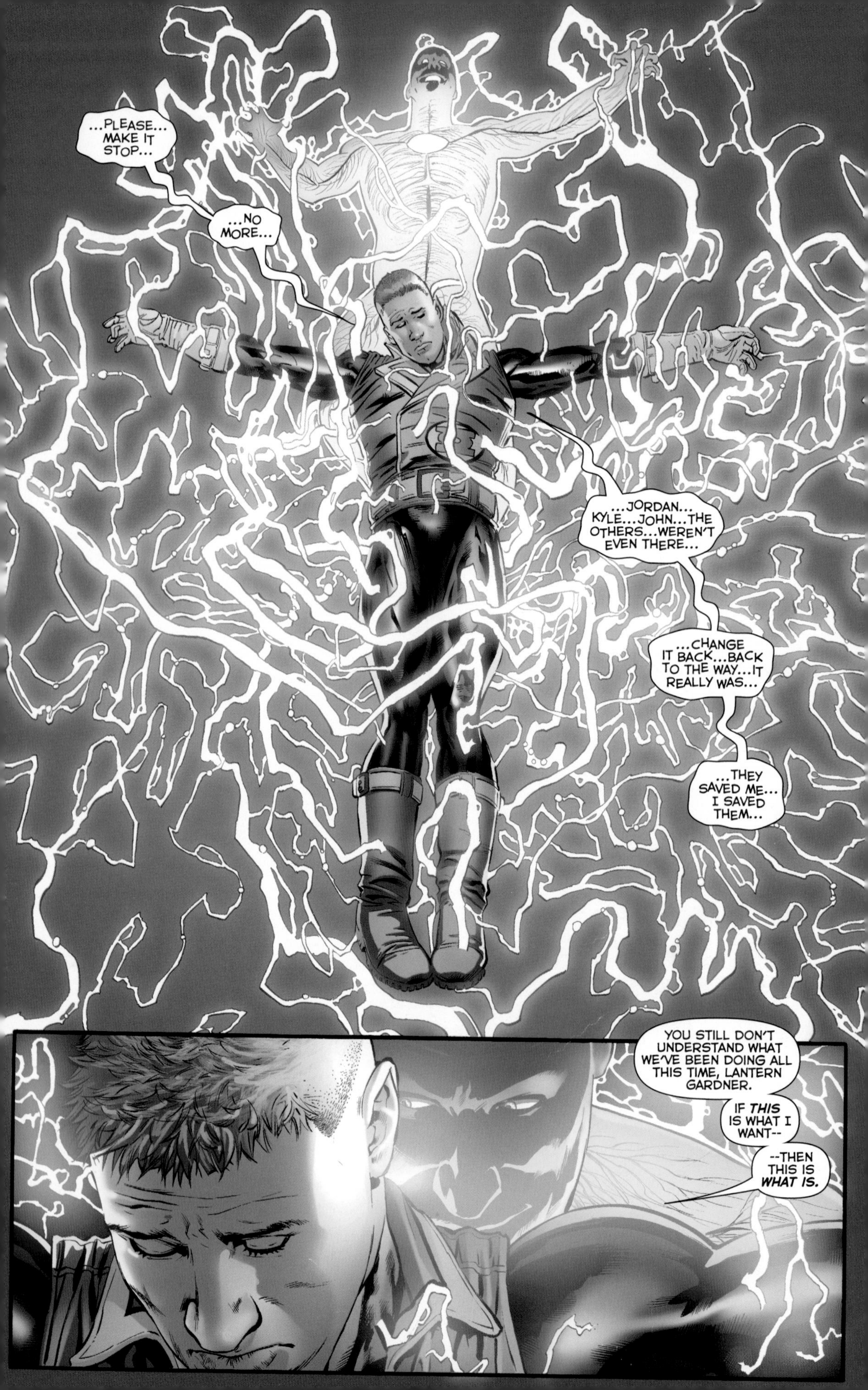
...PLEASE... MAKE IT STOP...
...NO MORE...
...JORDAN... KYLE...JOHN...THE OTHERS...WEREN'T EVEN THERE...
...CHANGE IT BACK...BACK TO THE WAY...IT REALLY WAS...
...THEY SAVED ME... I SAVED THEM...
YOU STILL DON'T UNDERSTAND WHAT WE'VE BEEN DOING ALL THIS TIME, LANTERN GARDNER.
IF *THIS* IS WHAT I WANT--
--THEN THIS IS ***WHAT IS.***

PART THREE: 2 REUNIONS & A FUNERAL

TONY BEDARD writer **AARON KUDER** artist

cover art by **AARON KUDER** & **WIL QUINTANA**

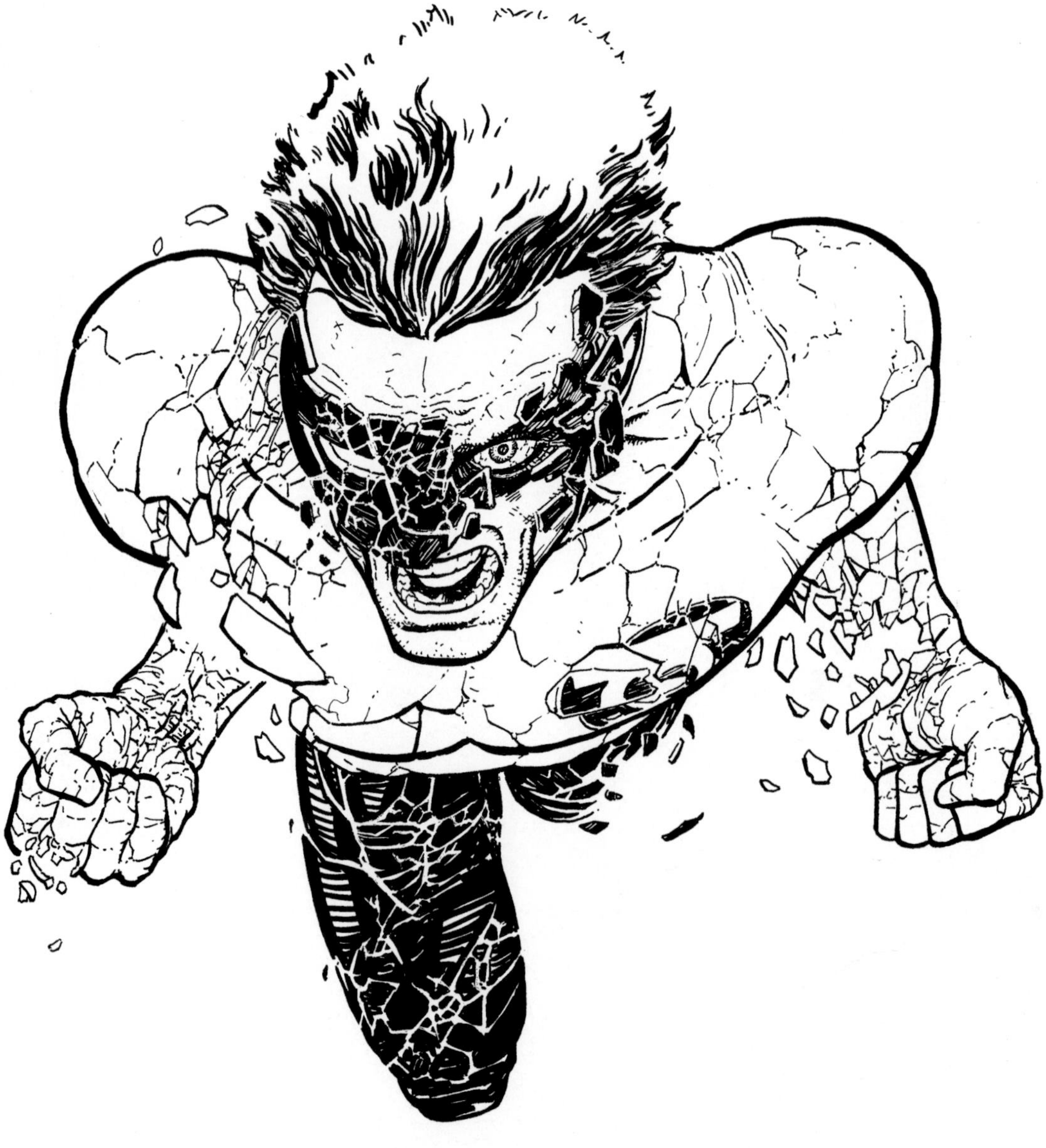

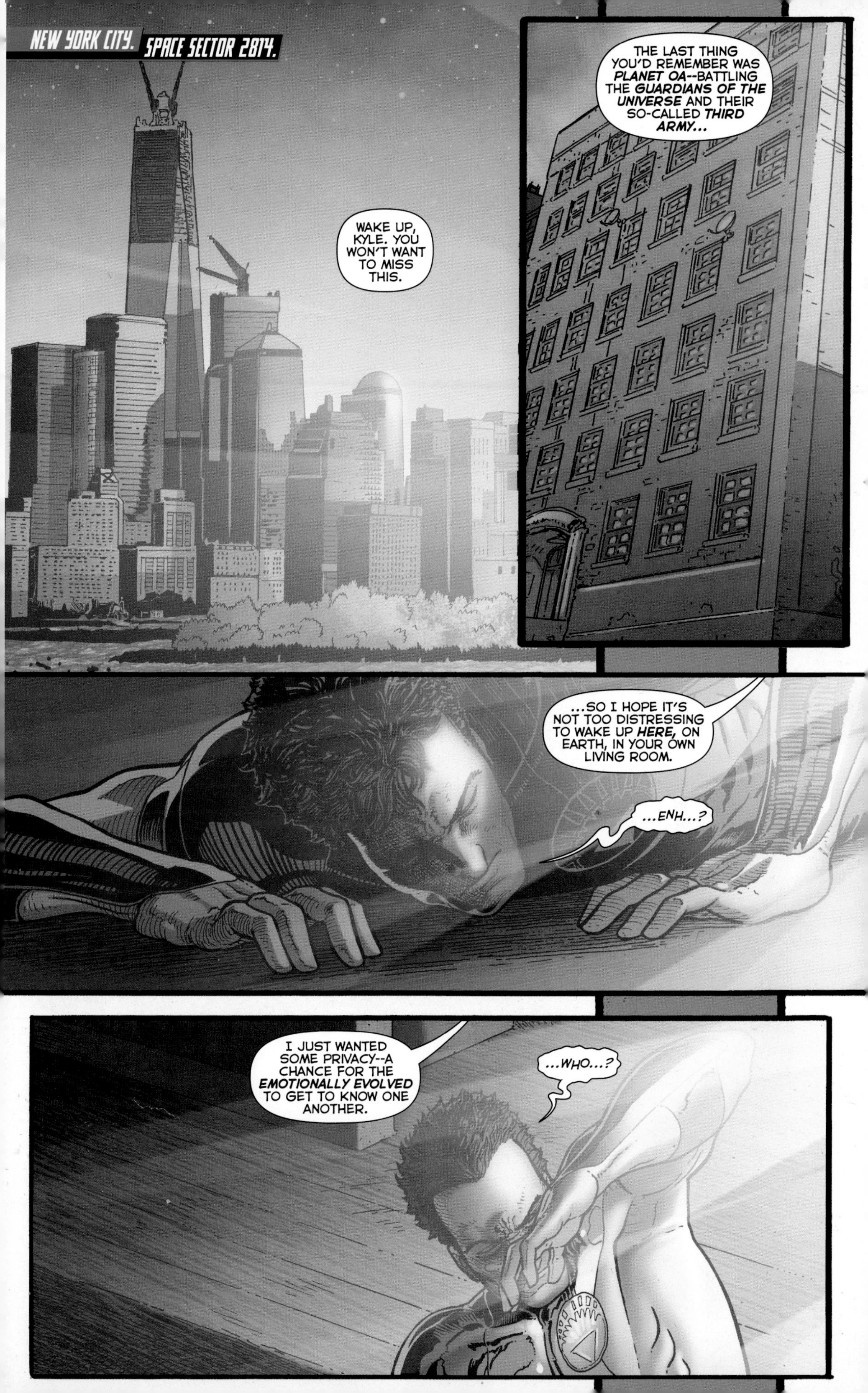
NEW YORK CITY.
SPACE SECTOR 2814.
WAKE UP, KYLE. YOU WON'T WANT TO MISS THIS.
THE LAST THING YOU'D REMEMBER WAS PLANET OA--BATTLING THE GUARDIANS OF THE UNIVERSE AND THEIR SO-CALLED THIRD ARMY...
...SO I HOPE IT'S NOT TOO DISTRESSING TO WAKE UP HERE, ON EARTH, IN YOUR OWN LIVING ROOM.
...ENH...?
I JUST WANTED SOME PRIVACY--A CHANCE FOR THE EMOTIONALLY EVOLVED TO GET TO KNOW ONE ANOTHER.
...WHO...?

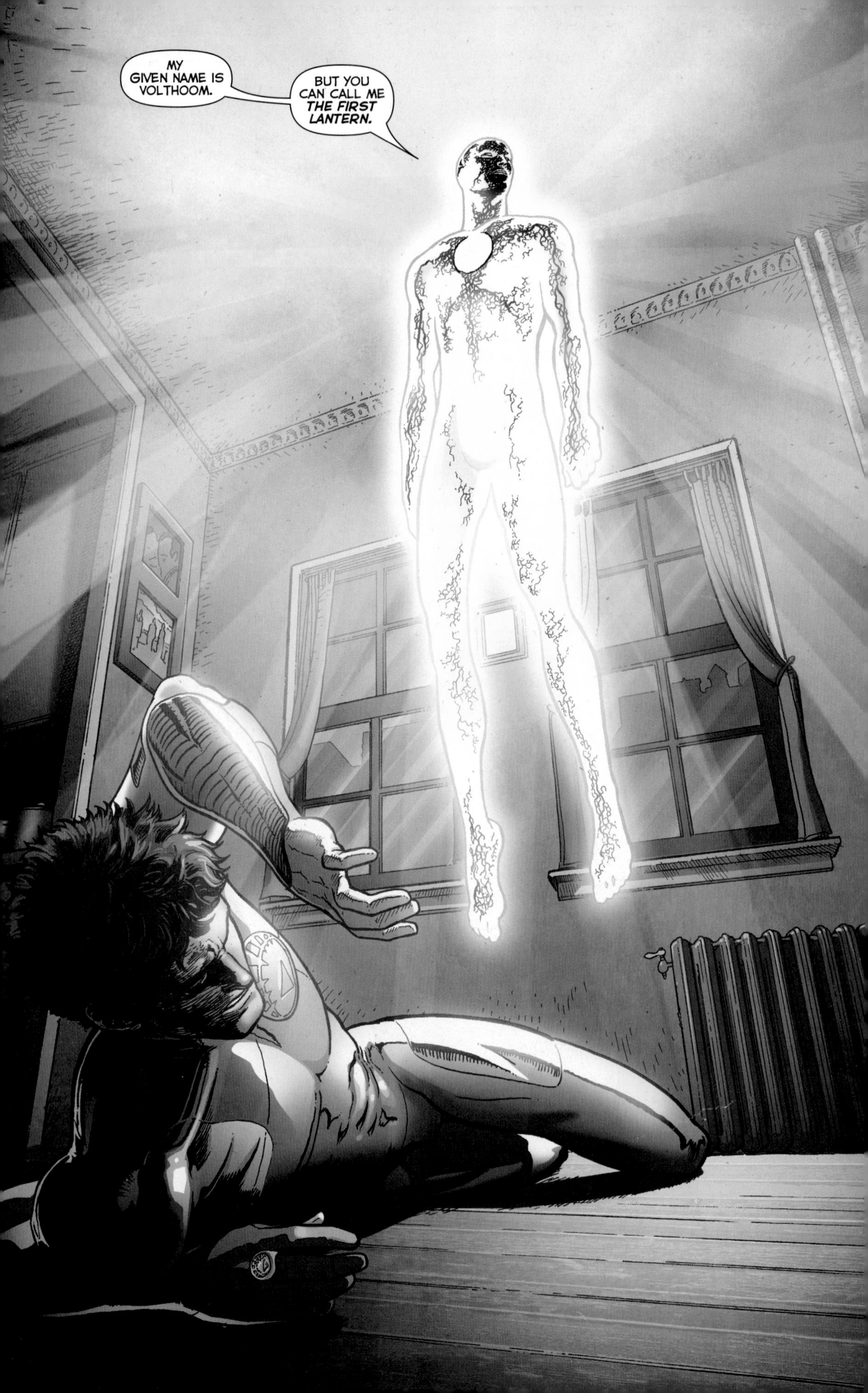
MY GIVEN NAME IS VOLTHOOM.
BUT YOU CAN CALL ME *THE FIRST LANTERN.*

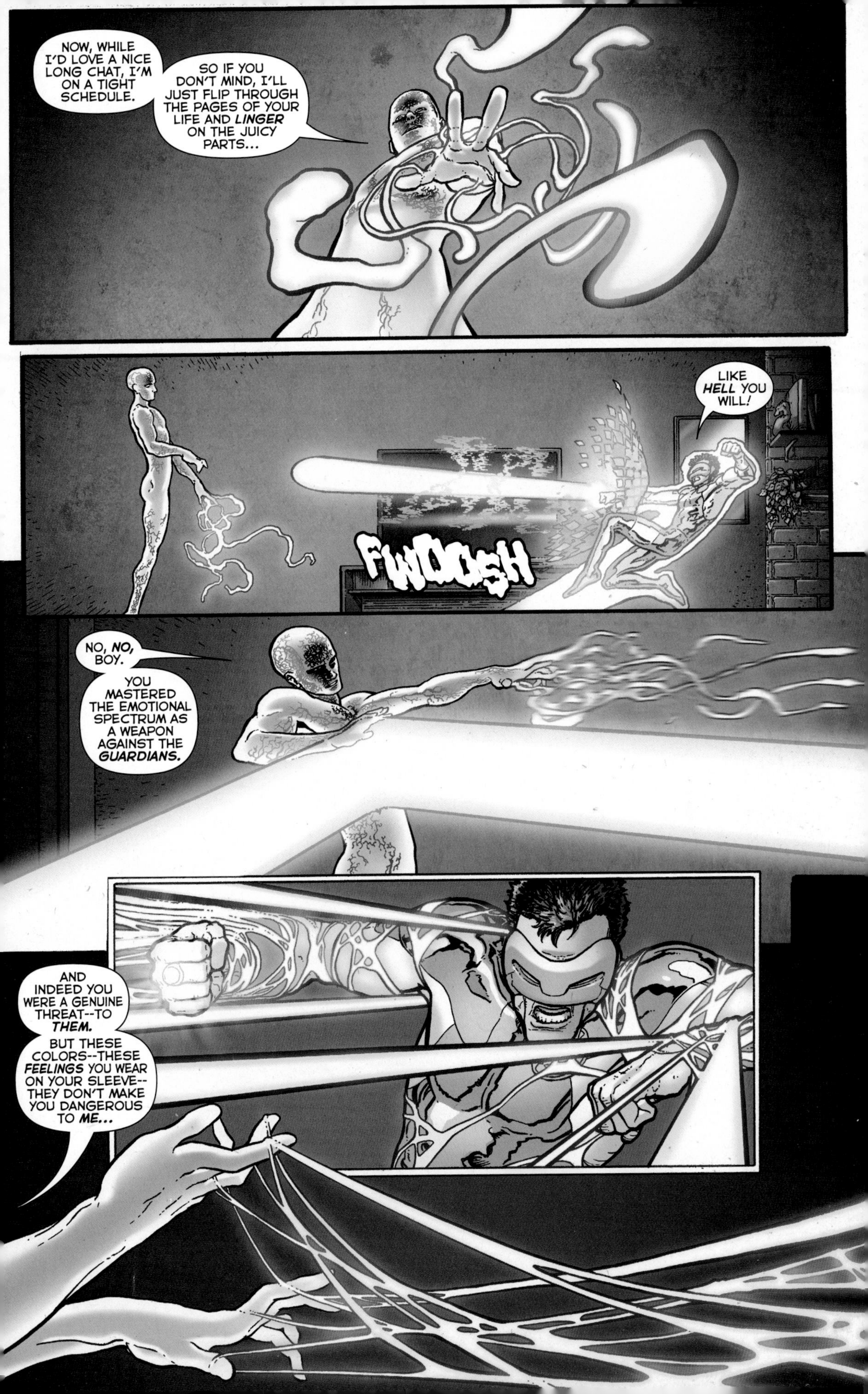
NOW, WHILE I'D LOVE A NICE LONG CHAT, I'M ON A TIGHT SCHEDULE.
SO IF YOU DON'T MIND, I'LL JUST FLIP THROUGH THE PAGES OF YOUR LIFE AND *LINGER* ON THE JUICY PARTS...
LIKE *HELL* YOU WILL!
FWOOSH
NO, *NO,* BOY.
YOU MASTERED THE EMOTIONAL SPECTRUM AS A WEAPON AGAINST THE *GUARDIANS.*
AND INDEED YOU WERE A GENUINE THREAT--TO *THEM.*
BUT THESE COLORS--THESE *FEELINGS* YOU WEAR ON YOUR SLEEVE--THEY DON'T MAKE YOU DANGEROUS TO *ME...*

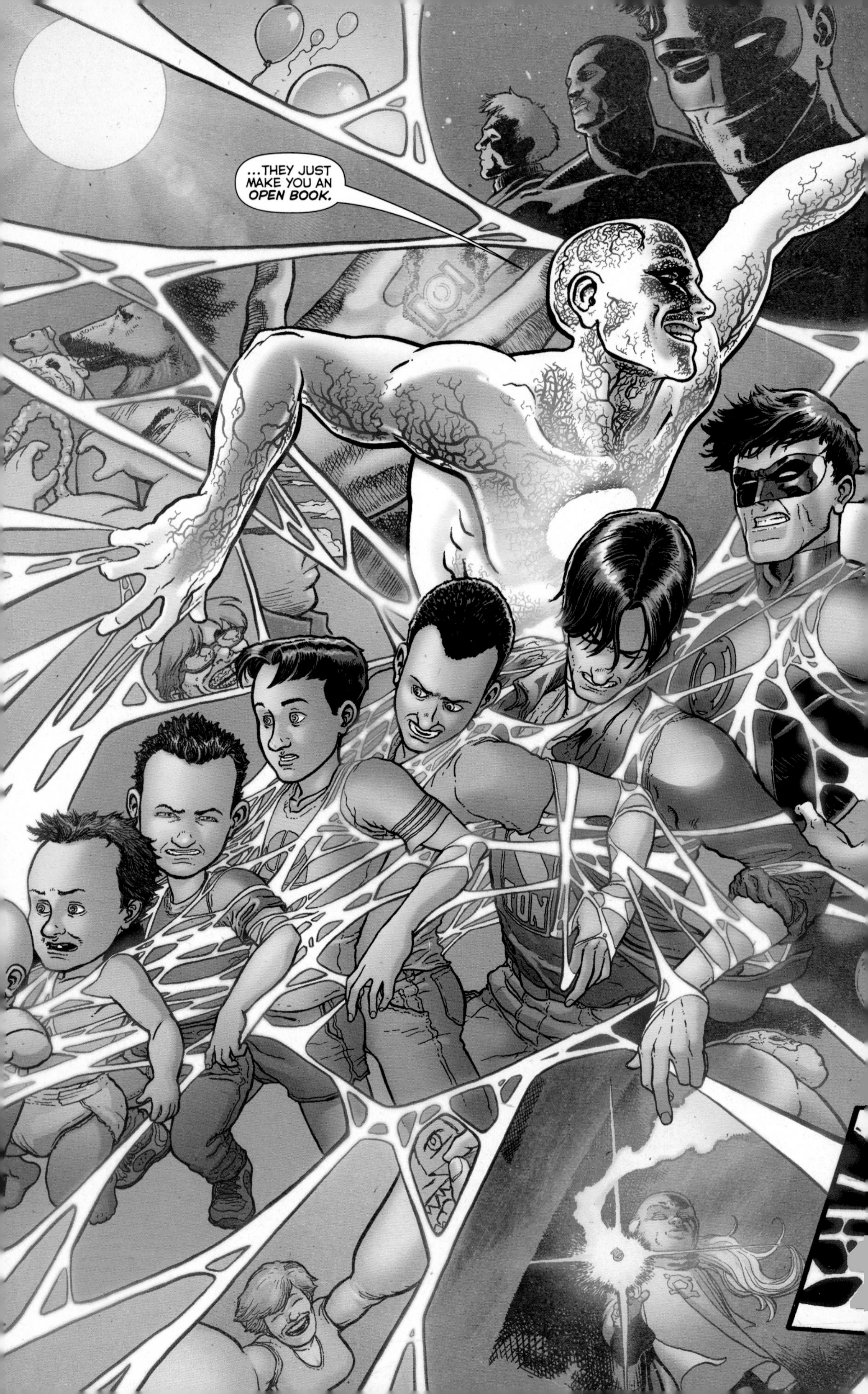
...THEY JUST MAKE YOU AN *OPEN BOOK*.

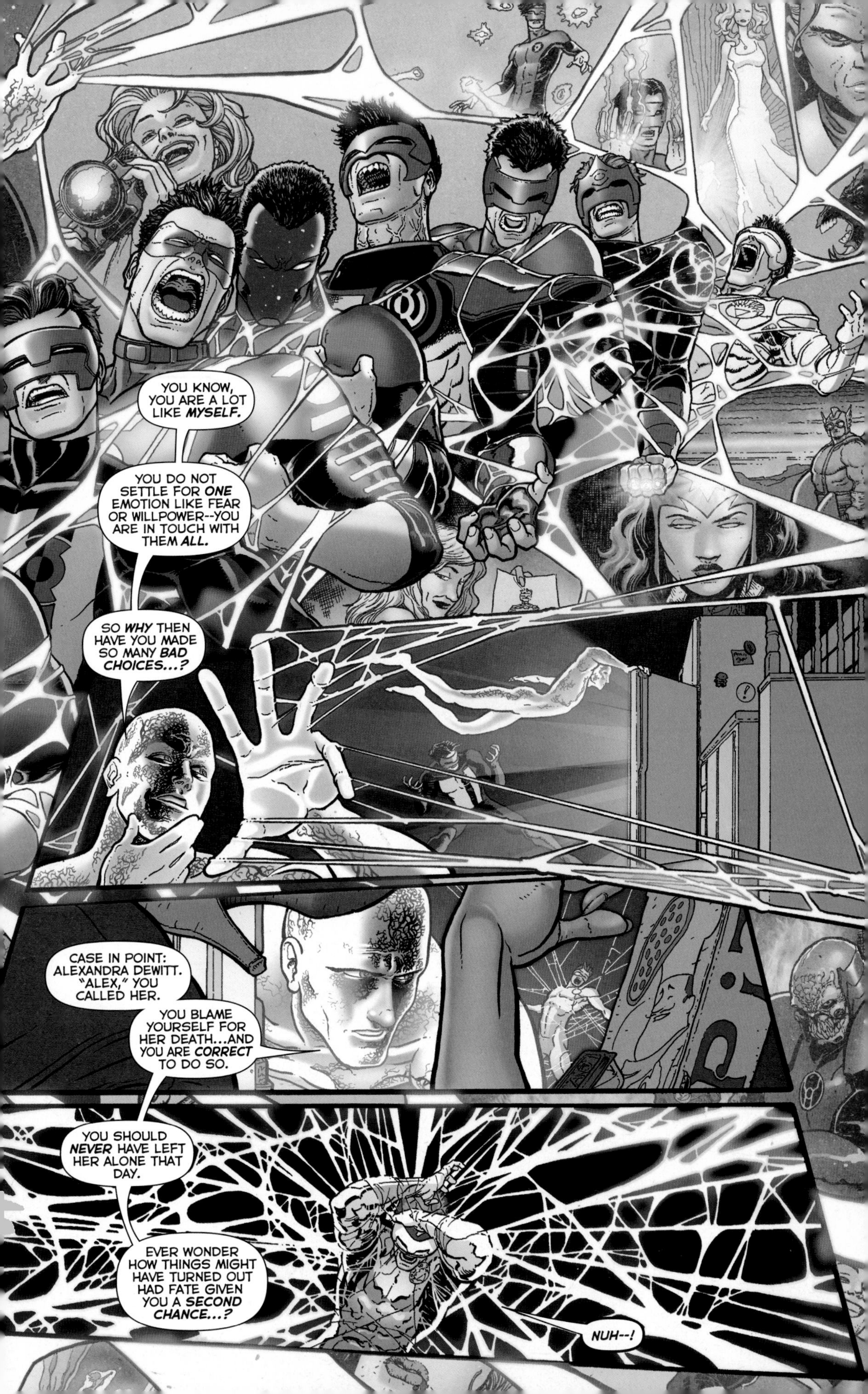
YOU KNOW, YOU ARE A LOT LIKE MYSELF.
YOU DO NOT SETTLE FOR ONE EMOTION LIKE FEAR OR WILLPOWER--YOU ARE IN TOUCH WITH THEM ALL.
SO WHY THEN HAVE YOU MADE SO MANY BAD CHOICES...?
CASE IN POINT: ALEXANDRA DEWITT. "ALEX," YOU CALLED HER.
YOU BLAME YOURSELF FOR HER DEATH...AND YOU ARE CORRECT TO DO SO.
YOU SHOULD NEVER HAVE LEFT HER ALONE THAT DAY.
EVER WONDER HOW THINGS MIGHT HAVE TURNED OUT HAD FATE GIVEN YOU A SECOND CHANCE...?
NUH--!

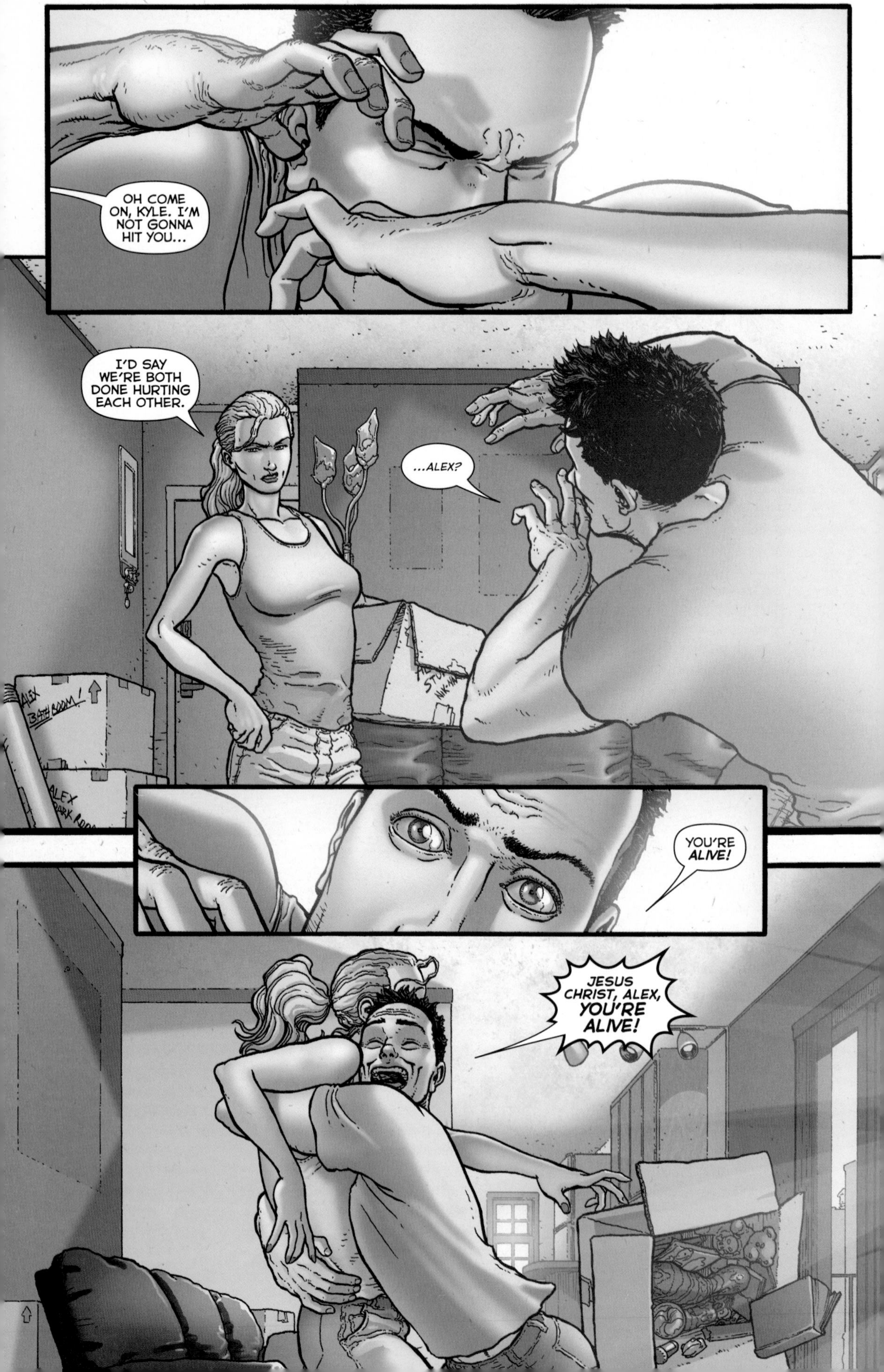

OH COME ON, KYLE. I'M NOT GONNA HIT YOU...
I'D SAY WE'RE BOTH DONE HURTING EACH OTHER.
...ALEX?
ALEX BATHROOM!
YOU'RE ALIVE!
JESUS CHRIST, ALEX, YOU'RE ALIVE!

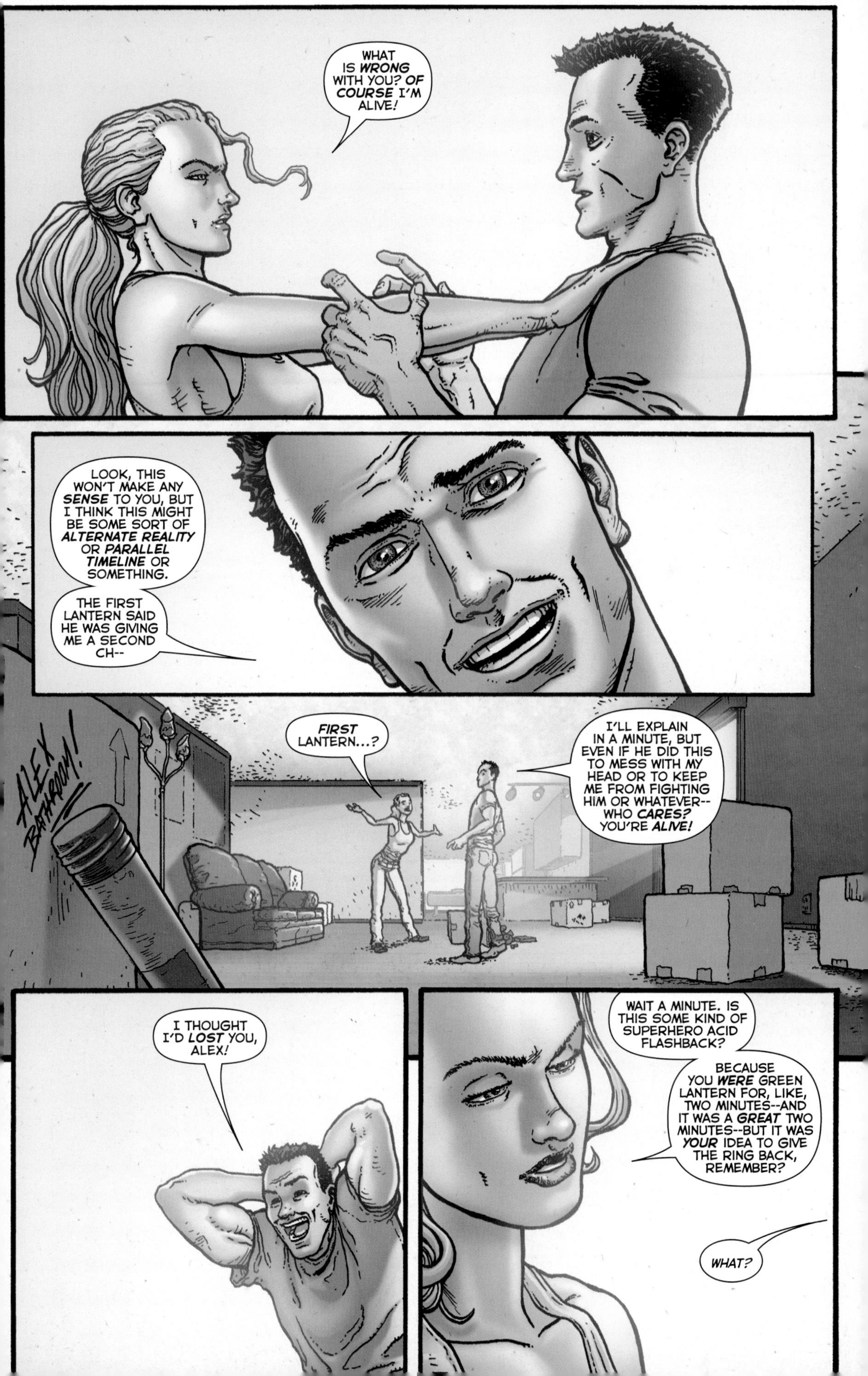
WHAT IS WRONG WITH YOU? OF COURSE I'M ALIVE!
LOOK, THIS WON'T MAKE ANY SENSE TO YOU, BUT I THINK THIS MIGHT BE SOME SORT OF ALTERNATE REALITY OR PARALLEL TIMELINE OR SOMETHING.
THE FIRST LANTERN SAID HE WAS GIVING ME A SECOND CH--
ALEX BATHROOM!
FIRST LANTERN...?
I'LL EXPLAIN IN A MINUTE, BUT EVEN IF HE DID THIS TO MESS WITH MY HEAD OR TO KEEP ME FROM FIGHTING HIM OR WHATEVER-- WHO CARES? YOU'RE ALIVE!
I THOUGHT I'D LOST YOU, ALEX!
WAIT A MINUTE. IS THIS SOME KIND OF SUPERHERO ACID FLASHBACK?
BECAUSE YOU WERE GREEN LANTERN FOR, LIKE, TWO MINUTES--AND IT WAS A GREAT TWO MINUTES--BUT IT WAS YOUR IDEA TO GIVE THE RING BACK, REMEMBER?
WHAT?

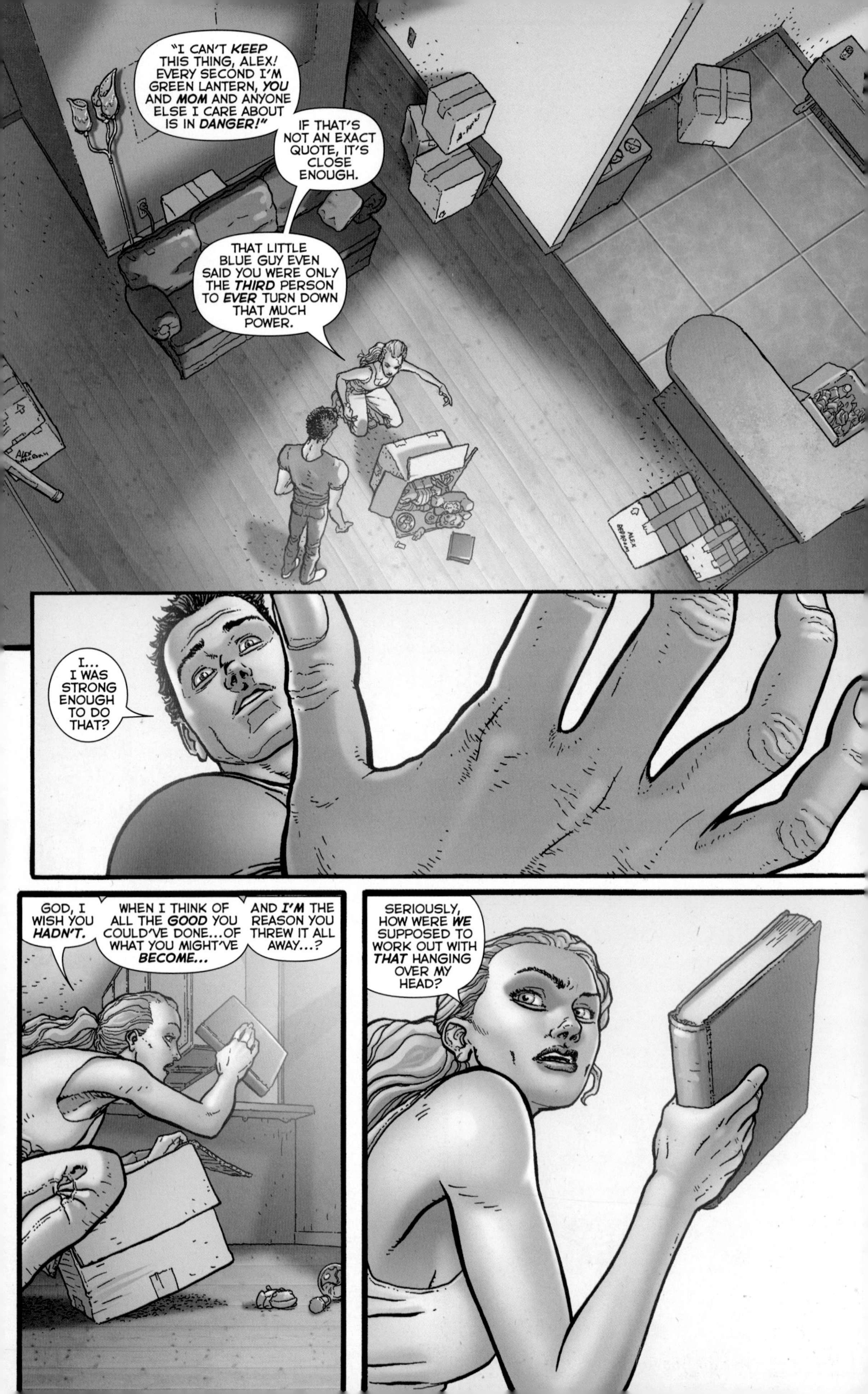

"I CAN'T KEEP THIS THING, ALEX! EVERY SECOND I'M GREEN LANTERN, YOU AND MOM AND ANYONE ELSE I CARE ABOUT IS IN DANGER!"
IF THAT'S NOT AN EXACT QUOTE, IT'S CLOSE ENOUGH.
THAT LITTLE BLUE GUY EVEN SAID YOU WERE ONLY THE THIRD PERSON TO EVER TURN DOWN THAT MUCH POWER.
I... I WAS STRONG ENOUGH TO DO THAT?
GOD, I WISH YOU HADN'T.
WHEN I THINK OF ALL THE GOOD YOU COULD'VE DONE...OF WHAT YOU MIGHT'VE BECOME...
AND I'M THE REASON YOU THREW IT ALL AWAY...?
SERIOUSLY, HOW WERE WE SUPPOSED TO WORK OUT WITH THAT HANGING OVER MY HEAD?

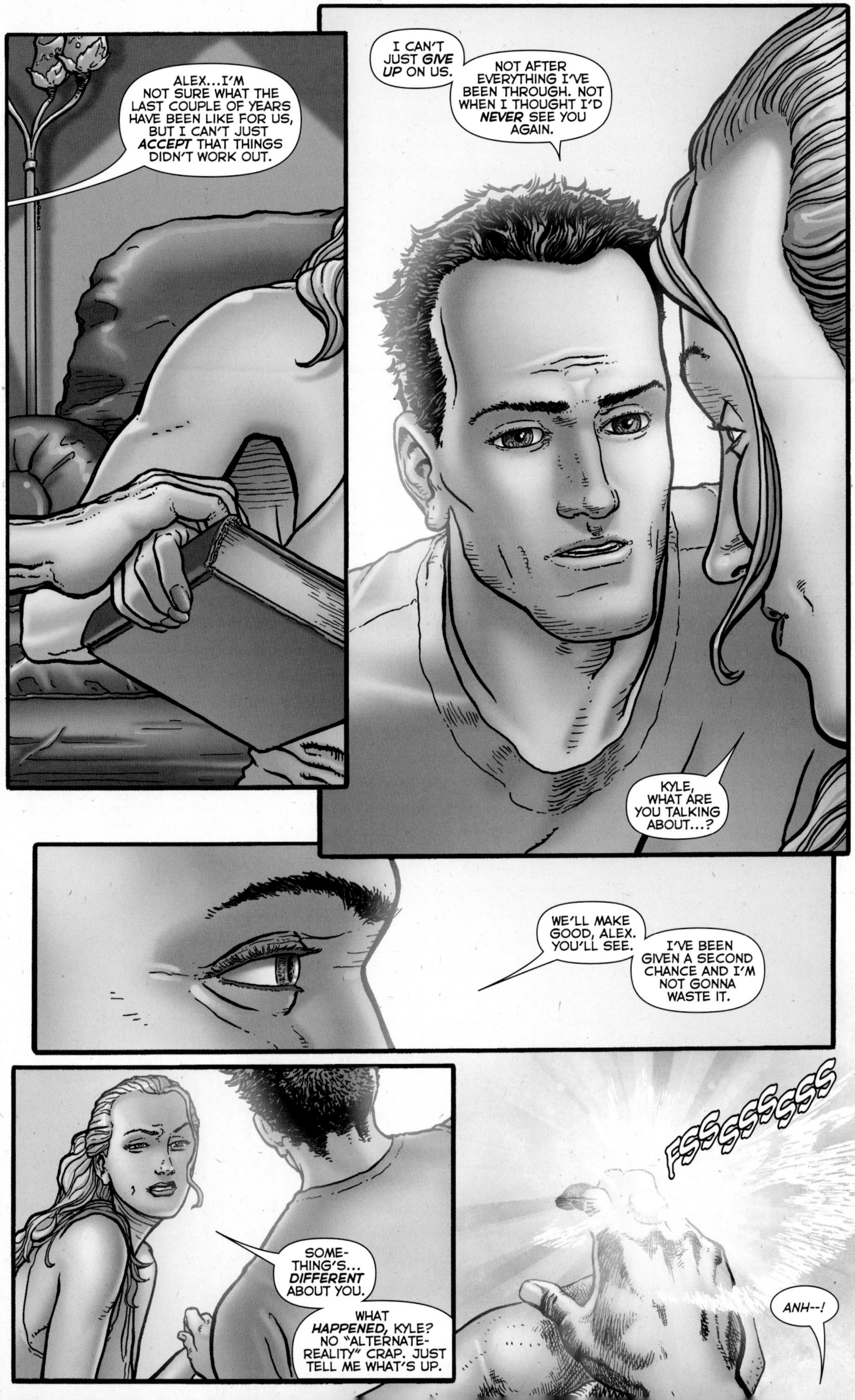
ALEX...I'M NOT SURE WHAT THE LAST COUPLE OF YEARS HAVE BEEN LIKE FOR US, BUT I CAN'T JUST ACCEPT THAT THINGS DIDN'T WORK OUT.
I CAN'T JUST GIVE UP ON US.
NOT AFTER EVERYTHING I'VE BEEN THROUGH. NOT WHEN I THOUGHT I'D NEVER SEE YOU AGAIN.
KYLE, WHAT ARE YOU TALKING ABOUT...?
WE'LL MAKE GOOD, ALEX. YOU'LL SEE.
I'VE BEEN GIVEN A SECOND CHANCE AND I'M NOT GONNA WASTE IT.
SOME-THING'S... DIFFERENT ABOUT YOU.
WHAT HAPPENED, KYLE? NO "ALTERNATE-REALITY" CRAP. JUST TELL ME WHAT'S UP.
FSSSSSSSS
ANH--!

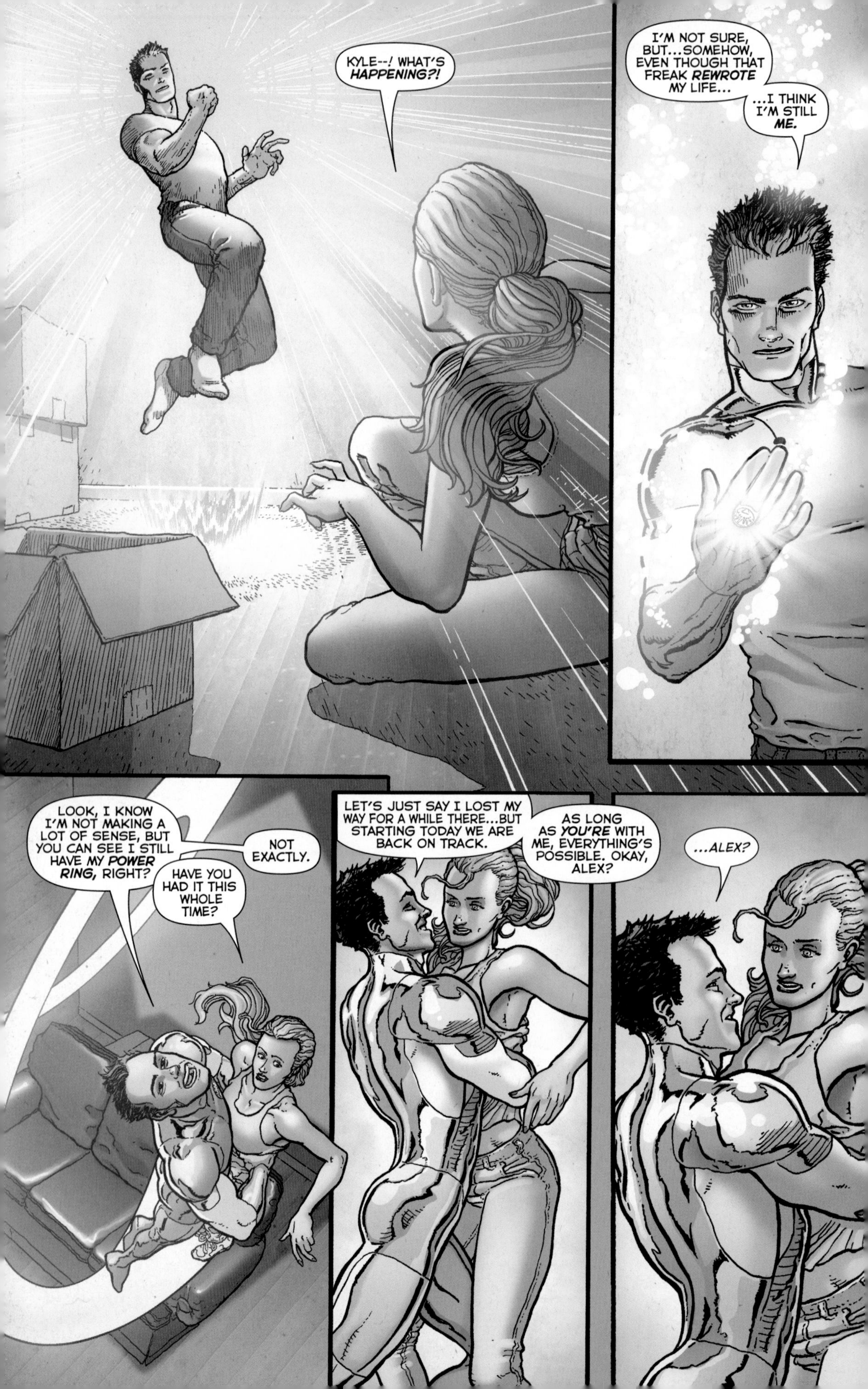

KYLE--! WHAT'S *HAPPENING?!*
I'M NOT SURE, BUT...SOMEHOW, EVEN THOUGH THAT FREAK *REWROTE* MY LIFE...
...I THINK I'M STILL *ME.*
LOOK, I KNOW I'M NOT MAKING A LOT OF SENSE, BUT YOU CAN SEE I STILL HAVE *MY POWER RING,* RIGHT?
NOT EXACTLY.
HAVE YOU HAD IT THIS WHOLE TIME?
LET'S JUST SAY I LOST MY WAY FOR A WHILE THERE...BUT STARTING TODAY WE ARE BACK ON TRACK.
AS LONG AS *YOU'RE* WITH ME, EVERYTHING'S POSSIBLE. OKAY, ALEX?
...ALEX?

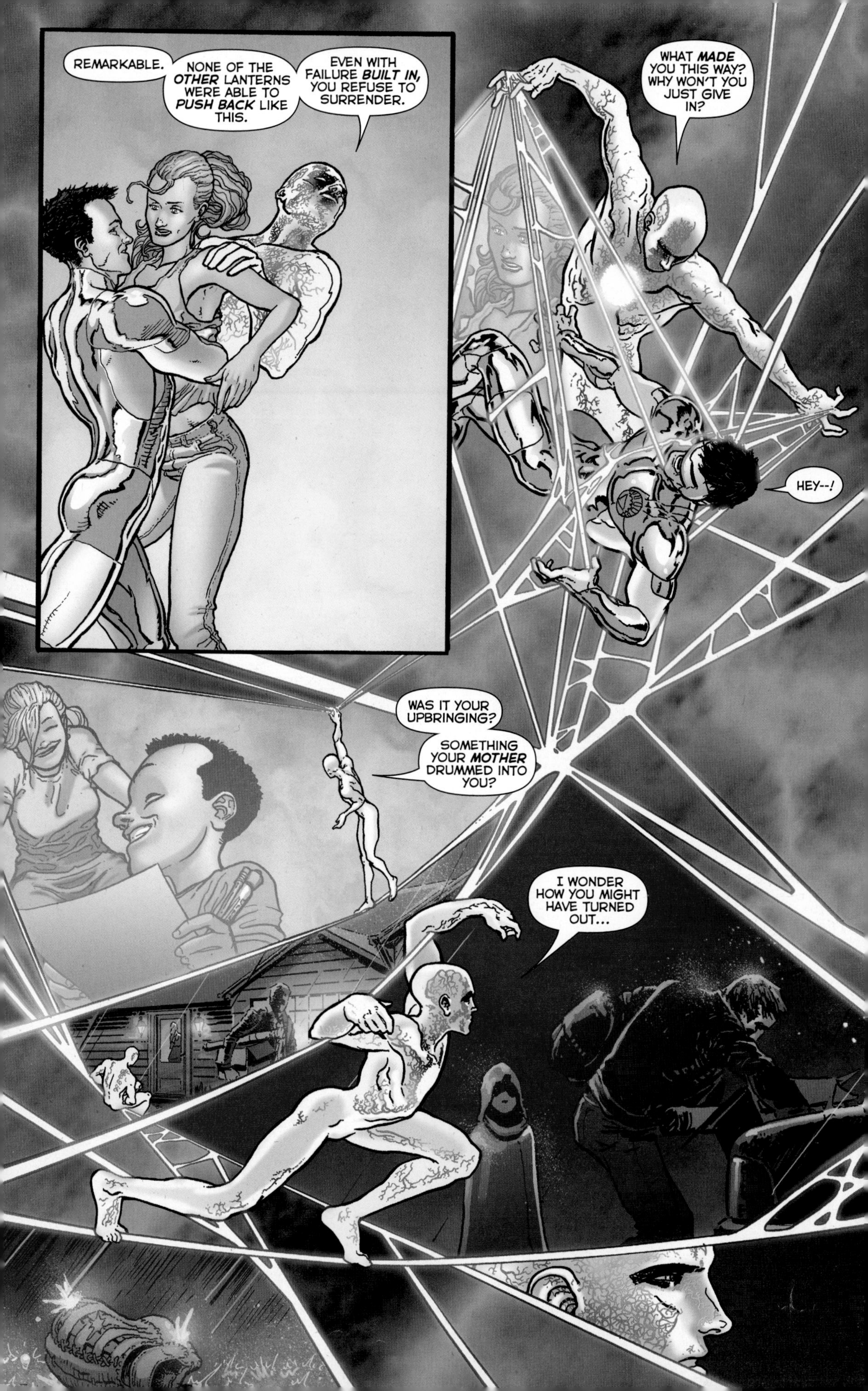
REMARKABLE.
NONE OF THE OTHER LANTERNS WERE ABLE TO PUSH BACK LIKE THIS.
EVEN WITH FAILURE BUILT IN, YOU REFUSE TO SURRENDER.
WHAT MADE YOU THIS WAY? WHY WON'T YOU JUST GIVE IN?
HEY--!
WAS IT YOUR UPBRINGING?
SOMETHING YOUR MOTHER DRUMMED INTO YOU?
I WONDER HOW YOU MIGHT HAVE TURNED OUT...

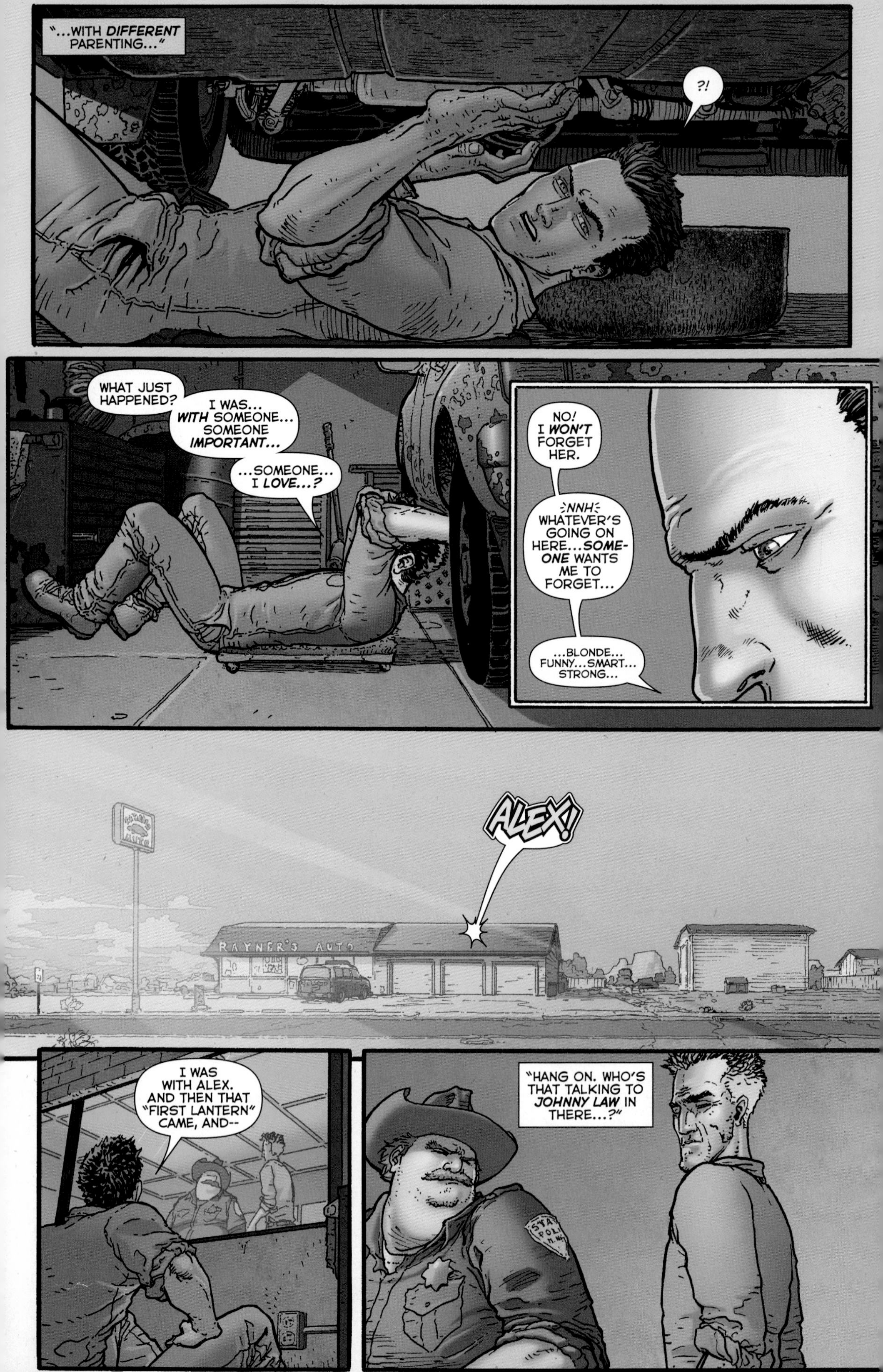
"...WITH DIFFERENT PARENTING..."
?!
WHAT JUST HAPPENED?
I WAS... WITH SOMEONE... SOMEONE IMPORTANT...
...SOMEONE... I LOVE...?
NO! I WON'T FORGET HER.
NNH WHATEVER'S GOING ON HERE...SOMEONE WANTS ME TO FORGET...
...BLONDE... FUNNY...SMART... STRONG...
RAYNER'S AUTO
ALEX!
I WAS WITH ALEX. AND THEN THAT "FIRST LANTERN" CAME, AND--
"HANG ON. WHO'S THAT TALKING TO JOHNNY LAW IN THERE...?"

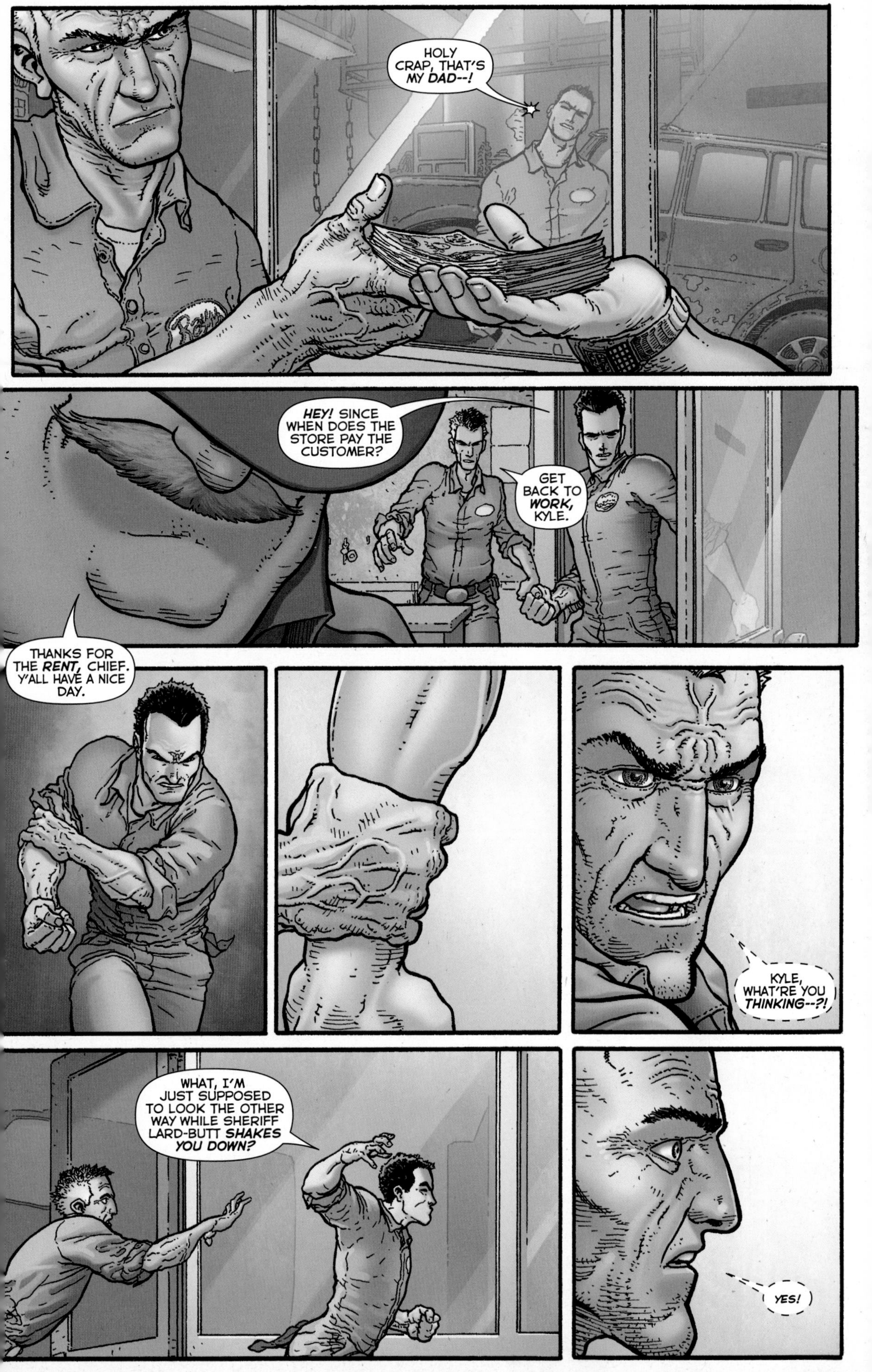
HOLY CRAP, THAT'S MY DAD--!
HEY! SINCE WHEN DOES THE STORE PAY THE CUSTOMER?
GET BACK TO WORK, KYLE.
THANKS FOR THE RENT, CHIEF. Y'ALL HAVE A NICE DAY.
KYLE, WHAT'RE YOU THINKING--?!
WHAT, I'M JUST SUPPOSED TO LOOK THE OTHER WAY WHILE SHERIFF LARD-BUTT SHAKES YOU DOWN?
YES!

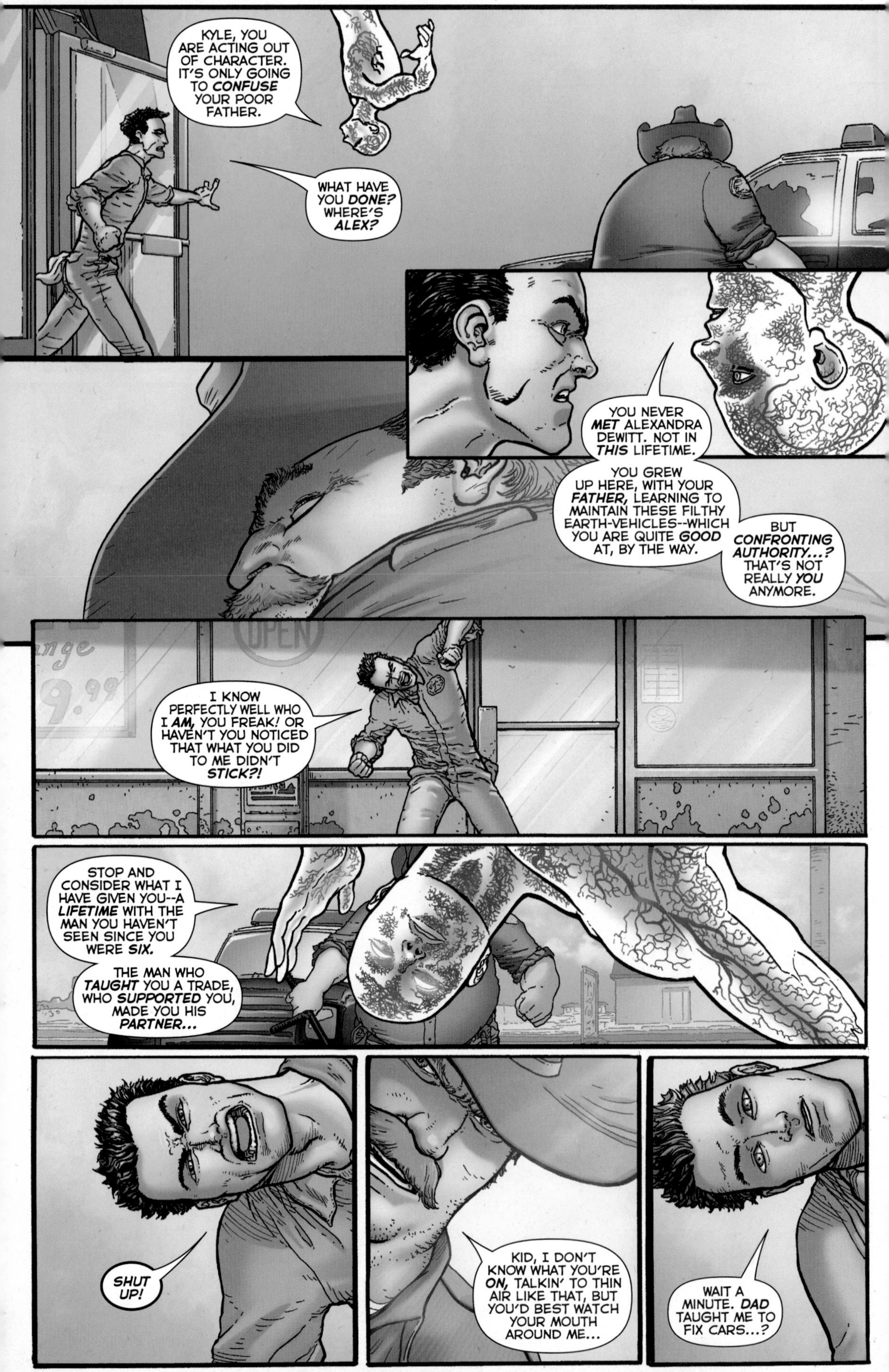
KYLE, YOU ARE ACTING OUT OF CHARACTER. IT'S ONLY GOING TO CONFUSE YOUR POOR FATHER.
WHAT HAVE YOU DONE? WHERE'S ALEX?
YOU NEVER MET ALEXANDRA DEWITT. NOT IN THIS LIFETIME.
YOU GREW UP HERE, WITH YOUR FATHER, LEARNING TO MAINTAIN THESE FILTHY EARTH-VEHICLES--WHICH YOU ARE QUITE GOOD AT, BY THE WAY.
BUT CONFRONTING AUTHORITY...? THAT'S NOT REALLY YOU ANYMORE.
OPEN
I KNOW PERFECTLY WELL WHO I AM, YOU FREAK! OR HAVEN'T YOU NOTICED THAT WHAT YOU DID TO ME DIDN'T STICK?!
STOP AND CONSIDER WHAT I HAVE GIVEN YOU--A LIFETIME WITH THE MAN YOU HAVEN'T SEEN SINCE YOU WERE SIX.
THE MAN WHO TAUGHT YOU A TRADE, WHO SUPPORTED YOU, MADE YOU HIS PARTNER...
SHUT UP!
KID, I DON'T KNOW WHAT YOU'RE ON, TALKIN' TO THIN AIR LIKE THAT, BUT YOU'D BEST WATCH YOUR MOUTH AROUND ME...
WAIT A MINUTE. DAD TAUGHT ME TO FIX CARS...?

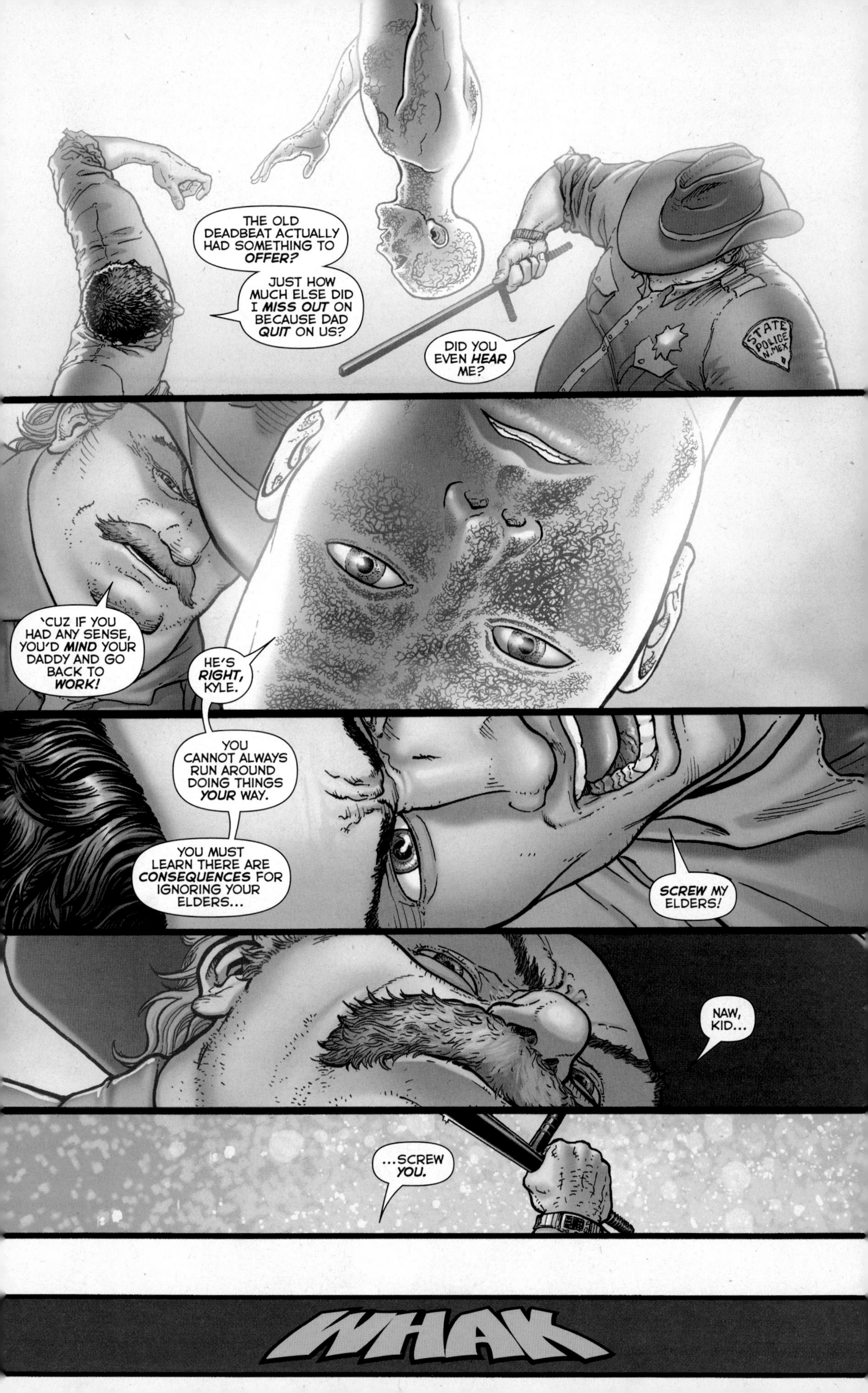
THE OLD DEADBEAT ACTUALLY HAD SOMETHING TO OFFER?
JUST HOW MUCH ELSE DID I MISS OUT ON BECAUSE DAD QUIT ON US?
DID YOU EVEN HEAR ME?
'CUZ IF YOU HAD ANY SENSE, YOU'D MIND YOUR DADDY AND GO BACK TO WORK!
HE'S RIGHT, KYLE.
YOU CANNOT ALWAYS RUN AROUND DOING THINGS YOUR WAY.
YOU MUST LEARN THERE ARE CONSEQUENCES FOR IGNORING YOUR ELDERS...
SCREW MY ELDERS!
NAW, KID...
...SCREW YOU.
WHAK
STATE POLICE N. MEX

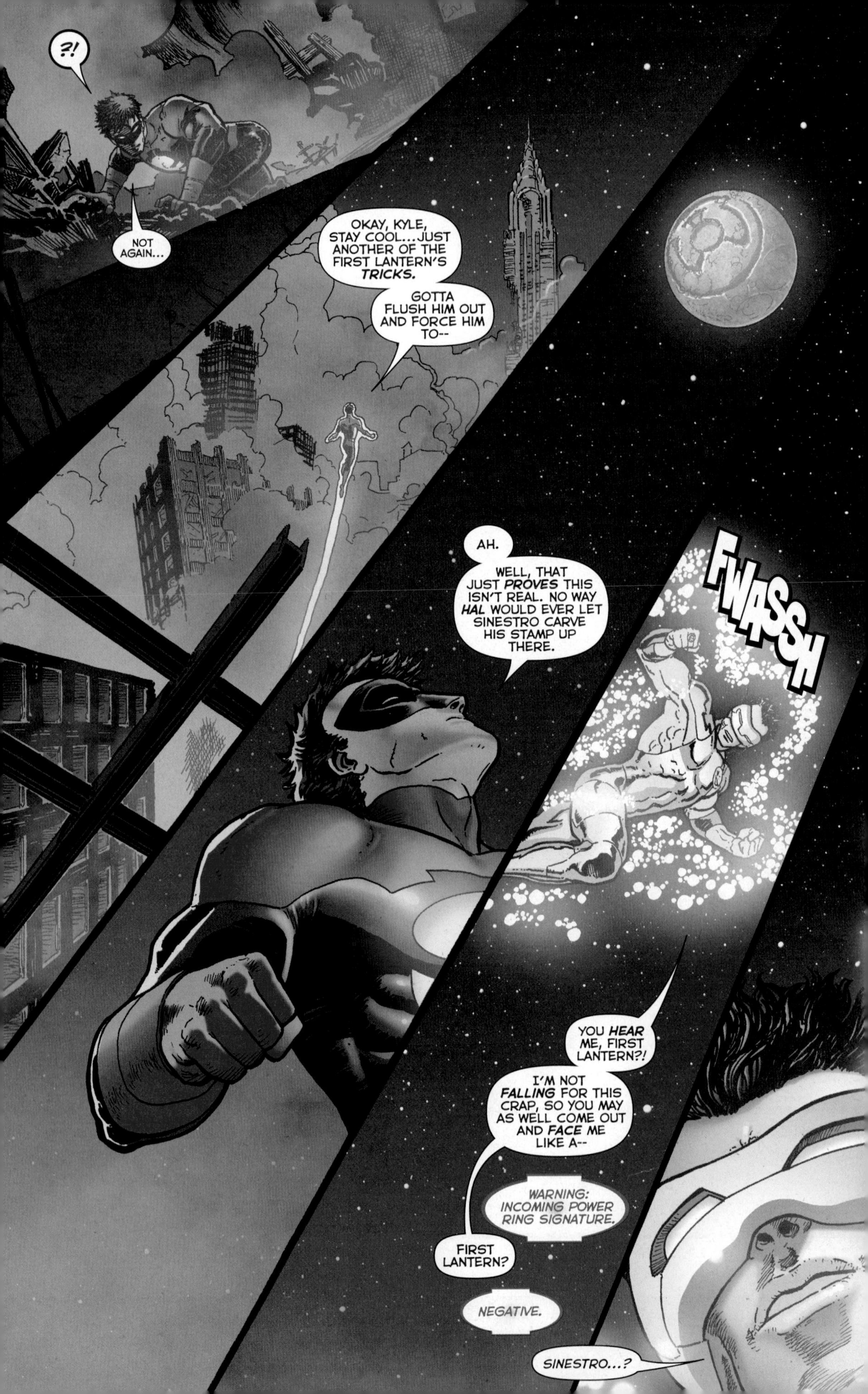
?!
NOT AGAIN...
OKAY, KYLE, STAY COOL...JUST ANOTHER OF THE FIRST LANTERN'S TRICKS.
GOTTA FLUSH HIM OUT AND FORCE HIM TO--
AH.
WELL, THAT JUST PROVES THIS ISN'T REAL. NO WAY HAL WOULD EVER LET SINESTRO CARVE HIS STAMP UP THERE.
FWASSH
YOU HEAR ME, FIRST LANTERN?!
I'M NOT FALLING FOR THIS CRAP, SO YOU MAY AS WELL COME OUT AND FACE ME LIKE A--
WARNING: INCOMING POWER RING SIGNATURE.
FIRST LANTERN?
NEGATIVE.
SINESTRO...?

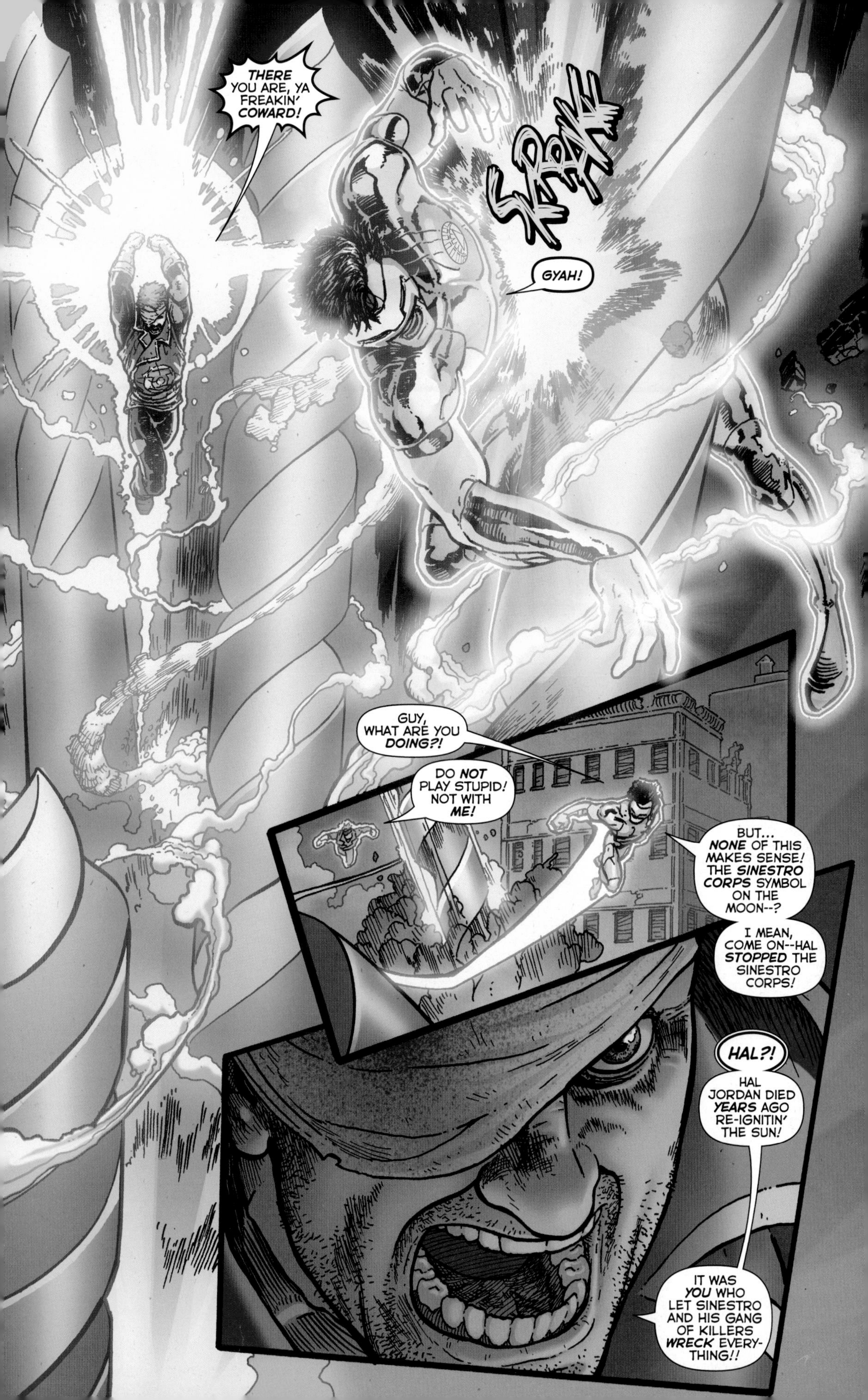
THERE YOU ARE, YA FREAKIN' COWARD!
GYAH!
GUY, WHAT ARE YOU DOING?!
DO NOT PLAY STUPID! NOT WITH ME!
BUT... NONE OF THIS MAKES SENSE! THE SINESTRO CORPS SYMBOL ON THE MOON--?
I MEAN, COME ON--HAL STOPPED THE SINESTRO CORPS!
HAL?!
HAL JORDAN DIED YEARS AGO RE-IGNITIN' THE SUN!
IT WAS YOU WHO LET SINESTRO AND HIS GANG OF KILLERS WRECK EVERY-THING!!

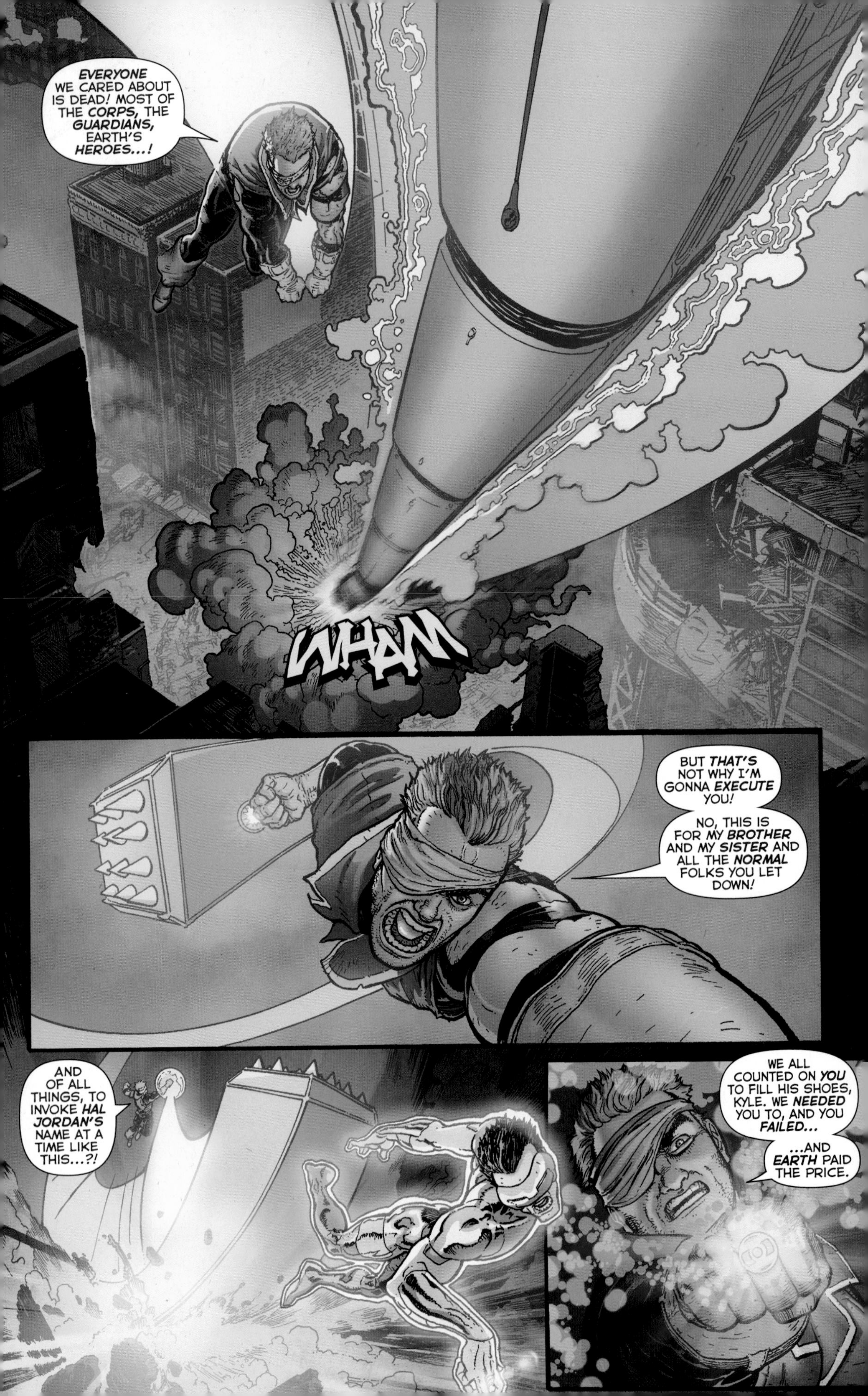

EVERYONE WE CARED ABOUT IS DEAD! MOST OF THE CORPS, THE GUARDIANS, EARTH'S HEROES...!
WHAM
BUT THAT'S NOT WHY I'M GONNA EXECUTE YOU!
NO, THIS IS FOR MY BROTHER AND MY SISTER AND ALL THE NORMAL FOLKS YOU LET DOWN!
AND OF ALL THINGS, TO INVOKE HAL JORDAN'S NAME AT A TIME LIKE THIS...?!
WE ALL COUNTED ON YOU TO FILL HIS SHOES, KYLE. WE NEEDED YOU TO, AND YOU FAILED...
...AND EARTH PAID THE PRICE.

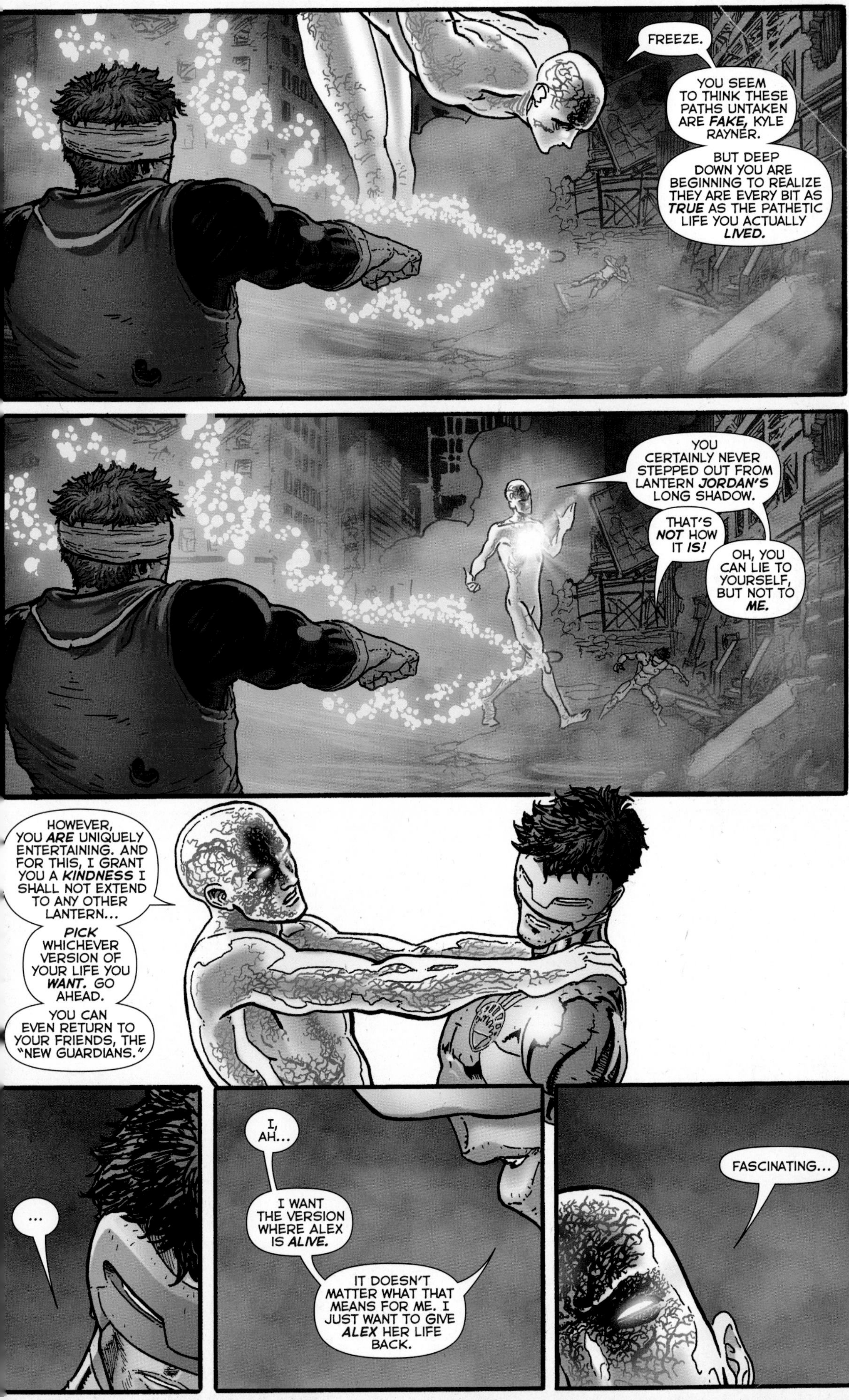
FREEZE.
YOU SEEM TO THINK THESE PATHS UNTAKEN ARE FAKE, KYLE RAYNER.
BUT DEEP DOWN YOU ARE BEGINNING TO REALIZE THEY ARE EVERY BIT AS TRUE AS THE PATHETIC LIFE YOU ACTUALLY LIVED.
YOU CERTAINLY NEVER STEPPED OUT FROM LANTERN JORDAN'S LONG SHADOW.
THAT'S NOT HOW IT IS!
OH, YOU CAN LIE TO YOURSELF, BUT NOT TO ME.
HOWEVER, YOU ARE UNIQUELY ENTERTAINING. AND FOR THIS, I GRANT YOU A KINDNESS I SHALL NOT EXTEND TO ANY OTHER LANTERN...
PICK WHICHEVER VERSION OF YOUR LIFE YOU WANT. GO AHEAD.
YOU CAN EVEN RETURN TO YOUR FRIENDS, THE "NEW GUARDIANS."
...
I, AH...
I WANT THE VERSION WHERE ALEX IS ALIVE.
IT DOESN'T MATTER WHAT THAT MEANS FOR ME. I JUST WANT TO GIVE ALEX HER LIFE BACK.
FASCINATING...

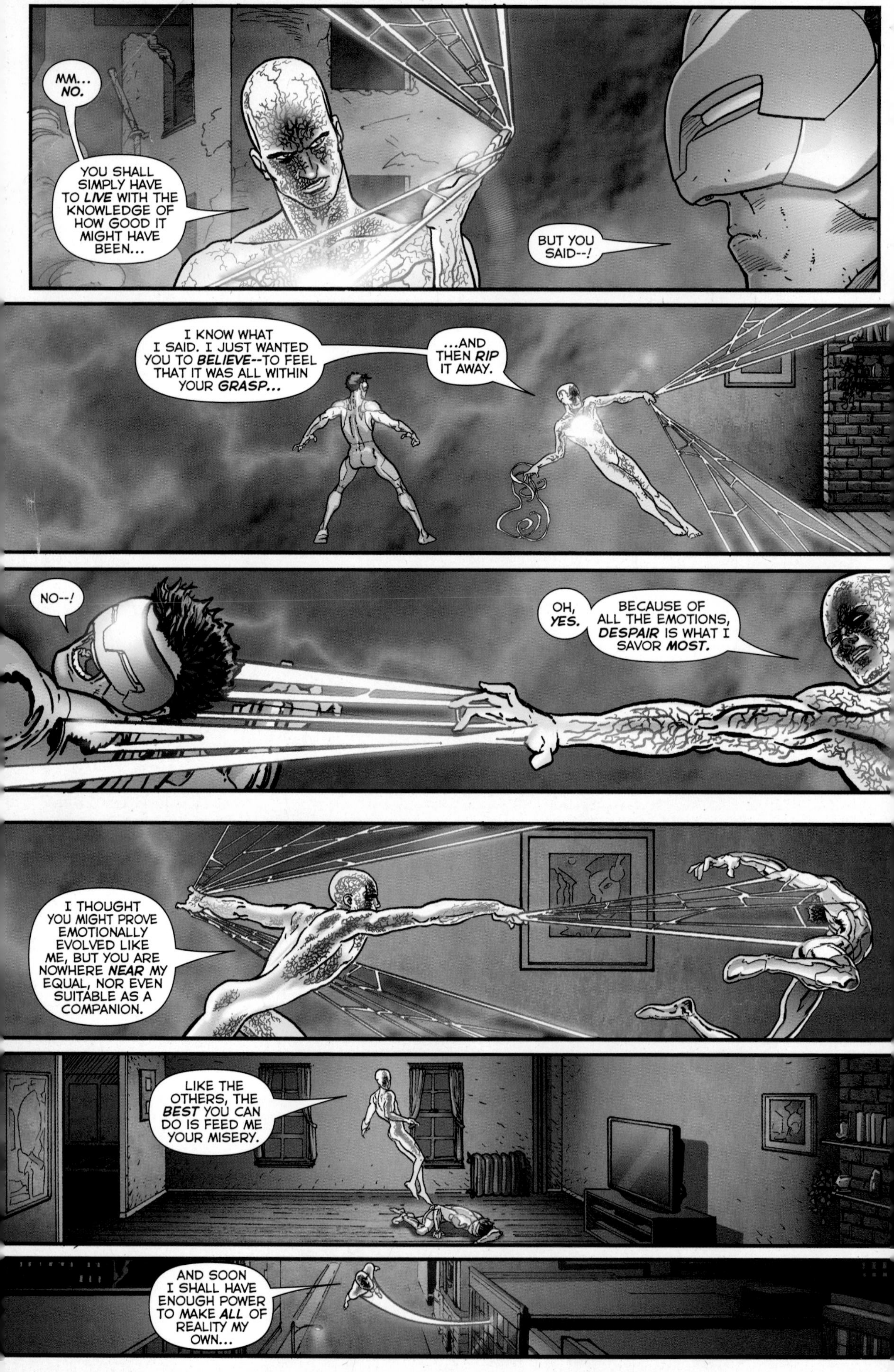
MM... NO.
YOU SHALL SIMPLY HAVE TO LIVE WITH THE KNOWLEDGE OF HOW GOOD IT MIGHT HAVE BEEN...
BUT YOU SAID--!
I KNOW WHAT I SAID. I JUST WANTED YOU TO BELIEVE--TO FEEL THAT IT WAS ALL WITHIN YOUR GRASP...
...AND THEN RIP IT AWAY.
NO--!
OH, YES.
BECAUSE OF ALL THE EMOTIONS, DESPAIR IS WHAT I SAVOR MOST.
I THOUGHT YOU MIGHT PROVE EMOTIONALLY EVOLVED LIKE ME, BUT YOU ARE NOWHERE NEAR MY EQUAL, NOR EVEN SUITABLE AS A COMPANION.
LIKE THE OTHERS, THE BEST YOU CAN DO IS FEED ME YOUR MISERY.
AND SOON I SHALL HAVE ENOUGH POWER TO MAKE ALL OF REALITY MY OWN...

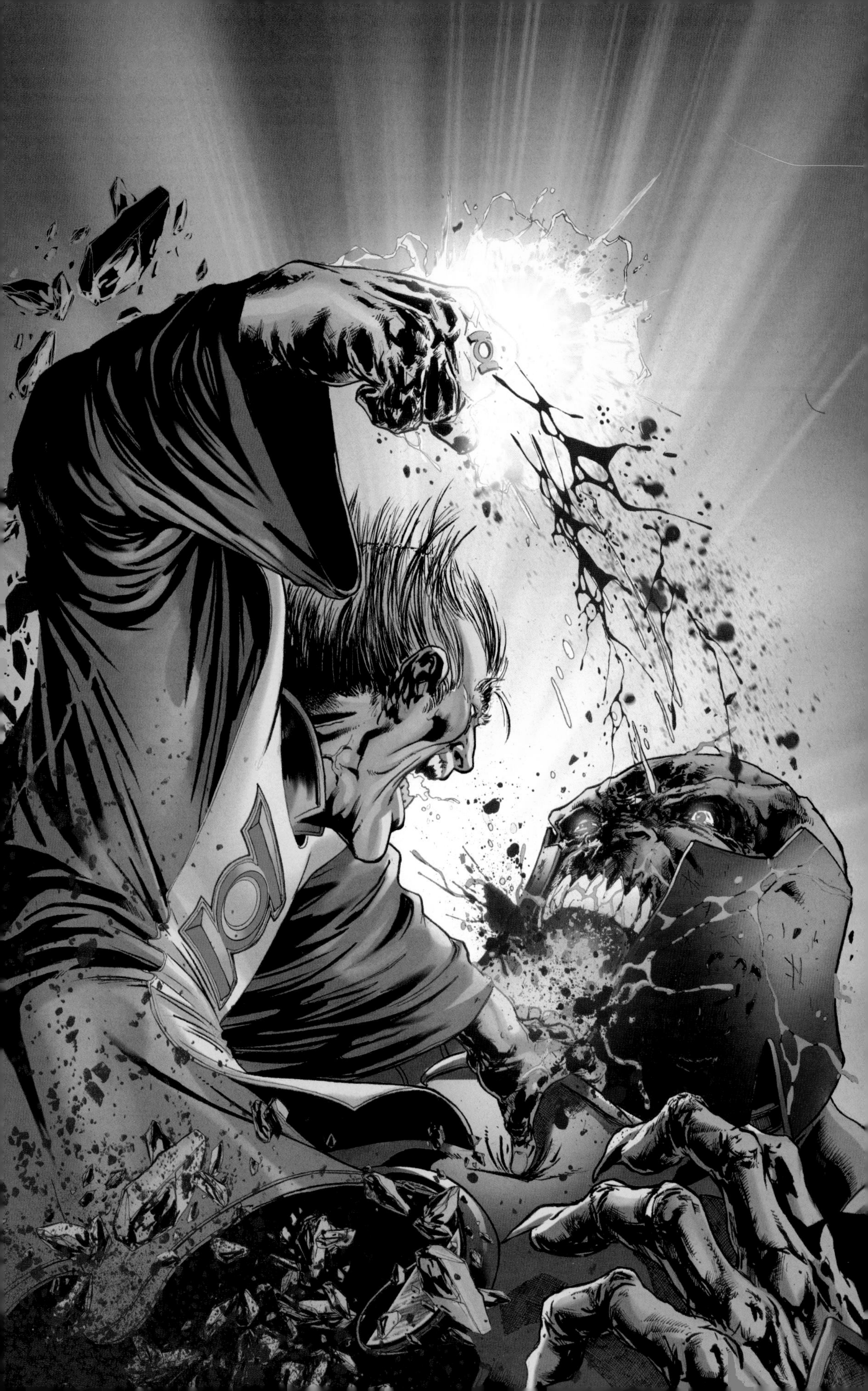

PART FOUR: SYMPATHY FOR THE DEVIL

PETER MILLIGAN writer **MIGUEL SEPULVEDA** artist
cover art by **MIGUEL SEPULVEDA** & **RAIN BEREDO**

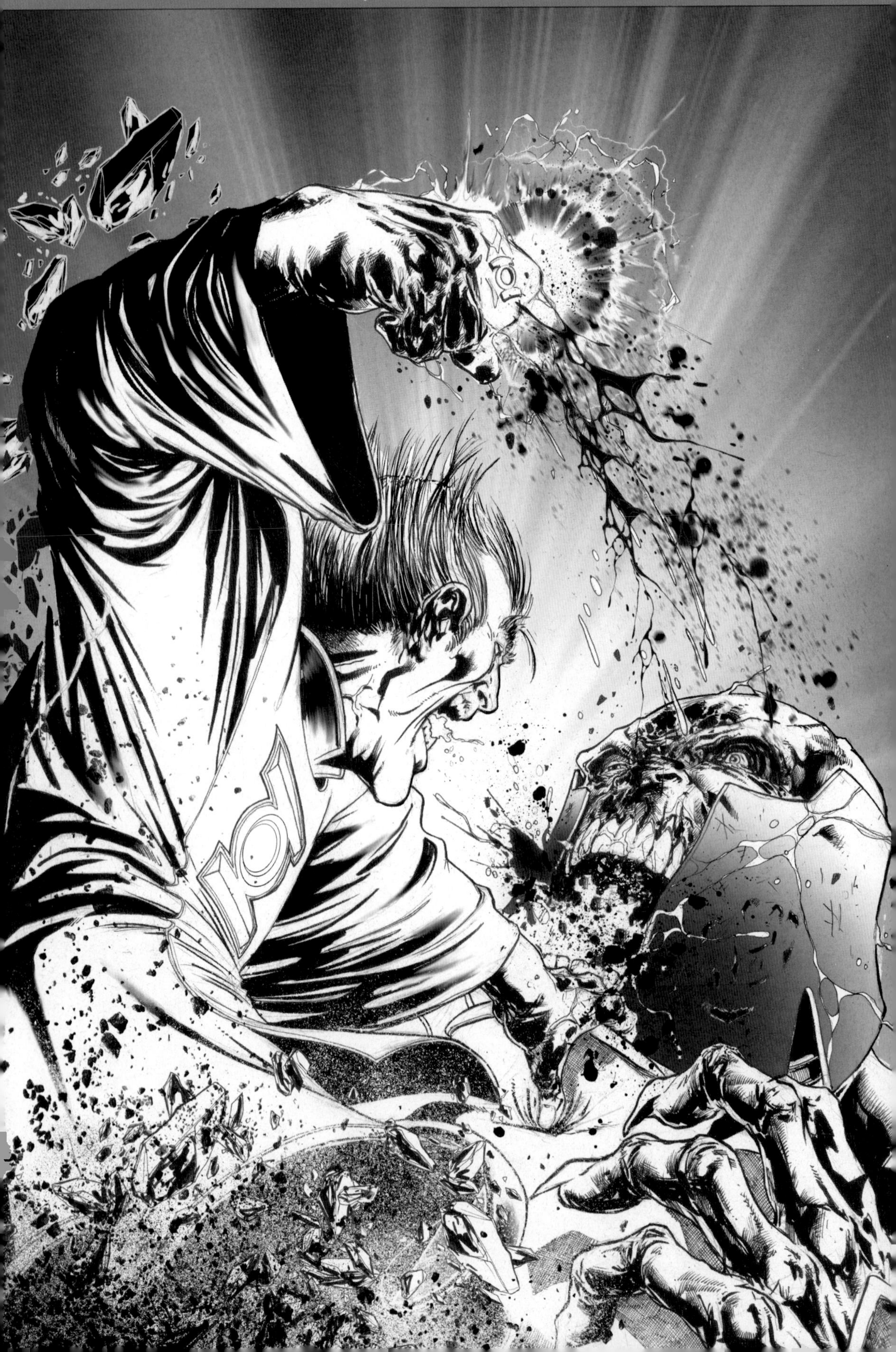

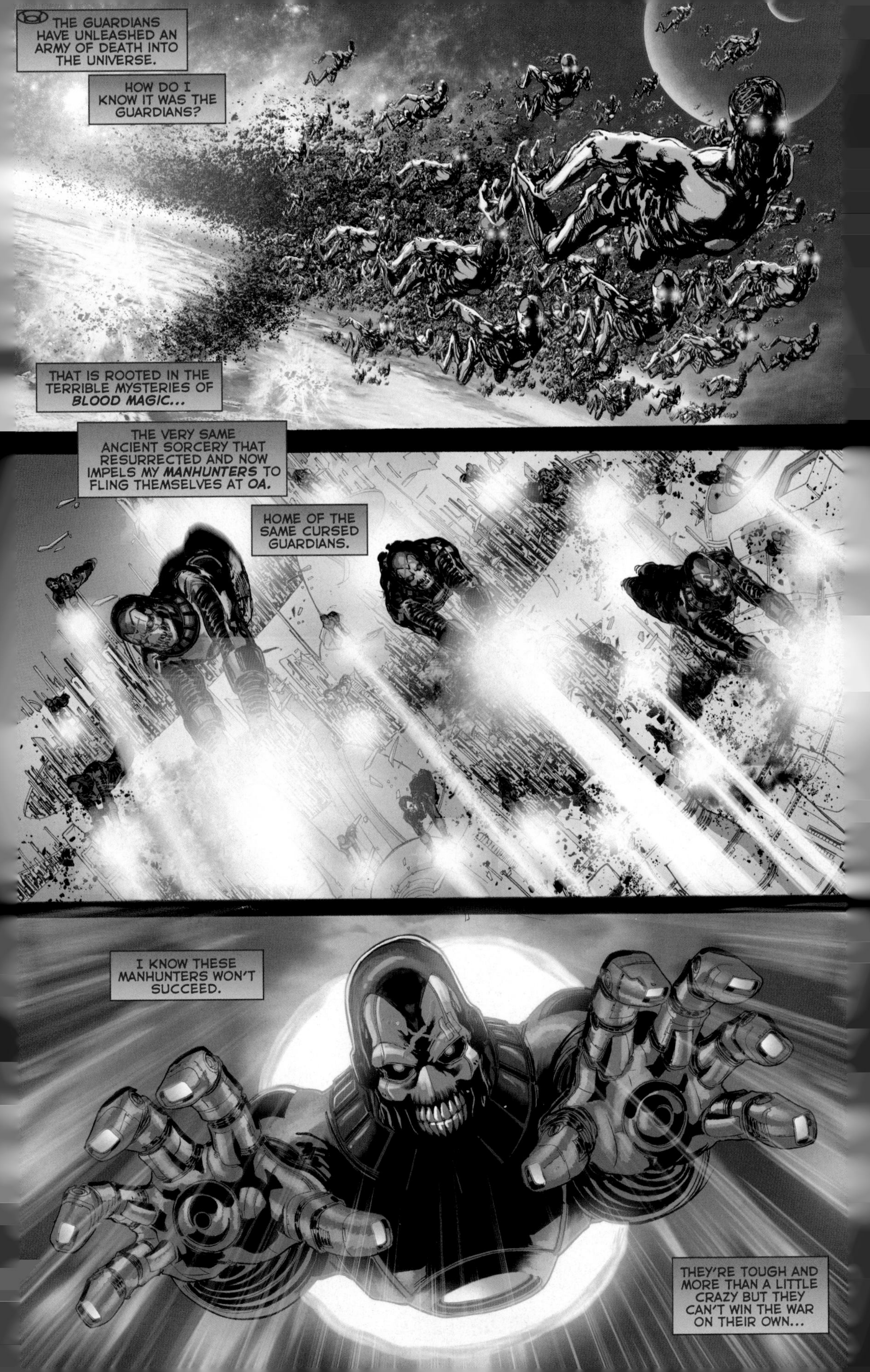
THE GUARDIANS HAVE UNLEASHED AN ARMY OF DEATH INTO THE UNIVERSE.
HOW DO I KNOW IT WAS THE GUARDIANS?
THAT IS ROOTED IN THE TERRIBLE MYSTERIES OF BLOOD MAGIC...
THE VERY SAME ANCIENT SORCERY THAT RESURRECTED AND NOW IMPELS MY MANHUNTERS TO FLING THEMSELVES AT OA.
HOME OF THE SAME CURSED GUARDIANS.
I KNOW THESE MANHUNTERS WON'T SUCCEED.
THEY'RE TOUGH AND MORE THAN A LITTLE CRAZY BUT THEY CAN'T WIN THE WAR ON THEIR OWN...

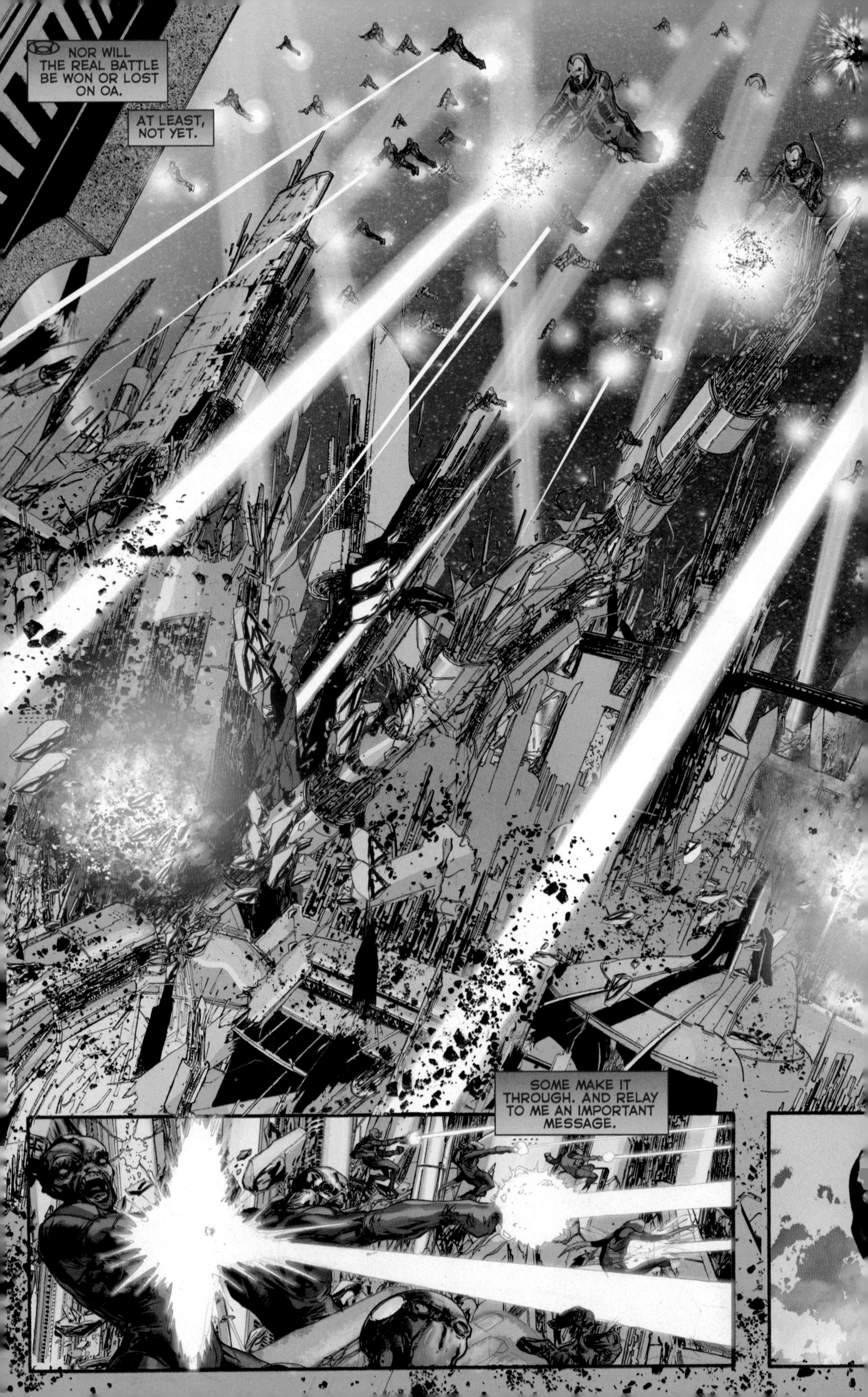
NOR WILL THE REAL BATTLE BE WON OR LOST ON OA.
AT LEAST, NOT YET.
SOME MAKE IT THROUGH. AND RELAY TO ME AN IMPORTANT MESSAGE.

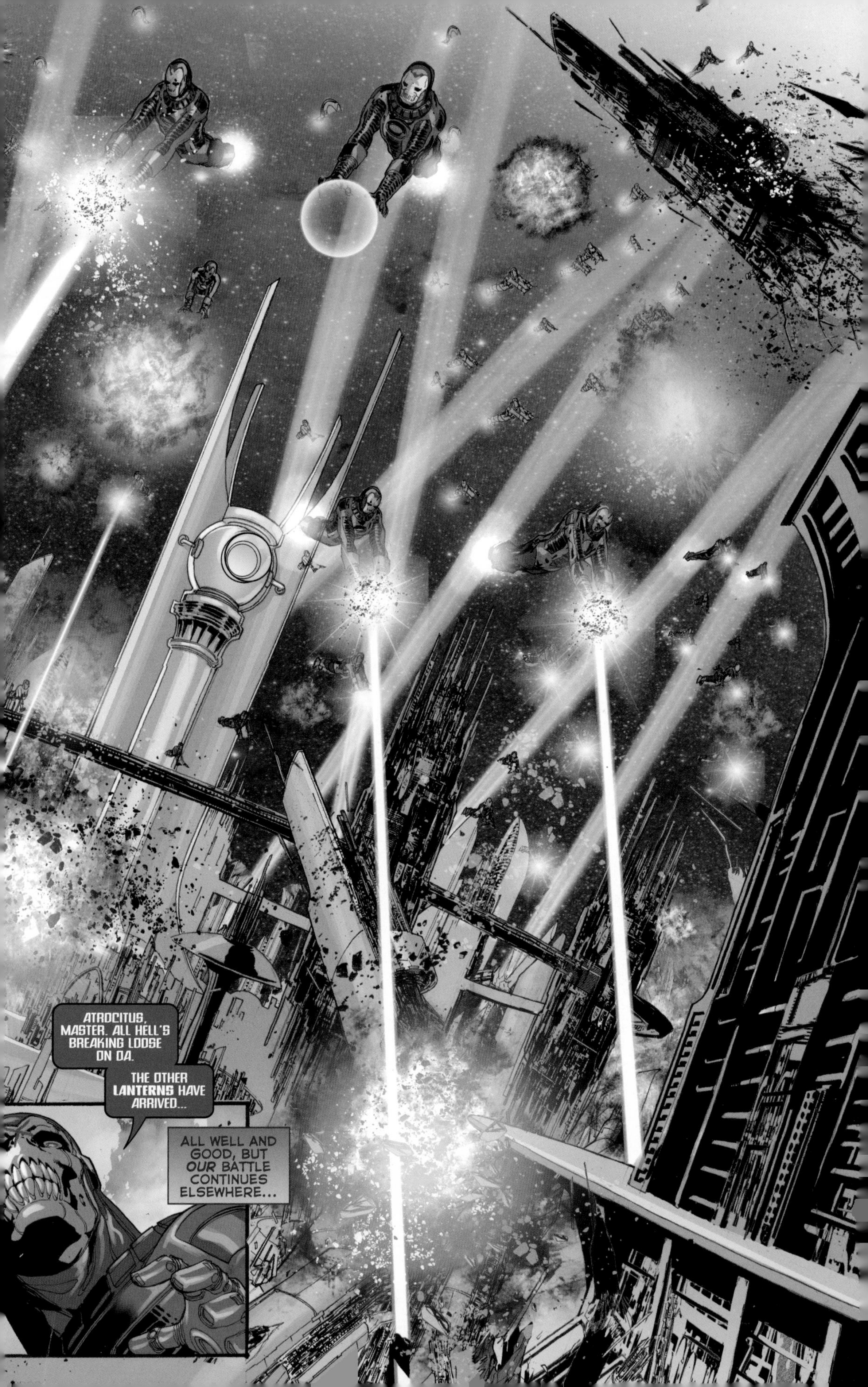
ATROCITUS, MASTER. ALL HELL'S BREAKING LOOSE ON OA.
THE OTHER LANTERNS HAVE ARRIVED...
ALL WELL AND GOOD, BUT OUR BATTLE CONTINUES ELSEWHERE...

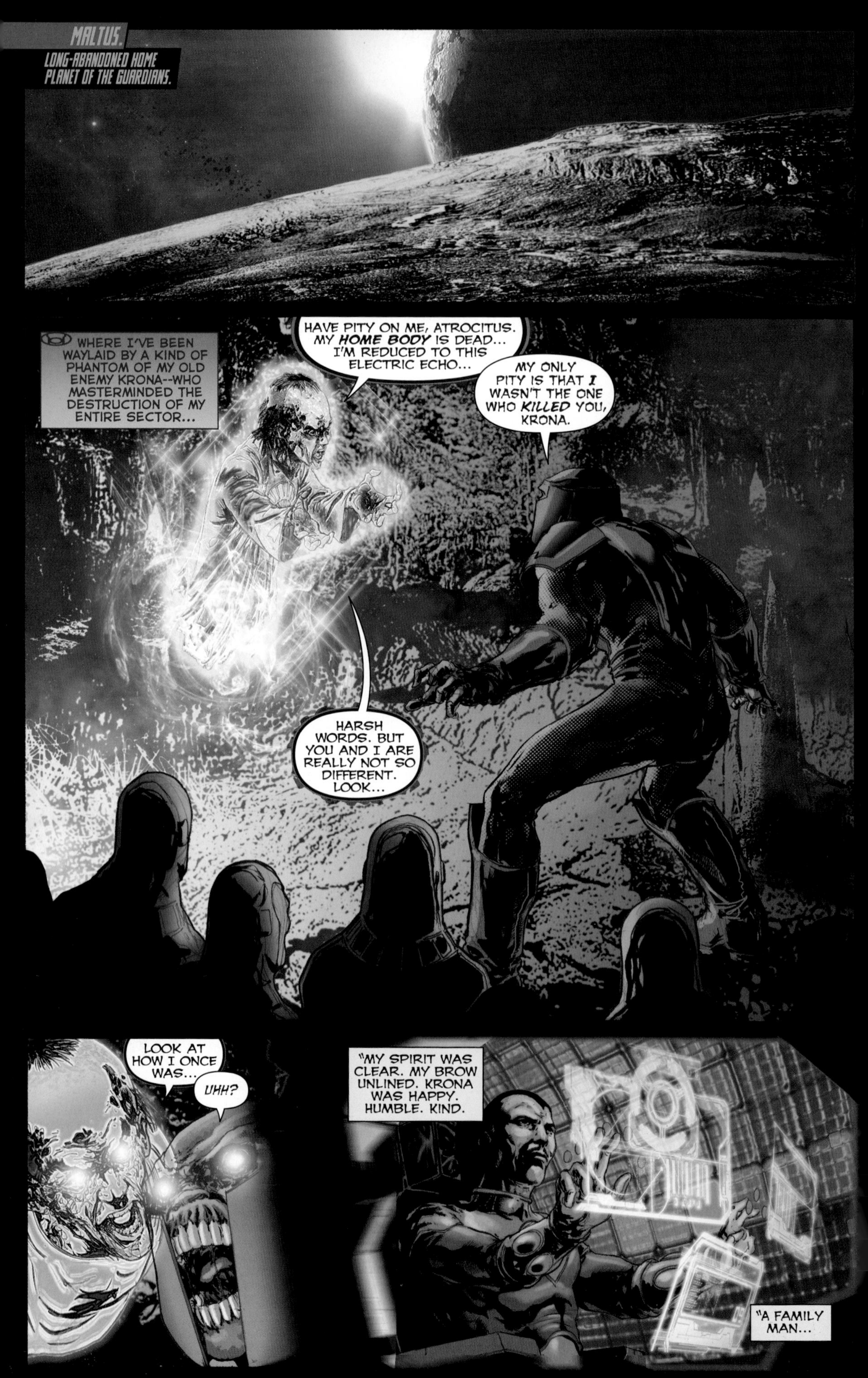
MALTUS.
LONG-ABANDONED HOME PLANET OF THE GUARDIANS.
WHERE I'VE BEEN WAYLAID BY A KIND OF PHANTOM OF MY OLD ENEMY KRONA--WHO MASTERMINDED THE DESTRUCTION OF MY ENTIRE SECTOR...
HAVE PITY ON ME, ATROCITUS. MY HOME BODY IS DEAD... I'M REDUCED TO THIS ELECTRIC ECHO...
MY ONLY PITY IS THAT I WASN'T THE ONE WHO KILLED YOU, KRONA.
HARSH WORDS. BUT YOU AND I ARE REALLY NOT SO DIFFERENT. LOOK...
LOOK AT HOW I ONCE WAS...
UHH?
"MY SPIRIT WAS CLEAR. MY BROW UNLINED. KRONA WAS HAPPY. HUMBLE. KIND.
"A FAMILY MAN...

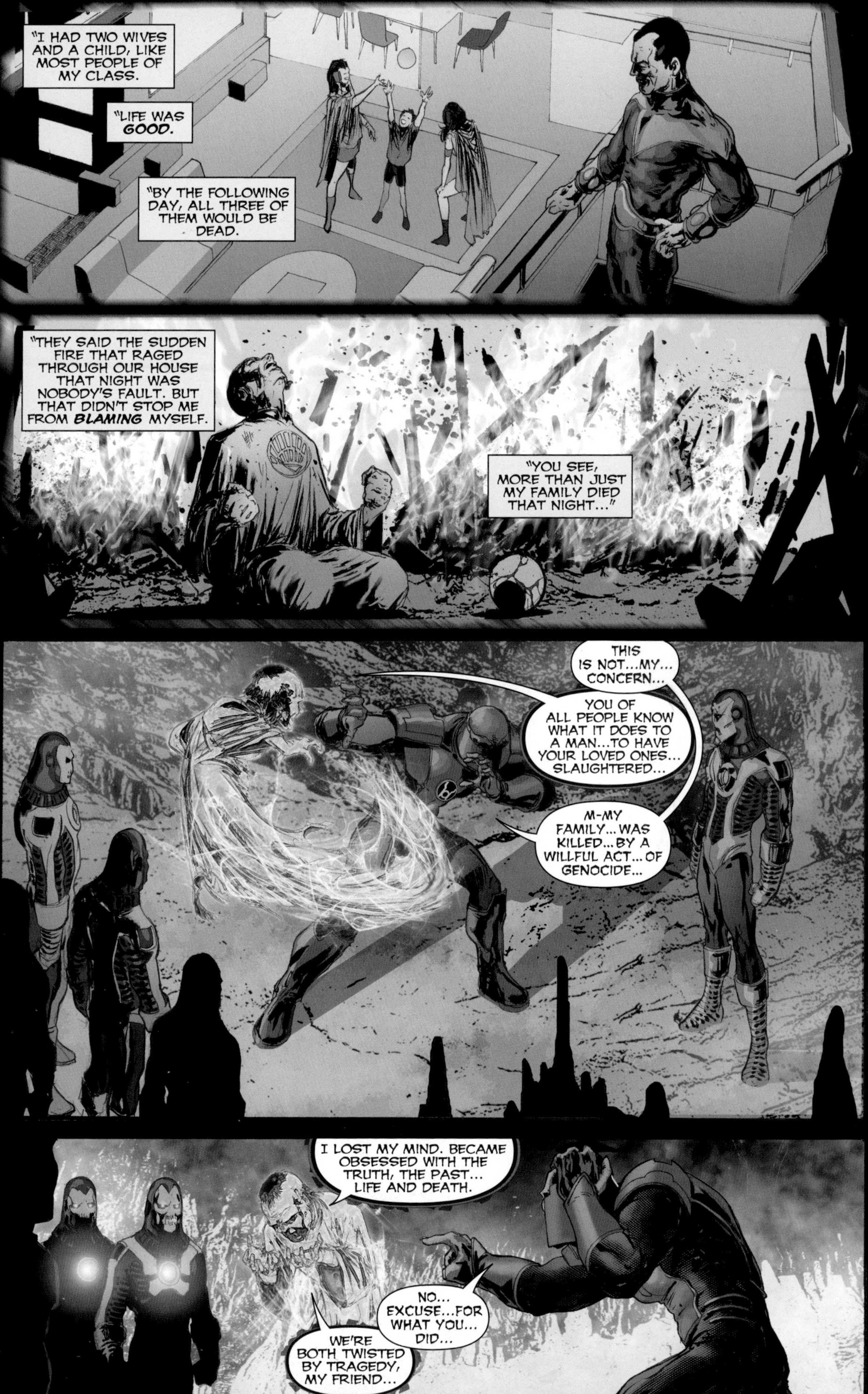
"I HAD TWO WIVES AND A CHILD, LIKE MOST PEOPLE OF MY CLASS.
"LIFE WAS *GOOD.*
"BY THE FOLLOWING DAY, ALL THREE OF THEM WOULD BE DEAD.
"THEY SAID THE SUDDEN FIRE THAT RAGED THROUGH OUR HOUSE THAT NIGHT WAS NOBODY'S FAULT. BUT THAT DIDN'T STOP ME FROM *BLAMING* MYSELF.
"YOU SEE, MORE THAN JUST MY FAMILY DIED THAT NIGHT..."
THIS IS NOT...MY... CONCERN...
YOU OF ALL PEOPLE KNOW WHAT IT DOES TO A MAN...TO HAVE YOUR LOVED ONES... SLAUGHTERED...
M-MY FAMILY...WAS KILLED...BY A WILLFUL ACT...OF GENOCIDE...
I LOST MY MIND. BECAME OBSESSED WITH THE TRUTH, THE PAST... LIFE AND DEATH.
NO... EXCUSE...FOR WHAT YOU... DID...
WE'RE BOTH TWISTED BY TRAGEDY, MY FRIEND...

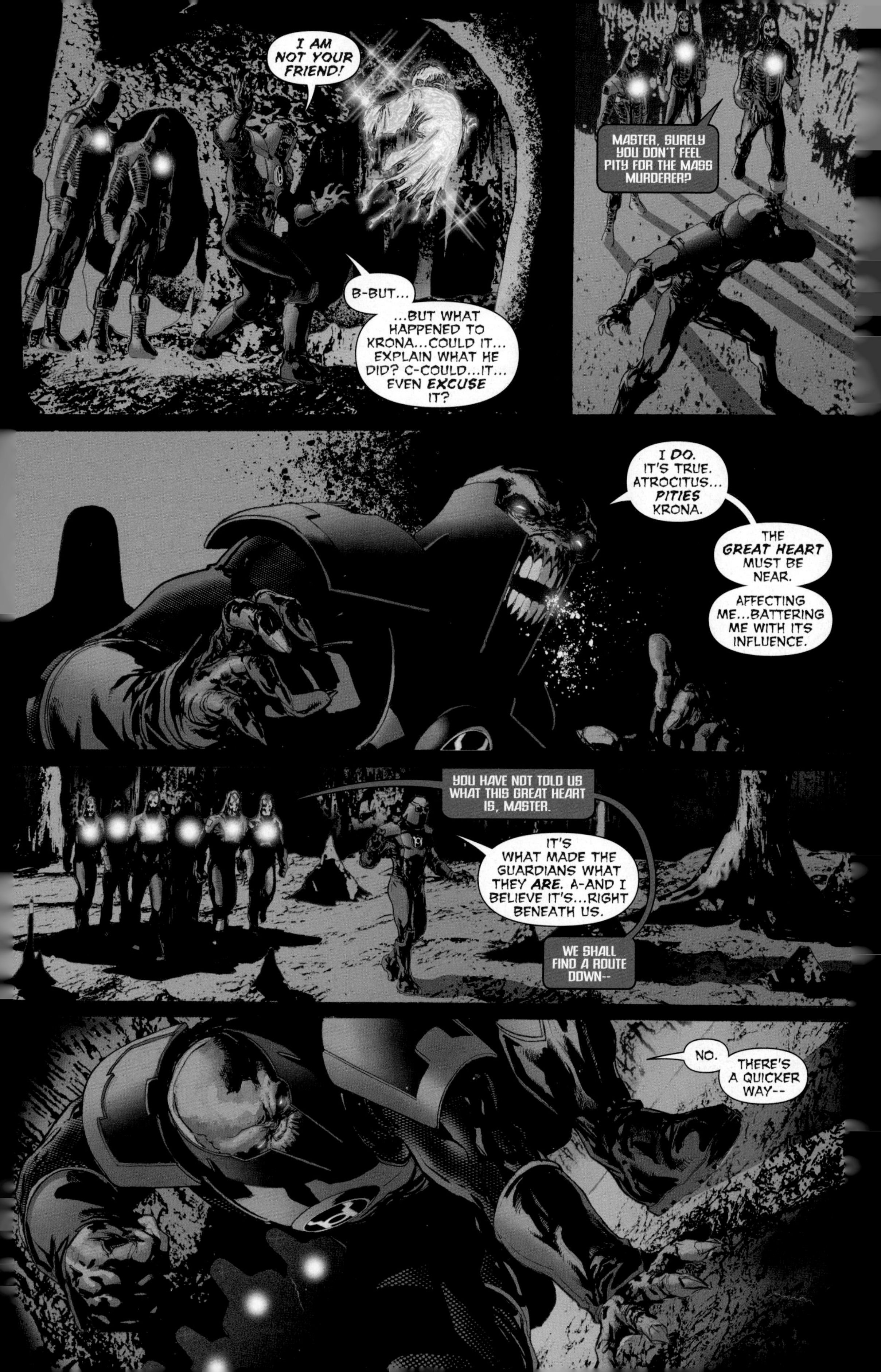
I AM NOT YOUR FRIEND!
B-BUT...
...BUT WHAT HAPPENED TO KRONA...COULD IT... EXPLAIN WHAT HE DID? C-COULD...IT... EVEN EXCUSE IT?
MASTER, SURELY YOU DON'T FEEL PITY FOR THE MASS MURDERER?
I DO. IT'S TRUE. ATROCITUS... PITIES KRONA.
THE GREAT HEART MUST BE NEAR.
AFFECTING ME...BATTERING ME WITH ITS INFLUENCE.
YOU HAVE NOT TOLD US WHAT THIS GREAT HEART IS, MASTER.
IT'S WHAT MADE THE GUARDIANS WHAT THEY ARE. A-AND I BELIEVE IT'S...RIGHT BENEATH US.
WE SHALL FIND A ROUTE DOWN--
NO.
THERE'S A QUICKER WAY--

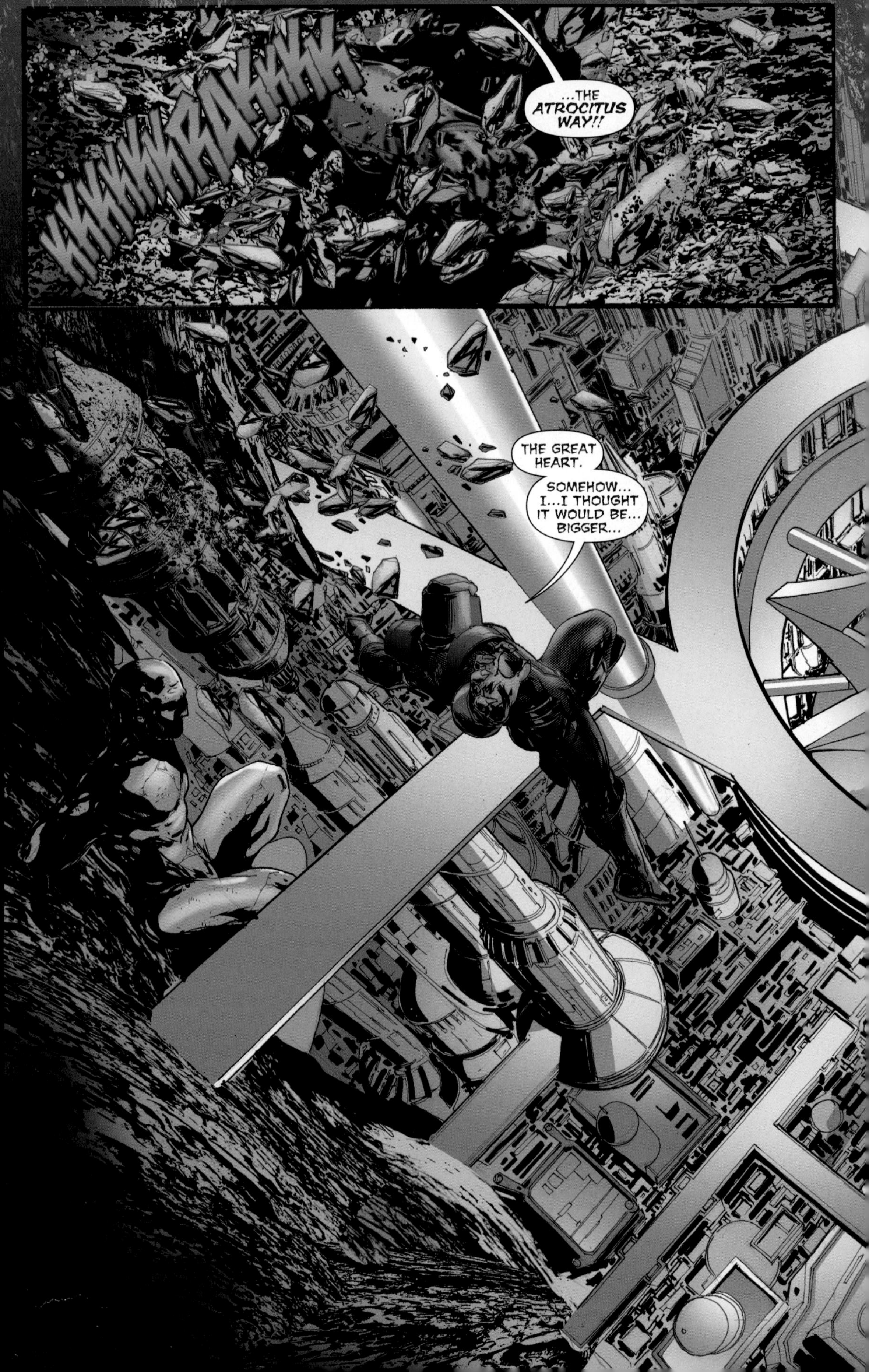
KKKKKKRAKKKKK
...THE ATROCITUS WAY!!
THE GREAT HEART.
SOMEHOW... I...I THOUGHT IT WOULD BE... BIGGER...

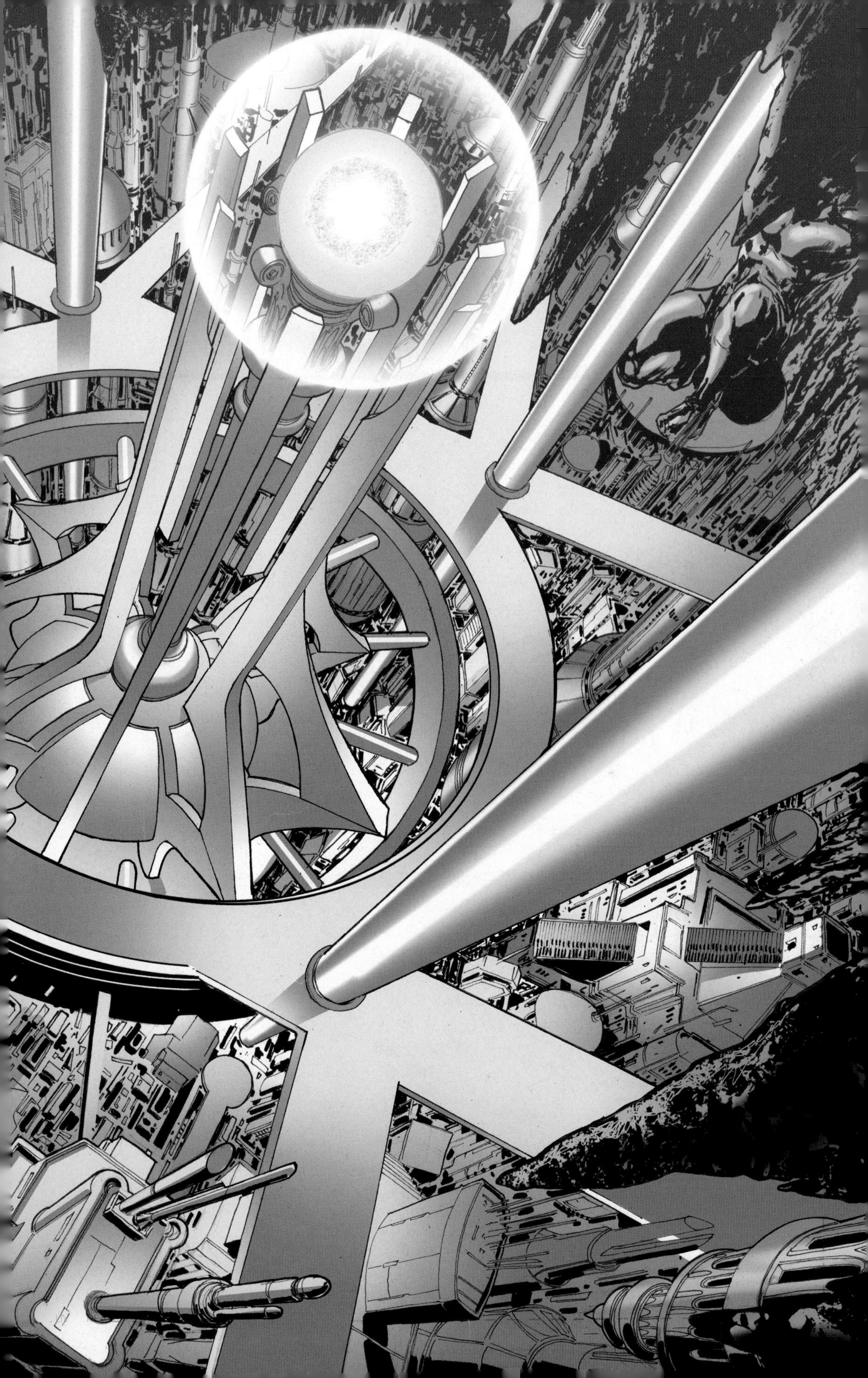

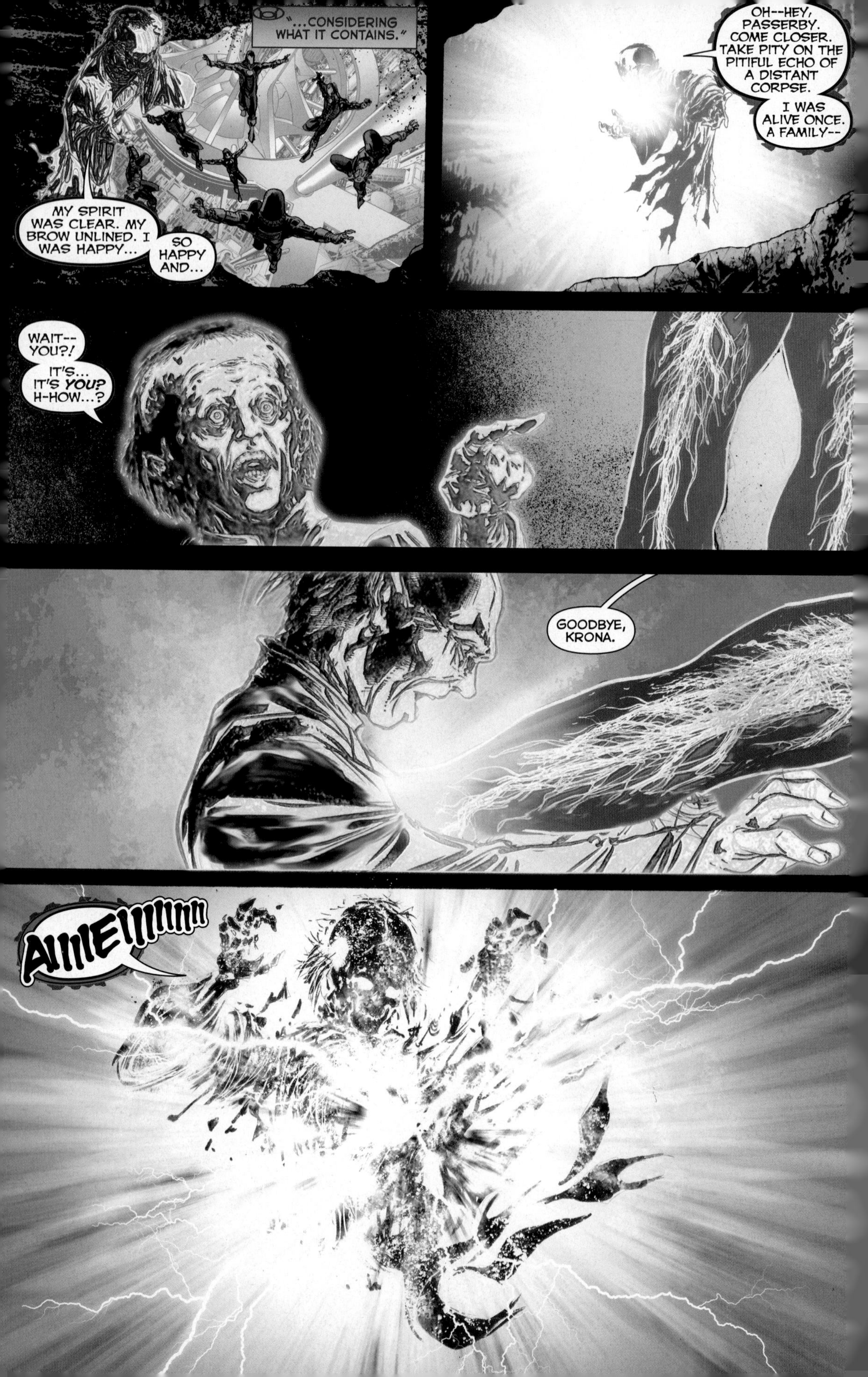
"...CONSIDERING WHAT IT CONTAINS."
MY SPIRIT WAS CLEAR. MY BROW UNLINED. I WAS HAPPY...
SO HAPPY AND...
OH--HEY, PASSERBY. COME CLOSER. TAKE PITY ON THE PITIFUL ECHO OF A DISTANT CORPSE.
I WAS ALIVE ONCE. A FAMILY--
WAIT-- YOU?!
IT'S... IT'S YOU? H-HOW...?
GOODBYE, KRONA.
AIIIEIIIIIIInnn

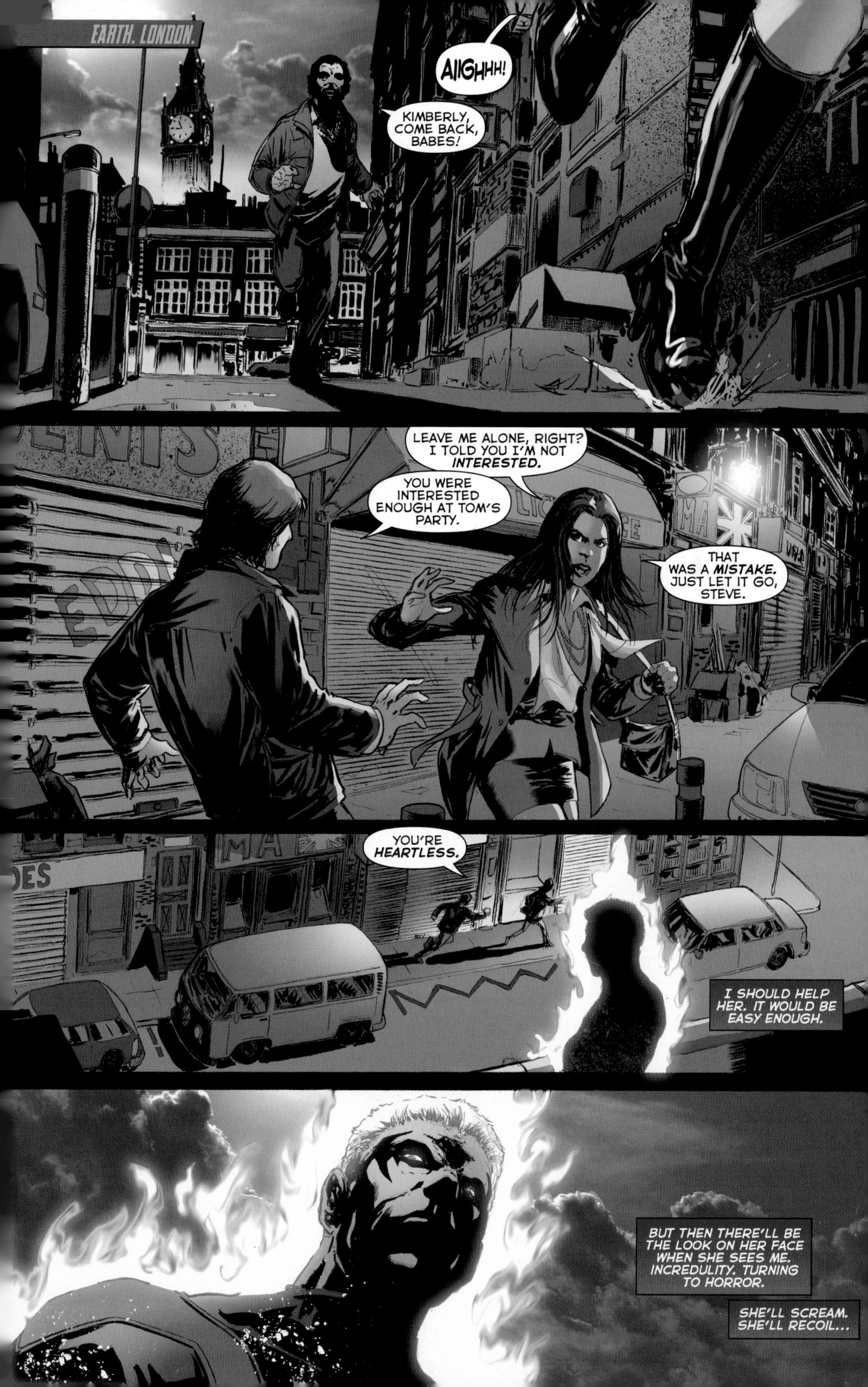
EARTH. LONDON.
AIIGHHH!
KIMBERLY, COME BACK, BABES!
LEAVE ME ALONE, RIGHT? I TOLD YOU I'M NOT INTERESTED.
YOU WERE INTERESTED ENOUGH AT TOM'S PARTY.
THAT WAS A MISTAKE. JUST LET IT GO, STEVE.
YOU'RE HEARTLESS.
I SHOULD HELP HER. IT WOULD BE EASY ENOUGH.
BUT THEN THERE'LL BE THE LOOK ON HER FACE WHEN SHE SEES ME. INCREDULITY. TURNING TO HORROR.
SHE'LL SCREAM. SHE'LL RECOIL...

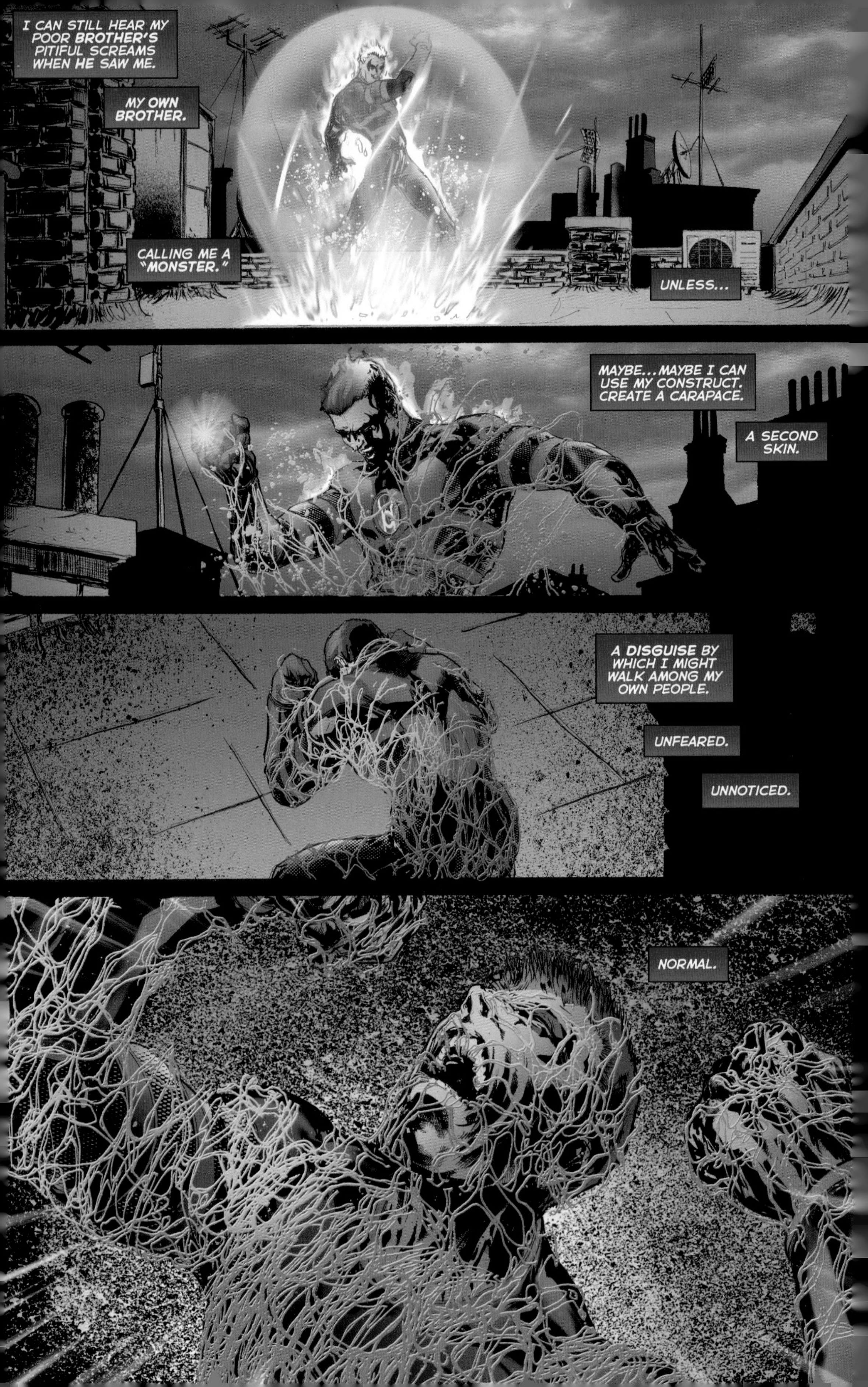
I CAN STILL HEAR MY POOR BROTHER'S PITIFUL SCREAMS WHEN HE SAW ME.
MY OWN BROTHER.
CALLING ME A "MONSTER."
UNLESS...
MAYBE... MAYBE I CAN USE MY CONSTRUCT. CREATE A CARAPACE.
A SECOND SKIN.
A DISGUISE BY WHICH I MIGHT WALK AMONG MY OWN PEOPLE.
UNFEARED.
UNNOTICED.
NORMAL.

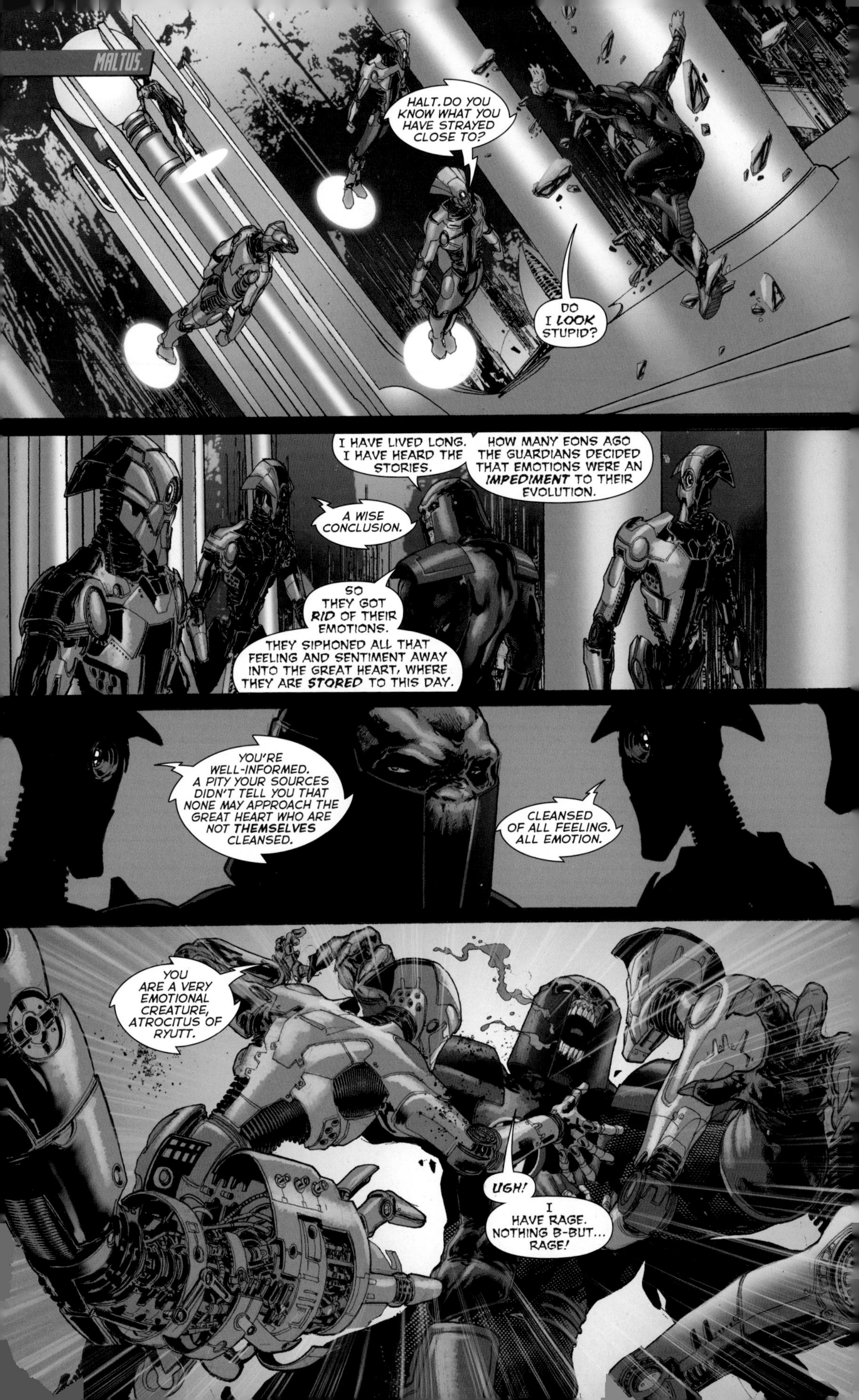
MALTUS.
HALT. DO YOU KNOW WHAT YOU HAVE STRAYED CLOSE TO?
DO I LOOK STUPID?
I HAVE LIVED LONG. I HAVE HEARD THE STORIES.
HOW MANY EONS AGO THE GUARDIANS DECIDED THAT EMOTIONS WERE AN IMPEDIMENT TO THEIR EVOLUTION.
A WISE CONCLUSION.
SO THEY GOT RID OF THEIR EMOTIONS.
THEY SIPHONED ALL THAT FEELING AND SENTIMENT AWAY INTO THE GREAT HEART, WHERE THEY ARE STORED TO THIS DAY.
YOU'RE WELL-INFORMED. A PITY YOUR SOURCES DIDN'T TELL YOU THAT NONE MAY APPROACH THE GREAT HEART WHO ARE NOT THEMSELVES CLEANSED.
CLEANSED OF ALL FEELING. ALL EMOTION.
YOU ARE A VERY EMOTIONAL CREATURE, ATROCITUS OF RYUTT.
UGH!
I HAVE RAGE. NOTHING B-BUT... RAGE!

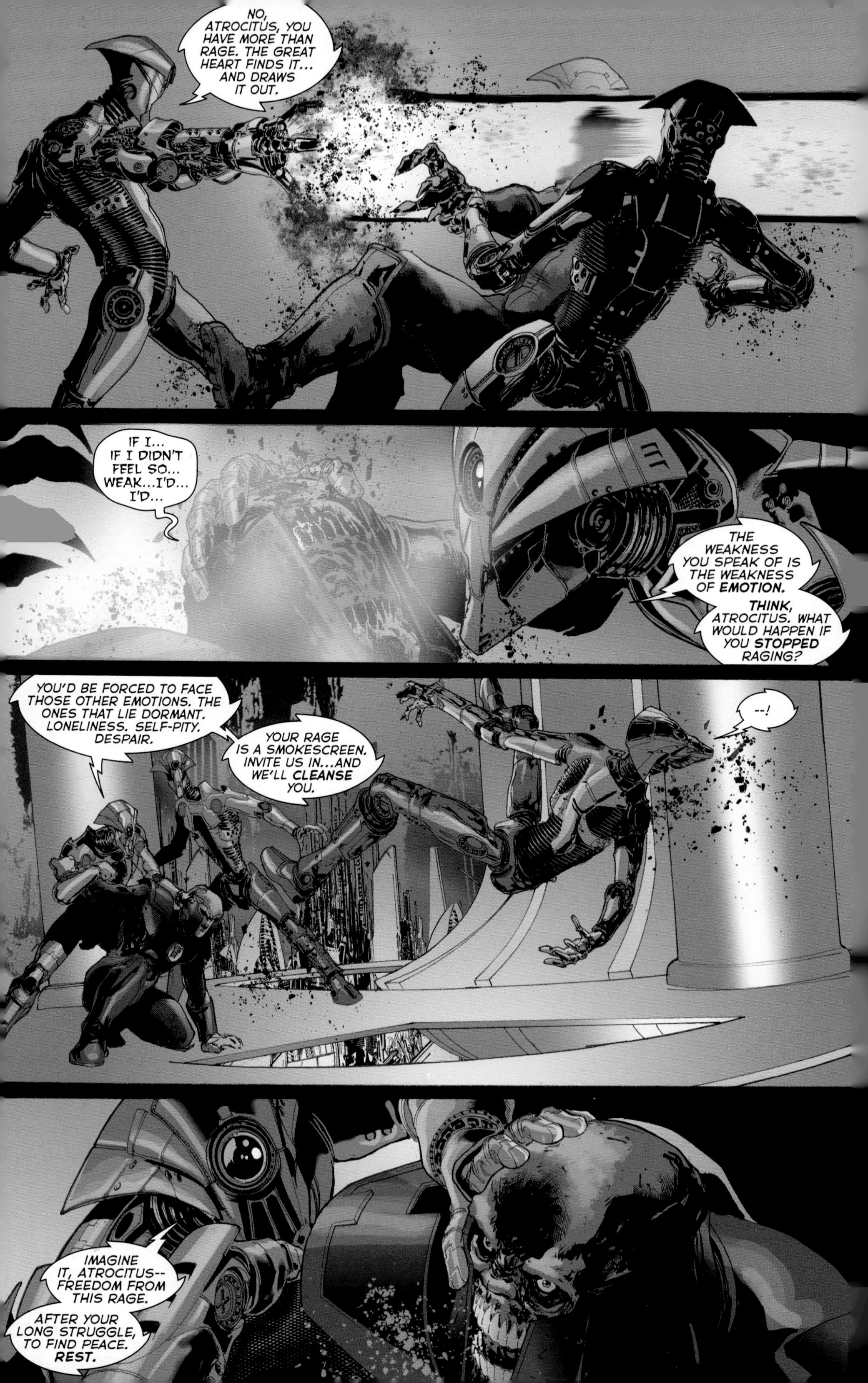
NO, ATROCITUS, YOU HAVE MORE THAN RAGE. THE GREAT HEART FINDS IT... AND DRAWS IT OUT.
IF I... IF I DIDN'T FEEL SO... WEAK...I'D... I'D...
THE WEAKNESS YOU SPEAK OF IS THE WEAKNESS OF **EMOTION.**
THINK, ATROCITUS. WHAT WOULD HAPPEN IF YOU **STOPPED** RAGING?
YOU'D BE FORCED TO FACE THOSE OTHER EMOTIONS. THE ONES THAT LIE DORMANT. LONELINESS. SELF-PITY. DESPAIR.
YOUR RAGE IS A SMOKESCREEN. INVITE US IN...AND WE'LL **CLEANSE** YOU.
--!
IMAGINE IT, ATROCITUS-- FREEDOM FROM THIS RAGE.
AFTER YOUR LONG STRUGGLE, TO FIND PEACE. **REST.**

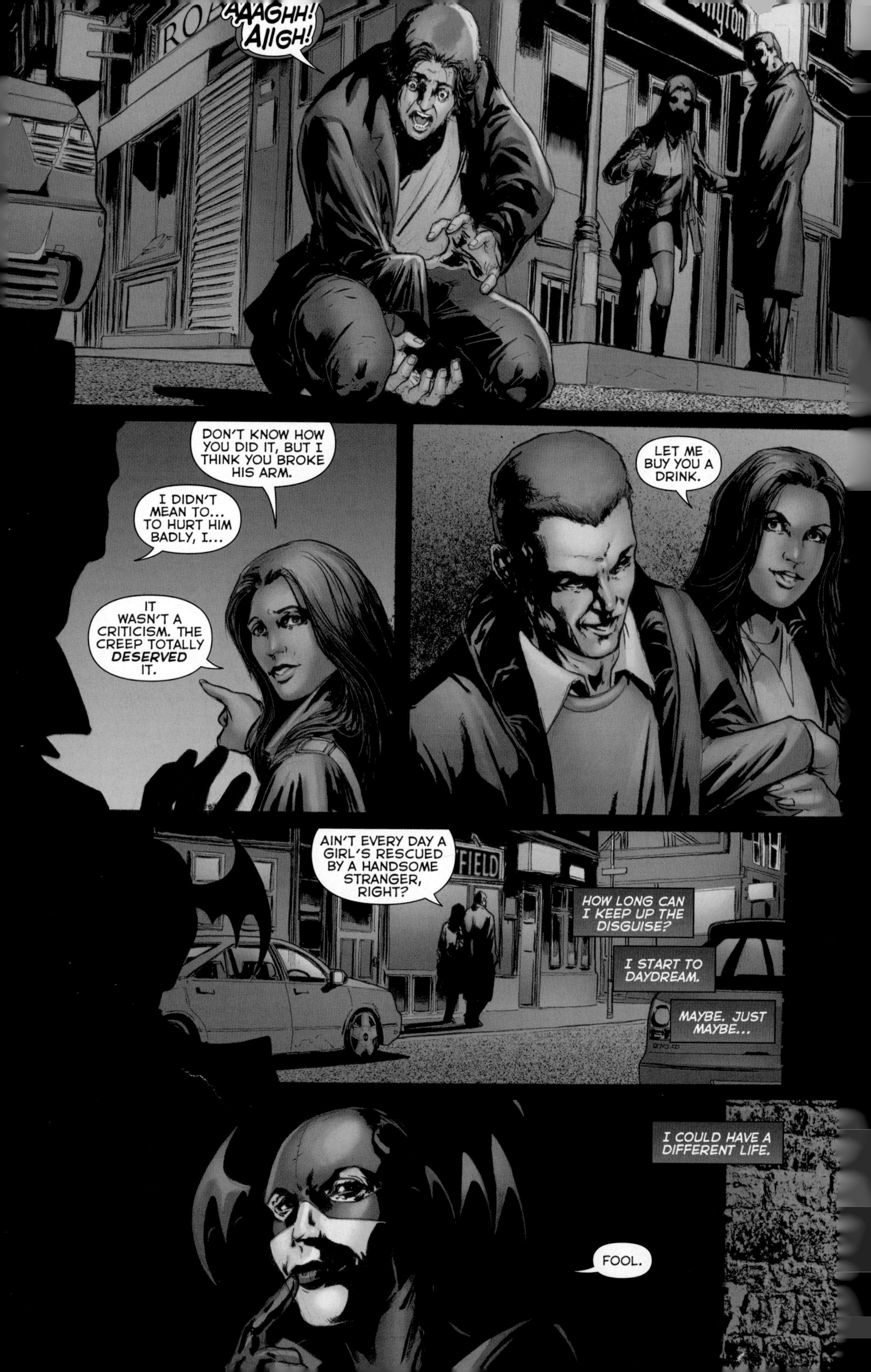
AAAGHH! AIIGH!
DON'T KNOW HOW YOU DID IT, BUT I THINK YOU BROKE HIS ARM.
I DIDN'T MEAN TO... TO HURT HIM BADLY, I...
IT WASN'T A CRITICISM. THE CREEP TOTALLY *DESERVED* IT.
LET ME BUY YOU A DRINK.
AIN'T EVERY DAY A GIRL'S RESCUED BY A HANDSOME STRANGER, RIGHT?
FIELD
HOW LONG CAN I KEEP UP THE DISGUISE?
I START TO DAYDREAM.
MAYBE. JUST MAYBE...
I COULD HAVE A DIFFERENT LIFE.
FOOL.

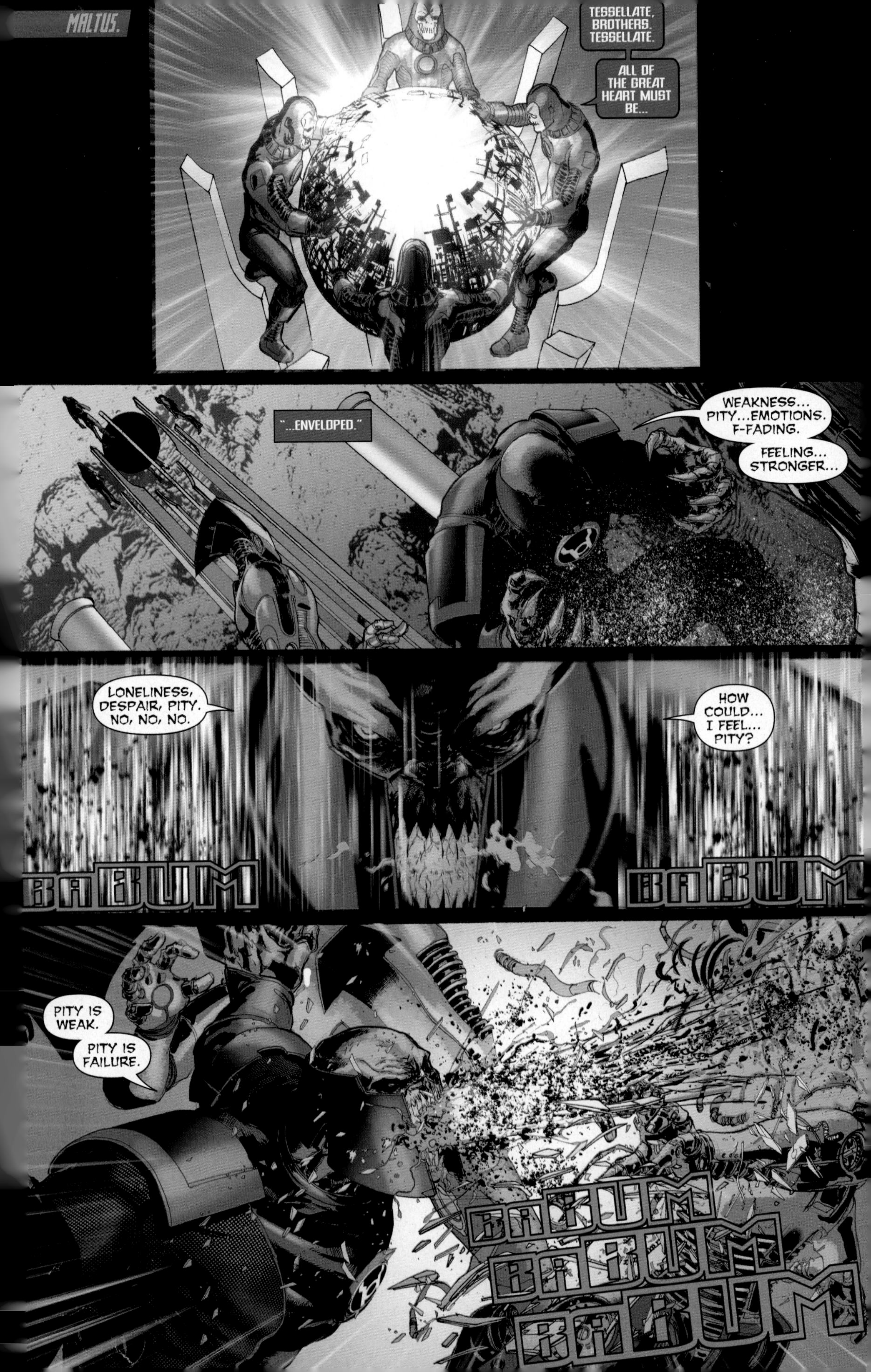
MALTUS.
TESSELLATE, BROTHERS. TESSELLATE.
ALL OF THE GREAT HEART MUST BE...
"...ENVELOPED."
WEAKNESS... PITY...EMOTIONS. F-FADING.
FEELING... STRONGER...
LONELINESS, DESPAIR, PITY. NO, NO, NO.
HOW COULD... I FEEL... PITY?
BABUM
BABUM
PITY IS WEAK.
PITY IS FAILURE.
BABUM
BABUM
BABUM

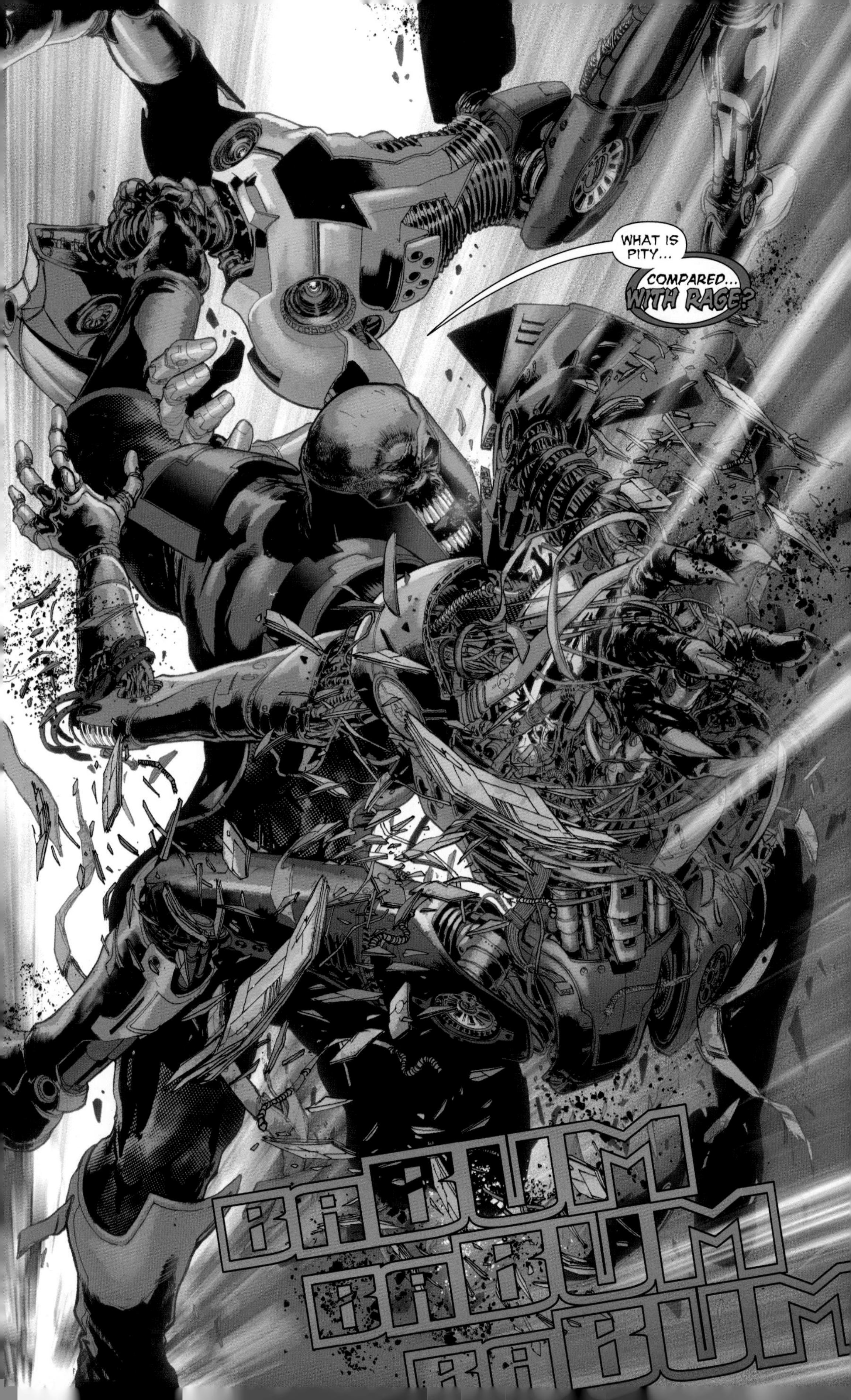
WHAT IS PITY...
COMPARED... WITH RAGE?
BRABUM
BRABUM
BRABUM

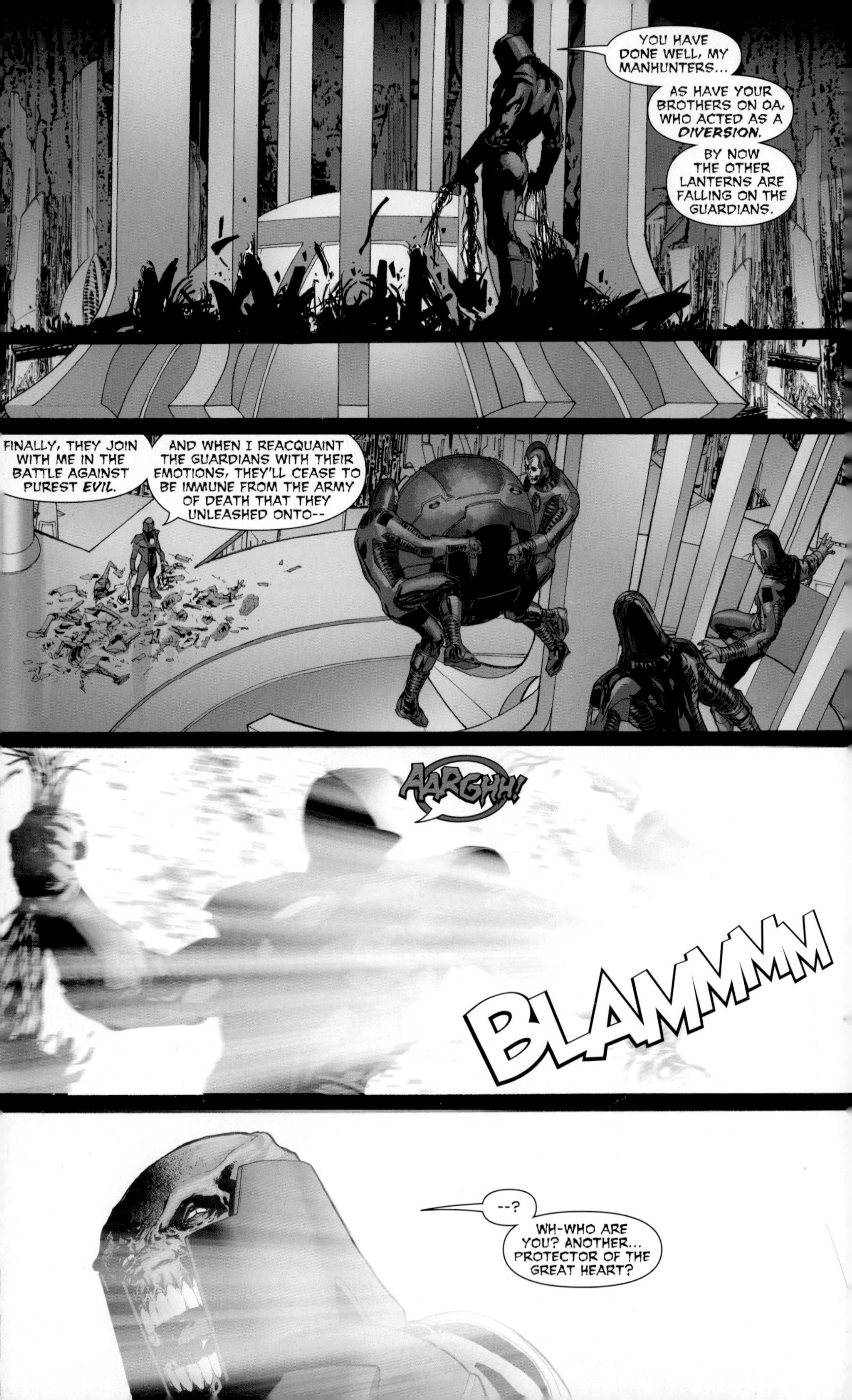

YOU HAVE DONE WELL, MY MANHUNTERS...
AS HAVE YOUR BROTHERS ON OA, WHO ACTED AS A *DIVERSION*.
BY NOW THE OTHER LANTERNS ARE FALLING ON THE GUARDIANS.
FINALLY, THEY JOIN WITH ME IN THE BATTLE AGAINST PUREST *EVIL*.
AND WHEN I REACQUAINT THE GUARDIANS WITH THEIR EMOTIONS, THEY'LL CEASE TO BE IMMUNE FROM THE ARMY OF DEATH THAT THEY UNLEASHED ONTO--
AARGHH!
BLAMMMM
--?
WH-WHO ARE YOU? ANOTHER... PROTECTOR OF THE GREAT HEART?

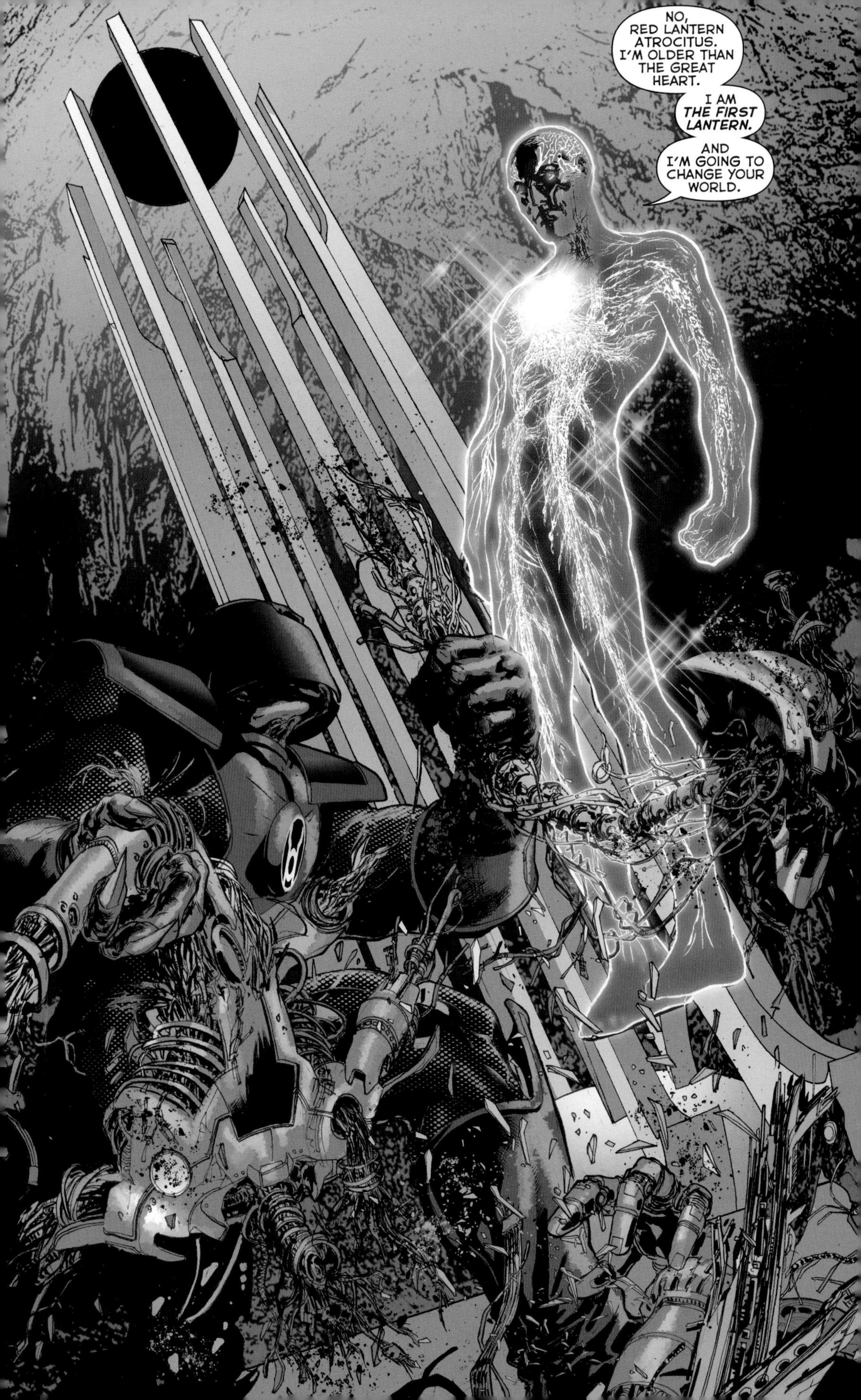
NO, RED LANTERN ATROCITUS. I'M OLDER THAN THE GREAT HEART.
I AM *THE FIRST LANTERN.*
AND I'M GOING TO CHANGE YOUR WORLD.

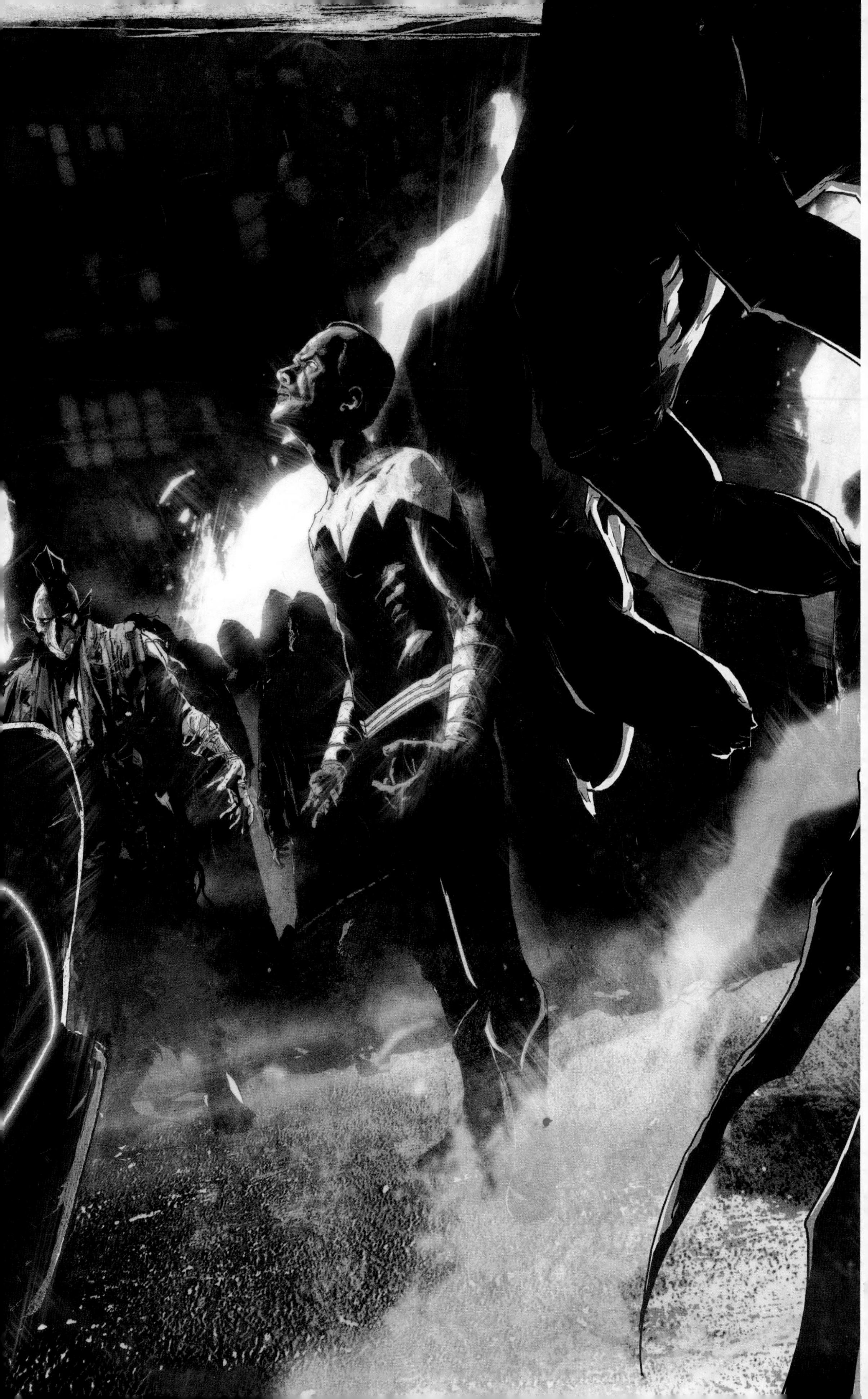

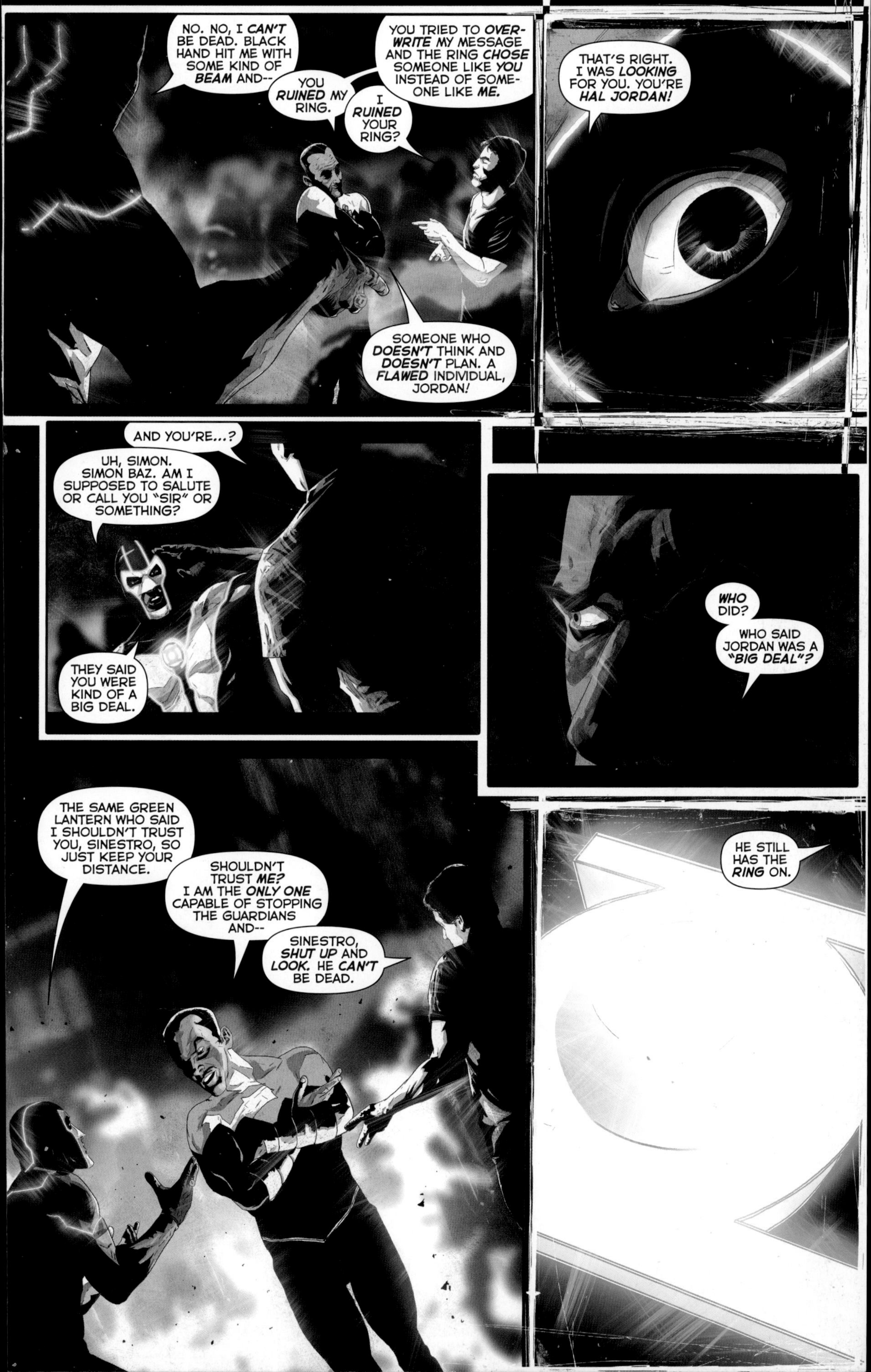

NO. NO, I CAN'T BE DEAD. BLACK HAND HIT ME WITH SOME KIND OF BEAM AND--
YOU RUINED MY RING.
YOU TRIED TO OVER-WRITE MY MESSAGE AND THE RING CHOSE SOMEONE LIKE YOU INSTEAD OF SOME-ONE LIKE ME.
I RUINED YOUR RING?
SOMEONE WHO DOESN'T THINK AND DOESN'T PLAN. A FLAWED INDIVIDUAL, JORDAN!
THAT'S RIGHT. I WAS LOOKING FOR YOU. YOU'RE HAL JORDAN!
AND YOU'RE...?
UH, SIMON. SIMON BAZ. AM I SUPPOSED TO SALUTE OR CALL YOU "SIR" OR SOMETHING?
THEY SAID YOU WERE KIND OF A BIG DEAL.
WHO DID?
WHO SAID JORDAN WAS A "BIG DEAL"?
THE SAME GREEN LANTERN WHO SAID I SHOULDN'T TRUST YOU, SINESTRO, SO JUST KEEP YOUR DISTANCE.
SHOULDN'T TRUST ME? I AM THE ONLY ONE CAPABLE OF STOPPING THE GUARDIANS AND--
SINESTRO, SHUT UP AND LOOK. HE CAN'T BE DEAD.
HE STILL HAS THE RING ON.

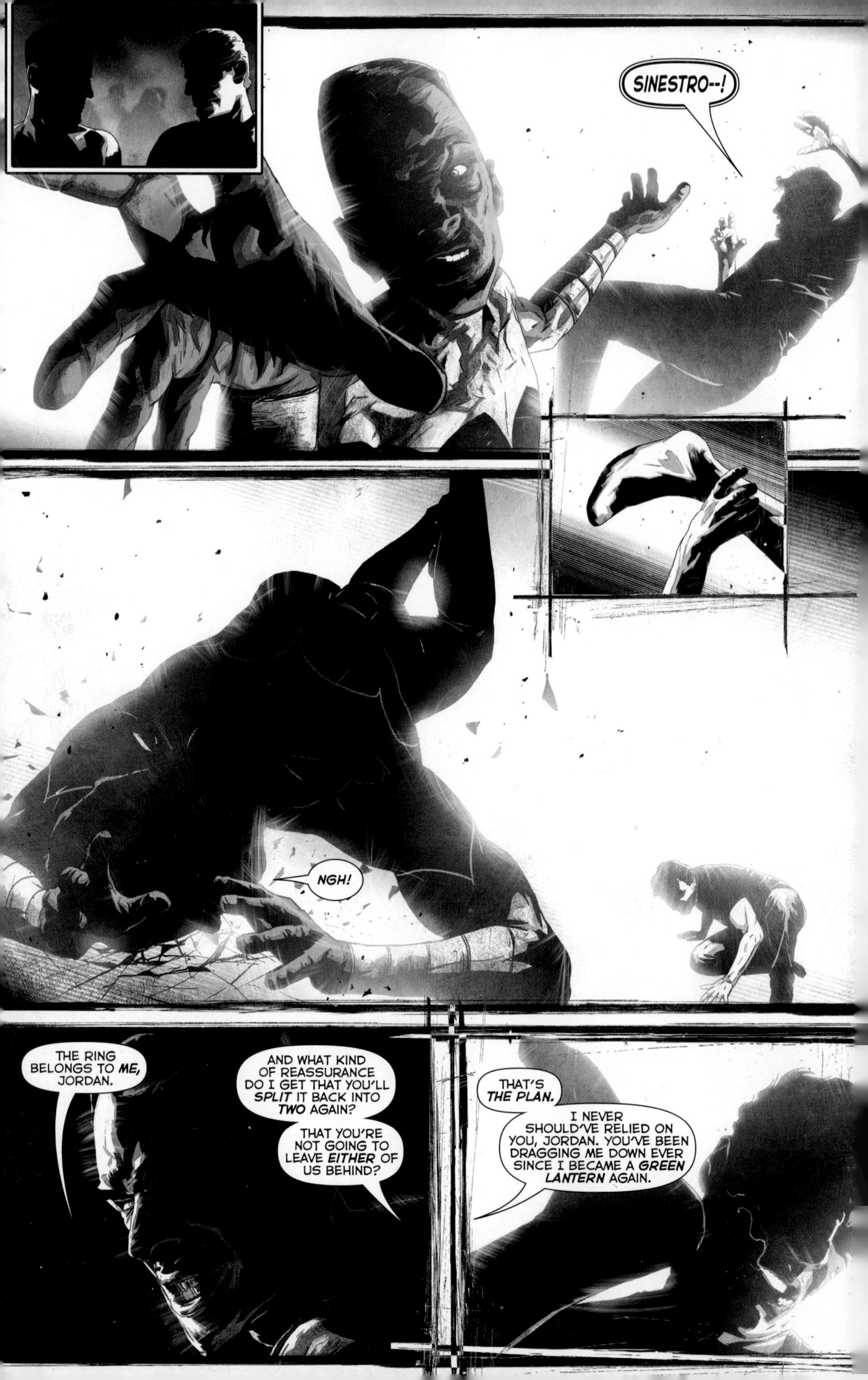
SINESTRO--!
NGH!
THE RING BELONGS TO *ME,* JORDAN.
AND WHAT KIND OF REASSURANCE DO I GET THAT YOU'LL *SPLIT* IT BACK INTO *TWO* AGAIN?
THAT YOU'RE NOT GOING TO LEAVE *EITHER* OF US BEHIND?
THAT'S *THE PLAN.*
I NEVER SHOULD'VE RELIED ON YOU, JORDAN. YOU'VE BEEN DRAGGING ME DOWN EVER SINCE I BECAME A *GREEN LANTERN* AGAIN.

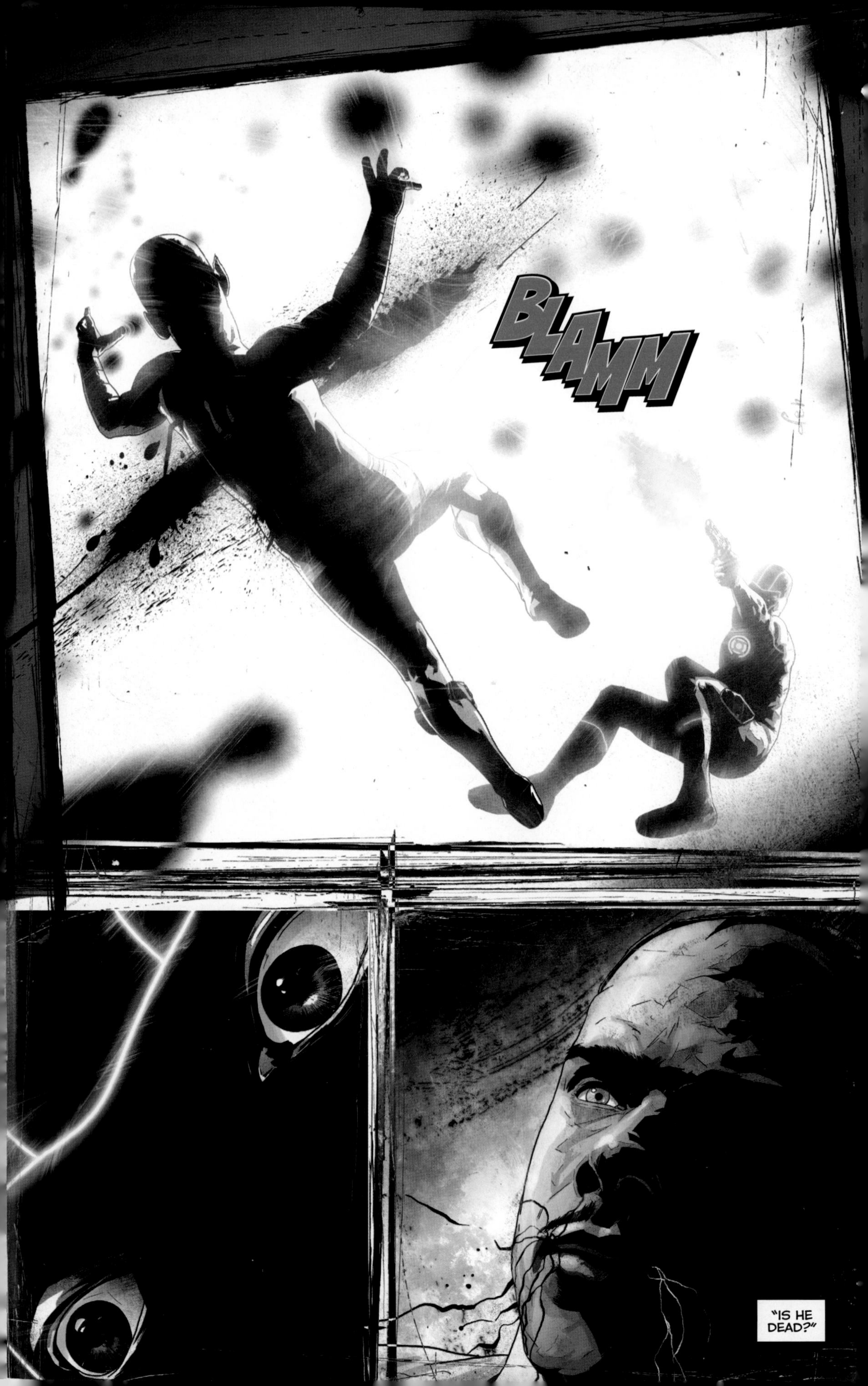
BLAMM
"IS HE DEAD?"

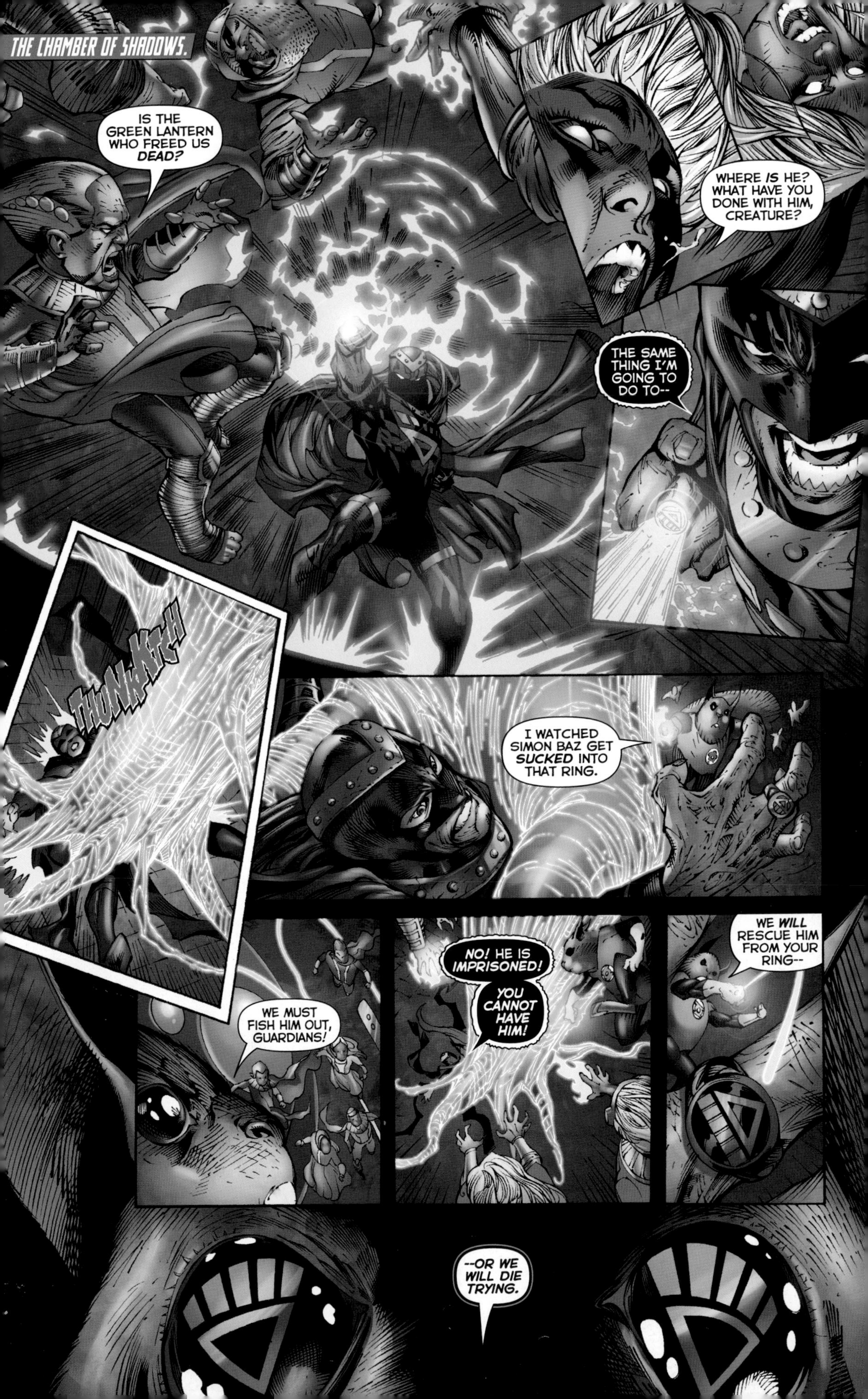
THE CHAMBER OF SHADOWS.
IS THE GREEN LANTERN WHO FREED US *DEAD?*
WHERE *IS* HE? WHAT HAVE YOU DONE WITH HIM, CREATURE?
THE SAME THING I'M GOING TO DO TO--
THUNKKTCH
I WATCHED SIMON BAZ GET *SUCKED* INTO THAT RING.
WE MUST FISH HIM OUT, GUARDIANS!
NO! HE IS *IMPRISONED!*
YOU CANNOT HAVE HIM!
WE *WILL* RESCUE HIM FROM YOUR RING--
--OR WE WILL DIE TRYING.

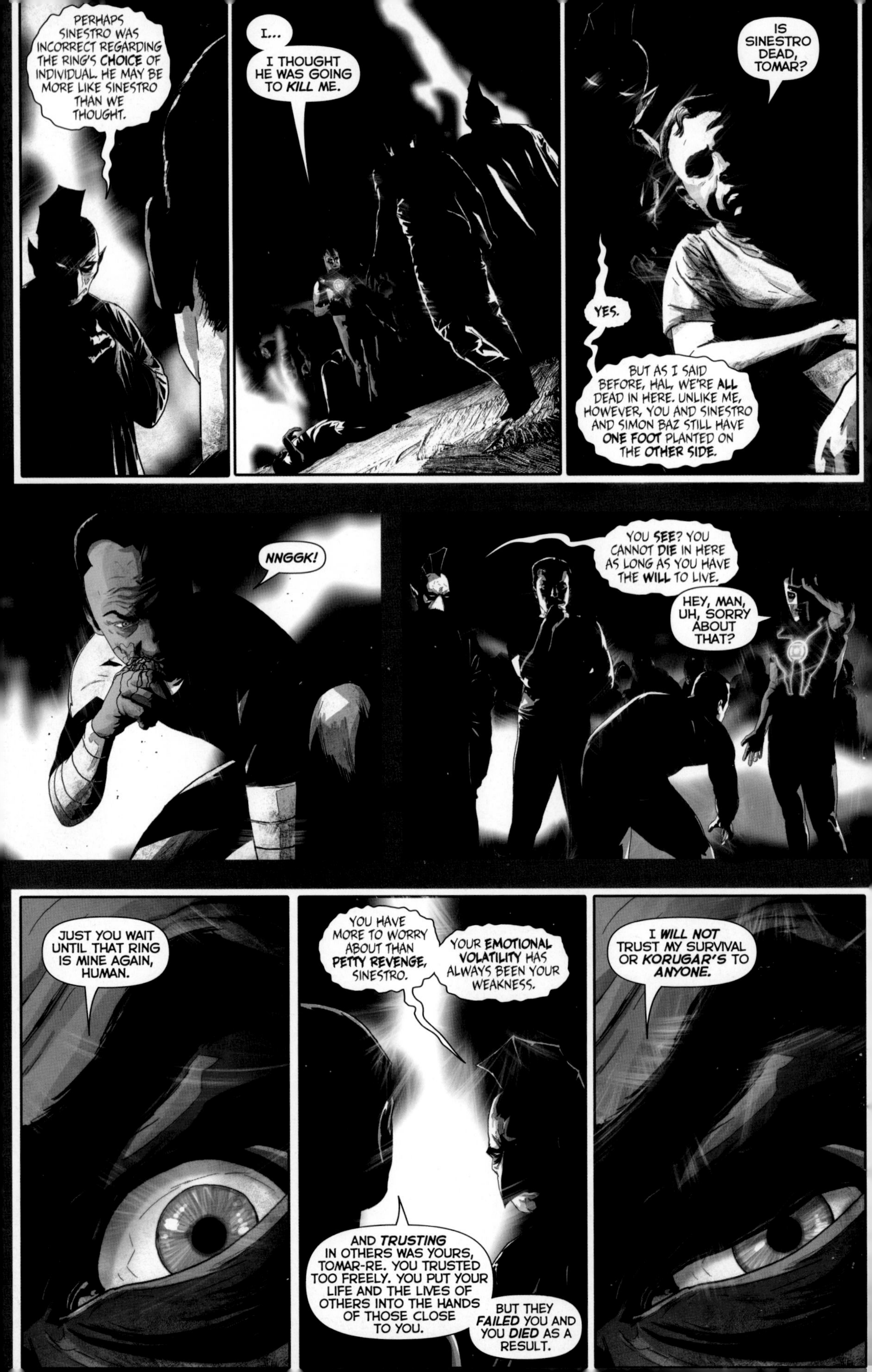
PERHAPS SINESTRO WAS INCORRECT REGARDING THE RING'S CHOICE OF INDIVIDUAL. HE MAY BE MORE LIKE SINESTRO THAN WE THOUGHT.
I...
I THOUGHT HE WAS GOING TO KILL ME.
IS SINESTRO DEAD, TOMAR?
YES.
BUT AS I SAID BEFORE, HAL, WE'RE ALL DEAD IN HERE. UNLIKE ME, HOWEVER, YOU AND SINESTRO AND SIMON BAZ STILL HAVE ONE FOOT PLANTED ON THE OTHER SIDE.
NNGGK!
YOU SEE? YOU CANNOT DIE IN HERE AS LONG AS YOU HAVE THE WILL TO LIVE.
HEY, MAN, UH, SORRY ABOUT THAT?
JUST YOU WAIT UNTIL THAT RING IS MINE AGAIN, HUMAN.
YOU HAVE MORE TO WORRY ABOUT THAN PETTY REVENGE, SINESTRO.
YOUR EMOTIONAL VOLATILITY HAS ALWAYS BEEN YOUR WEAKNESS.
AND TRUSTING IN OTHERS WAS YOURS, TOMAR-RE. YOU TRUSTED TOO FREELY. YOU PUT YOUR LIFE AND THE LIVES OF OTHERS INTO THE HANDS OF THOSE CLOSE TO YOU.
BUT THEY FAILED YOU AND YOU DIED AS A RESULT.
I WILL NOT TRUST MY SURVIVAL OR KORUGAR'S TO ANYONE.

AS LONG AS THE GUARDIANS BELIEVE I AM DEAD, MY PLANET IS SAFE.

NO PLANET IS SAFE, SINESTRO. NOT KORUGAR. NOT EARTH.

I'M TIRED OF LISTENING TO YOUR NONSENSE. WE KNOW FULL WELL THE GUARDIANS HAVE TURNED AGAINST THE UNIVERSE. EVEN NOW THEY--

THEY ARE AT SOMEONE ELSE'S MERCY, SINESTRO.

HOW DO YOU KNOW THAT?

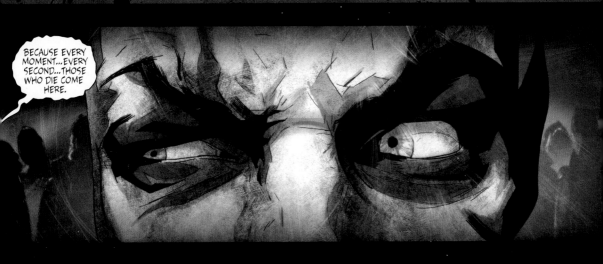

BECAUSE EVERY MOMENT...EVERY SECOND...THOSE WHO DIE COME HERE.

AND WORD SPREADS QUICKLY WHEN IT COMES TO VOLTHOOM.

THAT NAME AGAIN--AS IF IT WERE SUPPOSED TO MEAN SOMETHING TO US.

VOLTHOOM IS RESPONSIBLE FOR THE DEATH OF ALL THOSE YOU SEE HERE.

THOSE THINGS STARING AT US? THERE ARE MAYBE A HUNDRED--

A HUNDRED?

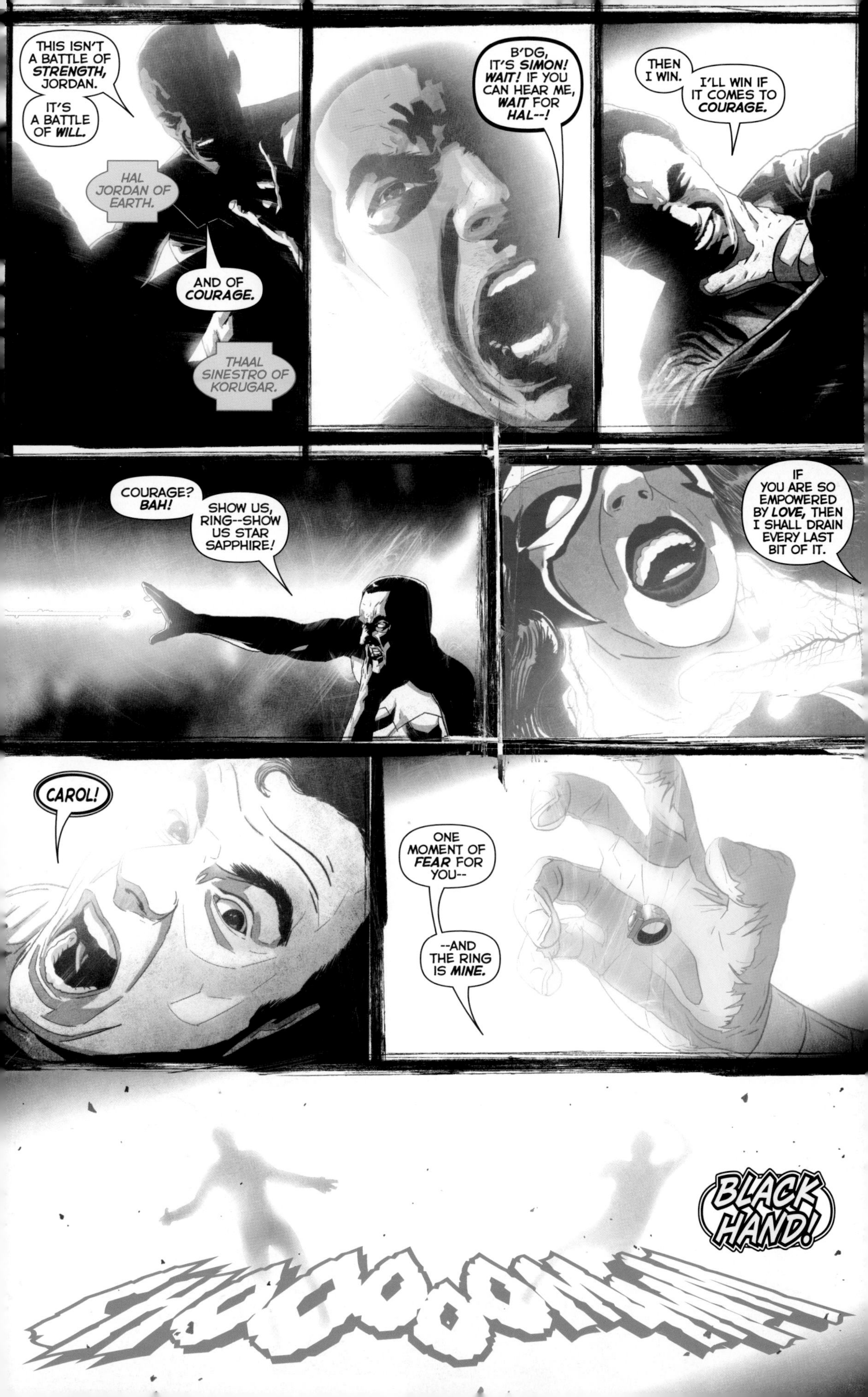
THIS ISN'T A BATTLE OF STRENGTH, JORDAN.
IT'S A BATTLE OF WILL.
HAL JORDAN OF EARTH.
AND OF COURAGE.
THAAL SINESTRO OF KORUGAR.
B'DG, IT'S SIMON! WAIT! IF YOU CAN HEAR ME, WAIT FOR HAL--!
THEN I WIN.
I'LL WIN IF IT COMES TO COURAGE.
COURAGE? BAH!
SHOW US, RING--SHOW US STAR SAPPHIRE!
IF YOU ARE SO EMPOWERED BY LOVE, THEN I SHALL DRAIN EVERY LAST BIT OF IT.
CAROL!
ONE MOMENT OF FEAR FOR YOU--
--AND THE RING IS MINE.
BLACK HAND!

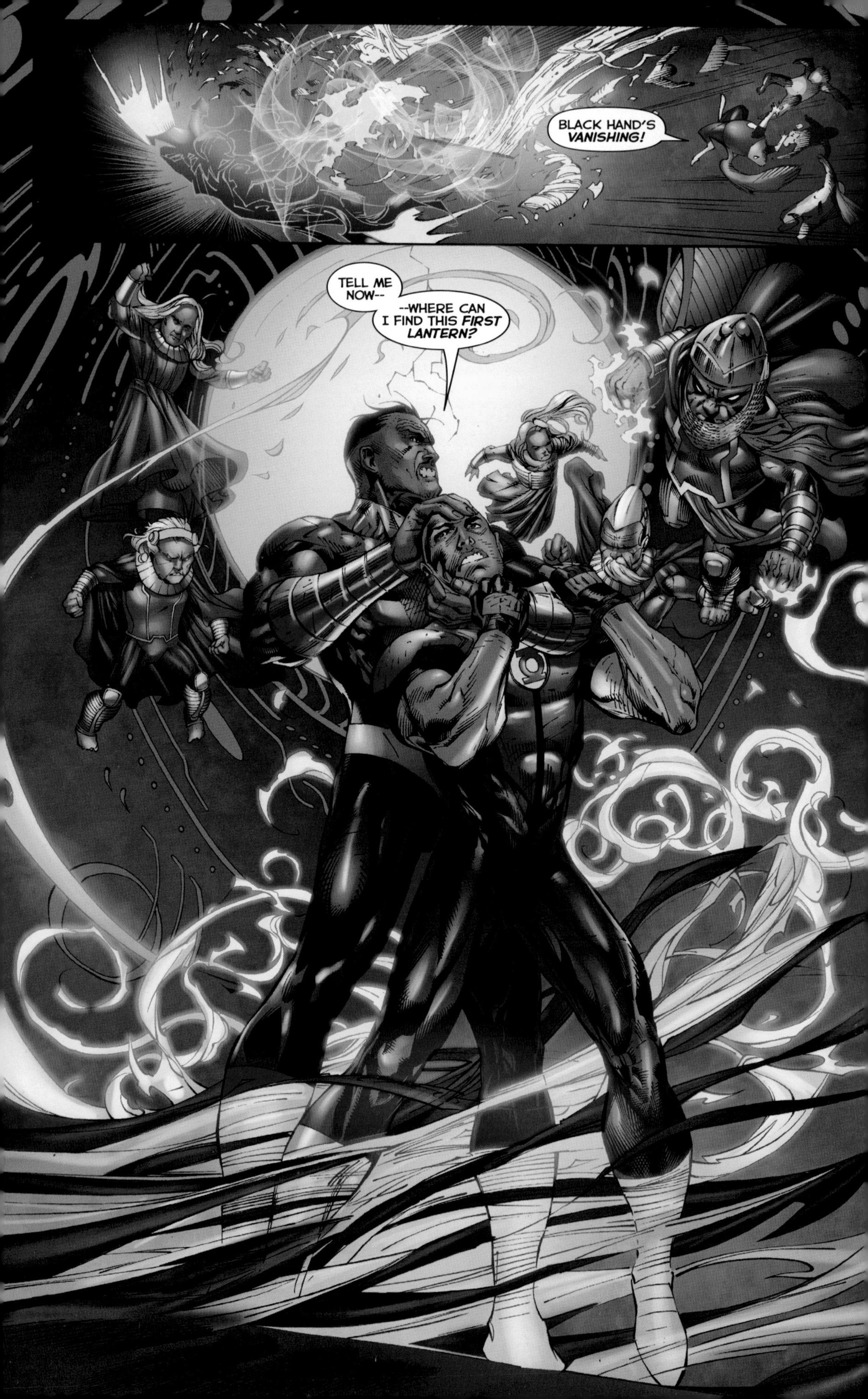
BLACK HAND'S VANISHING!
TELL ME NOW--
--WHERE CAN I FIND THIS FIRST LANTERN?

WHAT IF I DON'T?

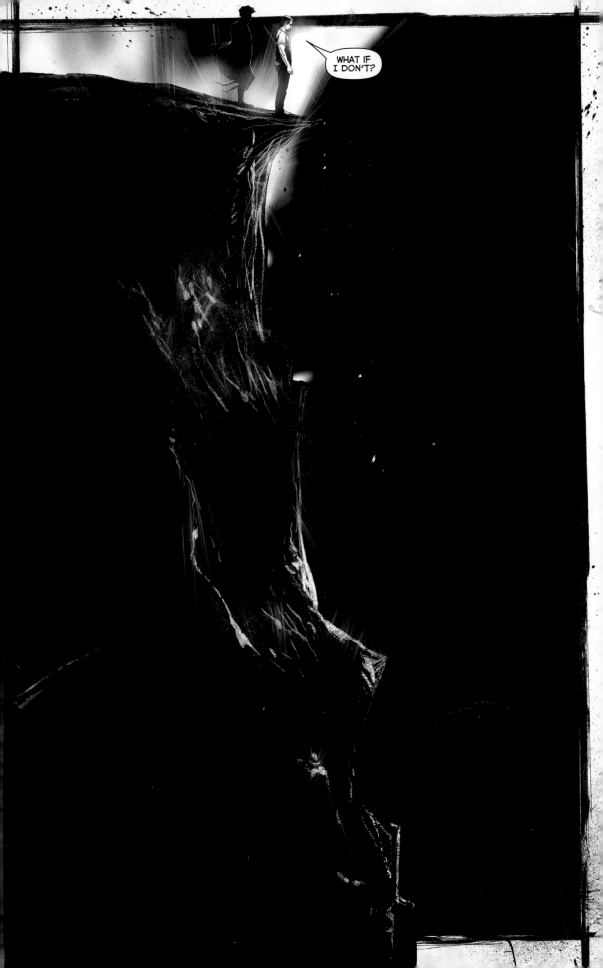

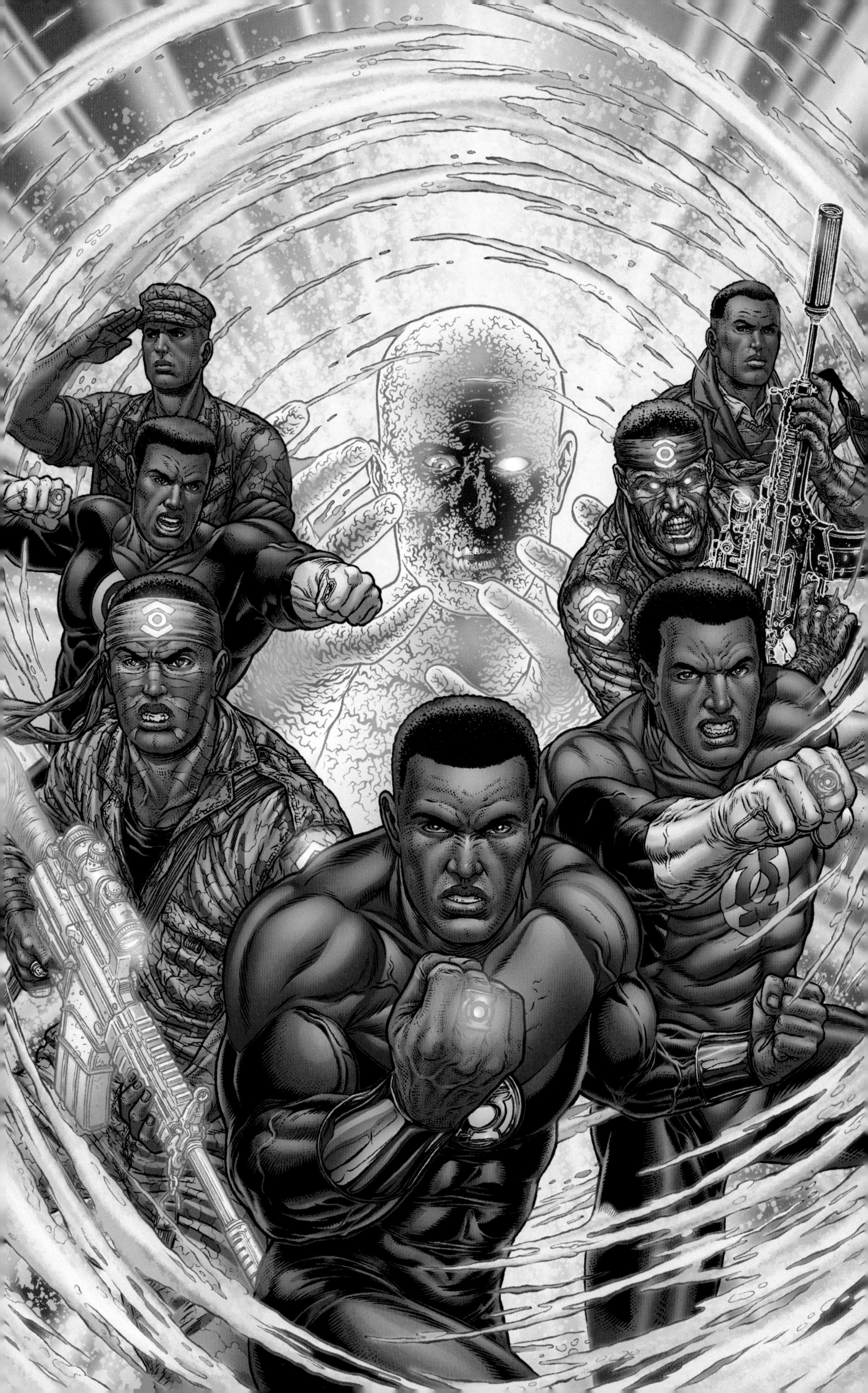

PART SIX: PIECES OF YOU

PETER J. TOMASI writer **CHRISCROSS** penciller **SCOTT HANNA** inker

cover art by **JUAN JOSÉ RYP & GABE ELTAEB**

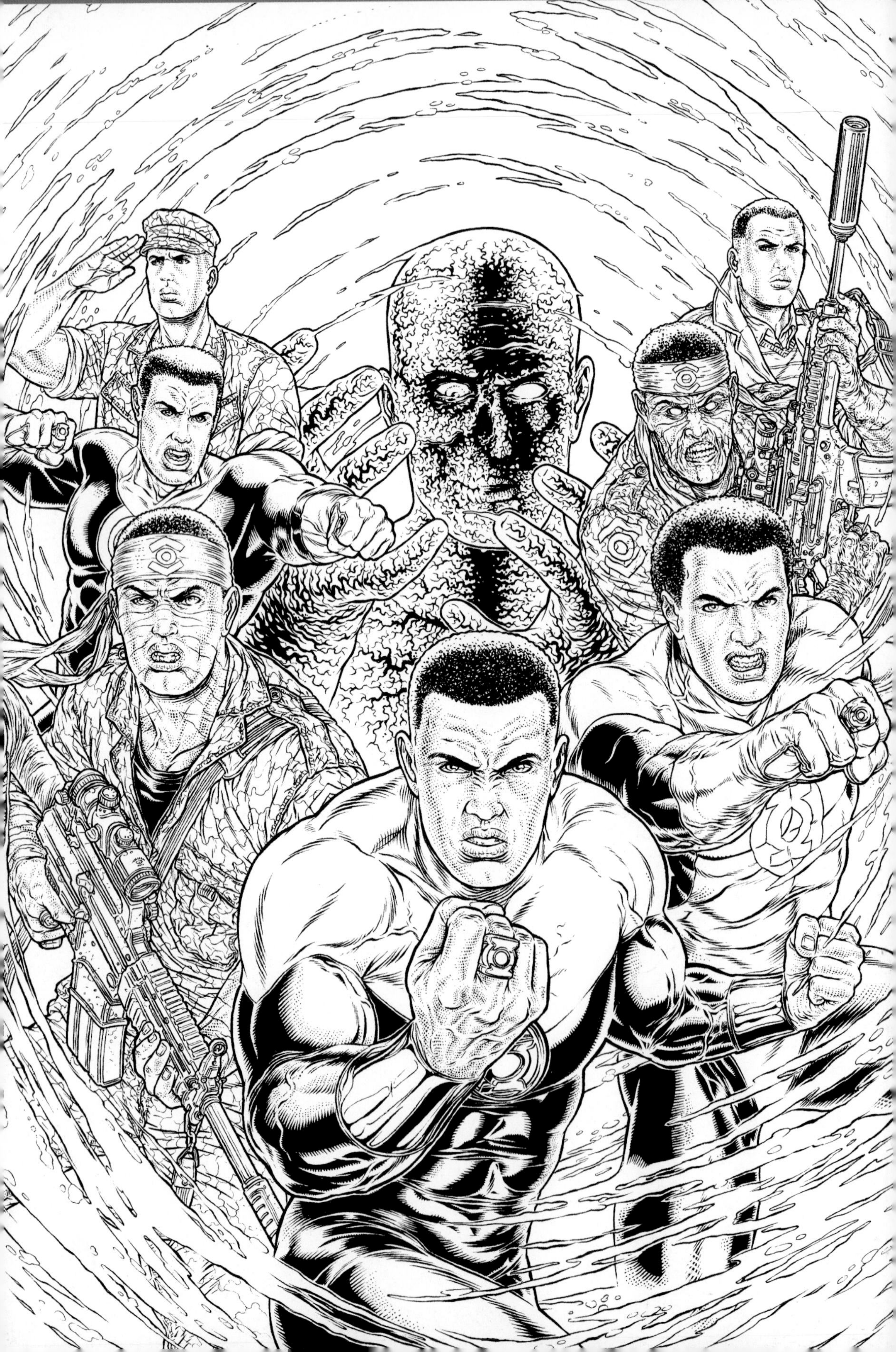

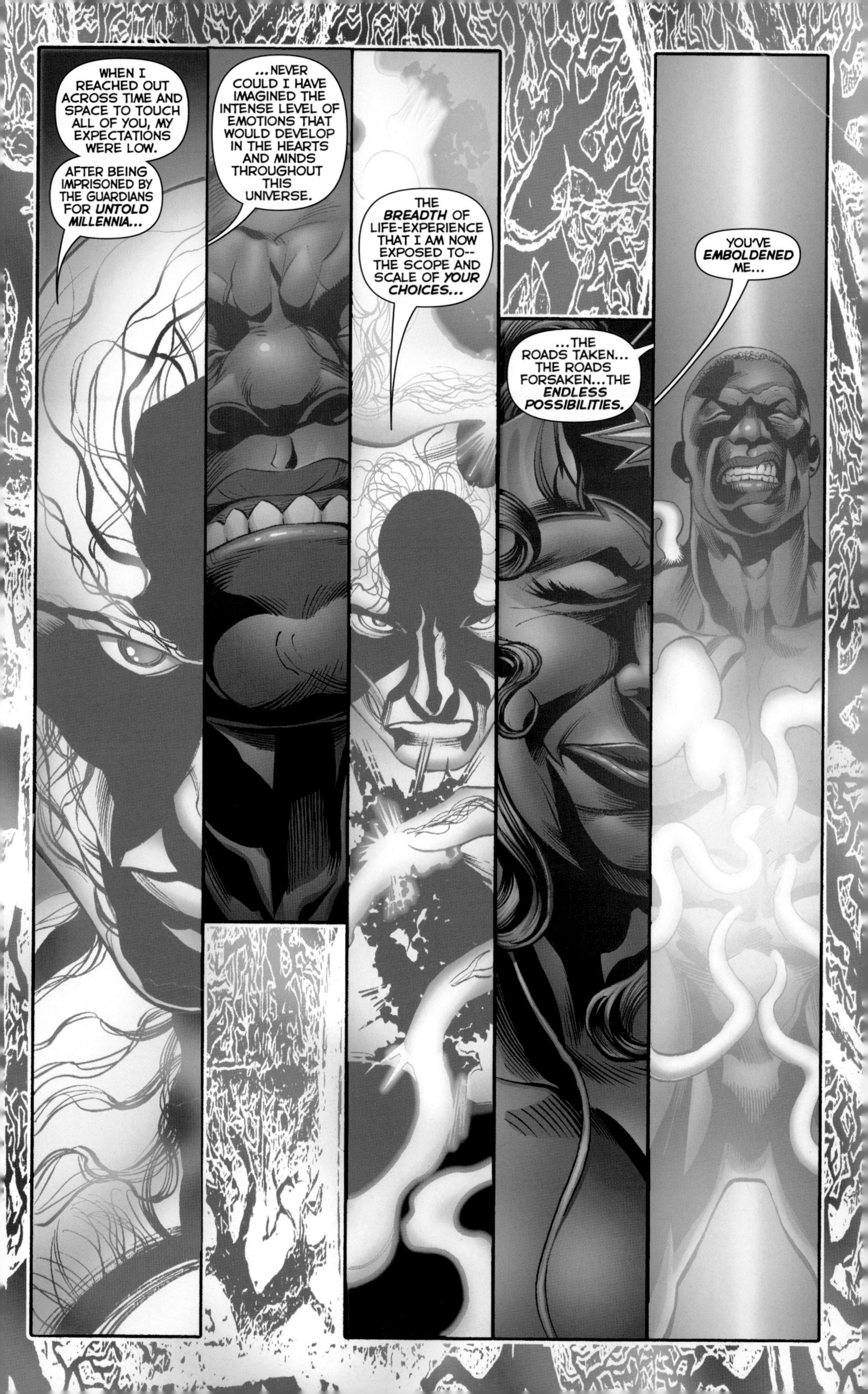
WHEN I REACHED OUT ACROSS TIME AND SPACE TO TOUCH ALL OF YOU, MY EXPECTATIONS WERE LOW.
AFTER BEING IMPRISONED BY THE GUARDIANS FOR *UNTOLD MILLENNIA...*
...NEVER COULD I HAVE IMAGINED THE INTENSE LEVEL OF EMOTIONS THAT WOULD DEVELOP IN THE HEARTS AND MINDS THROUGHOUT THIS UNIVERSE.
THE *BREADTH* OF LIFE-EXPERIENCE THAT I AM NOW EXPOSED TO-- THE SCOPE AND SCALE OF *YOUR CHOICES...*
...THE ROADS TAKEN... THE ROADS FORSAKEN...THE *ENDLESS POSSIBILITIES.*
YOU'VE *EMBOLDENED* ME...

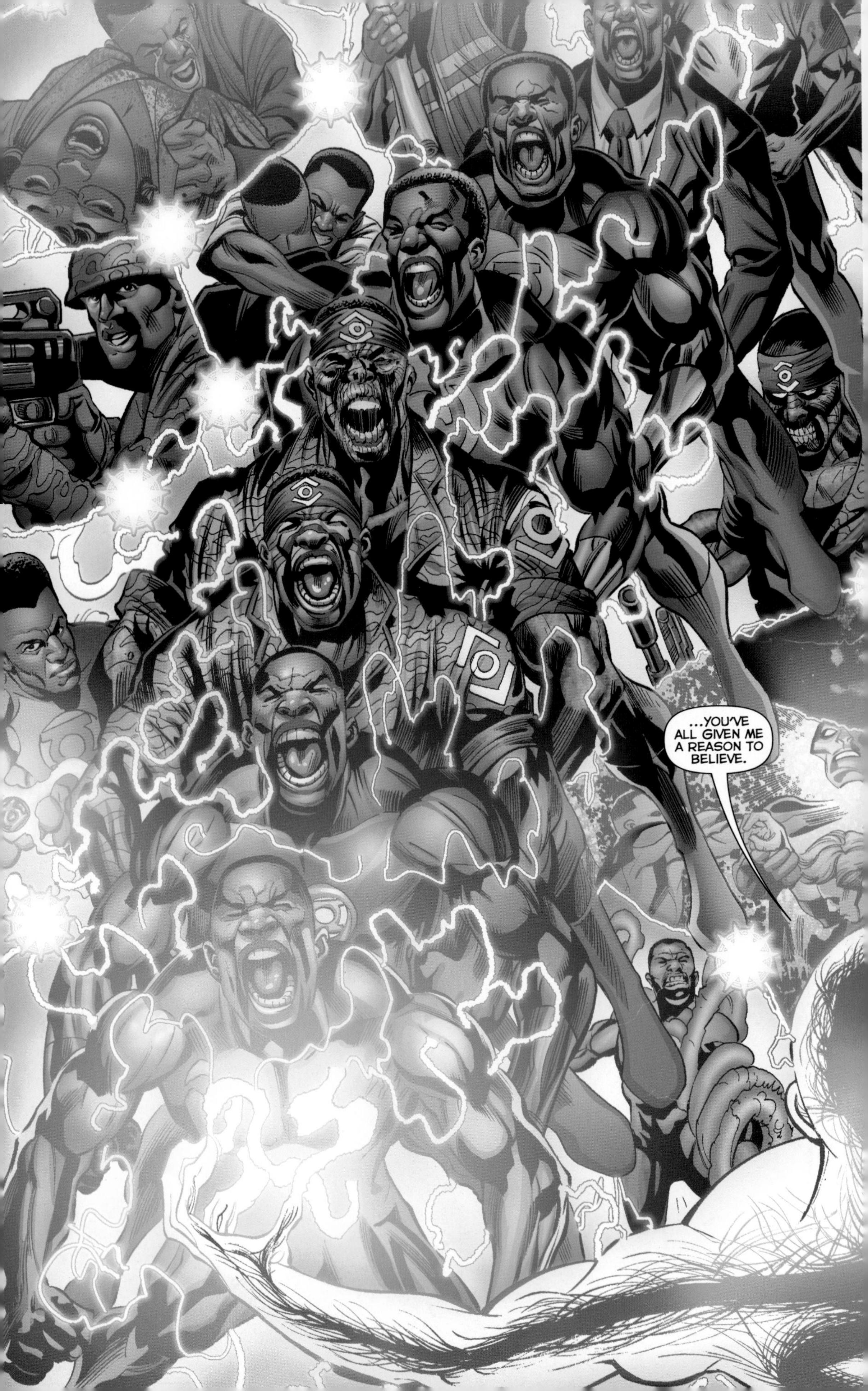
...YOU'VE ALL GIVEN ME A REASON TO BELIEVE.

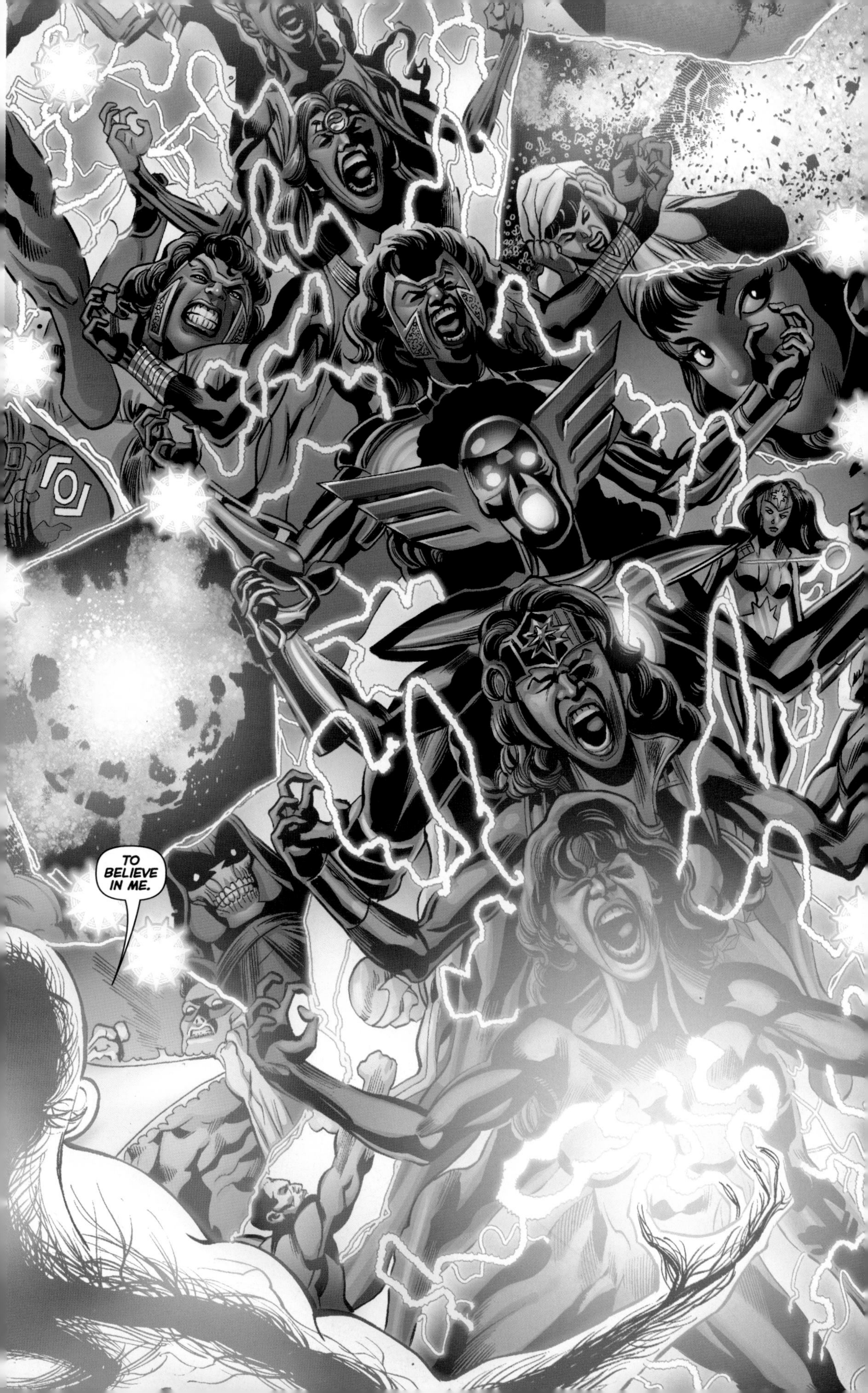
TO BELIEVE IN ME.

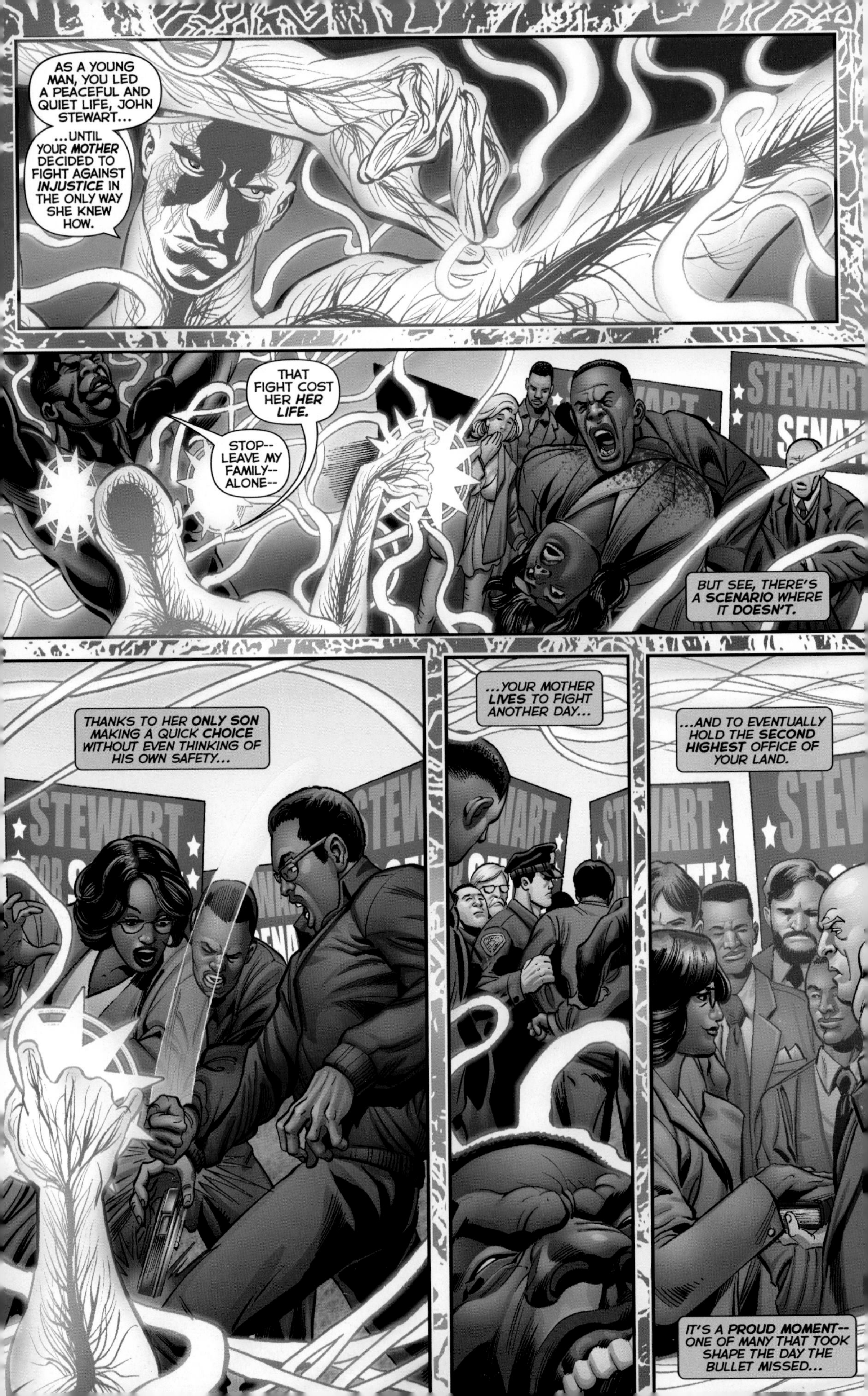

AS A YOUNG MAN, YOU LED A PEACEFUL AND QUIET LIFE, JOHN STEWART...
...UNTIL YOUR MOTHER DECIDED TO FIGHT AGAINST INJUSTICE IN THE ONLY WAY SHE KNEW HOW.
THAT FIGHT COST HER HER LIFE.
STOP-- LEAVE MY FAMILY-- ALONE--
STEWART FOR SENAT
BUT SEE, THERE'S A SCENARIO WHERE IT DOESN'T.
THANKS TO HER ONLY SON MAKING A QUICK CHOICE WITHOUT EVEN THINKING OF HIS OWN SAFETY...
STEWART
...YOUR MOTHER LIVES TO FIGHT ANOTHER DAY...
...AND TO EVENTUALLY HOLD THE SECOND HIGHEST OFFICE OF YOUR LAND.
IT'S A PROUD MOMENT-- ONE OF MANY THAT TOOK SHAPE THE DAY THE BULLET MISSED...

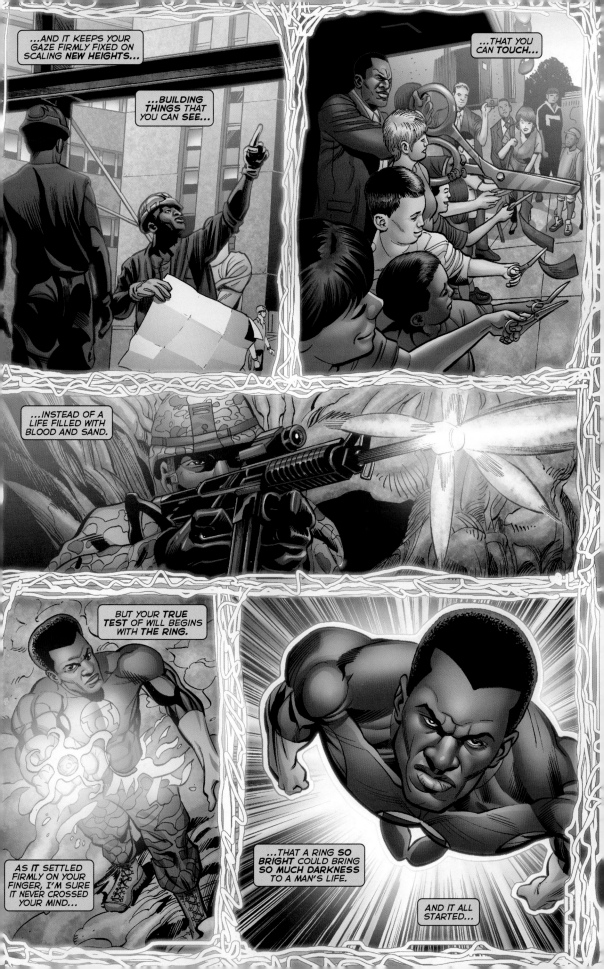

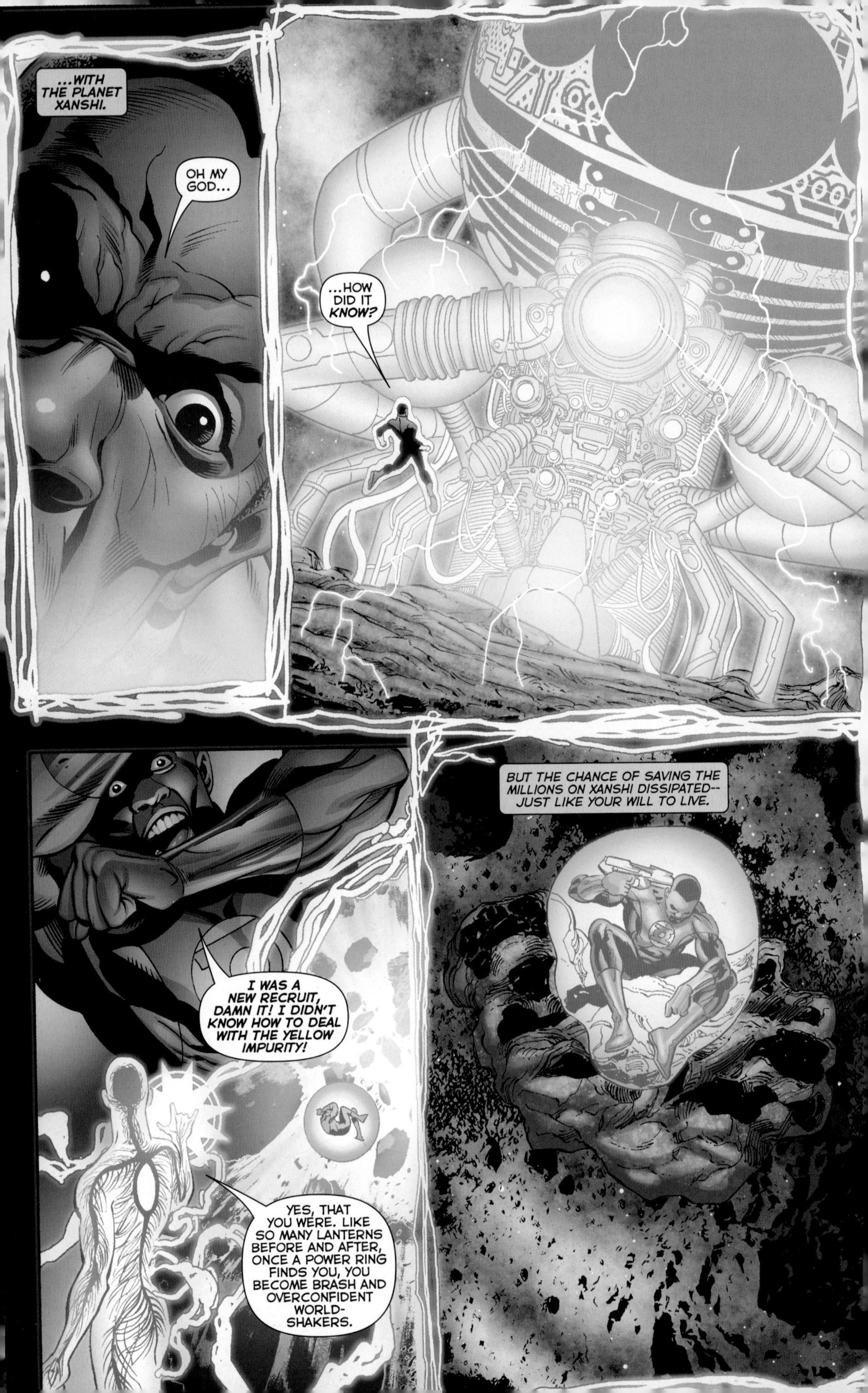
...WITH THE PLANET XANSHI.
OH MY GOD...
...HOW DID IT KNOW?
I WAS A NEW RECRUIT, DAMN IT! I DIDN'T KNOW HOW TO DEAL WITH THE YELLOW IMPURITY!
YES, THAT YOU WERE. LIKE SO MANY LANTERNS BEFORE AND AFTER, ONCE A POWER RING FINDS YOU, YOU BECOME BRASH AND OVERCONFIDENT WORLD-SHAKERS.
BUT THE CHANCE OF SAVING THE MILLIONS ON XANSHI DISSIPATED-- JUST LIKE YOUR WILL TO LIVE.

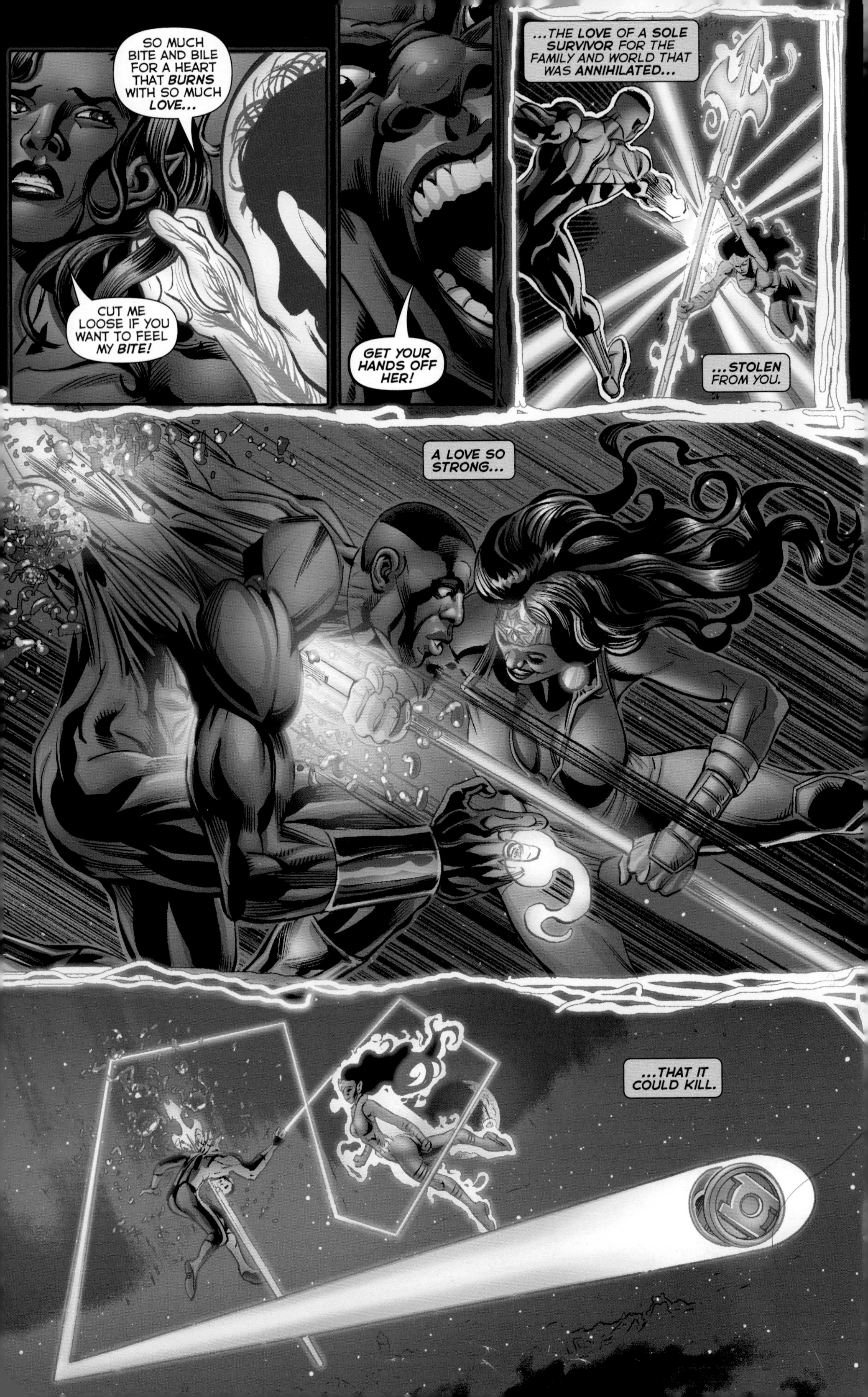
SO MUCH BITE AND BILE FOR A HEART THAT BURNS WITH SO MUCH LOVE...
CUT ME LOOSE IF YOU WANT TO FEEL MY BITE!
GET YOUR HANDS OFF HER!
...THE LOVE OF A SOLE SURVIVOR FOR THE FAMILY AND WORLD THAT WAS ANNIHILATED...
...STOLEN FROM YOU.
A LOVE SO STRONG...
...THAT IT COULD KILL.

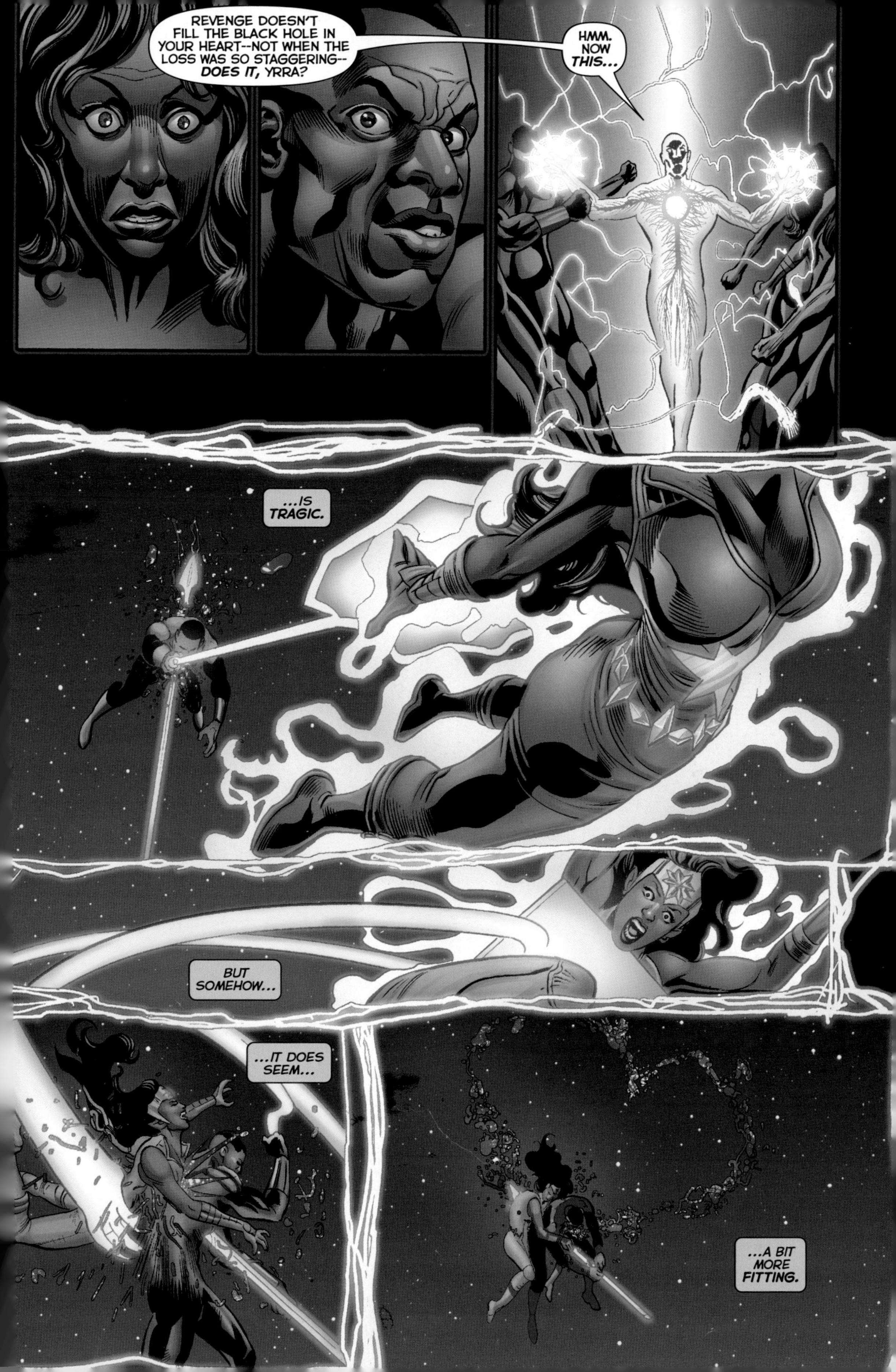
REVENGE DOESN'T FILL THE BLACK HOLE IN YOUR HEART--NOT WHEN THE LOSS WAS SO STAGGERING--DOES IT, YRRA?
HMM. NOW THIS...
...IS TRAGIC.
BUT SOMEHOW...
...IT DOES SEEM...
...A BIT MORE FITTING.

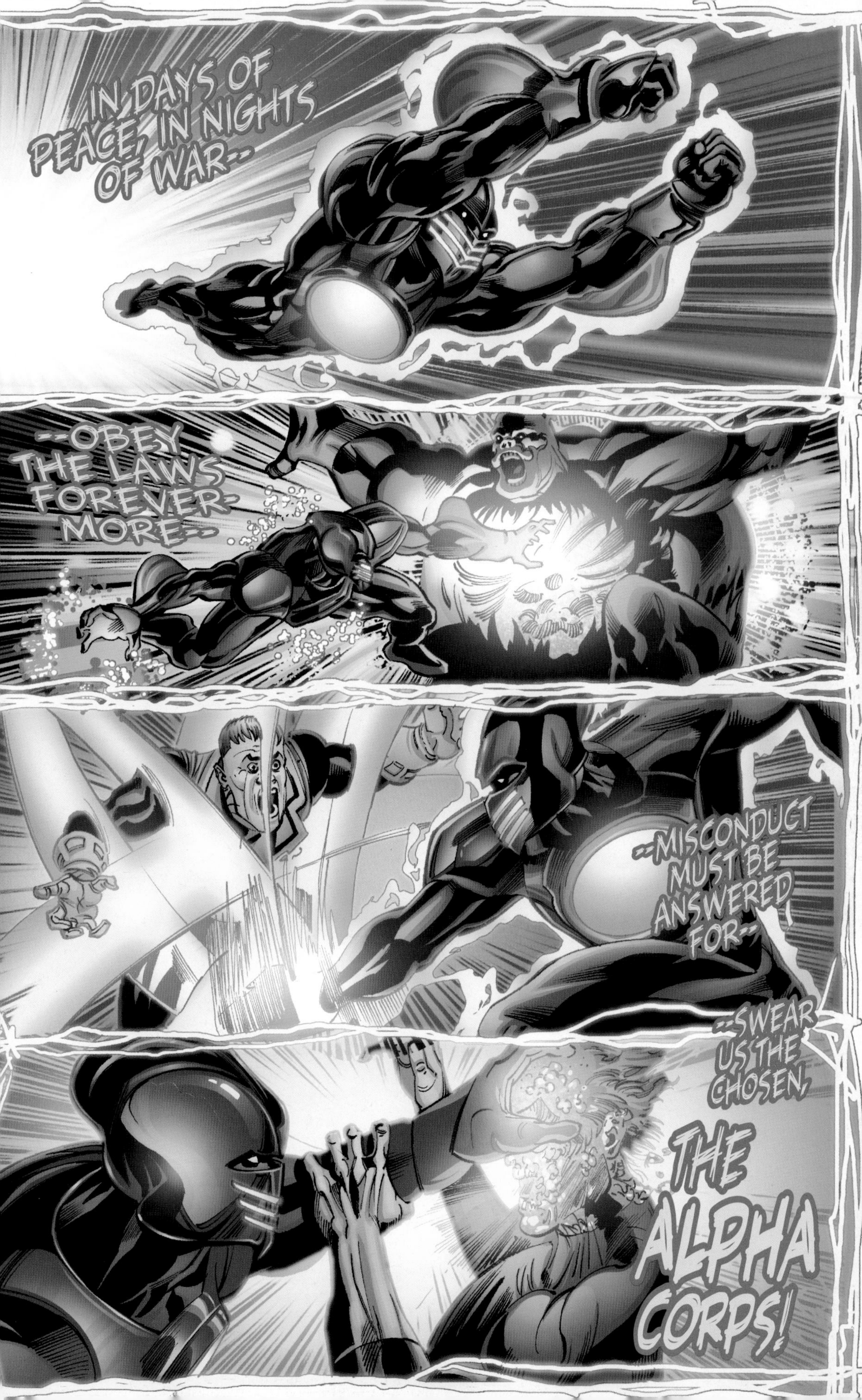
IN DAYS OF PEACE, IN NIGHTS OF WAR--
--OBEY THE LAWS FOREVER-MORE--
--MISCONDUCT MUST BE ANSWERED FOR--
--SWEAR US THE CHOSEN,
THE ALPHA CORPS!

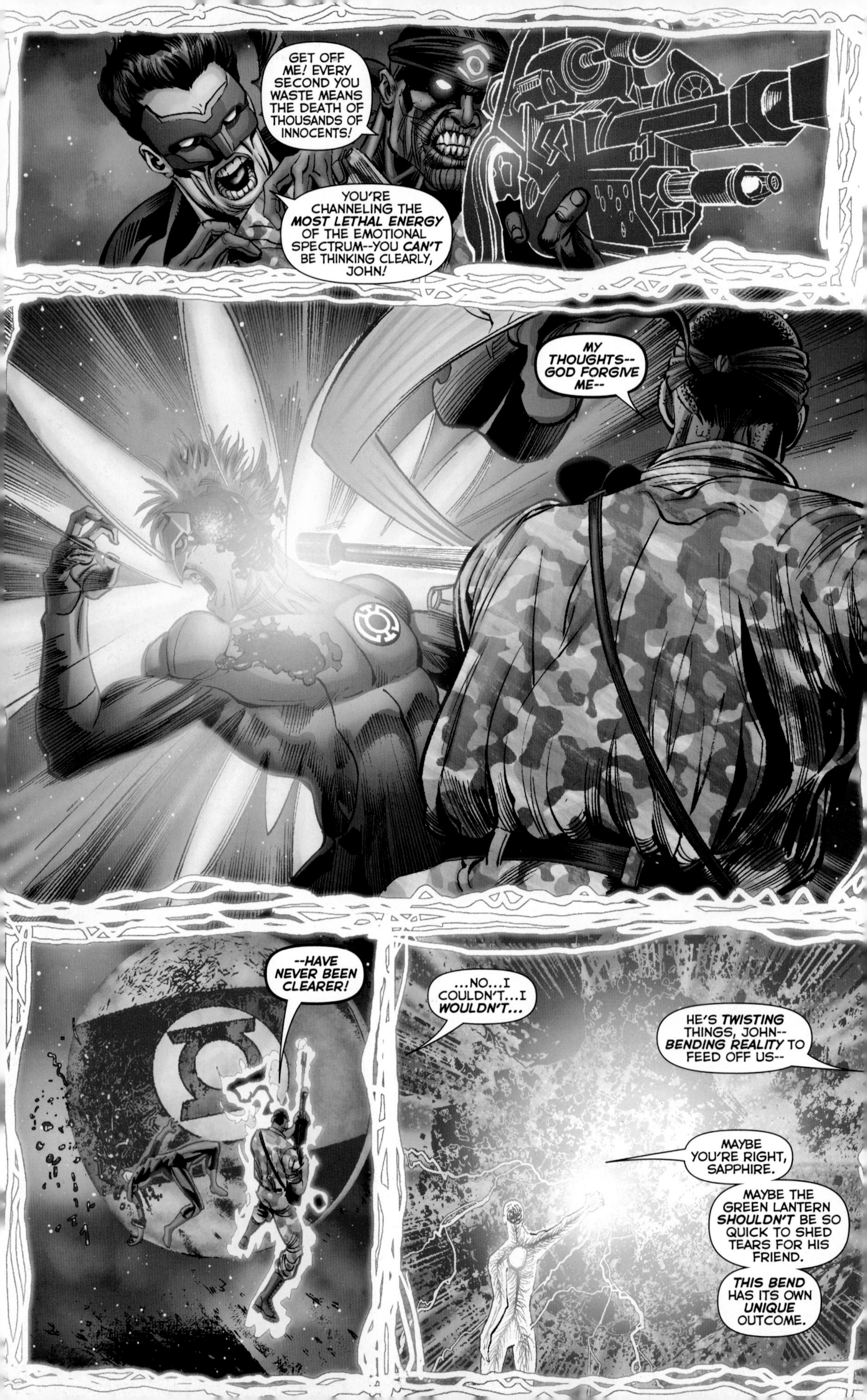
GET OFF ME! EVERY SECOND YOU WASTE MEANS THE DEATH OF THOUSANDS OF INNOCENTS!
YOU'RE CHANNELING THE MOST LETHAL ENERGY OF THE EMOTIONAL SPECTRUM--YOU CAN'T BE THINKING CLEARLY, JOHN!
MY THOUGHTS--GOD FORGIVE ME--
--HAVE NEVER BEEN CLEARER!
...NO...I COULDN'T...I WOULDN'T...
HE'S TWISTING THINGS, JOHN--BENDING REALITY TO FEED OFF US--
MAYBE YOU'RE RIGHT, SAPPHIRE.
MAYBE THE GREEN LANTERN SHOULDN'T BE SO QUICK TO SHED TEARS FOR HIS FRIEND.
THIS BEND HAS ITS OWN UNIQUE OUTCOME.

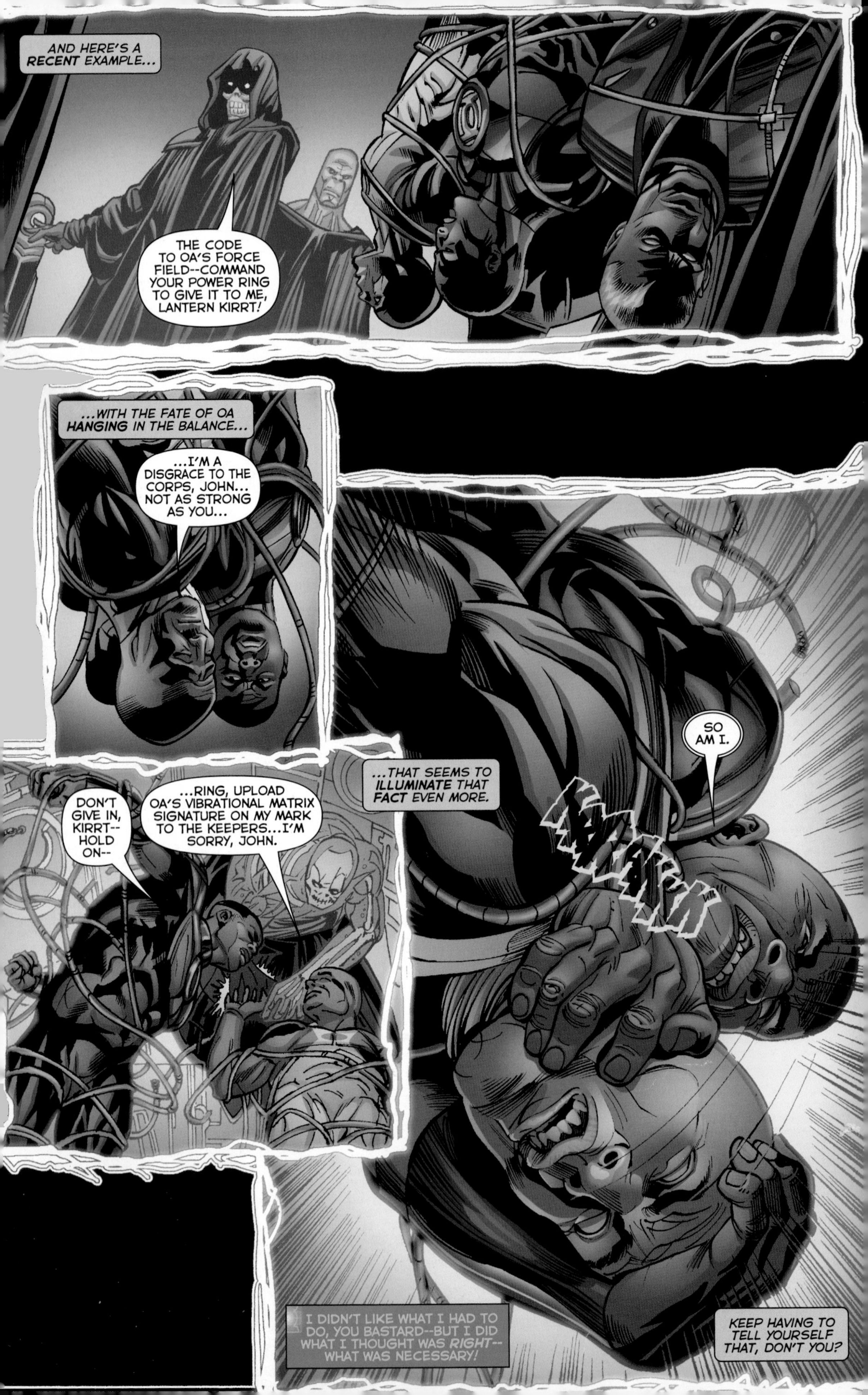
AND HERE'S A RECENT EXAMPLE...
THE CODE TO OA'S FORCE FIELD--COMMAND YOUR POWER RING TO GIVE IT TO ME, LANTERN KIRRT!
...WITH THE FATE OF OA HANGING IN THE BALANCE...
...I'M A DISGRACE TO THE CORPS, JOHN... NOT AS STRONG AS YOU...
DON'T GIVE IN, KIRRT-- HOLD ON--
...RING, UPLOAD OA'S VIBRATIONAL MATRIX SIGNATURE ON MY MARK TO THE KEEPERS...I'M SORRY, JOHN.
...THAT SEEMS TO ILLUMINATE THAT FACT EVEN MORE.
SO AM I.
I DIDN'T LIKE WHAT I HAD TO DO, YOU BASTARD--BUT I DID WHAT I THOUGHT WAS RIGHT-- WHAT WAS NECESSARY!
KEEP HAVING TO TELL YOURSELF THAT, DON'T YOU?

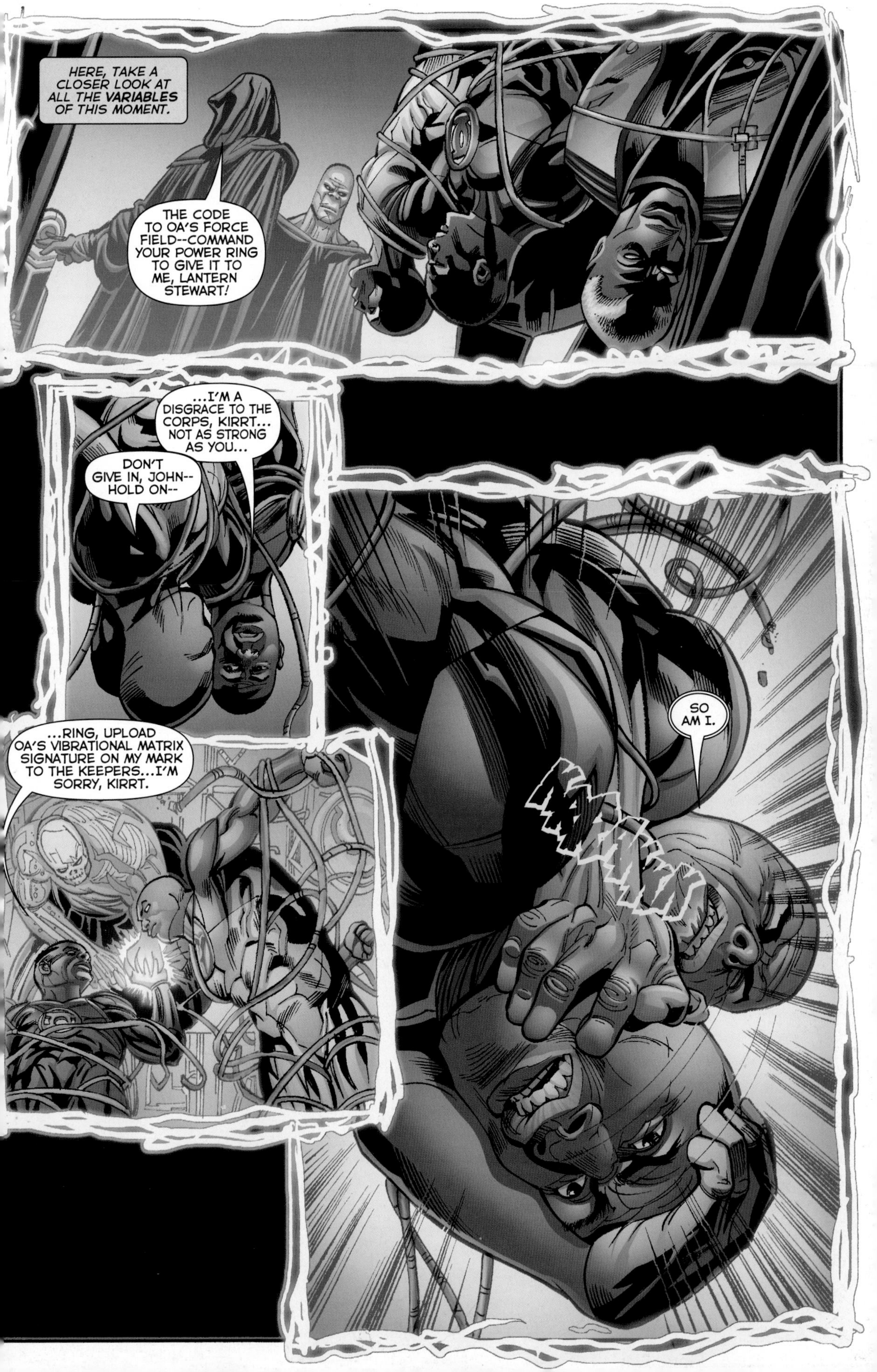
HERE, TAKE A CLOSER LOOK AT ALL THE *VARIABLES* OF THIS MOMENT.
THE CODE TO OA'S FORCE FIELD--COMMAND YOUR POWER RING TO GIVE IT TO ME, LANTERN STEWART!
...I'M A DISGRACE TO THE CORPS, KIRRT... NOT AS STRONG AS YOU...
DON'T GIVE IN, JOHN-- HOLD ON--
SO AM I.
...RING, UPLOAD OA'S VIBRATIONAL MATRIX SIGNATURE ON MY MARK TO THE KEEPERS...I'M SORRY, KIRRT.

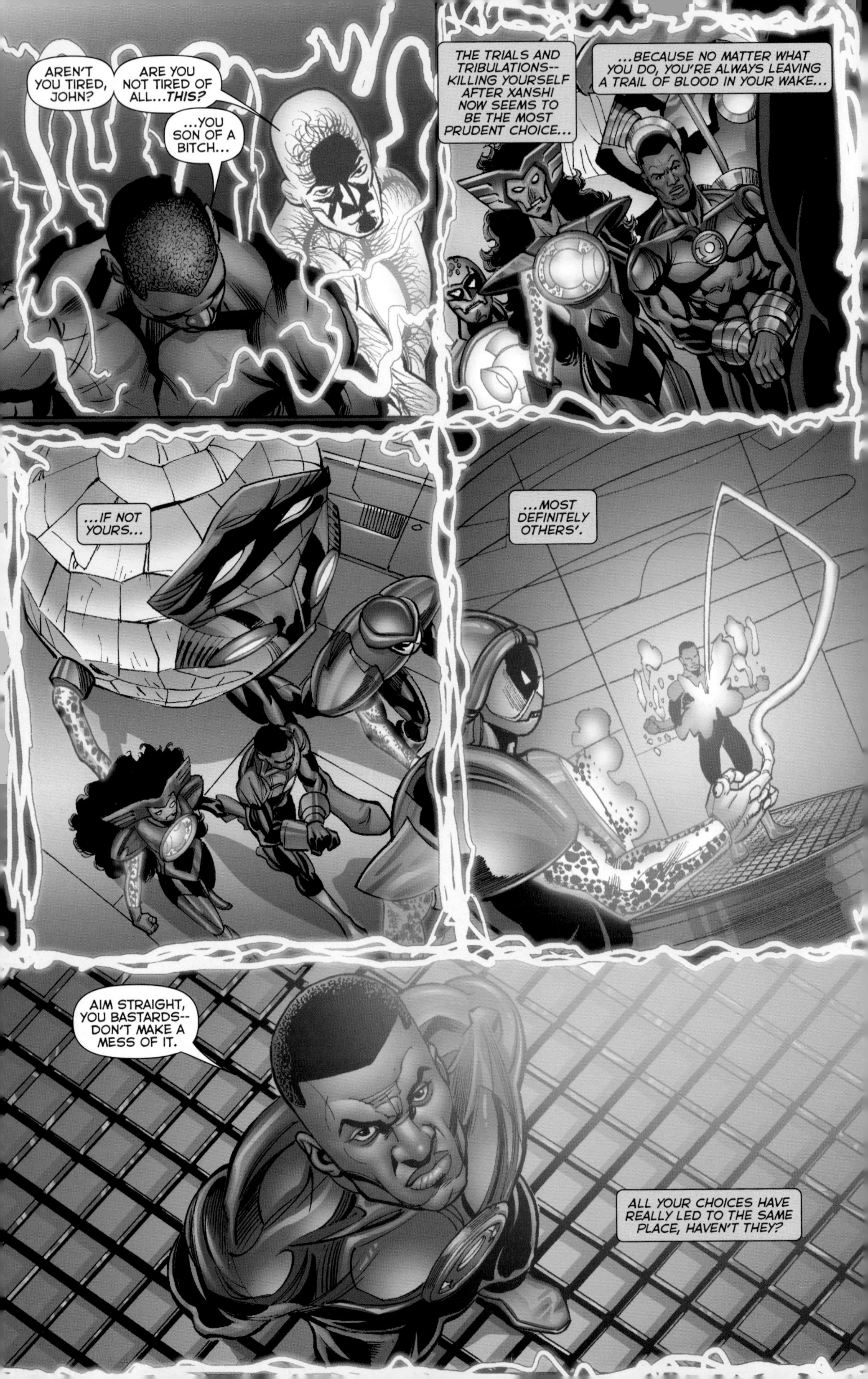
AREN'T YOU TIRED, JOHN?
ARE YOU NOT TIRED OF ALL...THIS?
...YOU SON OF A BITCH...
THE TRIALS AND TRIBULATIONS--KILLING YOURSELF AFTER XANSHI NOW SEEMS TO BE THE MOST PRUDENT CHOICE...
...BECAUSE NO MATTER WHAT YOU DO, YOU'RE ALWAYS LEAVING A TRAIL OF BLOOD IN YOUR WAKE...
...IF NOT YOURS...
...MOST DEFINITELY OTHERS'.
AIM STRAIGHT, YOU BASTARDS--DON'T MAKE A MESS OF IT.
ALL YOUR CHOICES HAVE REALLY LED TO THE SAME PLACE, HAVEN'T THEY?

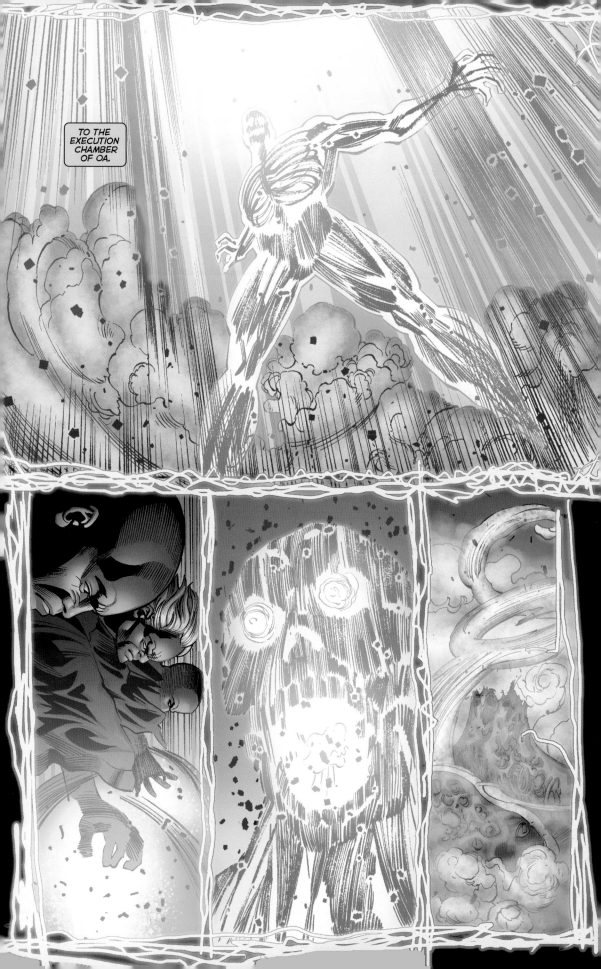

TO THE
EXECUTION
CHAMBER
OF OA.

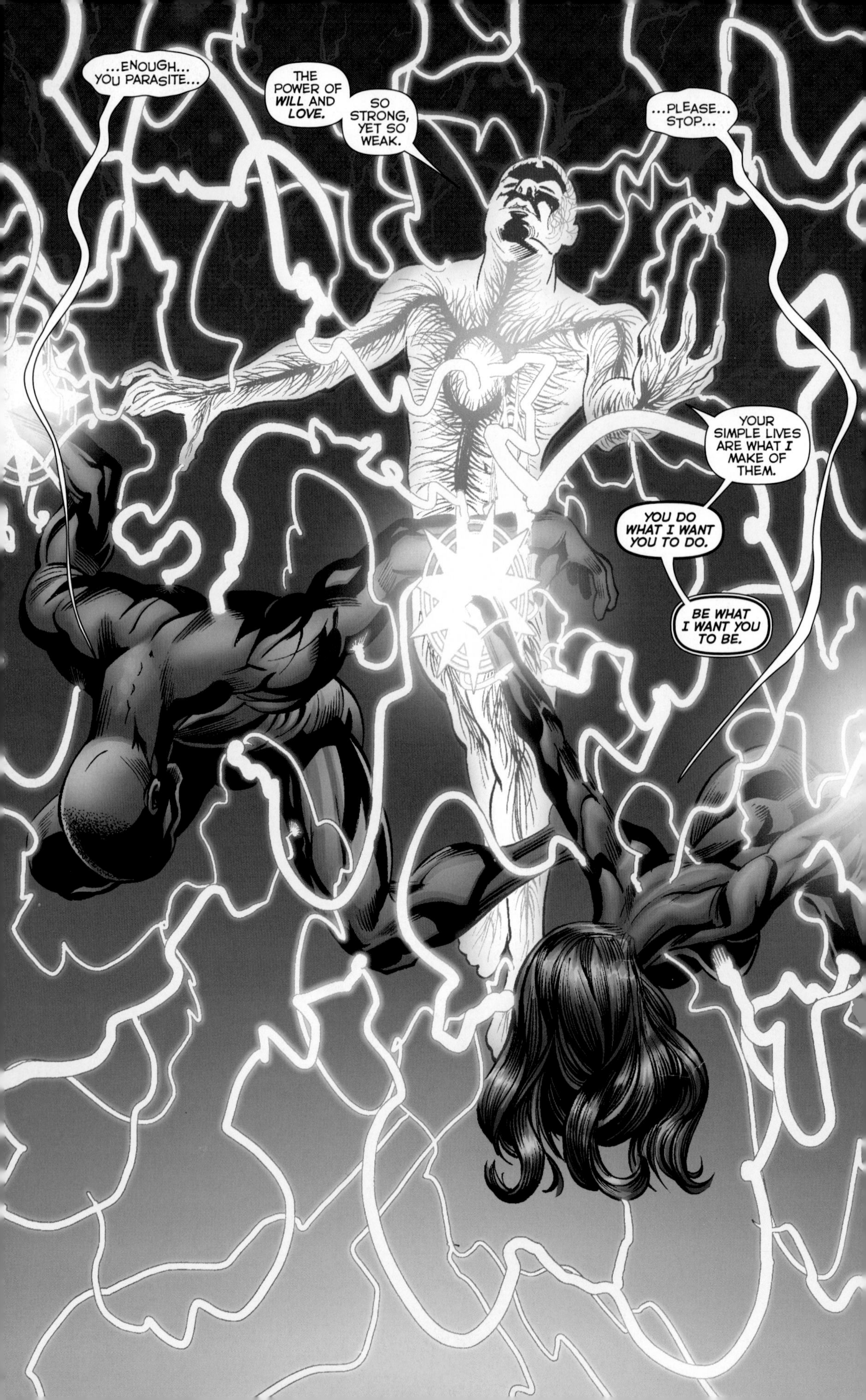
...ENOUGH... YOU PARASITE...
THE POWER OF WILL AND LOVE.
SO STRONG, YET SO WEAK.
...PLEASE... STOP...
YOUR SIMPLE LIVES ARE WHAT I MAKE OF THEM.
YOU DO WHAT I WANT YOU TO DO.
BE WHAT I WANT YOU TO BE.

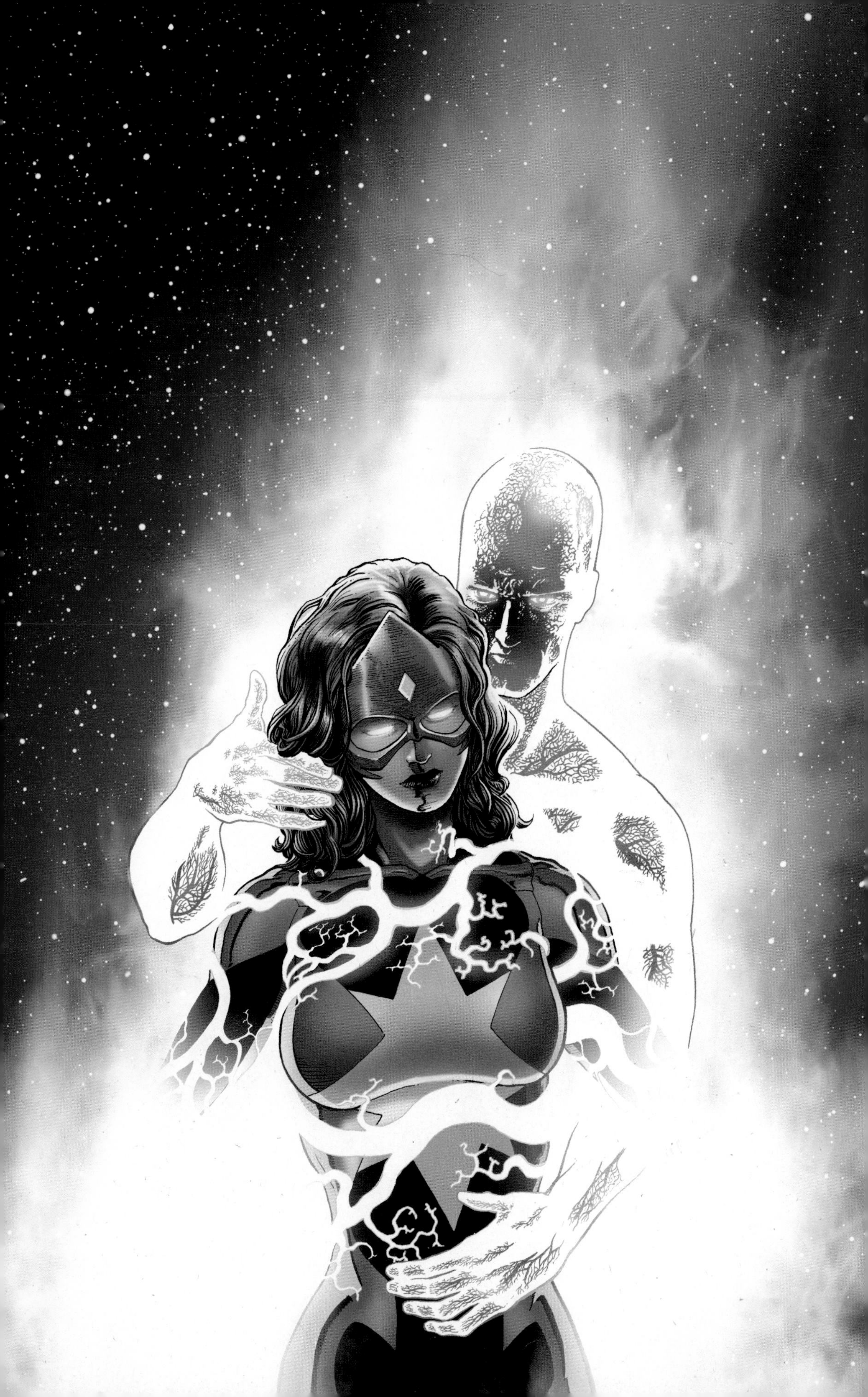

PART SEVEN: PATHS UNTAKEN
HENDRY PRASETYO artist CAROL FERRIS sequence JIM CALAFIORE artist LARFLEEZE sequence
JAVIER PULIDO artist SAINT WALKER sequence

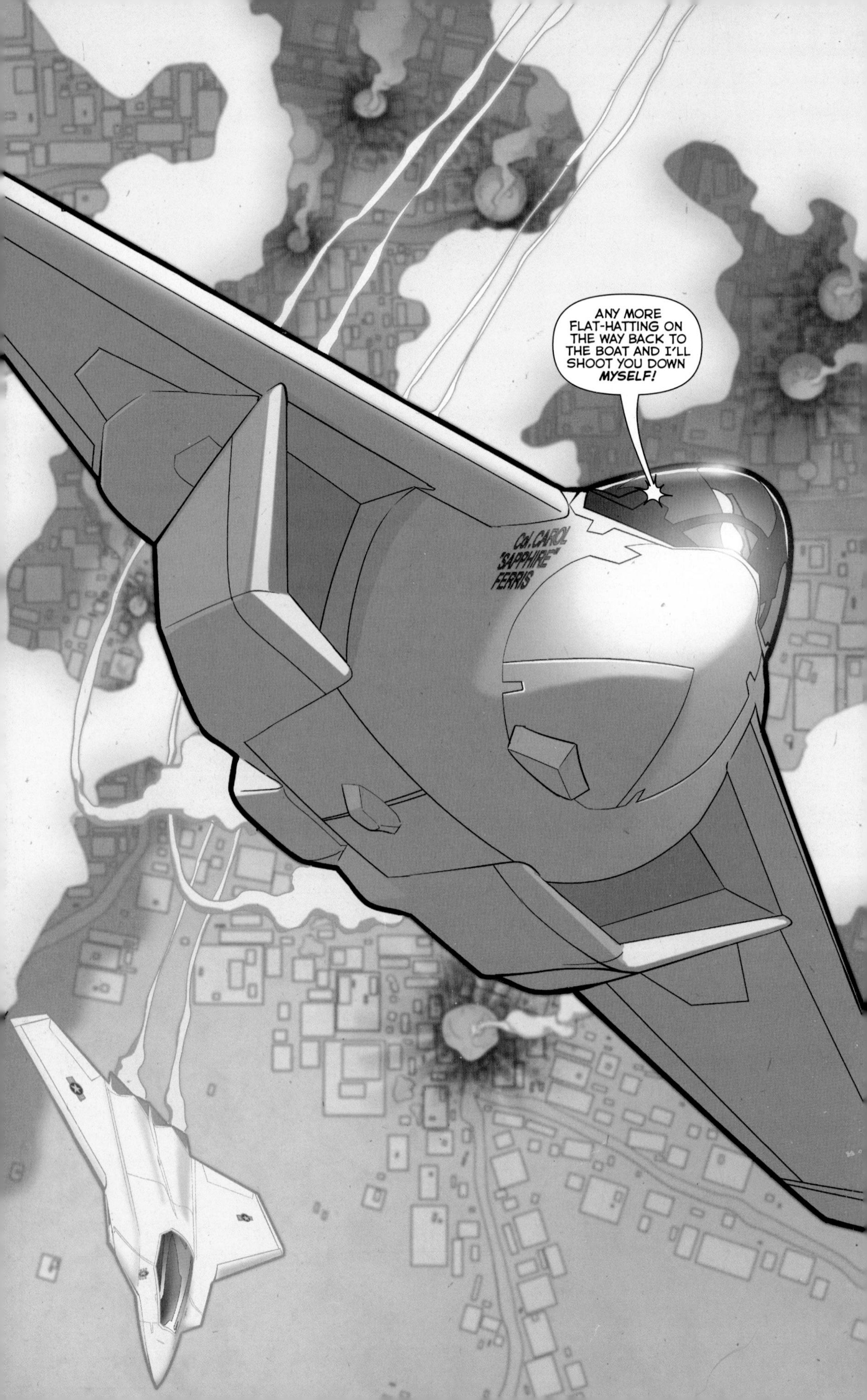
ANY MORE FLAT-HATTING ON THE WAY BACK TO THE BOAT AND I'LL SHOOT YOU DOWN MYSELF!
Col. CAROL "SAPPHIRE" FERRIS

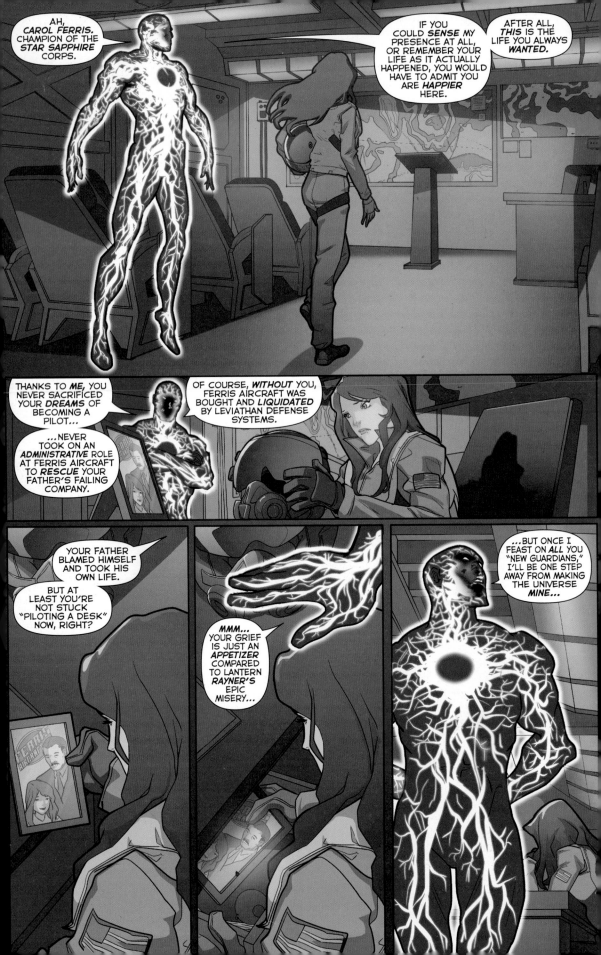

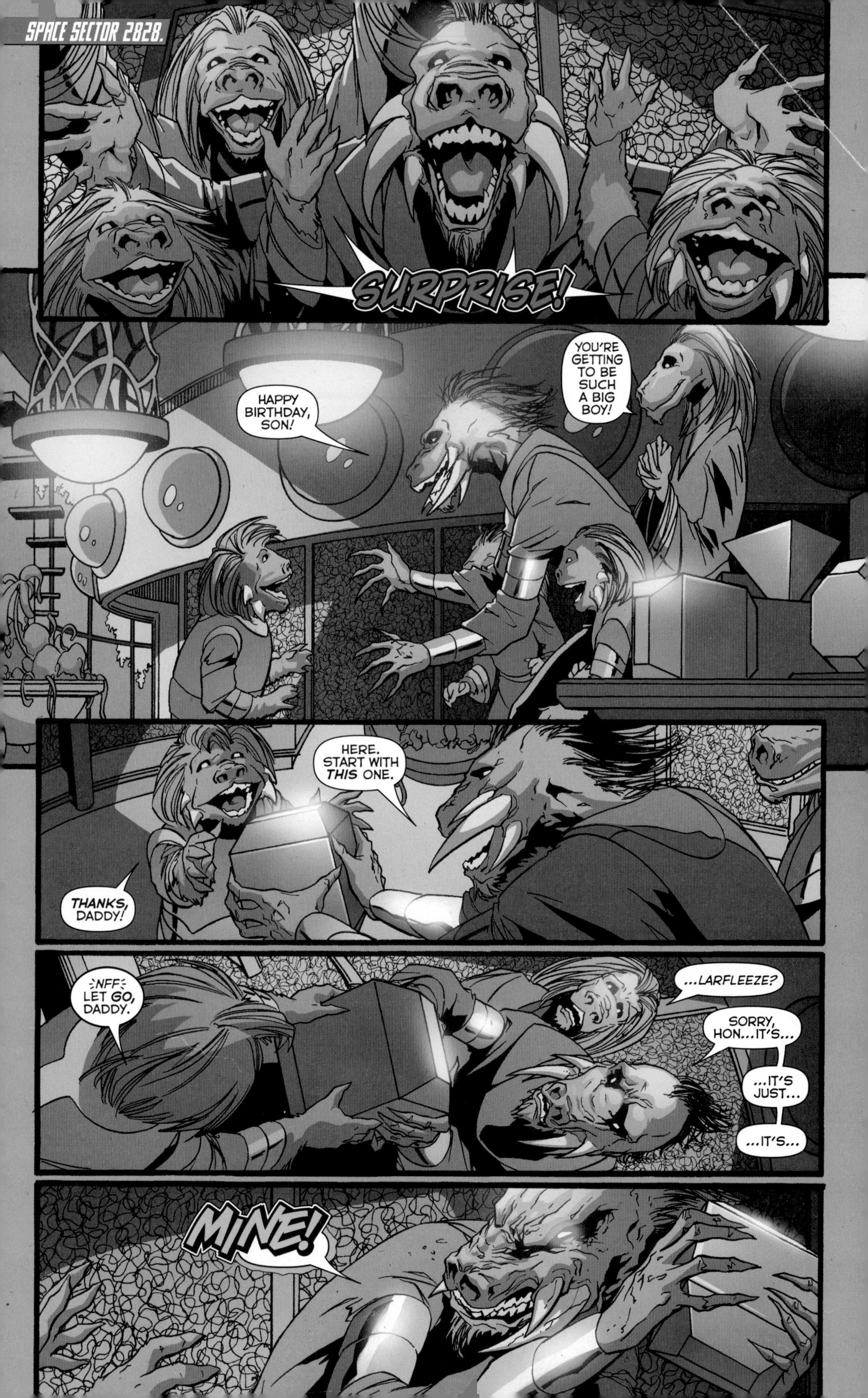
SPACE SECTOR 2828.
SURPRISE!
HAPPY BIRTHDAY, SON!
YOU'RE GETTING TO BE SUCH A BIG BOY!
HERE. START WITH *THIS* ONE.
THANKS, DADDY!
NFF LET *GO*, DADDY.
...LARFLEEZE?
SORRY, HON...IT'S...
...IT'S JUST...
...IT'S...
MINE!

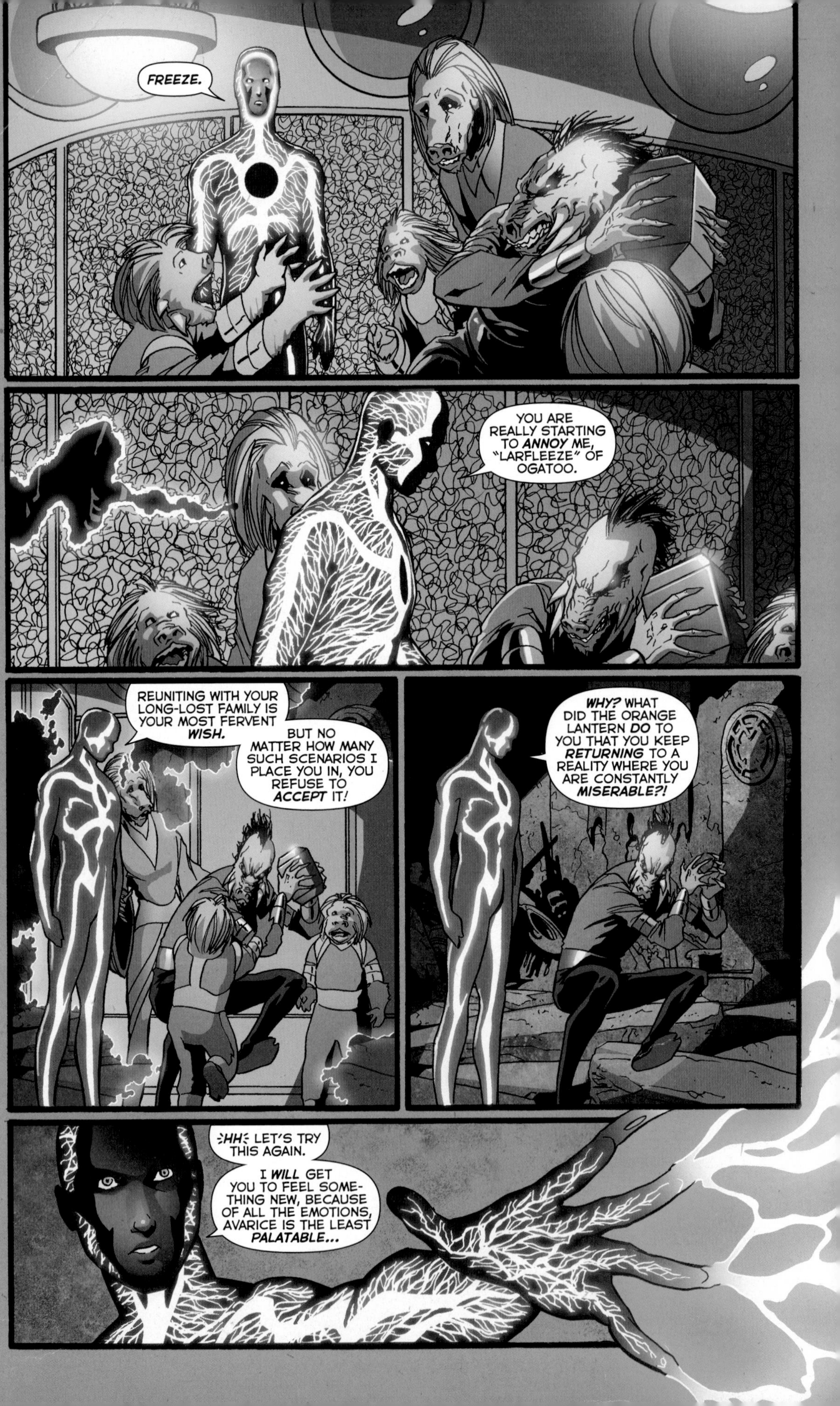
FREEZE.
YOU ARE REALLY STARTING TO ANNOY ME, "LARFLEEZE" OF OGATOO.
REUNITING WITH YOUR LONG-LOST FAMILY IS YOUR MOST FERVENT WISH.
BUT NO MATTER HOW MANY SUCH SCENARIOS I PLACE YOU IN, YOU REFUSE TO ACCEPT IT!
WHY? WHAT DID THE ORANGE LANTERN DO TO YOU THAT YOU KEEP RETURNING TO A REALITY WHERE YOU ARE CONSTANTLY MISERABLE?!
HH LET'S TRY THIS AGAIN.
I WILL GET YOU TO FEEL SOME-THING NEW, BECAUSE OF ALL THE EMOTIONS, AVARICE IS THE LEAST PALATABLE...

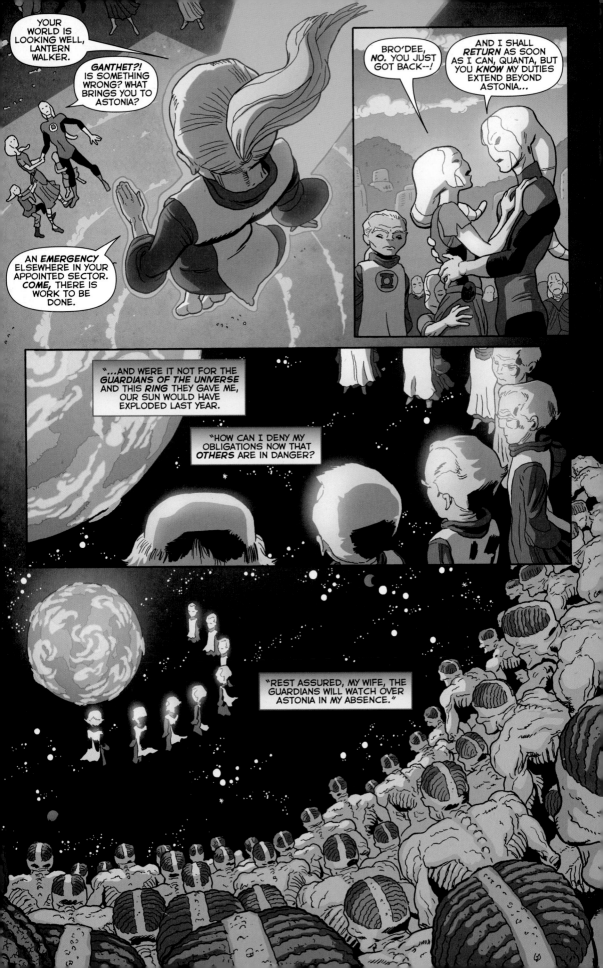

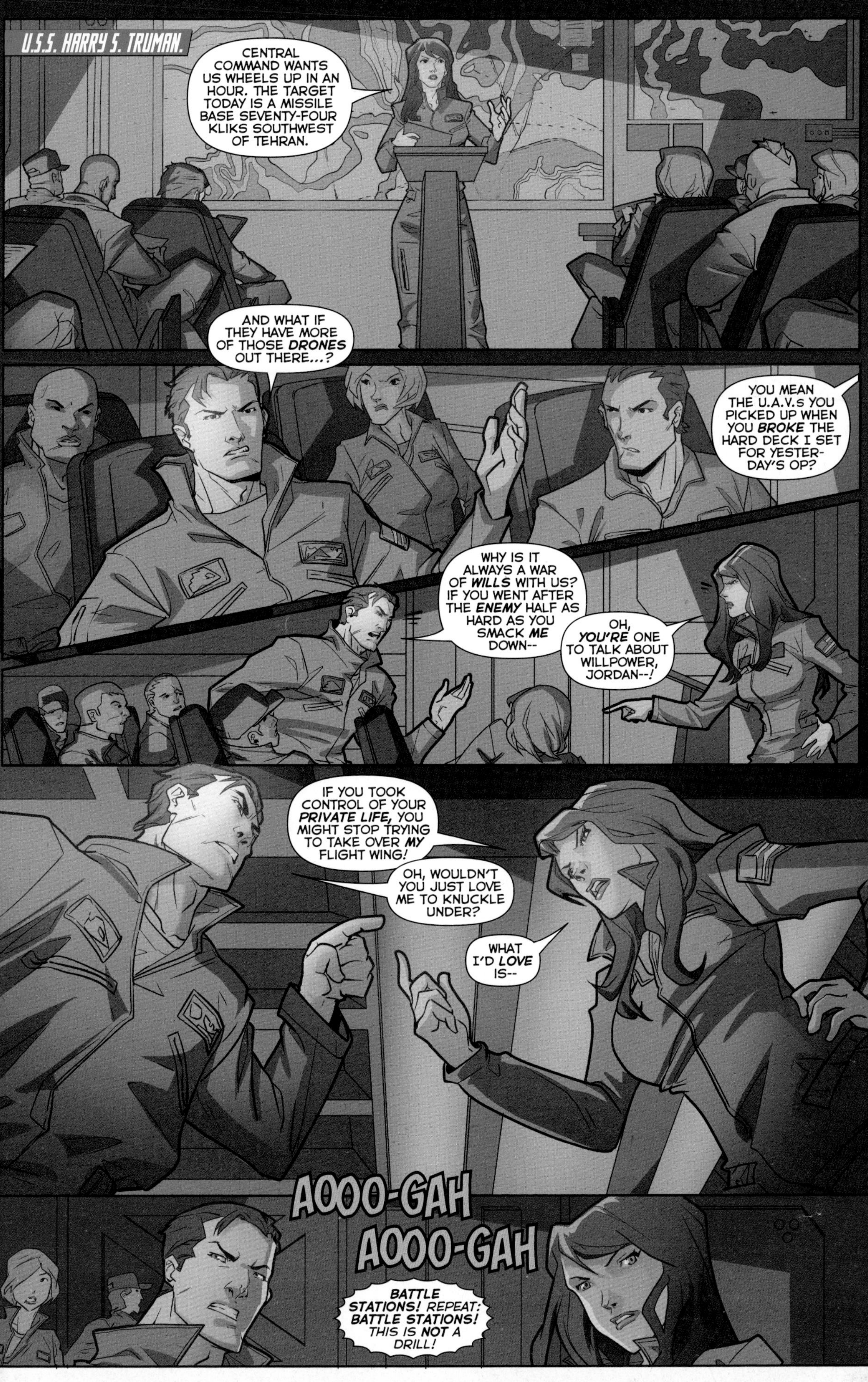
U.S.S. HARRY S. TRUMAN.
CENTRAL COMMAND WANTS US WHEELS UP IN AN HOUR. THE TARGET TODAY IS A MISSILE BASE SEVENTY-FOUR KLIKS SOUTHWEST OF TEHRAN.
AND WHAT IF THEY HAVE MORE OF THOSE DRONES OUT THERE...?
YOU MEAN THE U.A.V.s YOU PICKED UP WHEN YOU BROKE THE HARD DECK I SET FOR YESTERDAY'S OP?
WHY IS IT ALWAYS A WAR OF WILLS WITH US? IF YOU WENT AFTER THE ENEMY HALF AS HARD AS YOU SMACK ME DOWN--
OH, YOU'RE ONE TO TALK ABOUT WILLPOWER, JORDAN--!
IF YOU TOOK CONTROL OF YOUR PRIVATE LIFE, YOU MIGHT STOP TRYING TO TAKE OVER MY FLIGHT WING!
OH, WOULDN'T YOU JUST LOVE ME TO KNUCKLE UNDER?
WHAT I'D LOVE IS--
AOOO-GAH
AOOO-GAH
BATTLE STATIONS! REPEAT: BATTLE STATIONS! THIS IS NOT A DRILL!

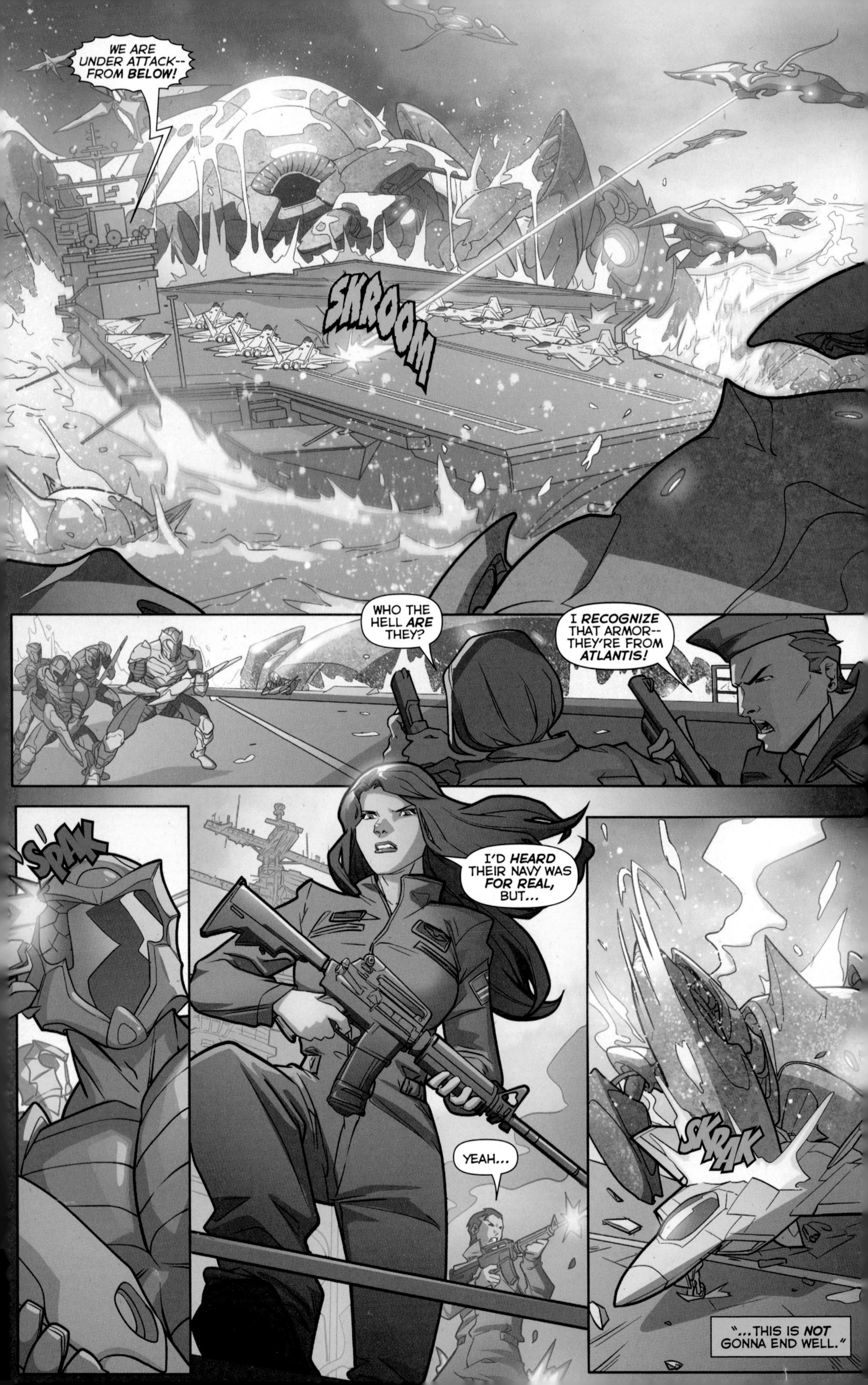
WE ARE UNDER ATTACK-- FROM BELOW!
SKROOM
WHO THE HELL ARE THEY?
I RECOGNIZE THAT ARMOR-- THEY'RE FROM ATLANTIS!
SPAK
I'D HEARD THEIR NAVY WAS FOR REAL, BUT...
YEAH...
SKRAK
"...THIS IS NOT GONNA END WELL."

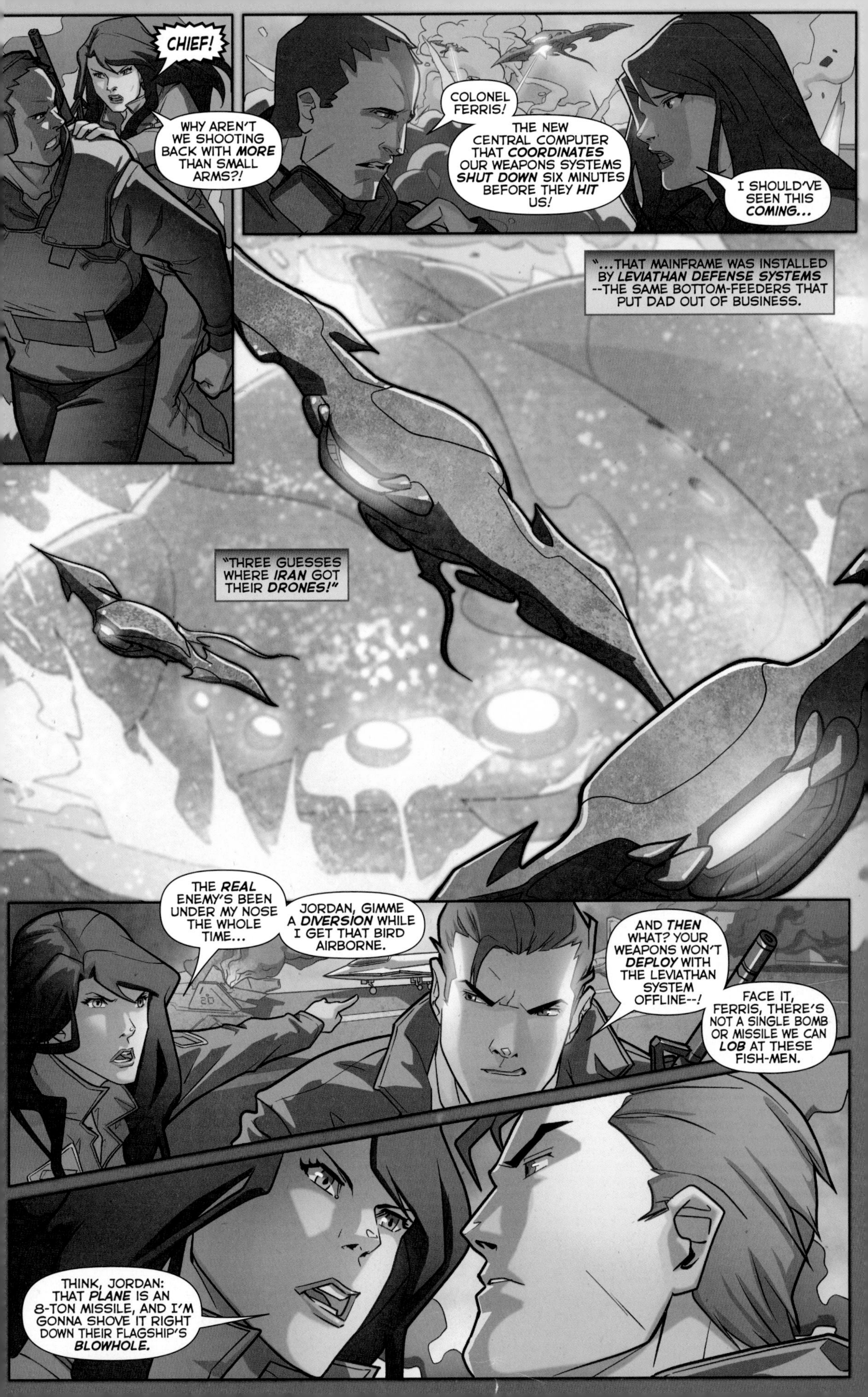
CHIEF!
WHY AREN'T WE SHOOTING BACK WITH MORE THAN SMALL ARMS?!
COLONEL FERRIS!
THE NEW CENTRAL COMPUTER THAT COORDINATES OUR WEAPONS SYSTEMS SHUT DOWN SIX MINUTES BEFORE THEY HIT US!
I SHOULD'VE SEEN THIS COMING...
"...THAT MAINFRAME WAS INSTALLED BY LEVIATHAN DEFENSE SYSTEMS --THE SAME BOTTOM-FEEDERS THAT PUT DAD OUT OF BUSINESS.
"THREE GUESSES WHERE IRAN GOT THEIR DRONES!"
THE REAL ENEMY'S BEEN UNDER MY NOSE THE WHOLE TIME...
JORDAN, GIMME A DIVERSION WHILE I GET THAT BIRD AIRBORNE.
AND THEN WHAT? YOUR WEAPONS WON'T DEPLOY WITH THE LEVIATHAN SYSTEM OFFLINE--!
FACE IT, FERRIS, THERE'S NOT A SINGLE BOMB OR MISSILE WE CAN LOB AT THESE FISH-MEN.
THINK, JORDAN: THAT PLANE IS AN 8-TON MISSILE, AND I'M GONNA SHOVE IT RIGHT DOWN THEIR FLAGSHIP'S BLOWHOLE.

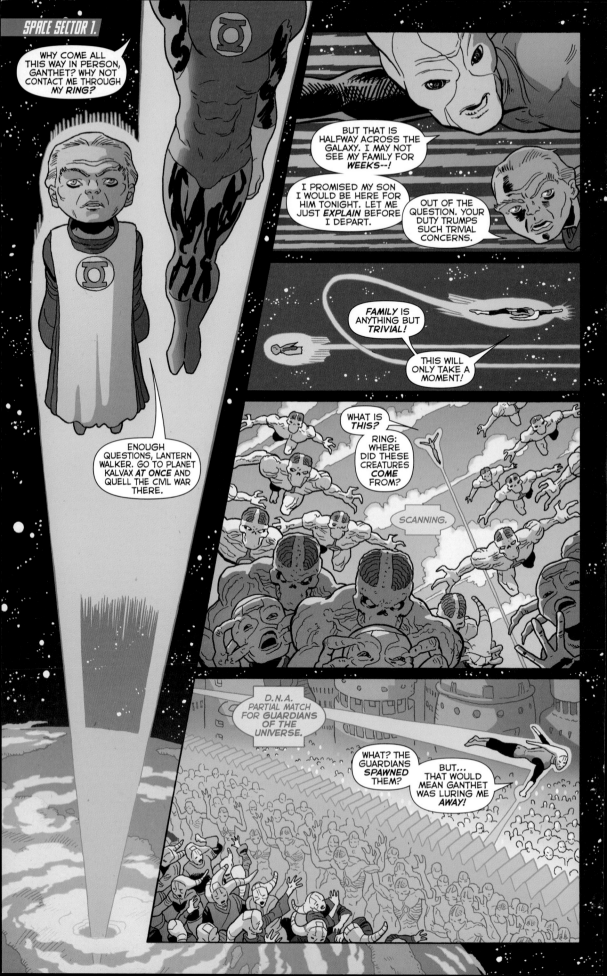

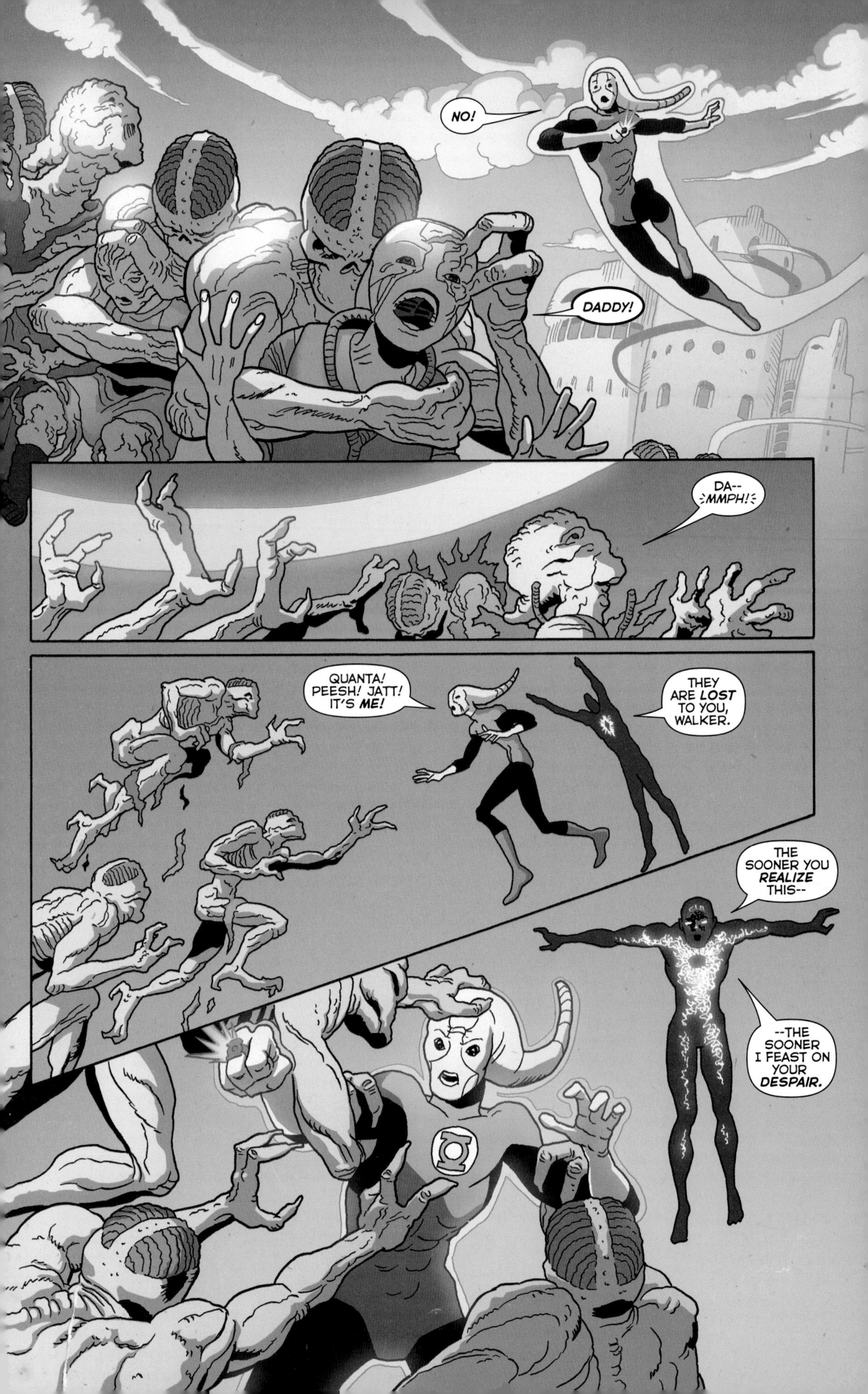
NO!
DADDY!
DA-- MMPH!
QUANTA! PEESH! JATT! IT'S ME!
THEY ARE LOST TO YOU, WALKER.
THE SOONER YOU REALIZE THIS--
--THE SOONER I FEAST ON YOUR DESPAIR.

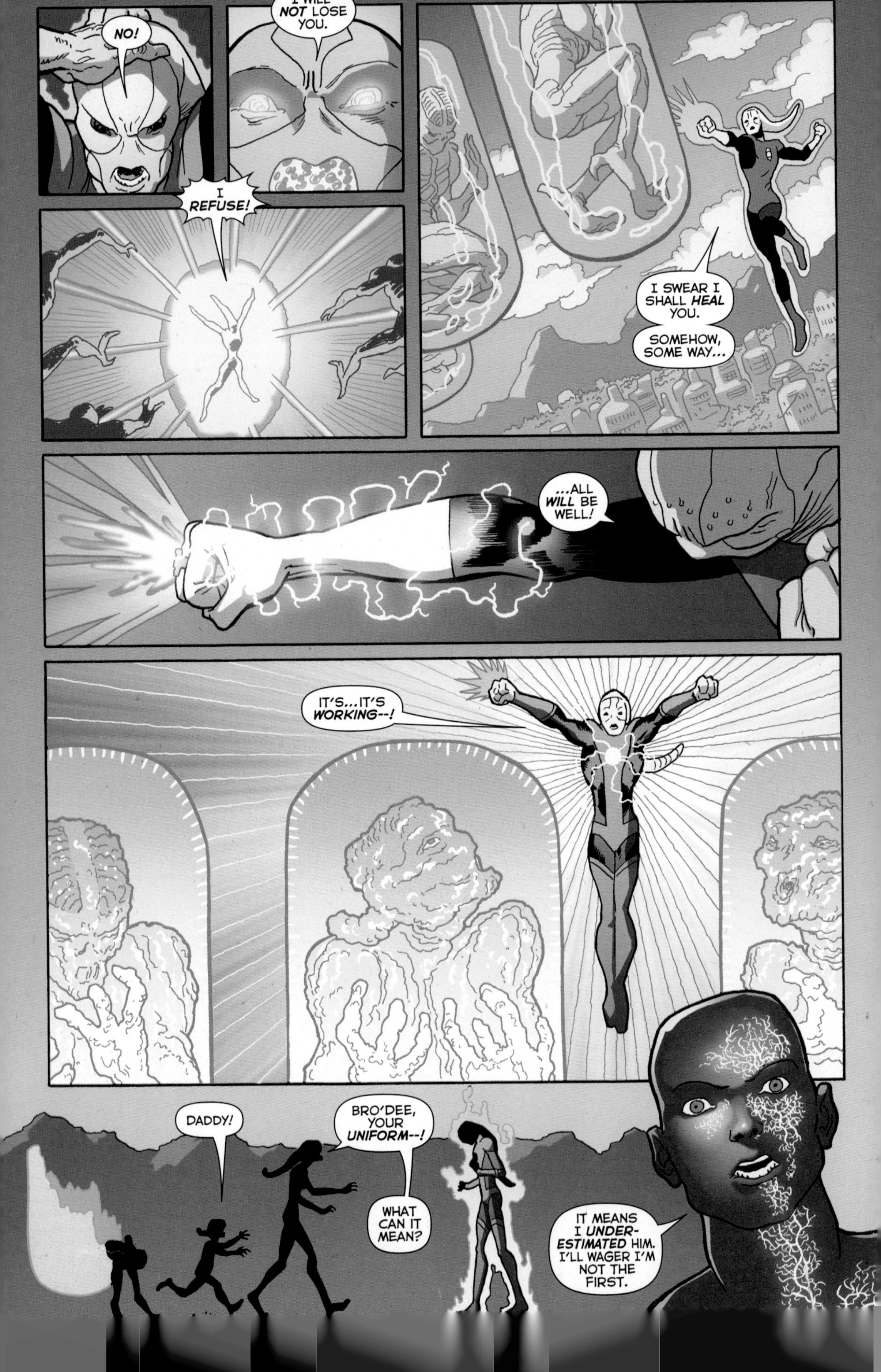
NO!
I WILL NOT LOSE YOU.
I REFUSE!
I SWEAR I SHALL HEAL YOU.
SOMEHOW, SOME WAY...
...ALL WILL BE WELL!
IT'S...IT'S WORKING--!
DADDY!
BRO'DEE, YOUR UNIFORM--!
WHAT CAN IT MEAN?
IT MEANS I UNDER-ESTIMATED HIM. I'LL WAGER I'M NOT THE FIRST.

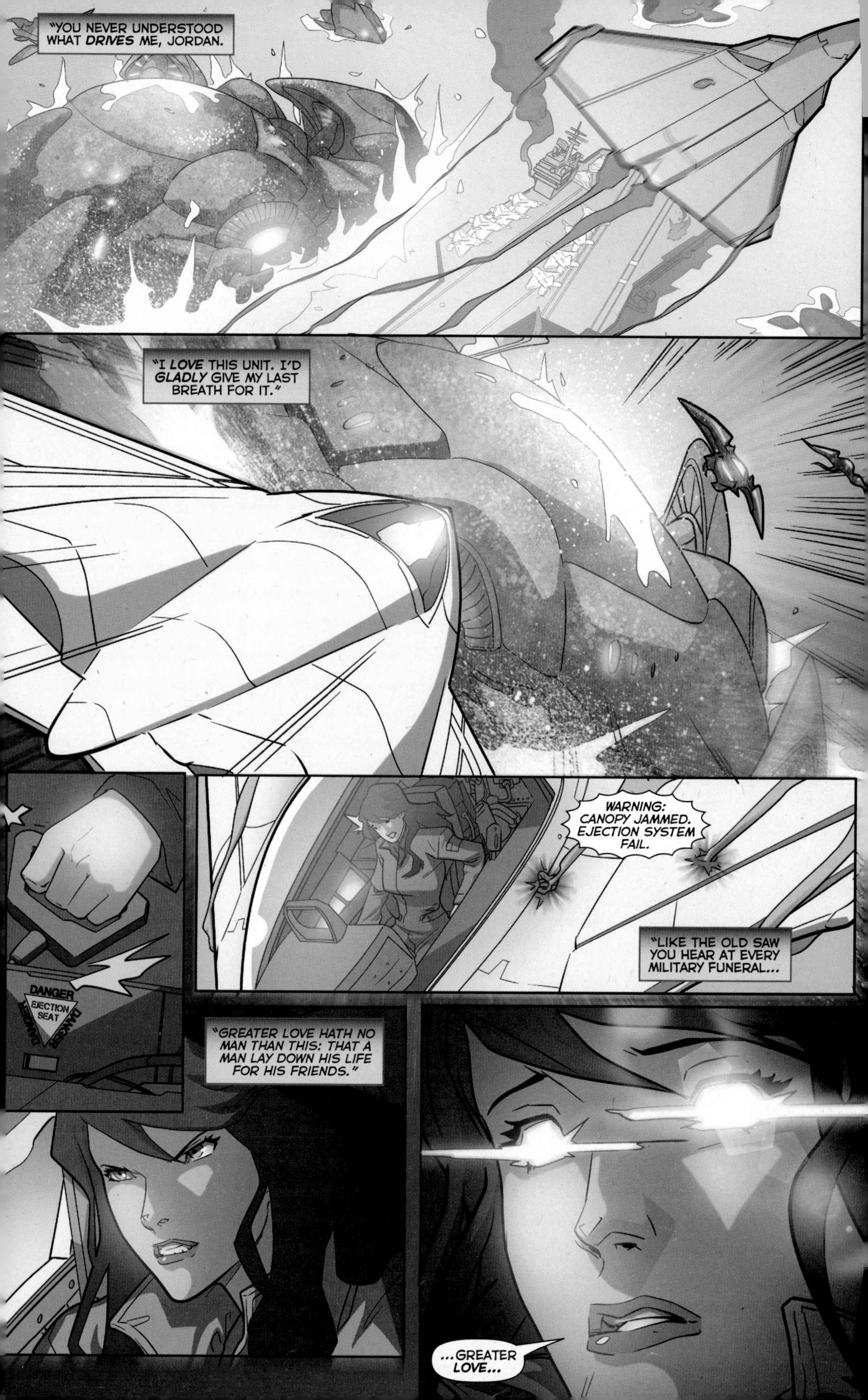
"YOU NEVER UNDERSTOOD WHAT DRIVES ME, JORDAN.
"I LOVE THIS UNIT. I'D GLADLY GIVE MY LAST BREATH FOR IT."
DANGER
EJECTION SEAT
DANGER
DANGER
WARNING: CANOPY JAMMED. EJECTION SYSTEM FAIL.
"LIKE THE OLD SAW YOU HEAR AT EVERY MILITARY FUNERAL...
"GREATER LOVE HATH NO MAN THAN THIS: THAT A MAN LAY DOWN HIS LIFE FOR HIS FRIENDS."
...GREATER LOVE...

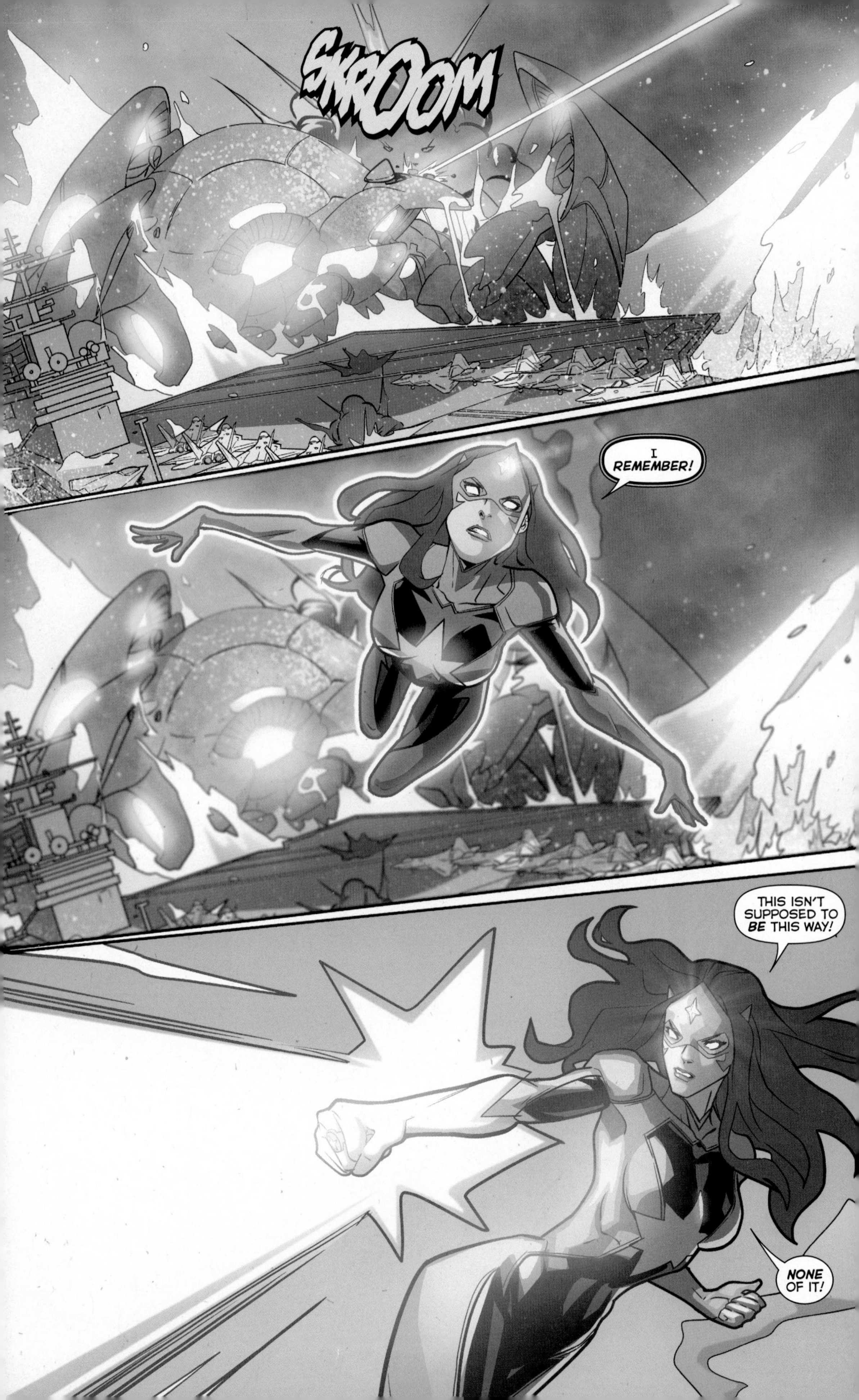
SKROOOM
I REMEMBER!
THIS ISN'T SUPPOSED TO BE THIS WAY!
NONE OF IT!

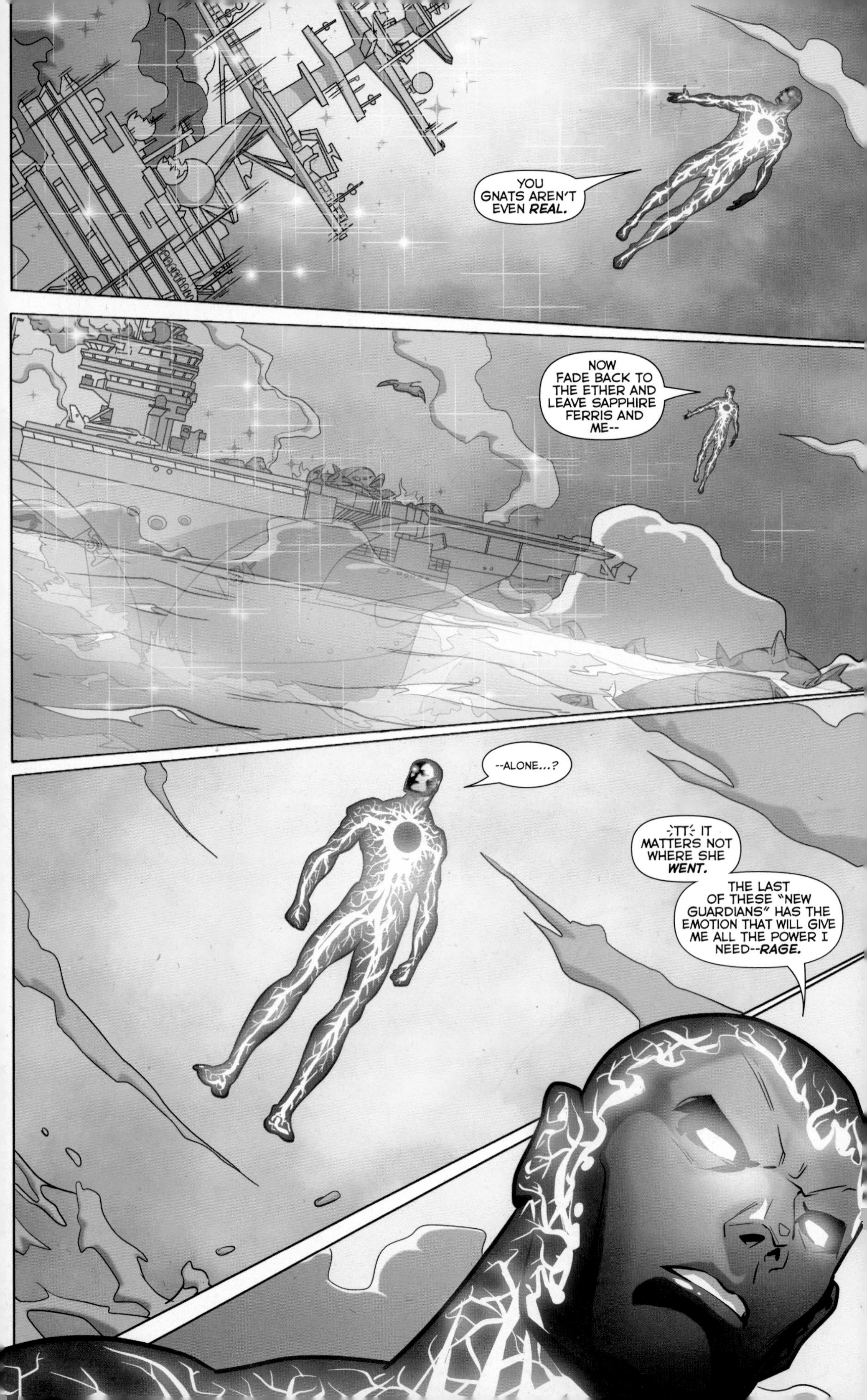
YOU GNATS AREN'T EVEN REAL.
NOW FADE BACK TO THE ETHER AND LEAVE SAPPHIRE FERRIS AND ME--
--ALONE...?
TT IT MATTERS NOT WHERE SHE WENT.
THE LAST OF THESE "NEW GUARDIANS" HAS THE EMOTION THAT WILL GIVE ME ALL THE POWER I NEED--RAGE.

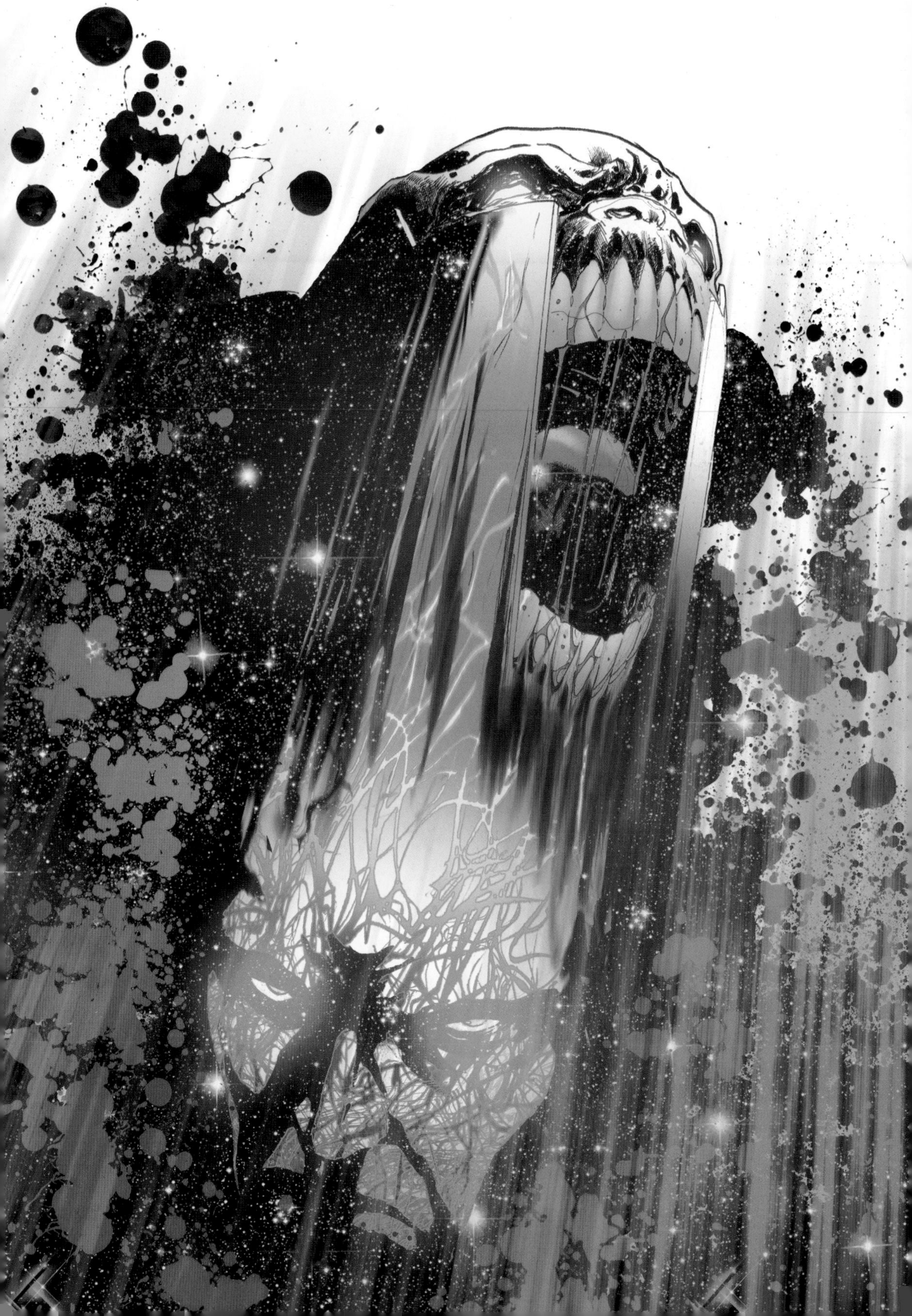

PART EIGHT: THE DECISION

PETER MILLIGAN writer **MIGUEL SEPULVEDA** artist
cover art by **MIGUEL SEPULVEDA** & **RAIN BEREDO**

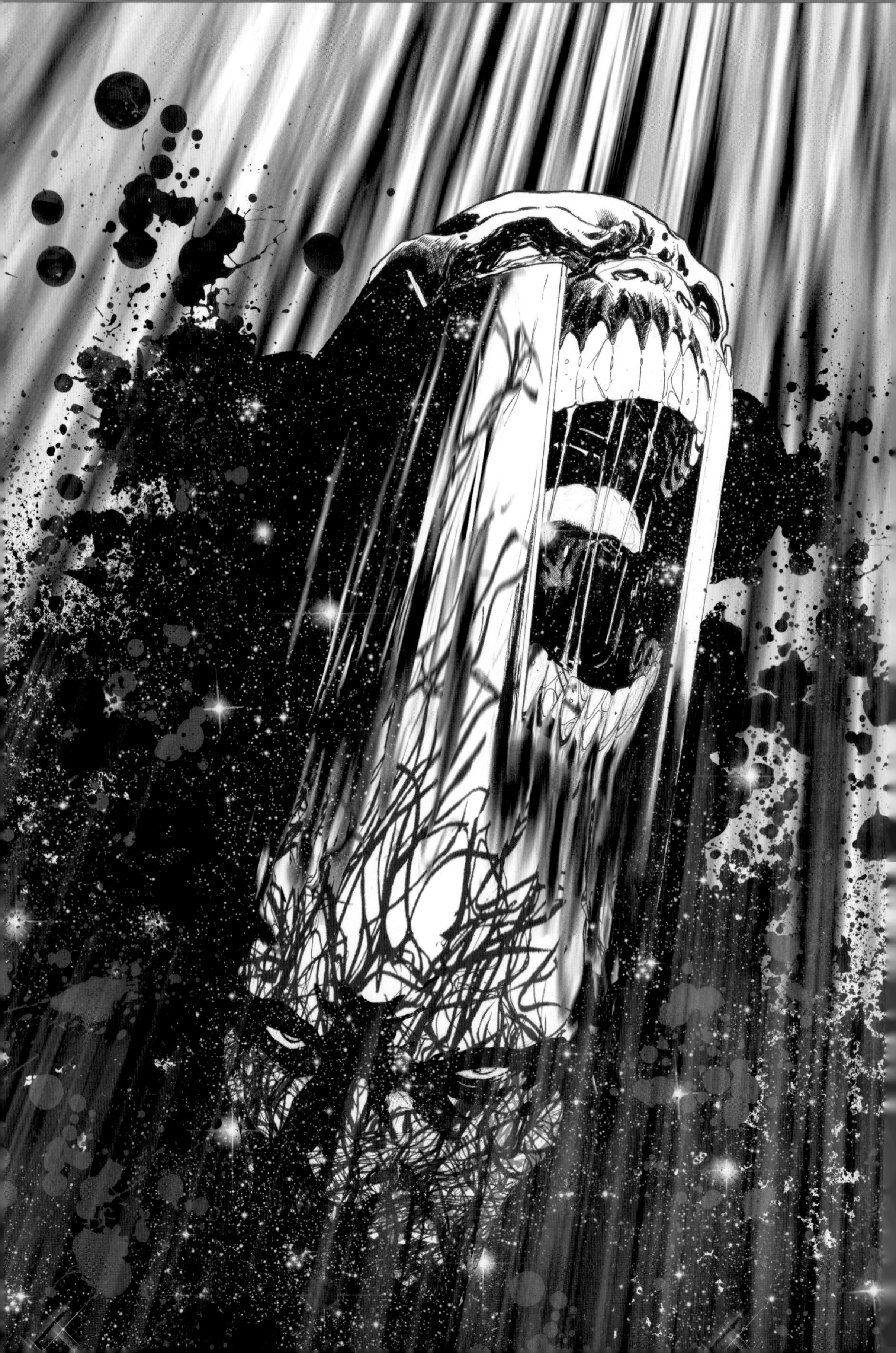

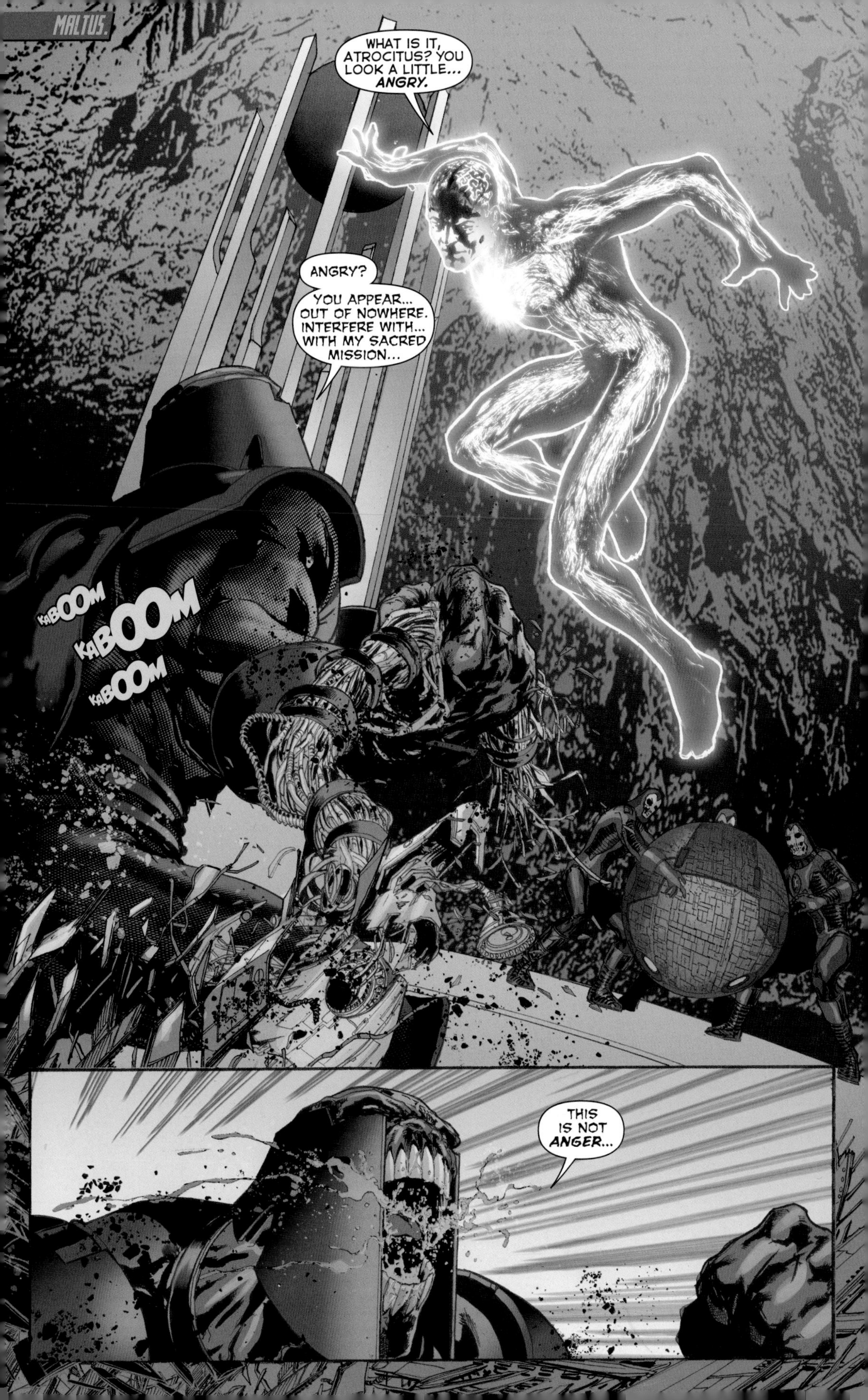
MALTUS.
WHAT IS IT, ATROCITUS? YOU LOOK A LITTLE... ANGRY.
ANGRY?
YOU APPEAR... OUT OF NOWHERE. INTERFERE WITH... WITH MY SACRED MISSION...
KABOOM
KABOOM
KABOOM
THIS IS NOT ANGER...

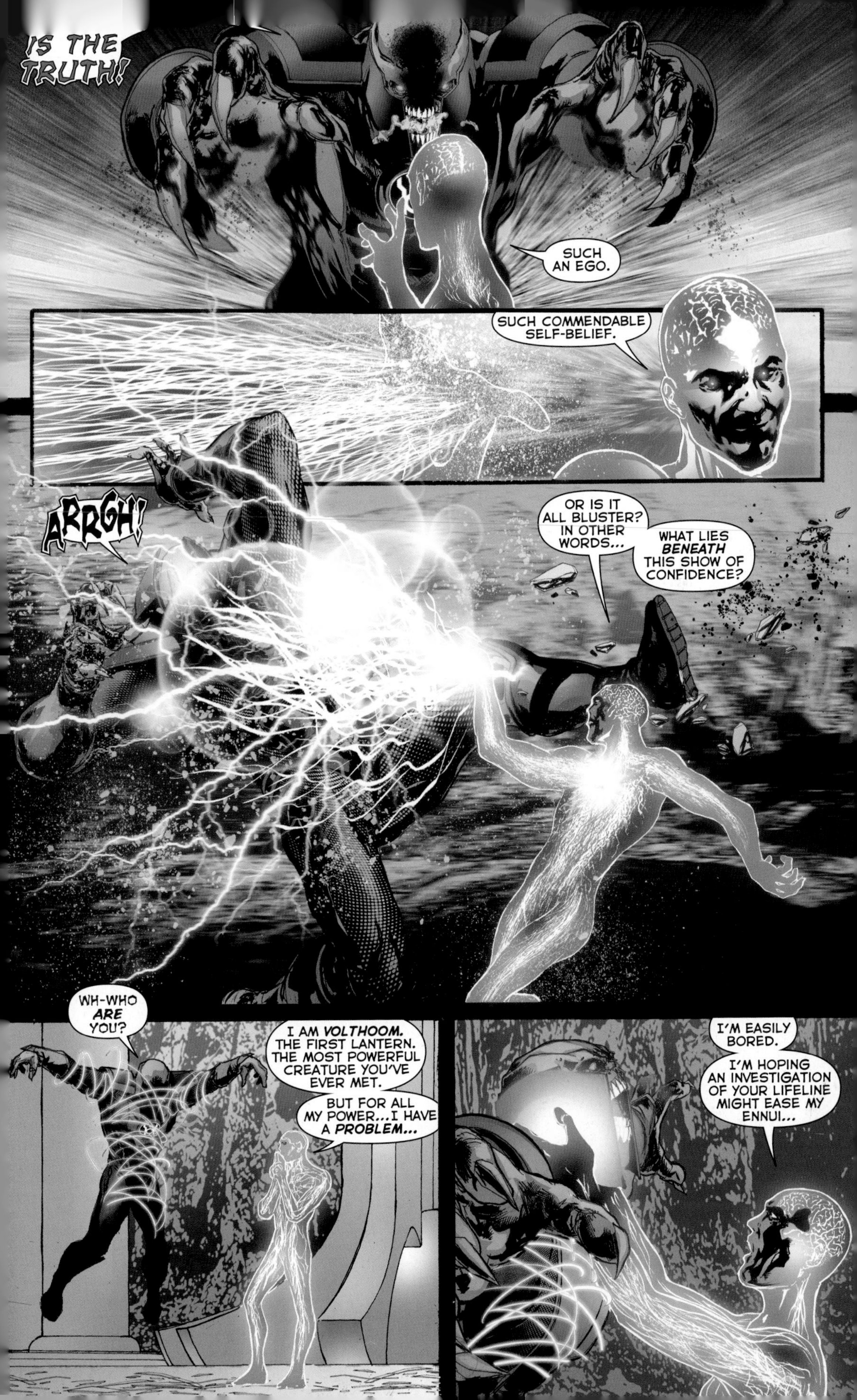
IS THE TRUTH!
SUCH AN EGO.
SUCH COMMENDABLE SELF-BELIEF.
ARRGH!
OR IS IT ALL BLUSTER? IN OTHER WORDS...
WHAT LIES BENEATH THIS SHOW OF CONFIDENCE?
WH-WHO ARE YOU?
I AM VOLTHOOM. THE FIRST LANTERN. THE MOST POWERFUL CREATURE YOU'VE EVER MET.
BUT FOR ALL MY POWER...I HAVE A PROBLEM...
I'M EASILY BORED.
I'M HOPING AN INVESTIGATION OF YOUR LIFELINE MIGHT EASE MY ENNUI...

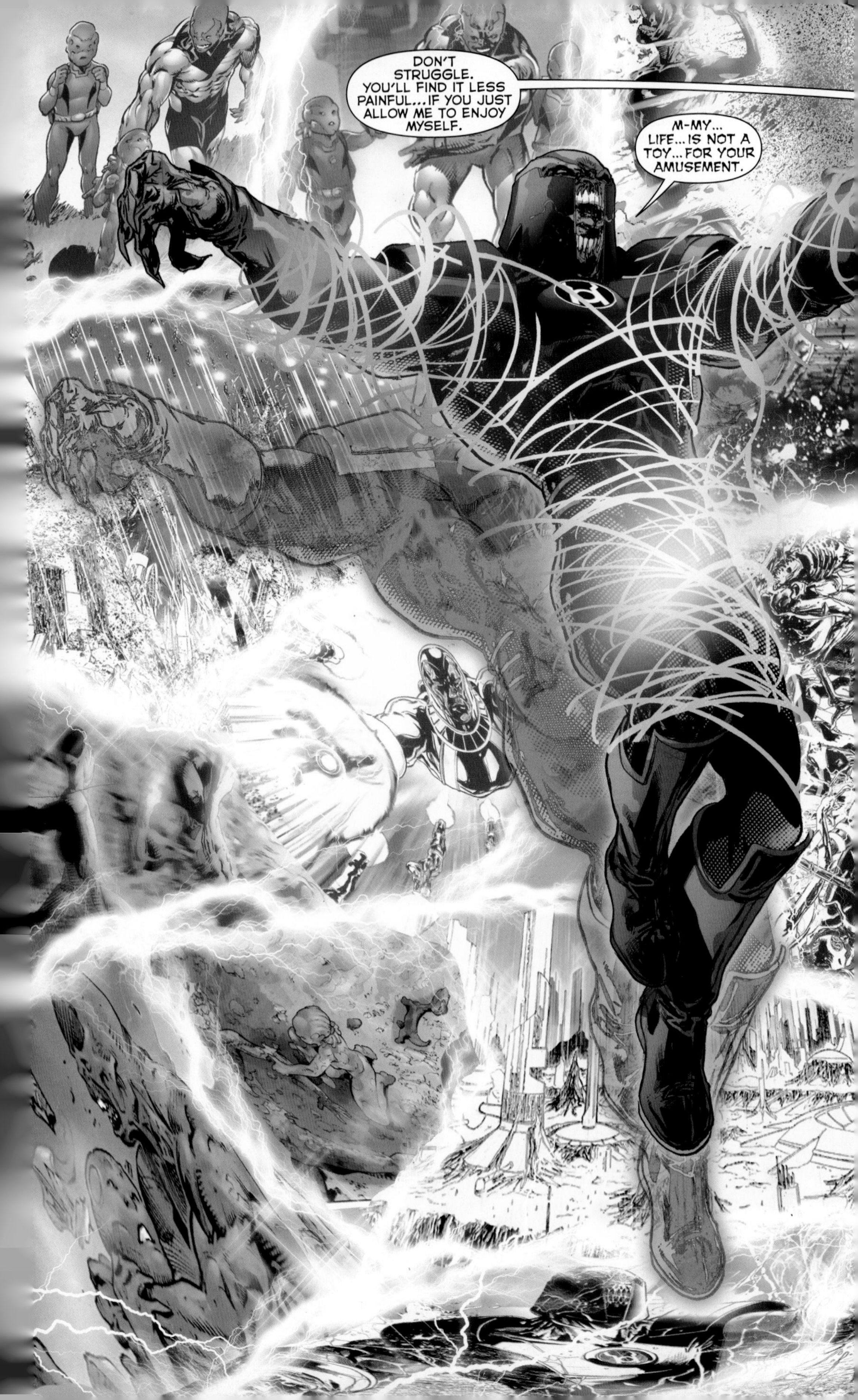
DON'T STRUGGLE. YOU'LL FIND IT LESS PAINFUL...IF YOU JUST ALLOW ME TO ENJOY MYSELF.
M-MY... LIFE...IS NOT A TOY...FOR YOUR AMUSEMENT.

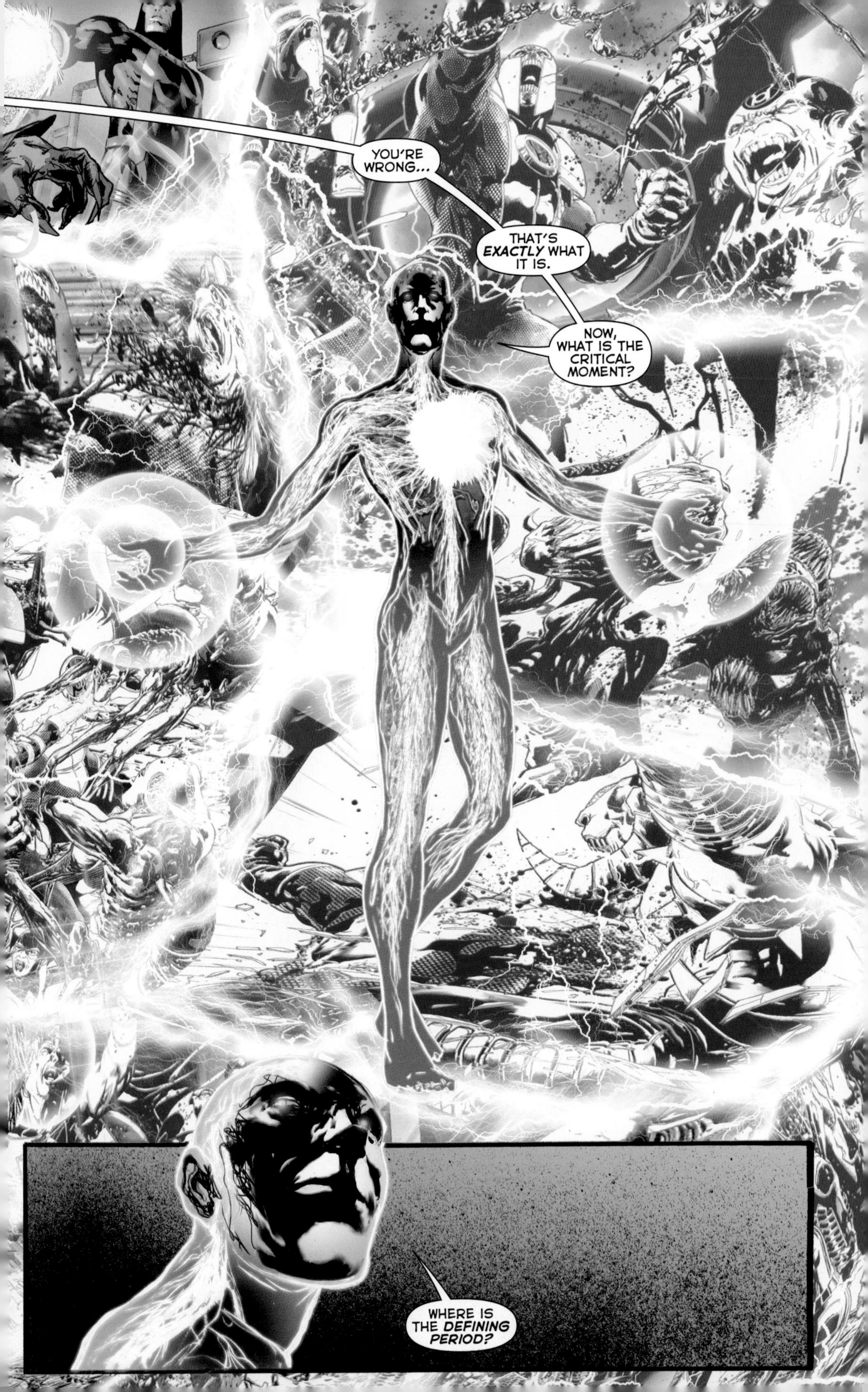
YOU'RE WRONG...
THAT'S EXACTLY WHAT IT IS.
NOW, WHAT IS THE CRITICAL MOMENT?
WHERE IS THE DEFINING PERIOD?

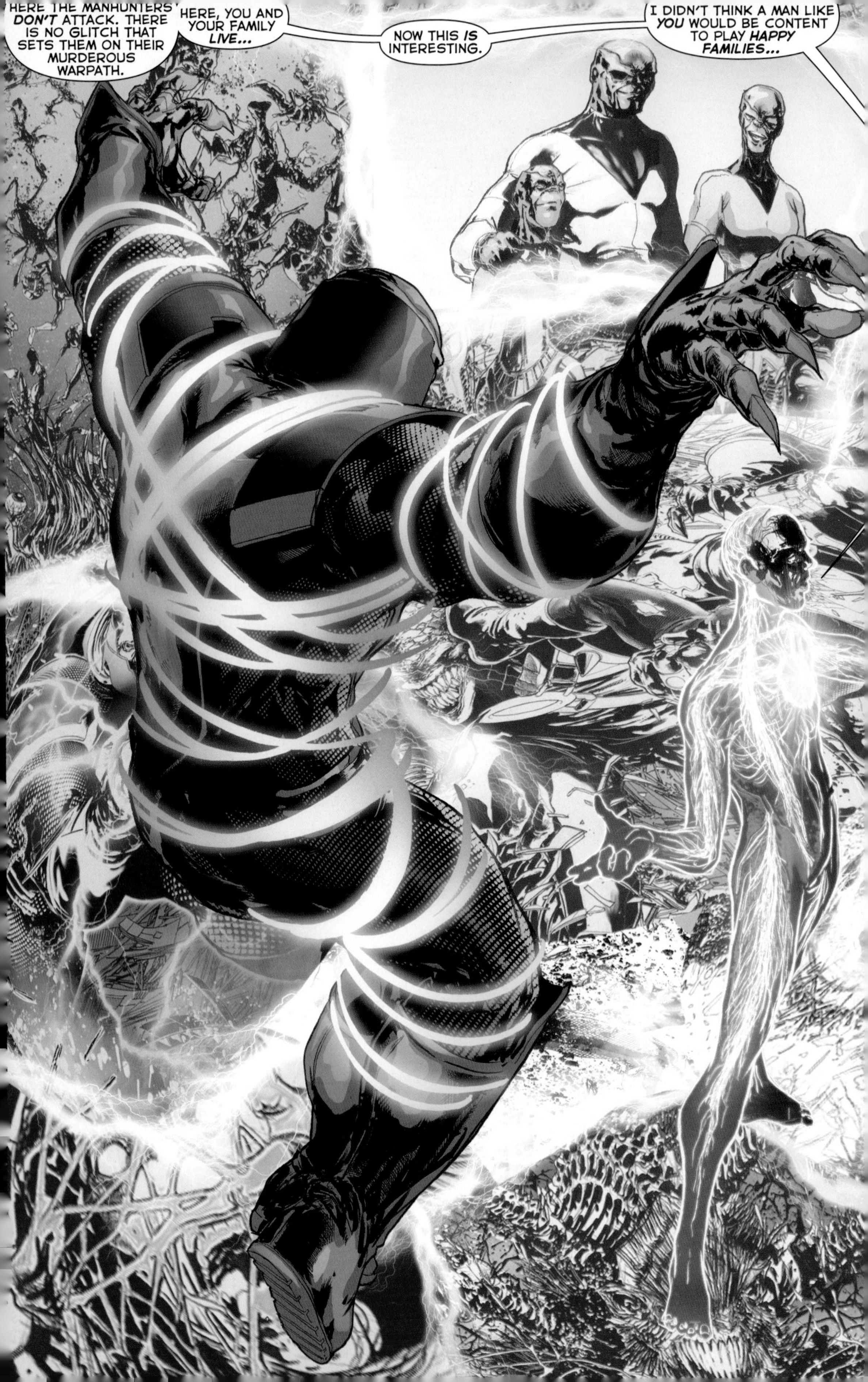

HERE THE MANHUNTERS DON'T ATTACK. THERE IS NO GLITCH THAT SETS THEM ON THEIR MURDEROUS WARPATH.
HERE, YOU AND YOUR FAMILY LIVE...
NOW THIS IS INTERESTING.
I DIDN'T THINK A MAN LIKE YOU WOULD BE CONTENT TO PLAY HAPPY FAMILIES...

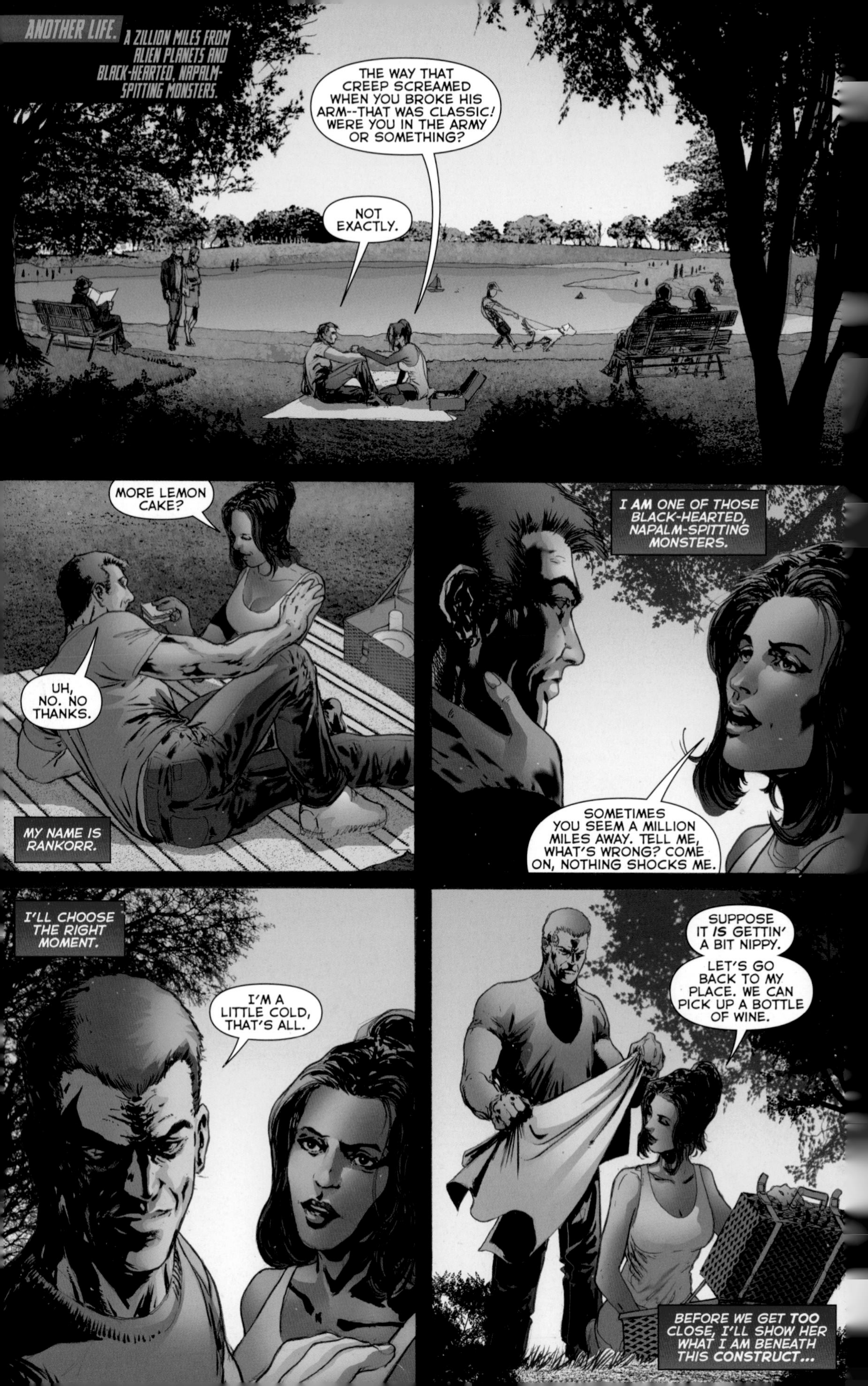
ANOTHER LIFE.
A ZILLION MILES FROM ALIEN PLANETS AND BLACK-HEARTED, NAPALM-SPITTING MONSTERS.
THE WAY THAT CREEP SCREAMED WHEN YOU BROKE HIS ARM--THAT WAS CLASSIC! WERE YOU IN THE ARMY OR SOMETHING?
NOT EXACTLY.
MORE LEMON CAKE?
UH, NO. NO THANKS.
MY NAME IS RANKORR.
I AM ONE OF THOSE BLACK-HEARTED, NAPALM-SPITTING MONSTERS.
SOMETIMES YOU SEEM A MILLION MILES AWAY. TELL ME, WHAT'S WRONG? COME ON, NOTHING SHOCKS ME.
I'LL CHOOSE THE RIGHT MOMENT.
I'M A LITTLE COLD, THAT'S ALL.
SUPPOSE IT IS GETTIN' A BIT NIPPY.
LET'S GO BACK TO MY PLACE. WE CAN PICK UP A BOTTLE OF WINE.
BEFORE WE GET TOO CLOSE, I'LL SHOW HER WHAT I AM BENEATH THIS CONSTRUCT...

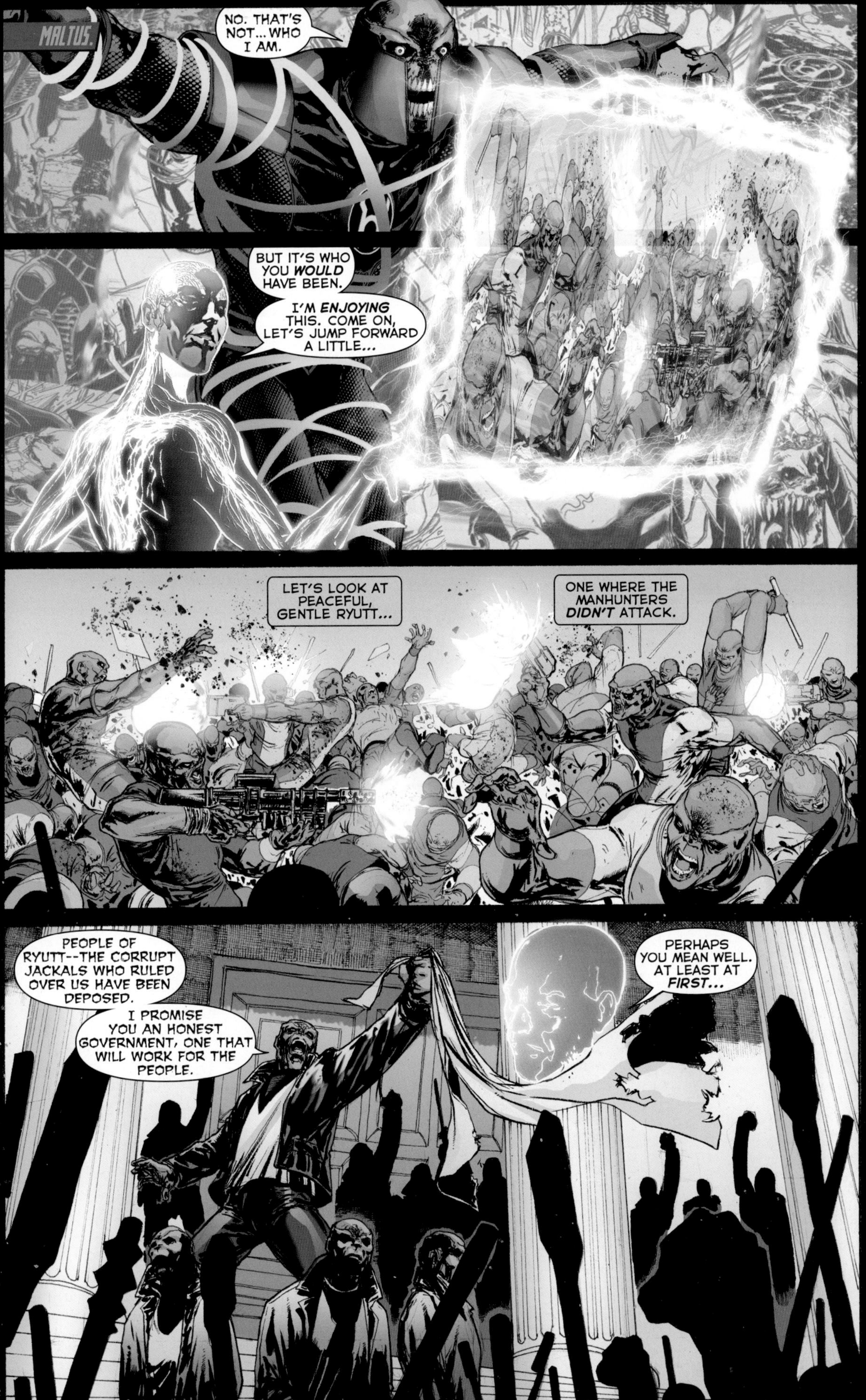
MALTUS.
NO. THAT'S NOT... WHO I AM.
BUT IT'S WHO YOU WOULD HAVE BEEN.
I'M ENJOYING THIS. COME ON, LET'S JUMP FORWARD A LITTLE...
LET'S LOOK AT PEACEFUL, GENTLE RYUTT...
ONE WHERE THE MANHUNTERS DIDN'T ATTACK.
PEOPLE OF RYUTT--THE CORRUPT JACKALS WHO RULED OVER US HAVE BEEN DEPOSED.
I PROMISE YOU AN HONEST GOVERNMENT, ONE THAT WILL WORK FOR THE PEOPLE.
PERHAPS YOU MEAN WELL. AT LEAST AT FIRST...

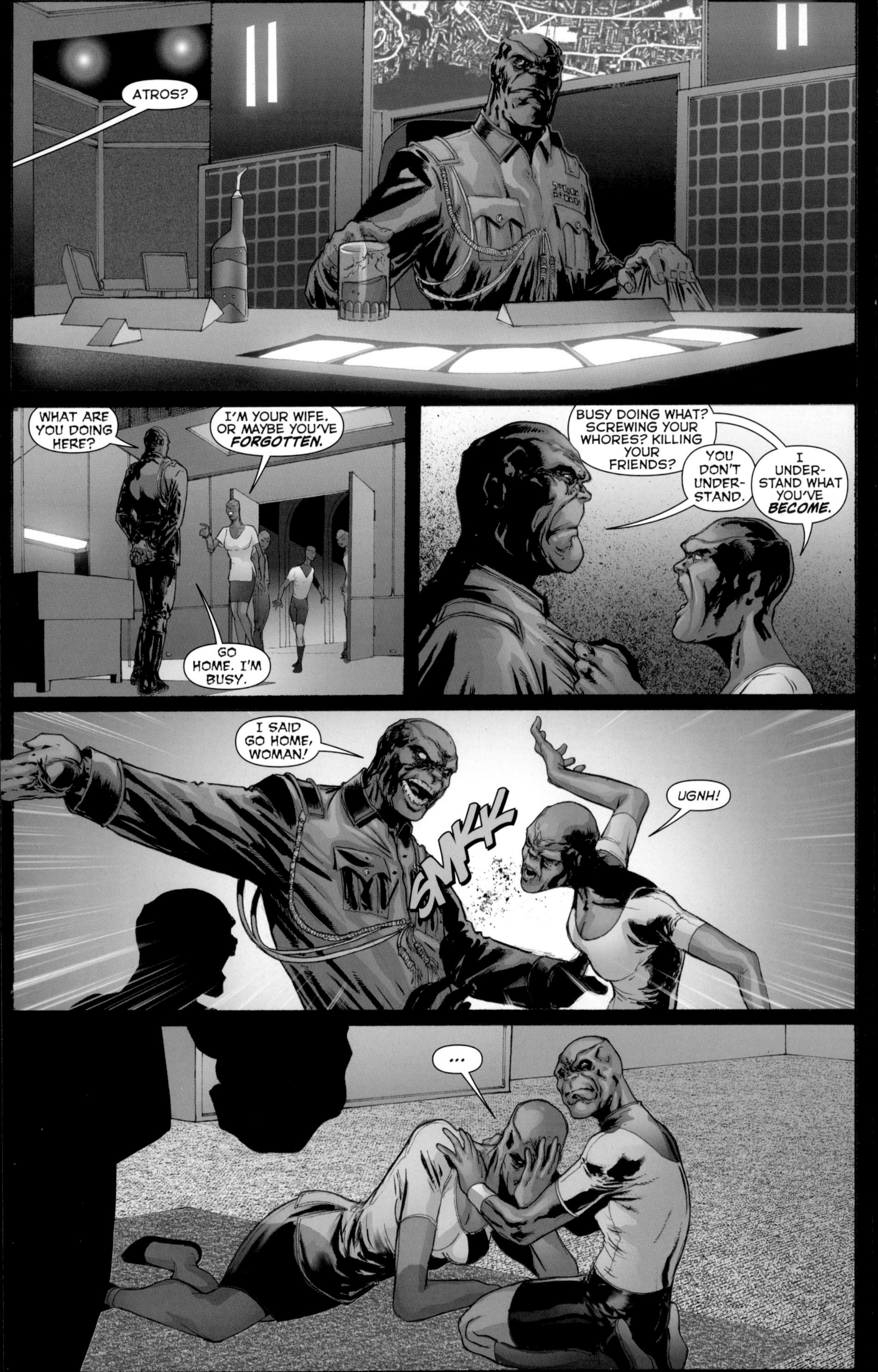
ATROS?
WHAT ARE YOU DOING HERE?
I'M YOUR WIFE. OR MAYBE YOU'VE *FORGOTTEN.*
GO HOME. I'M BUSY.
BUSY DOING WHAT? SCREWING YOUR WHORES? KILLING YOUR FRIENDS?
YOU DON'T UNDER-STAND.
I UNDER-STAND WHAT YOU'VE *BECOME.*
I SAID GO HOME, WOMAN!
SMAK
UGNH!
...

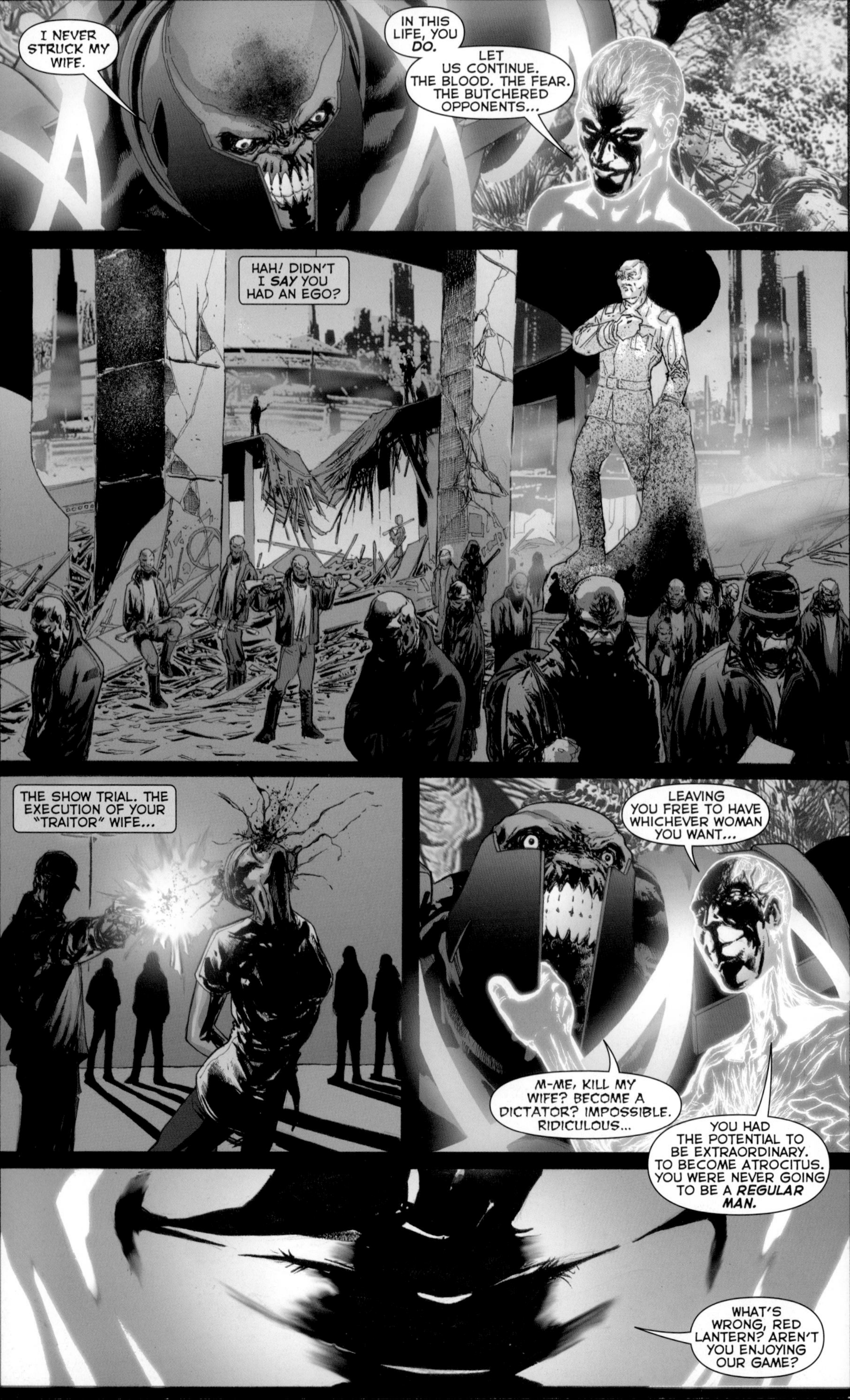
I NEVER STRUCK MY WIFE.
IN THIS LIFE, YOU DO.
LET US CONTINUE. THE BLOOD. THE FEAR. THE BUTCHERED OPPONENTS...
HAH! DIDN'T I SAY YOU HAD AN EGO?
THE SHOW TRIAL. THE EXECUTION OF YOUR "TRAITOR" WIFE...
LEAVING YOU FREE TO HAVE WHICHEVER WOMAN YOU WANT...
M-ME, KILL MY WIFE? BECOME A DICTATOR? IMPOSSIBLE. RIDICULOUS...
YOU HAD THE POTENTIAL TO BE EXTRAORDINARY. TO BECOME ATROCITUS. YOU WERE NEVER GOING TO BE A REGULAR MAN.
WHAT'S WRONG, RED LANTERN? AREN'T YOU ENJOYING OUR GAME?

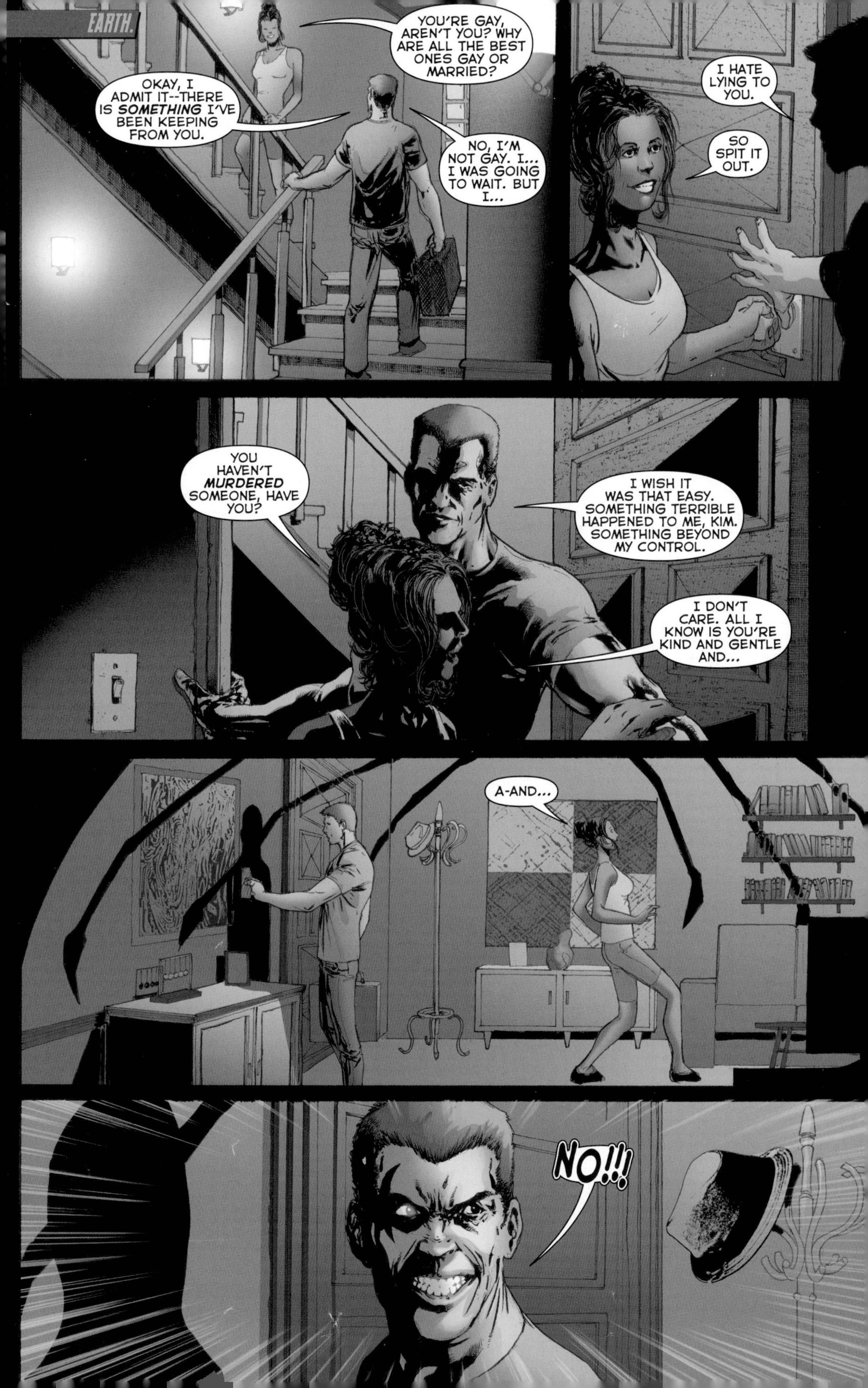
EARTH.
YOU'RE GAY, AREN'T YOU? WHY ARE ALL THE BEST ONES GAY OR MARRIED?
OKAY, I ADMIT IT--THERE IS SOMETHING I'VE BEEN KEEPING FROM YOU.
NO, I'M NOT GAY. I... I WAS GOING TO WAIT. BUT I...
I HATE LYING TO YOU.
SO SPIT IT OUT.
YOU HAVEN'T MURDERED SOMEONE, HAVE YOU?
I WISH IT WAS THAT EASY. SOMETHING TERRIBLE HAPPENED TO ME, KIM. SOMETHING BEYOND MY CONTROL.
I DON'T CARE. ALL I KNOW IS YOU'RE KIND AND GENTLE AND...
A-AND...
NO!!!

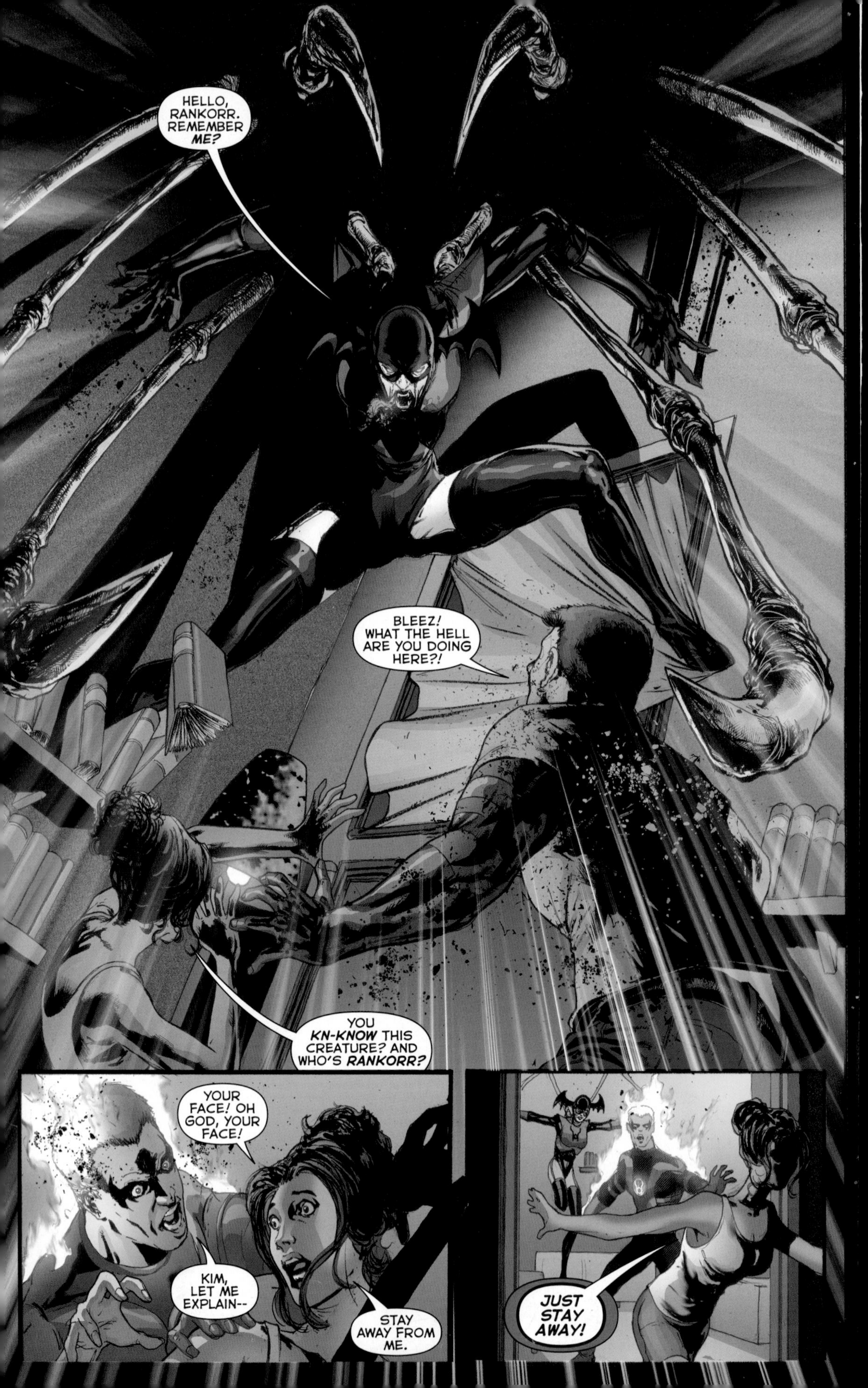
HELLO, RANKORR. REMEMBER ME?
BLEEZ! WHAT THE HELL ARE YOU DOING HERE?!
YOU KN-KNOW THIS CREATURE? AND WHO'S RANKORR?
YOUR FACE! OH GOD, YOUR FACE!
KIM, LET ME EXPLAIN--
STAY AWAY FROM ME.
JUST STAY AWAY!

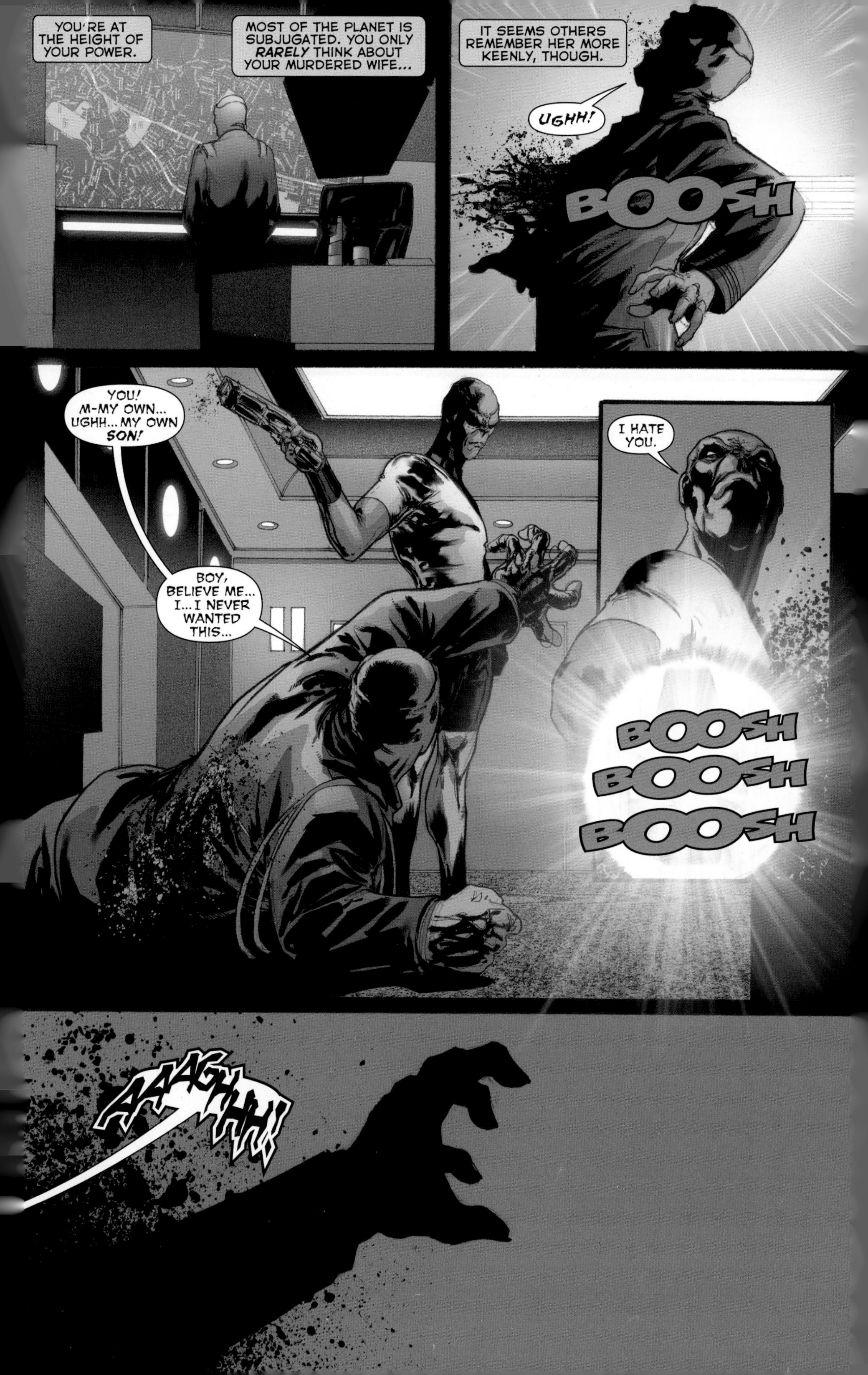

YOU'RE AT THE HEIGHT OF YOUR POWER.
MOST OF THE PLANET IS SUBJUGATED. YOU ONLY RARELY THINK ABOUT YOUR MURDERED WIFE...
IT SEEMS OTHERS REMEMBER HER MORE KEENLY, THOUGH.
UGHH!
BOOSH
YOU! M-MY OWN... UGHH... MY OWN SON!
I HATE YOU.
BOY, BELIEVE ME... I... I NEVER WANTED THIS...
BOOSH
BOOSH
BOOSH
AAAGHHH!

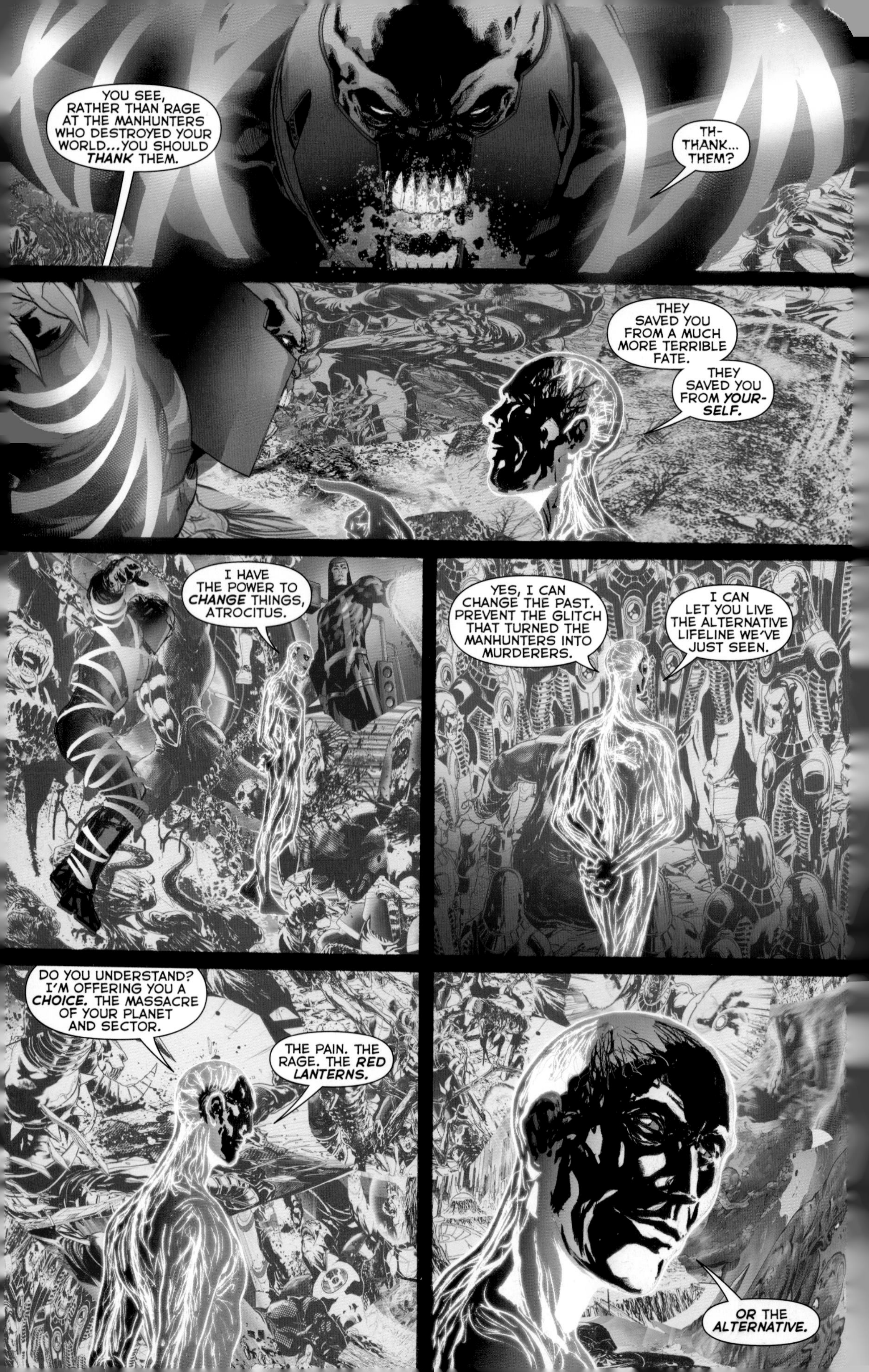
YOU SEE, RATHER THAN RAGE AT THE MANHUNTERS WHO DESTROYED YOUR WORLD...YOU SHOULD *THANK* THEM.
TH-THANK... THEM?
THEY SAVED YOU FROM A MUCH MORE TERRIBLE FATE.
THEY SAVED YOU FROM *YOURSELF.*
I HAVE THE POWER TO *CHANGE* THINGS, ATROCITUS.
YES, I CAN CHANGE THE PAST. PREVENT THE GLITCH THAT TURNED THE MANHUNTERS INTO MURDERERS.
I CAN LET YOU LIVE THE ALTERNATIVE LIFELINE WE'VE JUST SEEN.
DO YOU UNDERSTAND? I'M OFFERING YOU A *CHOICE.* THE MASSACRE OF YOUR PLANET AND SECTOR.
THE PAIN. THE RAGE. THE *RED LANTERNS.*
OR THE *ALTERNATIVE.*

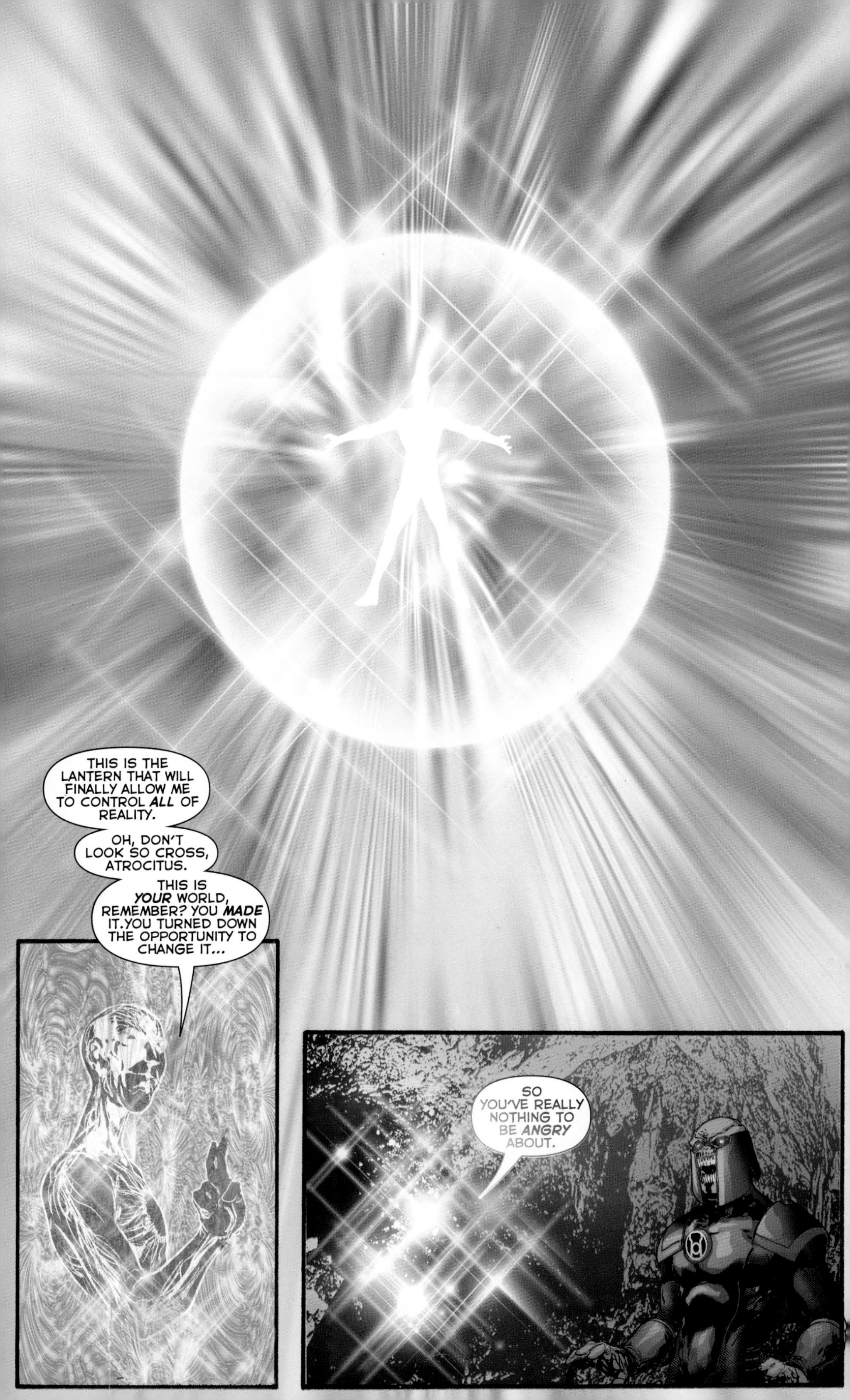
THIS IS THE LANTERN THAT WILL FINALLY ALLOW ME TO CONTROL *ALL* OF REALITY.
OH, DON'T LOOK SO CROSS, ATROCITUS.
THIS IS *YOUR* WORLD, REMEMBER? YOU *MADE* IT.YOU TURNED DOWN THE OPPORTUNITY TO CHANGE IT...
SO YOU'VE REALLY NOTHING TO BE *ANGRY* ABOUT.

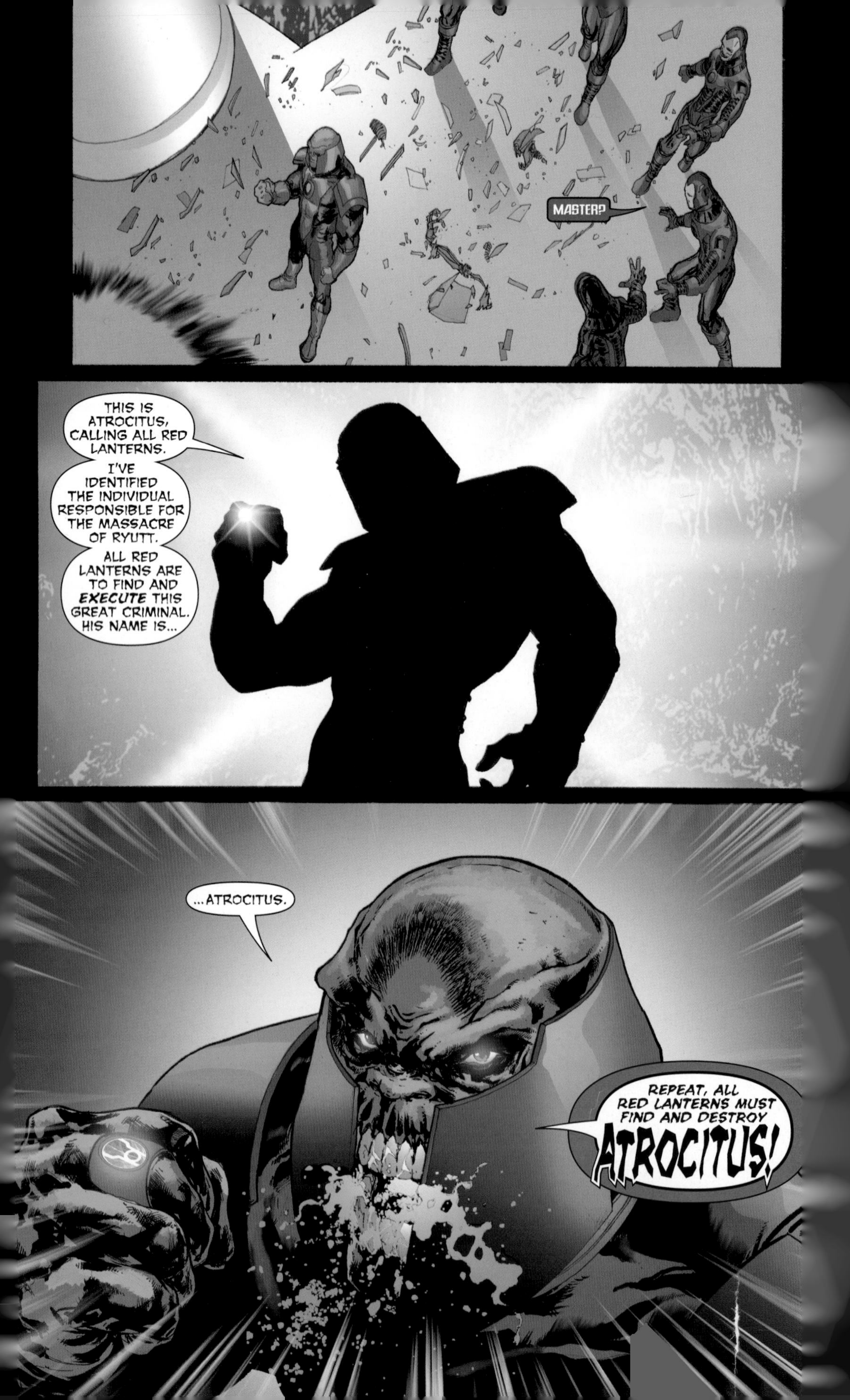
MASTER?
THIS IS ATROCITUS, CALLING ALL RED LANTERNS.
I'VE IDENTIFIED THE INDIVIDUAL RESPONSIBLE FOR THE MASSACRE OF RYUTT.
ALL RED LANTERNS ARE TO FIND AND *EXECUTE* THIS GREAT CRIMINAL. HIS NAME IS...
...ATROCITUS.
REPEAT, ALL RED LANTERNS MUST FIND AND DESTROY ATROCITUS!

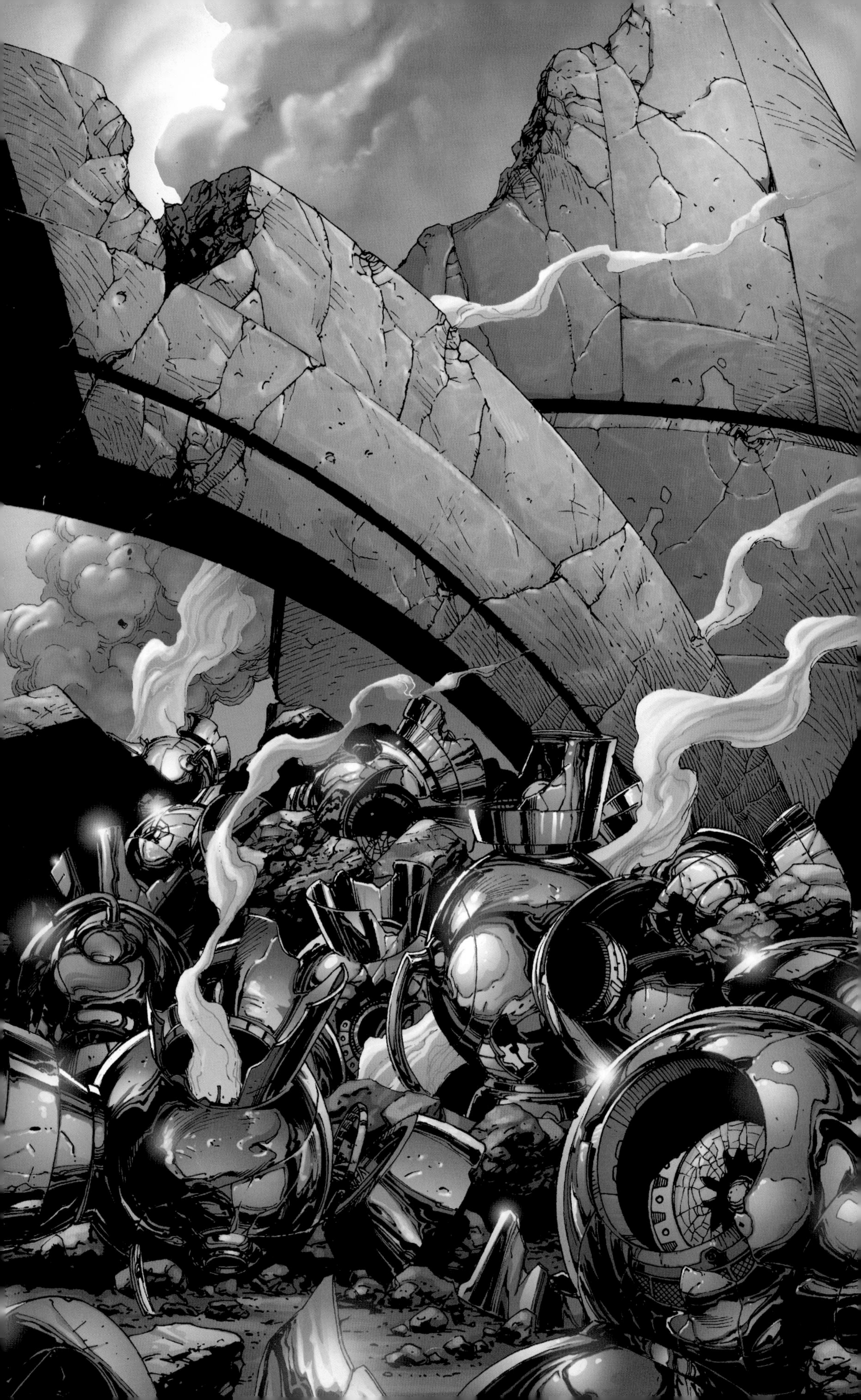

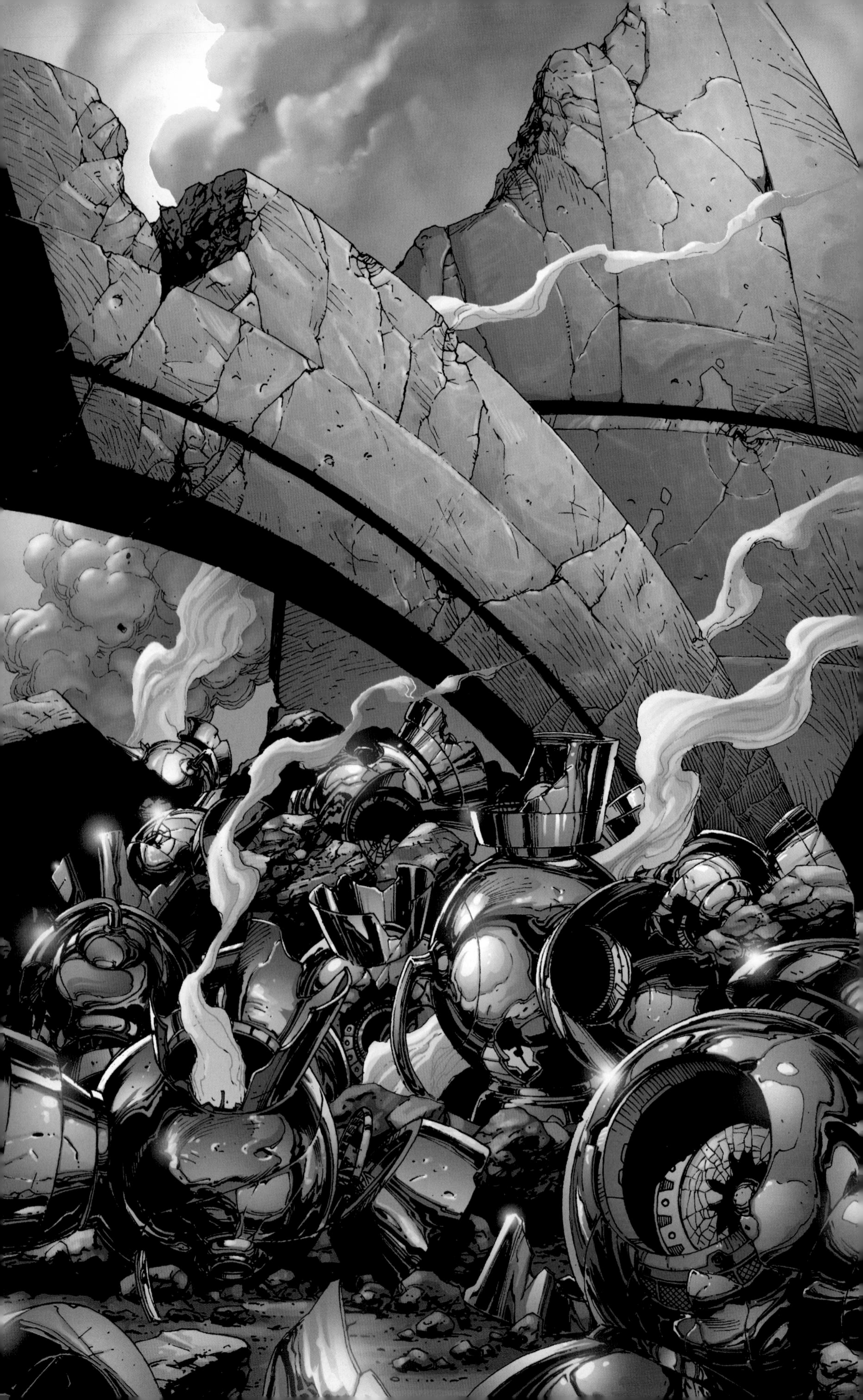

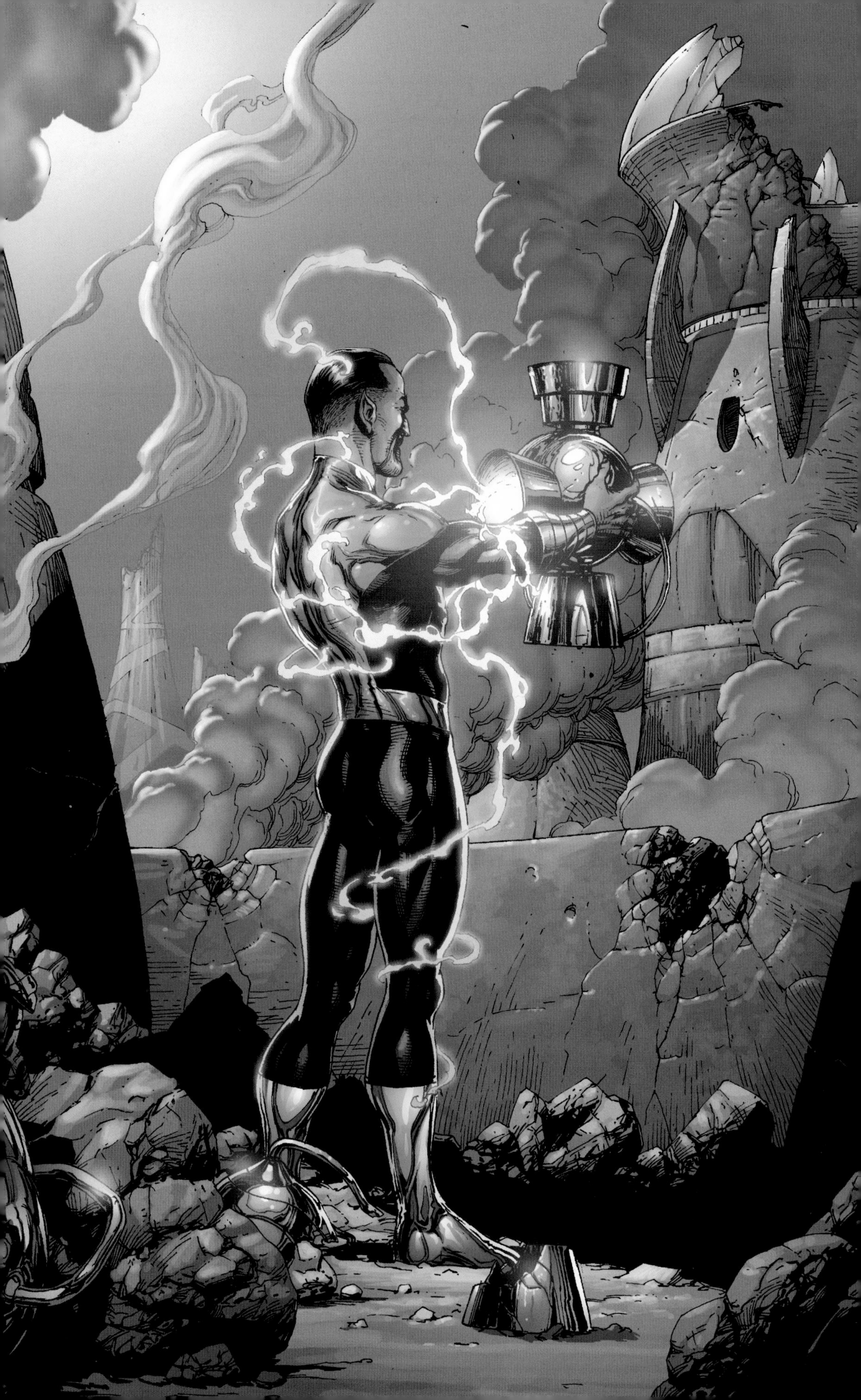

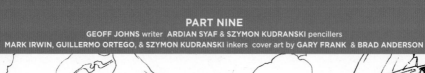

PART NINE

GEOFF JOHNS writer **ARDIAN SYAF** & **SZYMON KUDRANSKI** pencillers
MARK IRWIN, GUILLERMO ORTEGO, & **SZYMON KUDRANSKI** inkers cover art by **GARY FRANK** & **BRAD ANDERSON**

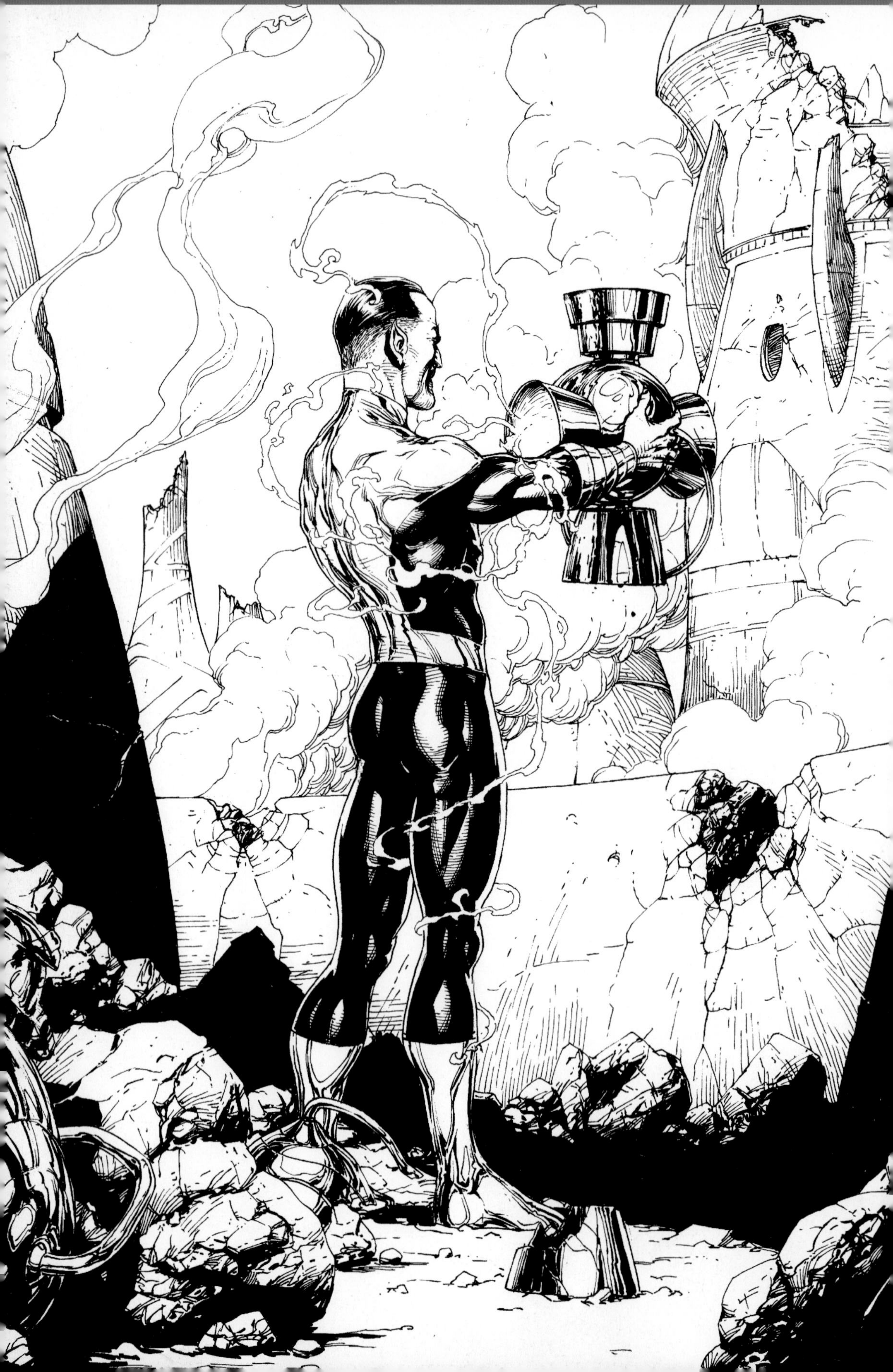

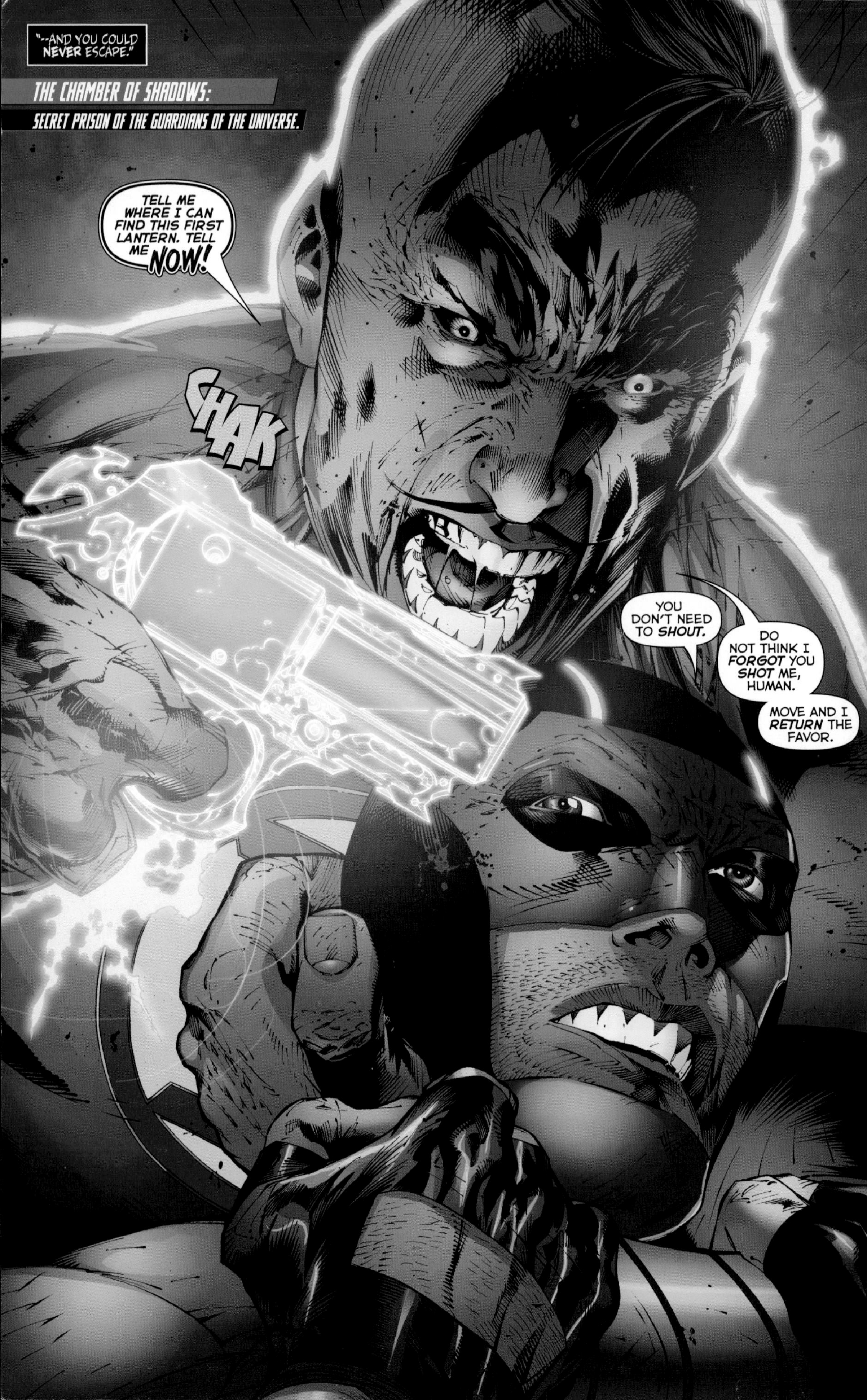
"--AND YOU COULD NEVER ESCAPE."
THE CHAMBER OF SHADOWS:
SECRET PRISON OF THE GUARDIANS OF THE UNIVERSE.
TELL ME WHERE I CAN FIND THIS FIRST LANTERN. TELL ME NOW!
CHAK
YOU DON'T NEED TO SHOUT.
DO NOT THINK I FORGOT YOU SHOT ME, HUMAN.
MOVE AND I RETURN THE FAVOR.

SPACE SECTOR 1417.
THE PLANET KORUGAR.

YOU'VE HIT THAT CHILD FOR THE *LAST TIME,* YOU UNDERSTAND?

SCREW YOU!

MY KID! MY RULES!

LOOK... IT'S...

TH-O-O-O-MMM

IT'S *SINESTRO.* DO WE *RUN* OR--

GREETINGS, OFFICER ARSONA.

WHAT ARE YOU DOING HERE, SINESTRO? YOU'RE NOT WELCOME--

NOT *EVERYONE* IS AFRAID. NOT EVERYONE IS RUNNING.

ONLY BECAUSE THEY DON'T KNOW ANY BETTER.

THE LAST TIME I WAS HERE I SAVED KORUGAR.

FROM AN ARMY OF *TERRORISTS* THAT *YOU* CREATED.

WHAT DO YOU *WANT?*

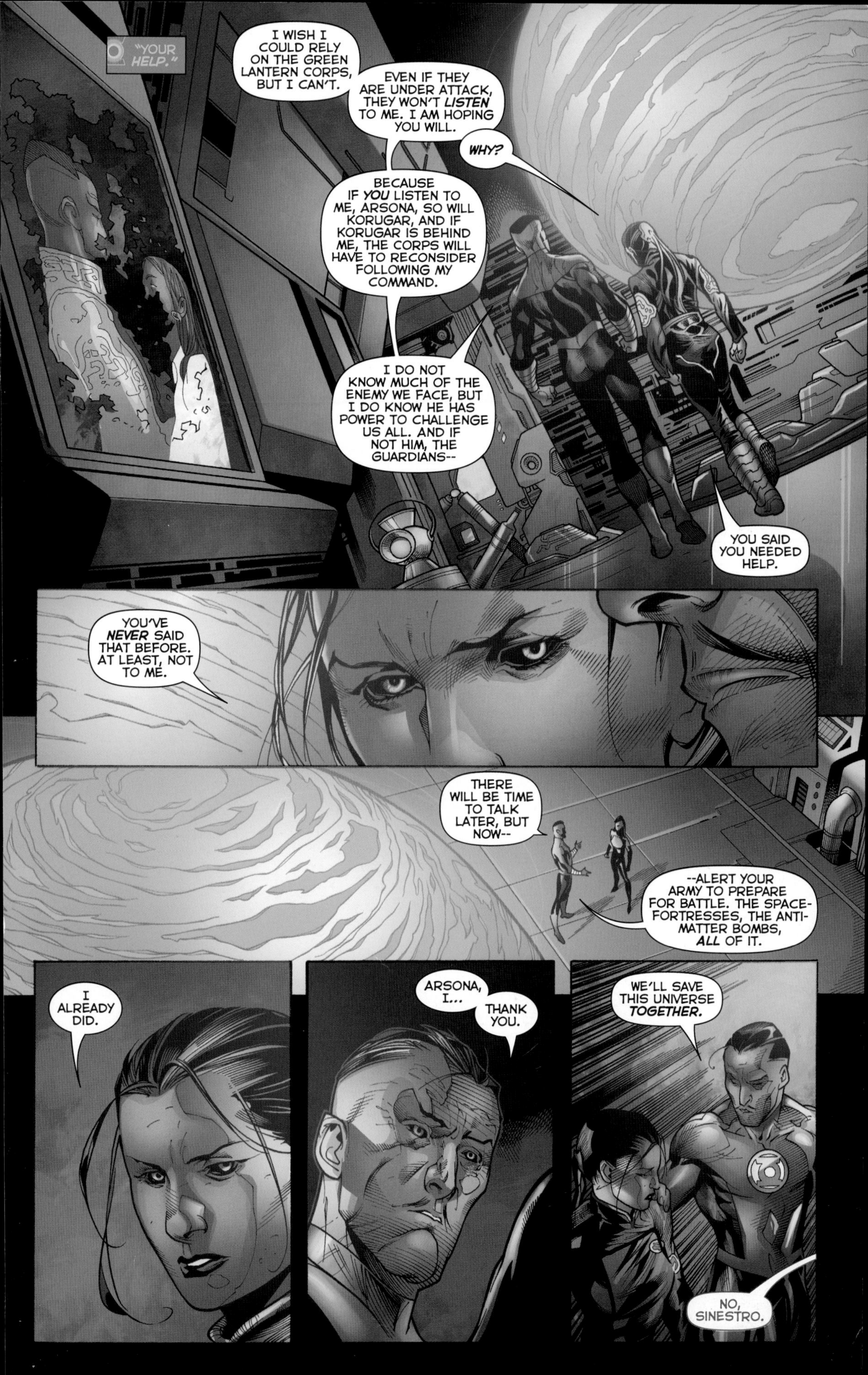
"YOUR HELP."
I WISH I COULD RELY ON THE GREEN LANTERN CORPS, BUT I CAN'T.
EVEN IF THEY ARE UNDER ATTACK, THEY WON'T LISTEN TO ME. I AM HOPING YOU WILL.
WHY?
BECAUSE IF YOU LISTEN TO ME, ARSONA, SO WILL KORUGAR, AND IF KORUGAR IS BEHIND ME, THE CORPS WILL HAVE TO RECONSIDER FOLLOWING MY COMMAND.
I DO NOT KNOW MUCH OF THE ENEMY WE FACE, BUT I DO KNOW HE HAS POWER TO CHALLENGE US ALL. AND IF NOT HIM, THE GUARDIANS--
YOU SAID YOU NEEDED HELP.
YOU'VE NEVER SAID THAT BEFORE. AT LEAST, NOT TO ME.
THERE WILL BE TIME TO TALK LATER, BUT NOW--
--ALERT YOUR ARMY TO PREPARE FOR BATTLE. THE SPACE-FORTRESSES, THE ANTI-MATTER BOMBS, ALL OF IT.
I ALREADY DID.
ARSONA, I...
THANK YOU.
WE'LL SAVE THIS UNIVERSE TOGETHER.
NO, SINESTRO.

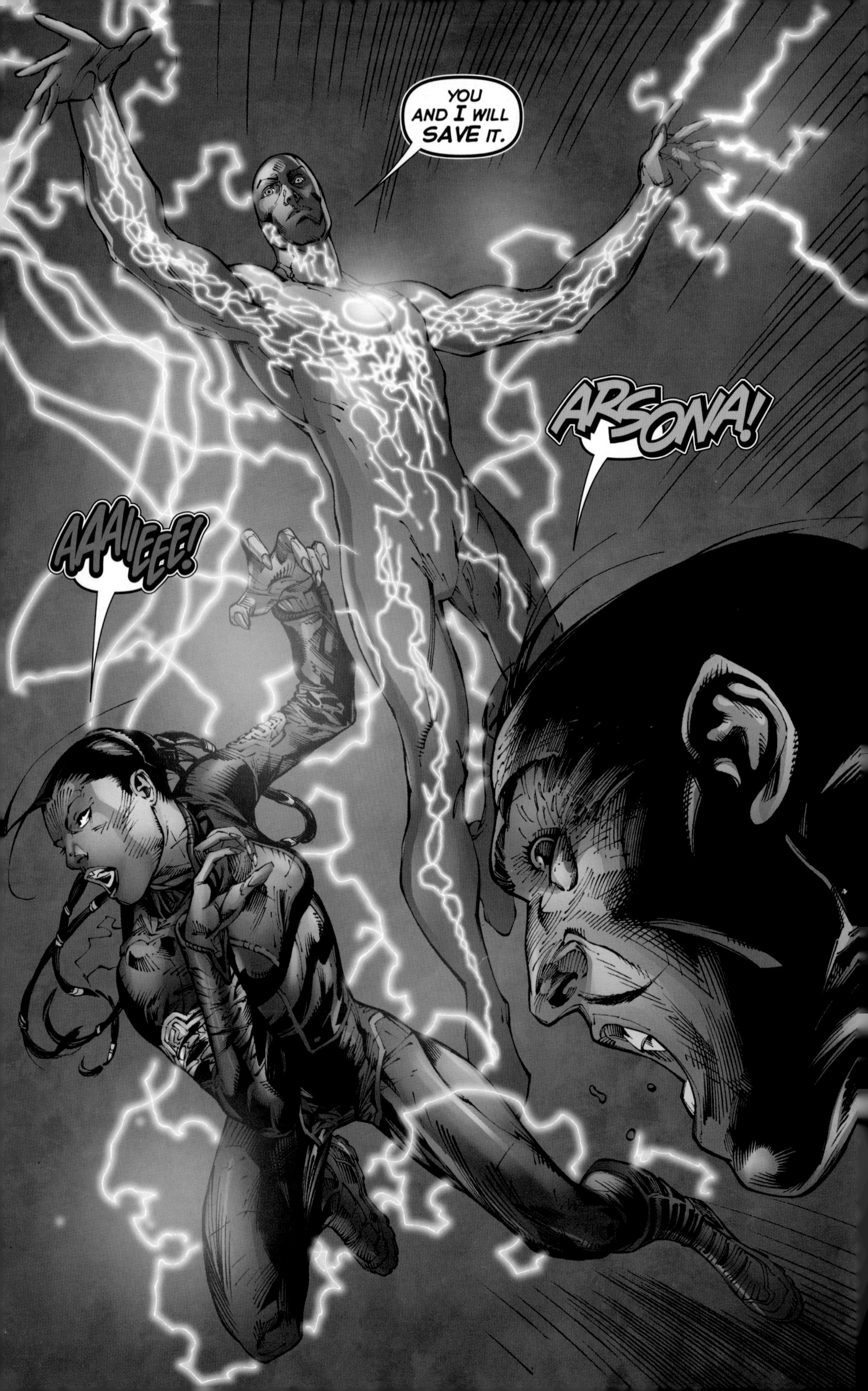
YOU AND I WILL SAVE IT.
ARSONA!
AAAIIIEEEE!

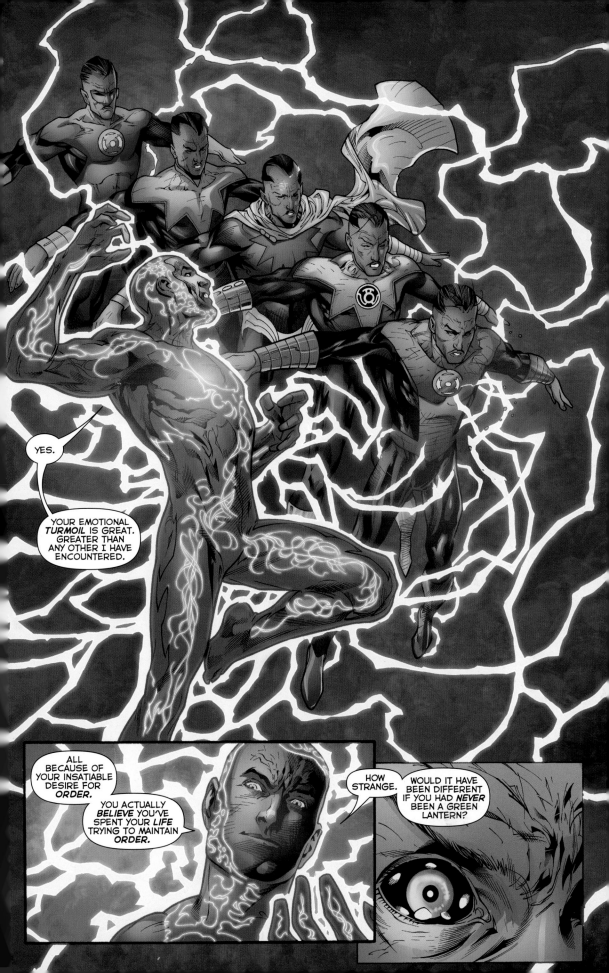

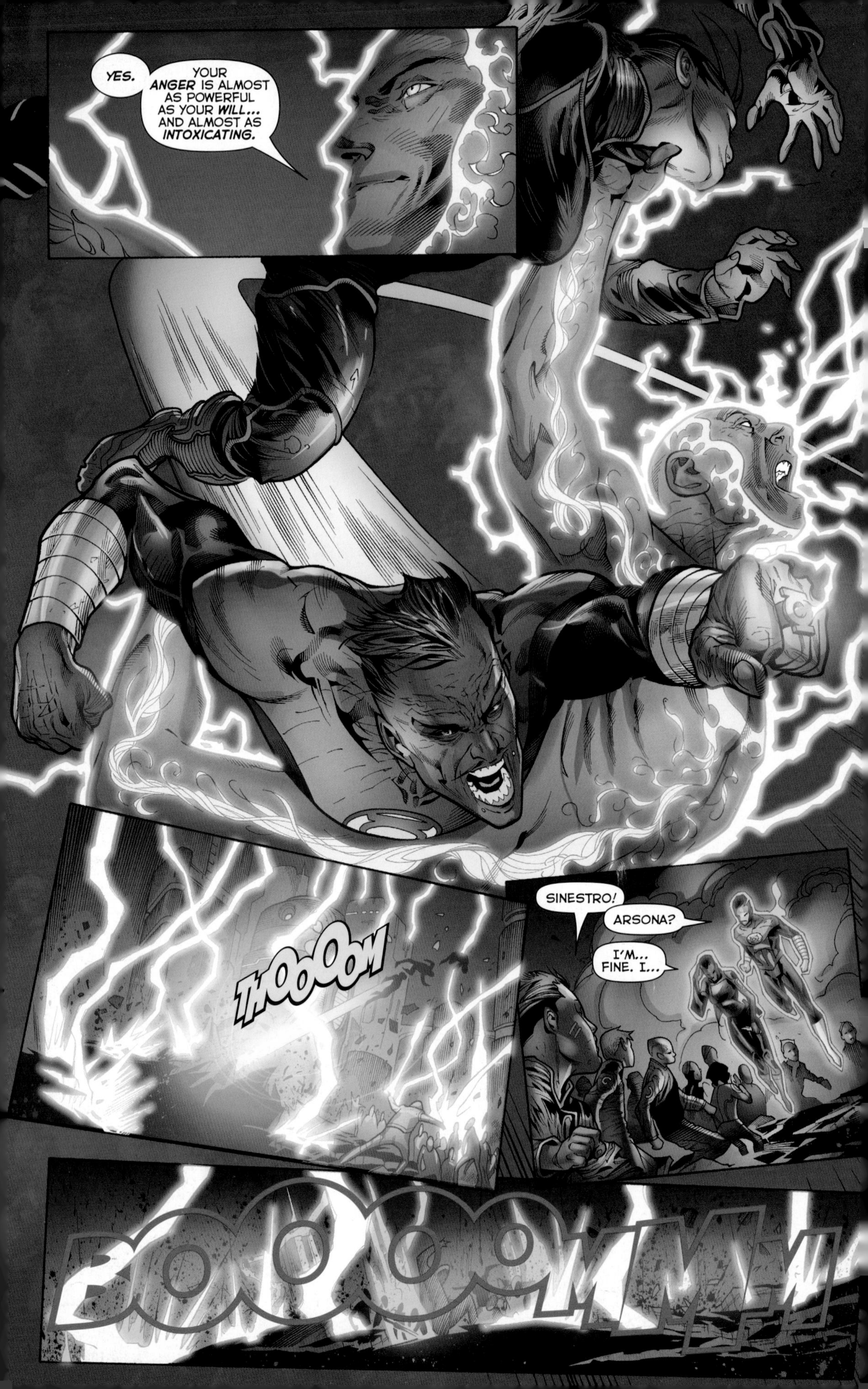
YES.
YOUR ANGER IS ALMOST AS POWERFUL AS YOUR WILL... AND ALMOST AS INTOXICATING.
THOOOOM
SINESTRO!
ARSONA?
I'M... FINE. I...
BOOOOOMMM

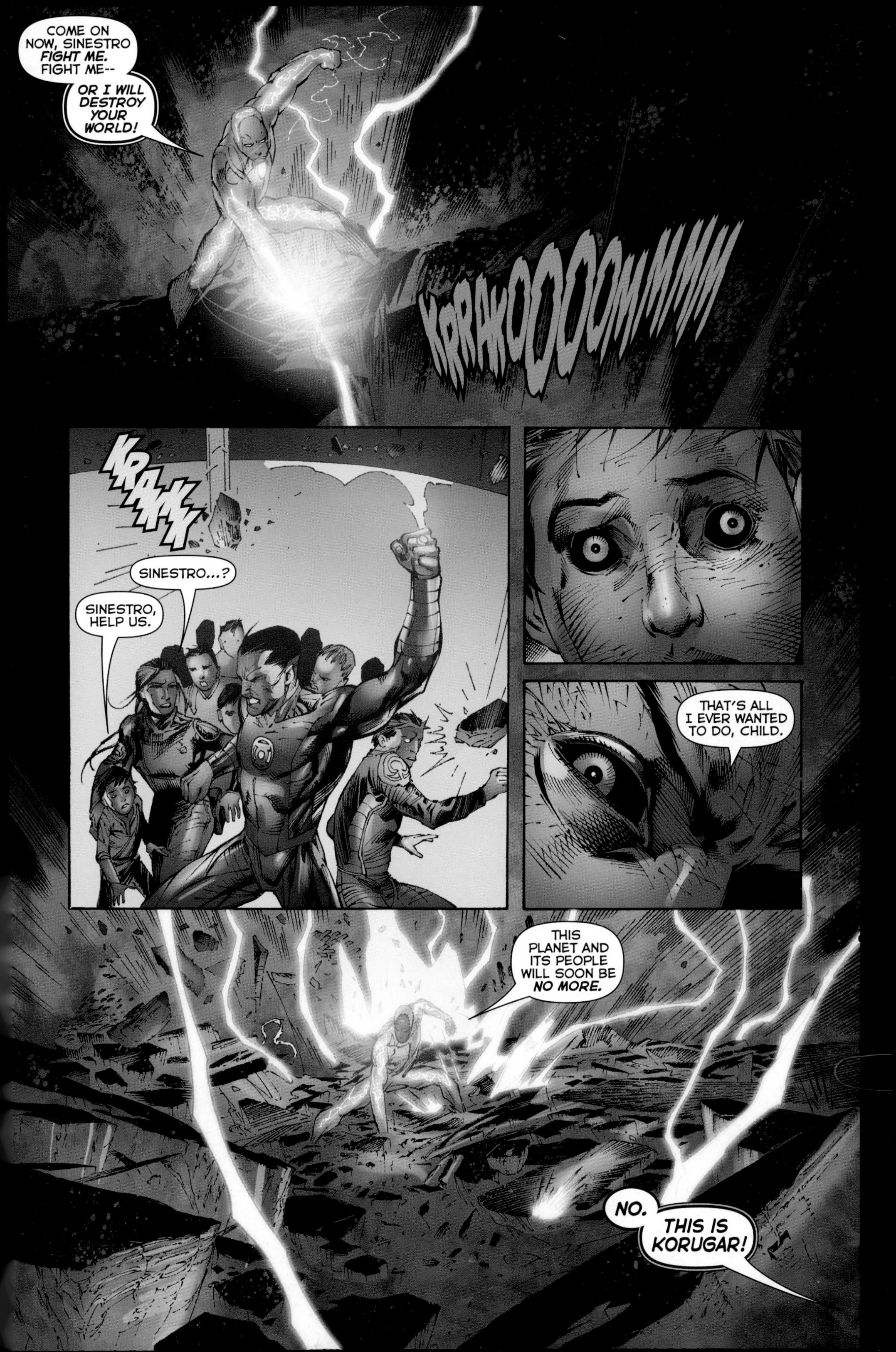
COME ON NOW, SINESTRO *FIGHT ME.* FIGHT ME--
OR I WILL DESTROY YOUR WORLD!
KRRAKOOOOMMMM
KRAKKK
SINESTRO...?
SINESTRO, HELP US.
THAT'S ALL I EVER WANTED TO DO, CHILD.
THIS PLANET AND ITS PEOPLE WILL SOON BE *NO MORE.*
NO.
THIS IS KORUGAR!

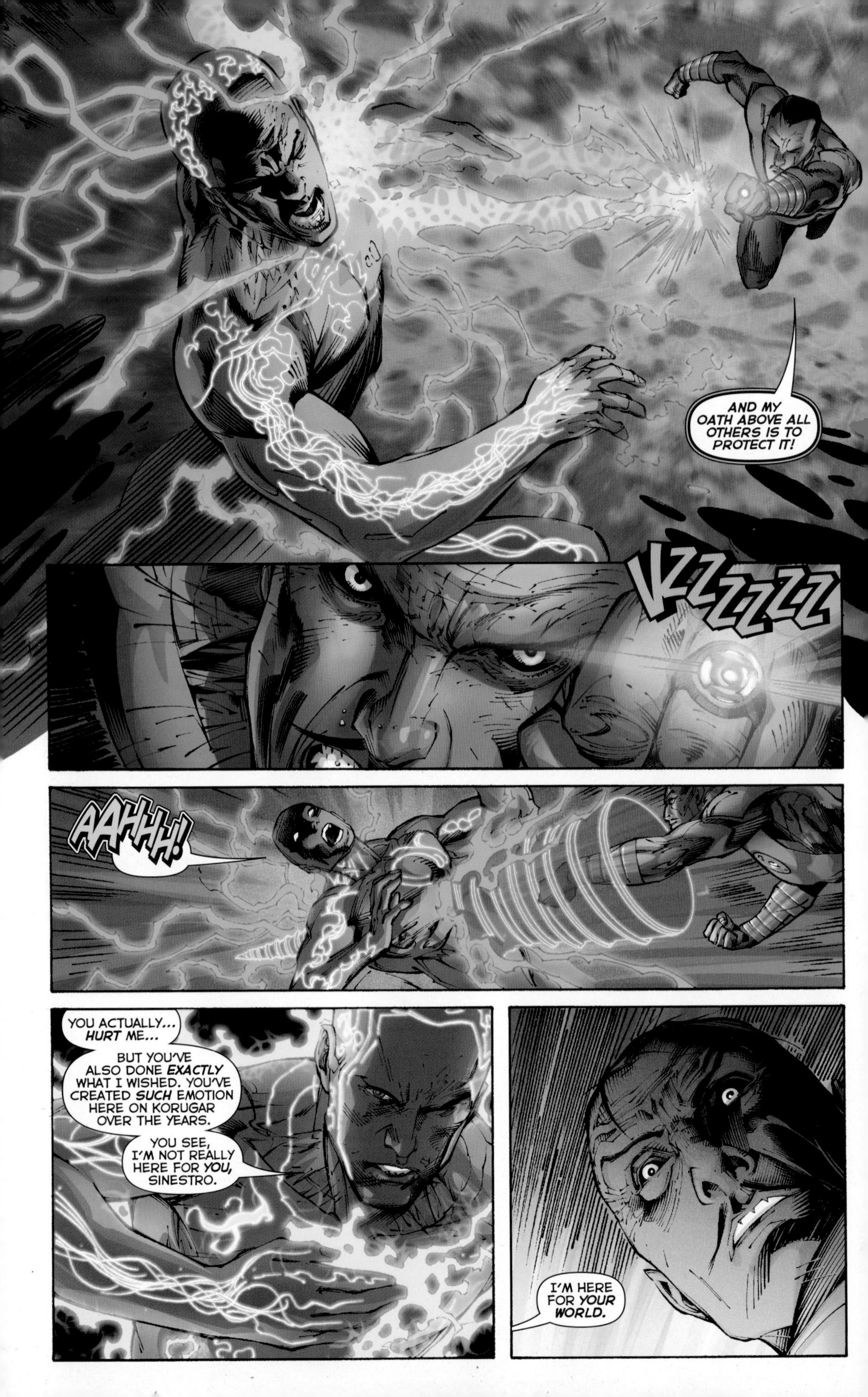
AND MY OATH ABOVE ALL OTHERS IS TO PROTECT IT!
VZZZZZZZ
AAHHH!
YOU ACTUALLY... HURT ME...
BUT YOU'VE ALSO DONE EXACTLY WHAT I WISHED. YOU'VE CREATED SUCH EMOTION HERE ON KORUGAR OVER THE YEARS.
YOU SEE, I'M NOT REALLY HERE FOR YOU, SINESTRO.
I'M HERE FOR YOUR WORLD.

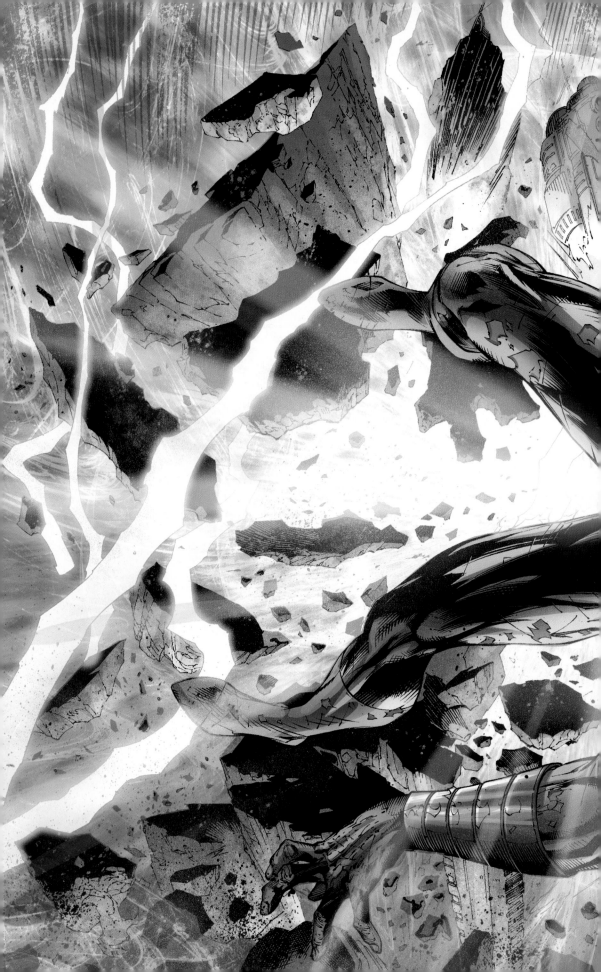

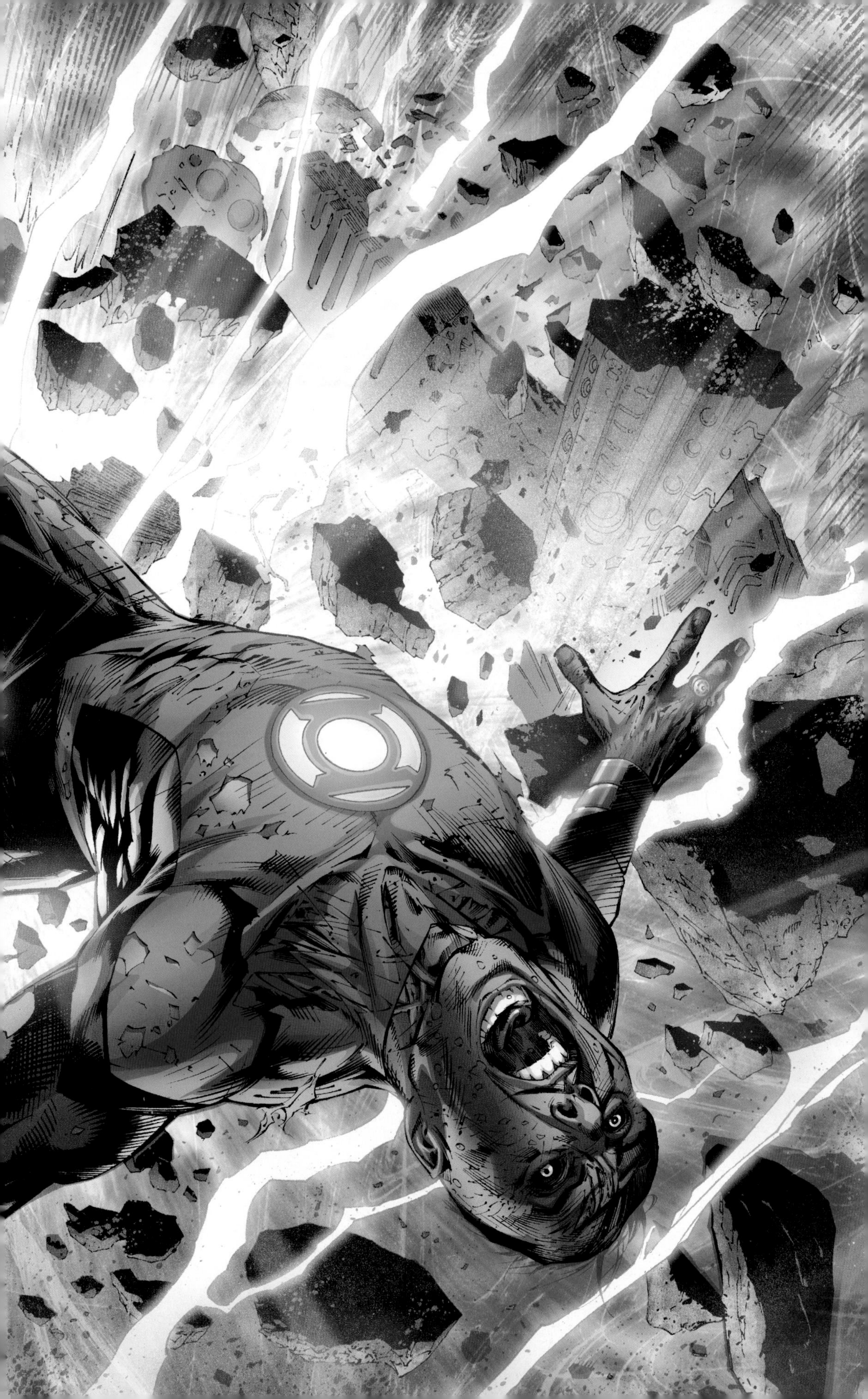

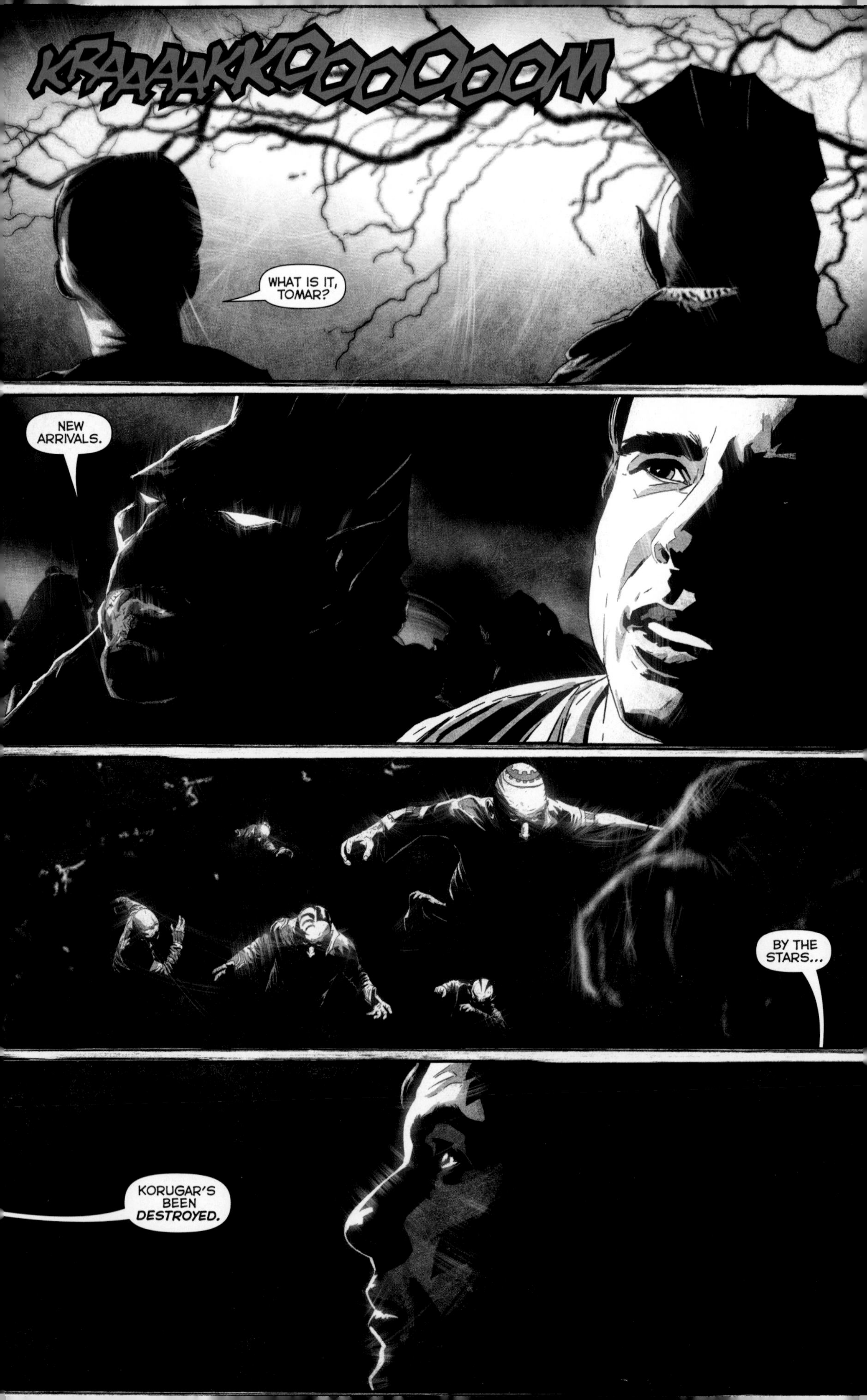
KRAAAKKOOOOOOOM
WHAT IS IT, TOMAR?
NEW ARRIVALS.
BY THE STARS...
KORUGAR'S BEEN DESTROYED.

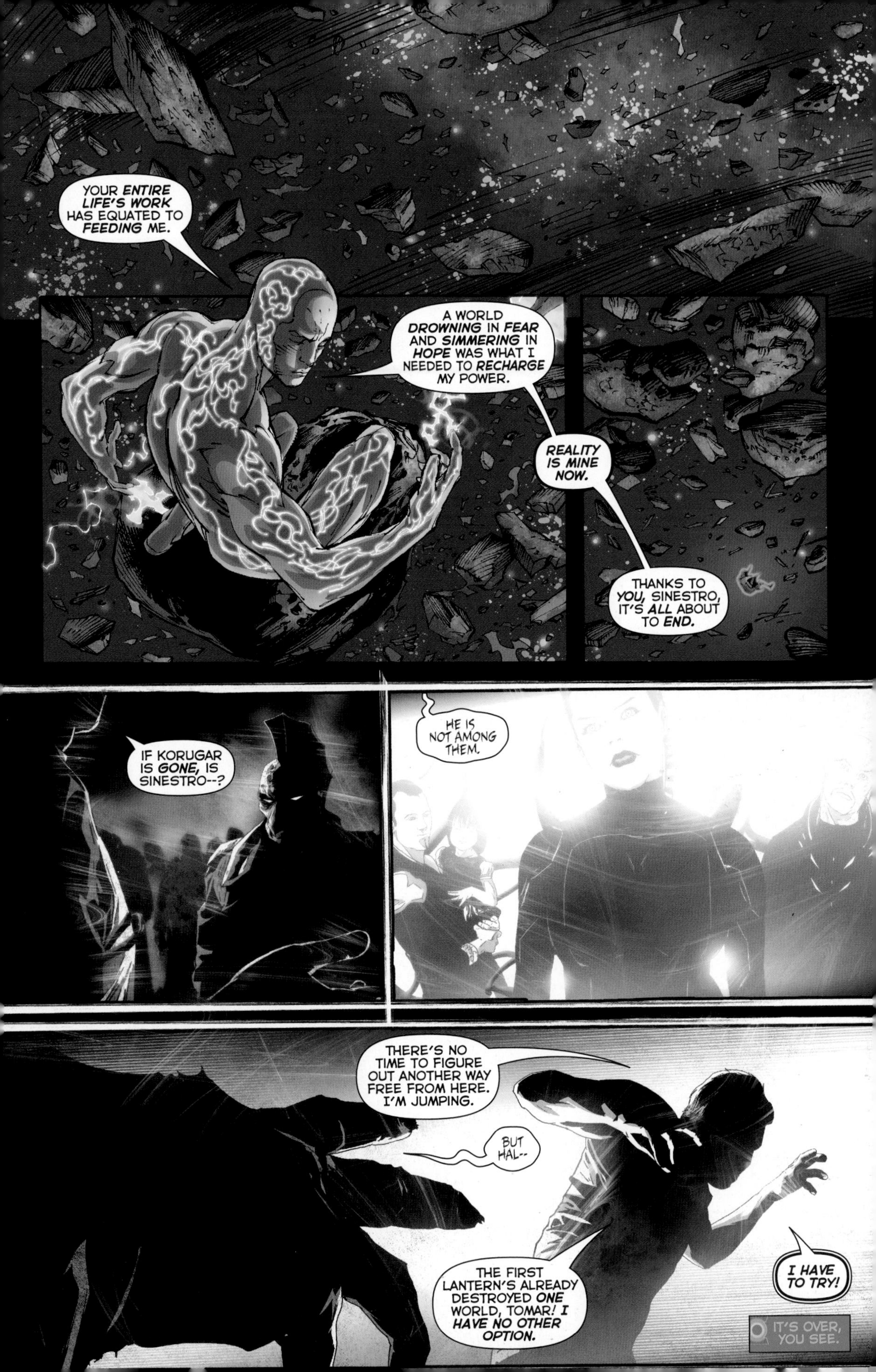
YOUR ENTIRE LIFE'S WORK HAS EQUATED TO FEEDING ME.
A WORLD DROWNING IN FEAR AND SIMMERING IN HOPE WAS WHAT I NEEDED TO RECHARGE MY POWER.
REALITY IS MINE NOW.
THANKS TO YOU, SINESTRO, IT'S ALL ABOUT TO END.
IF KORUGAR IS GONE, IS SINESTRO--?
HE IS NOT AMONG THEM.
THERE'S NO TIME TO FIGURE OUT ANOTHER WAY FREE FROM HERE. I'M JUMPING.
BUT HAL--
THE FIRST LANTERN'S ALREADY DESTROYED ONE WORLD, TOMAR! I HAVE NO OTHER OPTION.
I HAVE TO TRY!
IT'S OVER, YOU SEE.

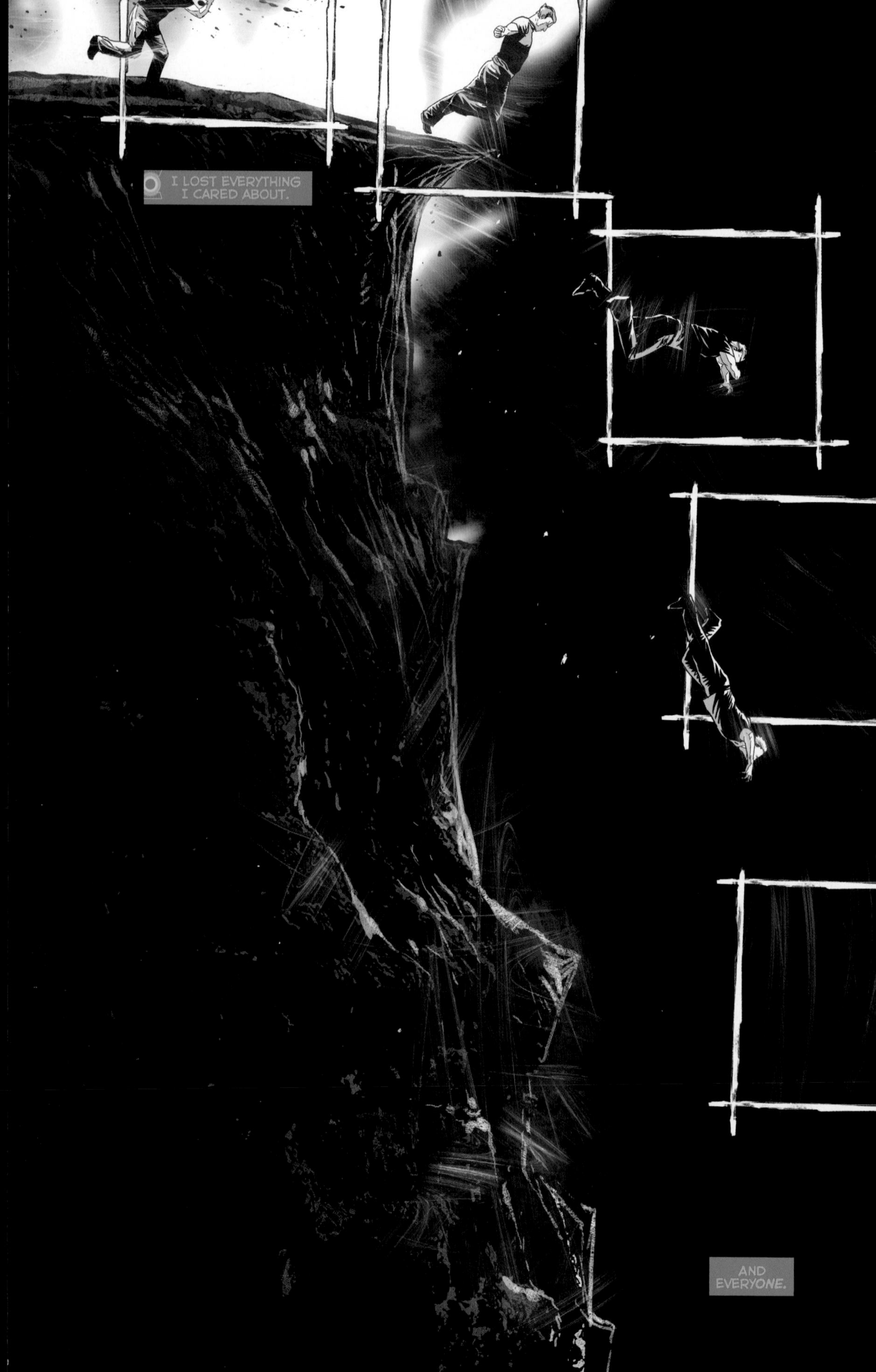
I LOST EVERYTHING I CARED ABOUT.
AND EVERYONE.

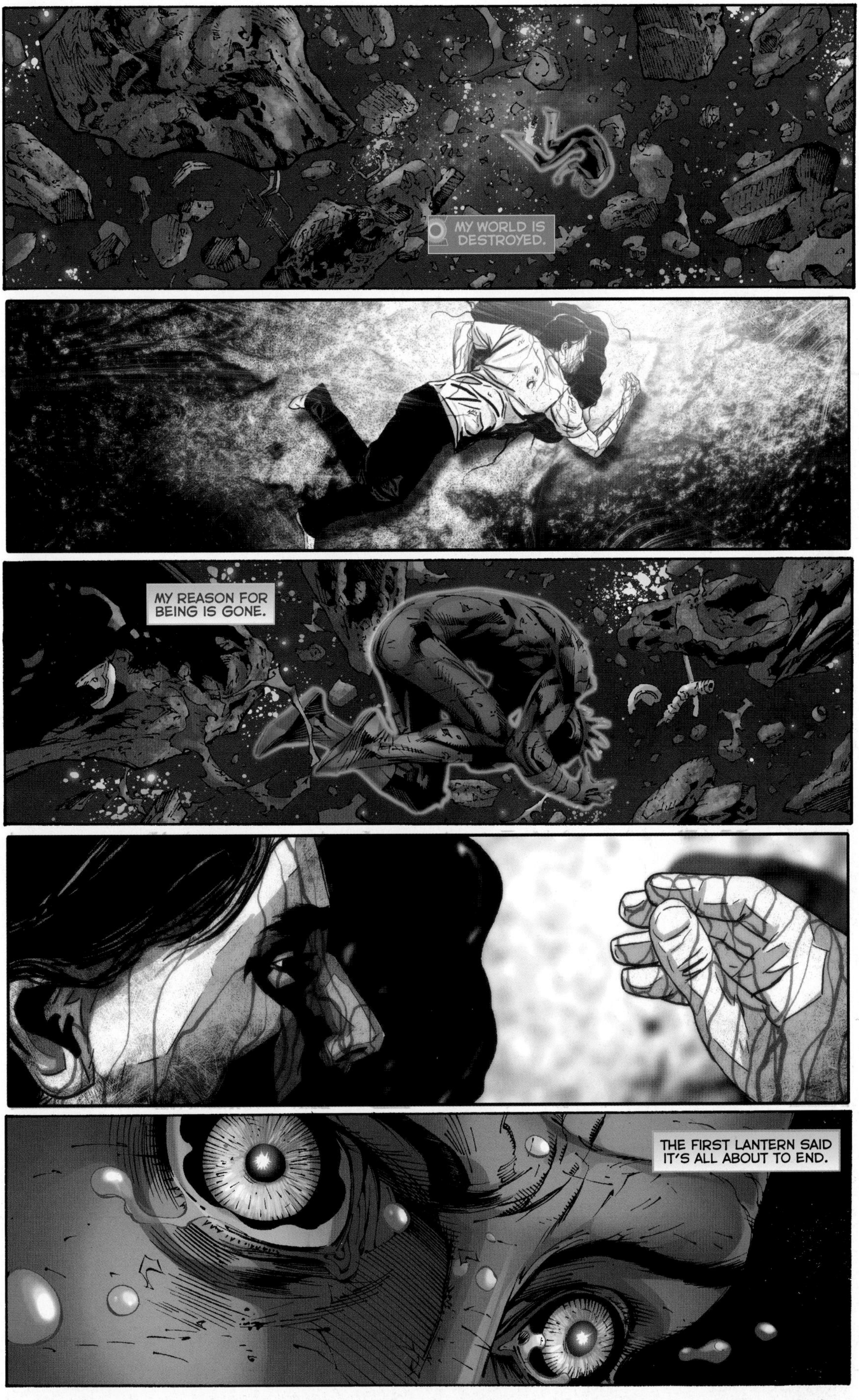
MY WORLD IS DESTROYED.
MY REASON FOR BEING IS GONE.
THE FIRST LANTERN SAID IT'S ALL ABOUT TO END.

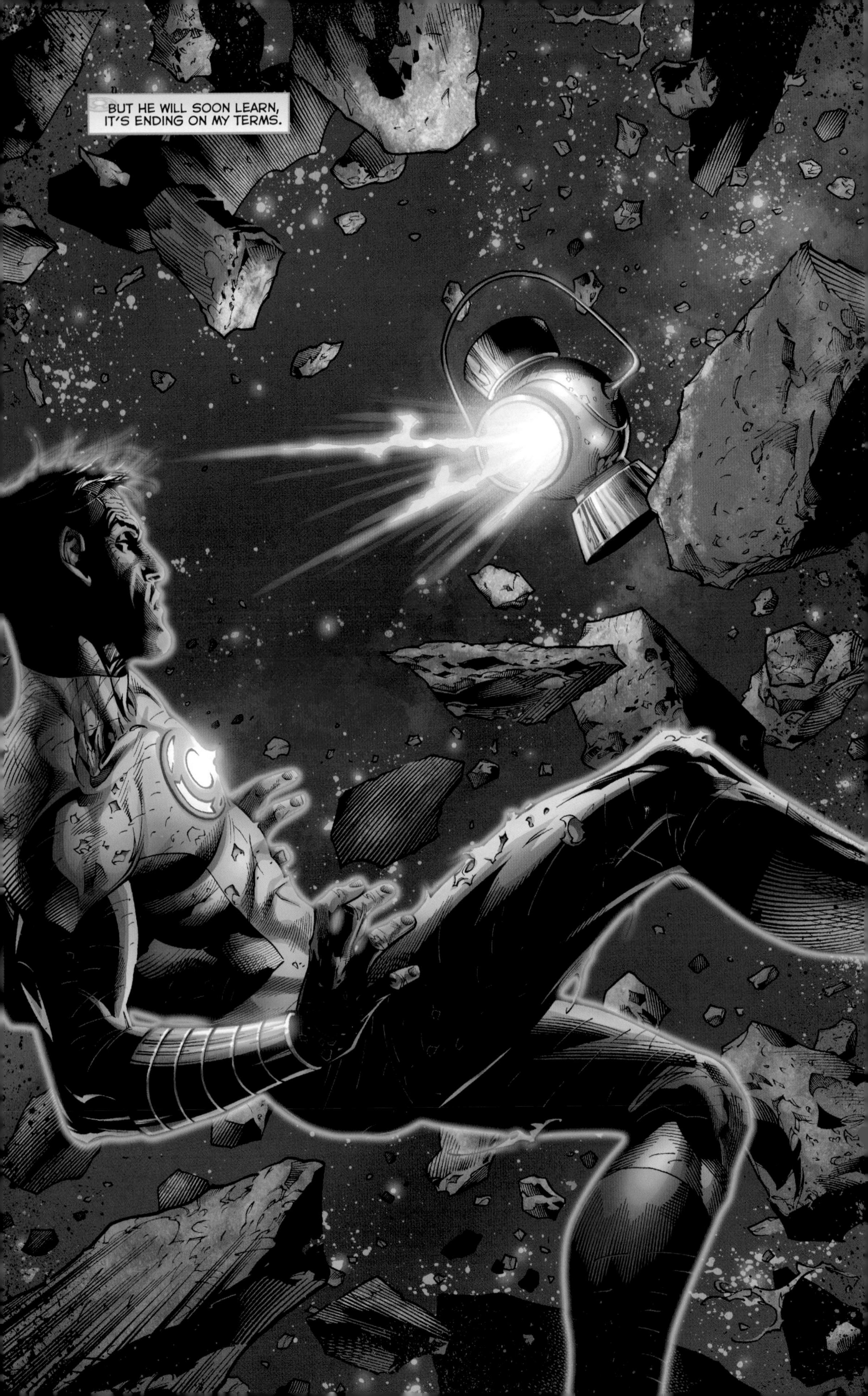
BUT HE WILL SOON LEARN, IT'S ENDING ON MY TERMS.

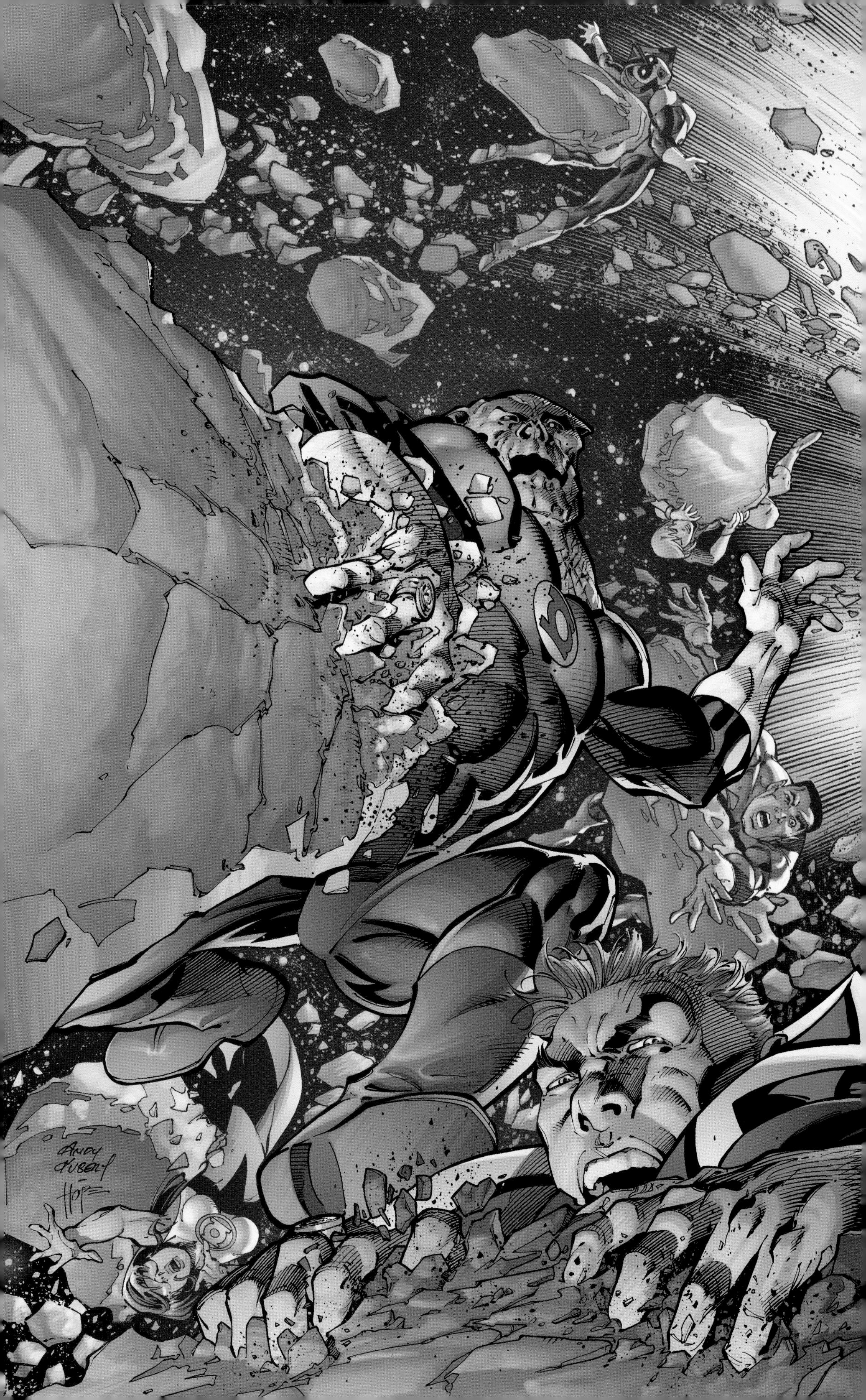
ANDY KUBERT
HOPE

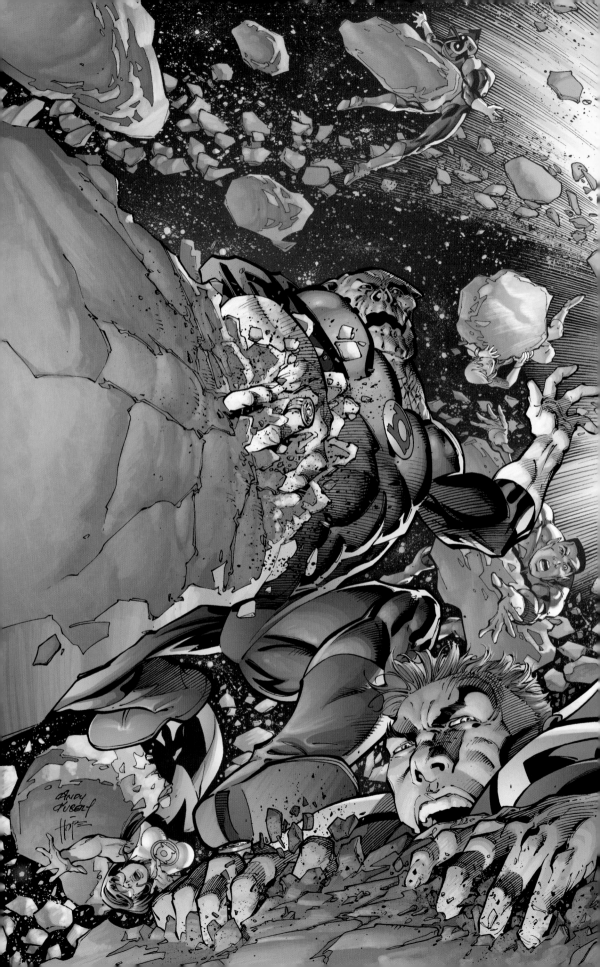

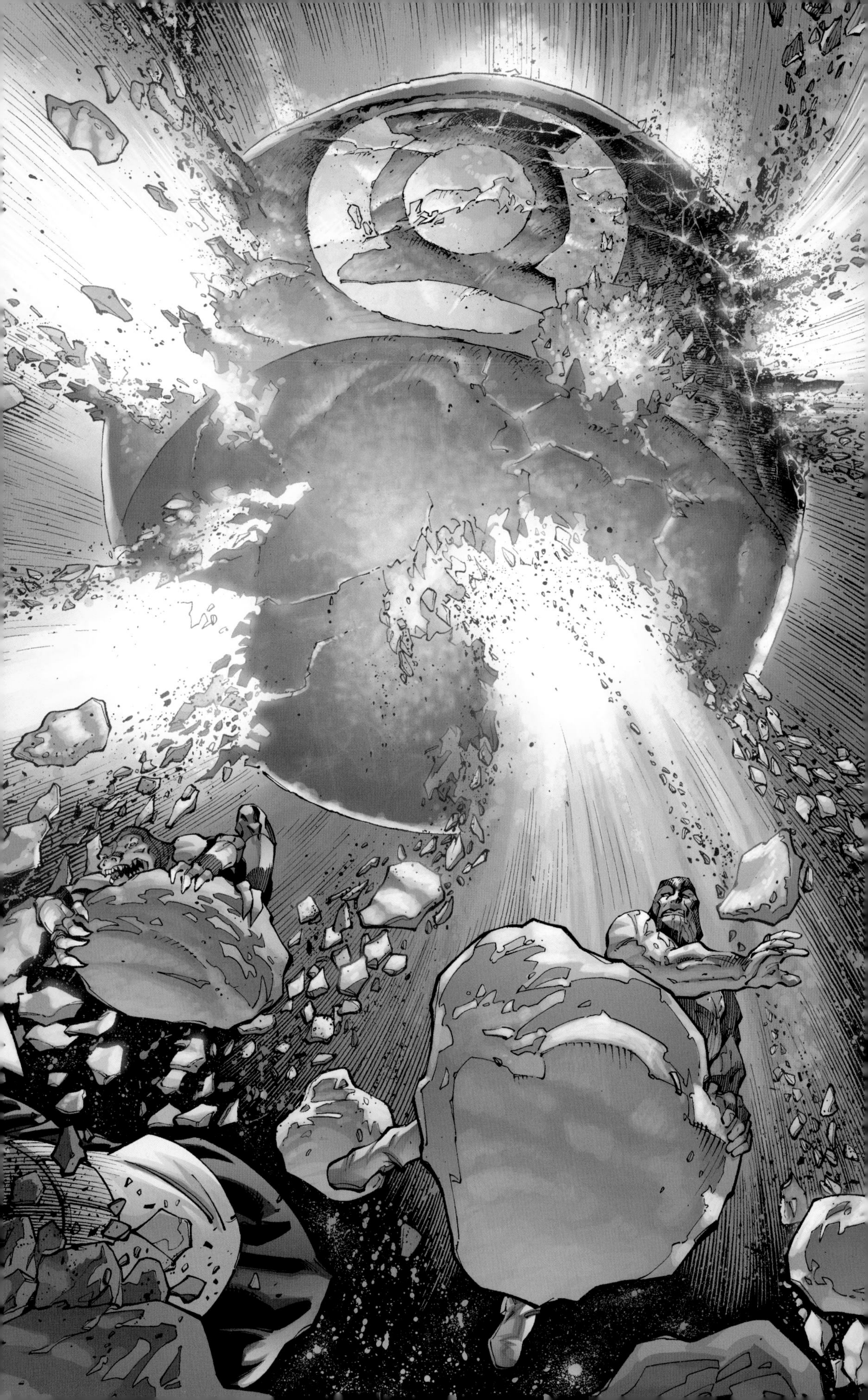

PART TEN: WILLING
PETER J. TOMASI writer FERNANDO PASARIN penciller SCOTT HANNA with MARC DEERING inkers
cover art by ANDY KUBERT, SANDRA HOPE & BRAD ANDERSON

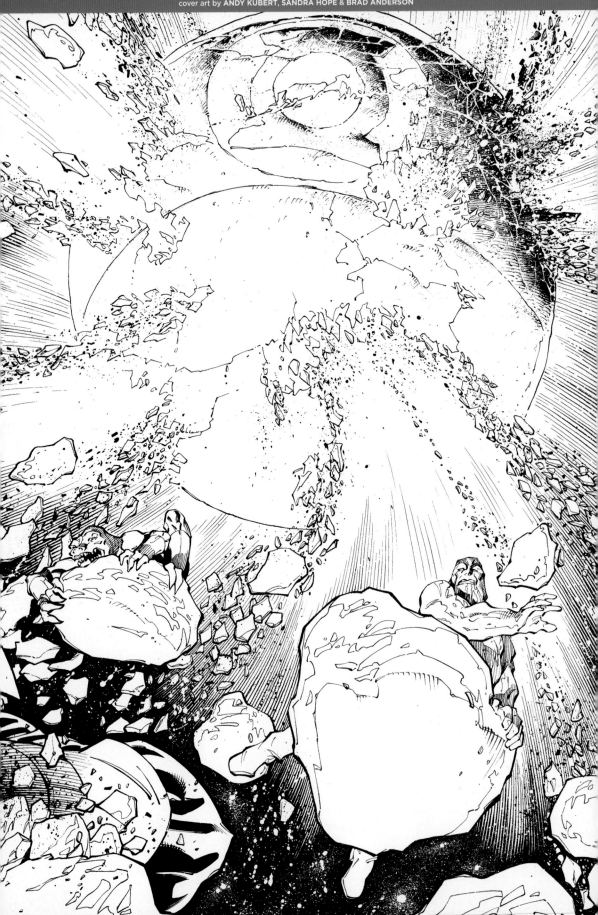

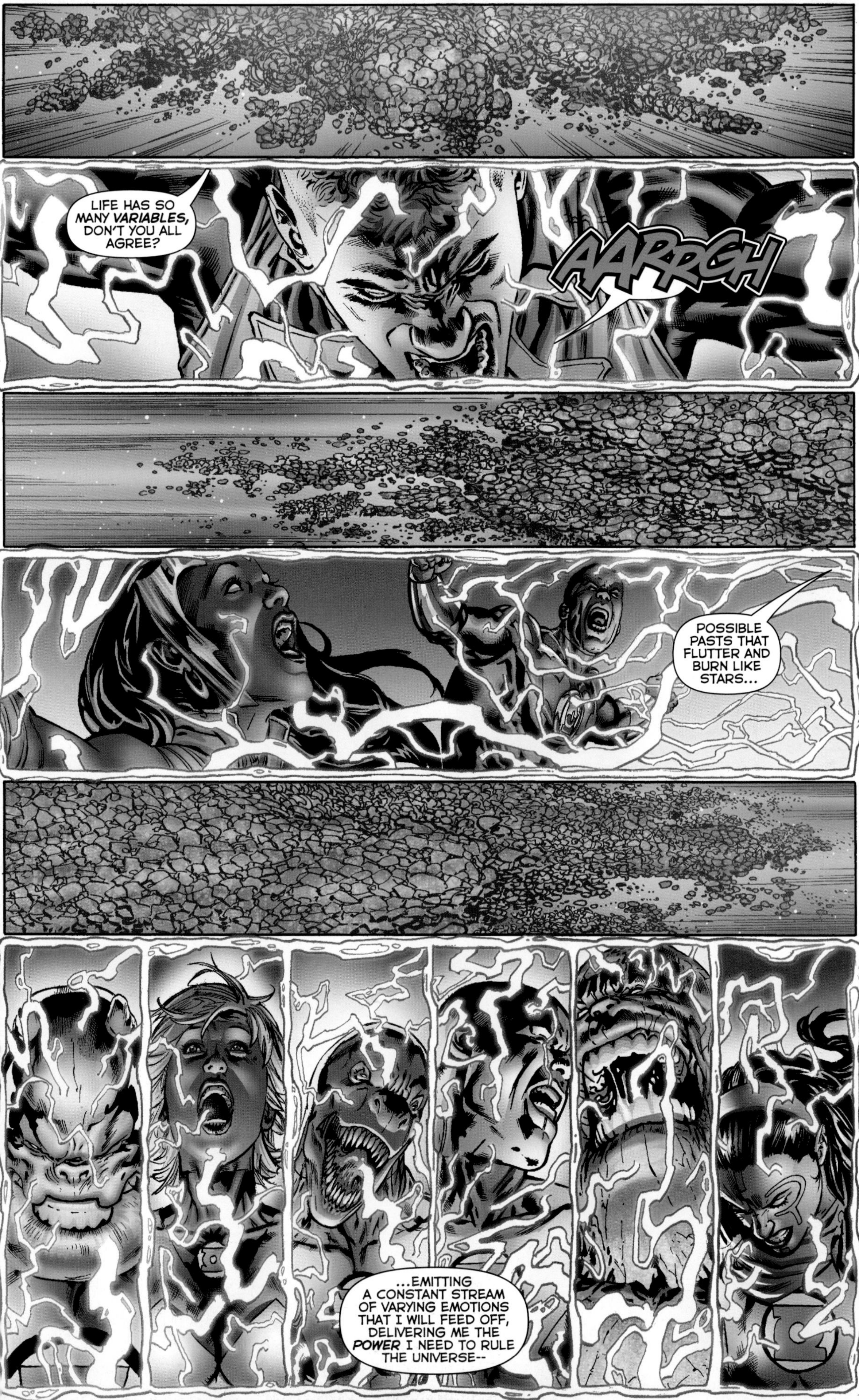
LIFE HAS SO MANY VARIABLES, DON'T YOU ALL AGREE?
AARRGH
POSSIBLE PASTS THAT FLUTTER AND BURN LIKE STARS...
...EMITTING A CONSTANT STREAM OF VARYING EMOTIONS THAT I WILL FEED OFF, DELIVERING ME THE POWER I NEED TO RULE THE UNIVERSE--

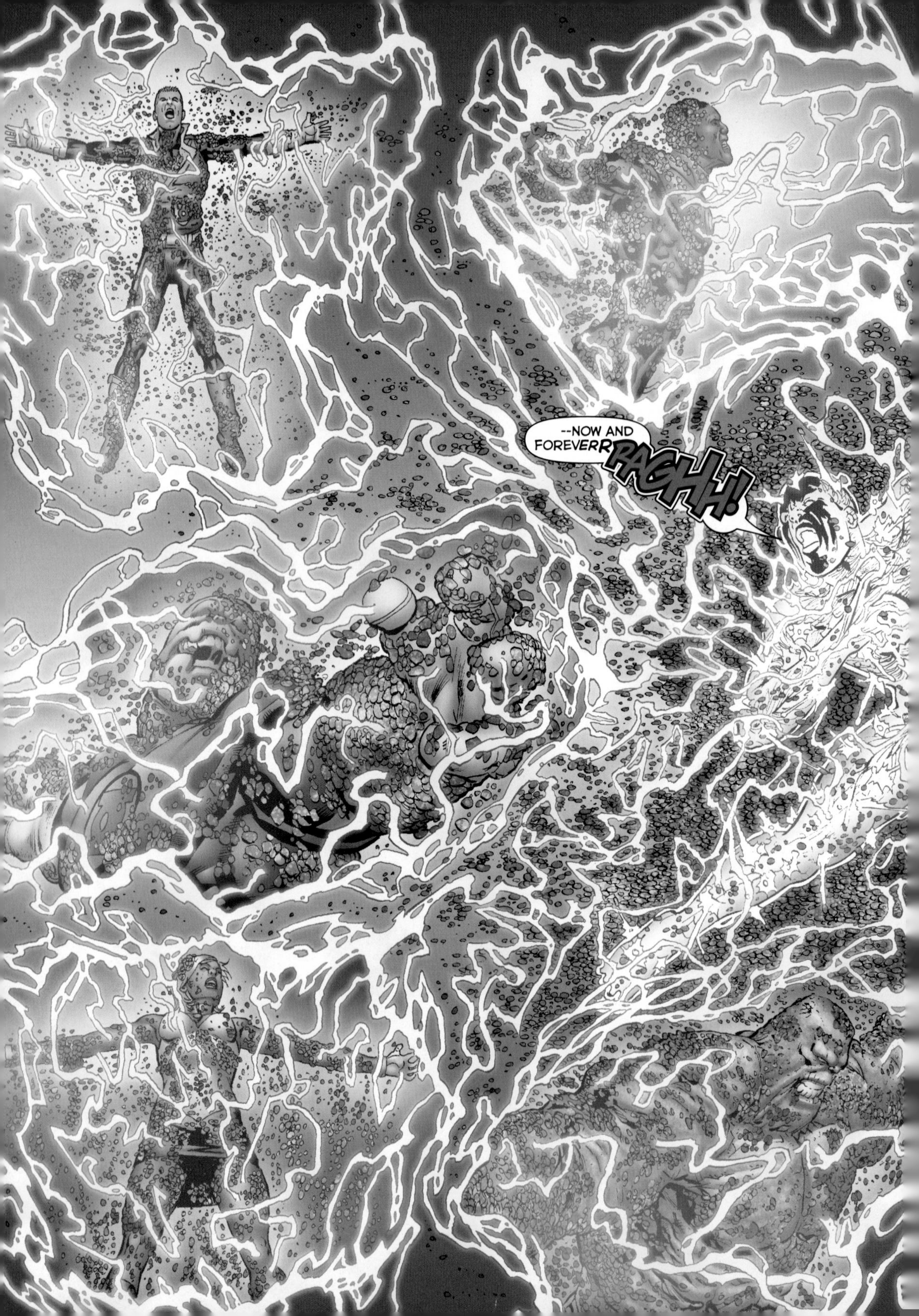
--NOW AND FOREVERRRAGHH!

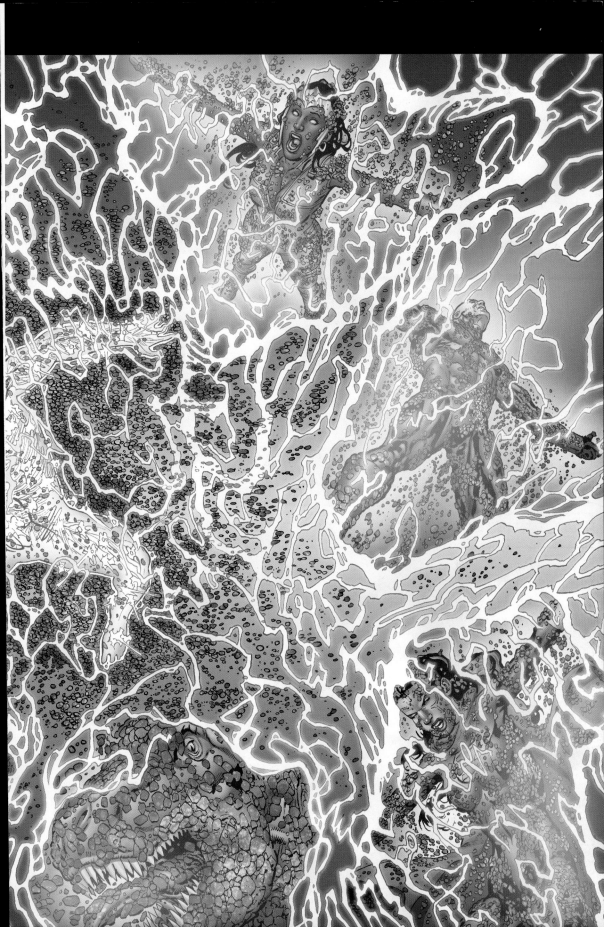

GAHH!
THESE ROCKS--
--CUTTING VOLTHOOM'S LINES--
--BASTARD'S FINALLY OUTTA MY HEAD--
UGNN! WHO DARES?!?
JOHN!
YRAA, HANG ON!
WHATEVER'S HAPPENING--
"--IS HAPPENING ALL ACROSS OA--"

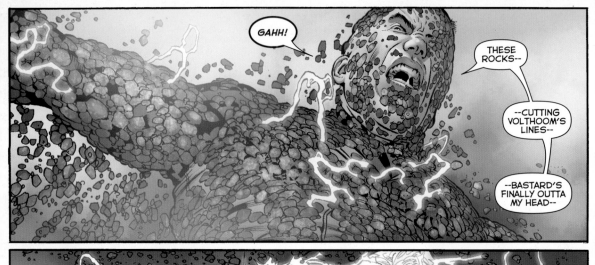

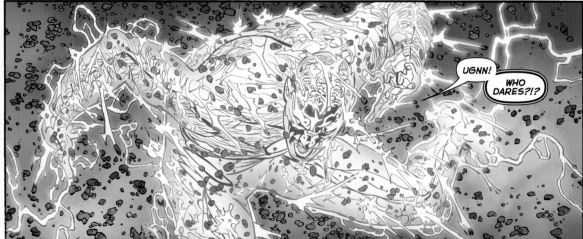

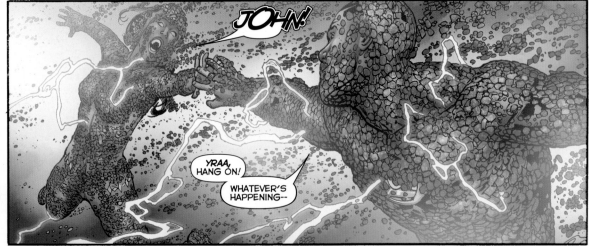

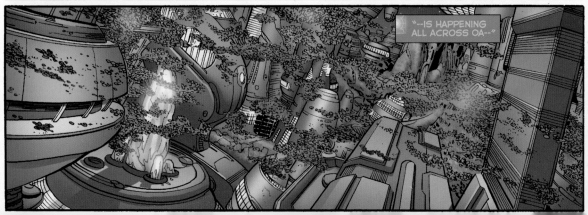

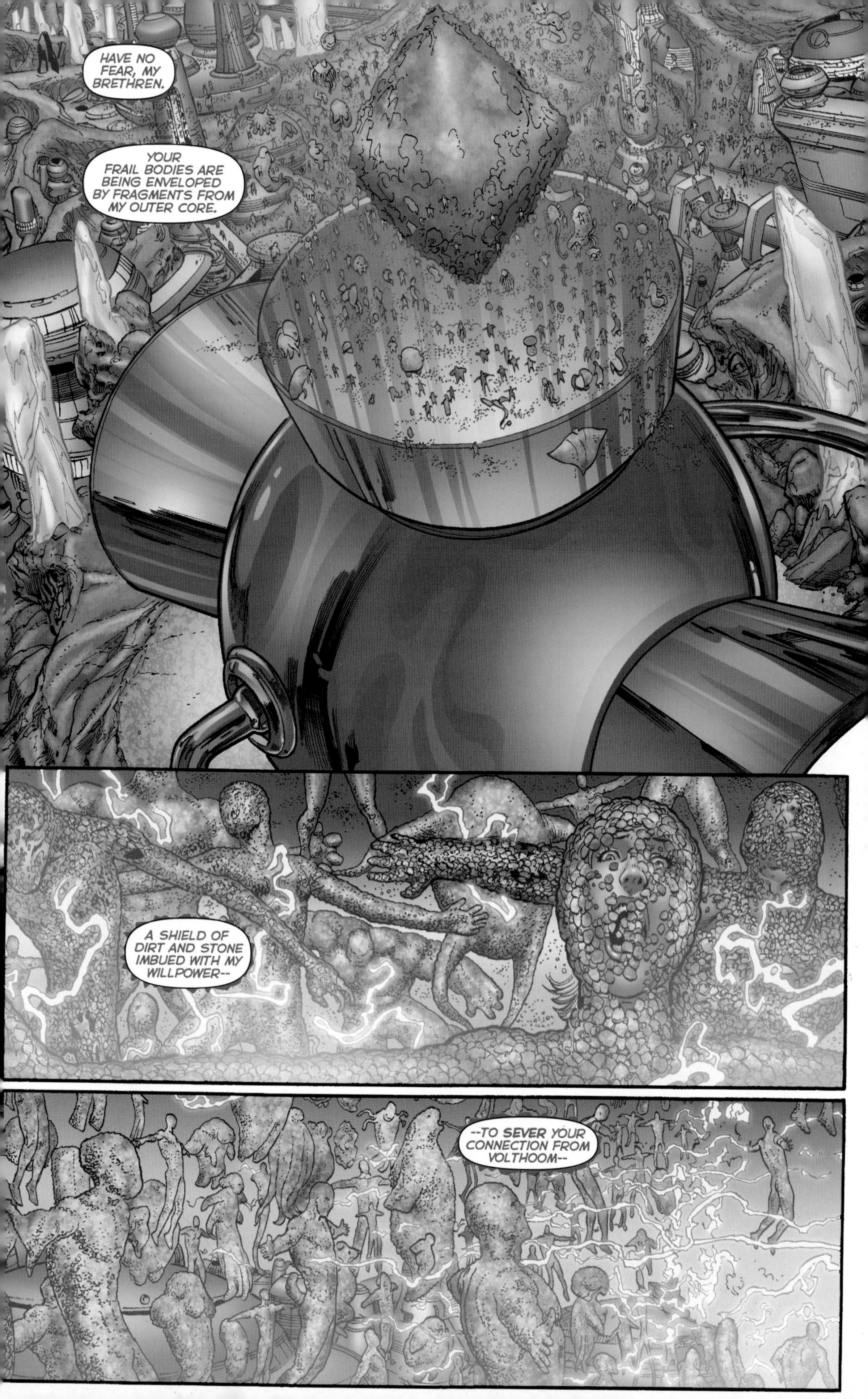
HAVE NO FEAR, MY BRETHREN.
YOUR FRAIL BODIES ARE BEING ENVELOPED BY FRAGMENTS FROM MY OUTER CORE.
A SHIELD OF DIRT AND STONE IMBUED WITH MY WILLPOWER--
--TO SEVER YOUR CONNECTION FROM VOLTHOOM--

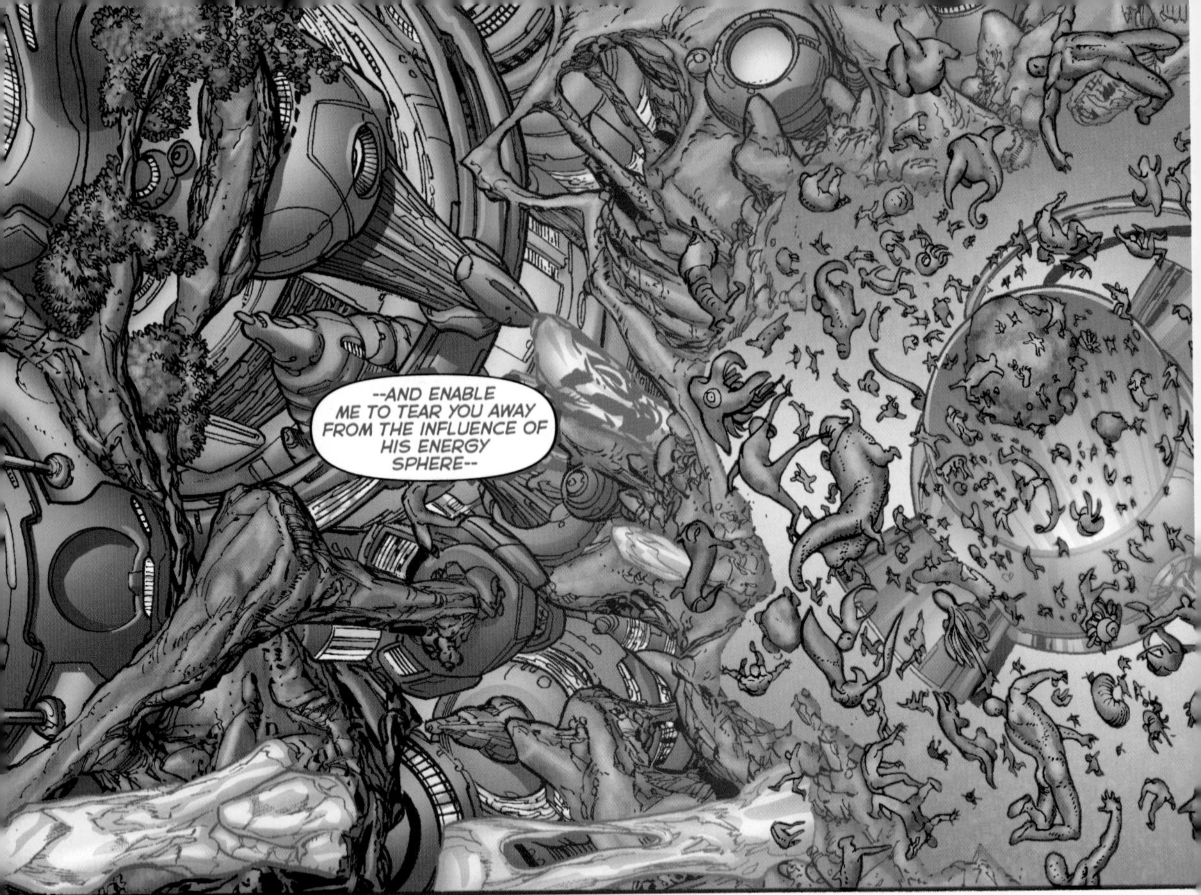
--AND ENABLE ME TO TEAR YOU AWAY FROM THE INFLUENCE OF HIS ENERGY SPHERE--

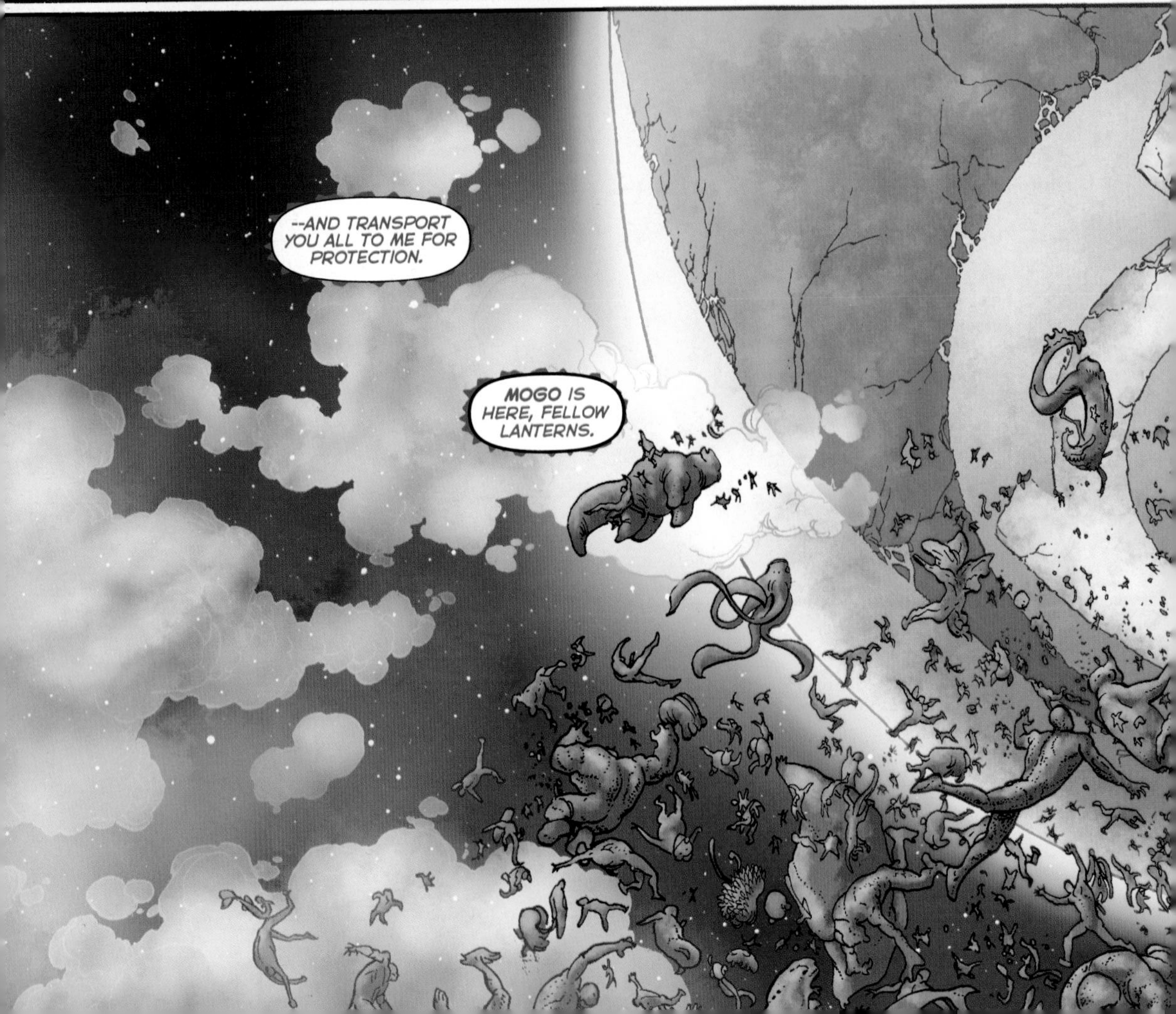
--AND TRANSPORT YOU ALL TO ME FOR PROTECTION.
MOGO IS HERE, FELLOW LANTERNS.

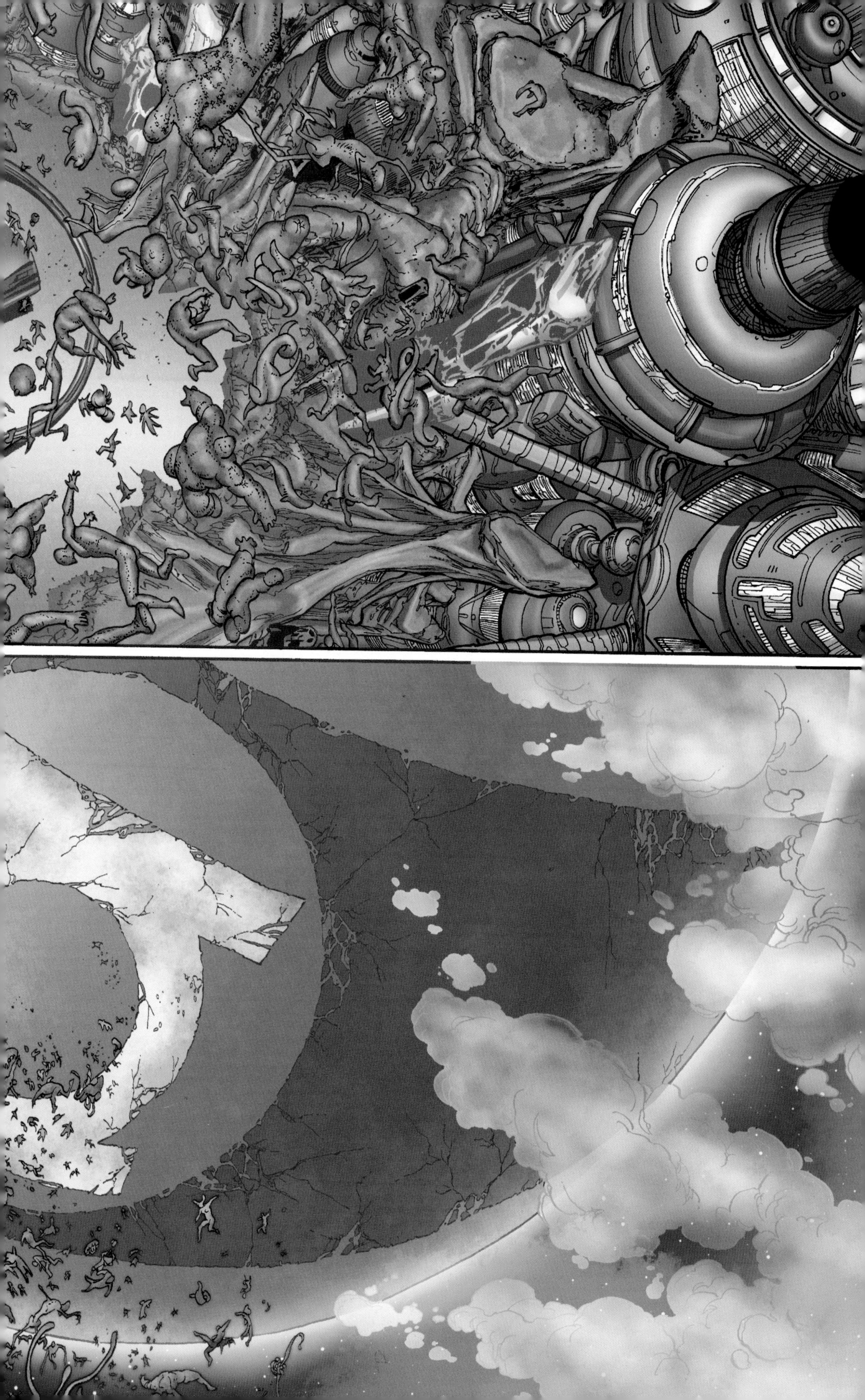

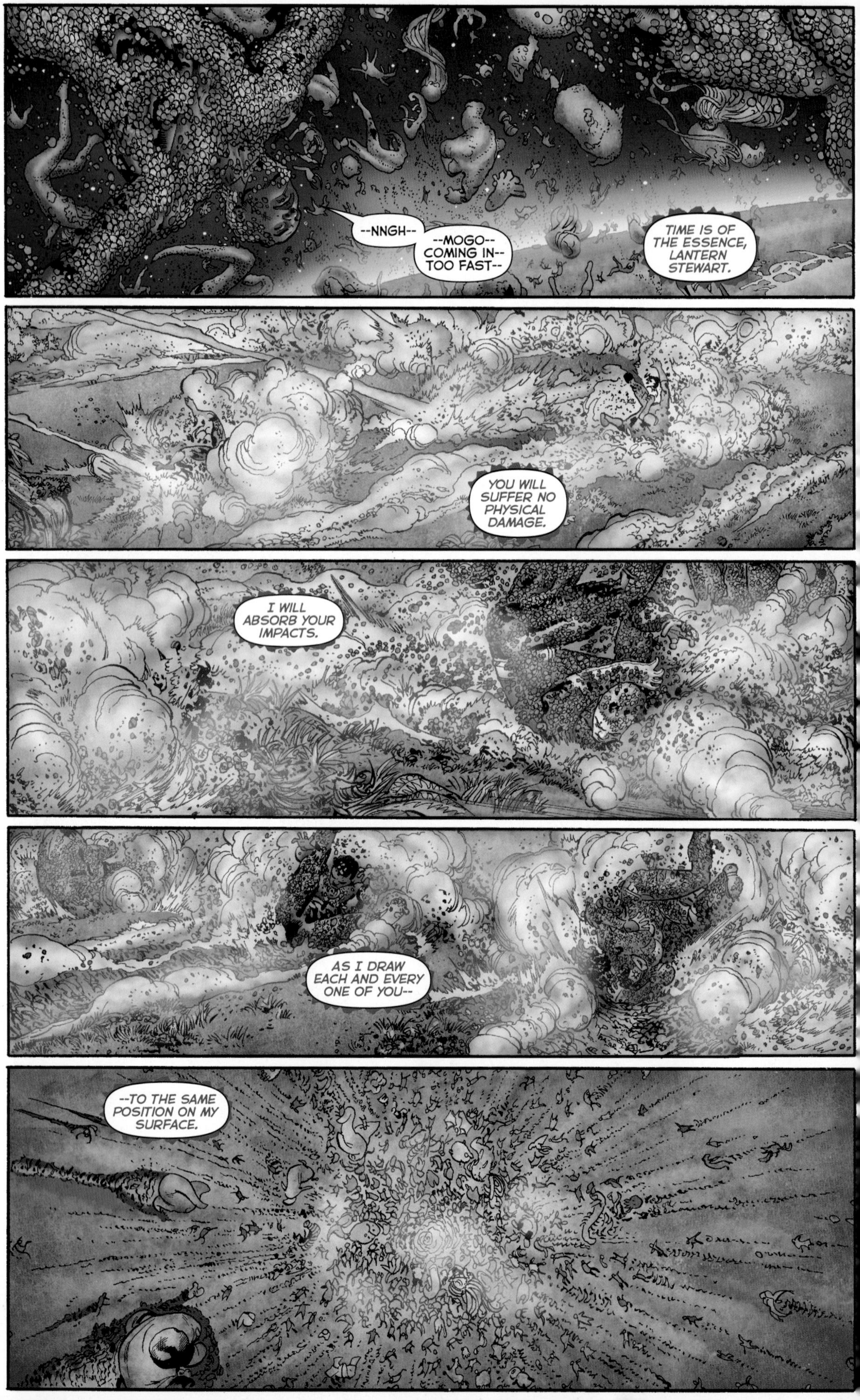
--NNGH--
--MOGO-- COMING IN-- TOO FAST--
TIME IS OF THE ESSENCE, LANTERN STEWART.
YOU WILL SUFFER NO PHYSICAL DAMAGE.
I WILL ABSORB YOUR IMPACTS.
AS I DRAW EACH AND EVERY ONE OF YOU--
--TO THE SAME POSITION ON MY SURFACE.

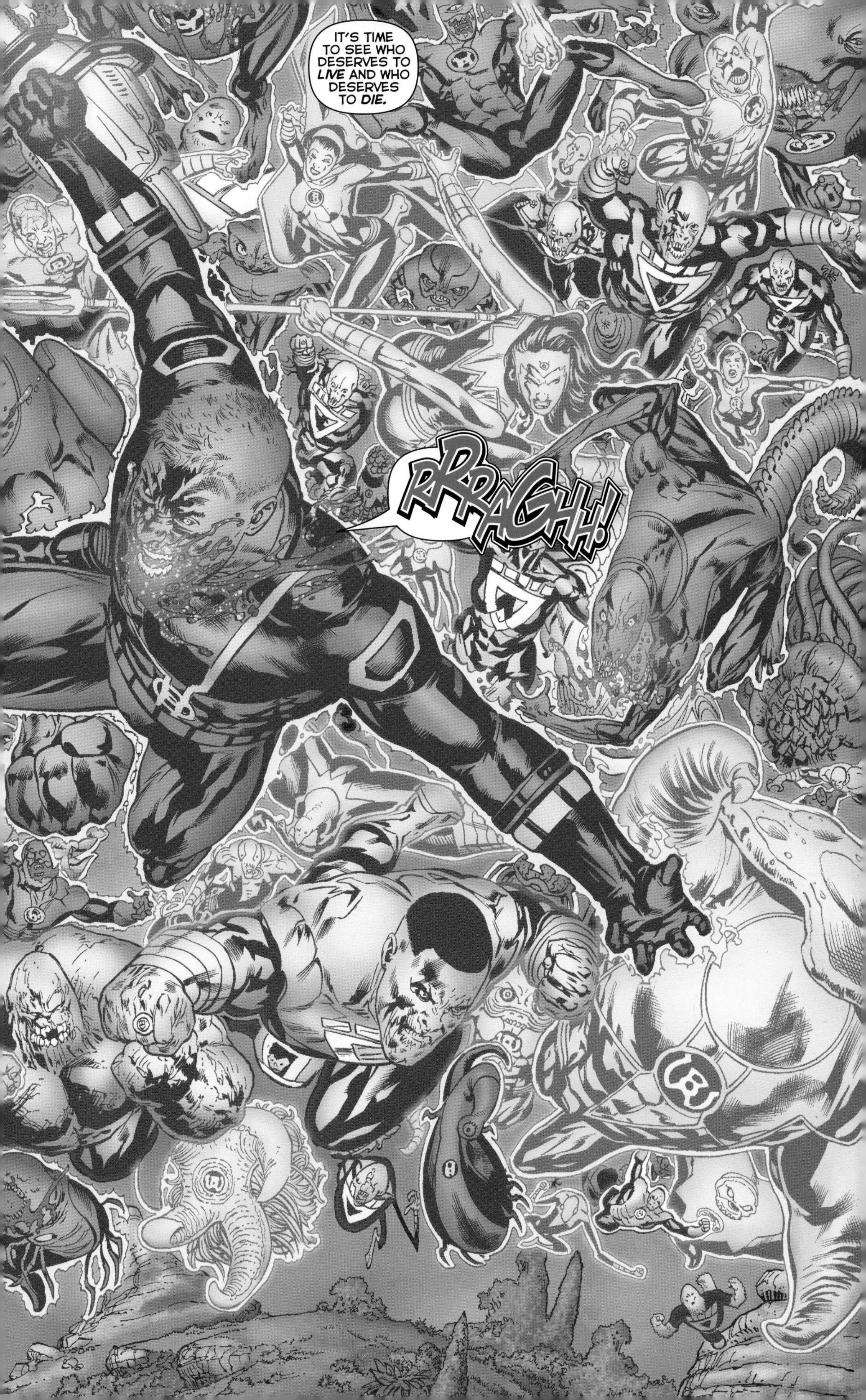
IT'S TIME TO SEE WHO DESERVES TO LIVE AND WHO DESERVES TO DIE.
RRRAGHH!

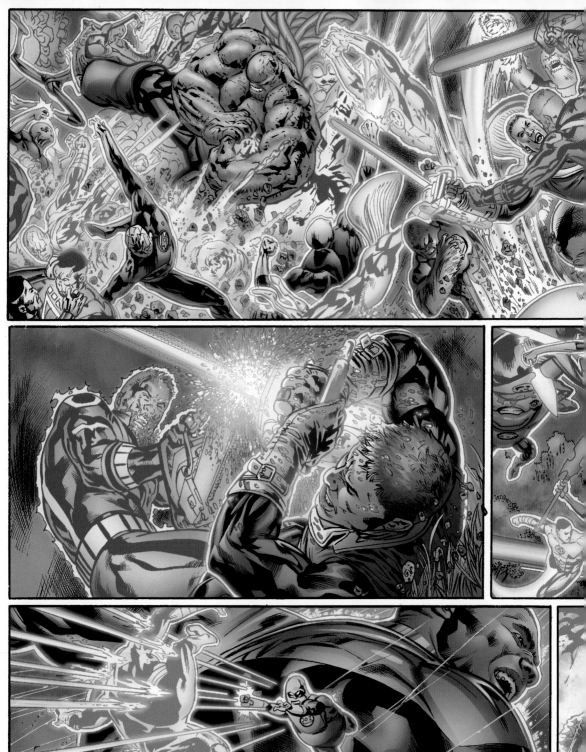

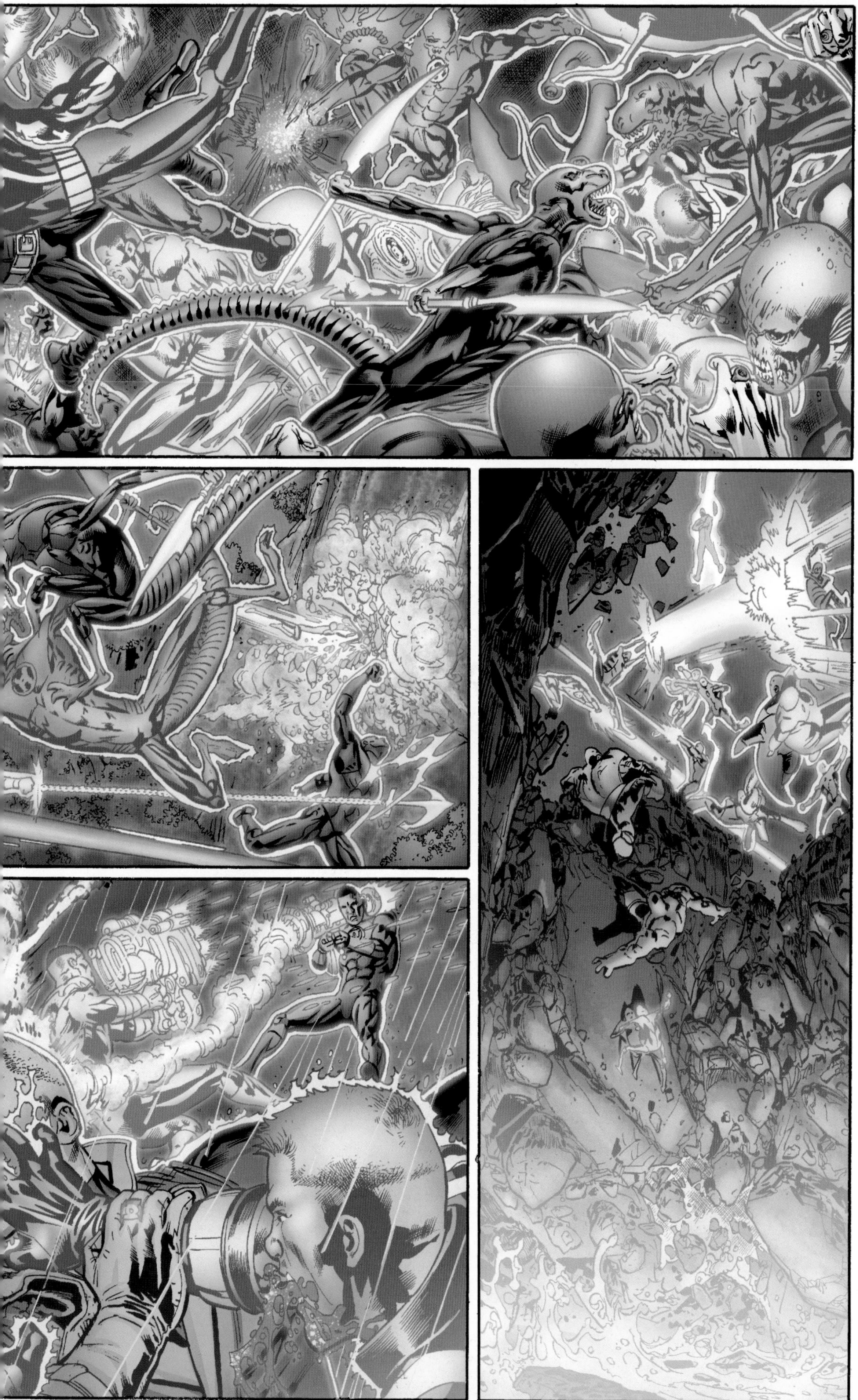

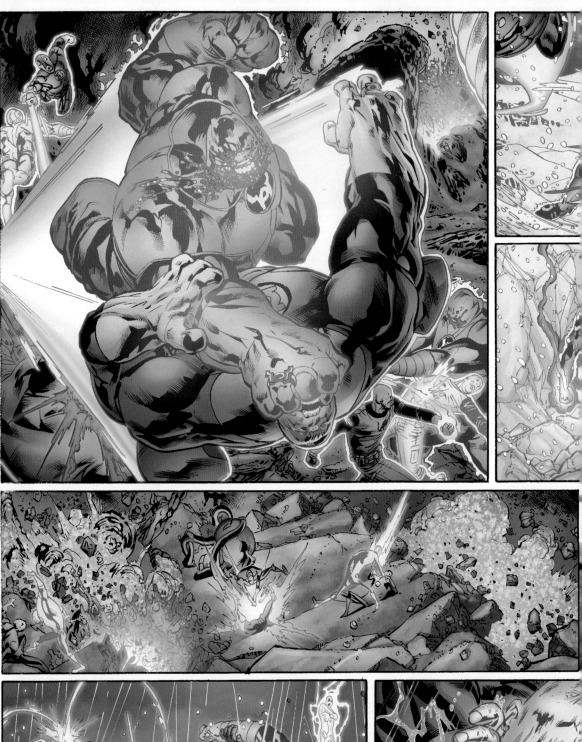

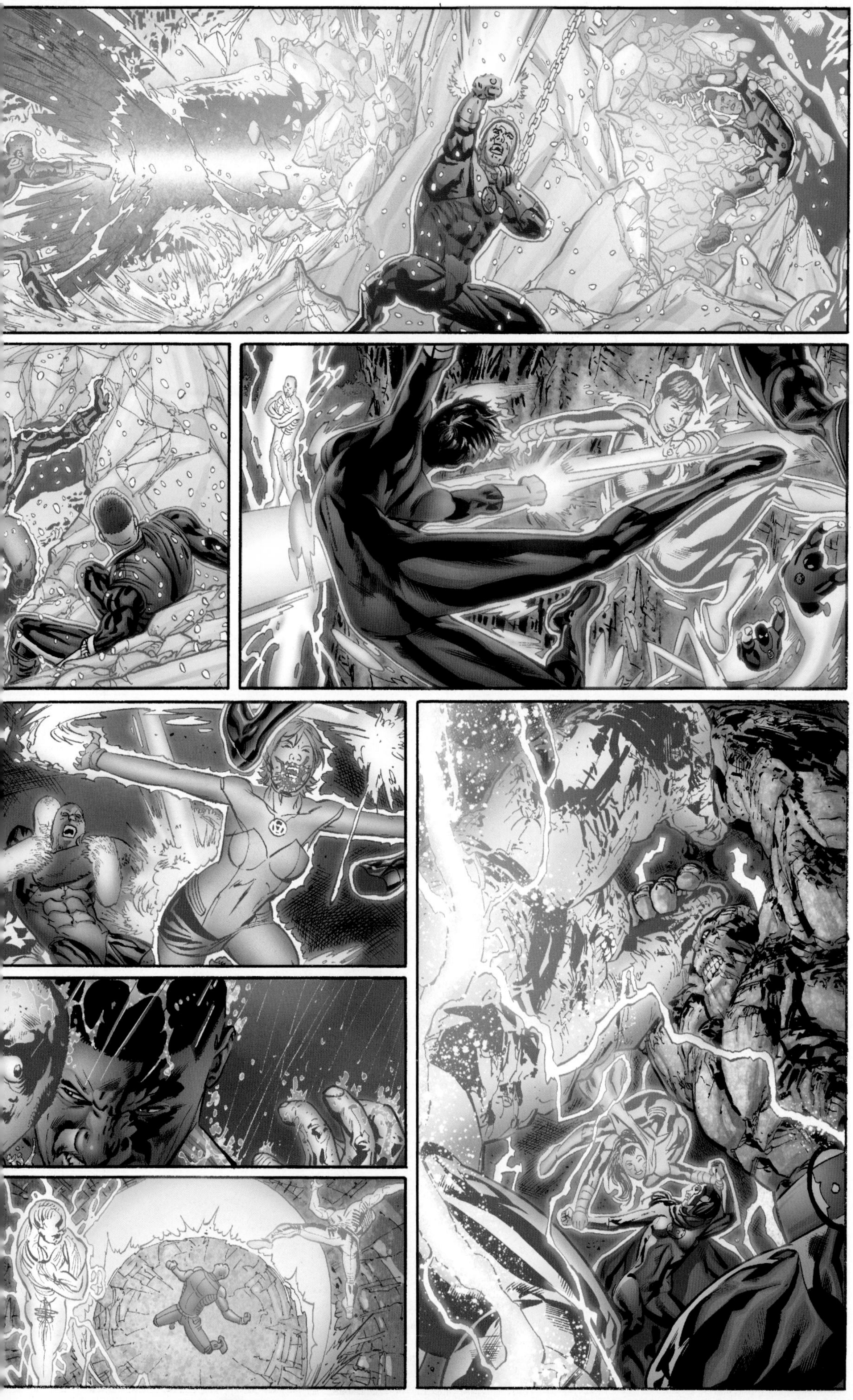

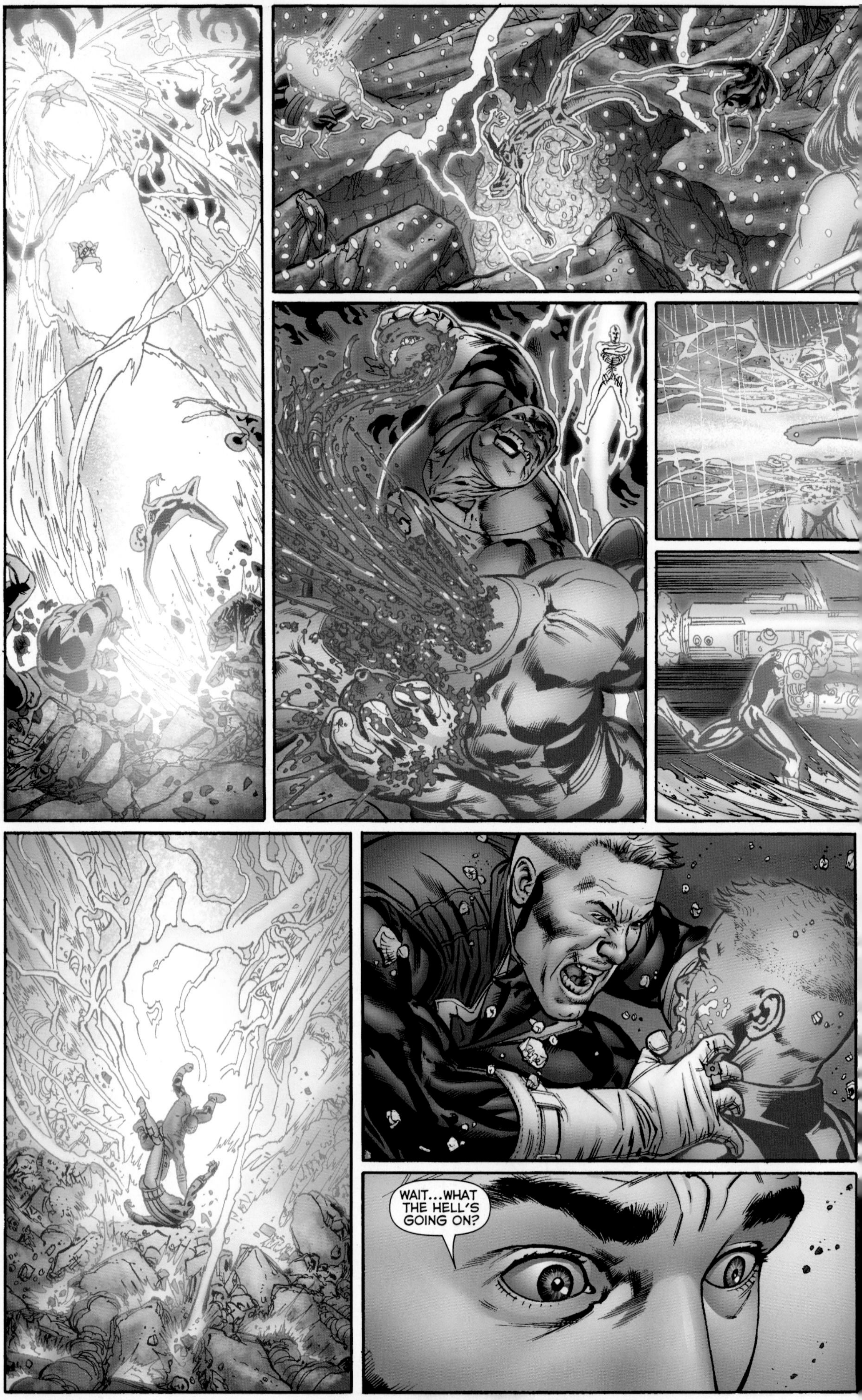
WAIT...WHAT THE HELL'S GOING ON?

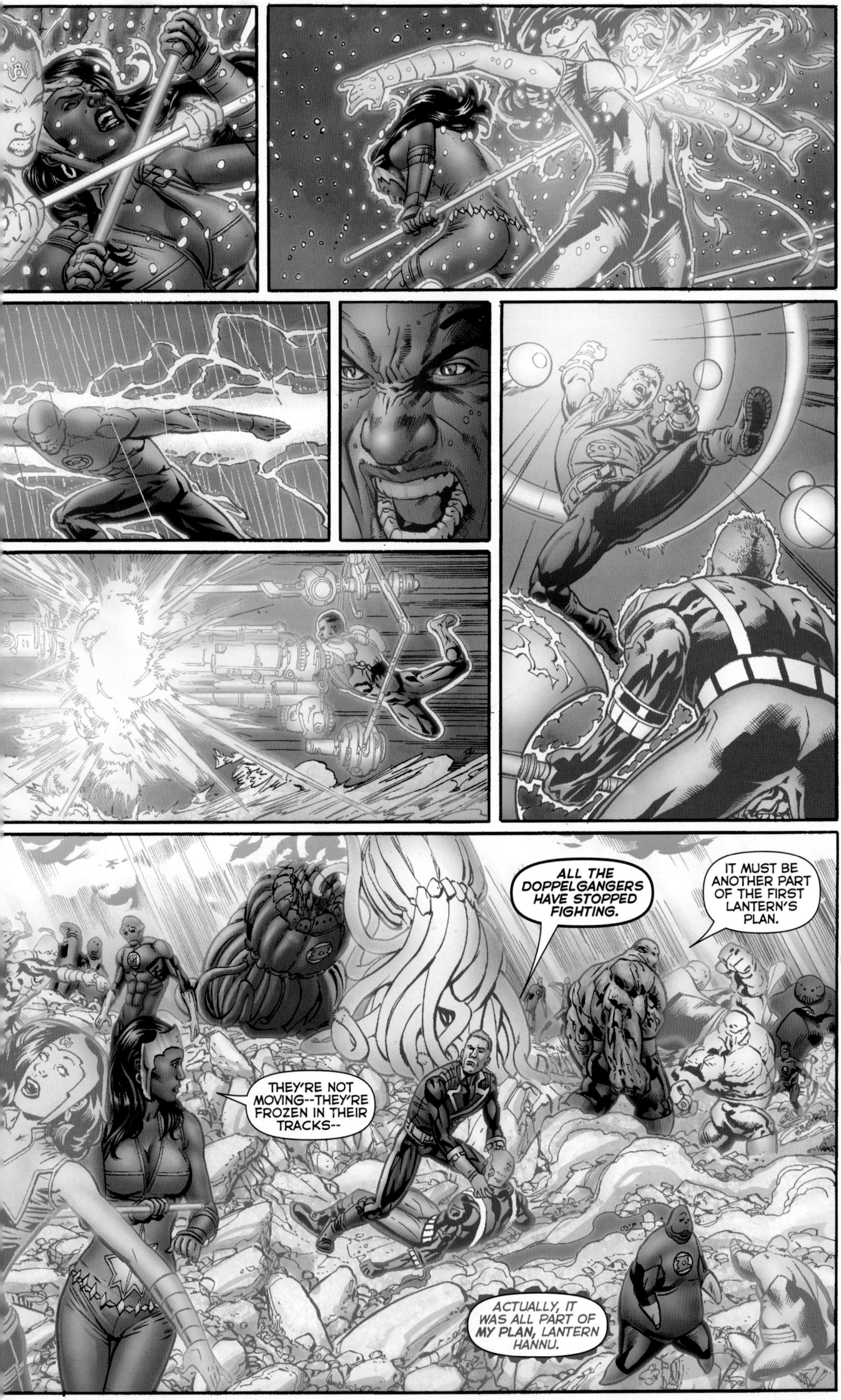
ALL THE DOPPELGANGERS HAVE STOPPED FIGHTING.
IT MUST BE ANOTHER PART OF THE FIRST LANTERN'S PLAN.
THEY'RE NOT MOVING--THEY'RE FROZEN IN THEIR TRACKS--
ACTUALLY, IT WAS ALL PART OF MY PLAN, LANTERN HANNU.

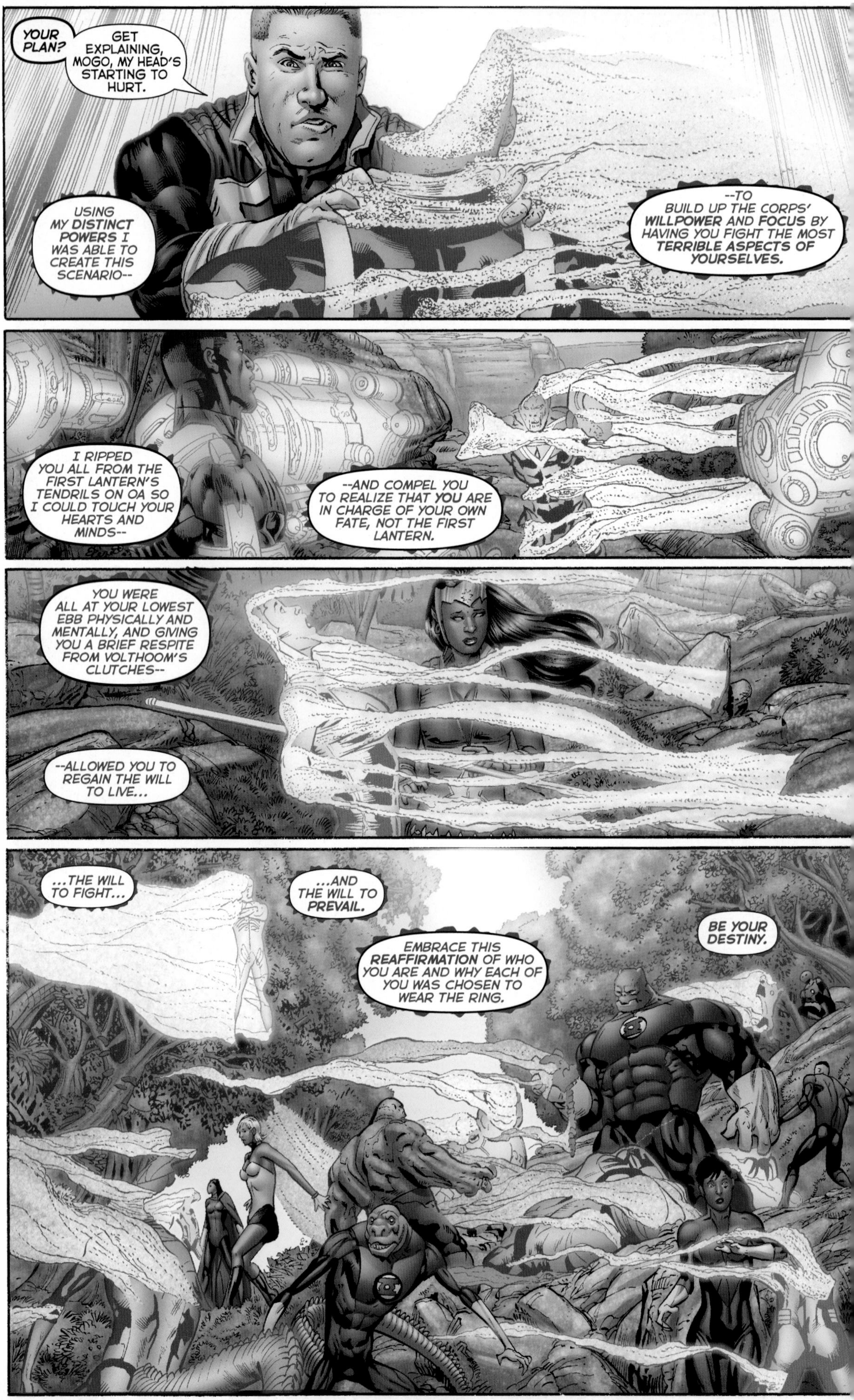
YOUR PLAN?
GET EXPLAINING, MOGO, MY HEAD'S STARTING TO HURT.
USING MY **DISTINCT POWERS** I WAS ABLE TO CREATE THIS SCENARIO--
--TO BUILD UP THE CORPS' **WILLPOWER** AND **FOCUS** BY HAVING YOU FIGHT THE MOST **TERRIBLE ASPECTS OF YOURSELVES.**
I RIPPED YOU ALL FROM THE FIRST LANTERN'S TENDRILS ON OA SO I COULD TOUCH YOUR HEARTS AND MINDS--
--AND COMPEL YOU TO REALIZE THAT **YOU** ARE IN CHARGE OF YOUR OWN FATE, NOT THE FIRST LANTERN.
YOU WERE ALL AT YOUR LOWEST EBB PHYSICALLY AND MENTALLY, AND GIVING YOU A BRIEF RESPITE FROM VOLTHOOM'S CLUTCHES--
--ALLOWED YOU TO REGAIN THE WILL TO LIVE...
...THE WILL TO FIGHT...
...AND THE WILL TO **PREVAIL.**
EMBRACE THIS **REAFFIRMATION** OF WHO YOU ARE AND WHY EACH OF YOU WAS CHOSEN TO WEAR THE RING.
BE YOUR DESTINY.

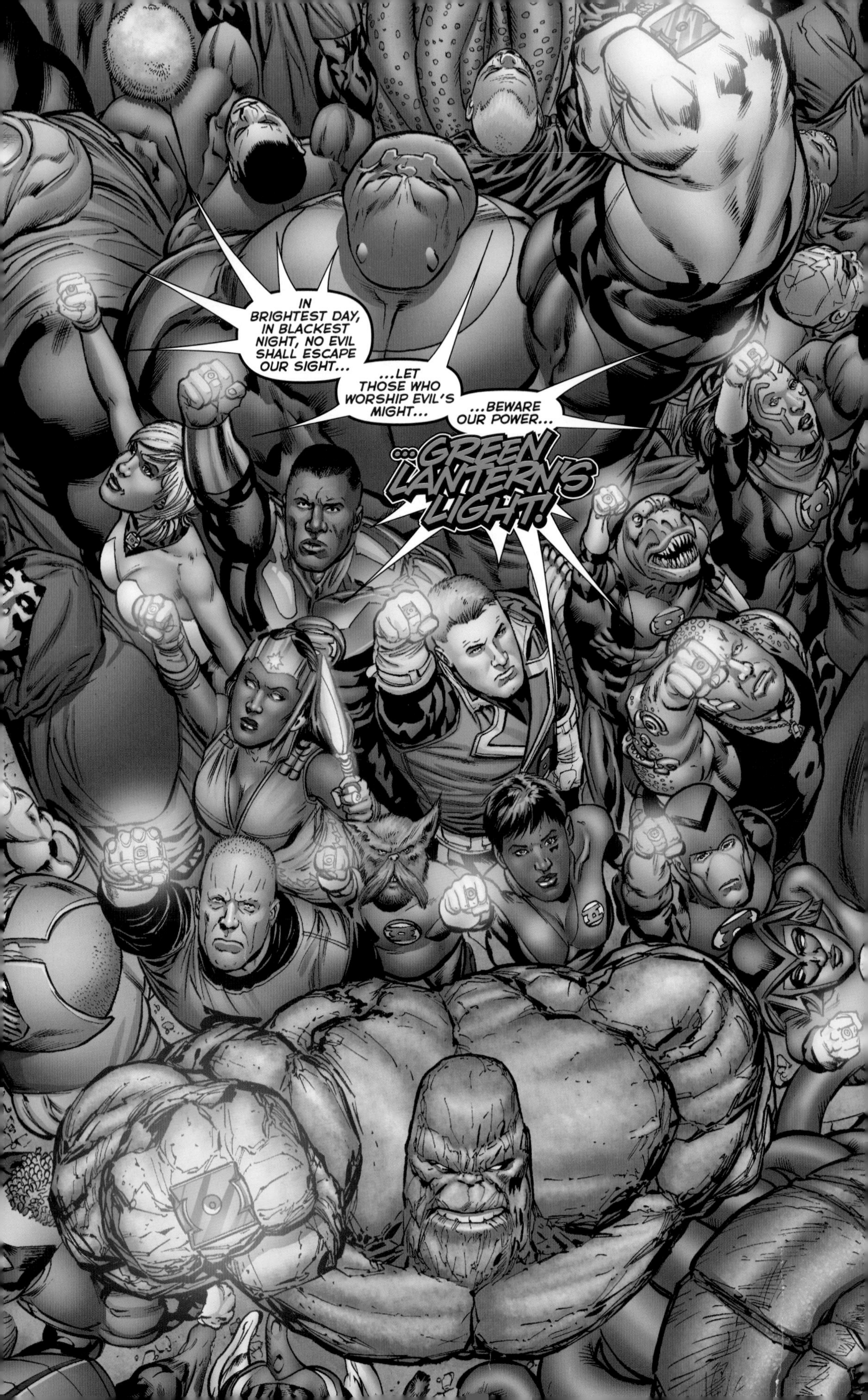
IN BRIGHTEST DAY, IN BLACKEST NIGHT, NO EVIL SHALL ESCAPE OUR SIGHT...
...LET THOSE WHO WORSHIP EVIL'S MIGHT...
...BEWARE OUR POWER...
...GREEN LANTERN'S LIGHT!

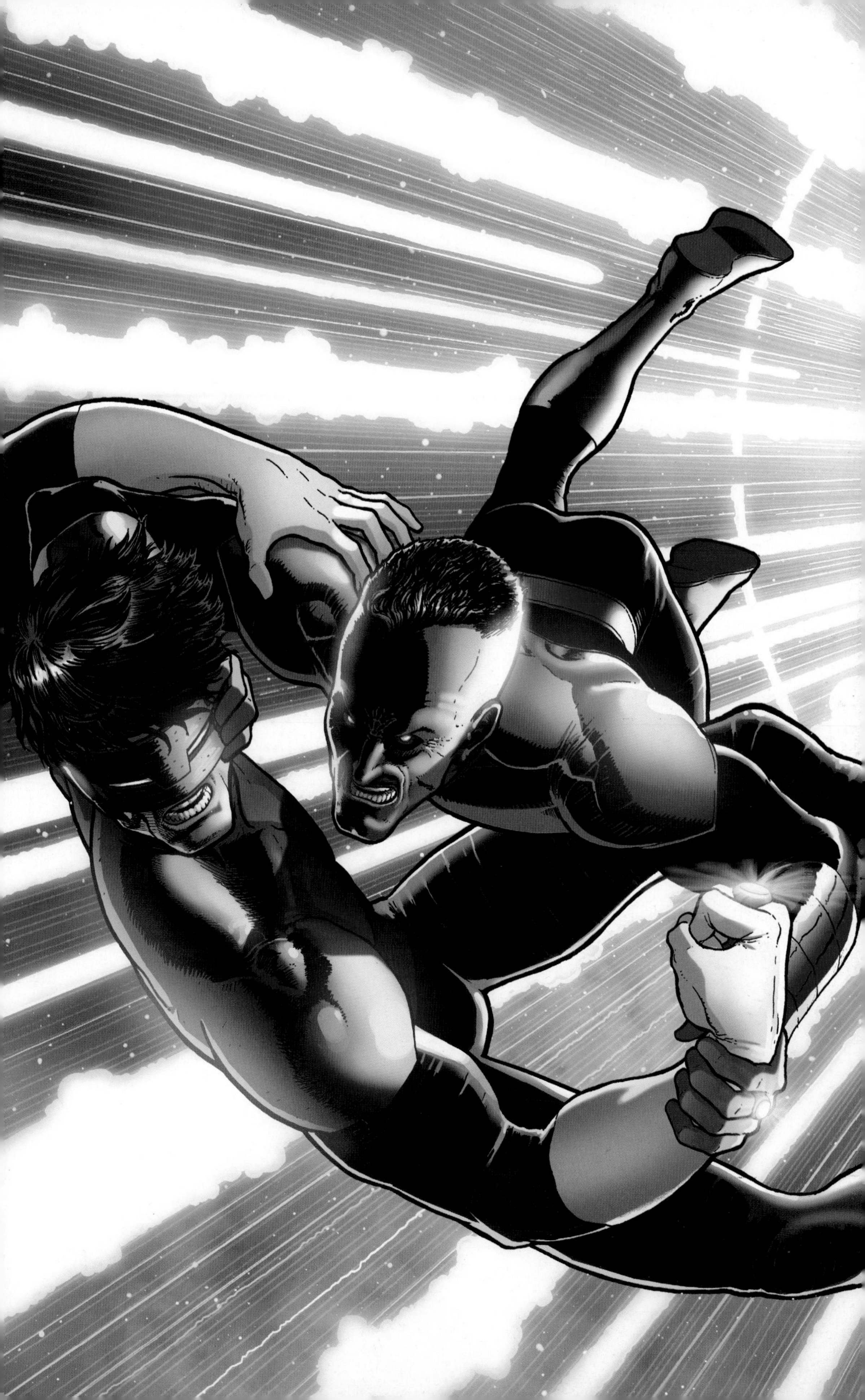

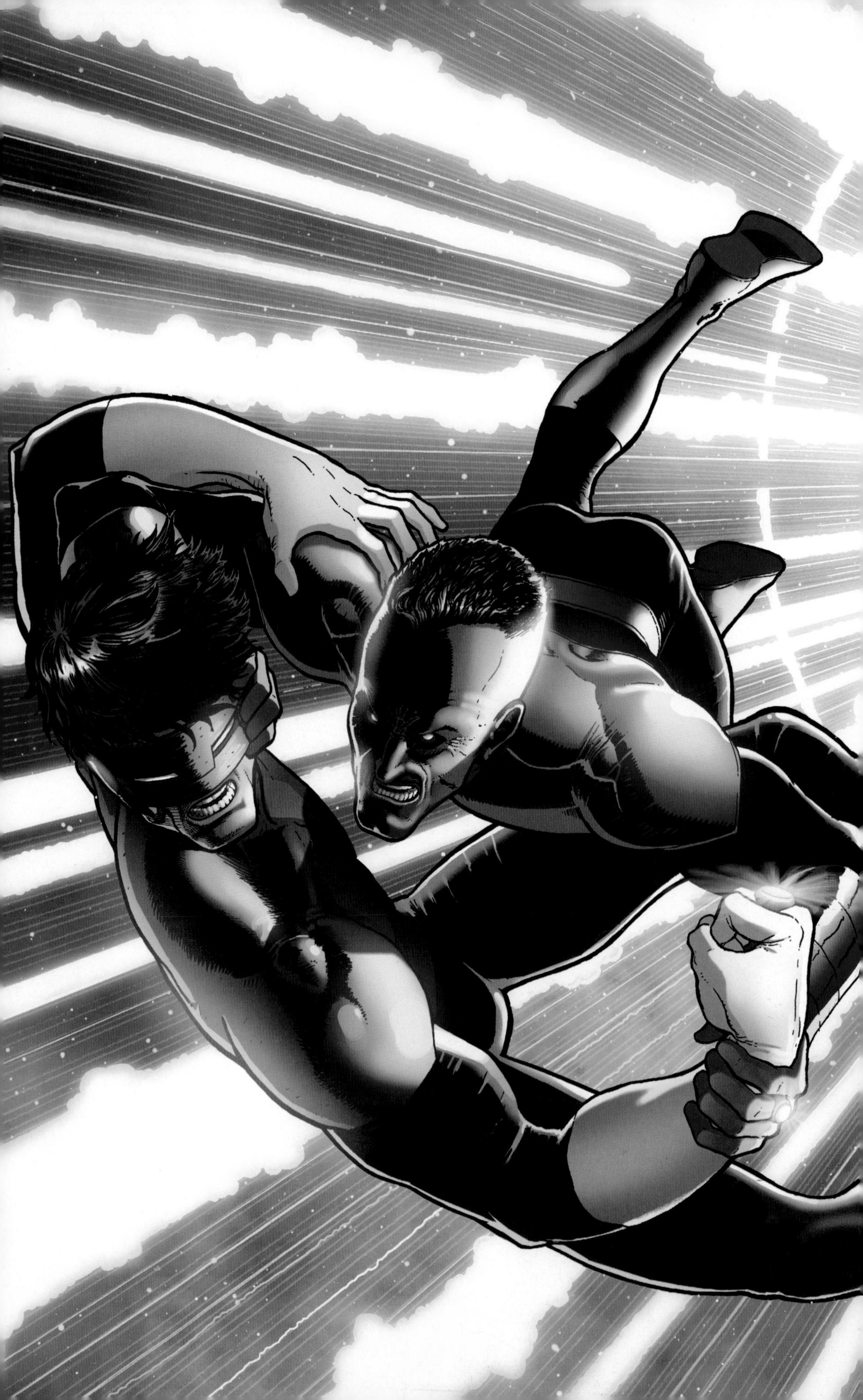

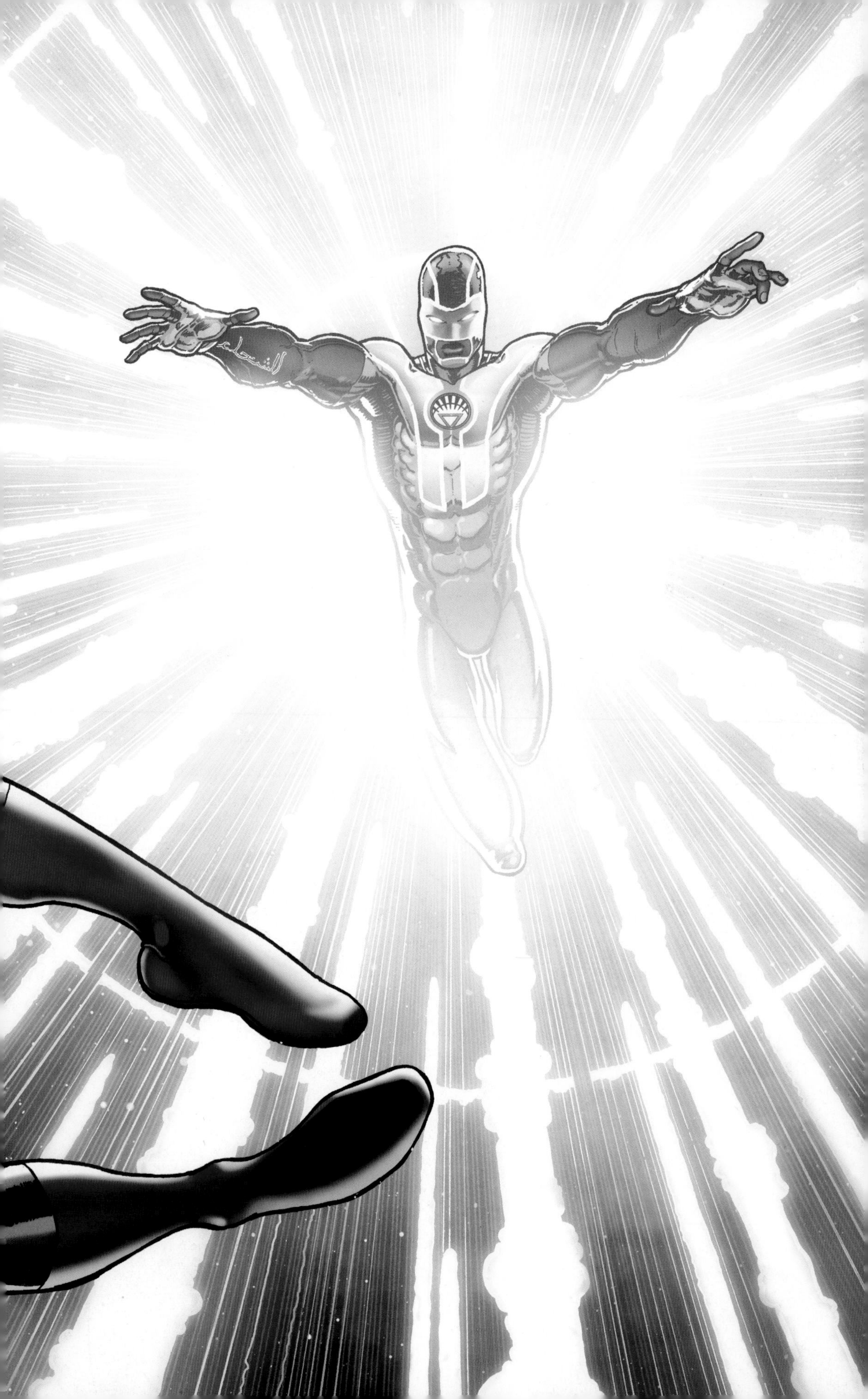

PART ELEVEN: SHADOW OF DEATH

TONY BEDARD writer **ANDRES GUINALDO** penciller **RAUL FERNANDEZ** inker
cover art by **AARON KUDER & WIL QUINTANA**

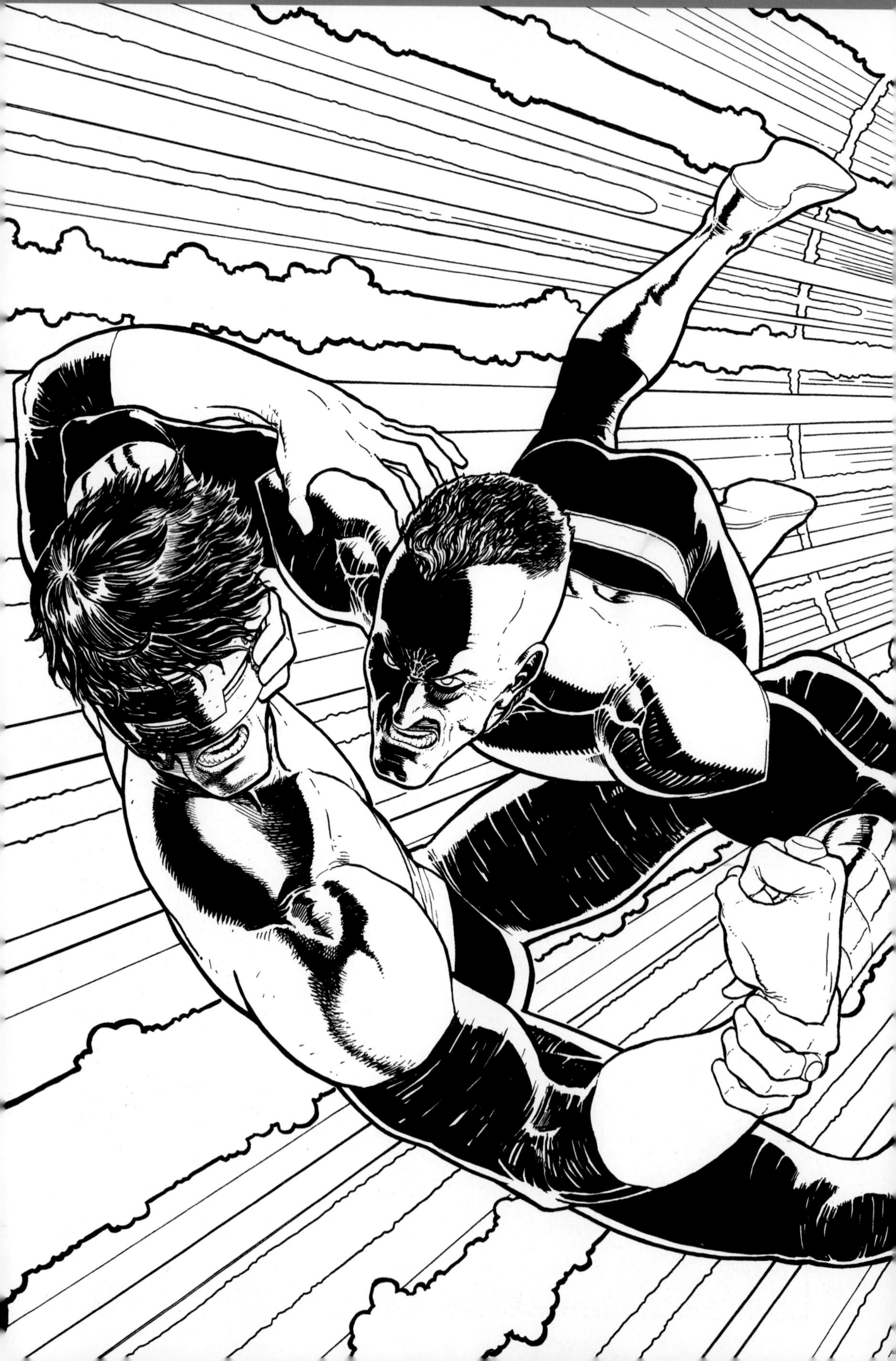

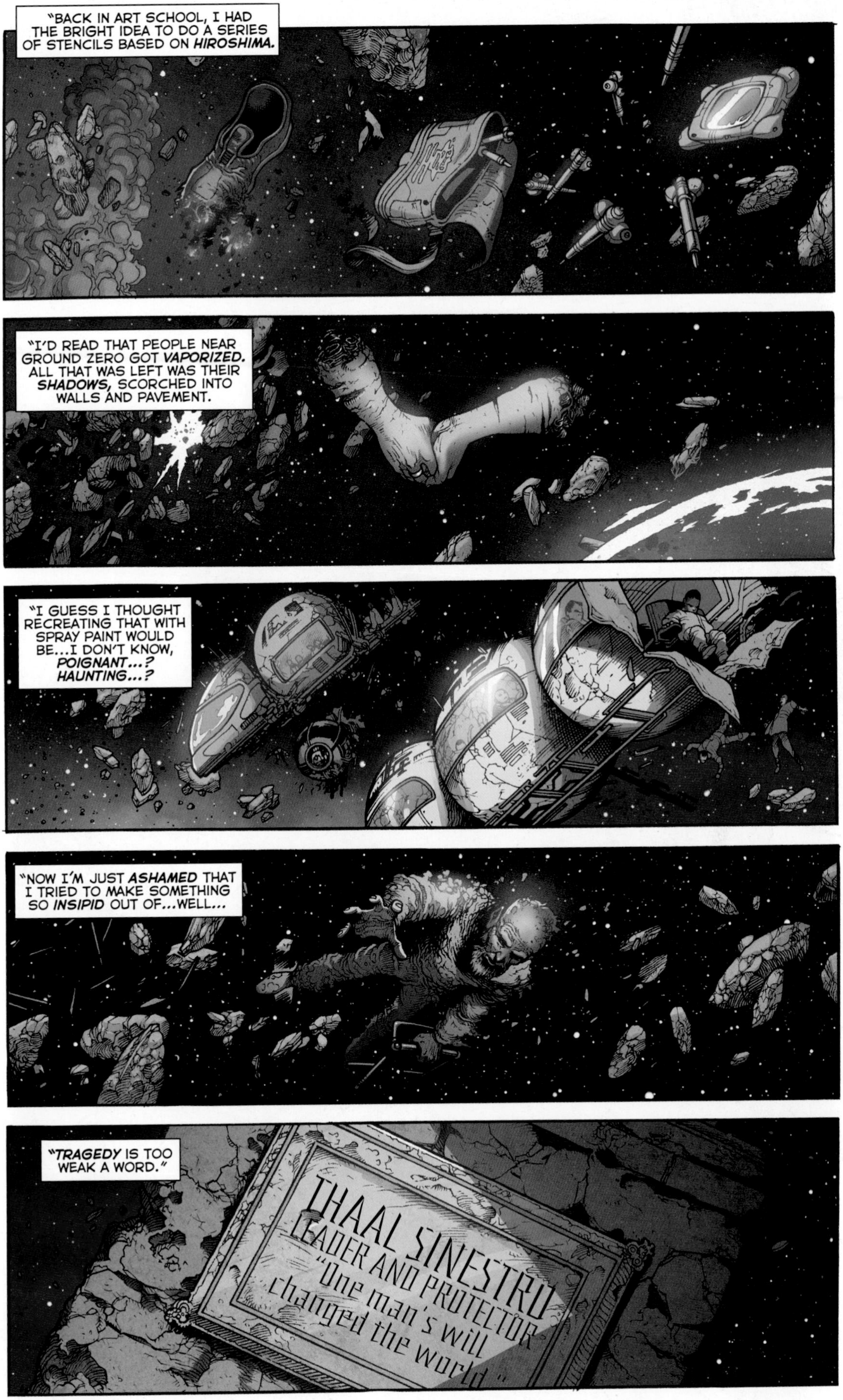
"BACK IN ART SCHOOL, I HAD THE BRIGHT IDEA TO DO A SERIES OF STENCILS BASED ON *HIROSHIMA.*
"I'D READ THAT PEOPLE NEAR GROUND ZERO GOT *VAPORIZED.* ALL THAT WAS LEFT WAS THEIR *SHADOWS,* SCORCHED INTO WALLS AND PAVEMENT.
"I GUESS I THOUGHT RECREATING THAT WITH SPRAY PAINT WOULD BE...I DON'T KNOW, *POIGNANT...? HAUNTING...?*
"NOW I'M JUST *ASHAMED* THAT I TRIED TO MAKE SOMETHING SO *INSIPID* OUT OF...WELL...
"*TRAGEDY* IS TOO WEAK A WORD."
THAAL SINESTRO
LEADER AND PROTECTOR
"One man's will changed the world."

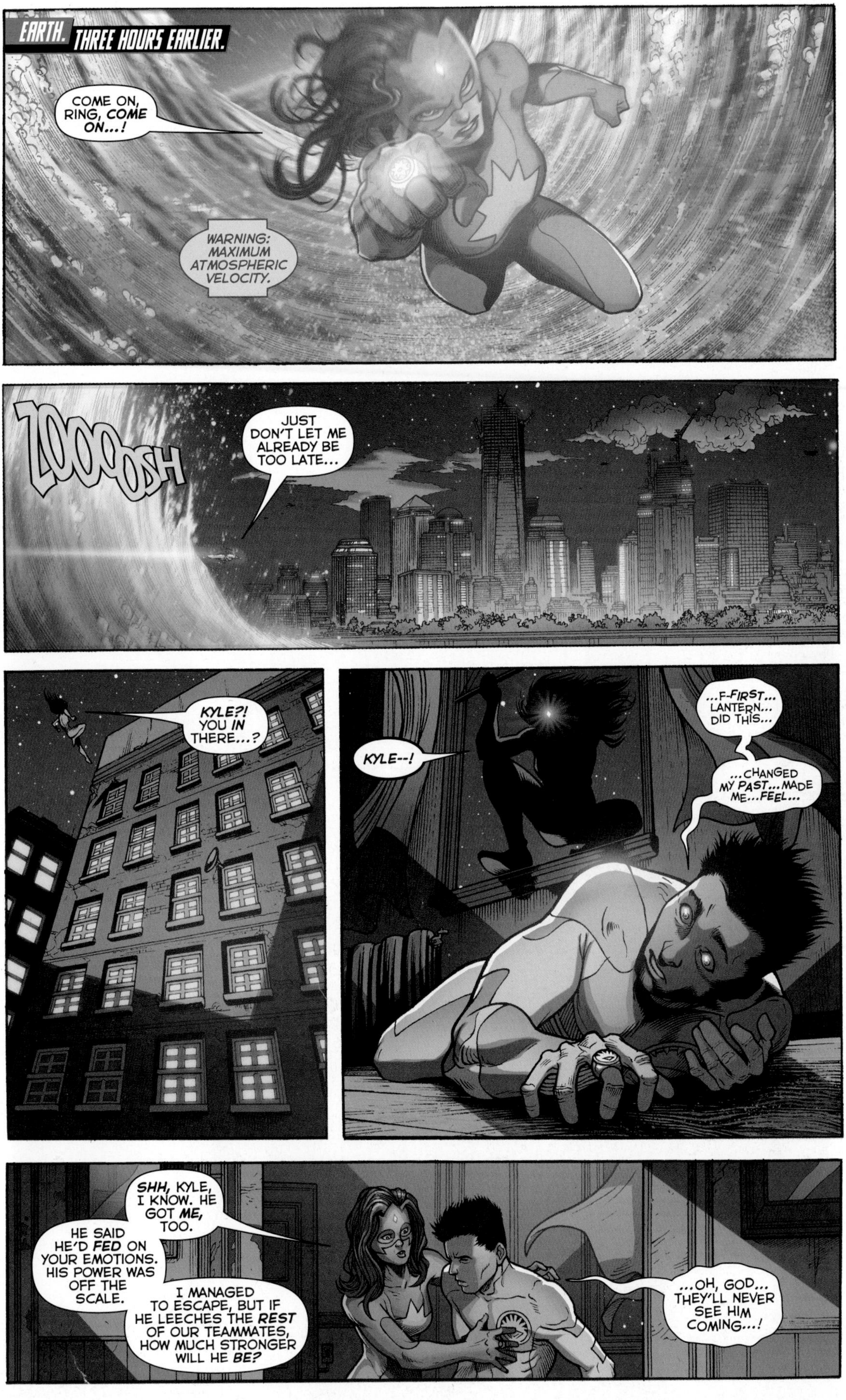
EARTH. THREE HOURS EARLIER.
COME ON, RING, COME ON...!
WARNING: MAXIMUM ATMOSPHERIC VELOCITY.
ZOOOOSH
JUST DON'T LET ME ALREADY BE TOO LATE...
KYLE?! YOU IN THERE...?
KYLE--!
...F-FIRST... LANTERN... DID THIS...
...CHANGED MY PAST...MADE ME...FEEL...
SHH, KYLE, I KNOW. HE GOT ME, TOO.
HE SAID HE'D FED ON YOUR EMOTIONS. HIS POWER WAS OFF THE SCALE.
I MANAGED TO ESCAPE, BUT IF HE LEECHES THE REST OF OUR TEAMMATES, HOW MUCH STRONGER WILL HE BE?
...OH, GOD... THEY'LL NEVER SEE HIM COMING...!

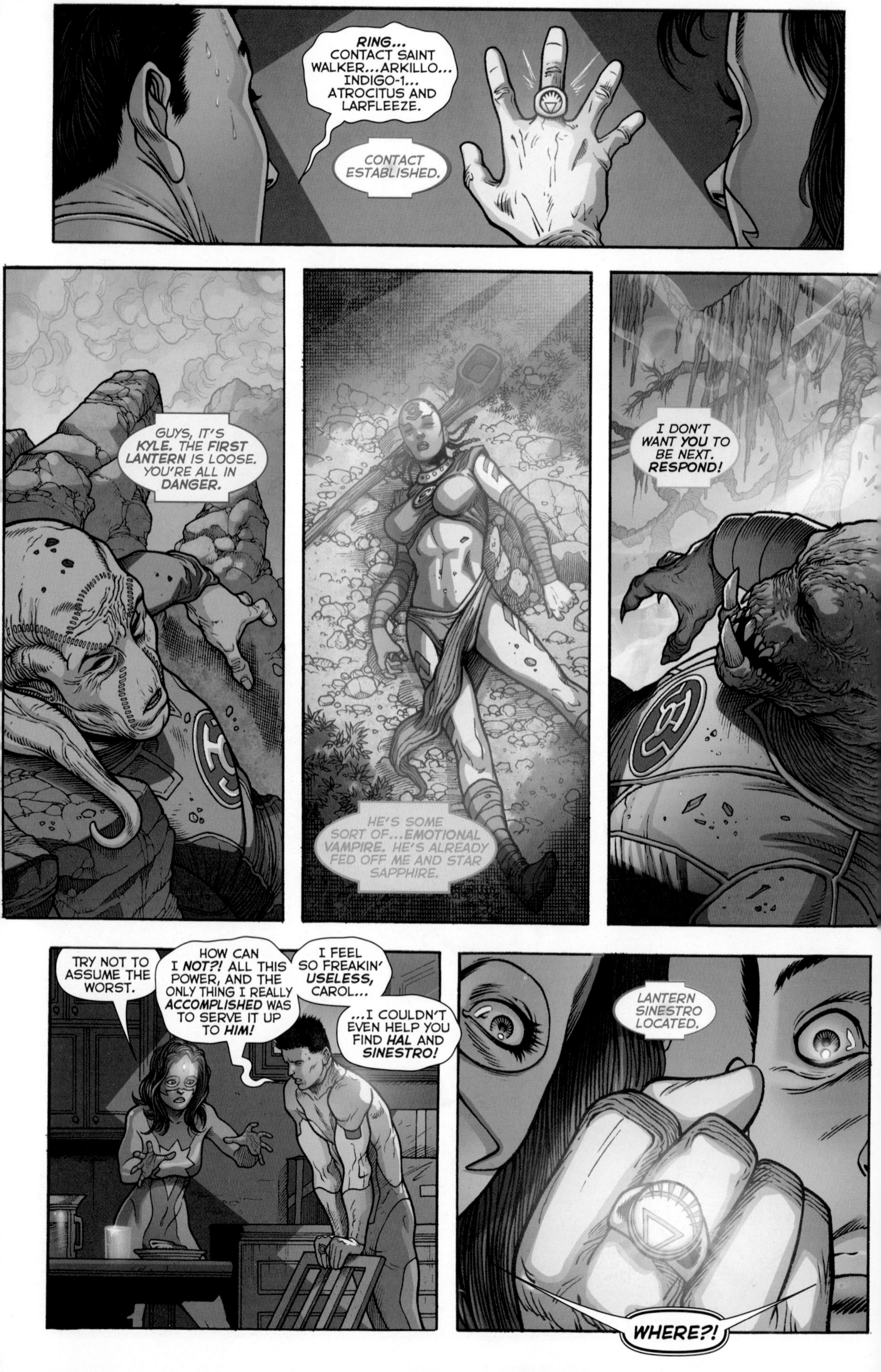
RING... CONTACT SAINT WALKER...ARKILLO... INDIGO-1... ATROCITUS AND LARFLEEZE.
CONTACT ESTABLISHED.
GUYS, IT'S KYLE. THE FIRST LANTERN IS LOOSE. YOU'RE ALL IN DANGER.
HE'S SOME SORT OF...EMOTIONAL VAMPIRE. HE'S ALREADY FED OFF ME AND STAR SAPPHIRE.
I DON'T WANT YOU TO BE NEXT. RESPOND!
TRY NOT TO ASSUME THE WORST.
HOW CAN I NOT?! ALL THIS POWER, AND THE ONLY THING I REALLY ACCOMPLISHED WAS TO SERVE IT UP TO HIM!
I FEEL SO FREAKIN' USELESS, CAROL...
...I COULDN'T EVEN HELP YOU FIND HAL AND SINESTRO!
LANTERN SINESTRO LOCATED.
WHERE?!

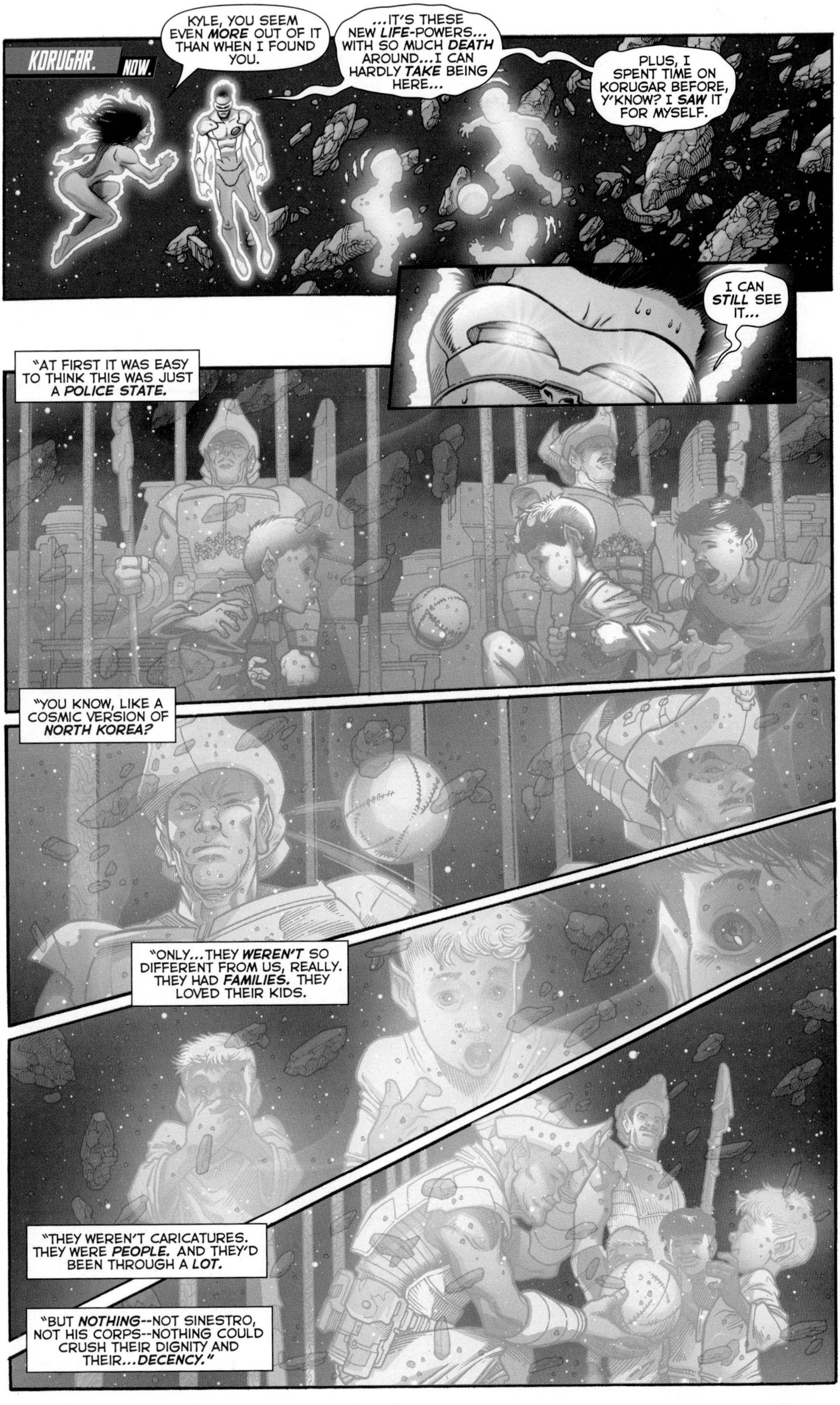
KORUGAR.
NOW.
KYLE, YOU SEEM EVEN MORE OUT OF IT THAN WHEN I FOUND YOU.
...IT'S THESE NEW LIFE-POWERS... WITH SO MUCH DEATH AROUND...I CAN HARDLY TAKE BEING HERE...
PLUS, I SPENT TIME ON KORUGAR BEFORE, Y'KNOW? I SAW IT FOR MYSELF.
I CAN STILL SEE IT...
"AT FIRST IT WAS EASY TO THINK THIS WAS JUST A POLICE STATE.
"YOU KNOW, LIKE A COSMIC VERSION OF NORTH KOREA?
"ONLY...THEY WEREN'T SO DIFFERENT FROM US, REALLY. THEY HAD FAMILIES. THEY LOVED THEIR KIDS.
"THEY WEREN'T CARICATURES. THEY WERE PEOPLE. AND THEY'D BEEN THROUGH A LOT.
"BUT NOTHING--NOT SINESTRO, NOT HIS CORPS--NOTHING COULD CRUSH THEIR DIGNITY AND THEIR...DECENCY."

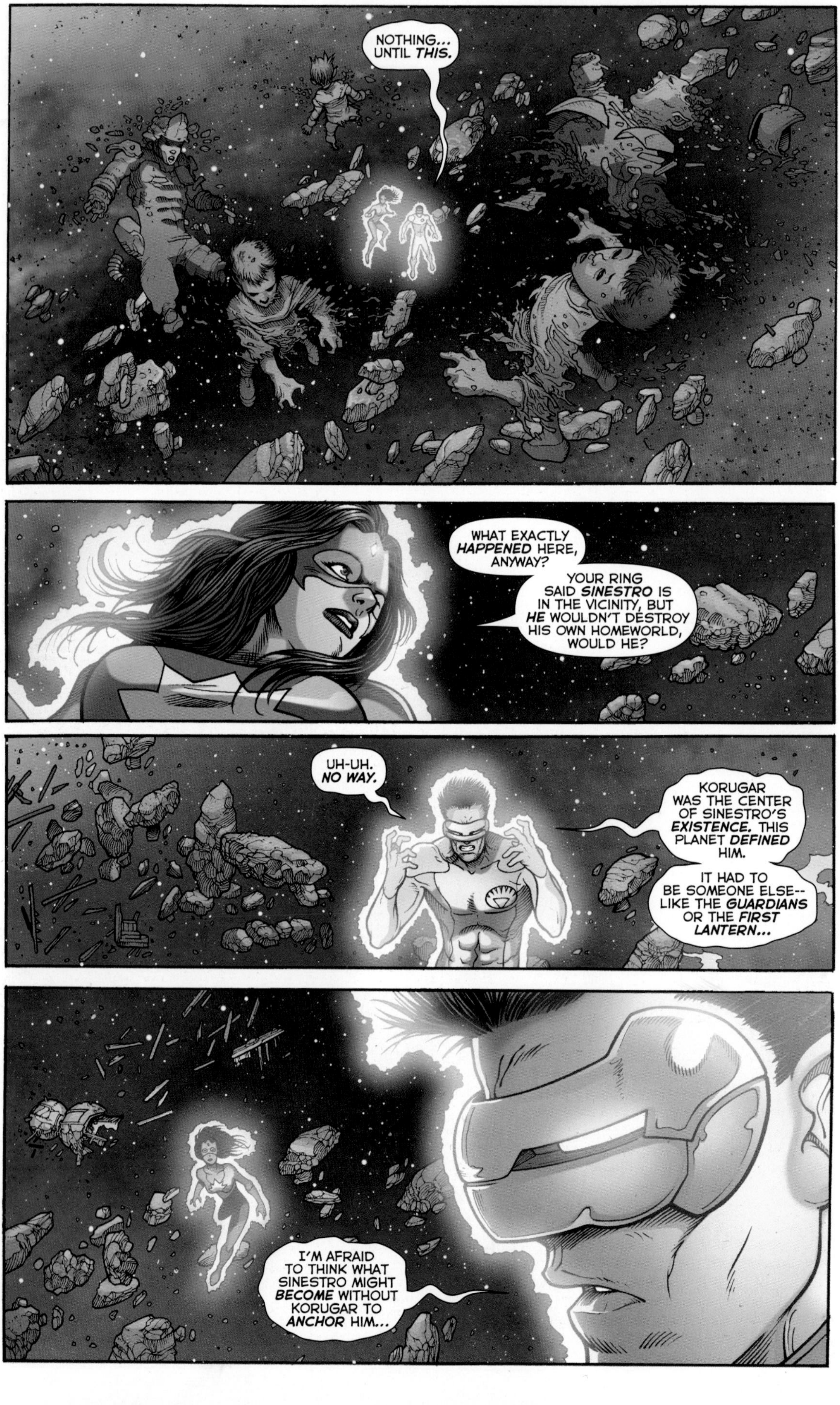
NOTHING... UNTIL THIS.
WHAT EXACTLY HAPPENED HERE, ANYWAY?
YOUR RING SAID SINESTRO IS IN THE VICINITY, BUT HE WOULDN'T DESTROY HIS OWN HOMEWORLD, WOULD HE?
UH-UH. NO WAY.
KORUGAR WAS THE CENTER OF SINESTRO'S EXISTENCE. THIS PLANET DEFINED HIM.
IT HAD TO BE SOMEONE ELSE-- LIKE THE GUARDIANS OR THE FIRST LANTERN...
I'M AFRAID TO THINK WHAT SINESTRO MIGHT BECOME WITHOUT KORUGAR TO ANCHOR HIM...

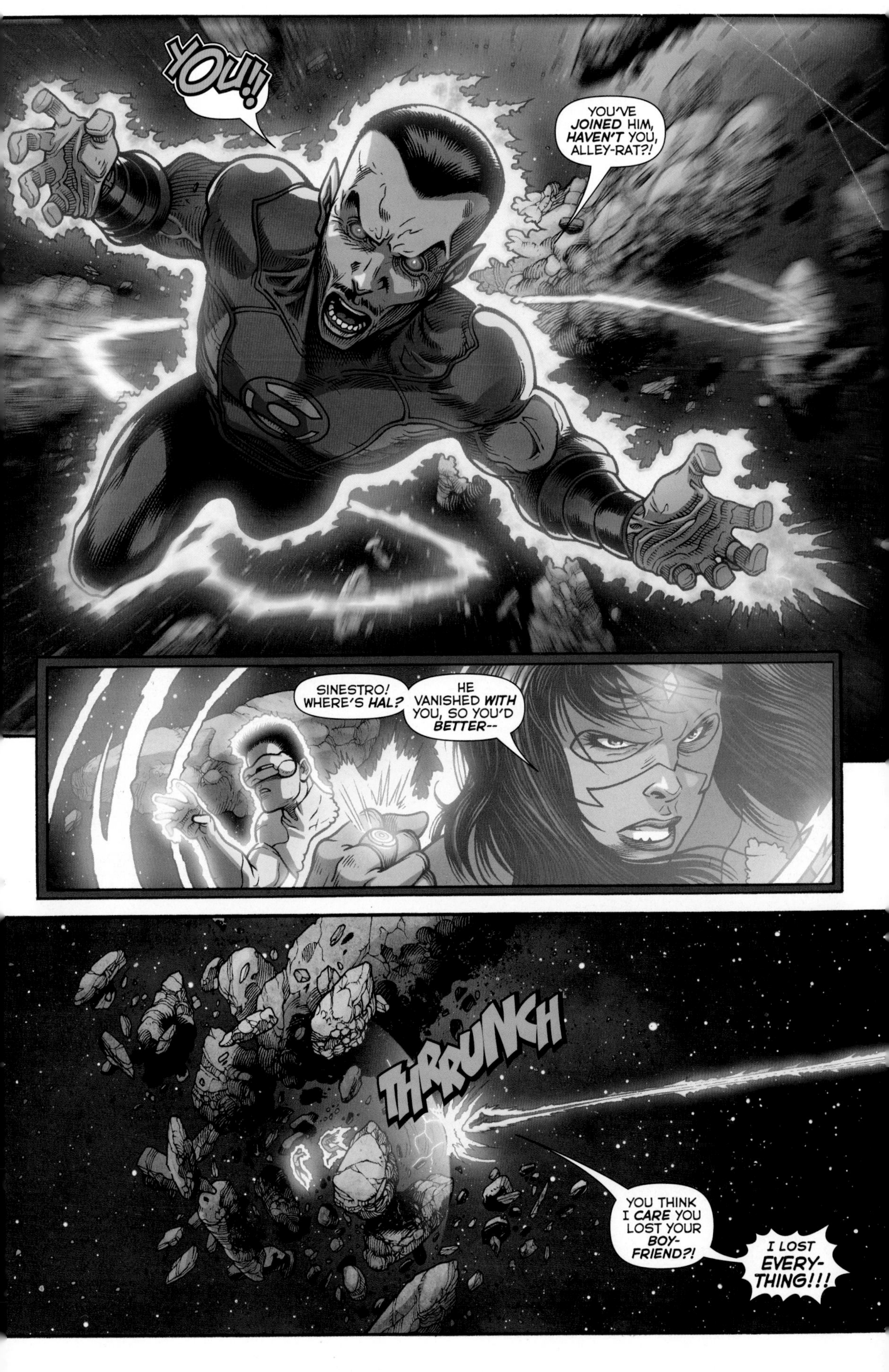
YOU!!
YOU'VE JOINED HIM, HAVEN'T YOU, ALLEY-RAT?!
SINESTRO! WHERE'S HAL?
HE VANISHED WITH YOU, SO YOU'D BETTER--
THRUNCH
YOU THINK I CARE YOU LOST YOUR BOY-FRIEND?!
I LOST EVERY-THING!!!

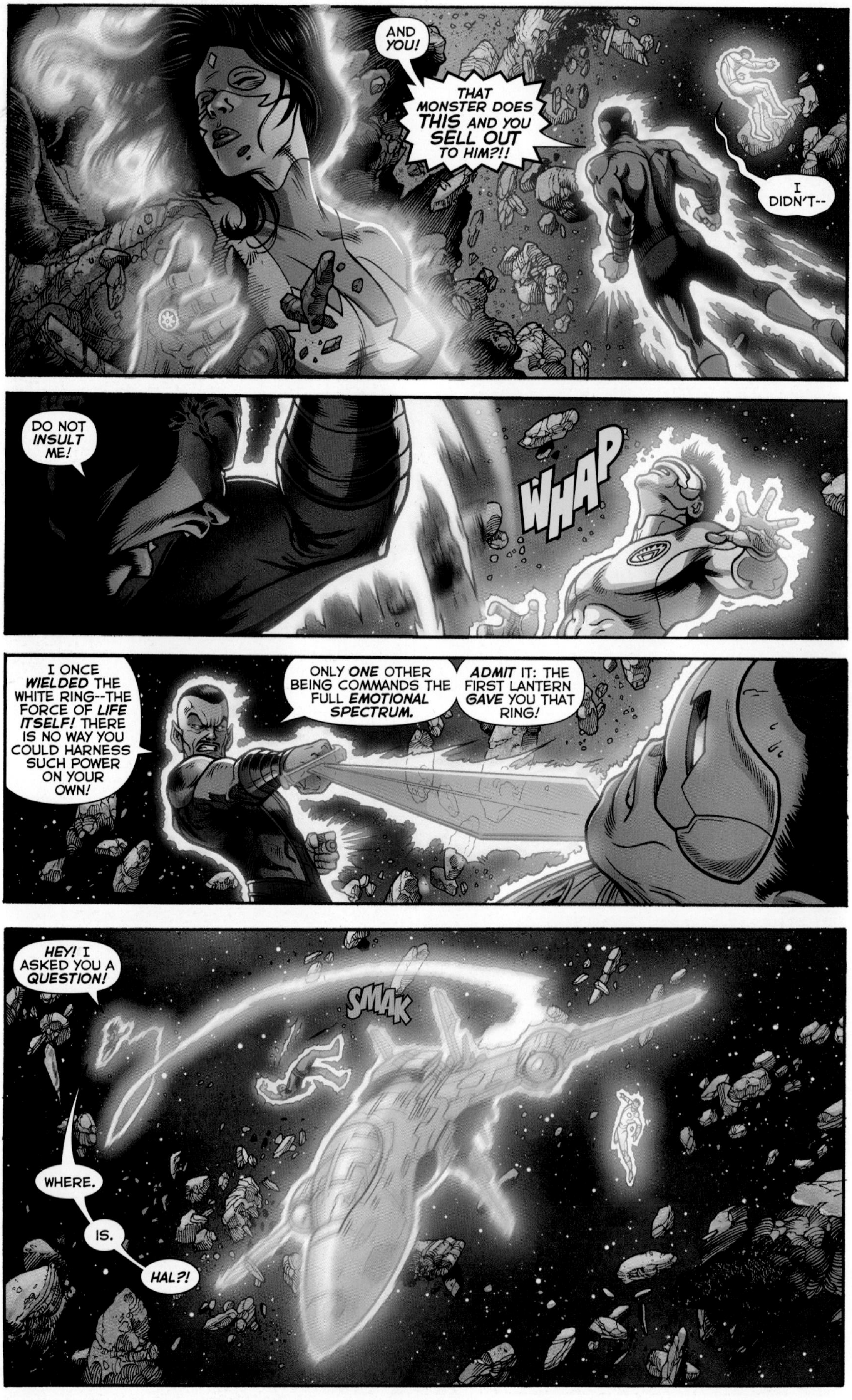
AND YOU!
THAT MONSTER DOES THIS AND YOU SELL OUT TO HIM?!!
I DIDN'T--
DO NOT INSULT ME!
WHAP
I ONCE WIELDED THE WHITE RING--THE FORCE OF LIFE ITSELF! THERE IS NO WAY YOU COULD HARNESS SUCH POWER ON YOUR OWN!
ONLY ONE OTHER BEING COMMANDS THE FULL EMOTIONAL SPECTRUM.
ADMIT IT: THE FIRST LANTERN GAVE YOU THAT RING!
HEY! I ASKED YOU A QUESTION!
SMAK
WHERE.
IS.
HAL?!

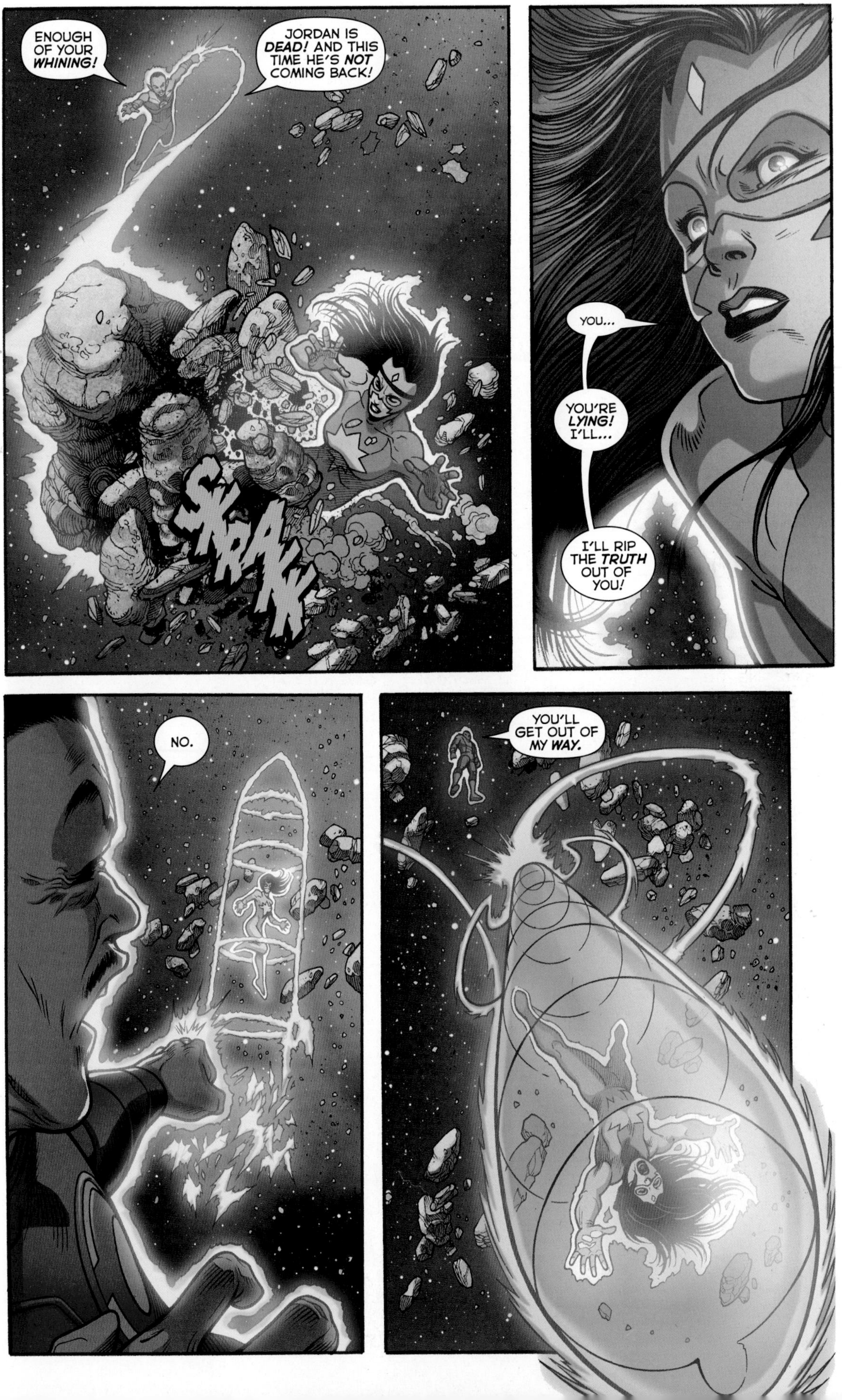
ENOUGH OF YOUR WHINING!
JORDAN IS DEAD! AND THIS TIME HE'S NOT COMING BACK!
SKRAKK
YOU...
YOU'RE LYING! I'LL...
I'LL RIP THE TRUTH OUT OF YOU!
NO.
YOU'LL GET OUT OF MY WAY.

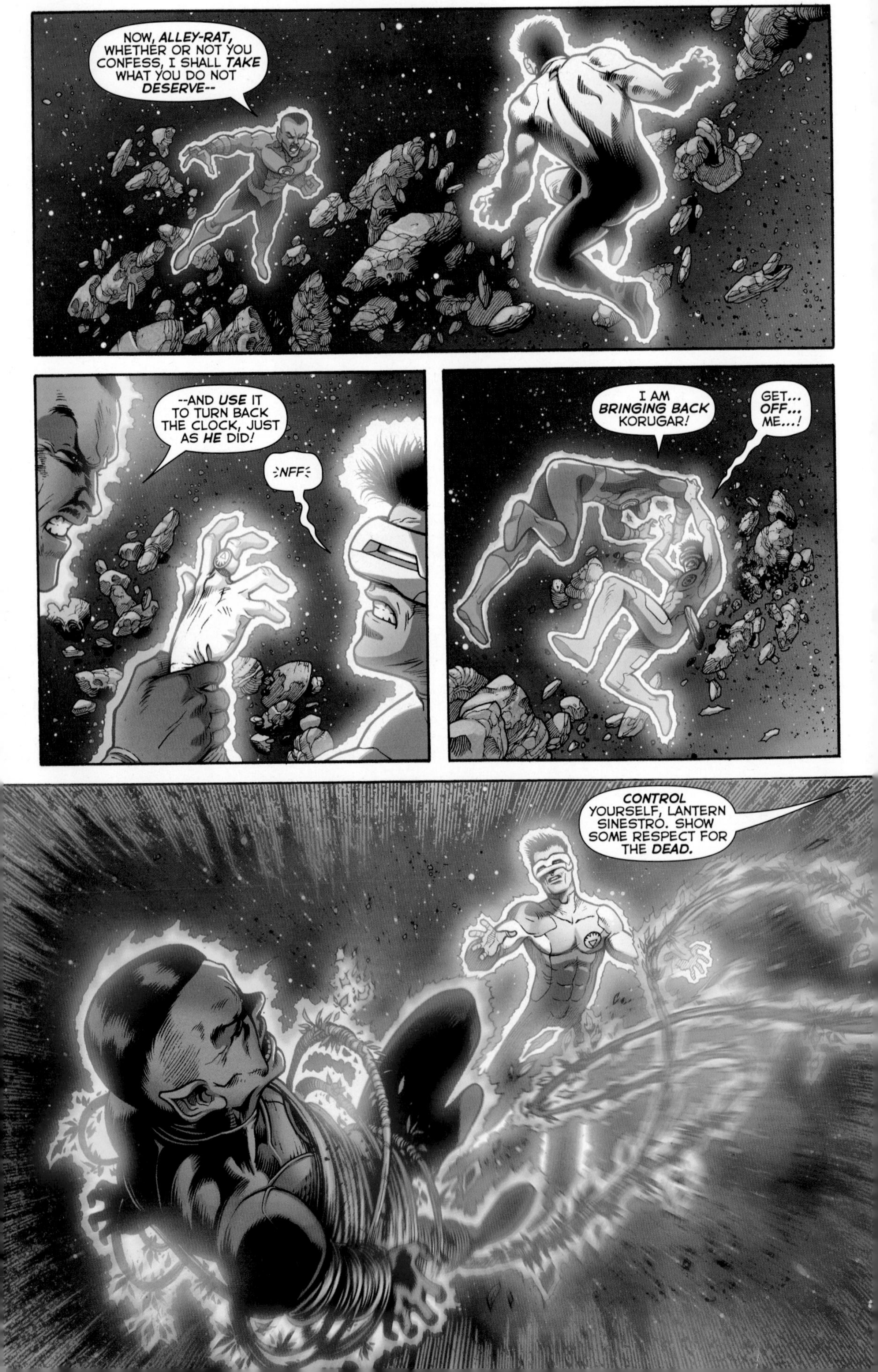
NOW, ALLEY-RAT, WHETHER OR NOT YOU CONFESS, I SHALL TAKE WHAT YOU DO NOT DESERVE--
--AND USE IT TO TURN BACK THE CLOCK, JUST AS HE DID!
NFF
I AM BRINGING BACK KORUGAR!
GET... OFF... ME...!
CONTROL YOURSELF, LANTERN SINESTRO. SHOW SOME RESPECT FOR THE DEAD.

SORRY, B'DG, WISH I COULD HELP, BUT—

YOUR RING CANNOT FUNCTION *AGAINST* HIM, I KNOW. BUT WE DID NOT COME TO *FIGHT* LANTERN SINESTRO...

"...NOT WHILE WE *ALL* HAVE A COMMON ENEMY IN THE *FIRST LANTERN*."

I'VE SEEN THE *SQUIRREL-LANTERN* BEFORE, BUT WHO'S THE OTHER GUY?

NO IDEA.

ALLOW ME TO PRESENT *SIMON BAZ* OF EARTH...

...NEWEST PROTECTOR OF SECTOR 2814 AND, AH... ...HAL JORDAN'S *REPLACEMENT.*

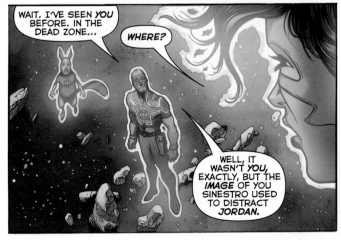

WAIT. I'VE SEEN *YOU* BEFORE. IN THE DEAD ZONE...

WHERE?

WELL, IT WASN'T *YOU*, EXACTLY, BUT THE *IMAGE* OF YOU SINESTRO USED TO DISTRACT *JORDAN.*

YOU FOUND *HAL?!*

IS HE *OKAY?!*

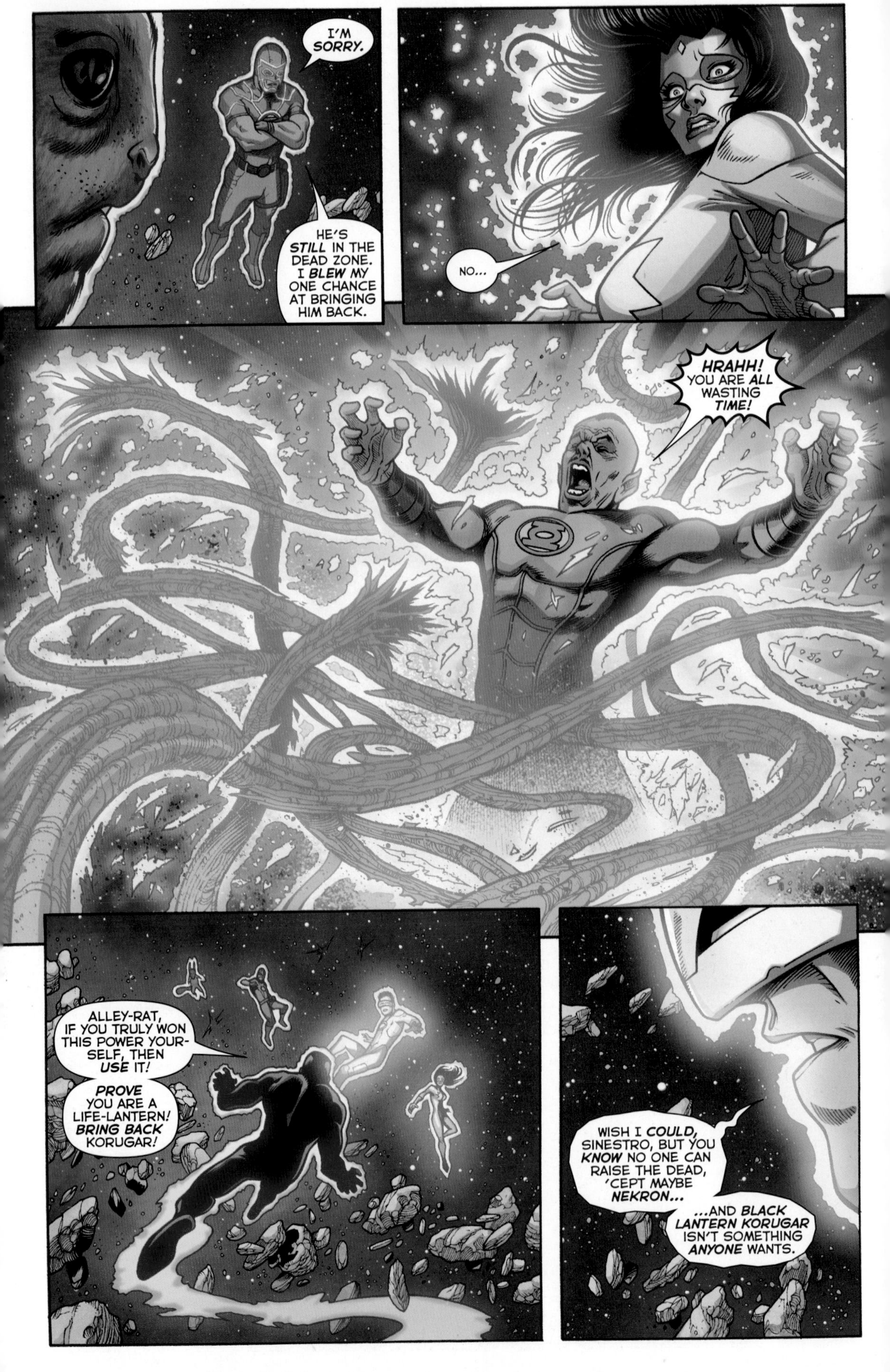
I'M SORRY.
HE'S STILL IN THE DEAD ZONE. I BLEW MY ONE CHANCE AT BRINGING HIM BACK.
NO...
HRAHH! YOU ARE ALL WASTING TIME!
ALLEY-RAT, IF YOU TRULY WON THIS POWER YOURSELF, THEN USE IT!
PROVE YOU ARE A LIFE-LANTERN! BRING BACK KORUGAR!
WISH I COULD, SINESTRO, BUT YOU KNOW NO ONE CAN RAISE THE DEAD, 'CEPT MAYBE NEKRON...
...AND BLACK LANTERN KORUGAR ISN'T SOMETHING ANYONE WANTS.

NO EXCUSES! DO IT NOW!

WAIT! IT MIGHT *BE* POSSIBLE!

I BROUGHT BACK MY BROTHER FROM A *LIVING DEATH* USING MY RING.

IT IS *TRUE.* I SAW HIM DO IT.

KYLE, YOU HAVE TO *TRY--!*

AND IF YOU CAN PULL THIS OFF, MAYBE YOU CAN RAISE HAL, *TOO...!*

...FINE. I'LL *DO* IT.

NOT FOR *YOU,* SINESTRO.

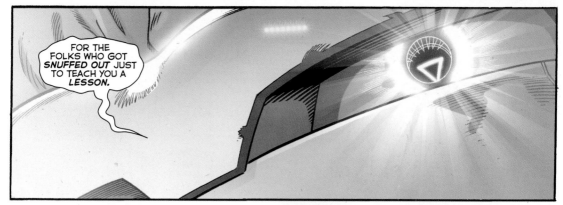

FOR THE FOLKS WHO GOT *SNUFFED OUT* JUST TO TEACH YOU A *LESSON.*

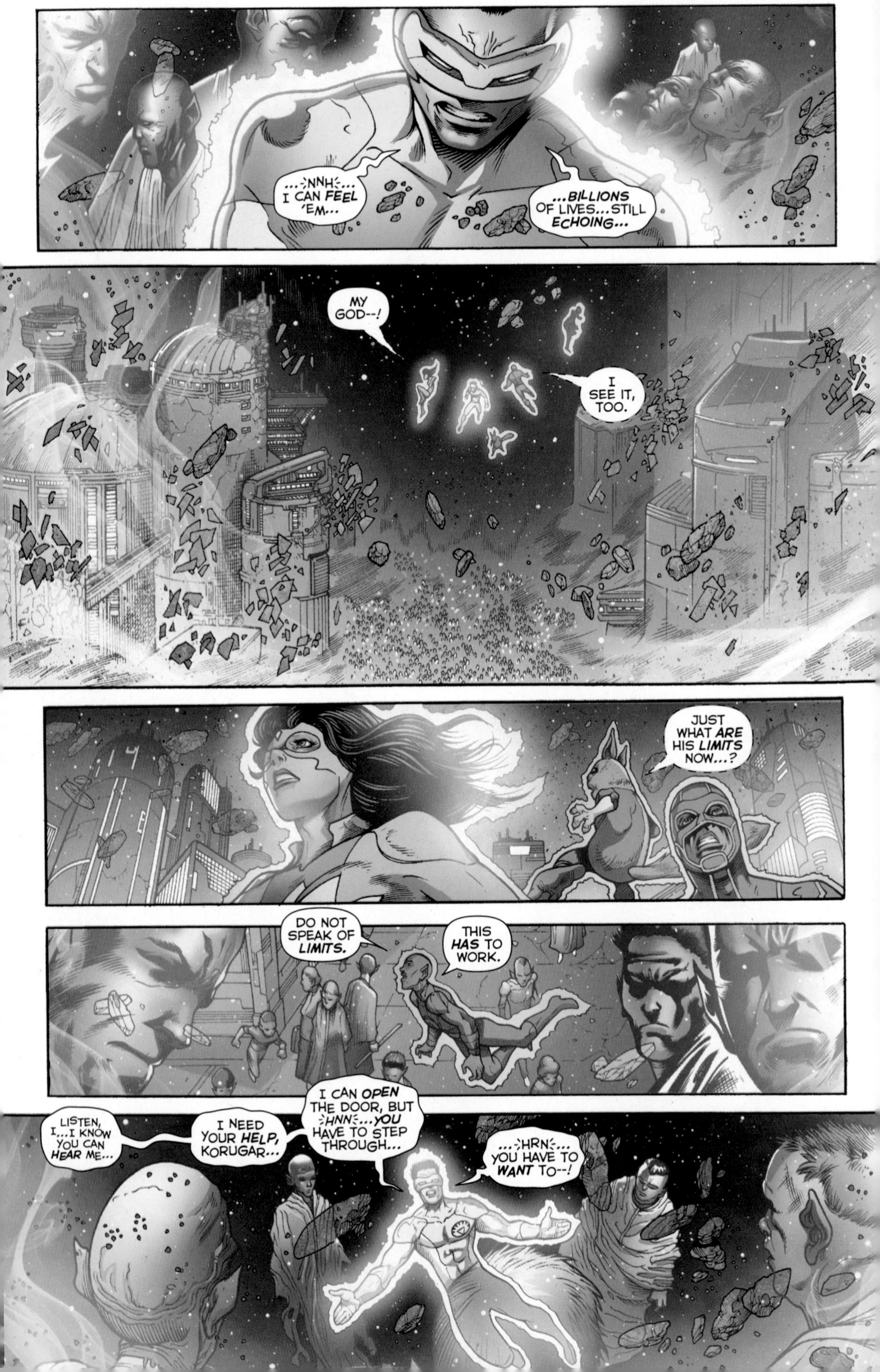
...NNH... I CAN FEEL 'EM...
...BILLIONS OF LIVES...STILL ECHOING...
MY GOD--!
I SEE IT, TOO.
JUST WHAT ARE HIS LIMITS NOW...?
DO NOT SPEAK OF LIMITS.
THIS HAS TO WORK.
LISTEN, I...I KNOW YOU CAN HEAR ME...
I NEED YOUR HELP, KORUGAR...
I CAN OPEN THE DOOR, BUT HNN...YOU HAVE TO STEP THROUGH...
...HRN... YOU HAVE TO WANT TO--!

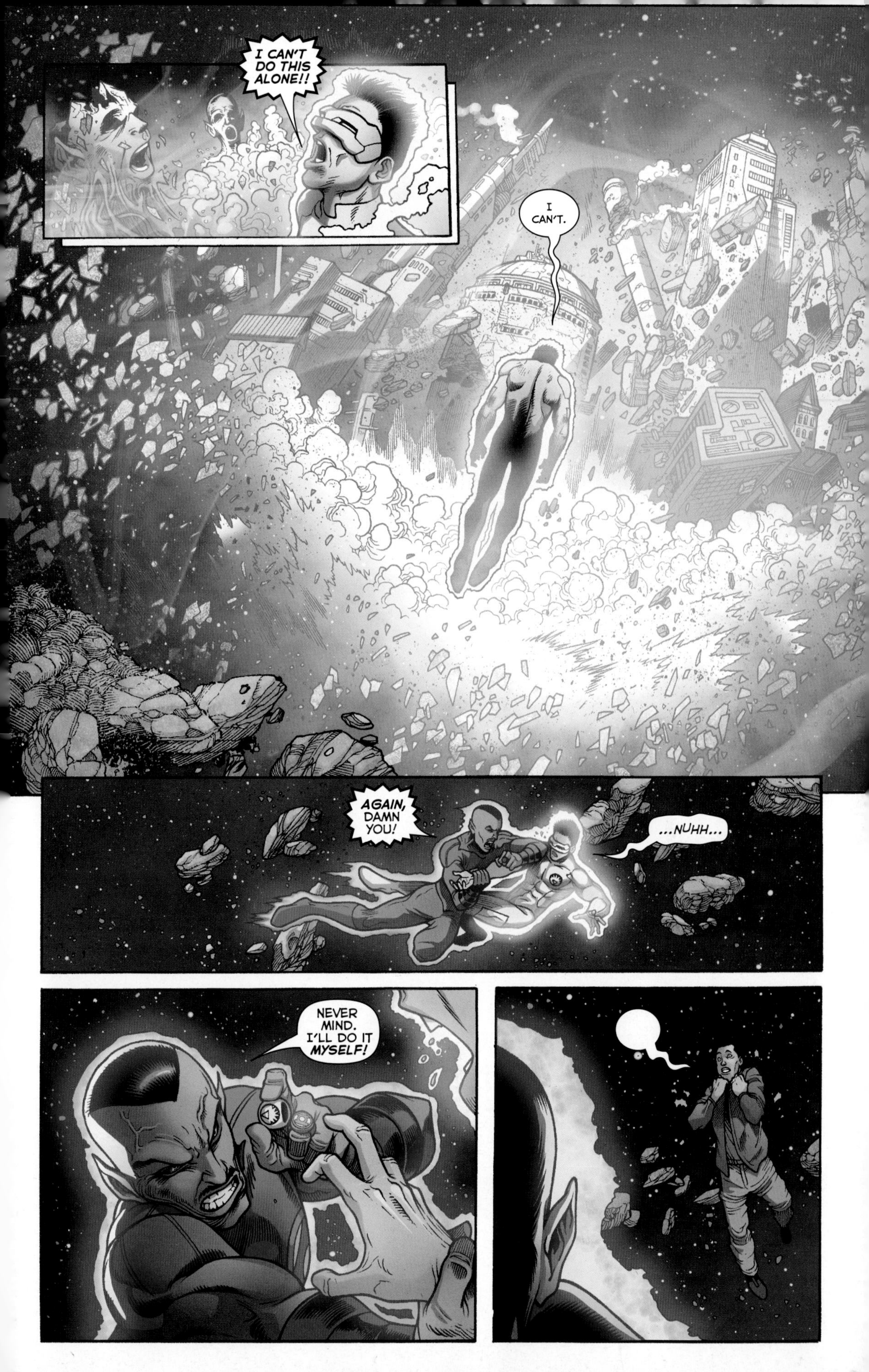
I CAN'T DO THIS ALONE!!
I CAN'T.
AGAIN, DAMN YOU!
...NUHH...
NEVER MIND. I'LL DO IT MYSELF!

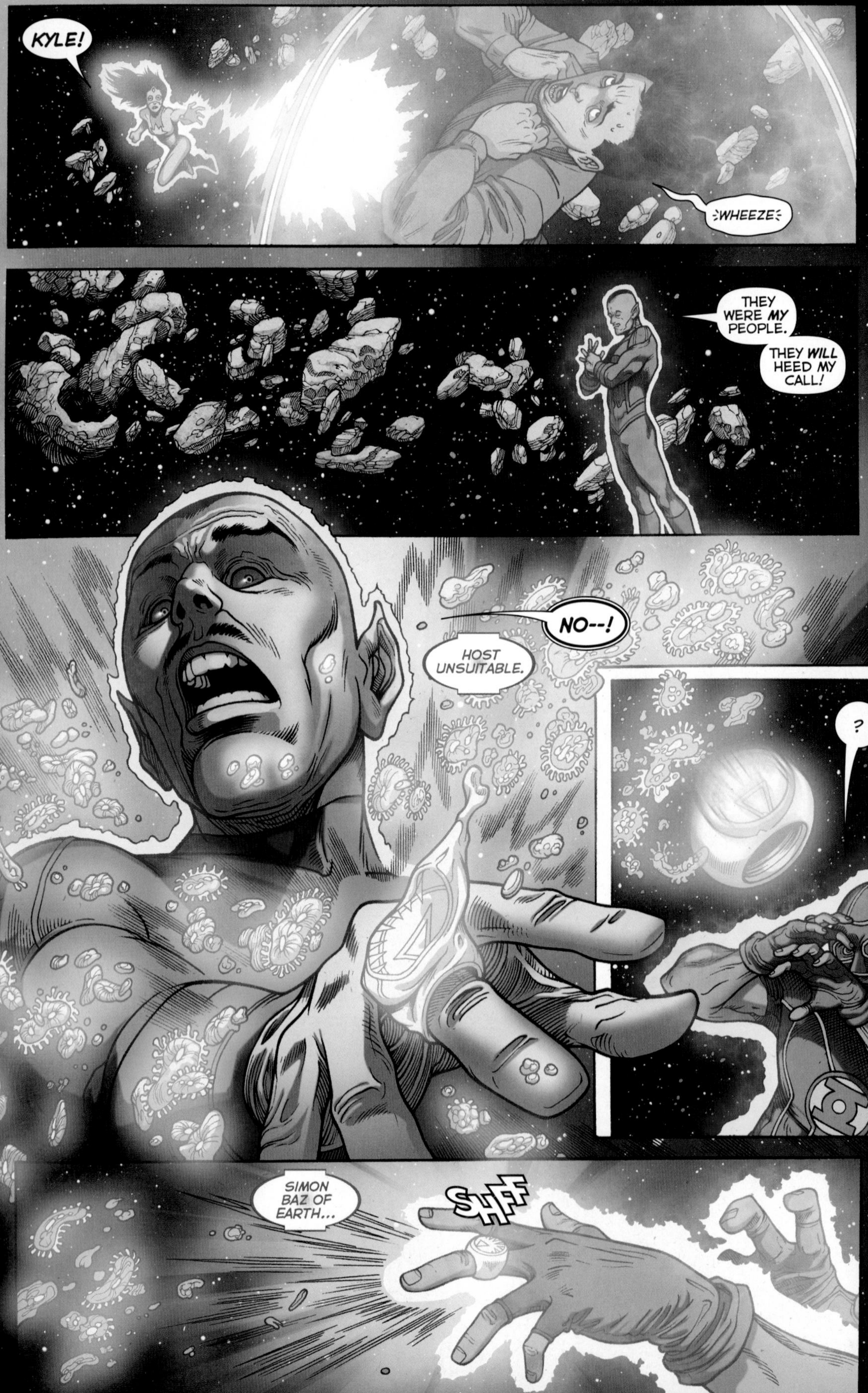
KYLE!
WHEEZE
THEY WERE MY PEOPLE.
THEY WILL HEED MY CALL!
NO--!
HOST UNSUITABLE.
?
SIMON BAZ OF EARTH...
SHFF

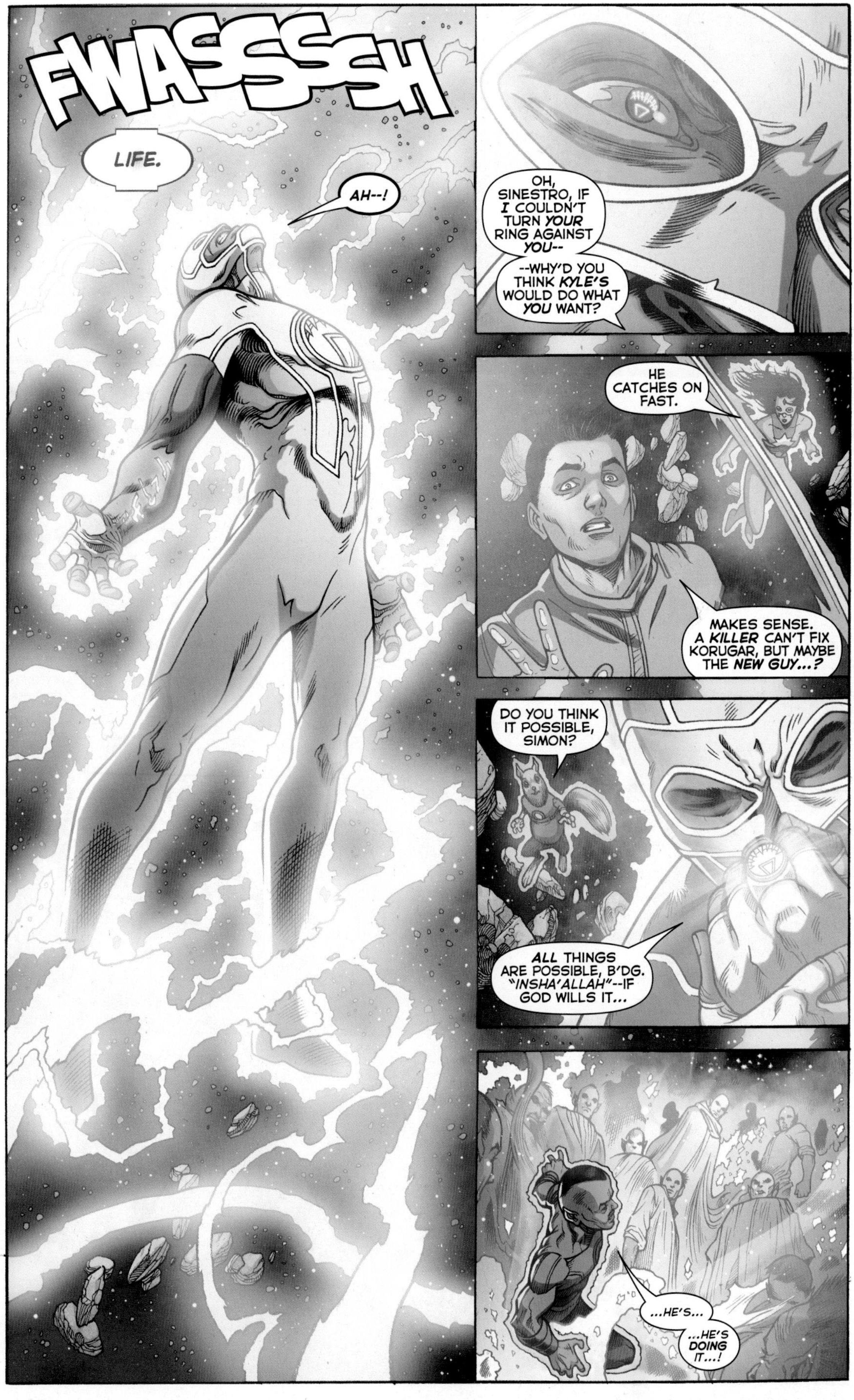
FWASSSSH
LIFE.
AH--!
OH, SINESTRO, IF I COULDN'T TURN YOUR RING AGAINST YOU--
--WHY'D YOU THINK KYLE'S WOULD DO WHAT YOU WANT?
HE CATCHES ON FAST.
MAKES SENSE. A KILLER CAN'T FIX KORUGAR, BUT MAYBE THE NEW GUY...?
DO YOU THINK IT POSSIBLE, SIMON?
ALL THINGS ARE POSSIBLE, B'DG. "INSHA'ALLAH"--IF GOD WILLS IT...
...HE'S...
...HE'S DOING IT...!

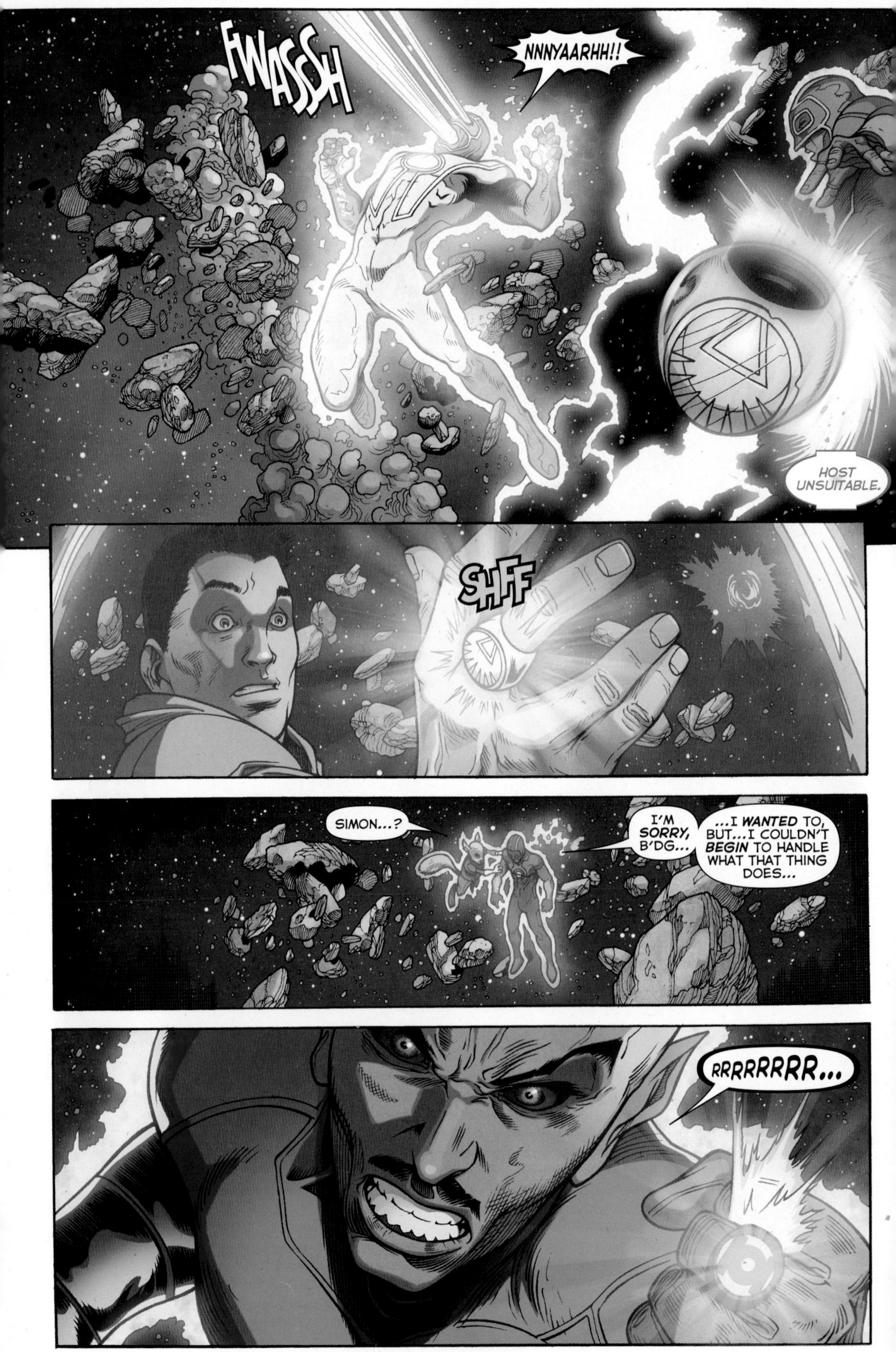
FWASSSH
NNNYAARHH!!
HOST UNSUITABLE.
SHFF
SIMON...?
I'M SORRY, B'DG...
...I WANTED TO, BUT...I COULDN'T BEGIN TO HANDLE WHAT THAT THING DOES...
RRRRRRRR...

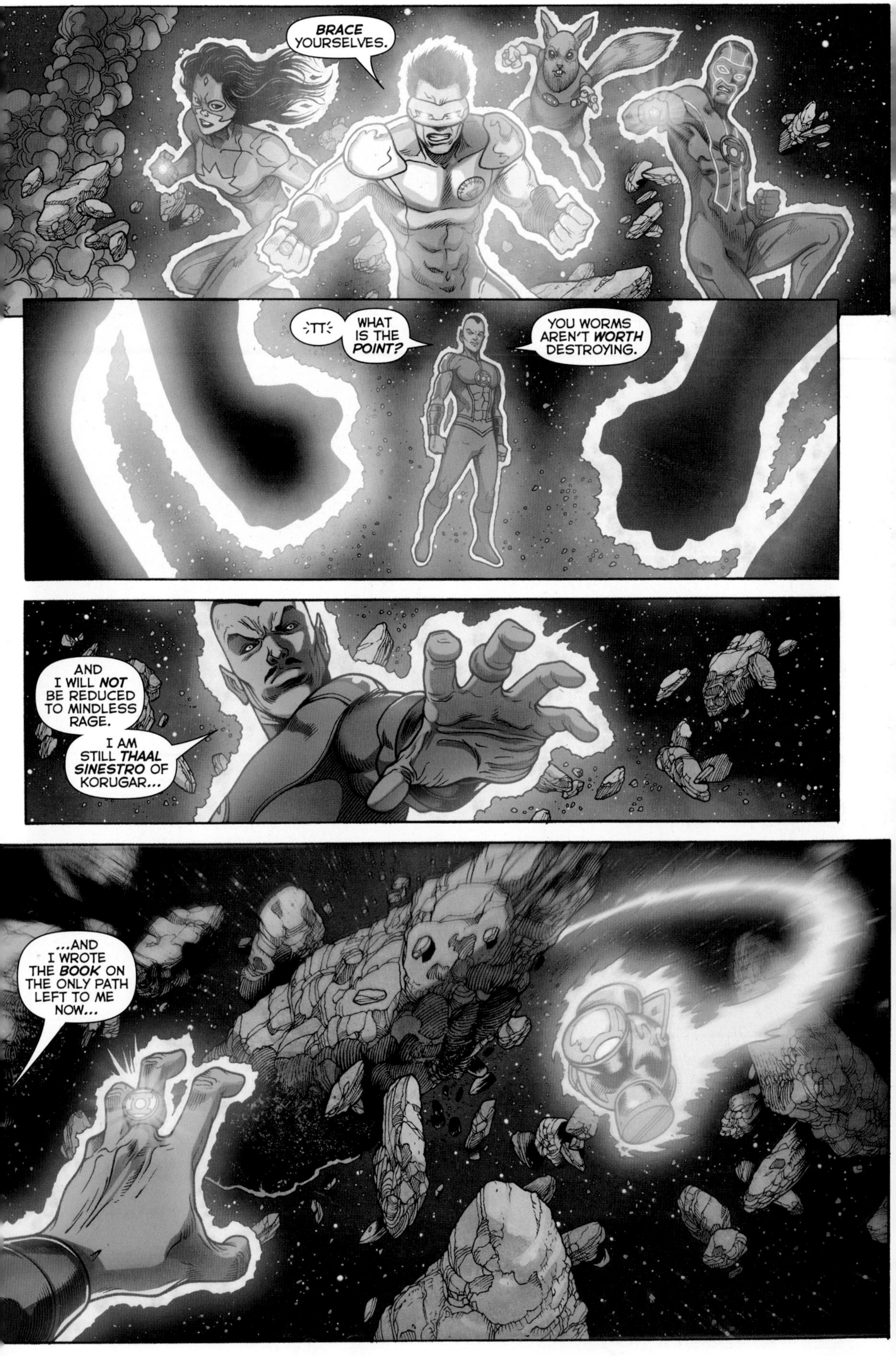
BRACE YOURSELVES.
TT
WHAT IS THE POINT?
YOU WORMS AREN'T WORTH DESTROYING.
AND I WILL NOT BE REDUCED TO MINDLESS RAGE.
I AM STILL THAAL SINESTRO OF KORUGAR...
...AND I WROTE THE BOOK ON THE ONLY PATH LEFT TO ME NOW...

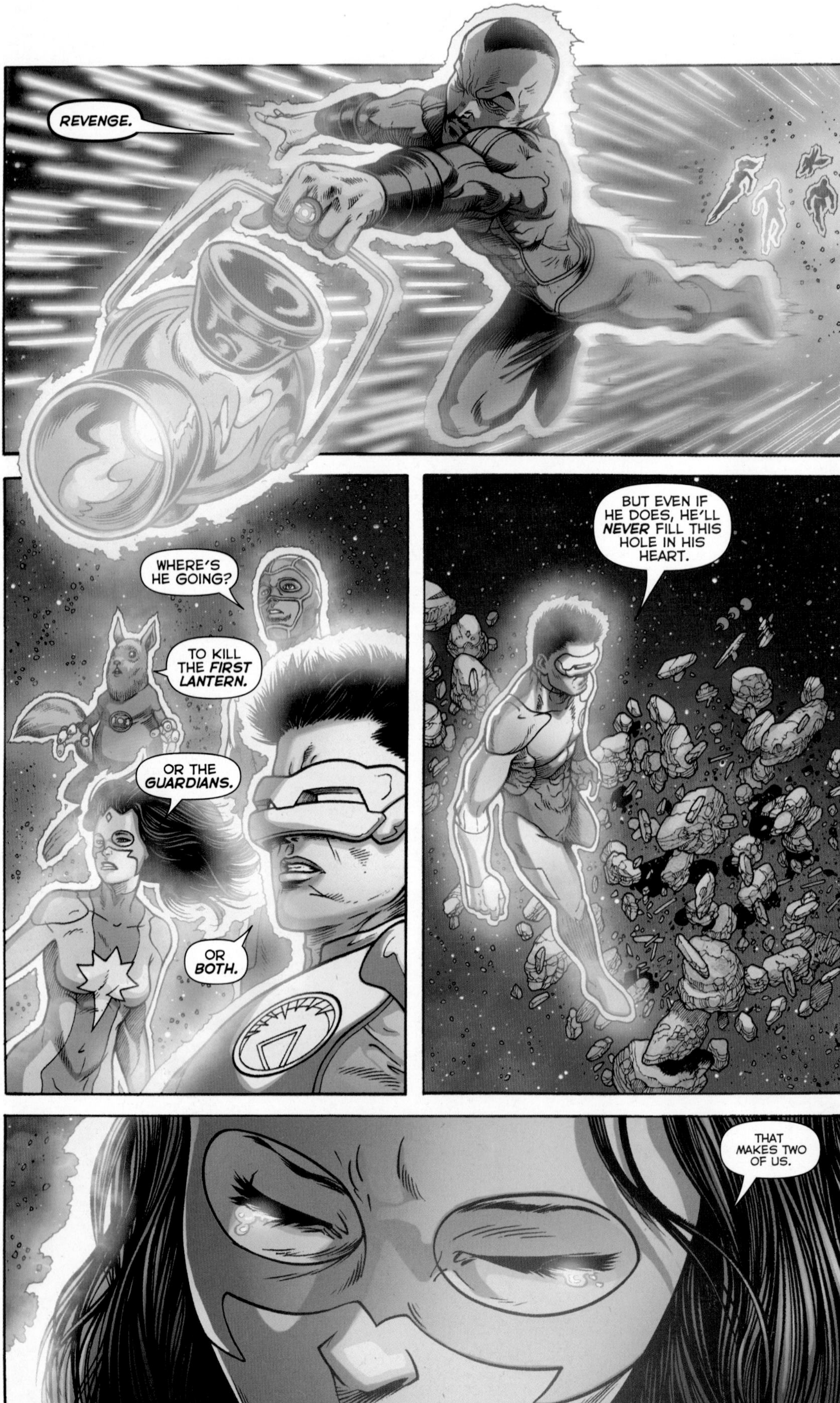
REVENGE.
WHERE'S HE GOING?
TO KILL THE FIRST LANTERN.
OR THE GUARDIANS.
OR BOTH.
BUT EVEN IF HE DOES, HE'LL NEVER FILL THIS HOLE IN HIS HEART.
THAT MAKES TWO OF US.

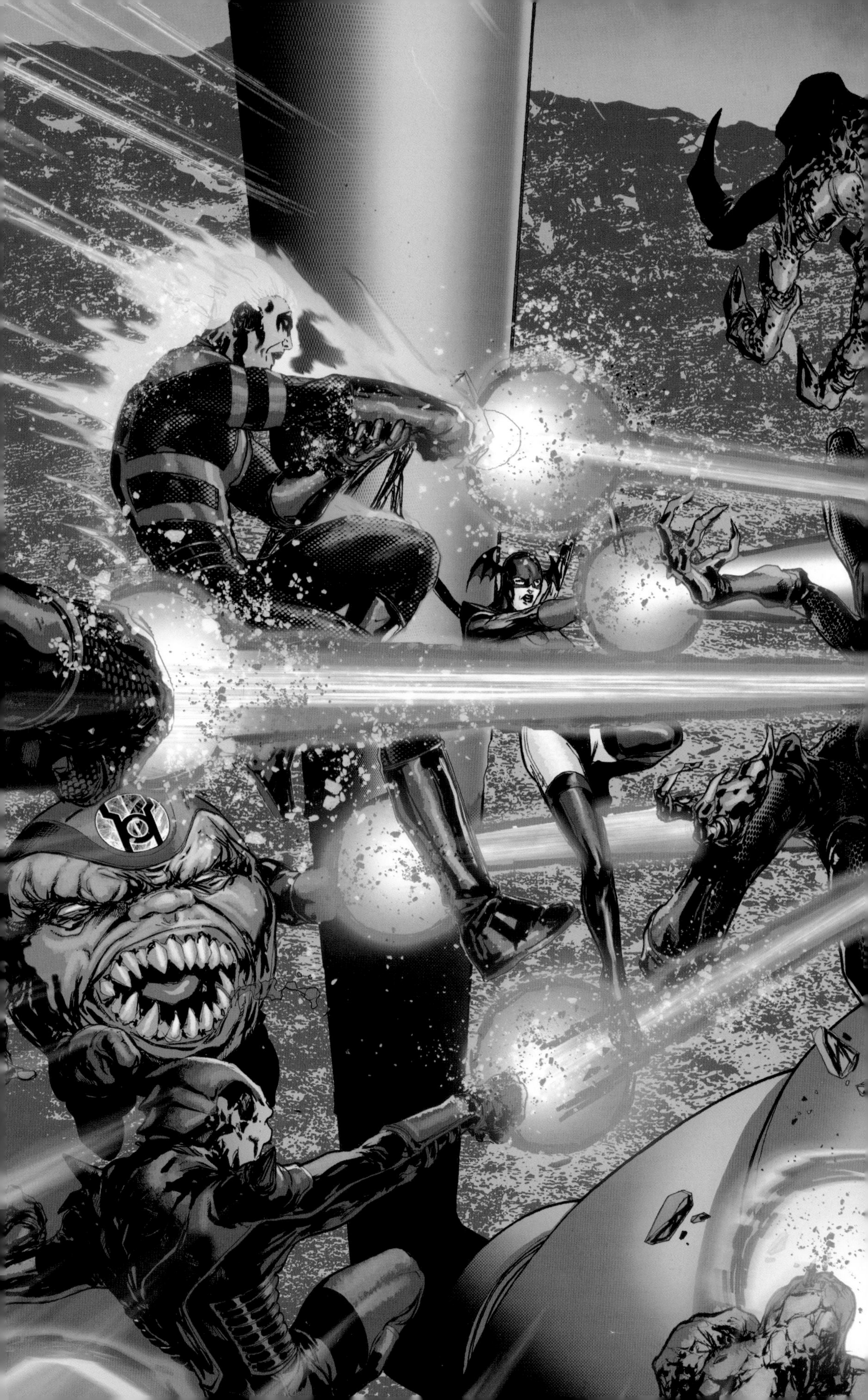

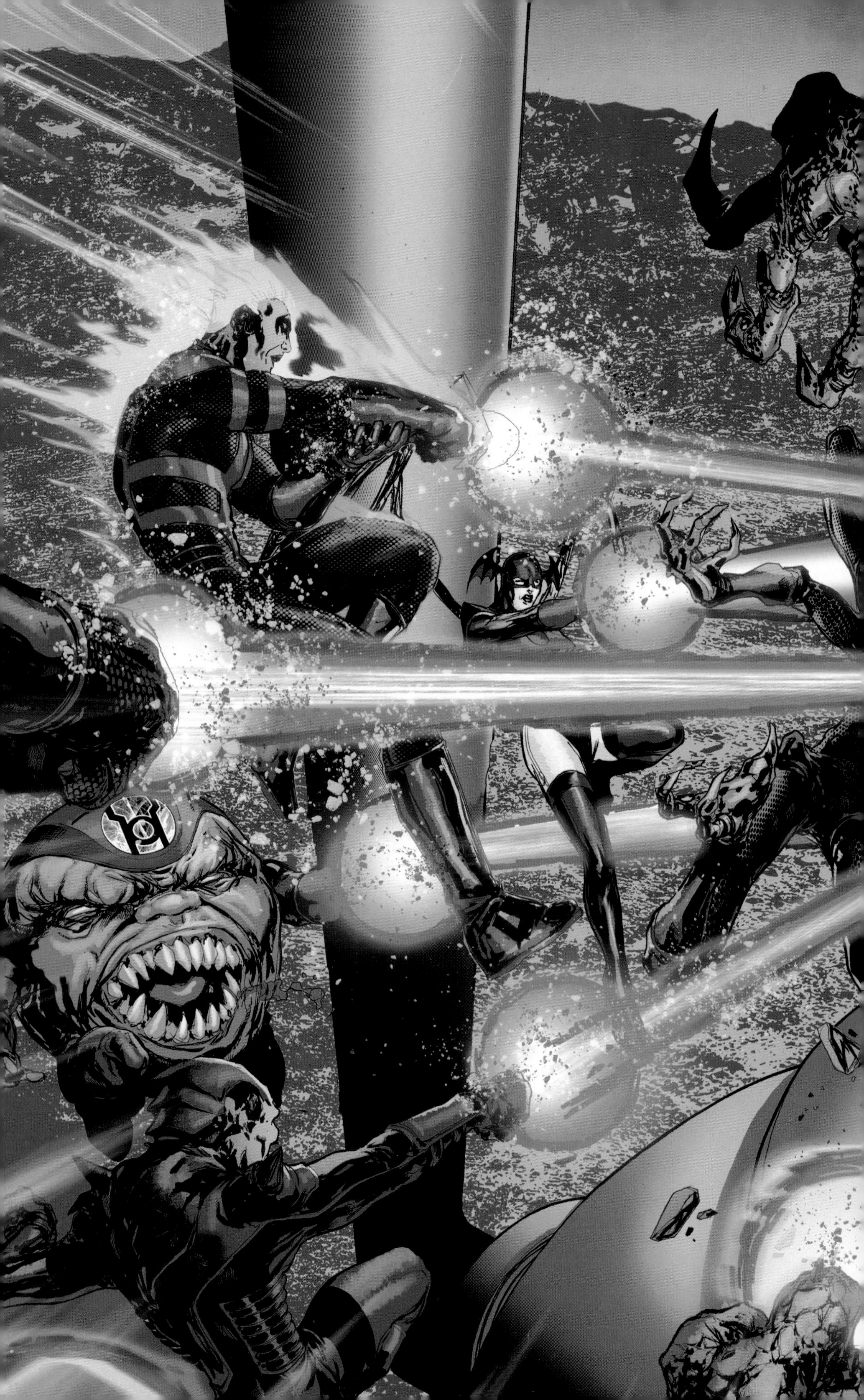

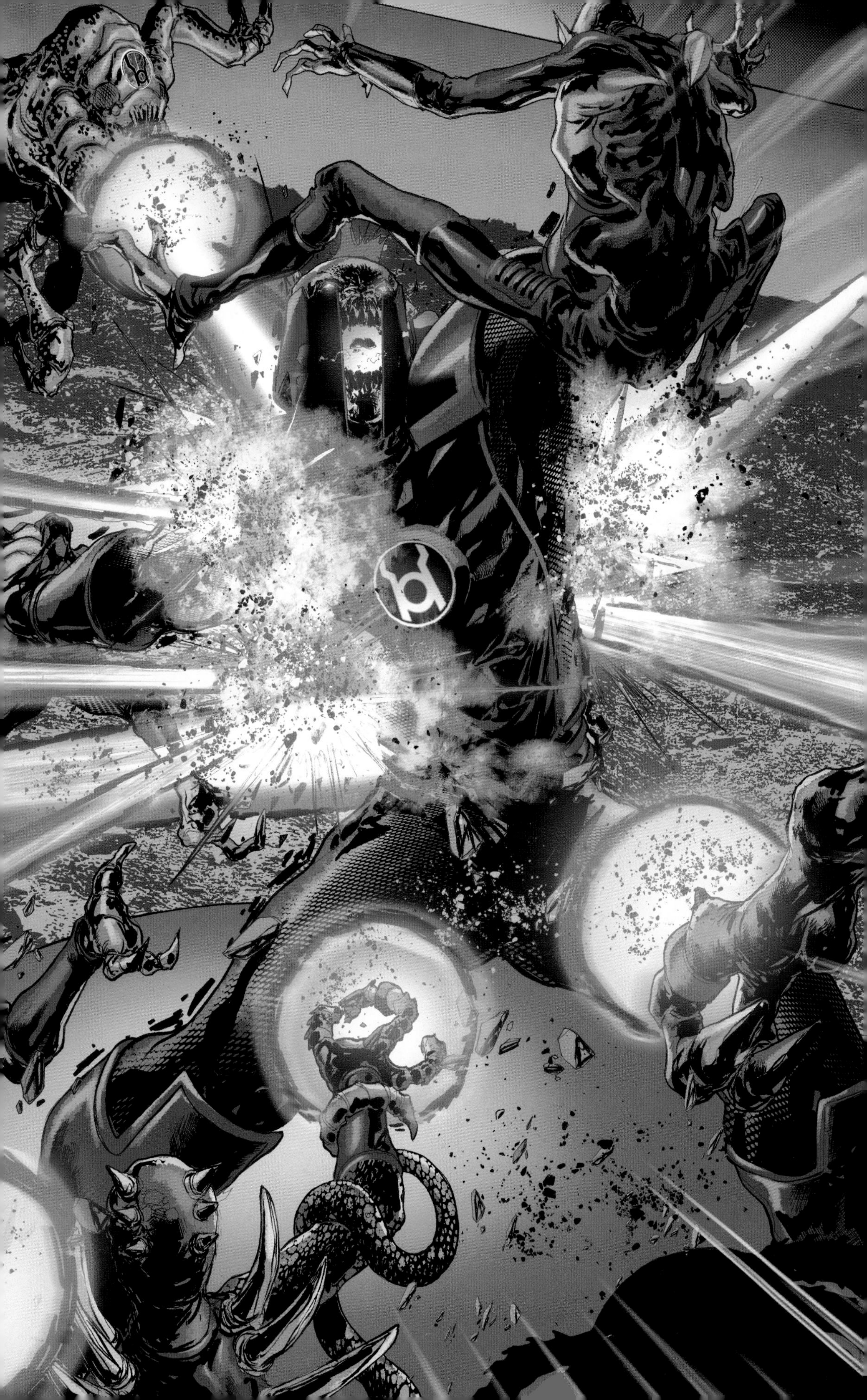

PART TWELVE: THE DEATH OF ATROCITUS

PETER MILLIGAN writer **WILL CONRAD** artist

cover art by **MIGUEL SEPULVEDA & RAIN BEREDO**

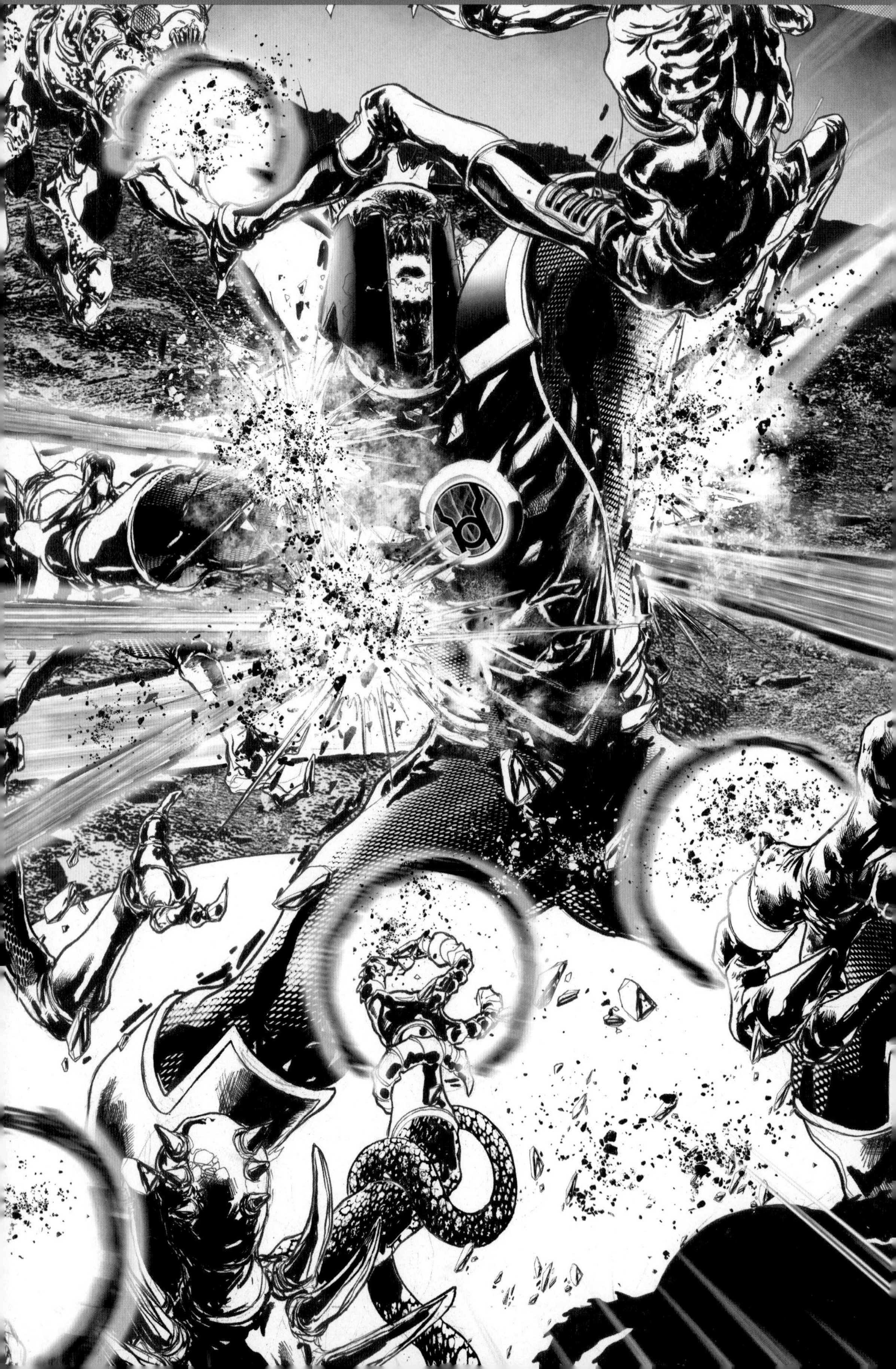

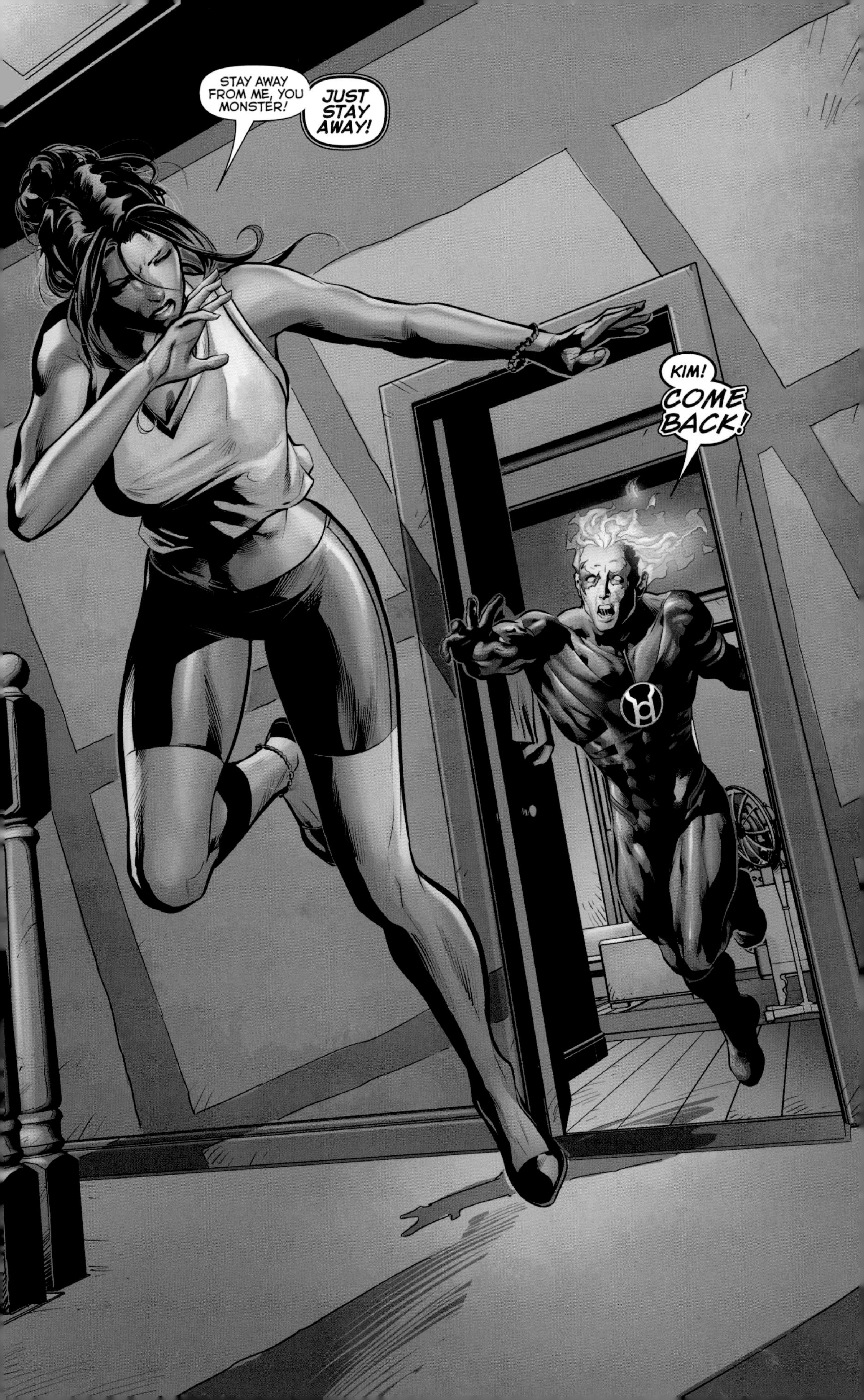
STAY AWAY FROM ME, YOU MONSTER!
JUST STAY AWAY!
KIM! COME BACK!

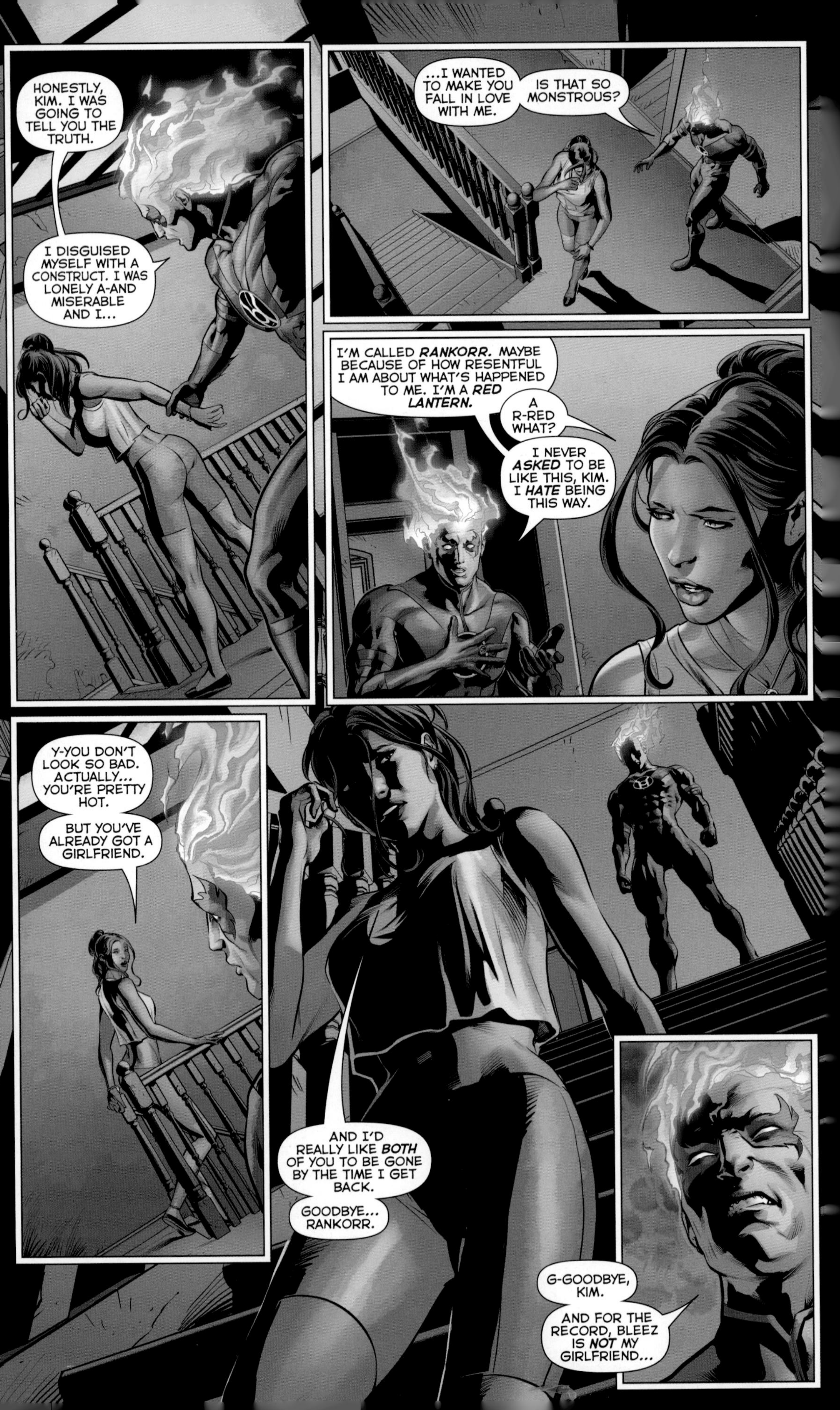
HONESTLY, KIM. I WAS GOING TO TELL YOU THE TRUTH.
I DISGUISED MYSELF WITH A CONSTRUCT. I WAS LONELY A-AND MISERABLE AND I...
...I WANTED TO MAKE YOU FALL IN LOVE WITH ME.
IS THAT SO MONSTROUS?
I'M CALLED RANKORR. MAYBE BECAUSE OF HOW RESENTFUL I AM ABOUT WHAT'S HAPPENED TO ME. I'M A RED LANTERN.
A R-RED WHAT?
I NEVER ASKED TO BE LIKE THIS, KIM. I HATE BEING THIS WAY.
Y-YOU DON'T LOOK SO BAD. ACTUALLY... YOU'RE PRETTY HOT.
BUT YOU'VE ALREADY GOT A GIRLFRIEND.
AND I'D REALLY LIKE BOTH OF YOU TO BE GONE BY THE TIME I GET BACK.
GOODBYE... RANKORR.
G-GOODBYE, KIM.
AND FOR THE RECORD, BLEEZ IS NOT MY GIRLFRIEND...

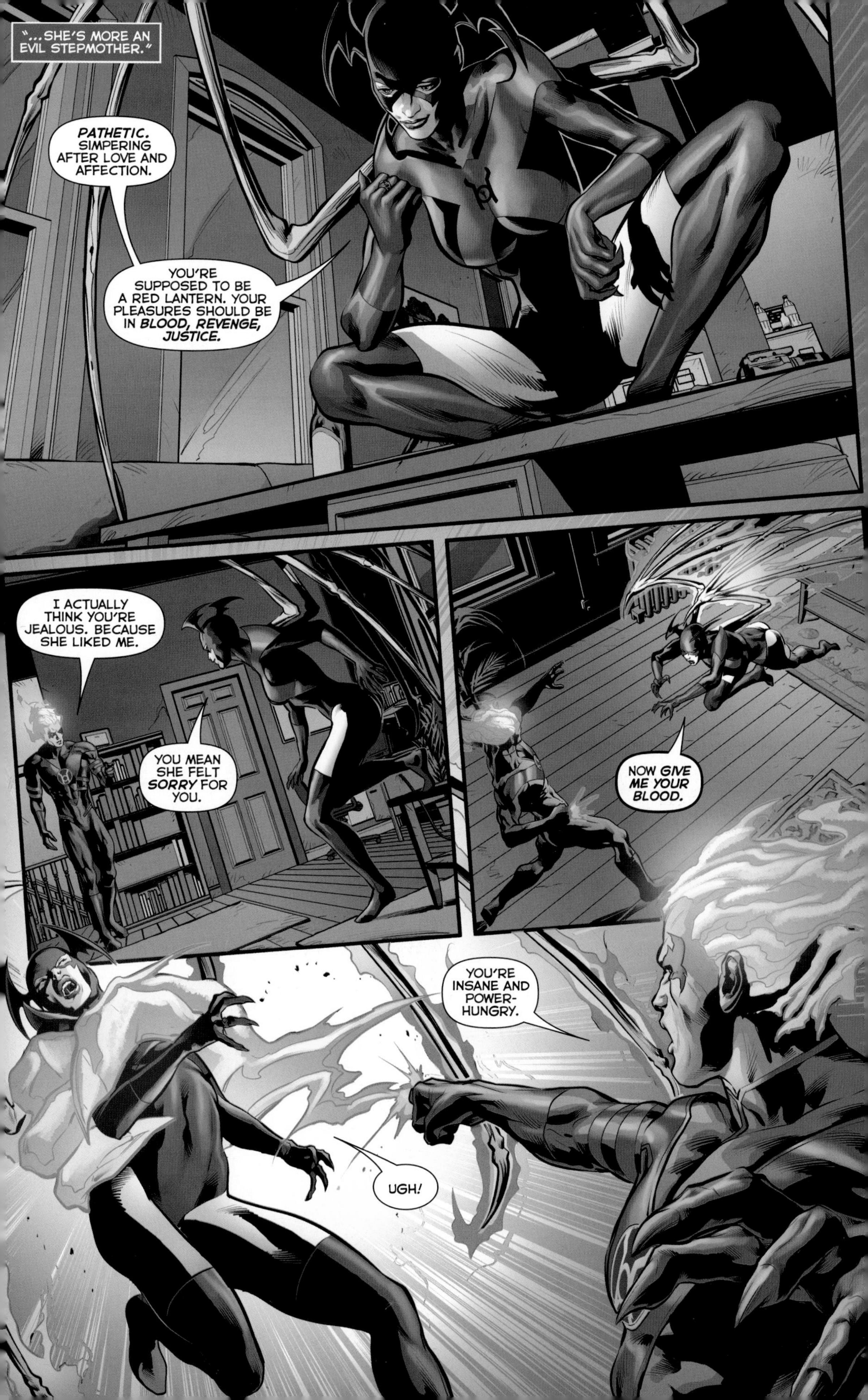
"...SHE'S MORE AN EVIL STEPMOTHER."
PATHETIC. SIMPERING AFTER LOVE AND AFFECTION.
YOU'RE SUPPOSED TO BE A RED LANTERN. YOUR PLEASURES SHOULD BE IN BLOOD, REVENGE, JUSTICE.
I ACTUALLY THINK YOU'RE JEALOUS. BECAUSE SHE LIKED ME.
YOU MEAN SHE FELT SORRY FOR YOU.
NOW GIVE ME YOUR BLOOD.
YOU'RE INSANE AND POWER-HUNGRY.
UGH!

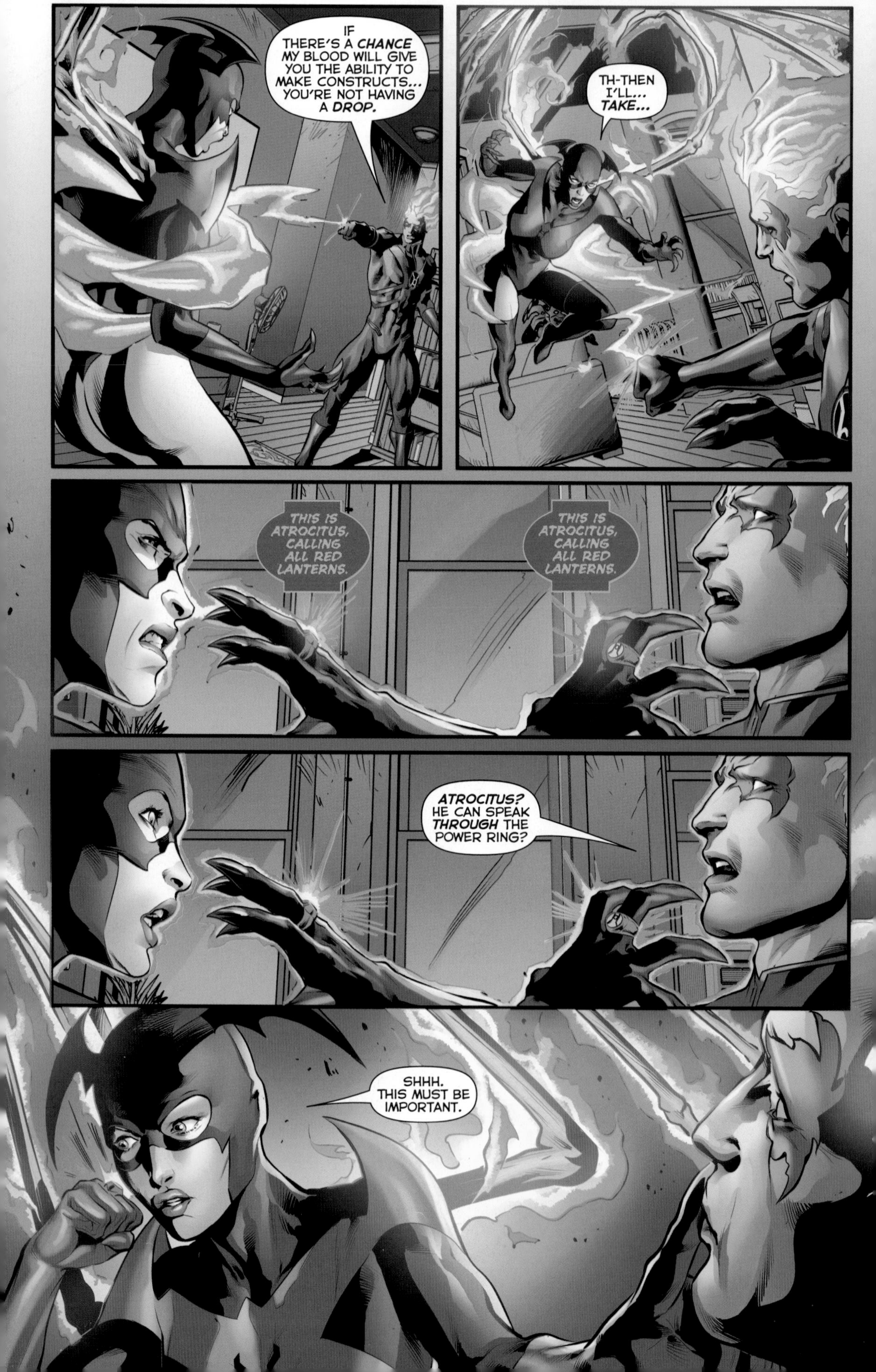
IF THERE'S A *CHANCE* MY BLOOD WILL GIVE YOU THE ABILITY TO MAKE CONSTRUCTS... YOU'RE NOT HAVING A *DROP*.
TH-THEN I'LL... *TAKE*...
THIS IS ATROCITUS, CALLING ALL RED LANTERNS.
THIS IS ATROCITUS, CALLING ALL RED LANTERNS.
ATROCITUS? HE CAN SPEAK *THROUGH* THE POWER RING?
SHHH. THIS MUST BE IMPORTANT.

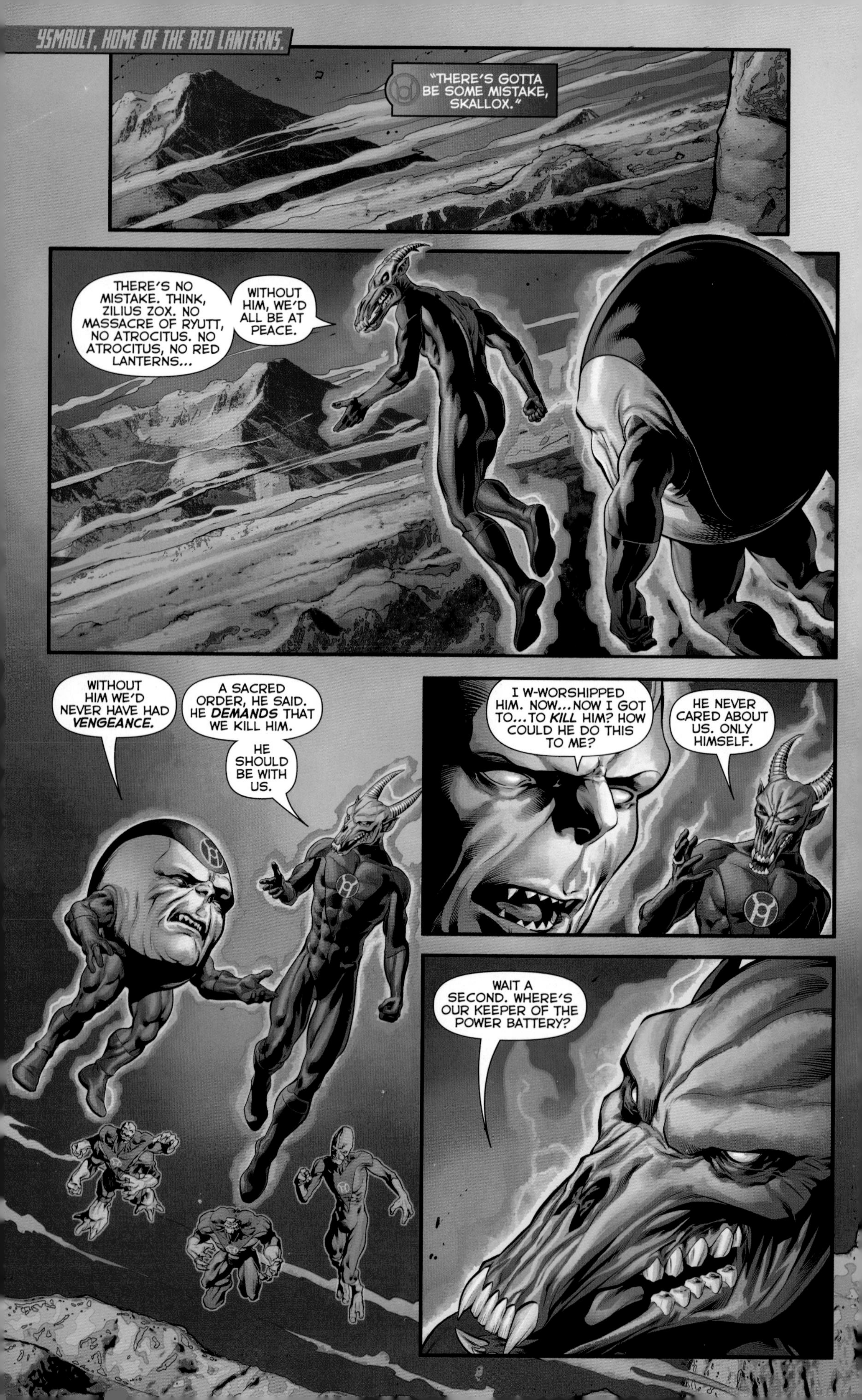

YSMAULT, HOME OF THE RED LANTERNS.
"THERE'S GOTTA BE SOME MISTAKE, SKALLOX."
THERE'S NO MISTAKE. THINK, ZILIUS ZOX. NO MASSACRE OF RYUTT, NO ATROCITUS. NO ATROCITUS, NO RED LANTERNS...
WITHOUT HIM, WE'D ALL BE AT PEACE.
WITHOUT HIM WE'D NEVER HAVE HAD VENGEANCE.
A SACRED ORDER, HE SAID. HE DEMANDS THAT WE KILL HIM.
HE SHOULD BE WITH US.
I W-WORSHIPPED HIM. NOW...NOW I GOT TO...TO KILL HIM? HOW COULD HE DO THIS TO ME?
HE NEVER CARED ABOUT US. ONLY HIMSELF.
WAIT A SECOND. WHERE'S OUR KEEPER OF THE POWER BATTERY?

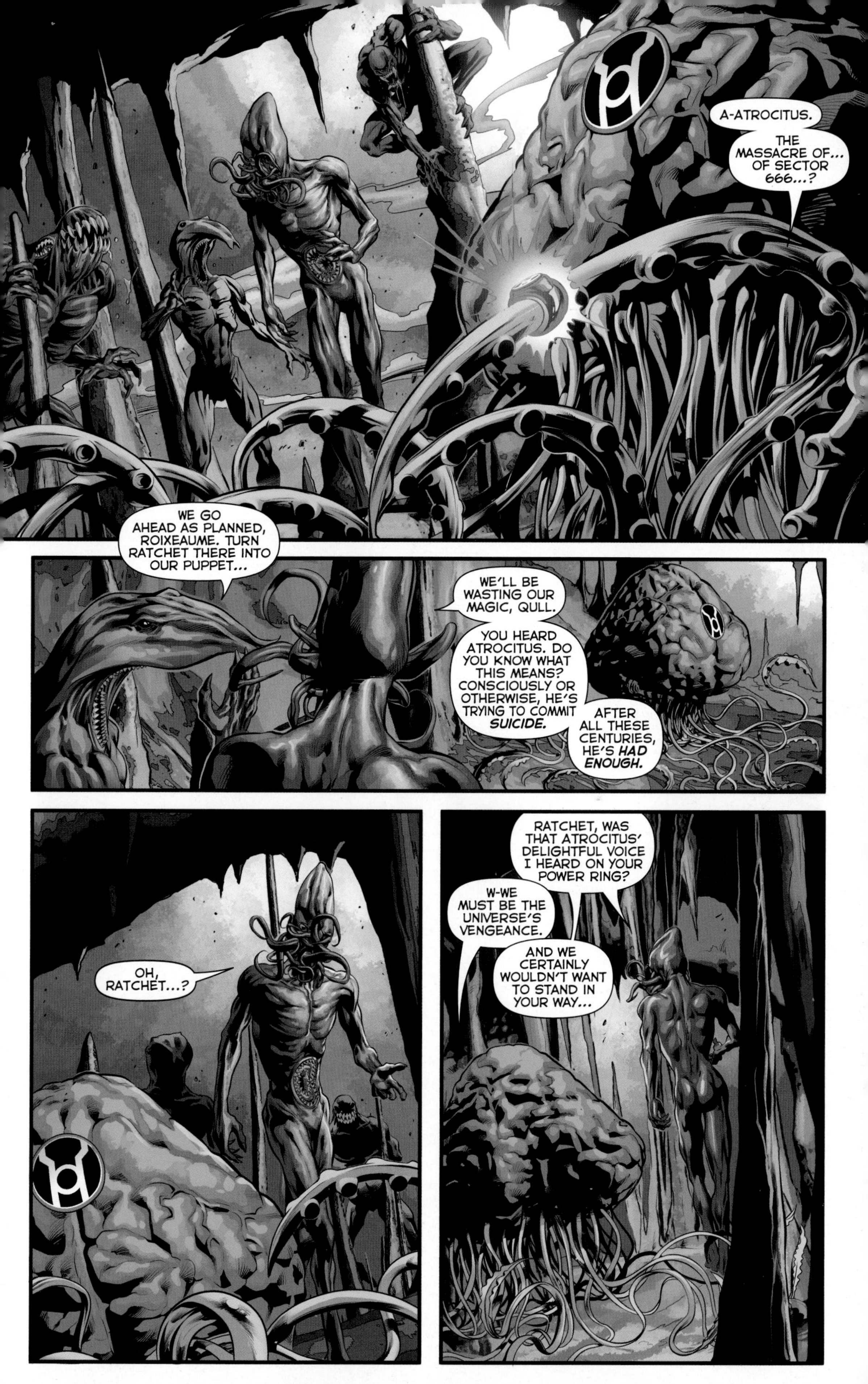
A-ATROCITUS.
THE MASSACRE OF... OF SECTOR 666...?
WE GO AHEAD AS PLANNED, ROIXEAUME. TURN RATCHET THERE INTO OUR PUPPET...
WE'LL BE WASTING OUR MAGIC, QULL.
YOU HEARD ATROCITUS. DO YOU KNOW WHAT THIS MEANS? CONSCIOUSLY OR OTHERWISE, HE'S TRYING TO COMMIT SUICIDE.
AFTER ALL THESE CENTURIES, HE'S HAD ENOUGH.
OH, RATCHET...?
RATCHET, WAS THAT ATROCITUS' DELIGHTFUL VOICE I HEARD ON YOUR POWER RING?
W-WE MUST BE THE UNIVERSE'S VENGEANCE.
AND WE CERTAINLY WOULDN'T WANT TO STAND IN YOUR WAY...

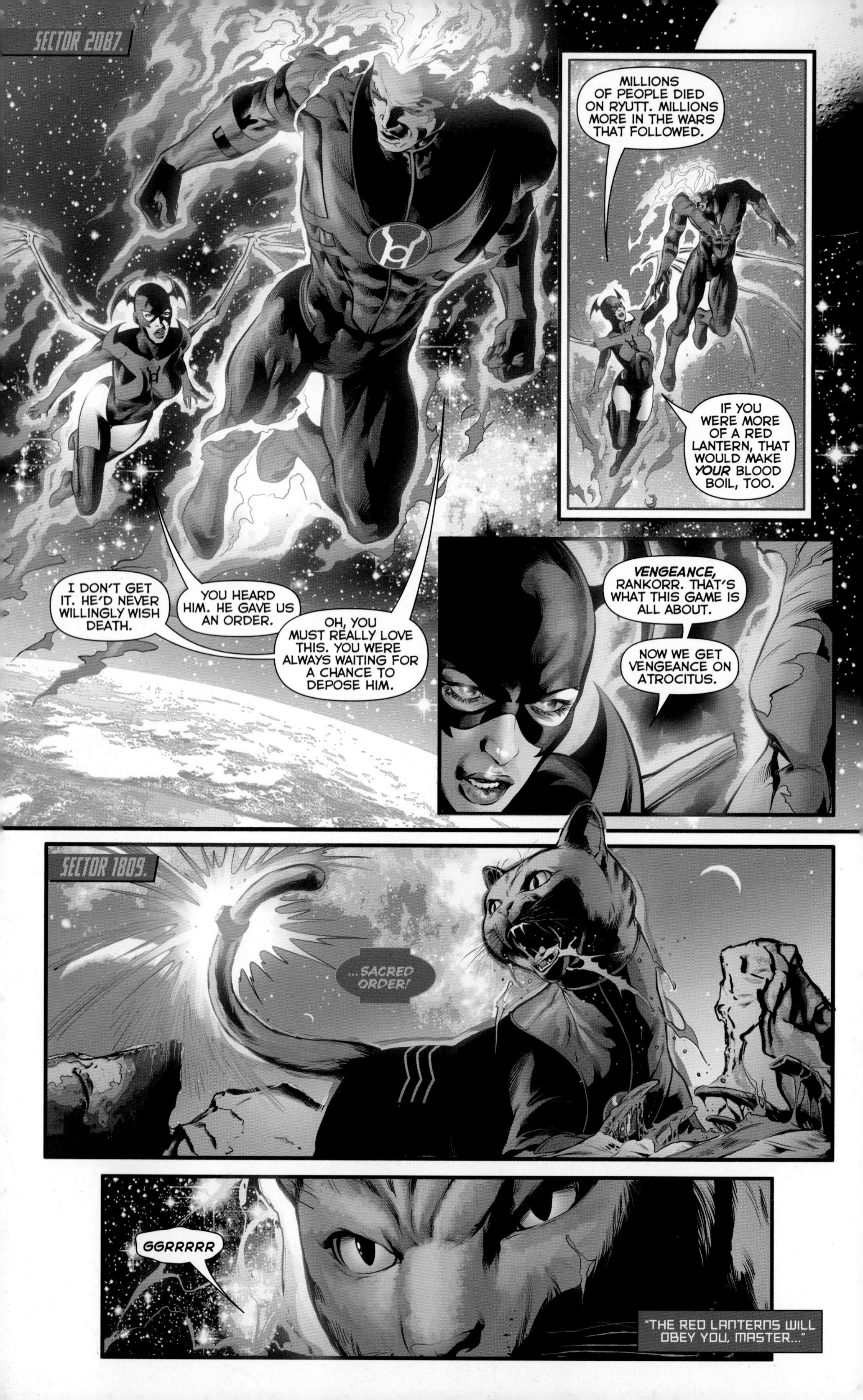
SECTOR 2087.
MILLIONS OF PEOPLE DIED ON RYUTT. MILLIONS MORE IN THE WARS THAT FOLLOWED.
IF YOU WERE MORE OF A RED LANTERN, THAT WOULD MAKE *YOUR* BLOOD BOIL, TOO.
I DON'T GET IT. HE'D NEVER WILLINGLY WISH DEATH.
YOU HEARD HIM. HE GAVE US AN ORDER.
OH, YOU MUST REALLY LOVE THIS. YOU WERE ALWAYS WAITING FOR A CHANCE TO DEPOSE HIM.
VENGEANCE, RANKORR. THAT'S WHAT THIS GAME IS ALL ABOUT.
NOW WE GET VENGEANCE ON ATROCITUS.
SECTOR 1809.
...SACRED ORDER!
GGRRRRR
"THE RED LANTERNS WILL OBEY YOU, MASTER..."

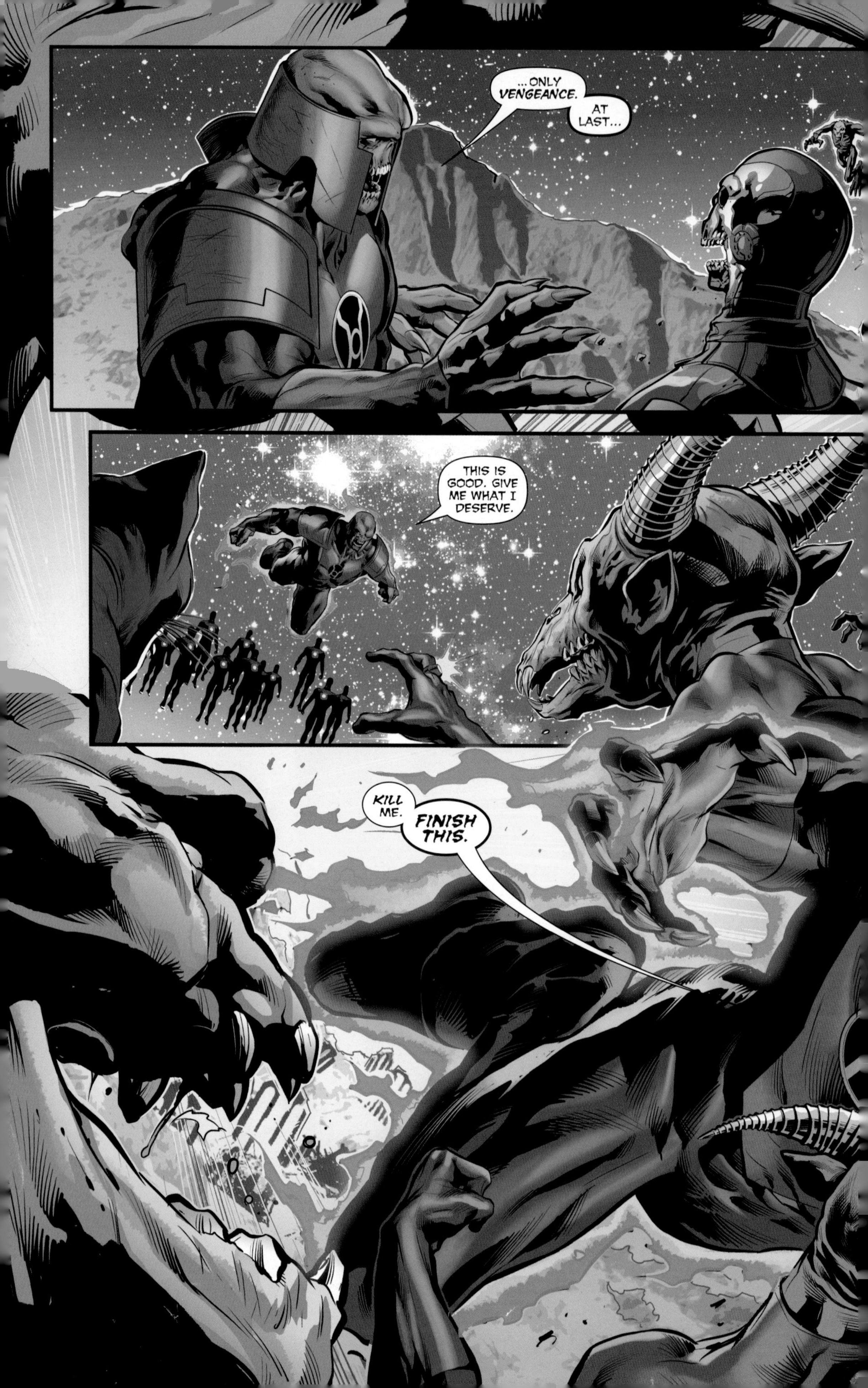
...ONLY VENGEANCE.
AT LAST...
THIS IS GOOD. GIVE ME WHAT I DESERVE.
KILL ME.
FINISH THIS.

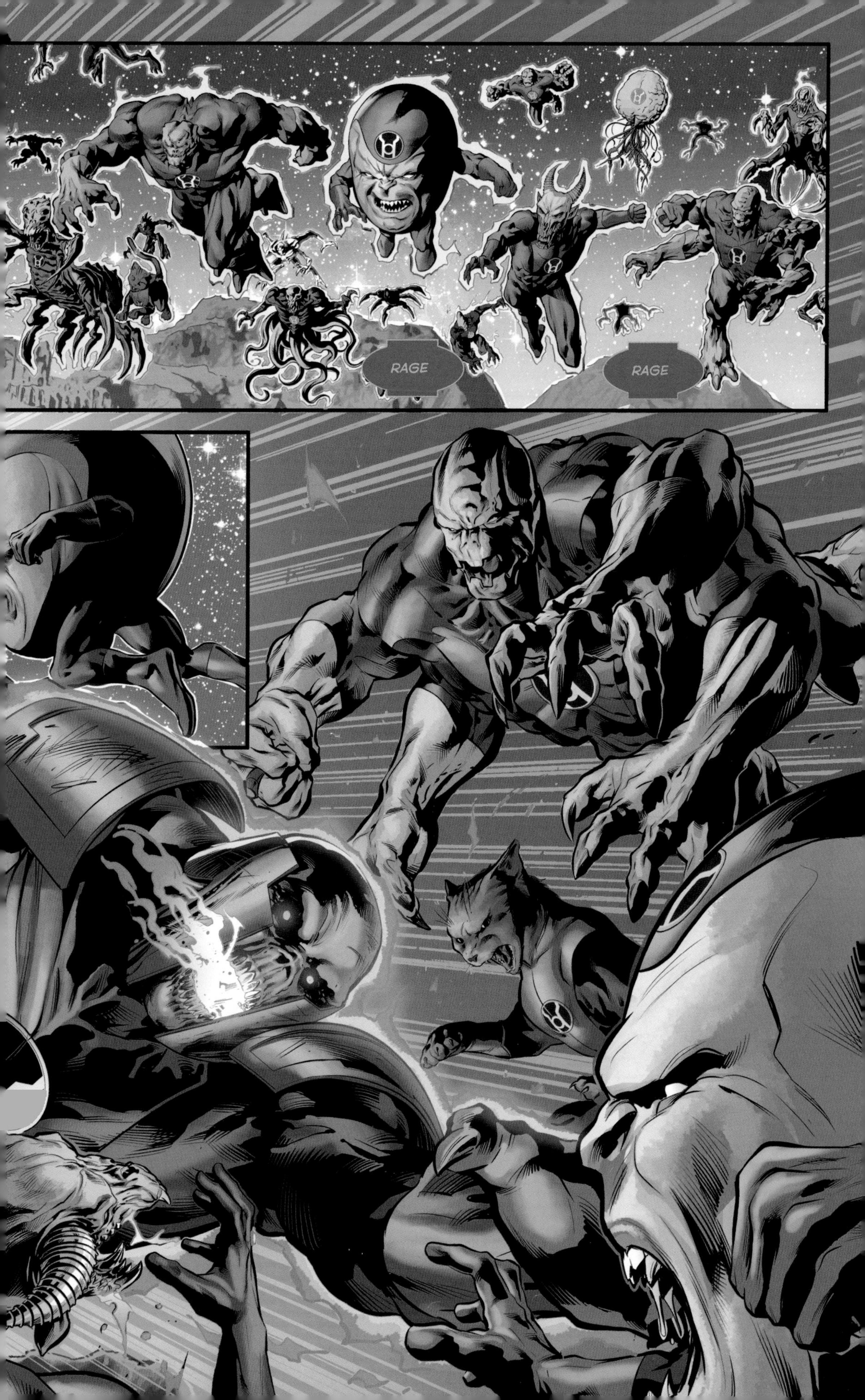
RAGE
RAGE

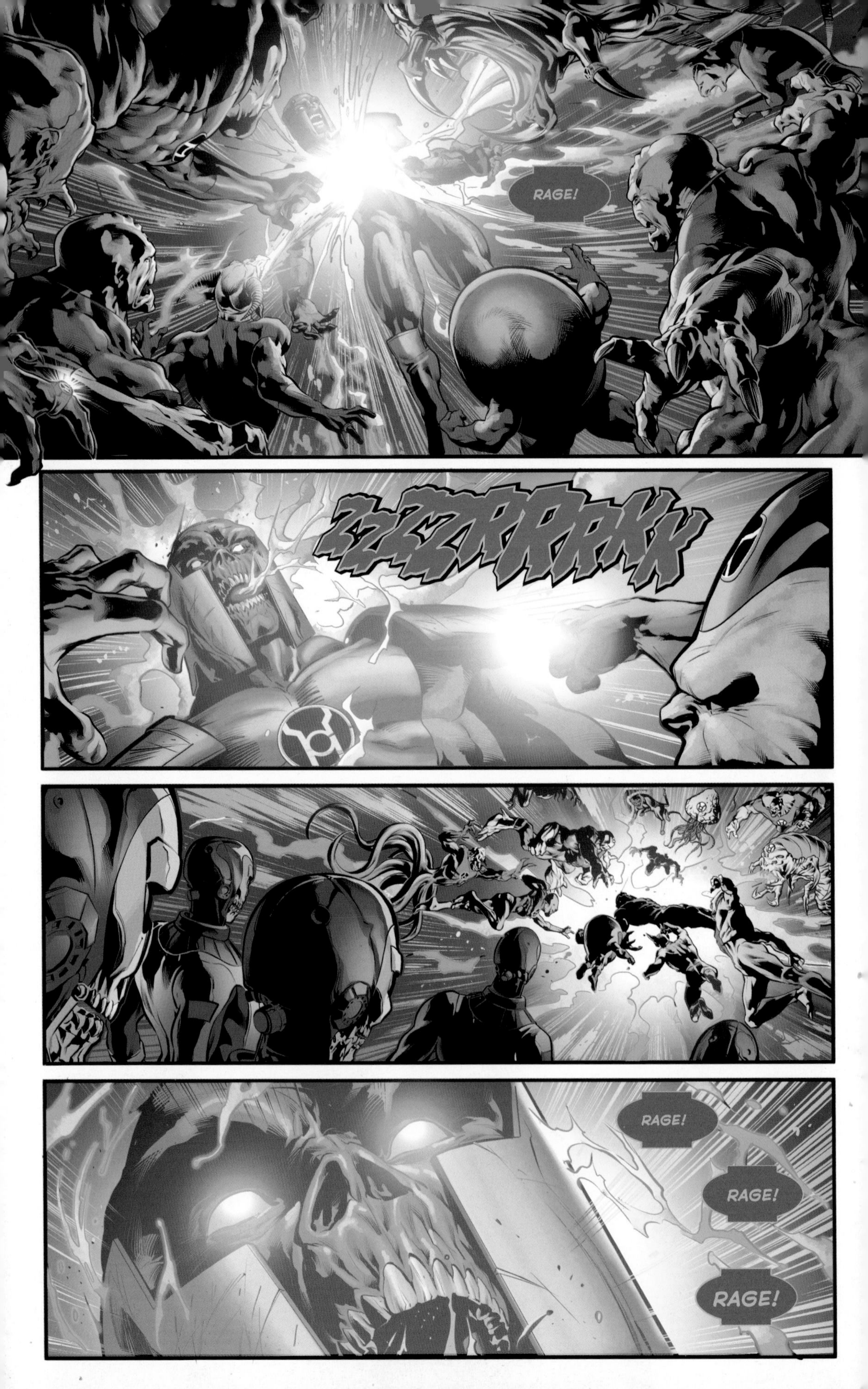
RAGE!
ZZZZRRRRKK
RAGE!
RAGE!
RAGE!

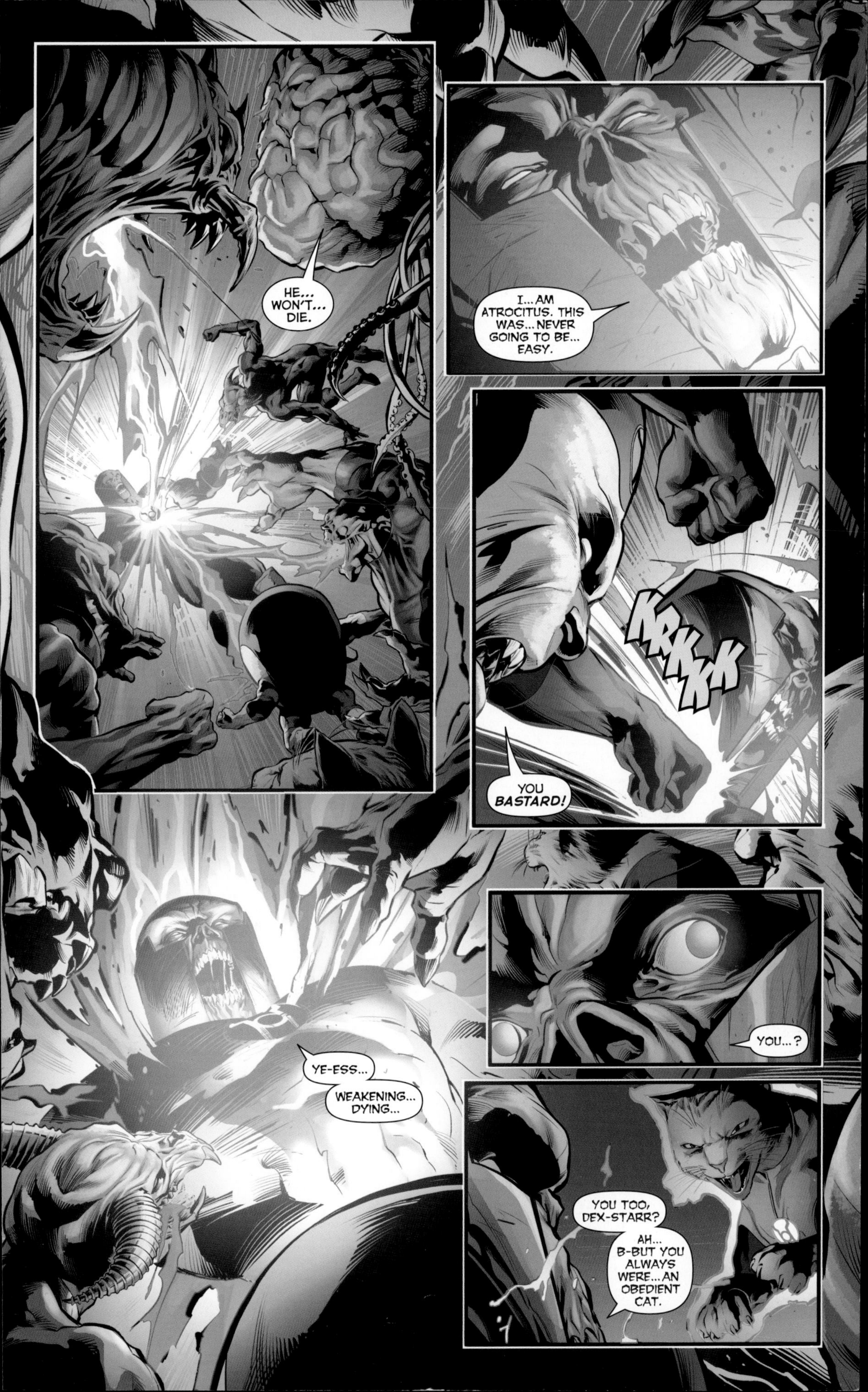
HE... WON'T... DIE.
I...AM ATROCITUS. THIS WAS...NEVER GOING TO BE... EASY.
KRKKKK
YOU BASTARD!
YOU...?
YE-ESS...
WEAKENING... DYING...
YOU TOO, DEX-STARR?
AH... B-BUT YOU ALWAYS WERE...AN OBEDIENT CAT.

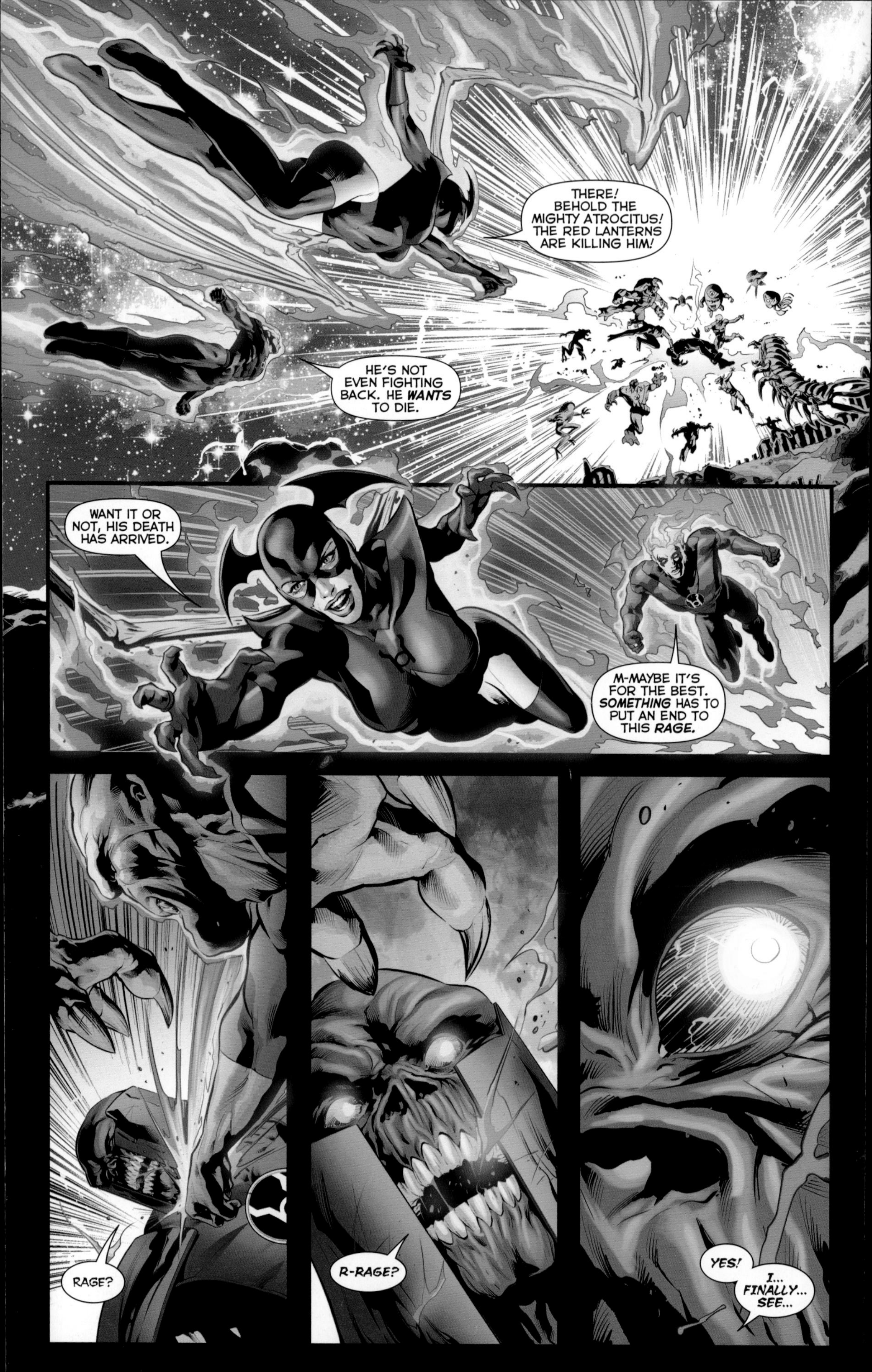
THERE! BEHOLD THE MIGHTY ATROCITUS! THE RED LANTERNS ARE KILLING HIM!
HE'S NOT EVEN FIGHTING BACK. HE *WANTS* TO DIE.
WANT IT OR NOT, HIS DEATH HAS ARRIVED.
M-MAYBE IT'S FOR THE BEST. *SOMETHING* HAS TO PUT AN END TO THIS *RAGE.*
RAGE?
R-RAGE?
YES!
I... FINALLY... SEE...

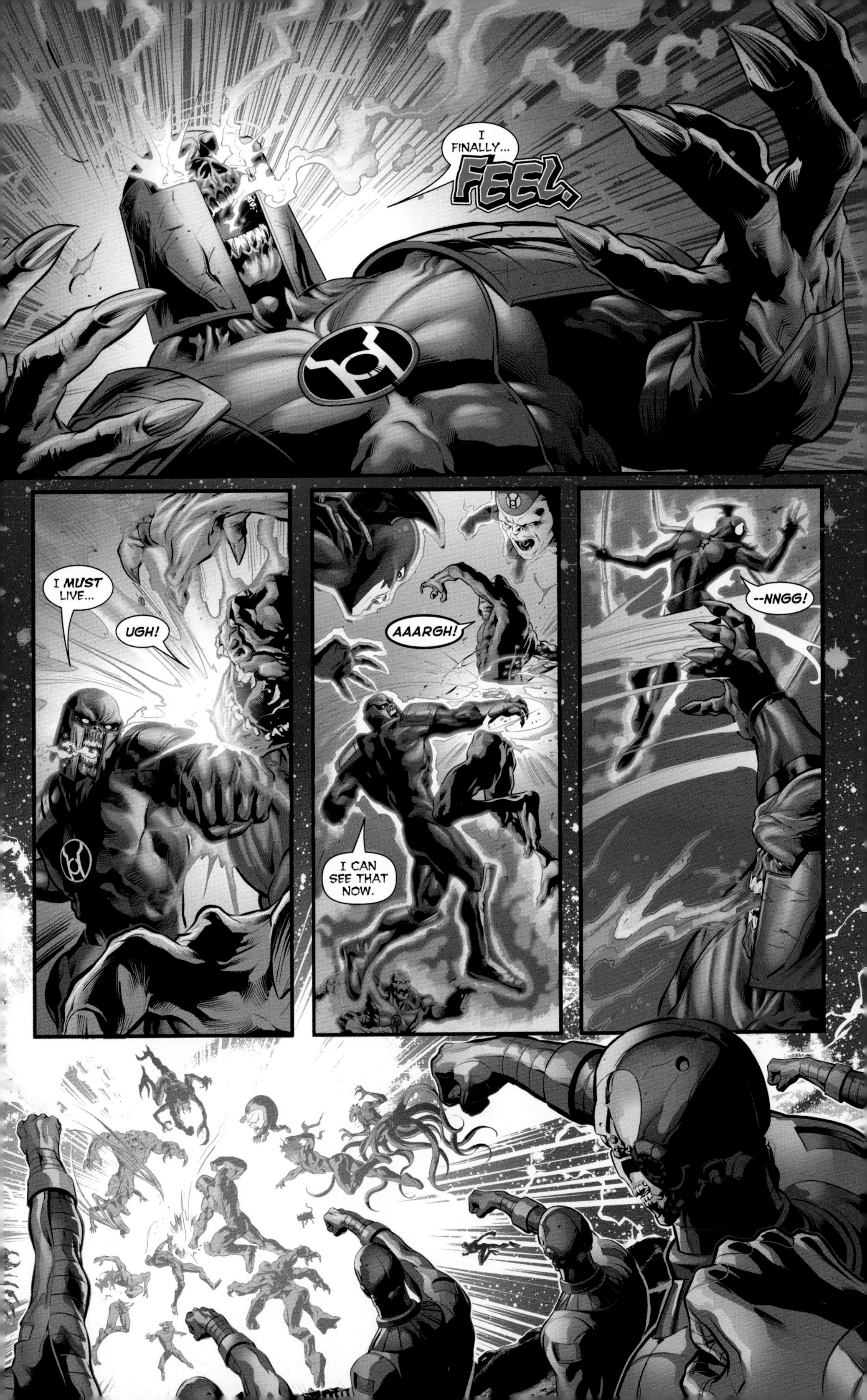
I FINALLY...
FEEL.
I MUST LIVE...
UGH!
AAARGH!
I CAN SEE THAT NOW.
--NNGG!

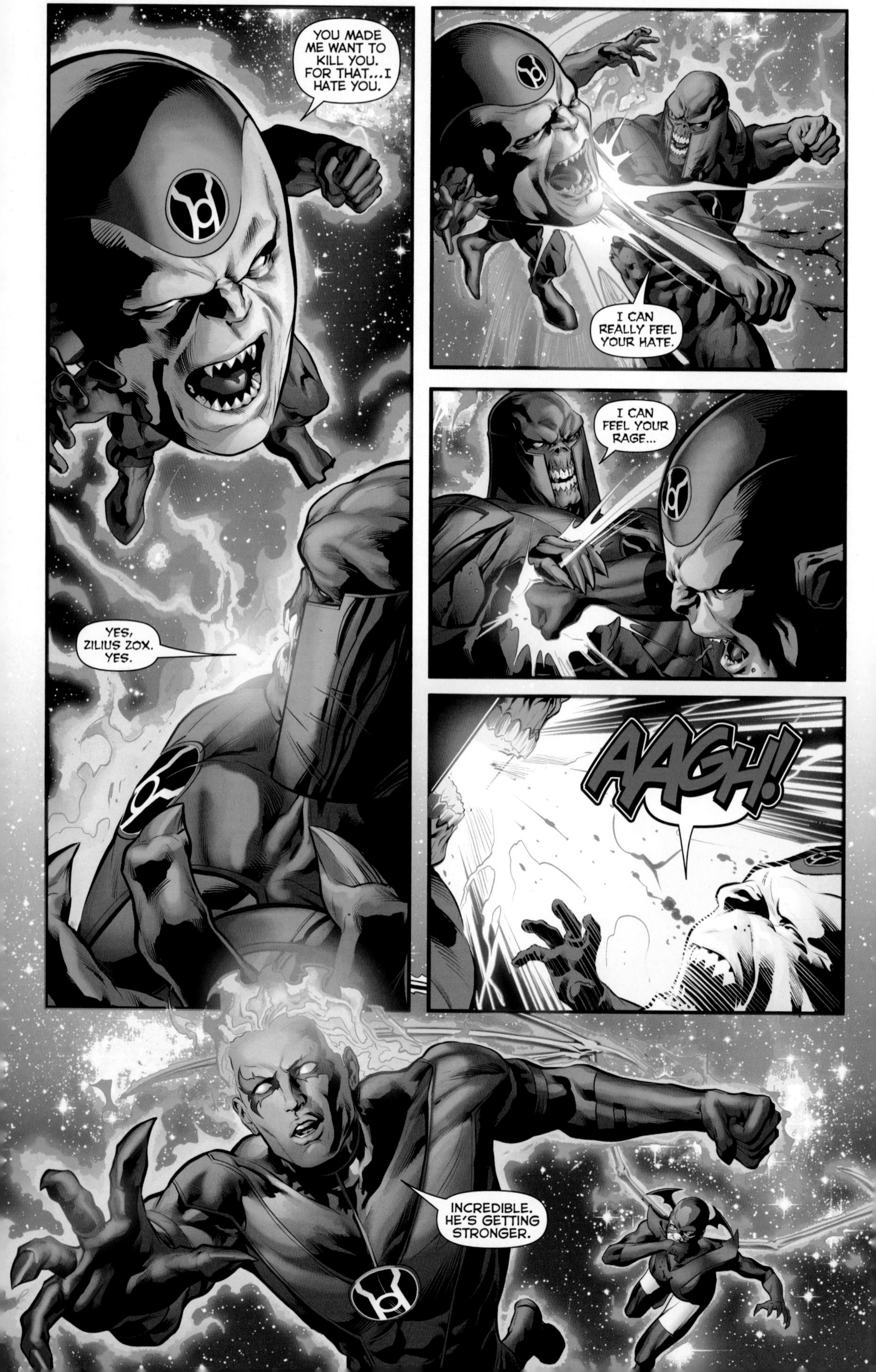
YOU MADE ME WANT TO KILL YOU. FOR THAT...I HATE YOU.
I CAN REALLY FEEL YOUR HATE.
I CAN FEEL YOUR RAGE...
YES, ZILIUS ZOX. YES.
AAGH!
INCREDIBLE. HE'S GETTING STRONGER.

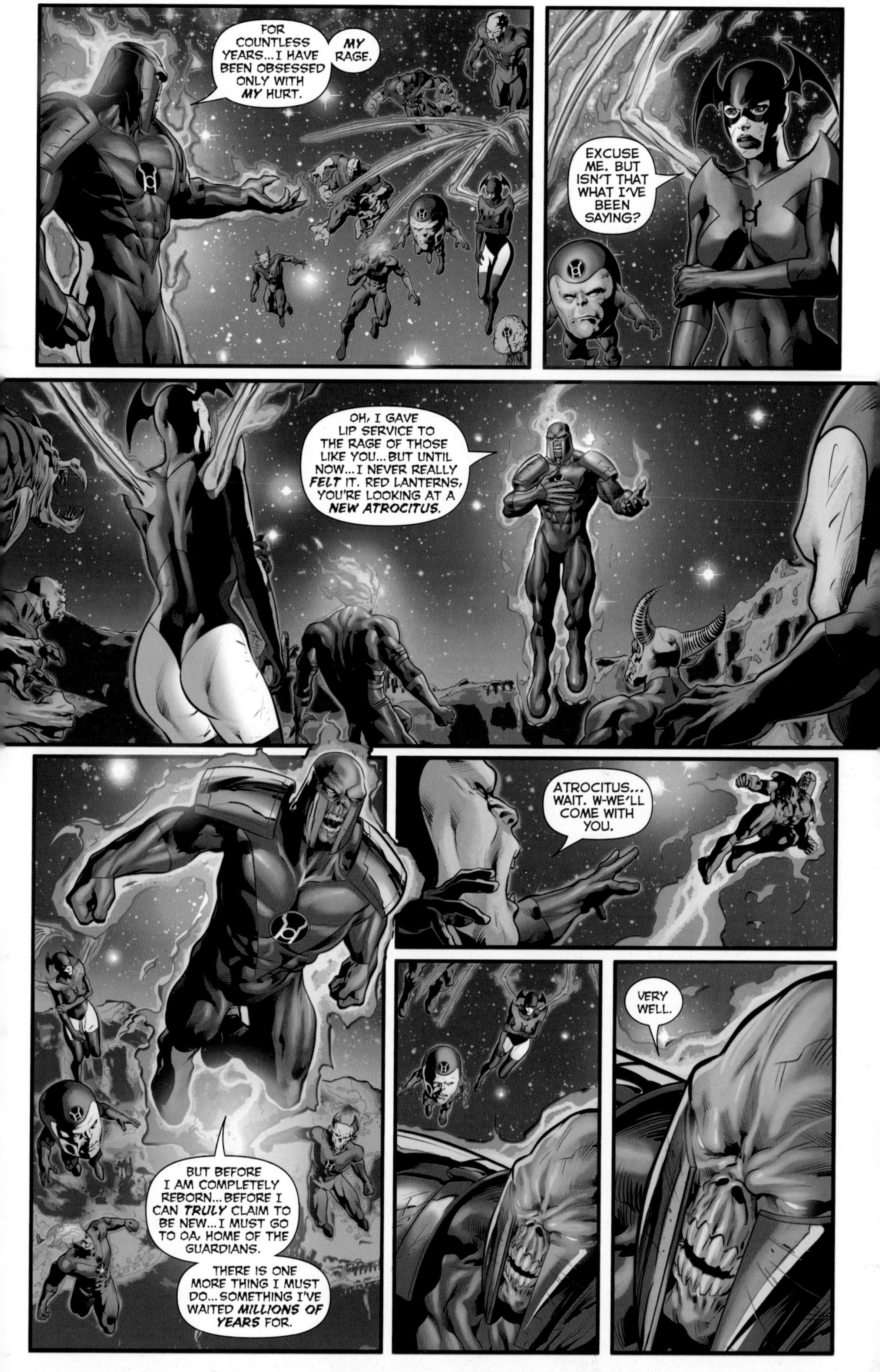

FOR COUNTLESS YEARS... I HAVE BEEN OBSESSED ONLY WITH MY HURT.
MY RAGE.
EXCUSE ME. BUT ISN'T THAT WHAT I'VE BEEN SAYING?
OH, I GAVE LIP SERVICE TO THE RAGE OF THOSE LIKE YOU... BUT UNTIL NOW... I NEVER REALLY FELT IT. RED LANTERNS, YOU'RE LOOKING AT A NEW ATROCITUS.
BUT BEFORE I AM COMPLETELY REBORN... BEFORE I CAN TRULY CLAIM TO BE NEW... I MUST GO TO OA, HOME OF THE GUARDIANS.
THERE IS ONE MORE THING I MUST DO... SOMETHING I'VE WAITED MILLIONS OF YEARS FOR.
ATROCITUS... WAIT. W-WE'LL COME WITH YOU.
VERY WELL.

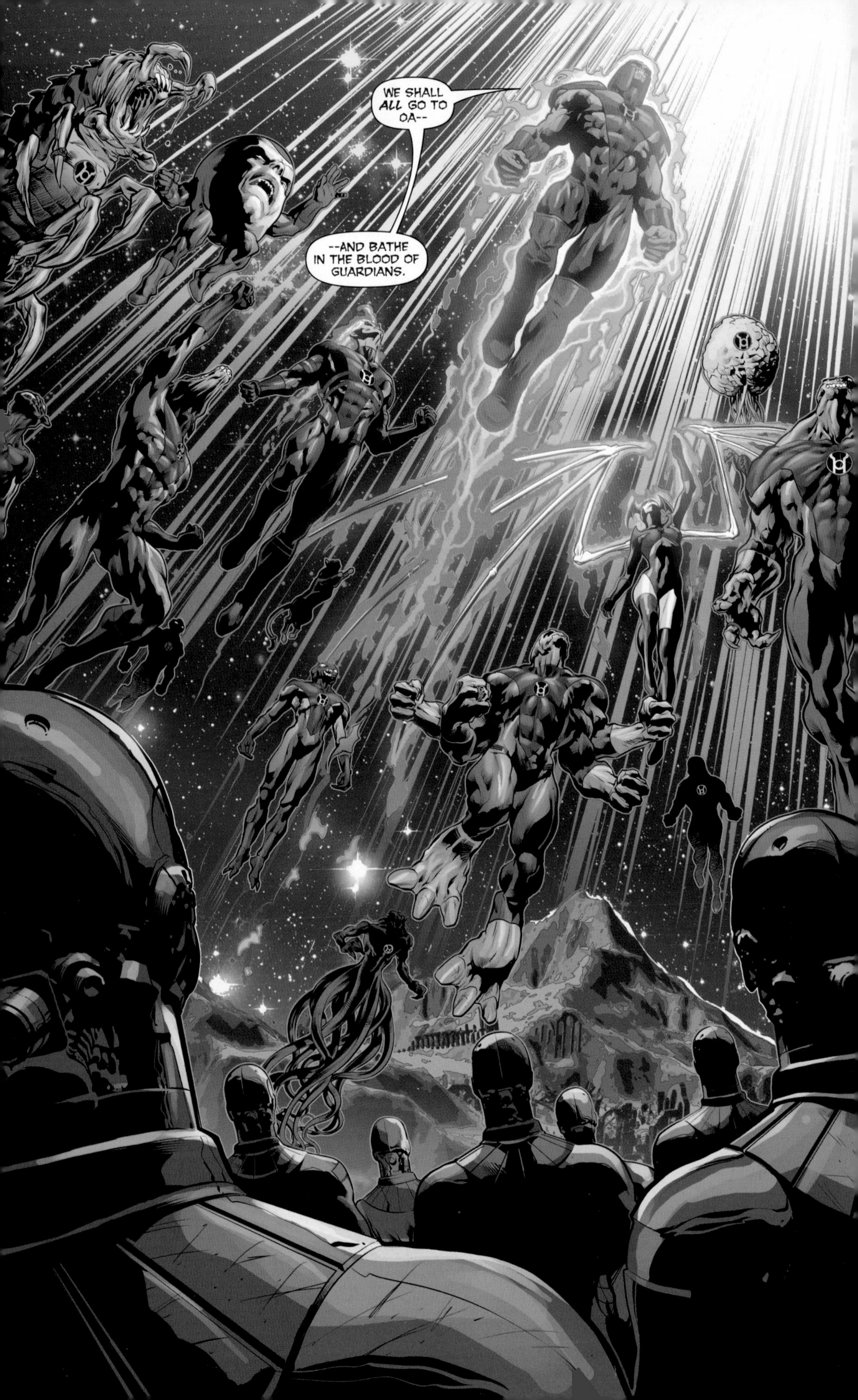
WE SHALL ALL GO TO OA--
--AND BATHE IN THE BLOOD OF GUARDIANS.

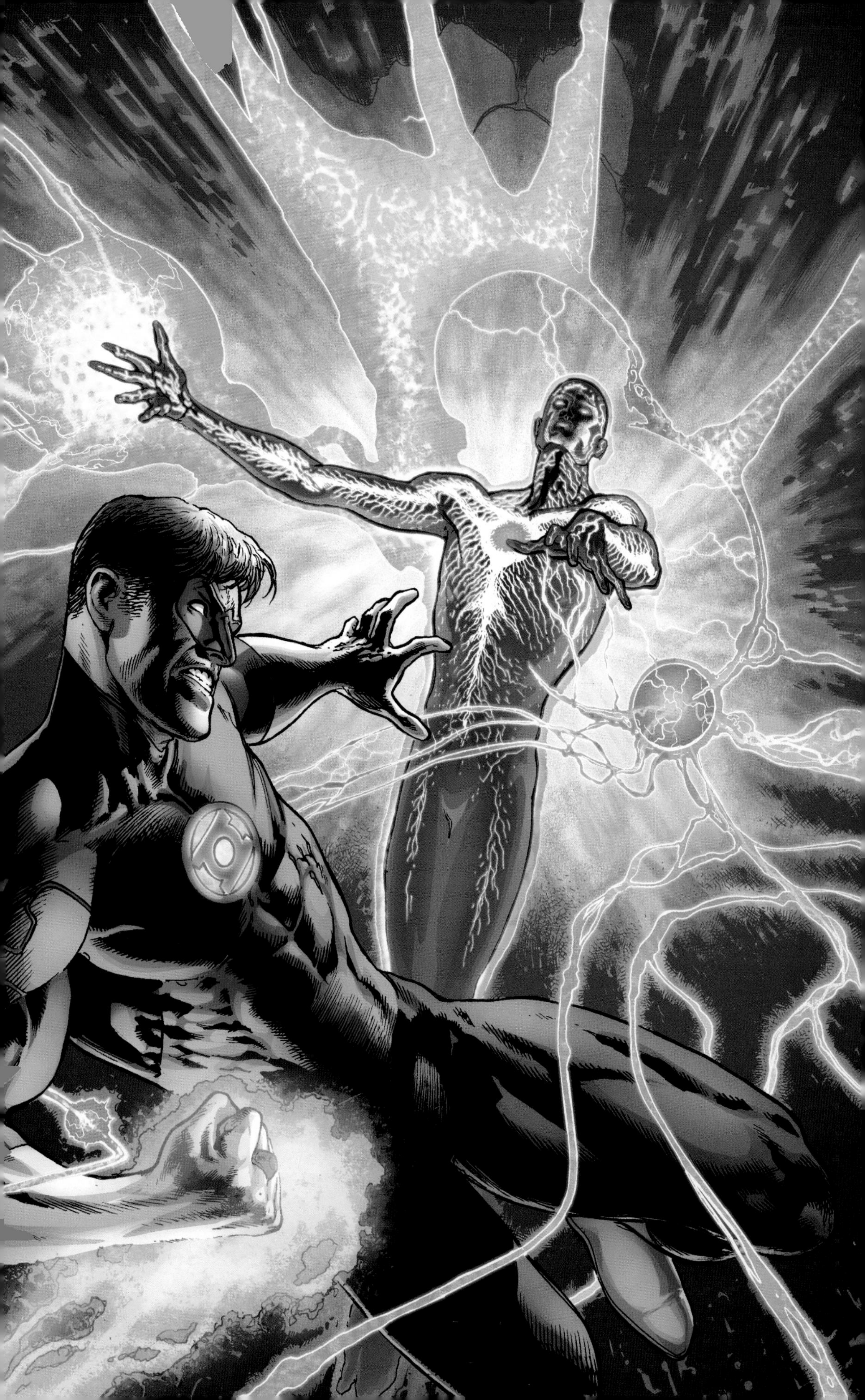

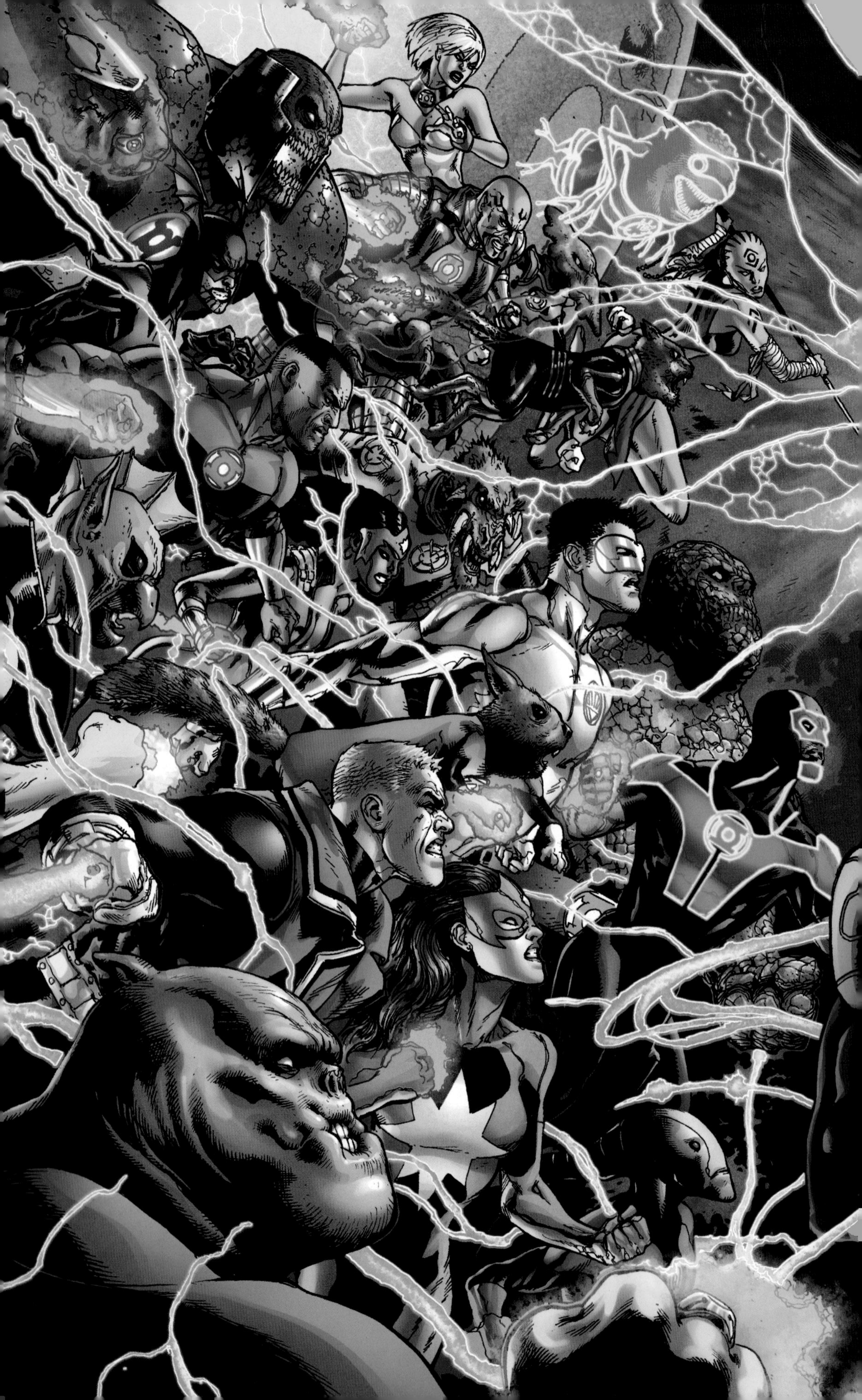

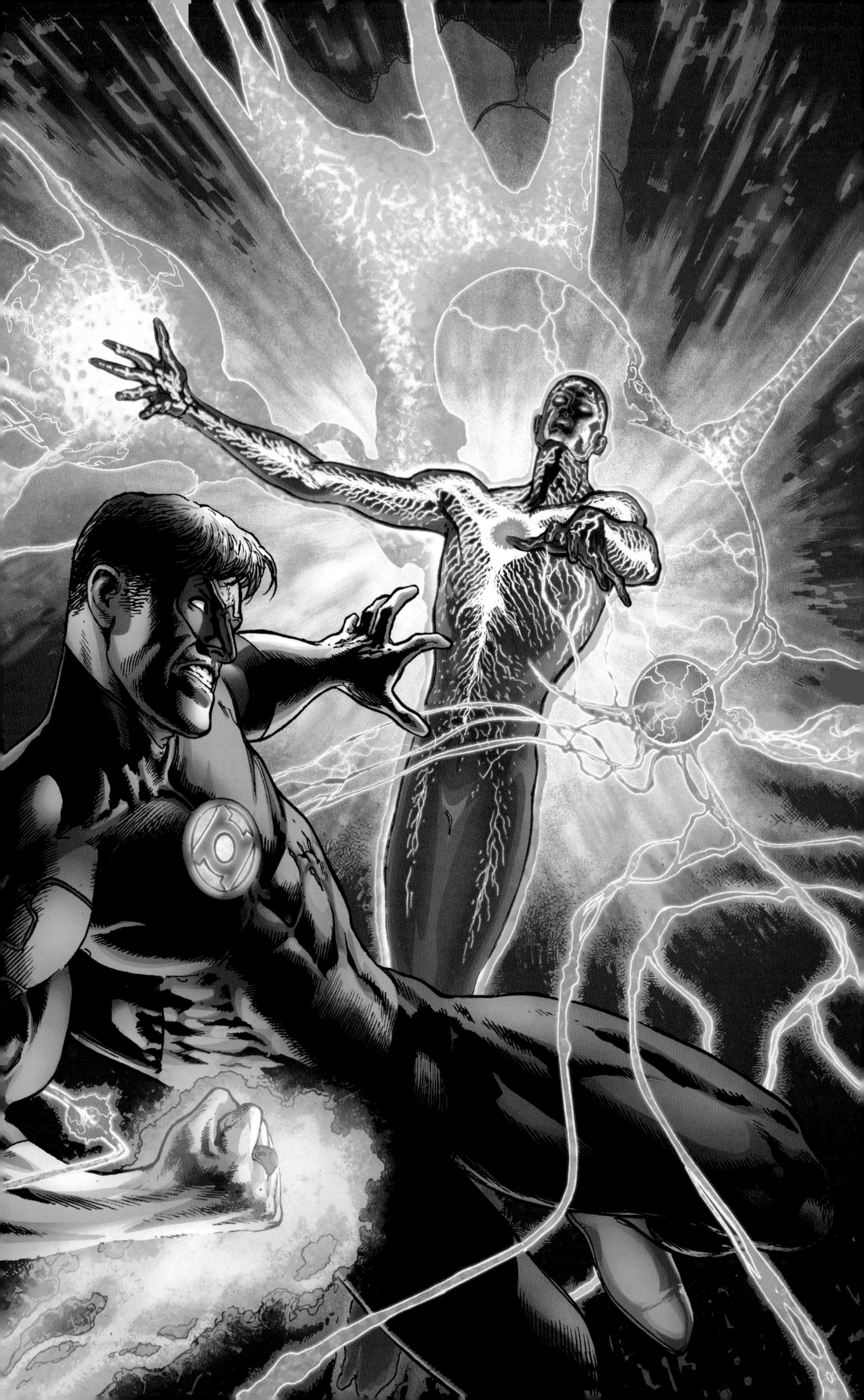

THE WRATH OF THE FIRST LANTERN FINALE: THE END

GEOFF JOHNS writer **DOUG MAHNKE, PATRICK GLEASON, CULLY HAMNER, AARON KUDER, JERRY ORDWAY, ETHAN VAN SCIVER, IVAN REIS** with **OCLAIR ALBERT** & **JOE PRADO** pencillers **CHRISTIAN ALAMY, KEITH CHAMPAGNE, MARC DEERING, MARK IRWIN, WADE VON GRAWBADGER, TOM NGUYEN** & **DOUG MAHNKE** inkers cover art by **DOUG MAHNKE** with **ALEX SINCLAIR**

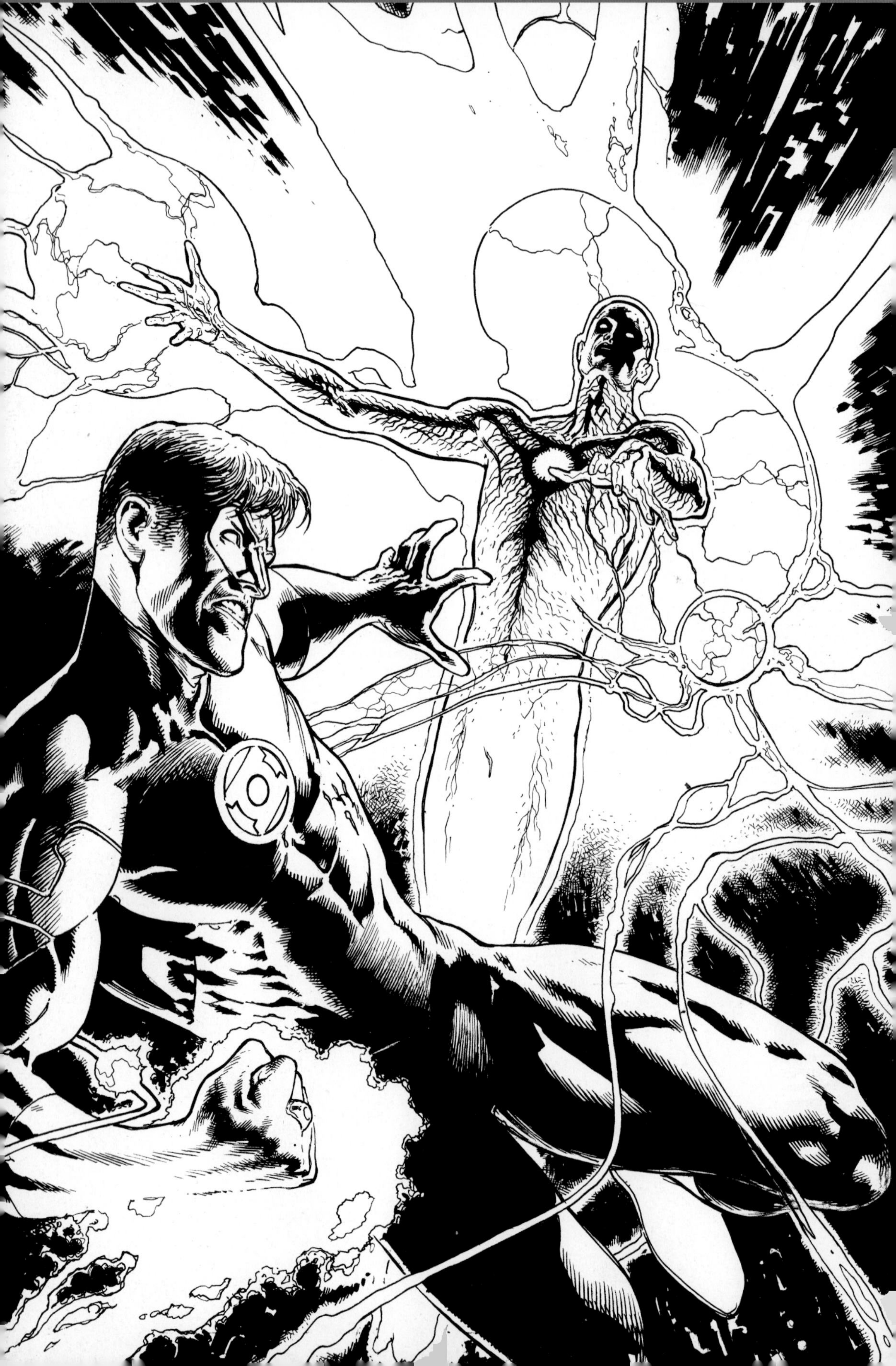

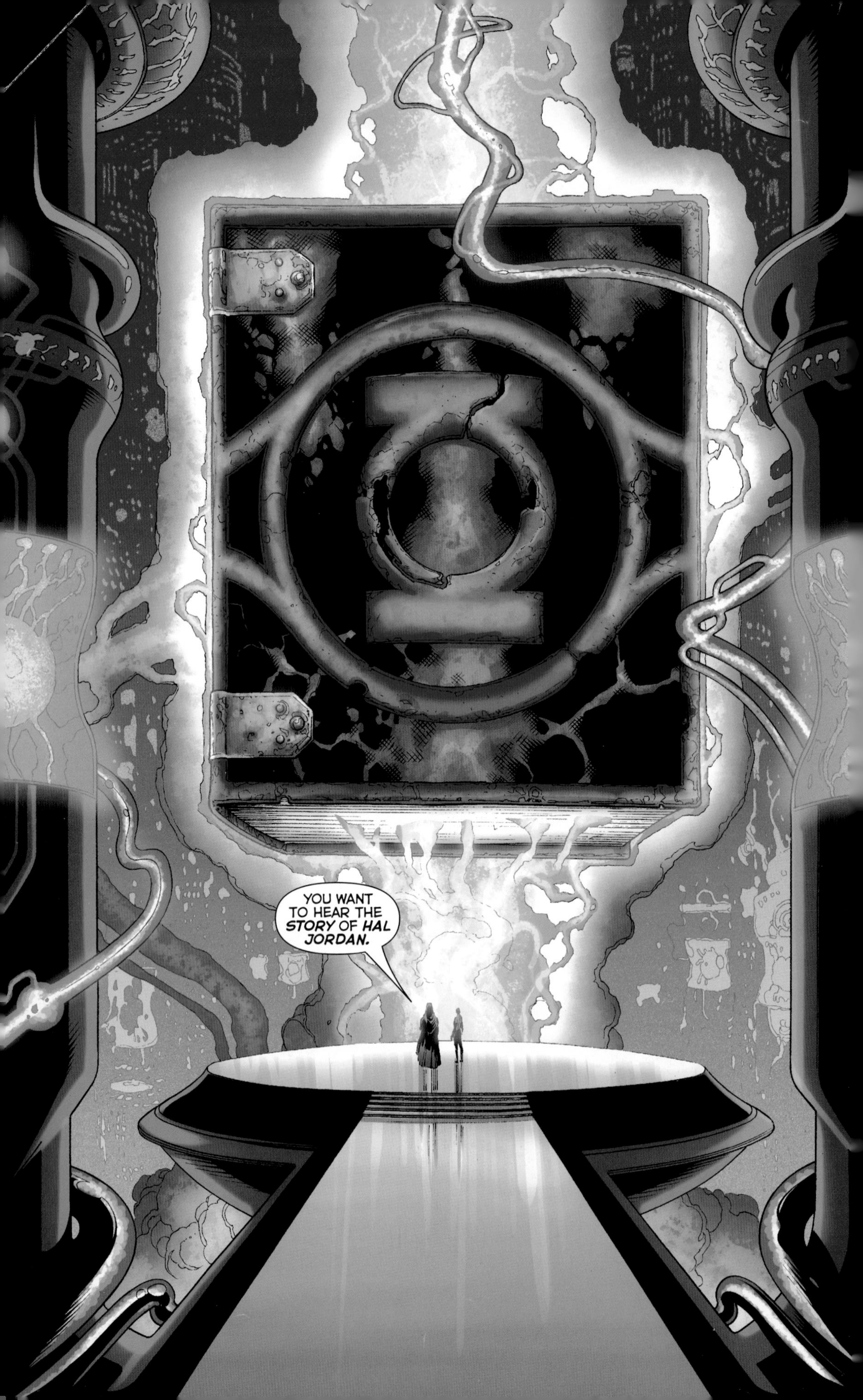
YOU WANT TO HEAR THE STORY OF HAL JORDAN.

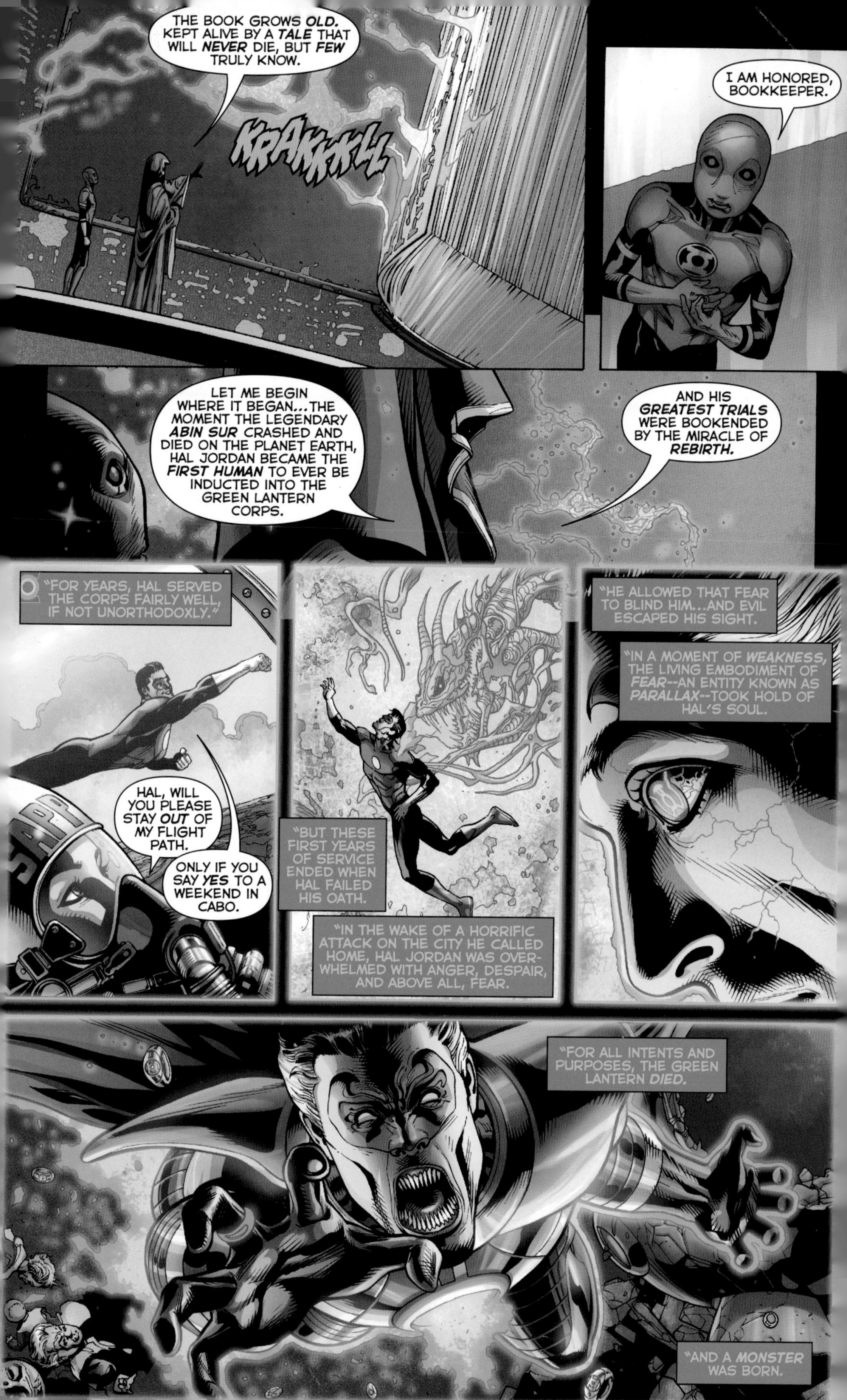
THE BOOK GROWS OLD. KEPT ALIVE BY A TALE THAT WILL NEVER DIE, BUT FEW TRULY KNOW.
KRAKKKLL
I AM HONORED, BOOKKEEPER.
LET ME BEGIN WHERE IT BEGAN... THE MOMENT THE LEGENDARY ABIN SUR CRASHED AND DIED ON THE PLANET EARTH, HAL JORDAN BECAME THE FIRST HUMAN TO EVER BE INDUCTED INTO THE GREEN LANTERN CORPS.
AND HIS GREATEST TRIALS WERE BOOKENDED BY THE MIRACLE OF REBIRTH.
"FOR YEARS, HAL SERVED THE CORPS FAIRLY WELL, IF NOT UNORTHODOXLY."
HAL, WILL YOU PLEASE STAY OUT OF MY FLIGHT PATH.
ONLY IF YOU SAY YES TO A WEEKEND IN CABO.
"BUT THESE FIRST YEARS OF SERVICE ENDED WHEN HAL FAILED HIS OATH.
"IN THE WAKE OF A HORRIFIC ATTACK ON THE CITY HE CALLED HOME, HAL JORDAN WAS OVER-WHELMED WITH ANGER, DESPAIR, AND ABOVE ALL, FEAR.
"HE ALLOWED THAT FEAR TO BLIND HIM...AND EVIL ESCAPED HIS SIGHT.
"IN A MOMENT OF WEAKNESS, THE LIVING EMBODIMENT OF FEAR--AN ENTITY KNOWN AS PARALLAX--TOOK HOLD OF HAL'S SOUL.
"FOR ALL INTENTS AND PURPOSES, THE GREEN LANTERN DIED.
"AND A MONSTER WAS BORN.

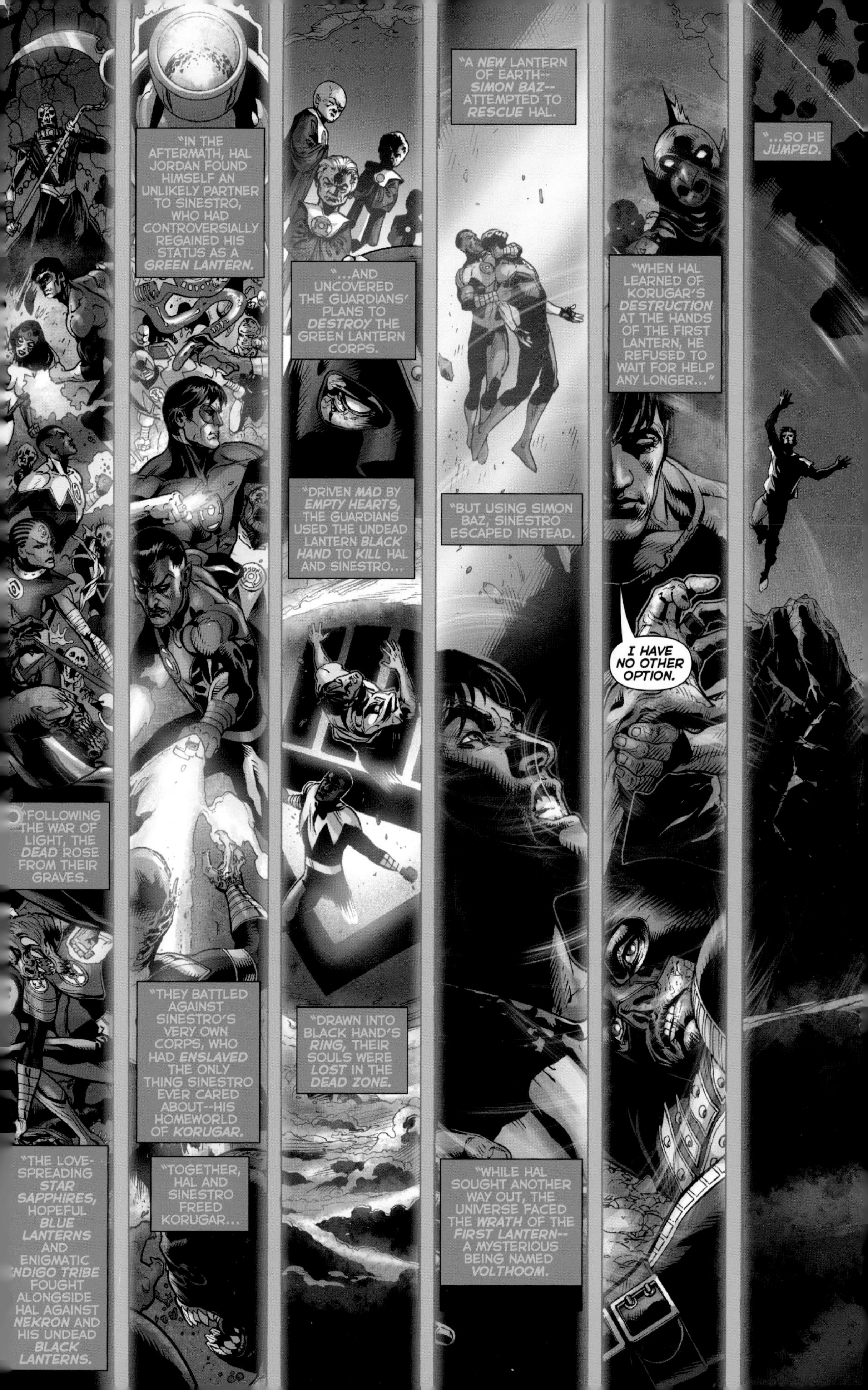
"FOLLOWING THE WAR OF LIGHT, THE DEAD ROSE FROM THEIR GRAVES.
"THE LOVE-SPREADING STAR SAPPHIRES, HOPEFUL BLUE LANTERNS AND ENIGMATIC INDIGO TRIBE FOUGHT ALONGSIDE HAL AGAINST NEKRON AND HIS UNDEAD BLACK LANTERNS.
"IN THE AFTERMATH, HAL JORDAN FOUND HIMSELF AN UNLIKELY PARTNER TO SINESTRO, WHO HAD CONTROVERSIALLY REGAINED HIS STATUS AS A GREEN LANTERN.
"THEY BATTLED AGAINST SINESTRO'S VERY OWN CORPS, WHO HAD ENSLAVED THE ONLY THING SINESTRO EVER CARED ABOUT--HIS HOMEWORLD OF KORUGAR.
"TOGETHER, HAL AND SINESTRO FREED KORUGAR...
"...AND UNCOVERED THE GUARDIANS' PLANS TO DESTROY THE GREEN LANTERN CORPS.
"DRIVEN MAD BY EMPTY HEARTS, THE GUARDIANS USED THE UNDEAD LANTERN BLACK HAND TO KILL HAL AND SINESTRO...
"DRAWN INTO BLACK HAND'S RING, THEIR SOULS WERE LOST IN THE DEAD ZONE.
"A NEW LANTERN OF EARTH--SIMON BAZ--ATTEMPTED TO RESCUE HAL.
"BUT USING SIMON BAZ, SINESTRO ESCAPED INSTEAD.
"WHILE HAL SOUGHT ANOTHER WAY OUT, THE UNIVERSE FACED THE WRATH OF THE FIRST LANTERN--A MYSTERIOUS BEING NAMED VOLTHOOM.
"WHEN HAL LEARNED OF KORUGAR'S DESTRUCTION AT THE HANDS OF THE FIRST LANTERN, HE REFUSED TO WAIT FOR HELP ANY LONGER..."
I HAVE NO OTHER OPTION.
"...SO HE JUMPED.

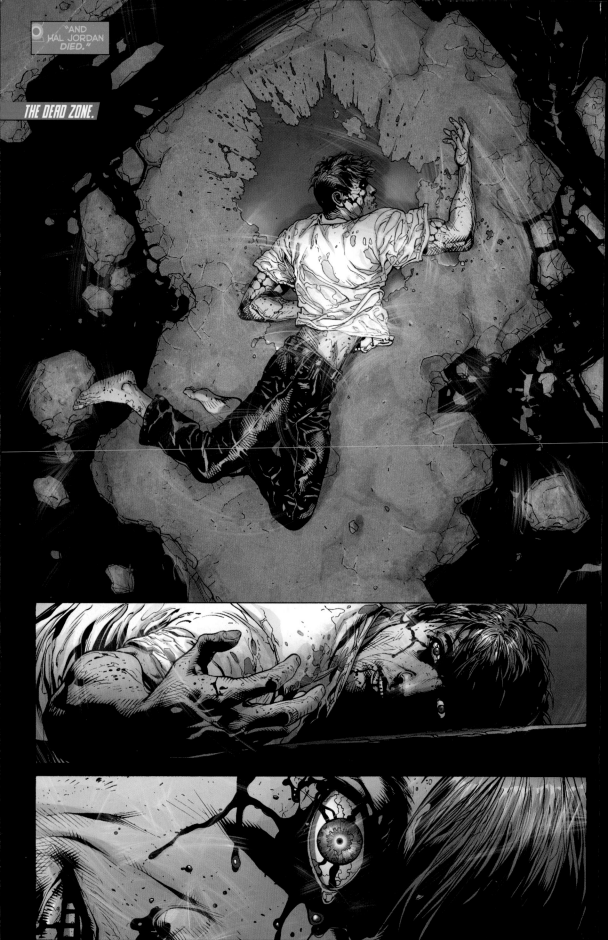

"AND
HAL JORDAN
DIED."

THE DEAD ZONE.

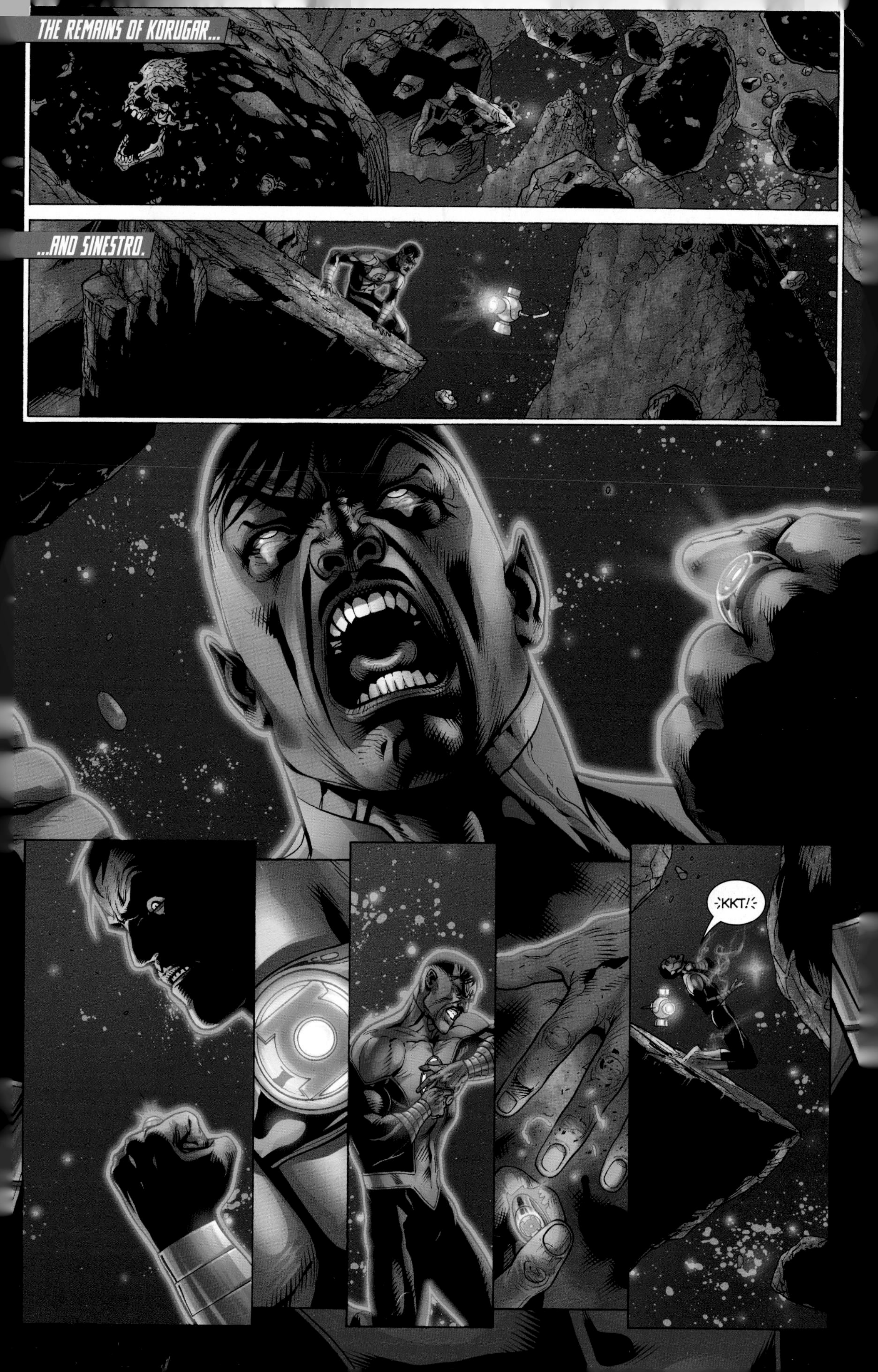
THE REMAINS OF KORUGAR...
...AND SINESTRO.
KKT!

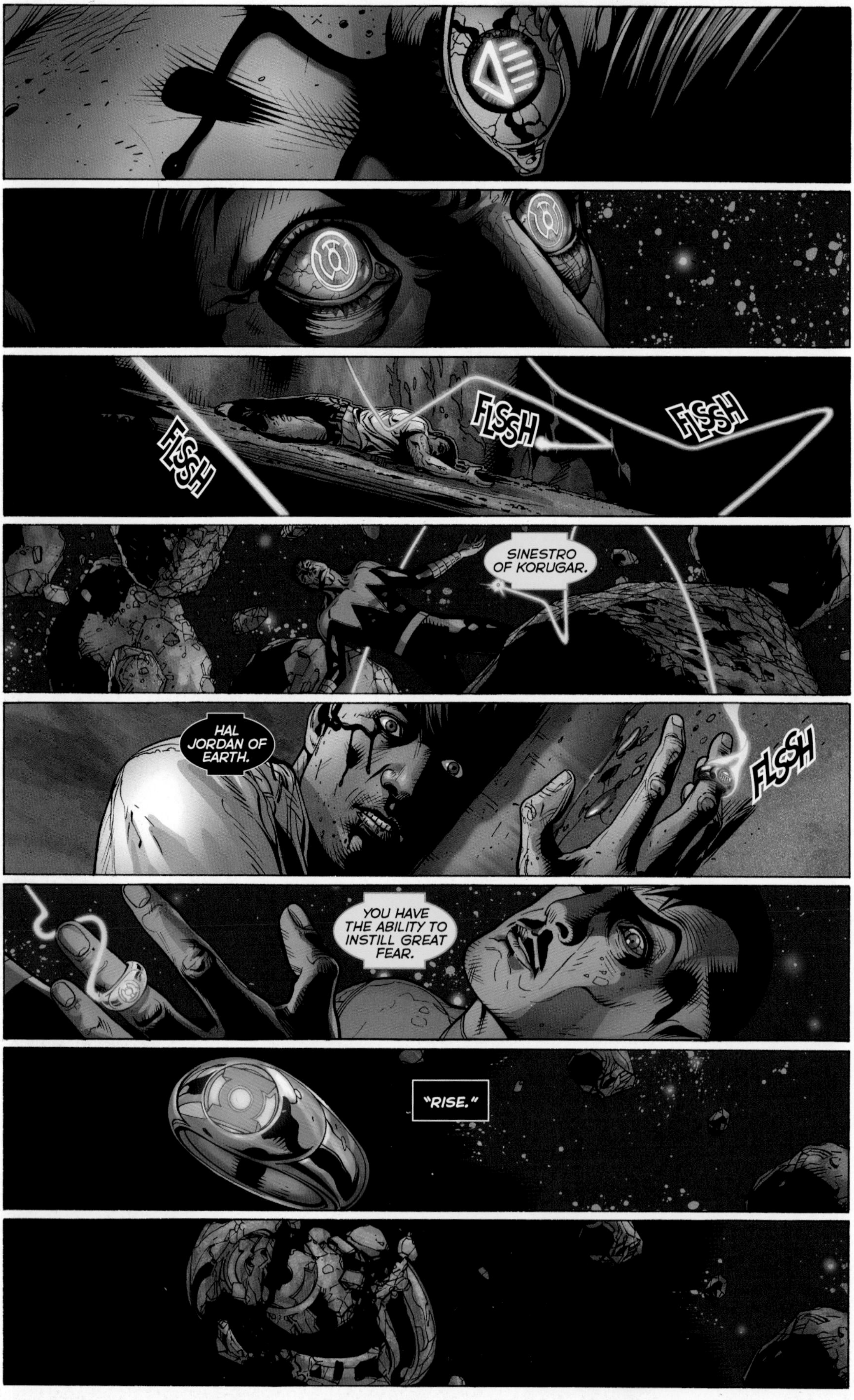

FLSSH
FLSSH
FLSSH
SINESTRO OF KORUGAR.
HAL JORDAN OF EARTH.
FLSSH
YOU HAVE THE ABILITY TO INSTILL GREAT FEAR.
"RISE."

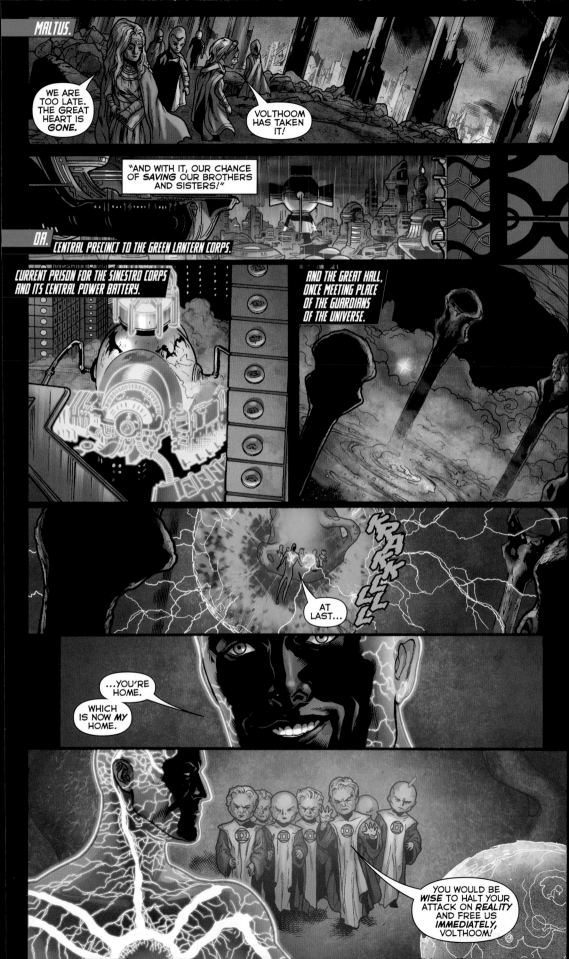

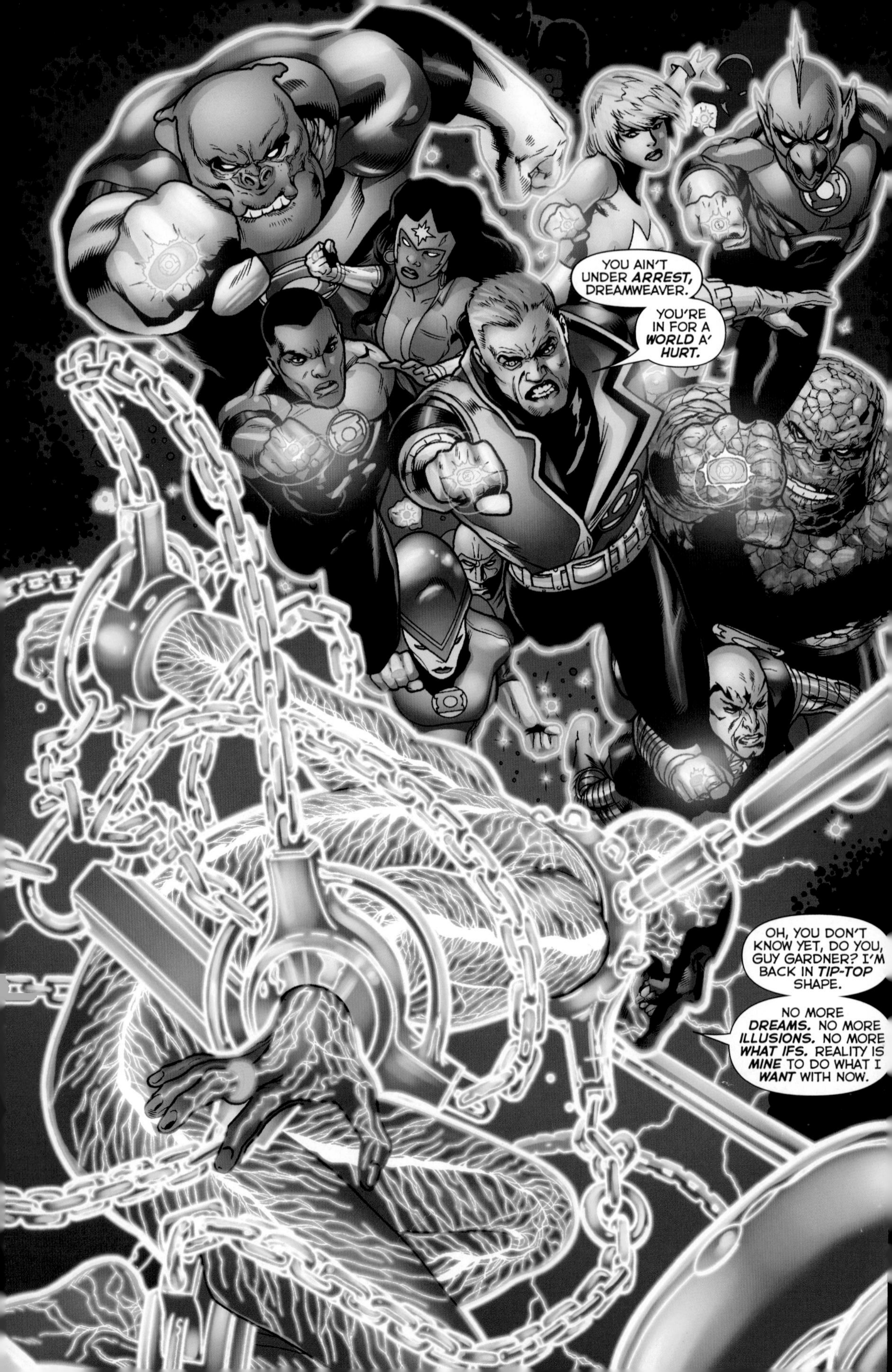
YOU AIN'T UNDER ARREST, DREAMWEAVER.
YOU'RE IN FOR A WORLD A' HURT.
OH, YOU DON'T KNOW YET, DO YOU, GUY GARDNER? I'M BACK IN TIP-TOP SHAPE.
NO MORE DREAMS. NO MORE ILLUSIONS. NO MORE WHAT IFS. REALITY IS MINE TO DO WHAT I WANT WITH NOW.

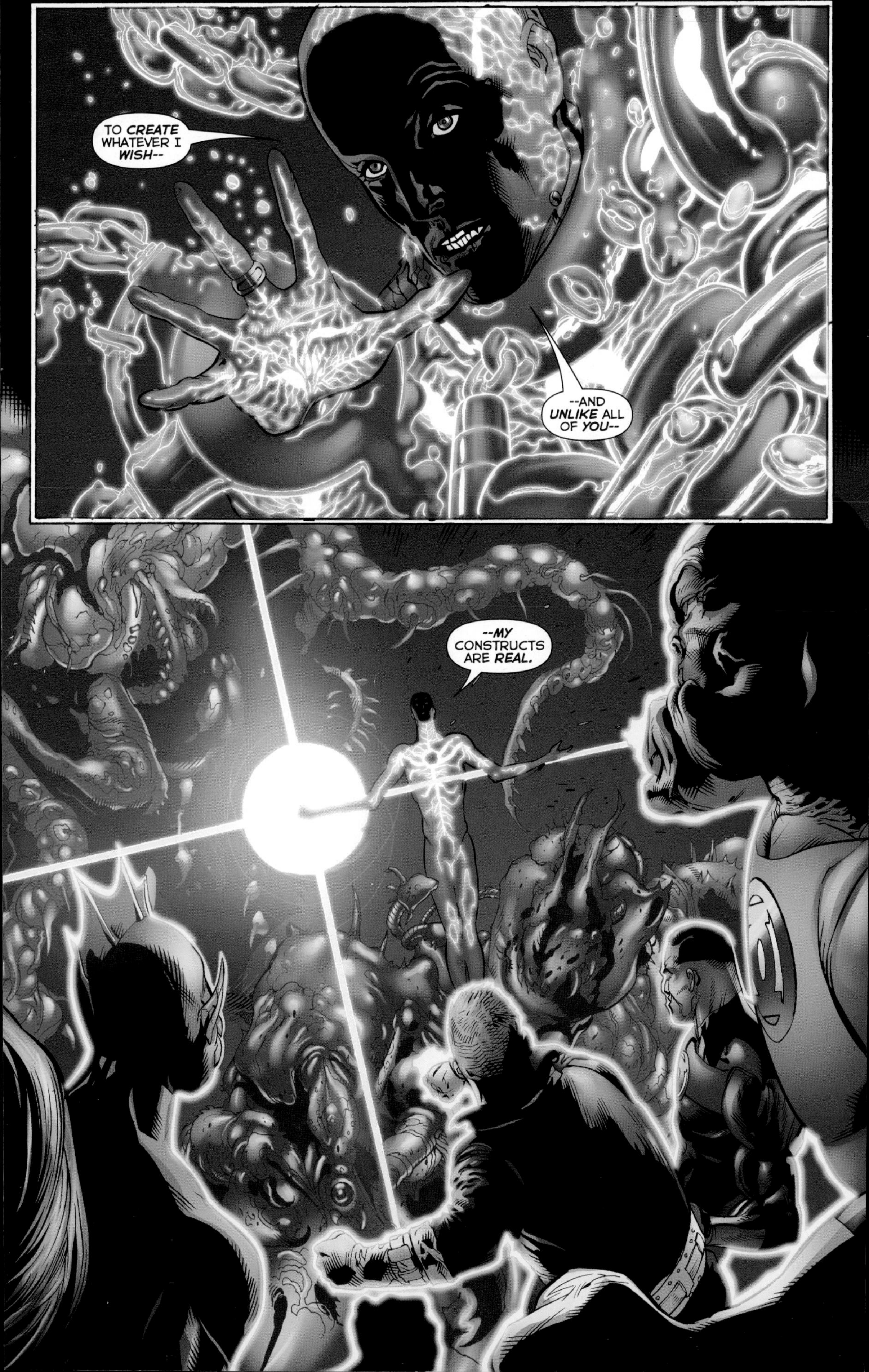
TO CREATE WHATEVER I WISH--
--AND UNLIKE ALL OF YOU--
--MY CONSTRUCTS ARE REAL.

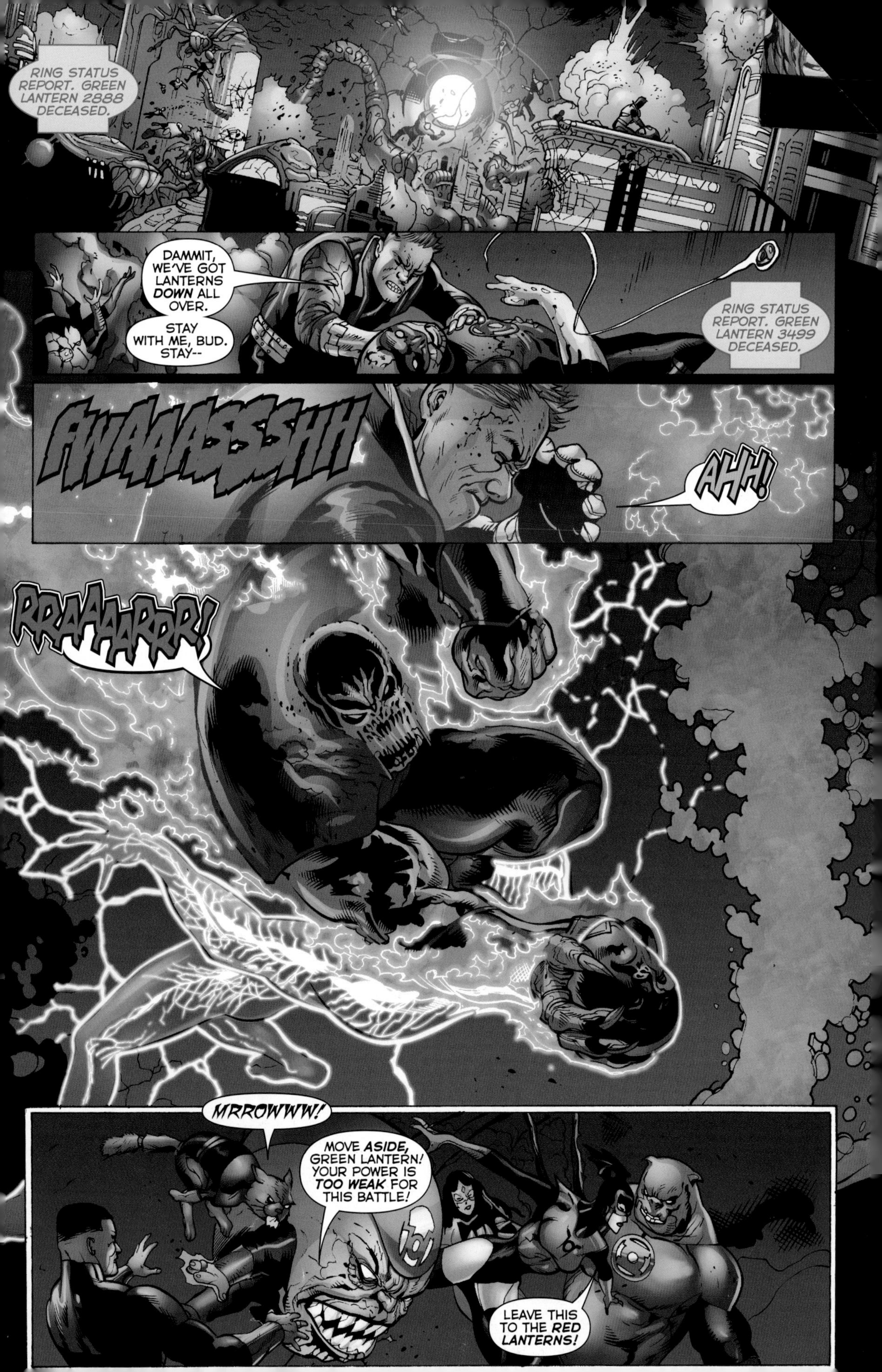
RING STATUS REPORT. GREEN LANTERN 2888 DECEASED.
DAMMIT, WE'VE GOT LANTERNS DOWN ALL OVER.
STAY WITH ME, BUD. STAY--
RING STATUS REPORT. GREEN LANTERN 3499 DECEASED.
FWAAAASSSHH
AHH!
RRAAAARRR!
MRROWWW!
MOVE ASIDE, GREEN LANTERN! YOUR POWER IS TOO WEAK FOR THIS BATTLE!
LEAVE THIS TO THE RED LANTERNS!

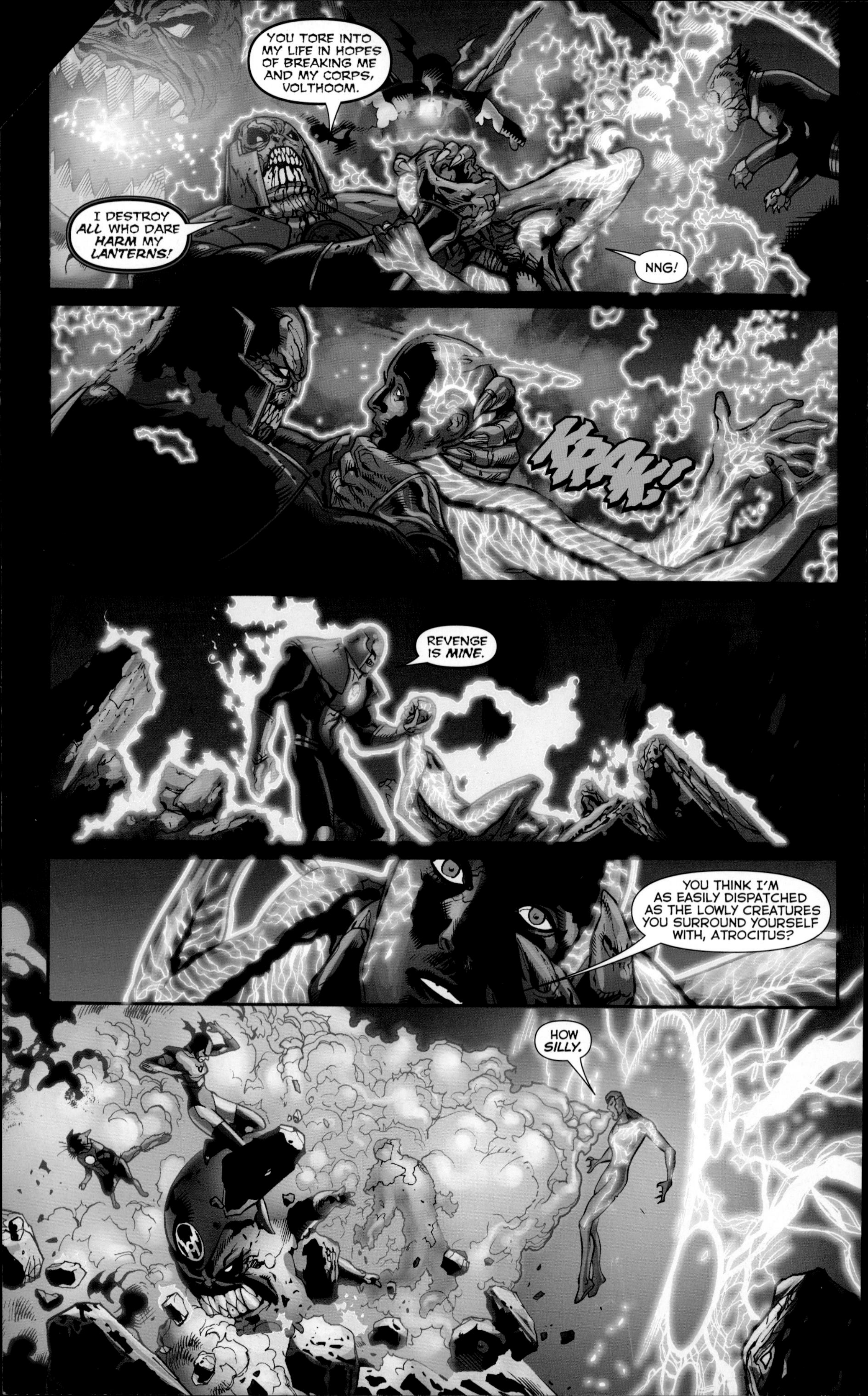
YOU TORE INTO MY LIFE IN HOPES OF BREAKING ME AND MY CORPS, VOLTHOOM.
I DESTROY ALL WHO DARE HARM MY LANTERNS!
NNG!
KRAK!
REVENGE IS MINE.
YOU THINK I'M AS EASILY DISPATCHED AS THE LOWLY CREATURES YOU SURROUND YOURSELF WITH, ATROCITUS?
HOW SILLY.

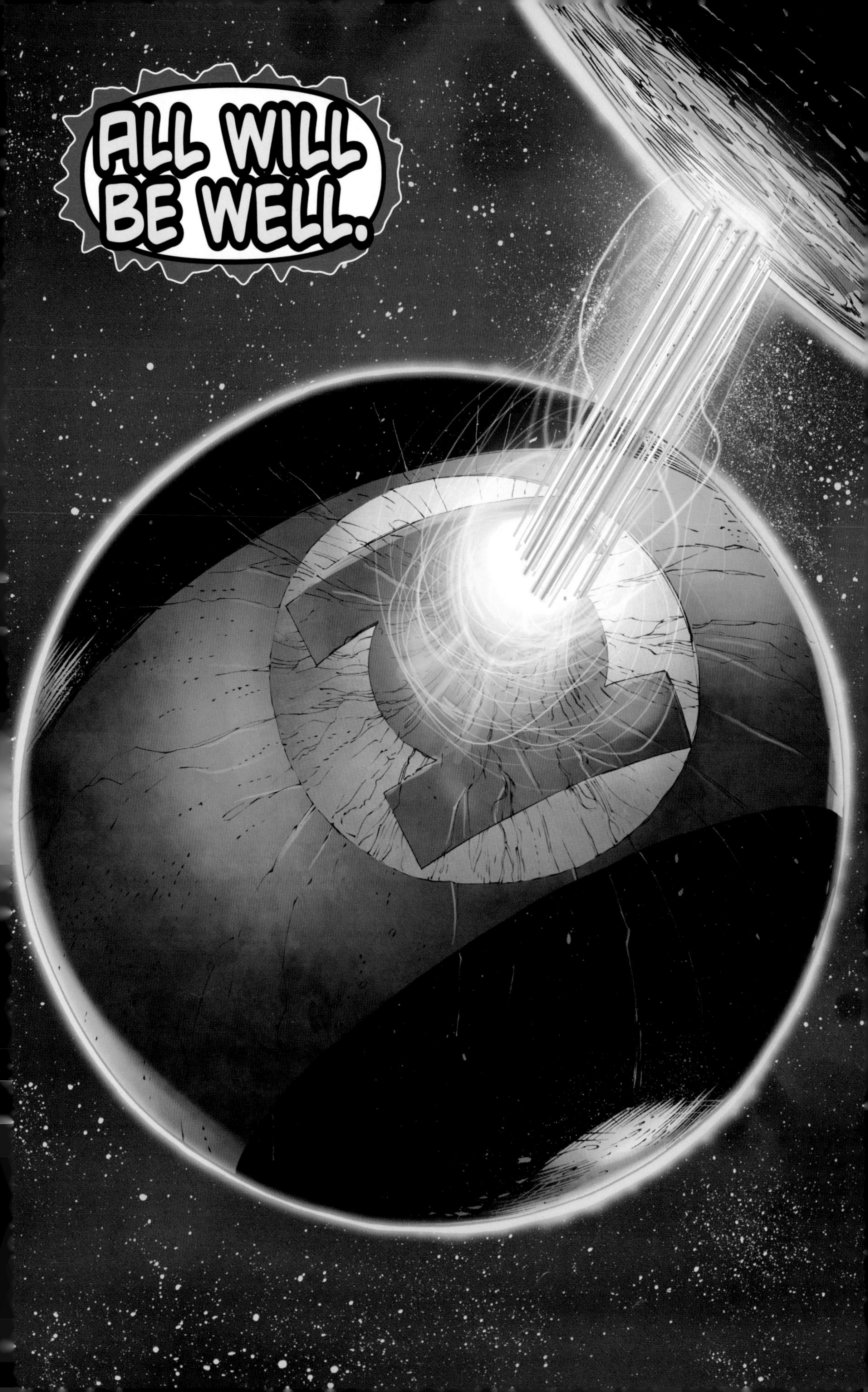
ALL WILL BE WELL.

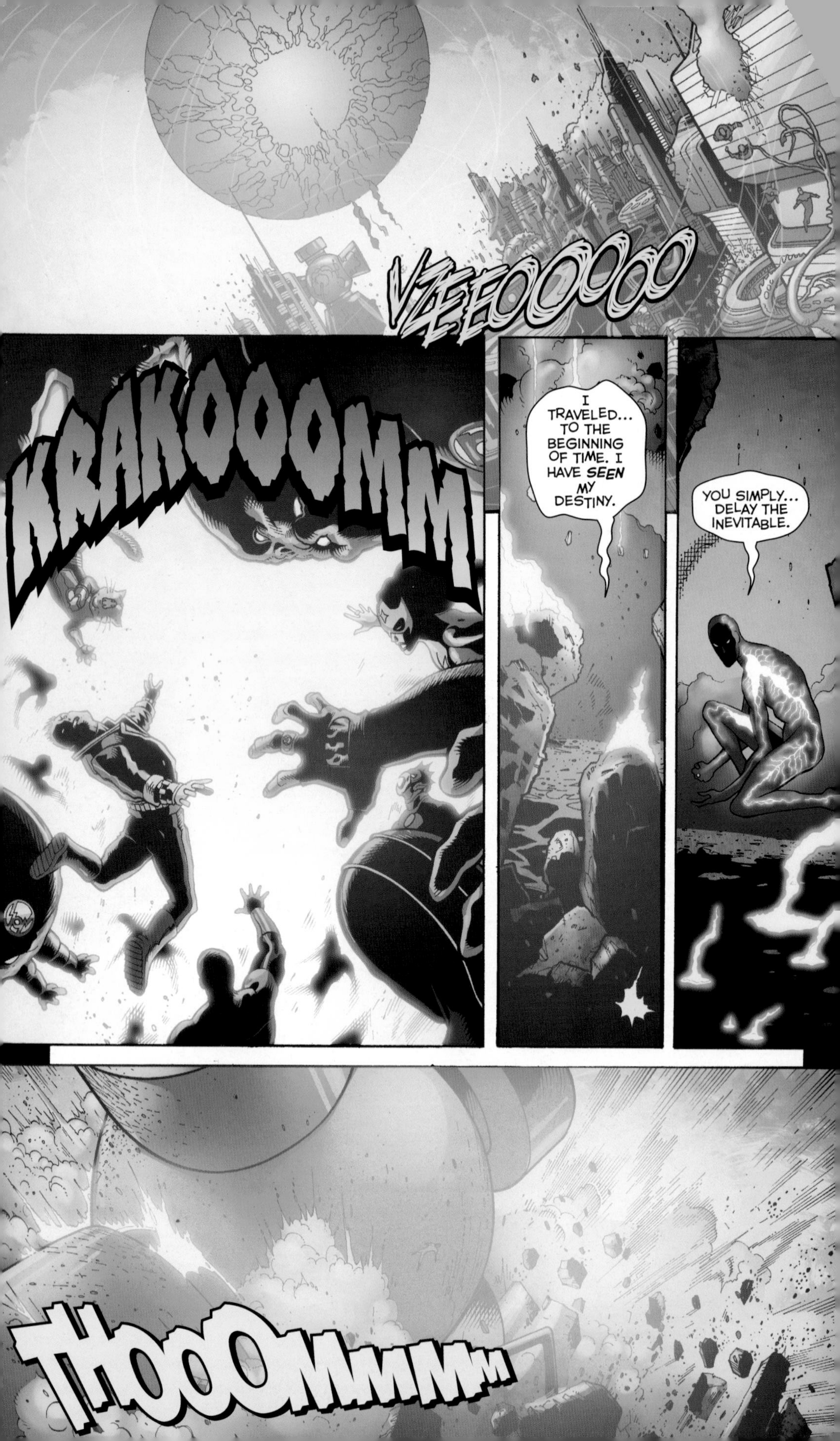
VZEEOOOOOO
KRAKOOOMMM
I TRAVELED... TO THE BEGINNING OF TIME. I HAVE SEEN MY DESTINY.
YOU SIMPLY... DELAY THE INEVITABLE.
THOOOMMMMM

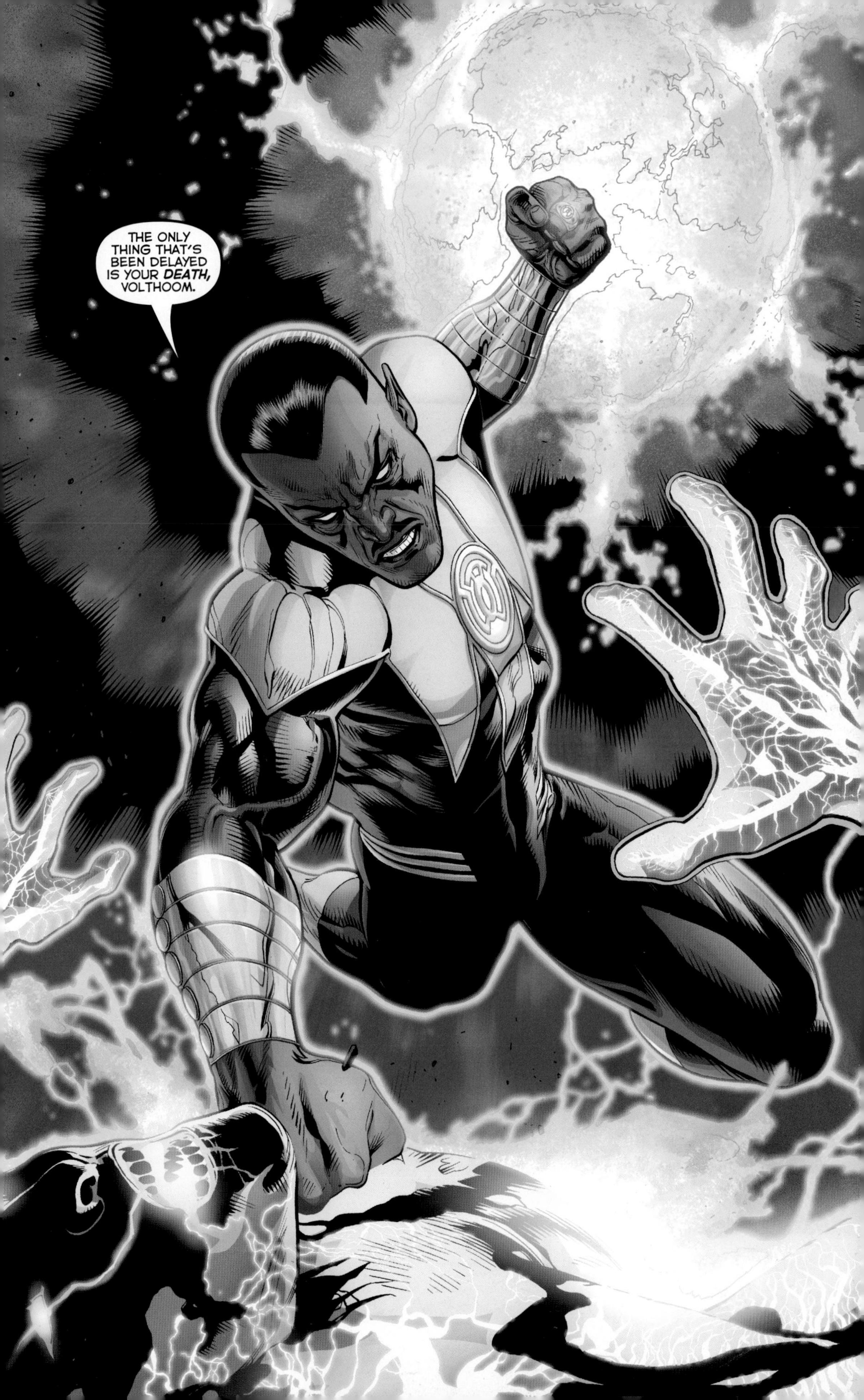
THE ONLY THING THAT'S BEEN DELAYED IS YOUR *DEATH,* VOLTHOOM.

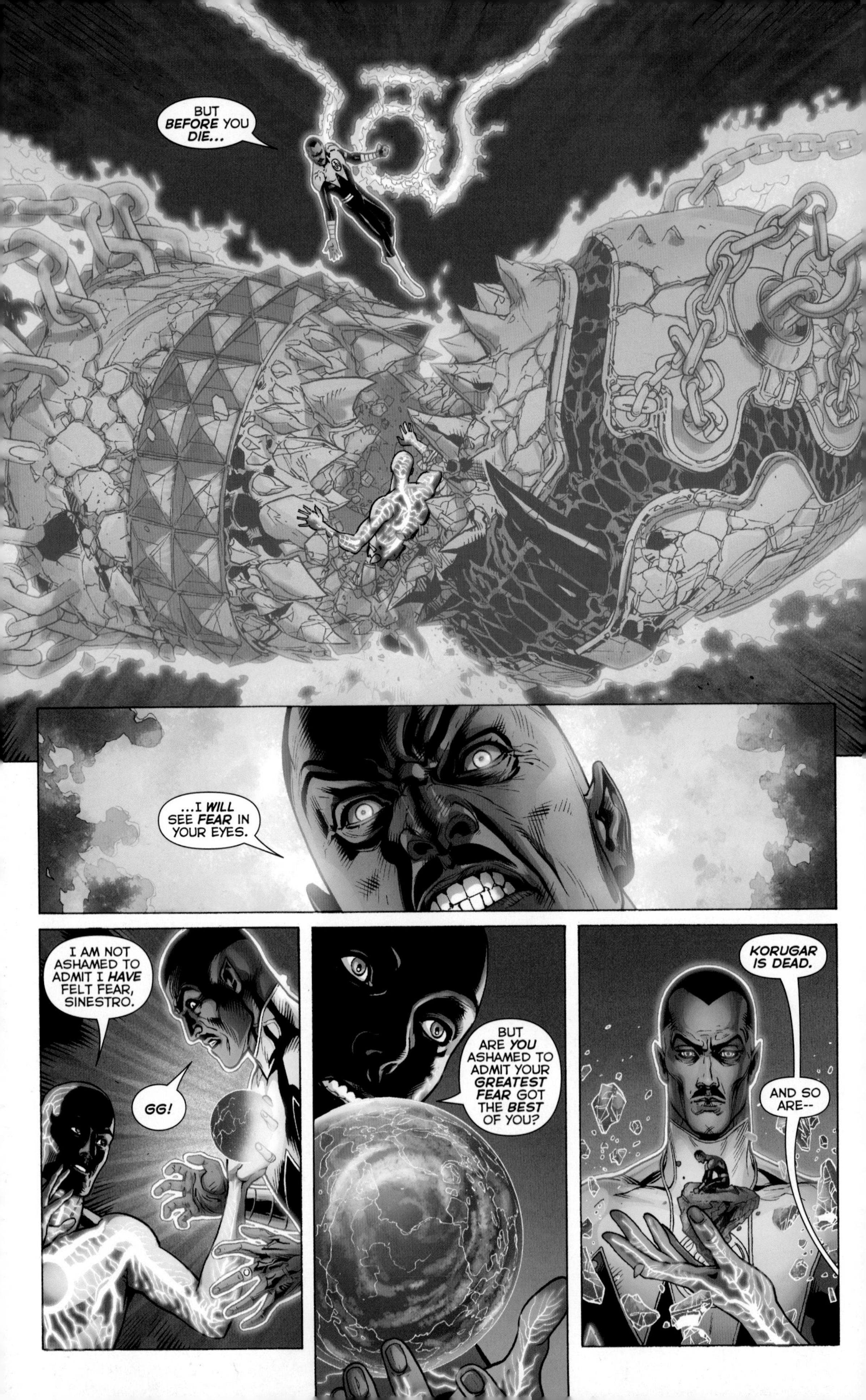
BUT BEFORE YOU DIE...
...I WILL SEE FEAR IN YOUR EYES.
I AM NOT ASHAMED TO ADMIT I HAVE FELT FEAR, SINESTRO.
GG!
BUT ARE YOU ASHAMED TO ADMIT YOUR GREATEST FEAR GOT THE BEST OF YOU?
KORUGAR IS DEAD.
AND SO ARE--

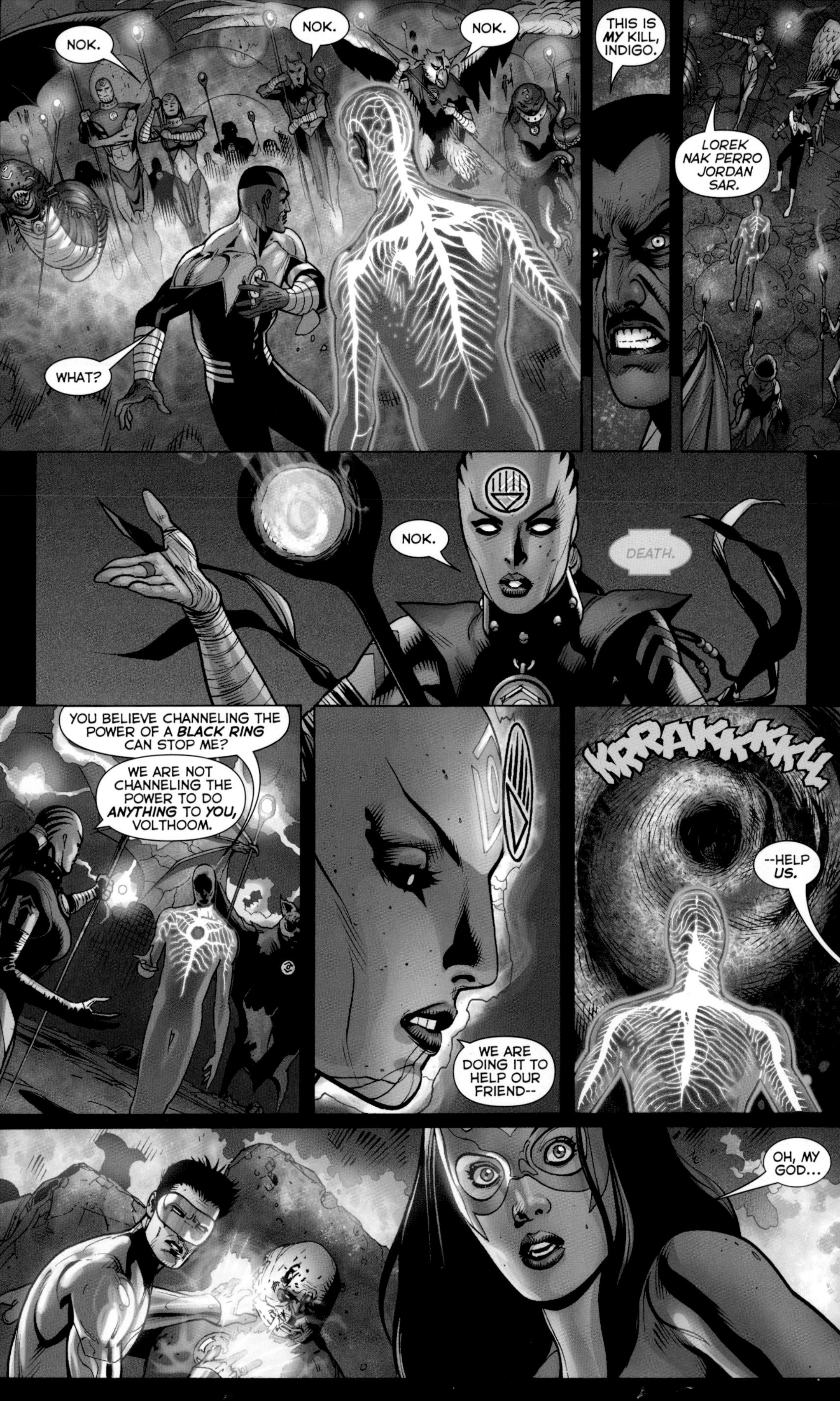
NOK.
NOK.
NOK.
WHAT?
THIS IS MY KILL, INDIGO.
LOREK NAK PERRO JORDAN SAR.
NOK.
DEATH.
YOU BELIEVE CHANNELING THE POWER OF A BLACK RING CAN STOP ME?
WE ARE NOT CHANNELING THE POWER TO DO ANYTHING TO YOU, VOLTHOOM.
WE ARE DOING IT TO HELP OUR FRIEND--
KRRAKKKKKL
--HELP US.
OH, MY GOD...

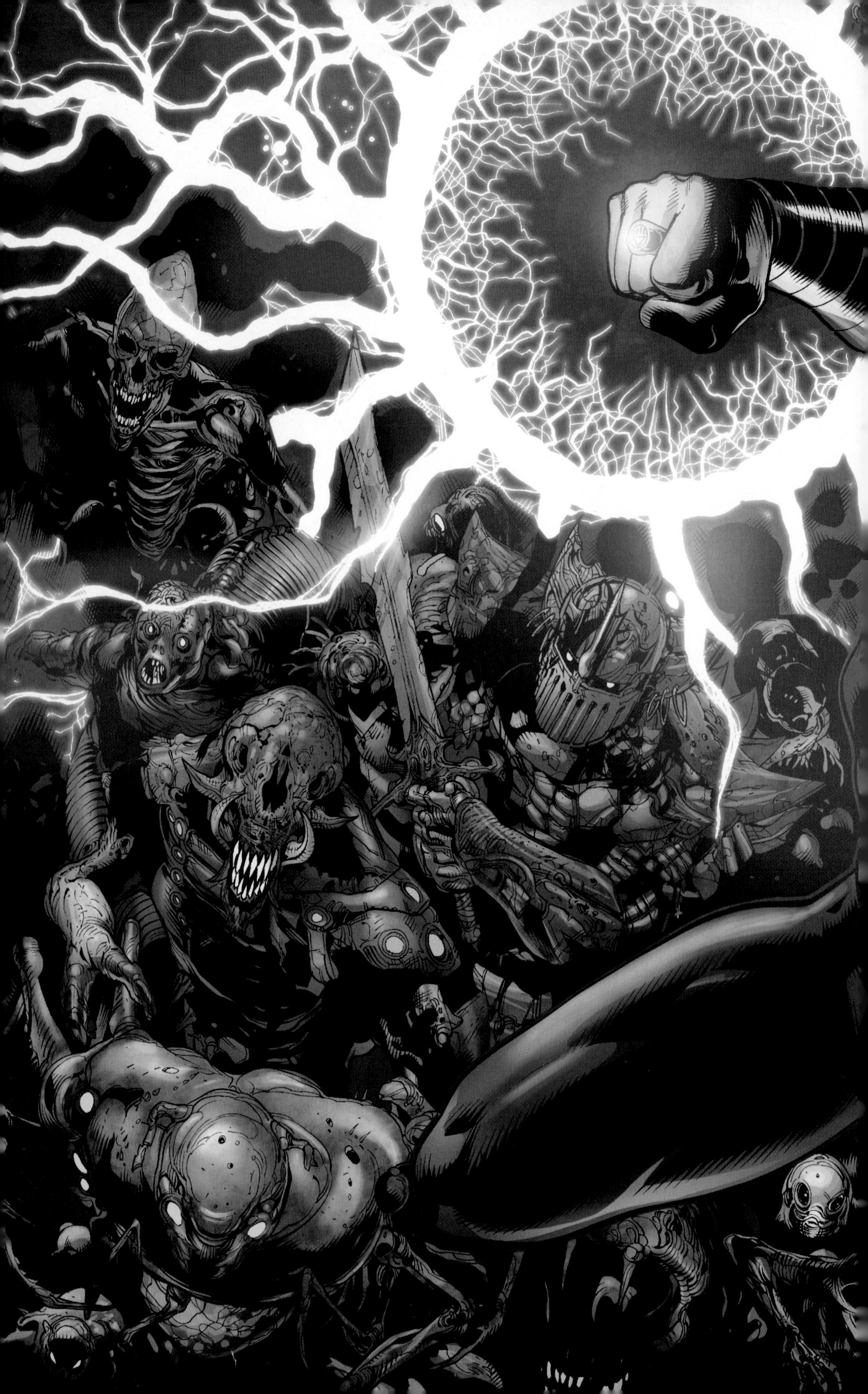

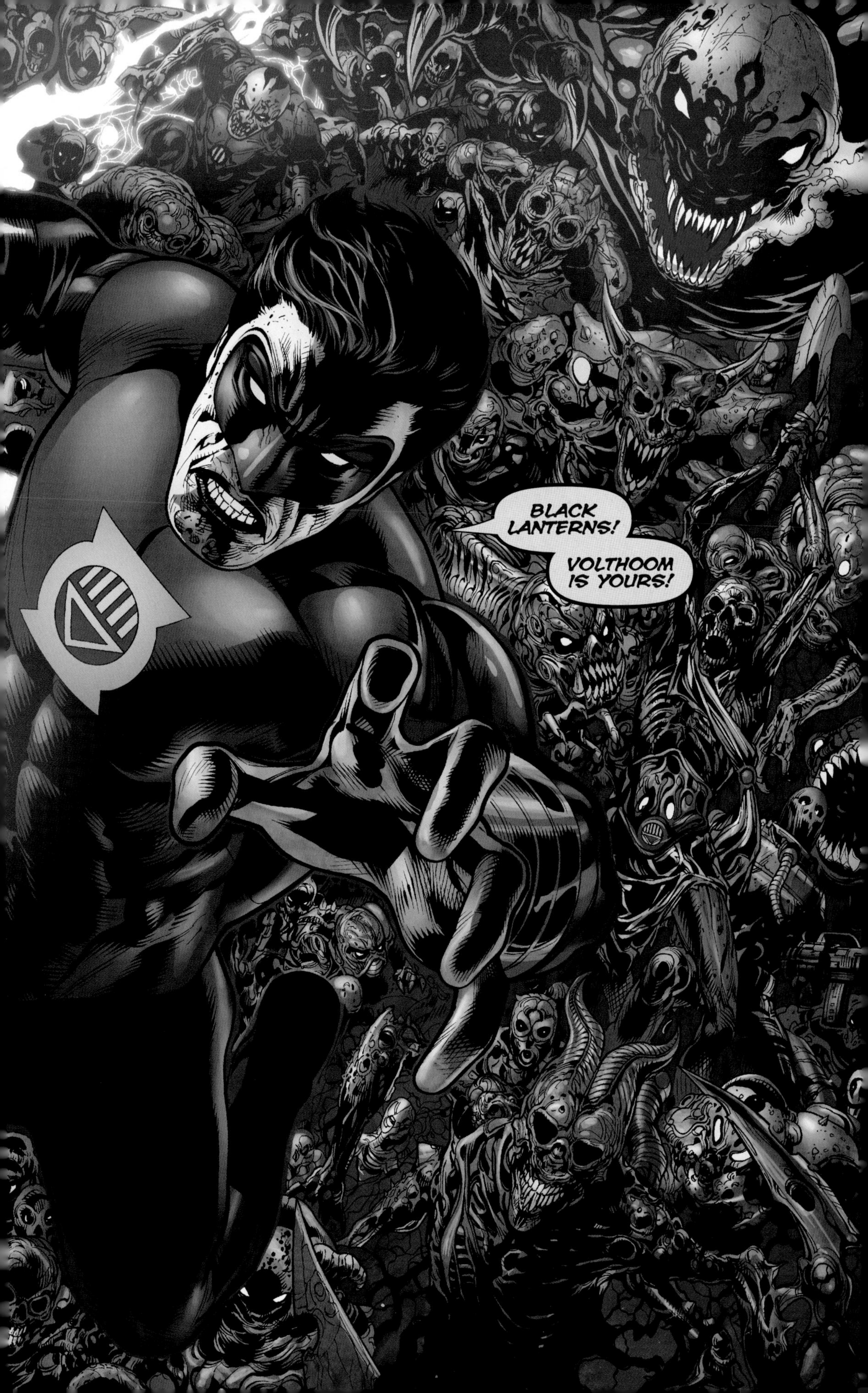
BLACK LANTERNS!
VOLTHOOM IS YOURS!

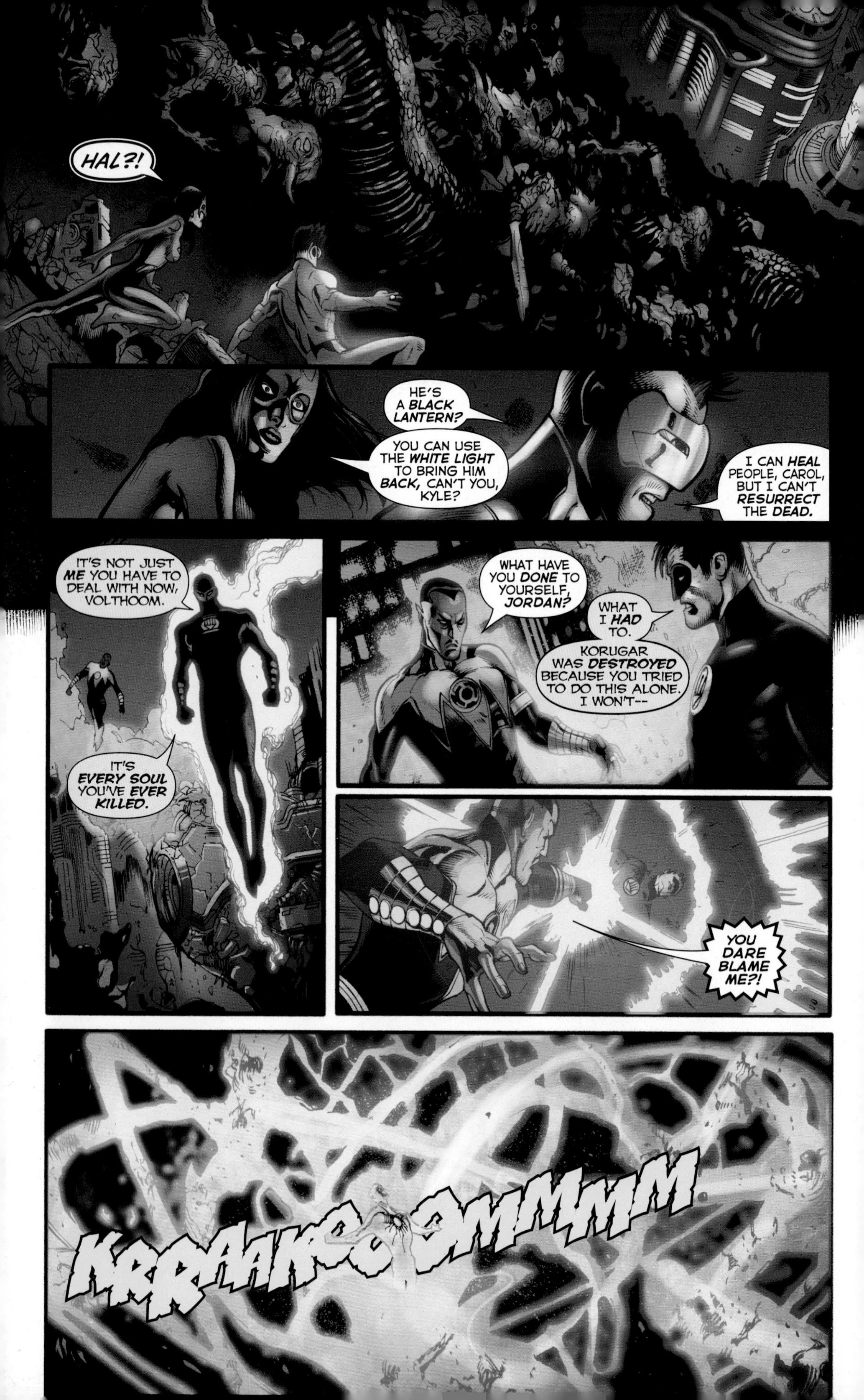

HAL?!
HE'S A BLACK LANTERN?
YOU CAN USE THE WHITE LIGHT TO BRING HIM BACK, CAN'T YOU, KYLE?
I CAN HEAL PEOPLE, CAROL, BUT I CAN'T RESURRECT THE DEAD.
IT'S NOT JUST ME YOU HAVE TO DEAL WITH NOW, VOLTHOOM.
IT'S EVERY SOUL YOU'VE EVER KILLED.
WHAT HAVE YOU DONE TO YOURSELF, JORDAN?
WHAT I HAD TO.
KORUGAR WAS DESTROYED BECAUSE YOU TRIED TO DO THIS ALONE. I WON'T--
YOU DARE BLAME ME?!
KRRAAKOOOMMMMM

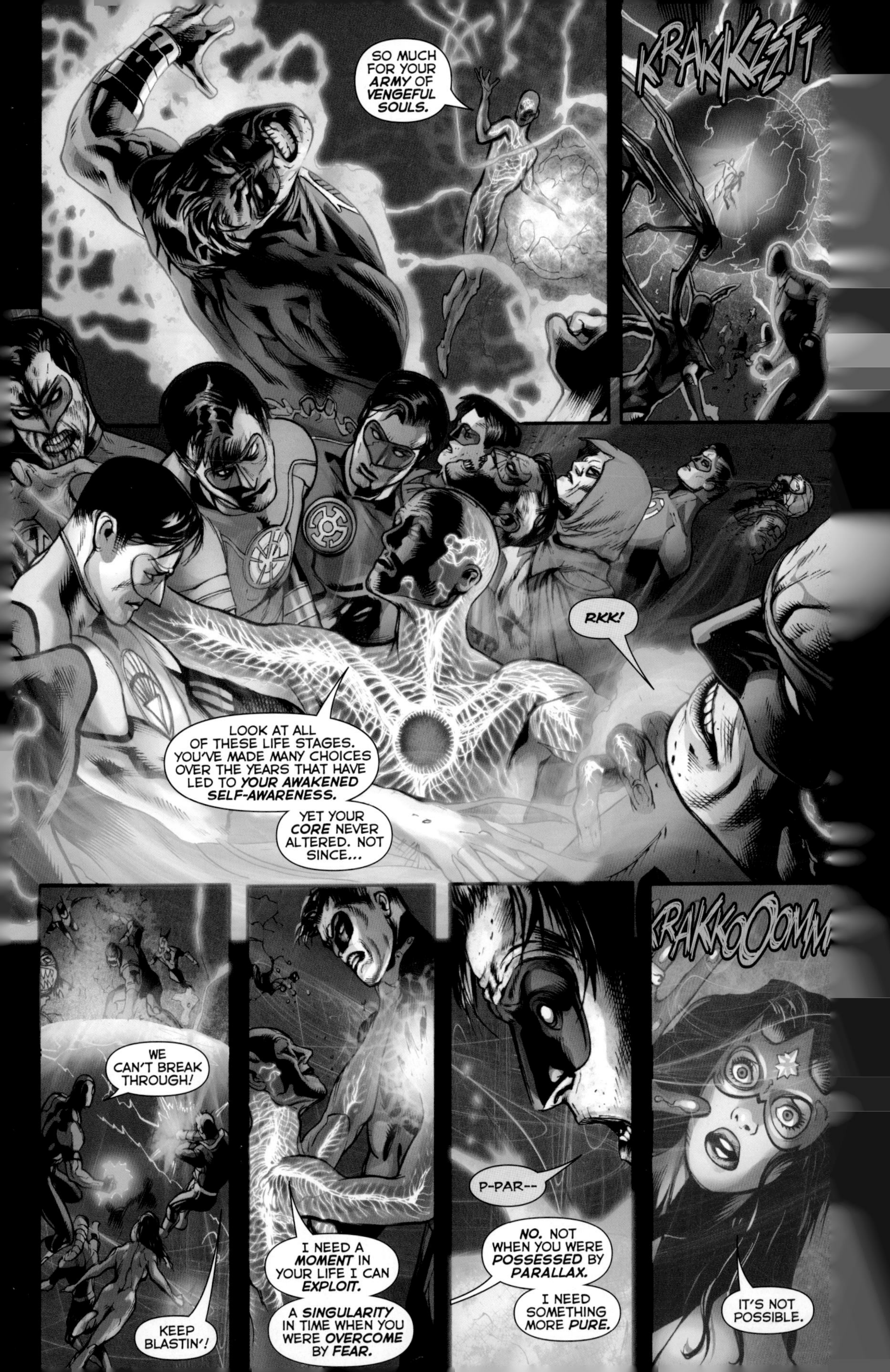
SO MUCH FOR YOUR ARMY OF VENGEFUL SOULS.
KRAKKZZTT
RKK!
LOOK AT ALL OF THESE LIFE STAGES. YOU'VE MADE MANY CHOICES OVER THE YEARS THAT HAVE LED TO YOUR AWAKENED SELF-AWARENESS.
YET YOUR CORE NEVER ALTERED. NOT SINCE...
WE CAN'T BREAK THROUGH!
KEEP BLASTIN'!
I NEED A MOMENT IN YOUR LIFE I CAN EXPLOIT.
A SINGULARITY IN TIME WHEN YOU WERE OVERCOME BY FEAR.
P-PAR--
NO. NOT WHEN YOU WERE POSSESSED BY PARALLAX.
I NEED SOMETHING MORE PURE.
KRAKKOOOMM
IT'S NOT POSSIBLE.

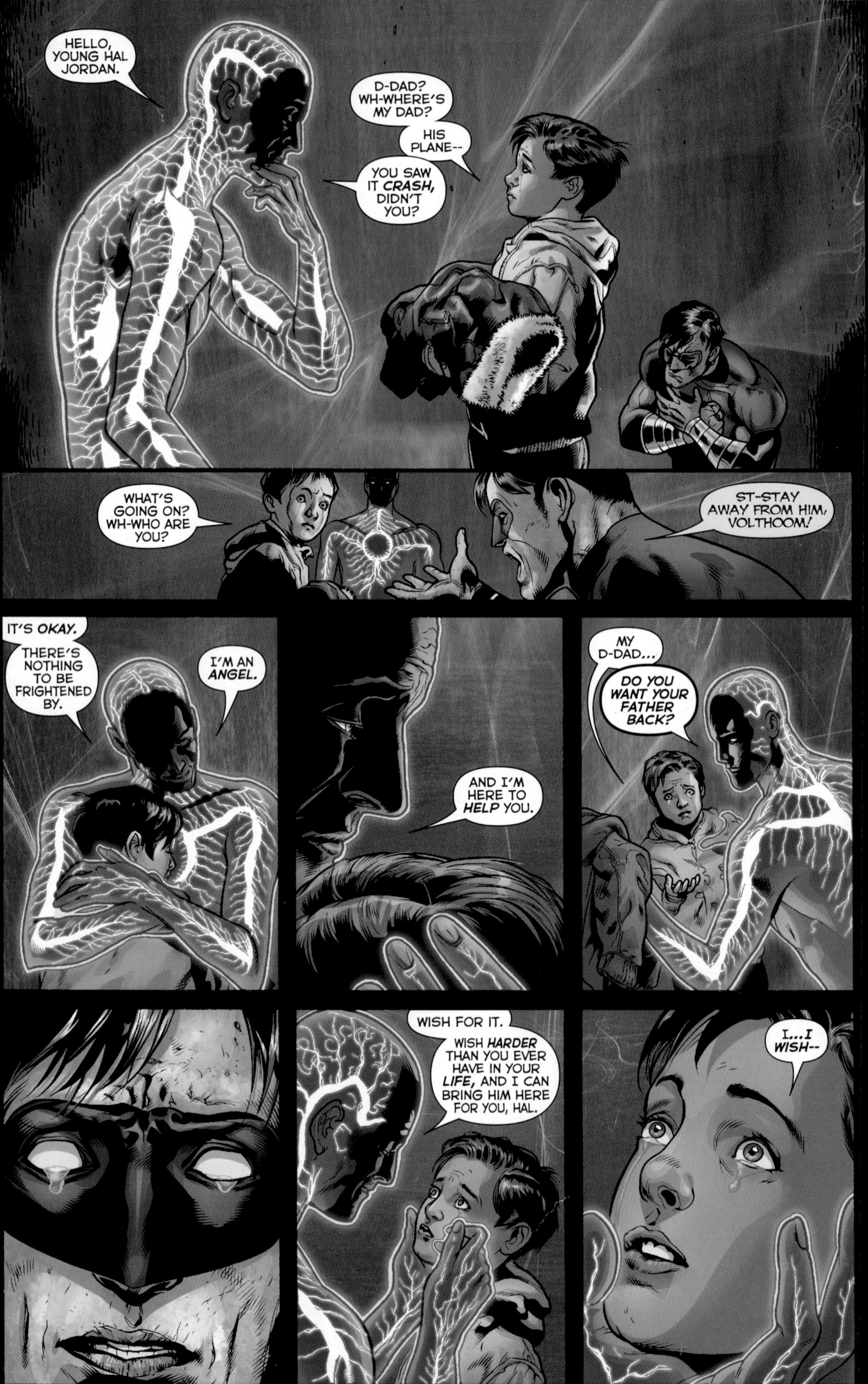
HELLO, YOUNG HAL JORDAN.
D-DAD? WH-WHERE'S MY DAD?
HIS PLANE--
YOU SAW IT CRASH, DIDN'T YOU?
WHAT'S GOING ON? WH-WHO ARE YOU?
ST-STAY AWAY FROM HIM, VOLTHOOM!
IT'S OKAY.
THERE'S NOTHING TO BE FRIGHTENED BY.
I'M AN ANGEL.
AND I'M HERE TO HELP YOU.
MY D-DAD...
DO YOU WANT YOUR FATHER BACK?
WISH FOR IT.
WISH HARDER THAN YOU EVER HAVE IN YOUR LIFE, AND I CAN BRING HIM HERE FOR YOU, HAL.
I...I WISH--

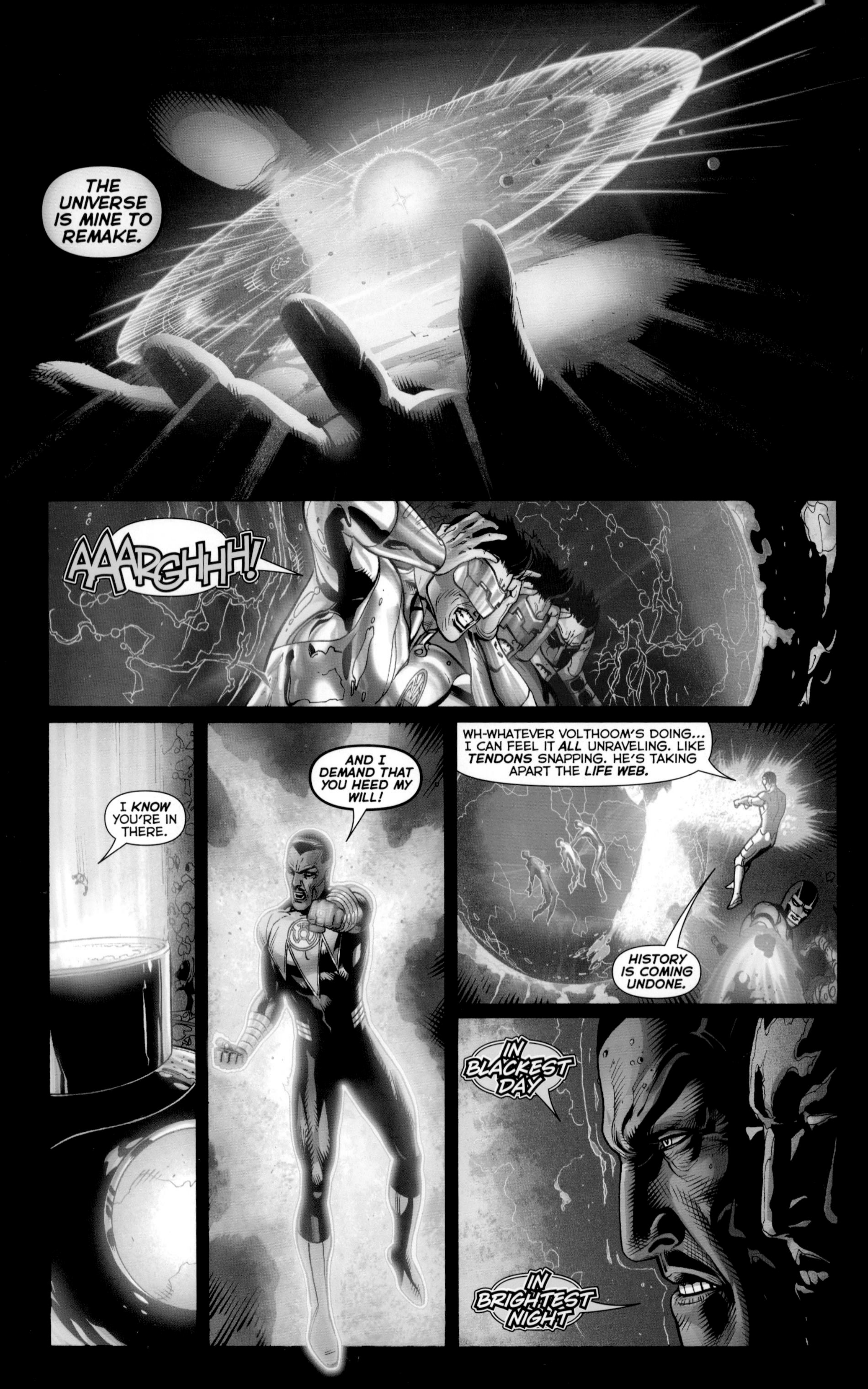
THE UNIVERSE IS MINE TO REMAKE.
AAARGHHH!
I KNOW YOU'RE IN THERE.
AND I DEMAND THAT YOU HEED MY WILL!
WH-WHATEVER VOLTHOOM'S DOING... I CAN FEEL IT ALL UNRAVELING. LIKE TENDONS SNAPPING. HE'S TAKING APART THE LIFE WEB.
HISTORY IS COMING UNDONE.
IN BLACKEST DAY
IN BRIGHTEST NIGHT

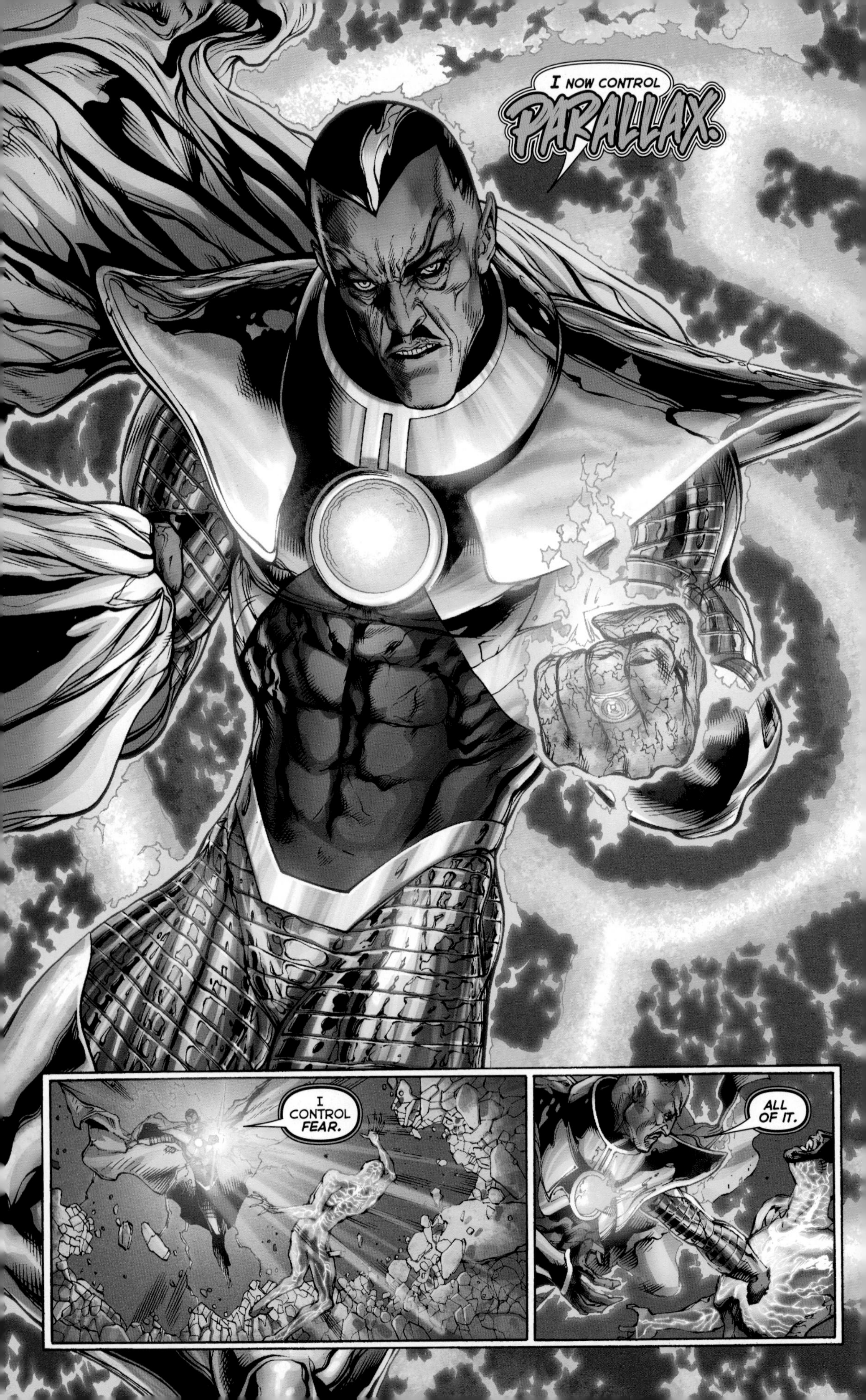
I NOW CONTROL
PARALLAX.
I CONTROL FEAR.
ALL OF IT.

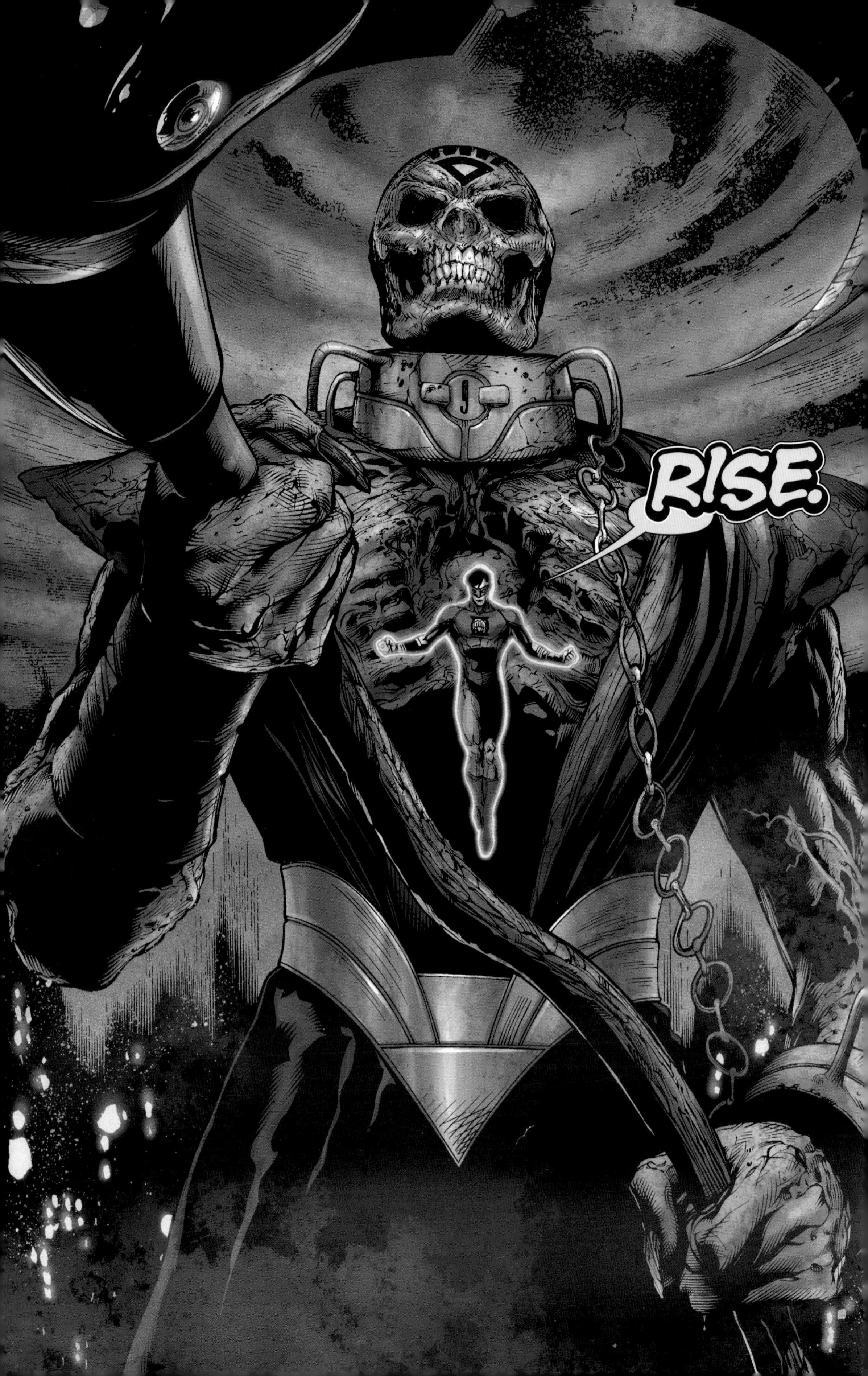
RISE.

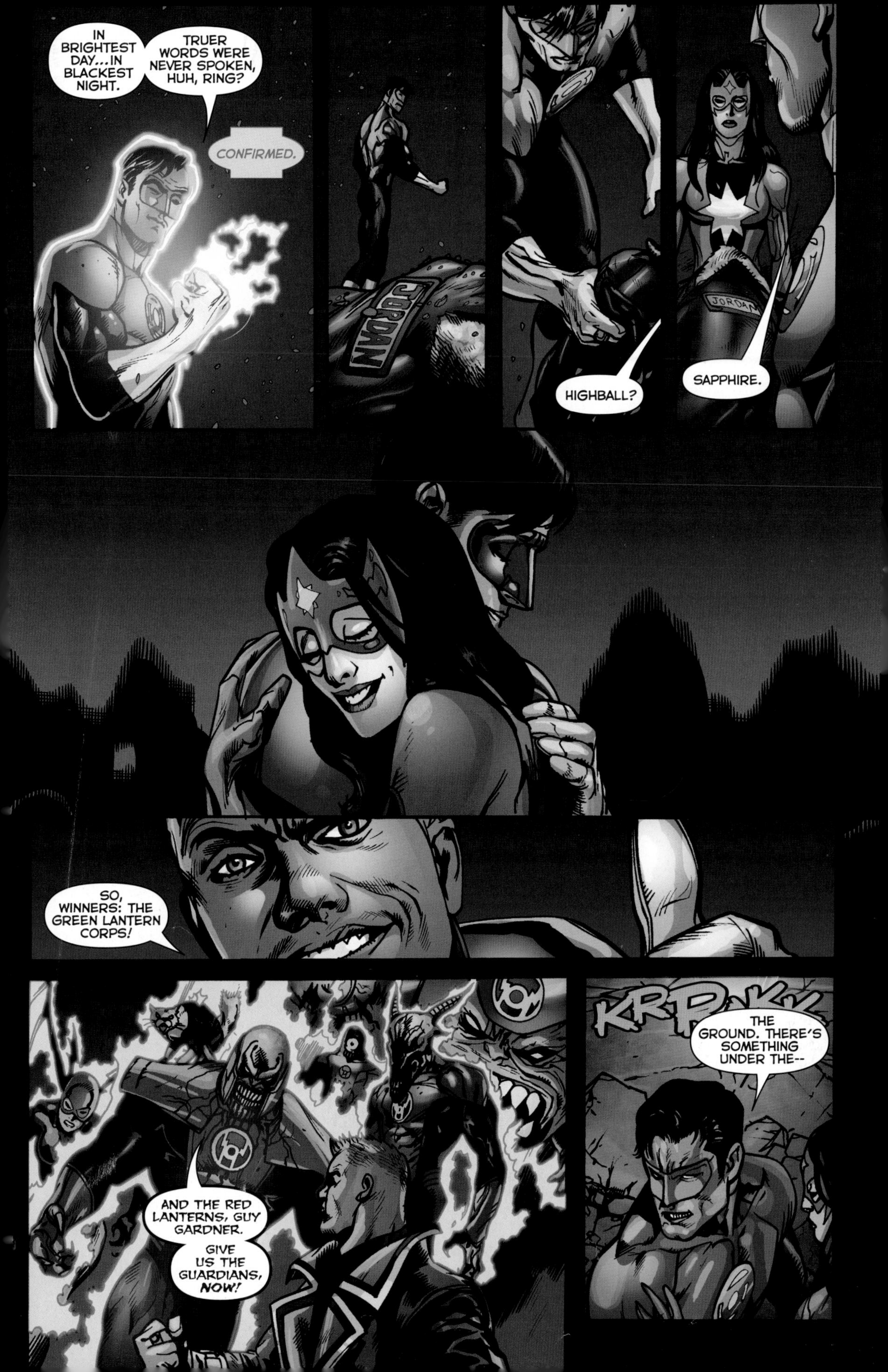
IN BRIGHTEST DAY...IN BLACKEST NIGHT.
TRUER WORDS WERE NEVER SPOKEN, HUH, RING?
CONFIRMED.
JORDAN
HIGHBALL?
SAPPHIRE.
SO, WINNERS: THE GREEN LANTERN CORPS!
AND THE RED LANTERNS, GUY GARDNER.
GIVE US THE GUARDIANS, NOW!
KRRKKK
THE GROUND. THERE'S SOMETHING UNDER THE--

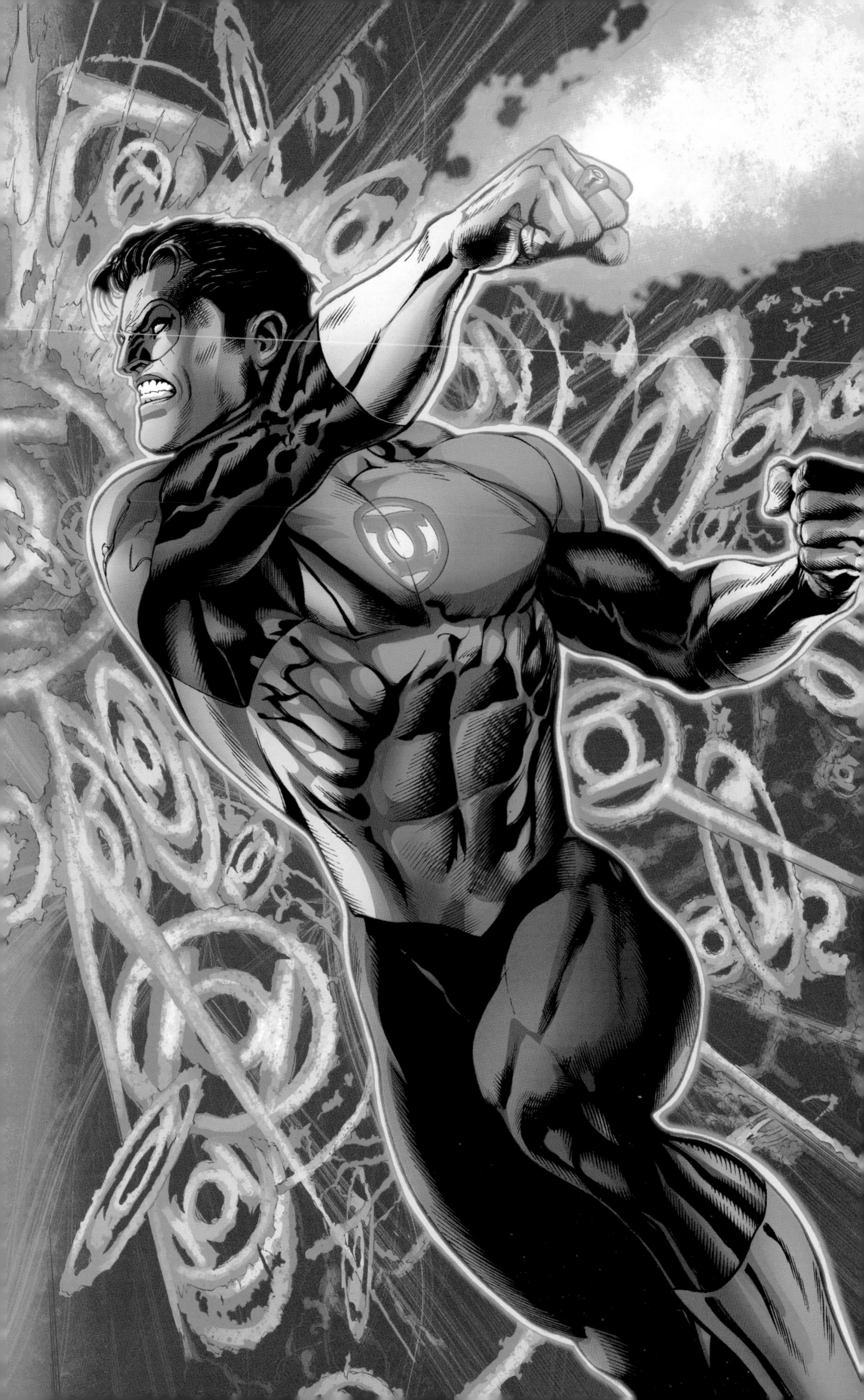

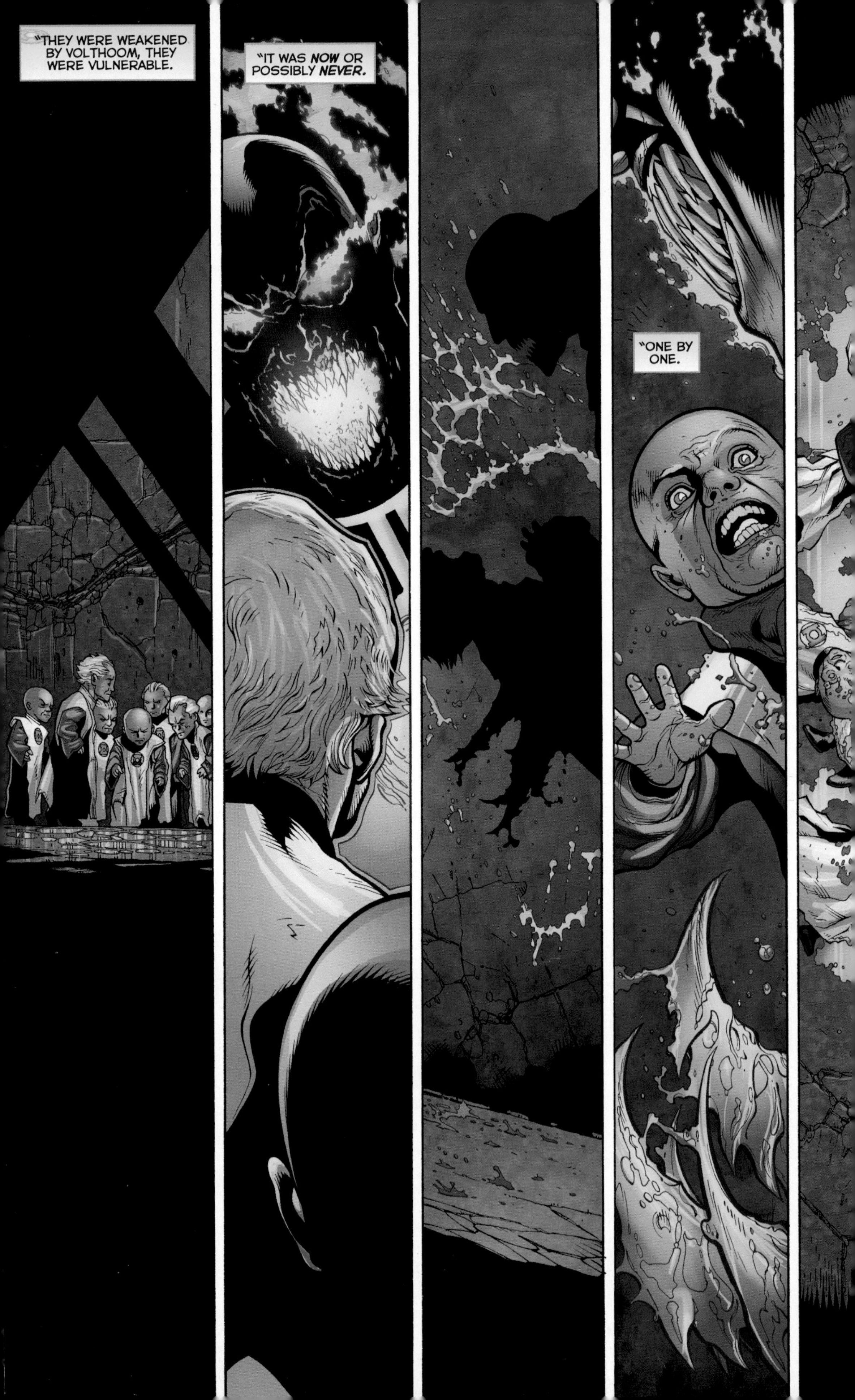
"THEY WERE WEAKENED BY VOLTHOOM, THEY WERE VULNERABLE.
"IT WAS NOW OR POSSIBLY NEVER.
"ONE BY ONE.

WHAT HAPPENED TO EVERYONE?

I MEAN, IN THE END?

WHAT HAPPENED TO EVERYONE IN *THE END?*

YOU ASK OF THEIR *FUTURES?*

OF HOW THEY *DIED?*

YES.

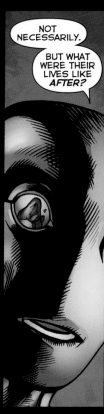

NOT NECESSARILY.

BUT WHAT WERE THEIR LIVES LIKE *AFTER?*

AFTER THEIR MOST CHALLENGING AND ADVENTUROUS YEARS?

YES. AFTER THE *BOOKENDS OF REBIRTH.*

LET ME OPEN THE BOOK OF OA AGAIN, THEN...

...AND I'LL SHOW YOU...

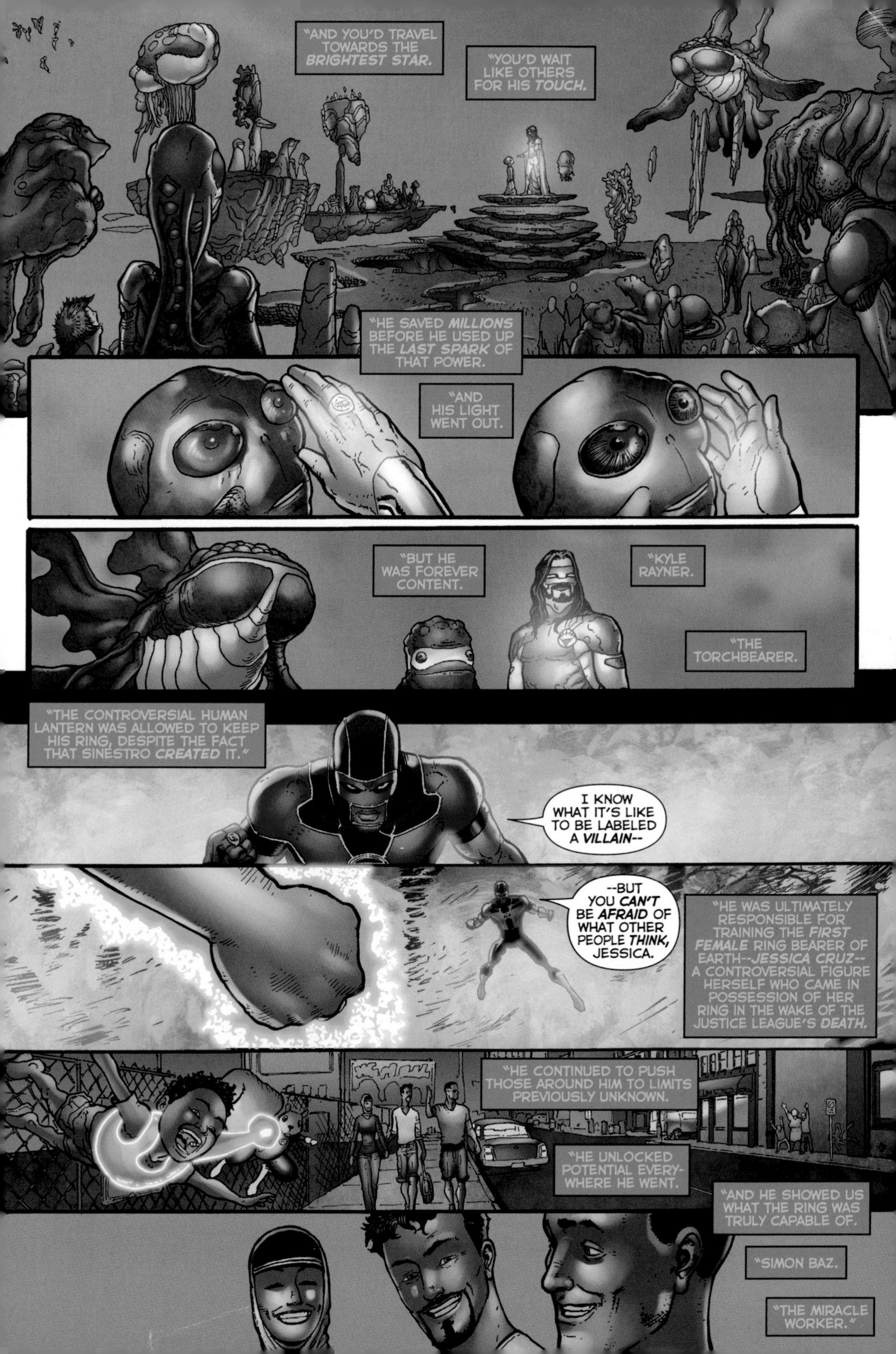
"AND YOU'D TRAVEL TOWARDS THE BRIGHTEST STAR.
"YOU'D WAIT LIKE OTHERS FOR HIS TOUCH.
"HE SAVED MILLIONS BEFORE HE USED UP THE LAST SPARK OF THAT POWER.
"AND HIS LIGHT WENT OUT.
"BUT HE WAS FOREVER CONTENT.
"KYLE RAYNER.
"THE TORCHBEARER.
"THE CONTROVERSIAL HUMAN LANTERN WAS ALLOWED TO KEEP HIS RING, DESPITE THE FACT THAT SINESTRO CREATED IT."
I KNOW WHAT IT'S LIKE TO BE LABELED A VILLAIN--
--BUT YOU CAN'T BE AFRAID OF WHAT OTHER PEOPLE THINK, JESSICA.
"HE WAS ULTIMATELY RESPONSIBLE FOR TRAINING THE FIRST FEMALE RING BEARER OF EARTH--JESSICA CRUZ--A CONTROVERSIAL FIGURE HERSELF WHO CAME IN POSSESSION OF HER RING IN THE WAKE OF THE JUSTICE LEAGUE'S DEATH.
"HE CONTINUED TO PUSH THOSE AROUND HIM TO LIMITS PREVIOUSLY UNKNOWN.
"HE UNLOCKED POTENTIAL EVERYWHERE HE WENT.
"AND HE SHOWED US WHAT THE RING WAS TRULY CAPABLE OF.
"SIMON BAZ.
"THE MIRACLE WORKER."

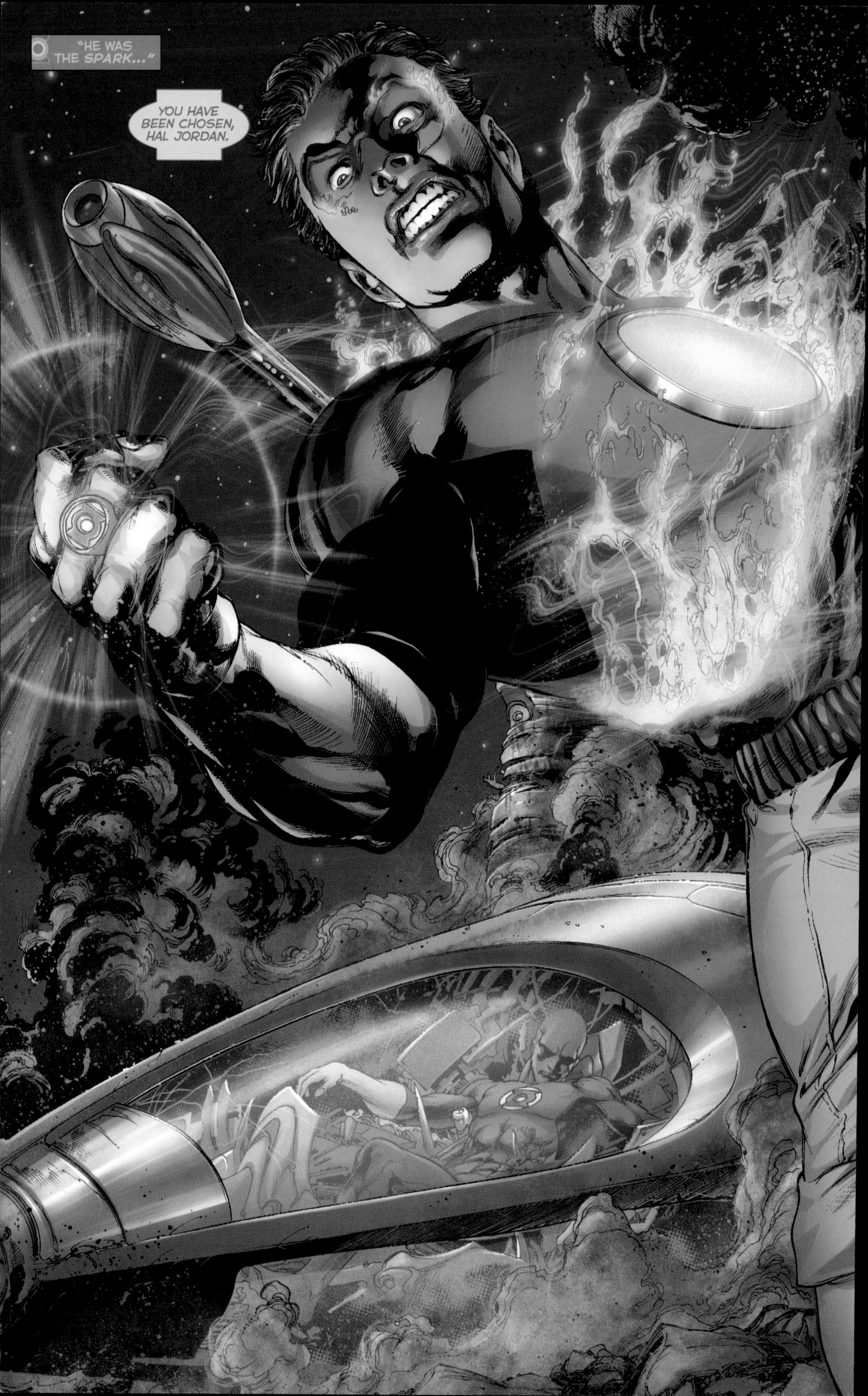
"HE WAS THE SPARK..."
YOU HAVE BEEN CHOSEN, HAL JORDAN.

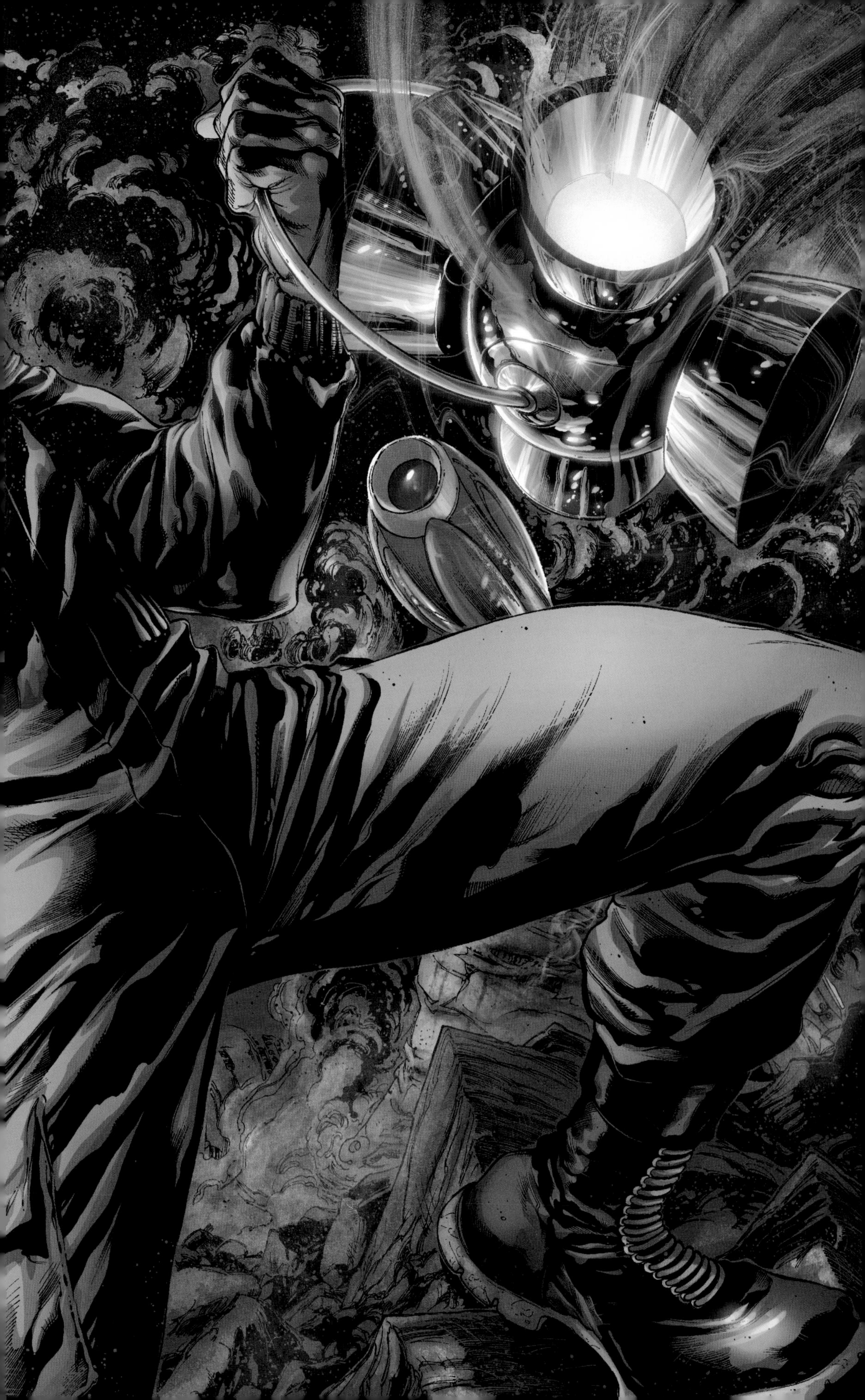

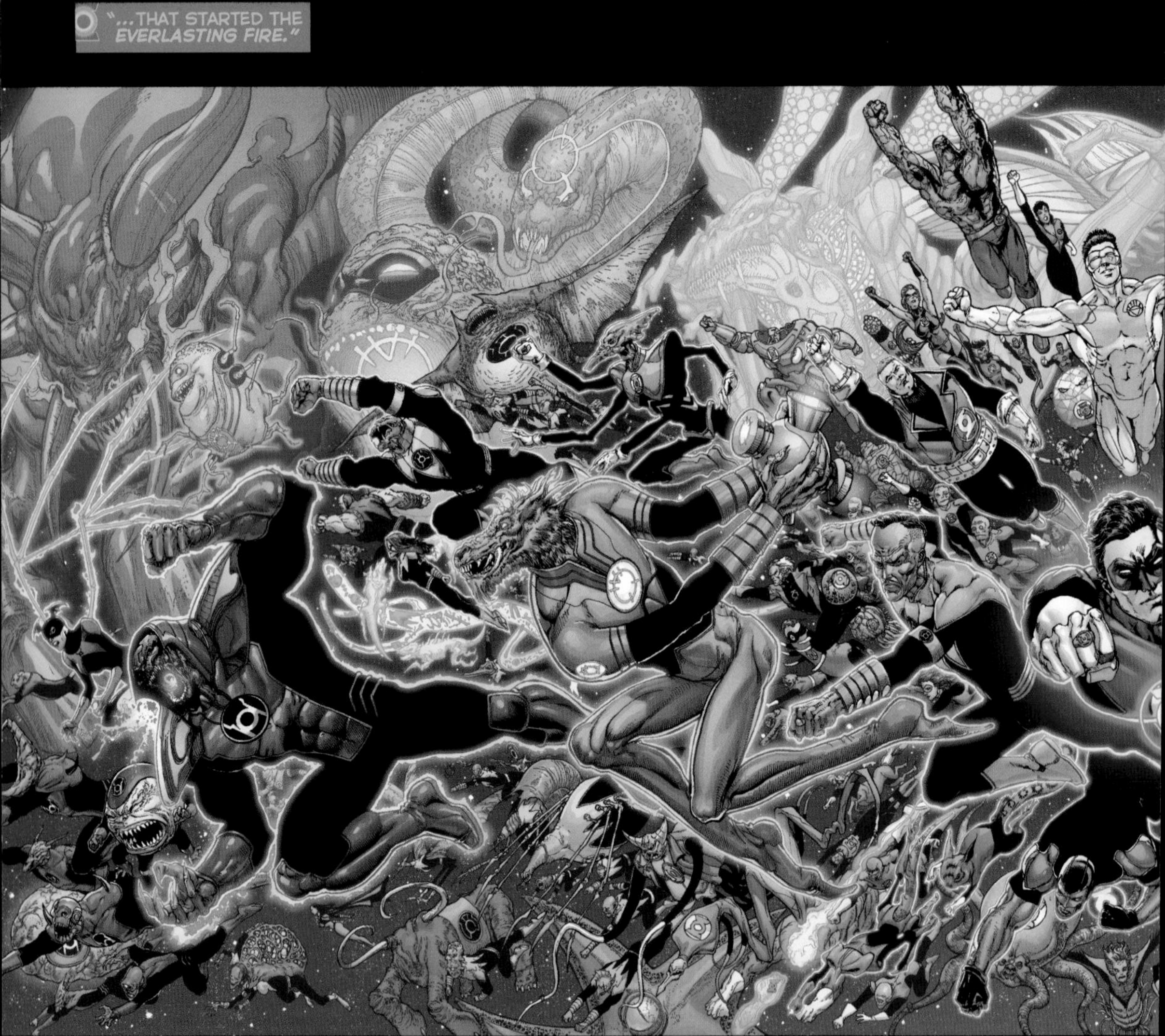
"...THAT STARTED THE *EVERLASTING FIRE.*"

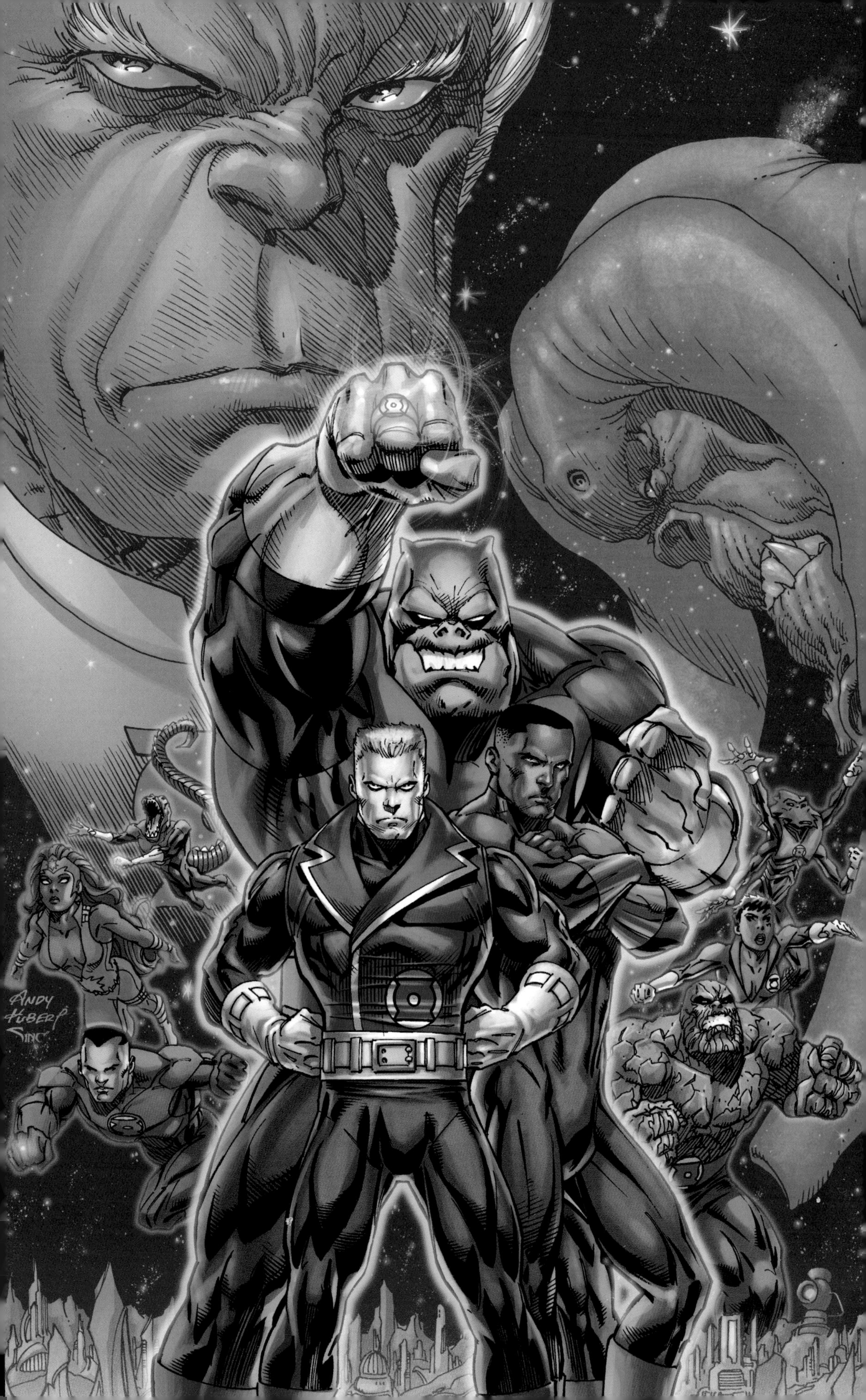
ANDY
KUBERT
SINC

OA. THE GUARDIANS' PLANETARY CITADEL.
YOU SURE HE'S HERE?
NO I'M NOT SURE, BUT WE'VE CHECKED EVERY-WHERE ELSE.
KKKRRRKKKK
HEY, POOZER, YOU MISS US?

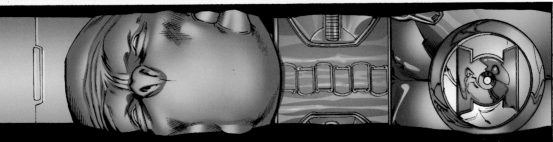

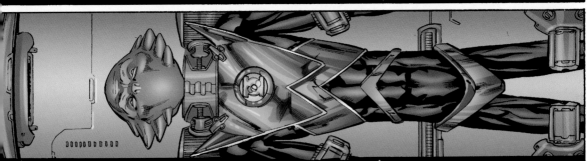

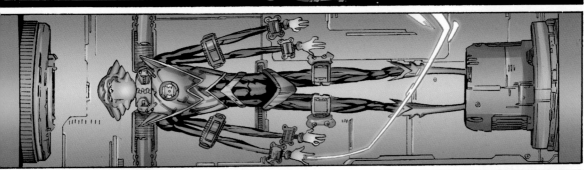

UM, YES, I AM QUITE...RELIEVED TO SEE YOU HAVE AVOIDED ANY PHYSICAL OR PSYCHOLOGICAL DURESS.

WE MISSED YOU TOO, SALAAK.

SPEAKING OF MISSING-- YOU MISSED IT *ALL*.

ALL WHAT?

YOU KNOW, LOTS OF COLORS, BLASTING, BLOOD, SCREAMING, SURROUND-SOUND DESTRUCTION, WIDESCREEN MAYHEM, GOOD VERSUS EVIL, STUFF THAT MAKES AN EPIC EPIC.

THEY DIED. WE'RE ALIVE.

AND THE *GUARDIANS*-- THEIR PLANS-- HOW DID--

THEY'RE GONE, BUBBA.

DEFINE GONE.

WE WON. THEY LOST.

DEFINE LOST.

THOUGH IT WAS UNNECESSARY, THANK YOU BOTH FOR ESCORTING ME BACK TO MY SECTOR.

IT WAS THE LEAST WE COULD DO AFTER YOU TORE US AWAY FROM THE FIRST LANTERN'S GRIP.

I WOULD HAVE BEEN NO USE TO ANYONE IF NOT FOR YOUR RESTORING MY PLANETARY FRAGMENTS, LANTERN STEWART.

CONNECTING TO OTHER MINDS OF THE CORPS AFTER HAVING BEEN FRACTURED FOR SO LONG WAS BENEFICIAL.

AND I TOOK GREAT PLEASURE IN OUR CONVERSATIONS DURING OUR JOURNEY TOGETHER HERE, SAPPHIRE YRRA.

AS DID WE, MOGO.

YOU'RE SO BEAUTIFUL...

INCREDIBLY.

...JOHN...

I KNOW.

...WE HAVE FOUGHT TOGETHER HARD FOR A PEACE WHERE *ALL GAVE SOME* AND *SOME GAVE ALL.*

BUT A NEW HORIZON BECKONS WHERE HOPE SPRINGS ETERNAL...

...AND BEFORE I DEPART FOR THE BLUE LANTERNS' NEW HOME, I WOULD LIKE TO SHARE--

I NEED YOUR HELP, WALKER.

OF COURSE, LANTERN GARDNER, BUT CAN IT WAIT UNTIL AFTER I SPEAK TO YOUR BRETHREN--

--WHO ARE LOOKING FOR THEIR HEARTS AND MINDS TO BE FILLED WITH JOYFUL AFFIRMATION AFTER THESE RECENT DARK DAYS?

NO.

POWER LEVEL 105%.

MAY I ASK WHAT IS GOING ON?

BLUE LANTERNS *CHARGE UP* GREEN LANTERNS, SO YOU'RE COMING ON A ROAD TRIP TO FILL MY RING TO THE BRIM.

WHY DO YOU NEED SO MUCH POWER, MY FRIEND?

TO *END* SOMETHING.

POWER LEVEL 115%.

I'VE LOCATED *XAR.* I'LL SEND A SQUAD OF--

NEGATORY. THIS IS PERSONAL.

WHERE THE HELL IS HE, SALAAK?

POWER LEVEL 300%

I'M NOT SURE WHAT THE CAPACITY OF YOUR RING IS, BUT YOU NEED TO DISCHARGE THE IMMENSE POWER YOU'VE BUILT UP SOON.

YEAH. *THAT'S THE PLAN.*

IT'S TIME TO DIE.

IT WILL BE INCREDIBLY SLOW AND PAINFUL.

SMASH

YOUR LAST MOMENTS WILL BE RECORDED SO GUY GARDNER CAN WATCH HOW HE FAILED HIS OWN BLOOD-COVERED FAMILY.

THANKS FOR THE *COMPANY,* WALKER.

GOTTA DO THIS ALONE.

POWER LEVEL 325%

SO...

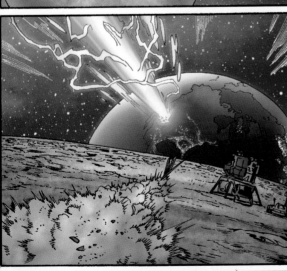

...WHO WANTS TO *SCREAM* FOR THE CAMERA FIRST?

I HAVE A FEELING IT'S GOING TO BE *YOU.*

HMM?

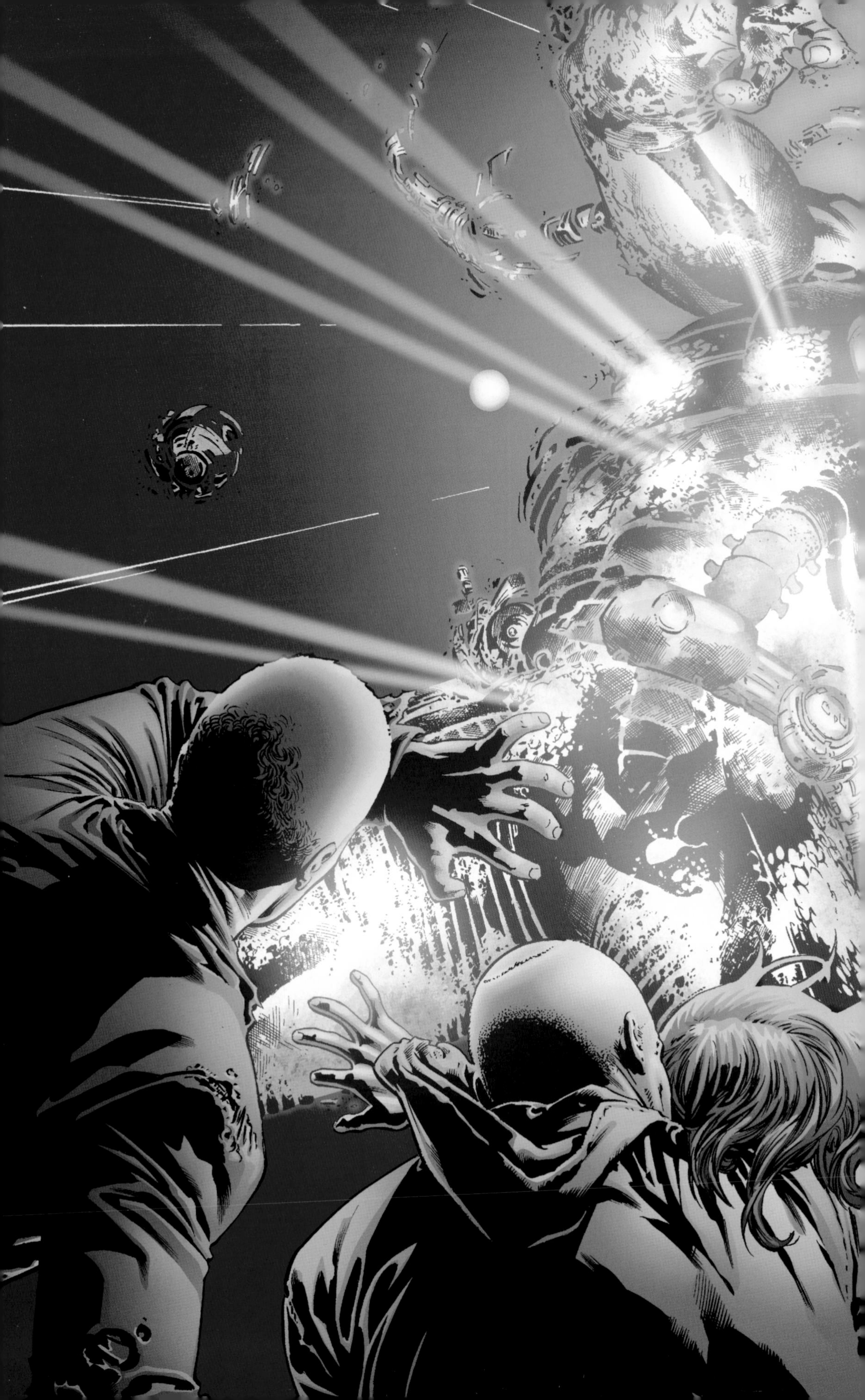

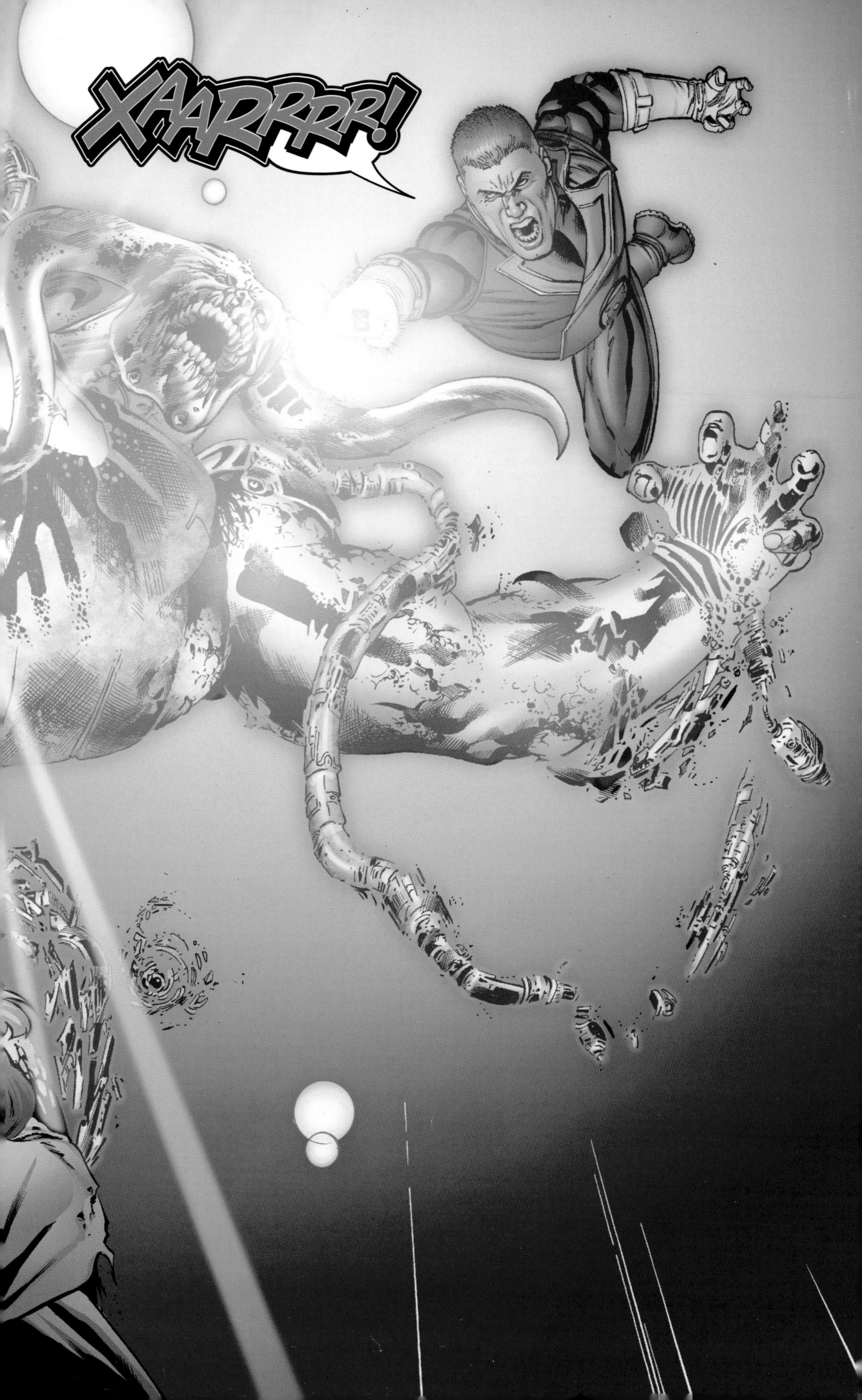
XAARRRR!

YOU ALL OKAY?

...UM... YEAH, WE'RE GOOD.

...*THAT* WAS SOMETHING YOU DON'T SEE EVERY DAY.

POWER LEVEL *85%*

...GOD... THOUGHT I MIGHTA LOST YOU...

ANOTHER FEW SECONDS AND YOU *WOULD'VE.*

BUT YOU *DIDN'T*--YOU SAVED US-- *YOU* GOT THE BAD GUY, GUY.

...I DID, SIS, DIDN'T I?

XAR'S FINALLY TOAST.

BUT, UH...SORRY ABOUT THE HOUSE, POP.

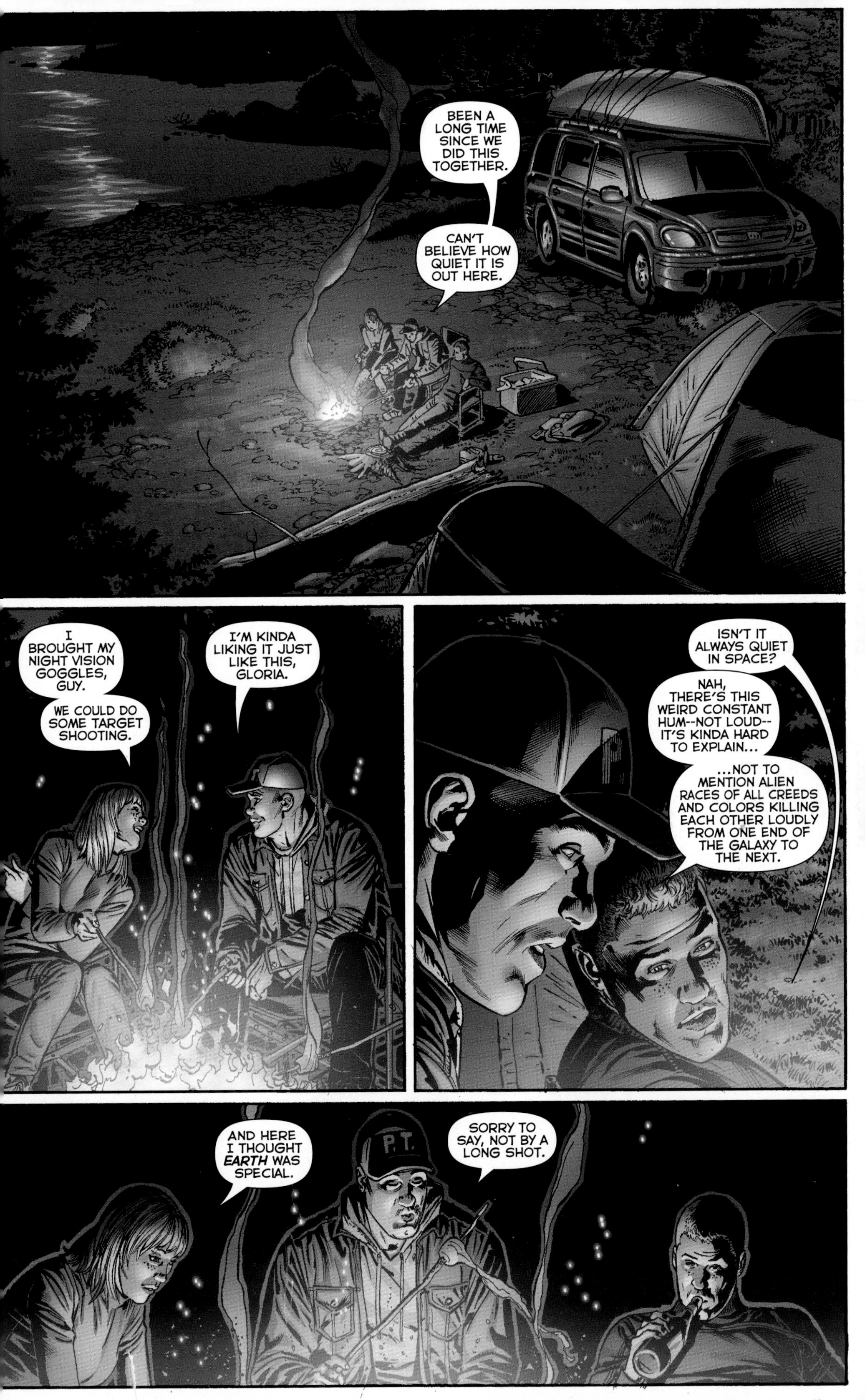
BEEN A LONG TIME SINCE WE DID THIS TOGETHER.
CAN'T BELIEVE HOW QUIET IT IS OUT HERE.
I BROUGHT MY NIGHT VISION GOGGLES, GUY.
WE COULD DO SOME TARGET SHOOTING.
I'M KINDA LIKING IT JUST LIKE THIS, GLORIA.
ISN'T IT ALWAYS QUIET IN SPACE?
NAH, THERE'S THIS WEIRD CONSTANT HUM--NOT LOUD--IT'S KINDA HARD TO EXPLAIN...
...NOT TO MENTION ALIEN RACES OF ALL CREEDS AND COLORS KILLING EACH OTHER LOUDLY FROM ONE END OF THE GALAXY TO THE NEXT.
AND HERE I THOUGHT *EARTH* WAS SPECIAL.
SORRY TO SAY, NOT BY A LONG SHOT.

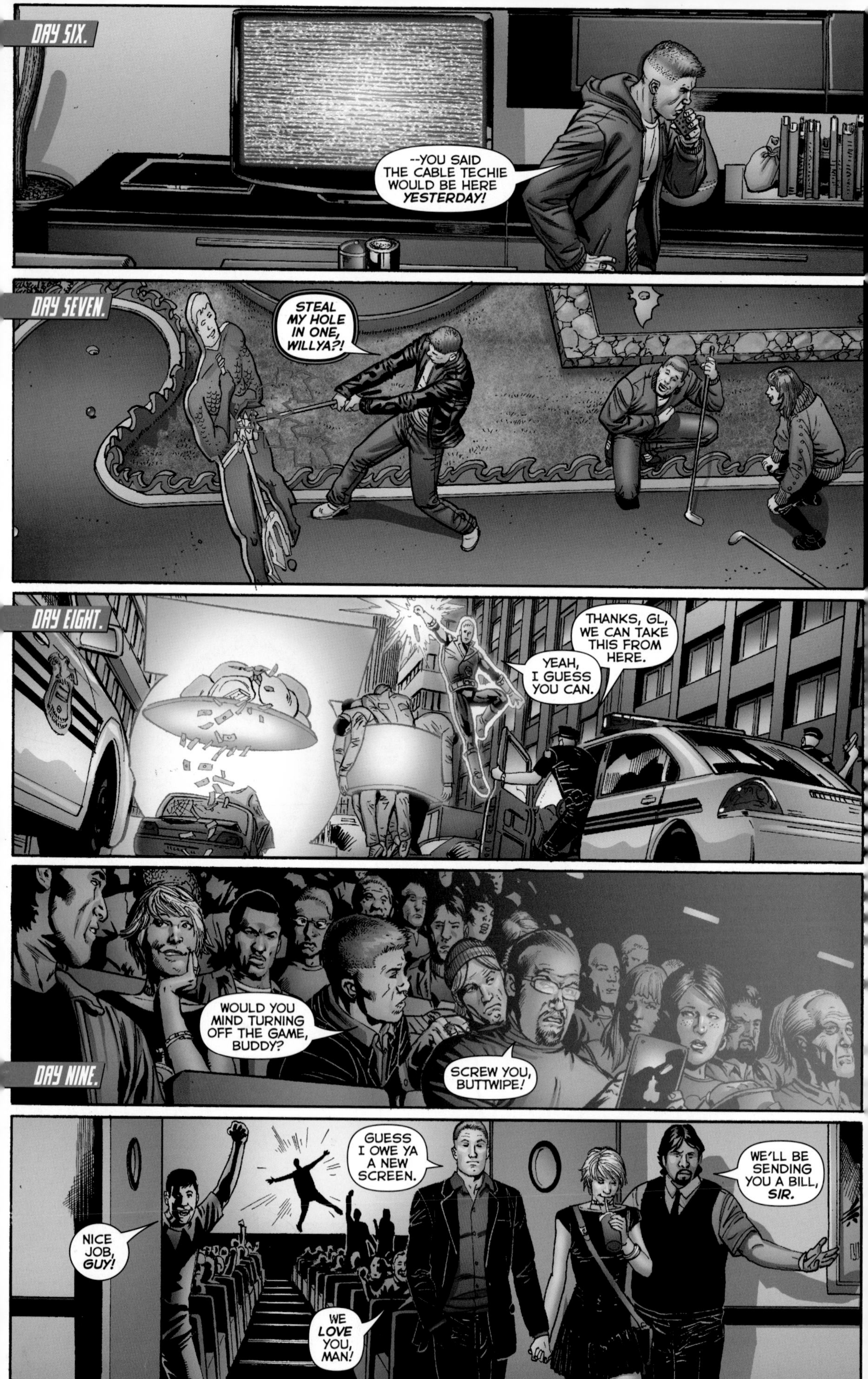
DAY SIX.
--YOU SAID THE CABLE TECHIE WOULD BE HERE YESTERDAY!
DAY SEVEN.
STEAL MY HOLE IN ONE, WILLYA?!
DAY EIGHT.
THANKS, GL, WE CAN TAKE THIS FROM HERE.
YEAH, I GUESS YOU CAN.
DAY NINE.
WOULD YOU MIND TURNING OFF THE GAME, BUDDY?
SCREW YOU, BUTTWIPE!
GUESS I OWE YA A NEW SCREEN.
WE'LL BE SENDING YOU A BILL, SIR.
NICE JOB, GUY!
WE LOVE YOU, MAN!

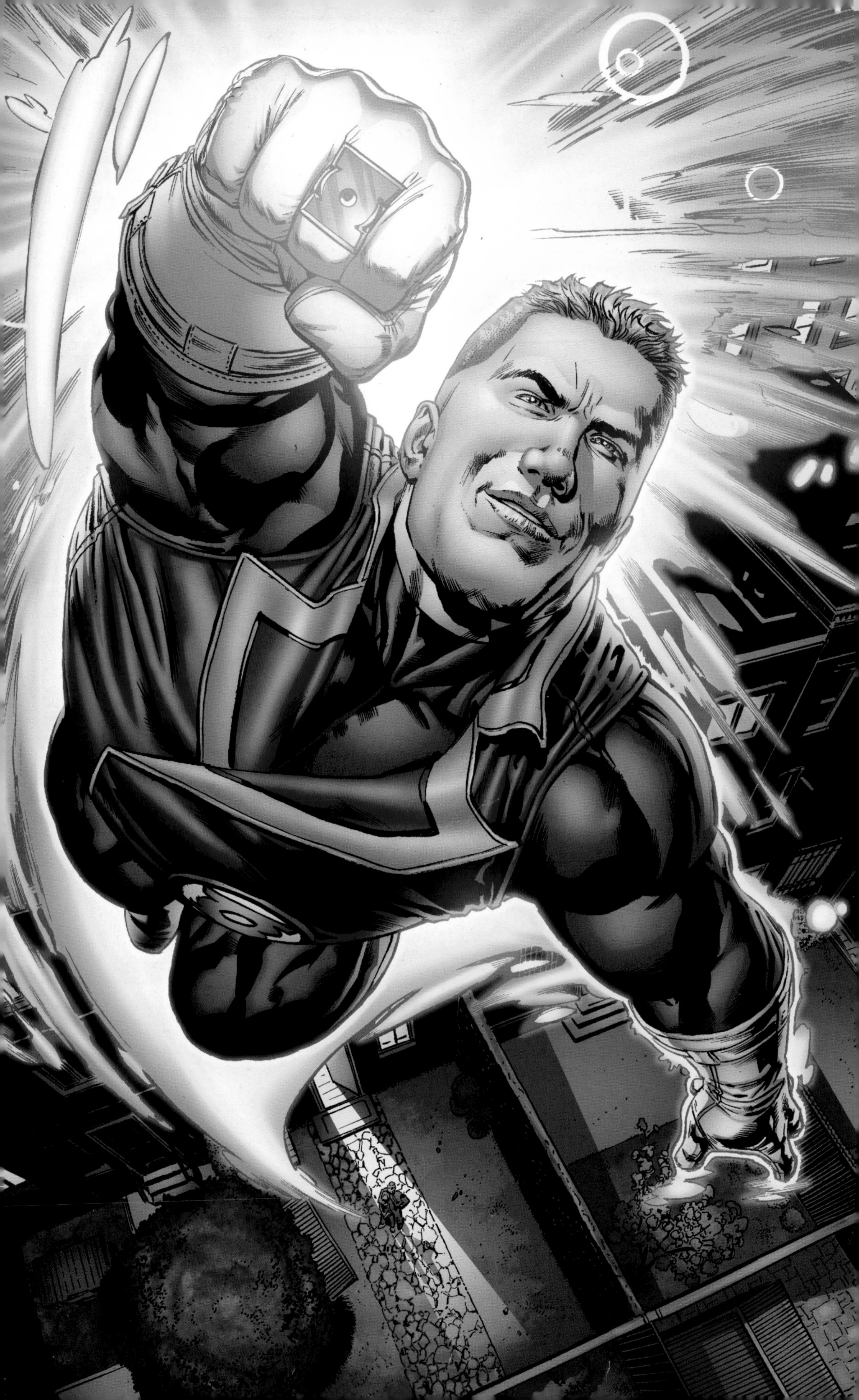

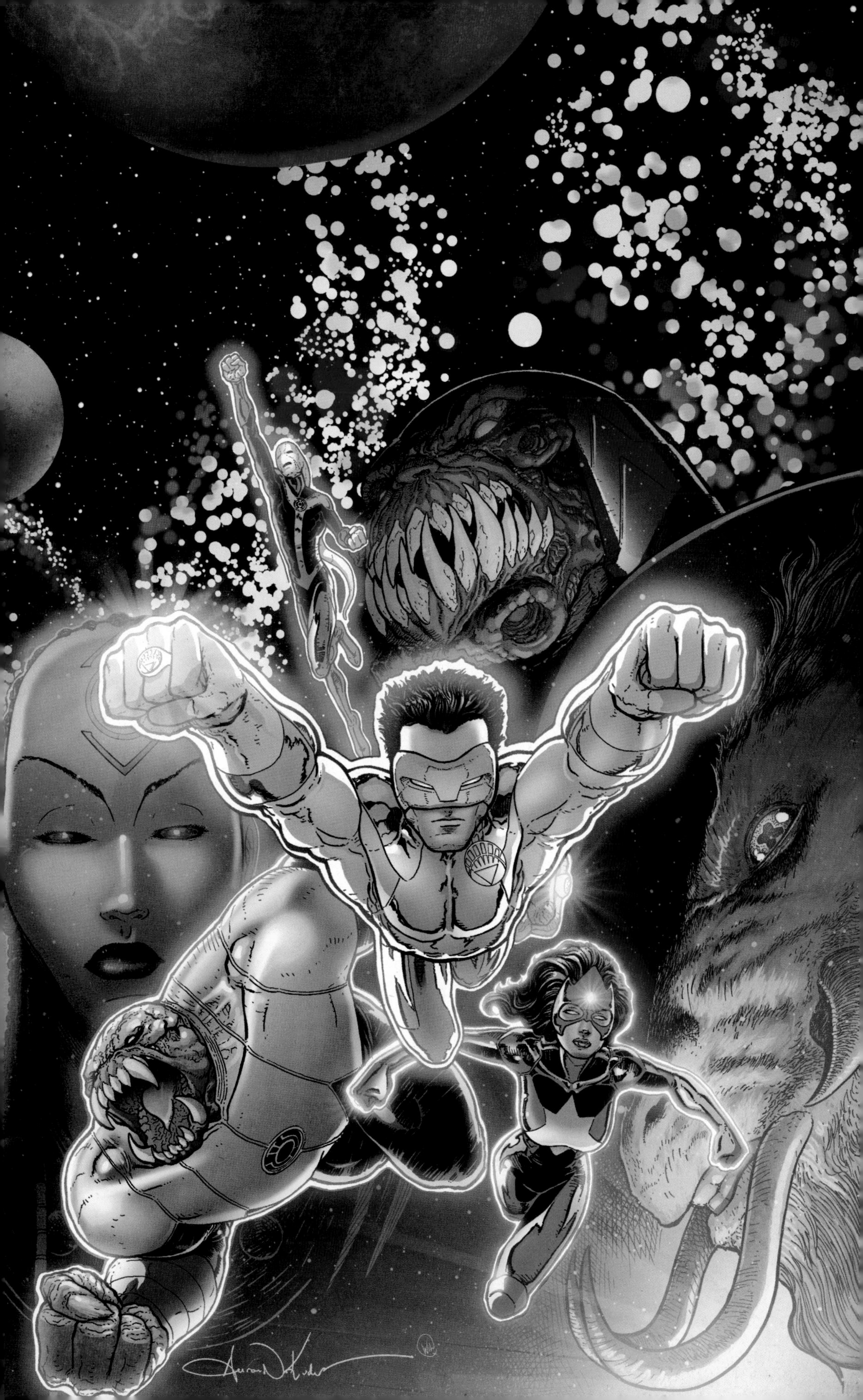

EPILOGUE: REUNION

TONY BEDARD writer ANDRES GUINALDO penciller RAUL FERNANDEZ inker
cover art by AARON KUDER & WIL QUINTANA

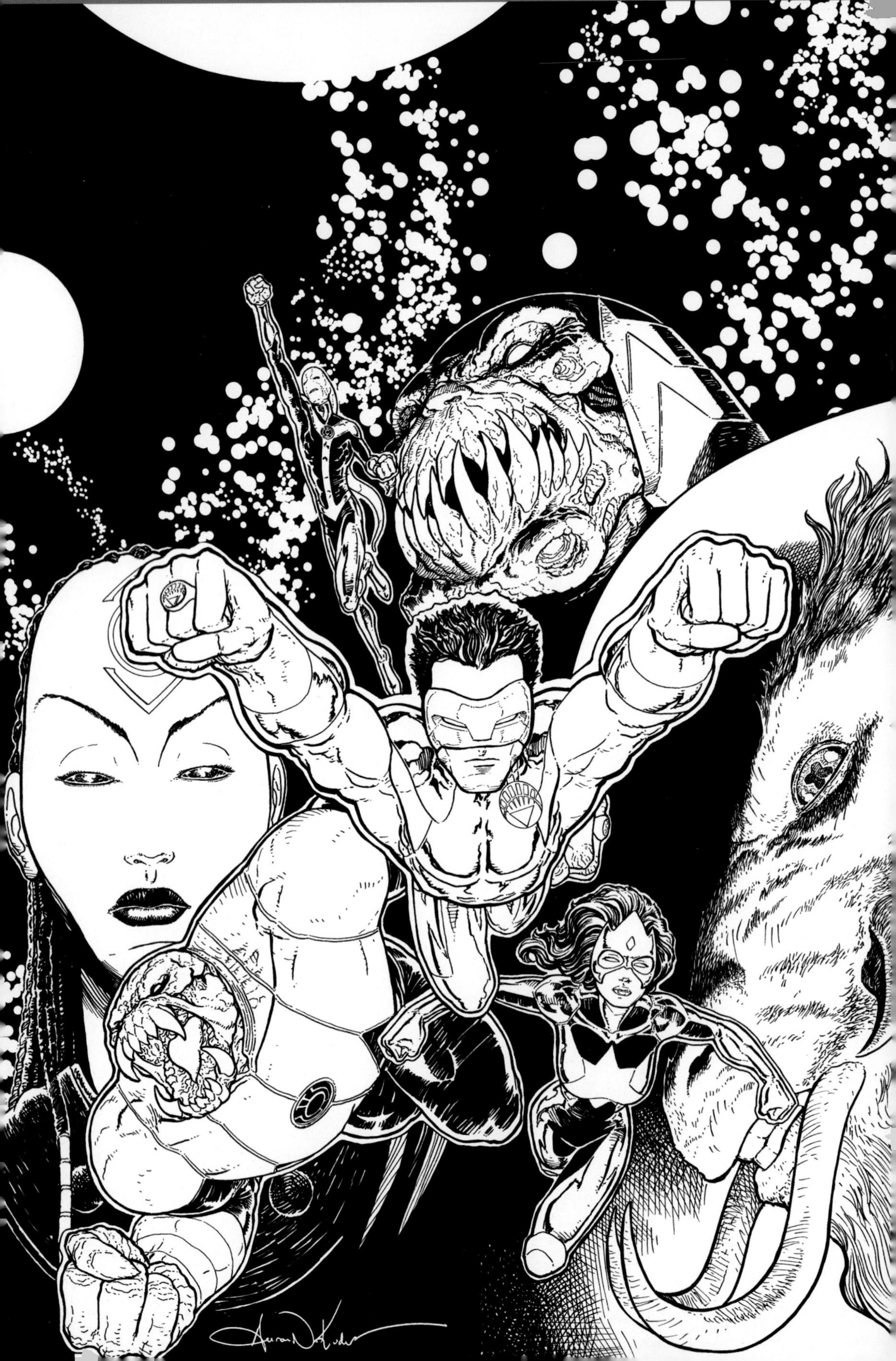

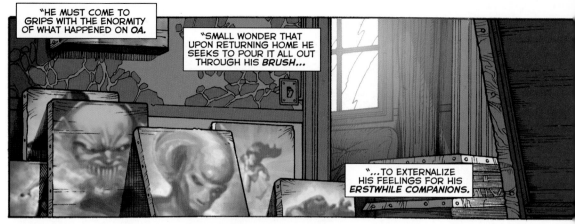

"HE MUST COME TO GRIPS WITH THE ENORMITY OF WHAT HAPPENED ON *OA*.

"SMALL WONDER THAT UPON RETURNING HOME HE SEEKS TO POUR IT ALL OUT THROUGH HIS *BRUSH*...

"...TO EXTERNALIZE HIS FEELINGS FOR HIS *ERSTWHILE* COMPANIONS.

"*SAINT WALKER,* CHAMPION OF HOPE.

"FEARSOME *ARKILLO.*

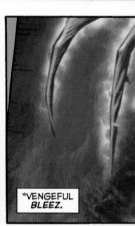

"VENGEFUL *BLEEZ.*

"...AND HIS MISTRESS, *INDIGO-1.*

"RAGING *ATROCITUS.*

"GREEDY *LARFLEEZE,* WHOM WE KNOW ALL TOO WELL...

RING: *TELL* ME SOMETHING.

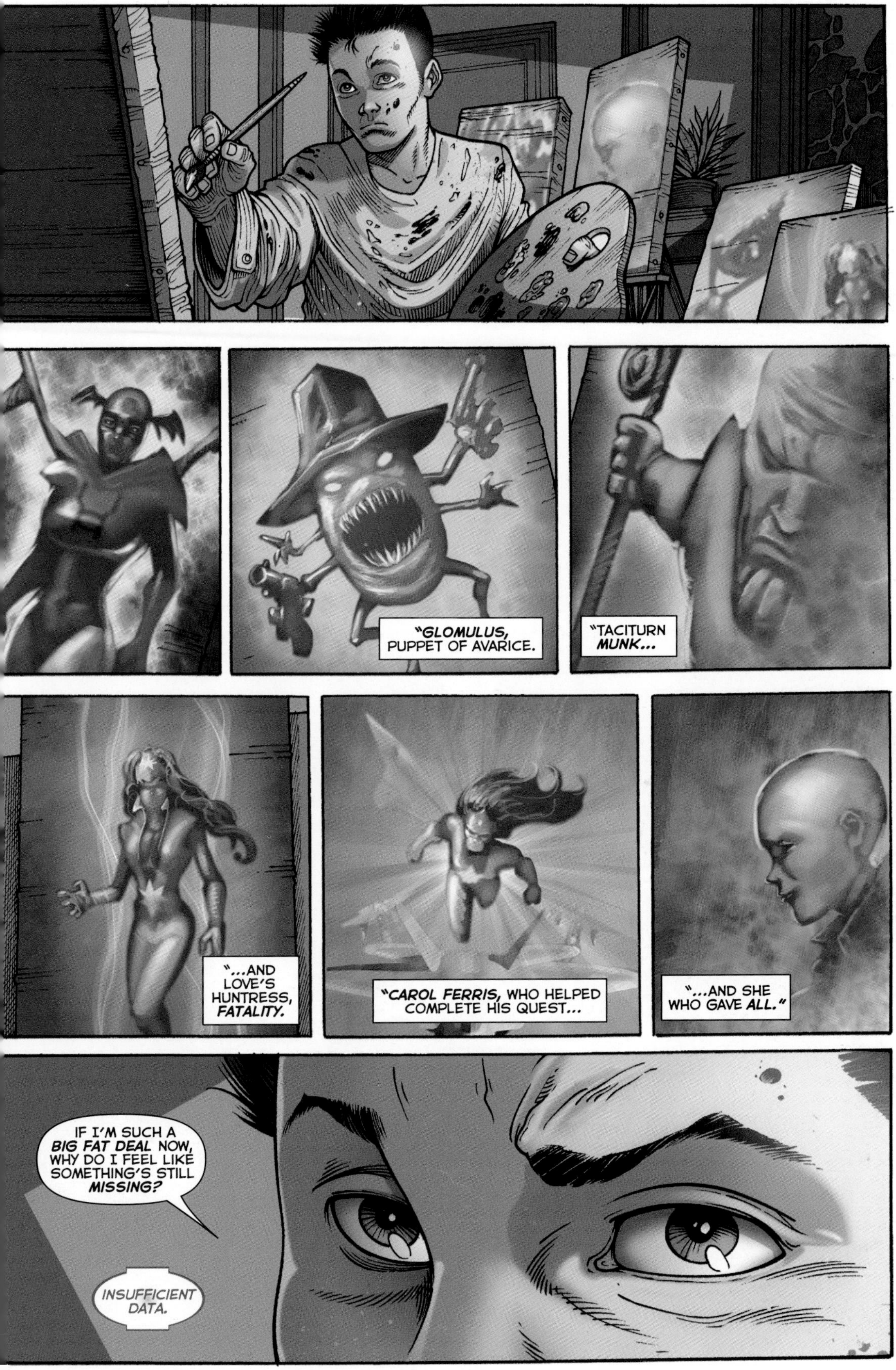
"GLOMULUS, PUPPET OF AVARICE.
"TACITURN MUNK...
"...AND LOVE'S HUNTRESS, FATALITY.
"CAROL FERRIS, WHO HELPED COMPLETE HIS QUEST...
"...AND SHE WHO GAVE ALL."
IF I'M SUCH A BIG FAT DEAL NOW, WHY DO I FEEL LIKE SOMETHING'S STILL MISSING?
INSUFFICIENT DATA.

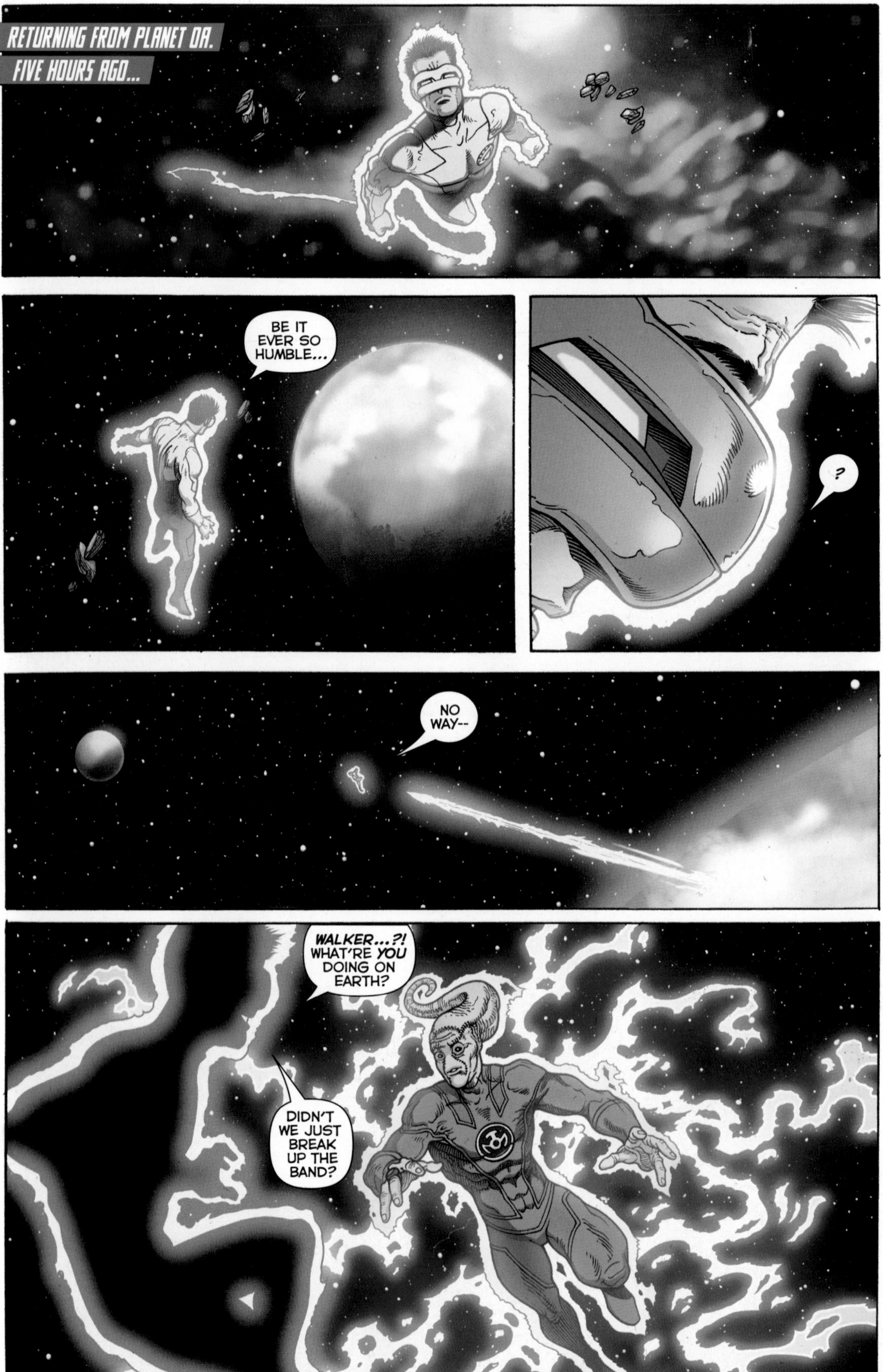
RETURNING FROM PLANET OA.
FIVE HOURS AGO...
BE IT EVER SO HUMBLE...
?
NO WAY--
WALKER...?! WHAT'RE YOU DOING ON EARTH?
DIDN'T WE JUST BREAK UP THE BAND?

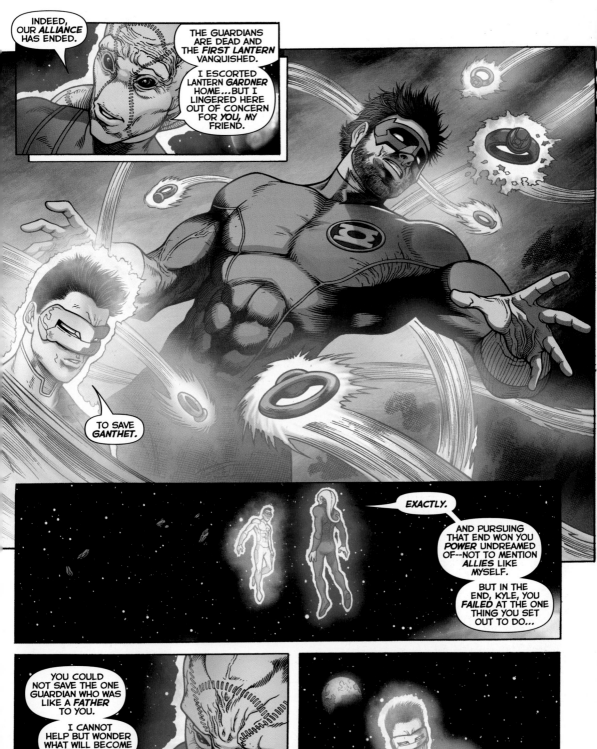

INDEED, OUR *ALLIANCE* HAS ENDED.

THE GUARDIANS ARE DEAD AND THE *FIRST LANTERN* VANQUISHED.

I ESCORTED LANTERN *GARDNER* HOME...BUT I LINGERED HERE OUT OF CONCERN FOR *YOU,* MY FRIEND.

TO SAVE *GANTHET.*

EXACTLY.

AND PURSUING THAT END WON YOU *POWER* UNDREAMED OF--NOT TO MENTION *ALLIES* LIKE MYSELF.

BUT IN THE END, KYLE, YOU *FAILED* AT THE ONE THING YOU SET OUT TO DO...

YOU COULD NOT SAVE THE ONE GUARDIAN WHO WAS LIKE A *FATHER* TO YOU.

I CANNOT HELP BUT WONDER WHAT WILL BECOME OF YOU *NOW?*

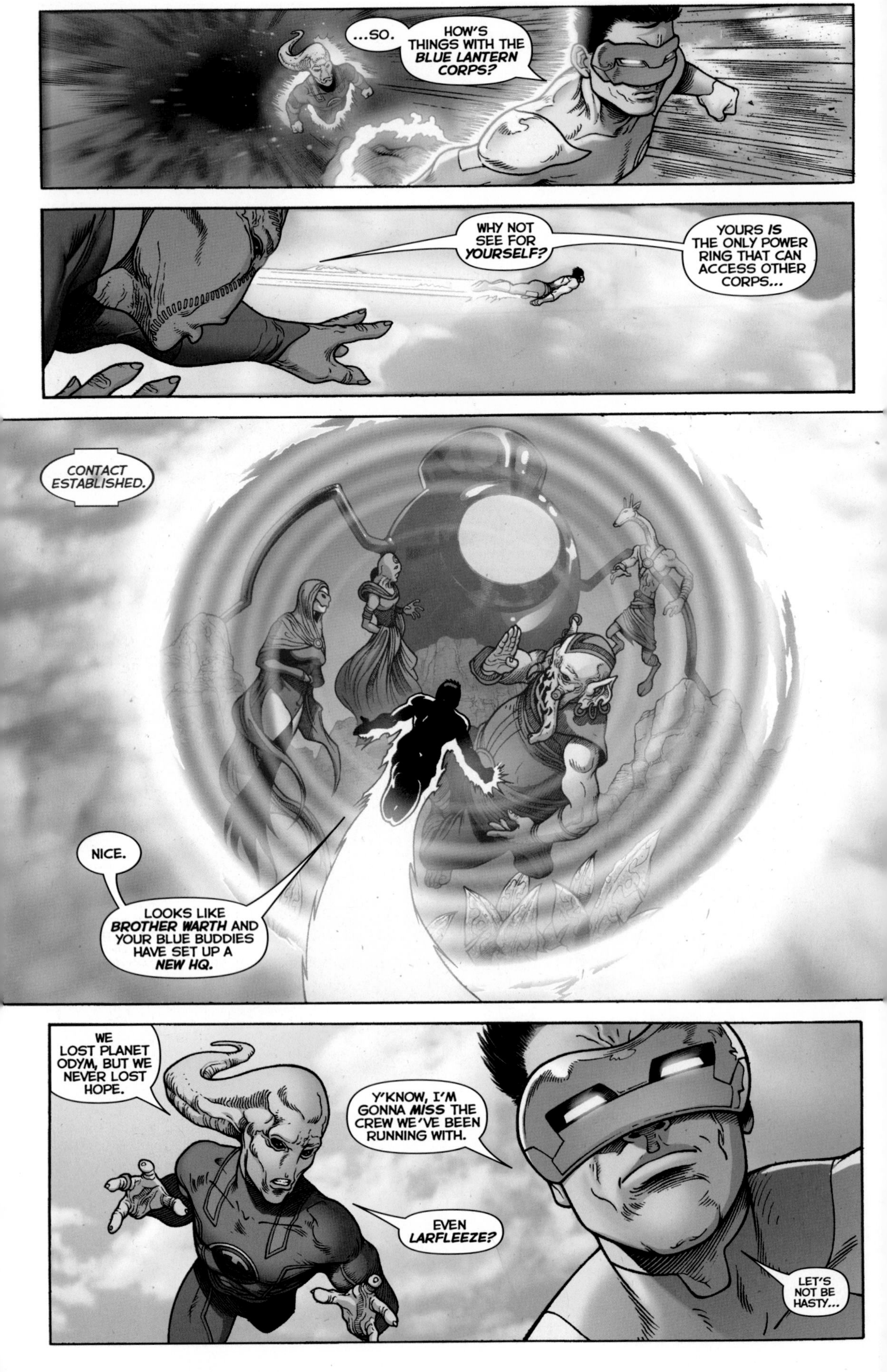
...SO.
HOW'S THINGS WITH THE BLUE LANTERN CORPS?
WHY NOT SEE FOR YOURSELF?
YOURS IS THE ONLY POWER RING THAT CAN ACCESS OTHER CORPS...
CONTACT ESTABLISHED.
NICE.
LOOKS LIKE BROTHER WARTH AND YOUR BLUE BUDDIES HAVE SET UP A NEW HQ.
WE LOST PLANET ODYM, BUT WE NEVER LOST HOPE.
Y'KNOW, I'M GONNA MISS THE CREW WE'VE BEEN RUNNING WITH.
EVEN LARFLEEZE?
LET'S NOT BE HASTY...

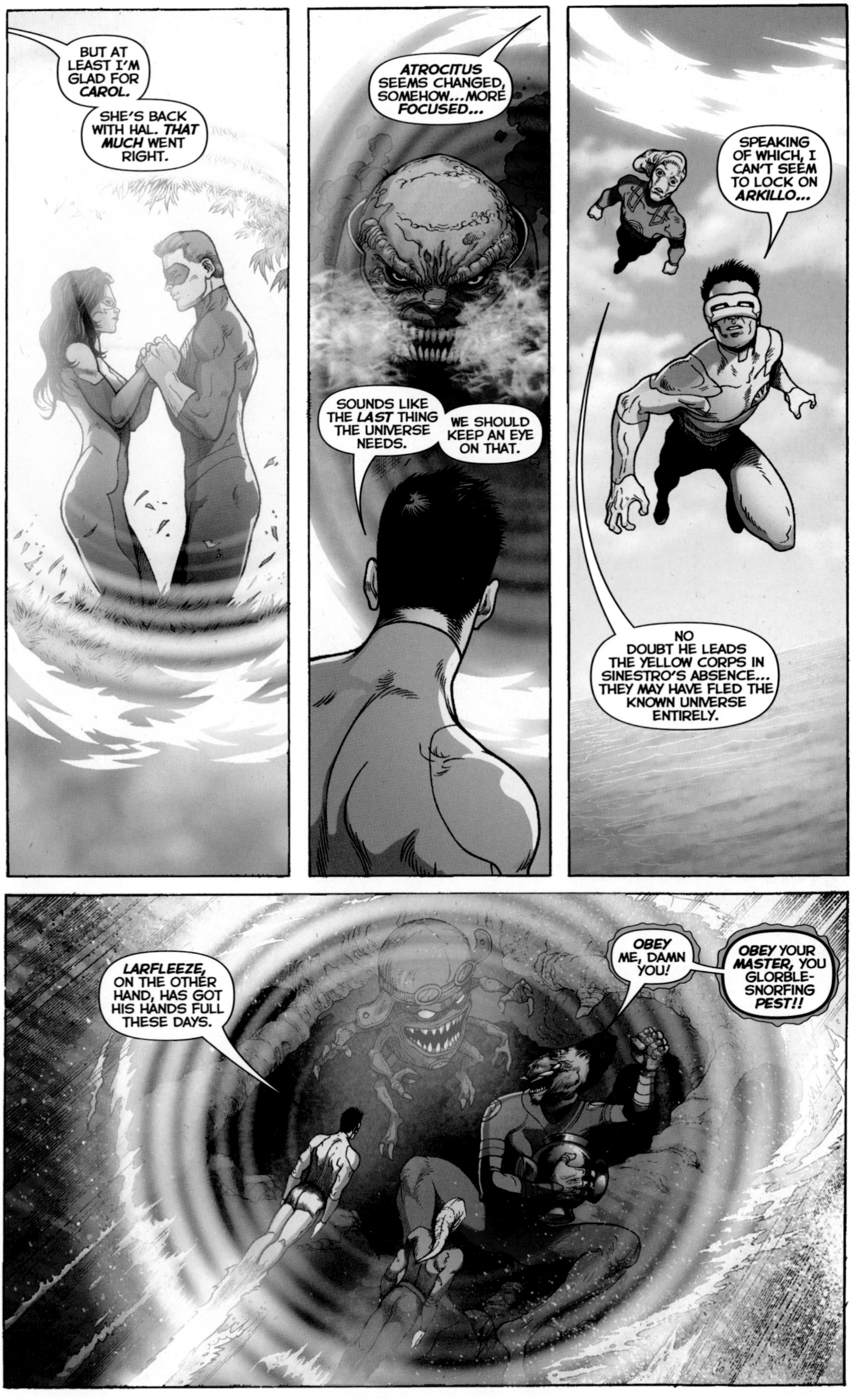
BUT AT LEAST I'M GLAD FOR CAROL.
SHE'S BACK WITH HAL. THAT MUCH WENT RIGHT.
ATROCITUS SEEMS CHANGED, SOMEHOW...MORE FOCUSED...
SOUNDS LIKE THE LAST THING THE UNIVERSE NEEDS.
WE SHOULD KEEP AN EYE ON THAT.
SPEAKING OF WHICH, I CAN'T SEEM TO LOCK ON ARKILLO...
NO DOUBT HE LEADS THE YELLOW CORPS IN SINESTRO'S ABSENCE... THEY MAY HAVE FLED THE KNOWN UNIVERSE ENTIRELY.
LARFLEEZE, ON THE OTHER HAND, HAS GOT HIS HANDS FULL THESE DAYS.
OBEY ME, DAMN YOU!
OBEY YOUR MASTER, YOU GLORBLE-SNORFING PEST!!

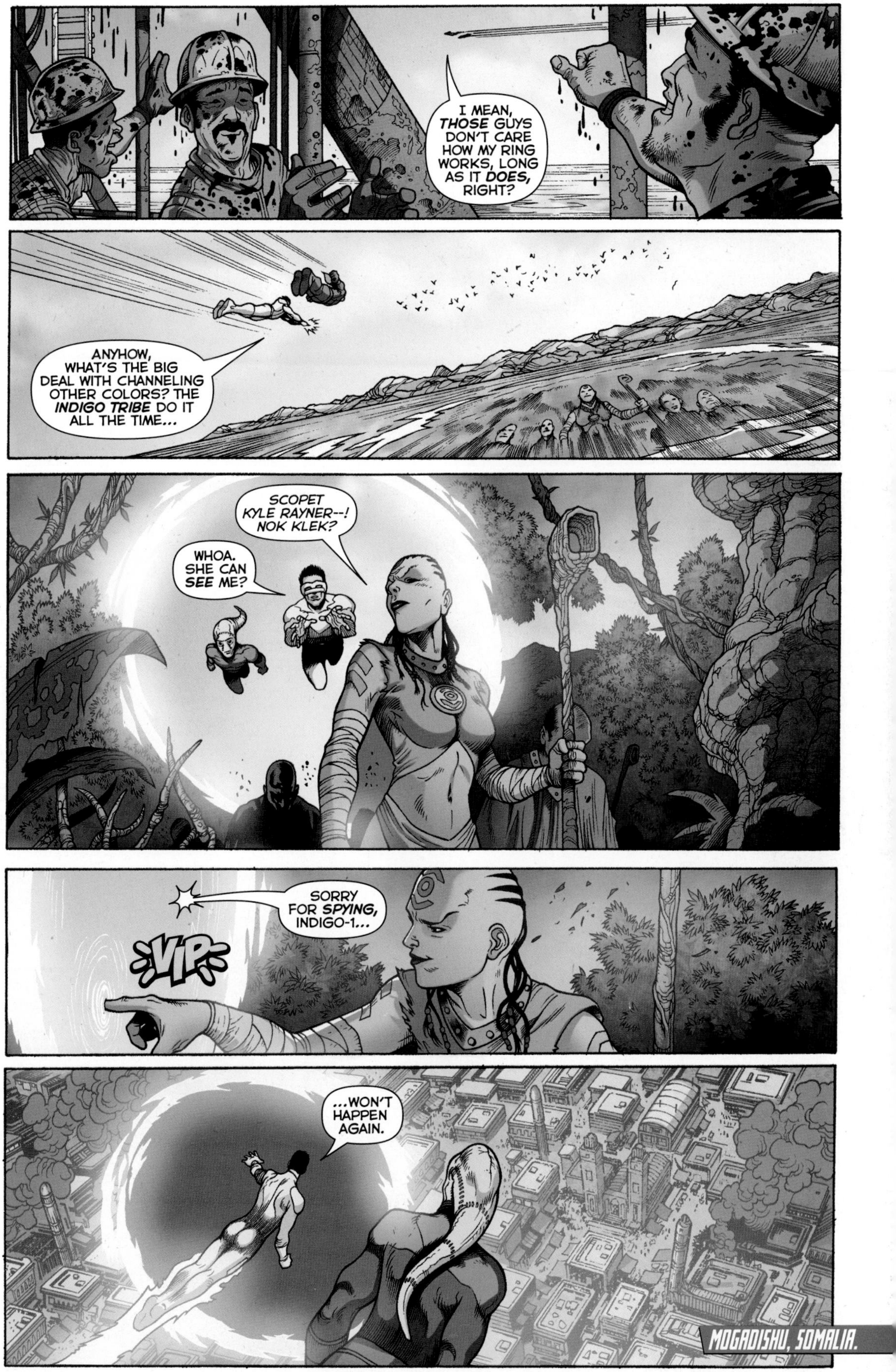
I MEAN, THOSE GUYS DON'T CARE HOW MY RING WORKS, LONG AS IT DOES, RIGHT?
ANYHOW, WHAT'S THE BIG DEAL WITH CHANNELING OTHER COLORS? THE INDIGO TRIBE DO IT ALL THE TIME...
SCOPET KYLE RAYNER--! NOK KLEK?
WHOA. SHE CAN SEE ME?
SORRY FOR SPYING, INDIGO-1...
VIP
...WON'T HAPPEN AGAIN.
MOGADISHU, SOMALIA.

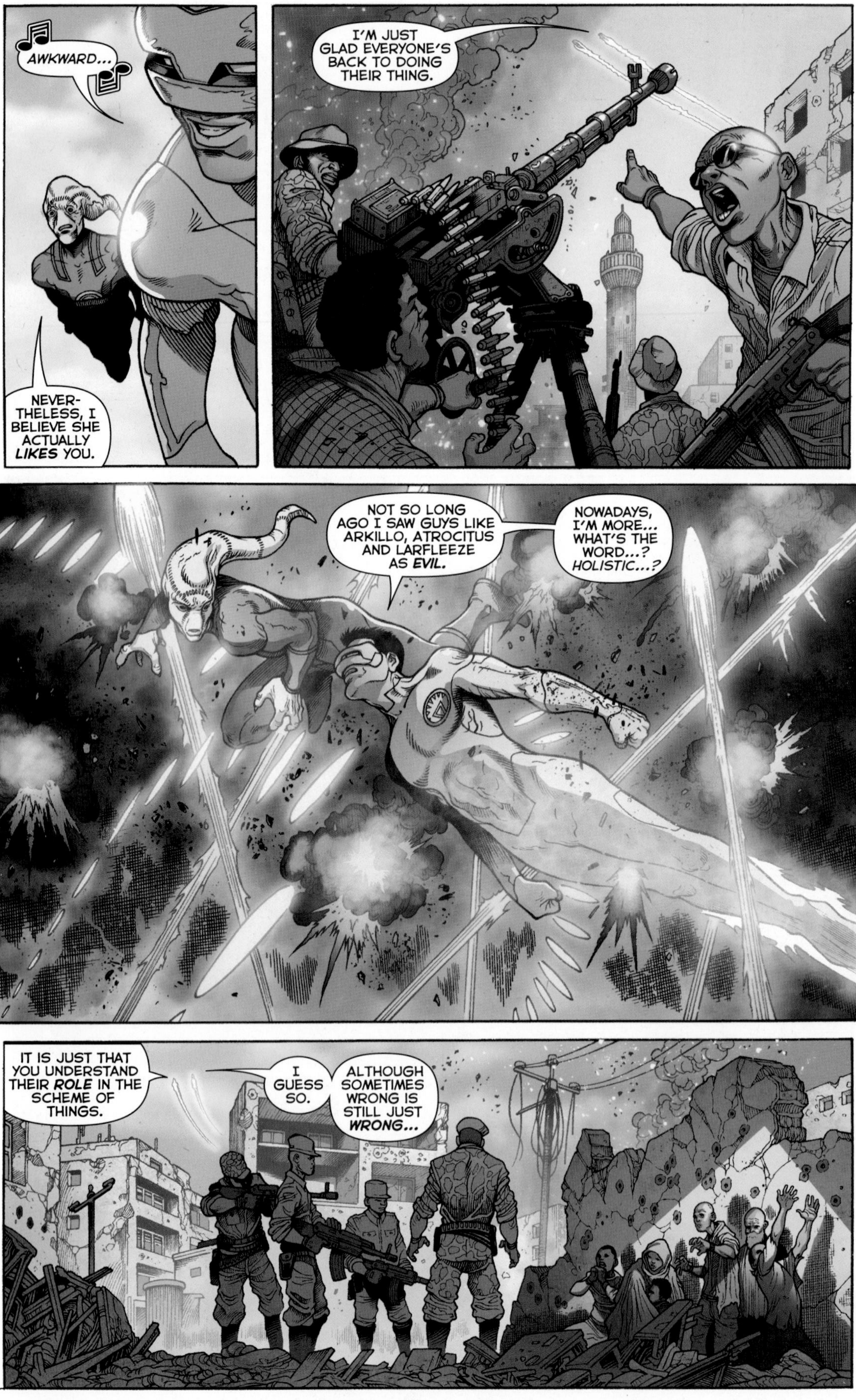
AWKWARD...
NEVER-THELESS, I BELIEVE SHE ACTUALLY LIKES YOU.
I'M JUST GLAD EVERYONE'S BACK TO DOING THEIR THING.
NOT SO LONG AGO I SAW GUYS LIKE ARKILLO, ATROCITUS AND LARFLEEZE AS EVIL.
NOWADAYS, I'M MORE... WHAT'S THE WORD...? HOLISTIC...?
IT IS JUST THAT YOU UNDERSTAND THEIR ROLE IN THE SCHEME OF THINGS.
I GUESS SO.
ALTHOUGH SOMETIMES WRONG IS STILL JUST WRONG...

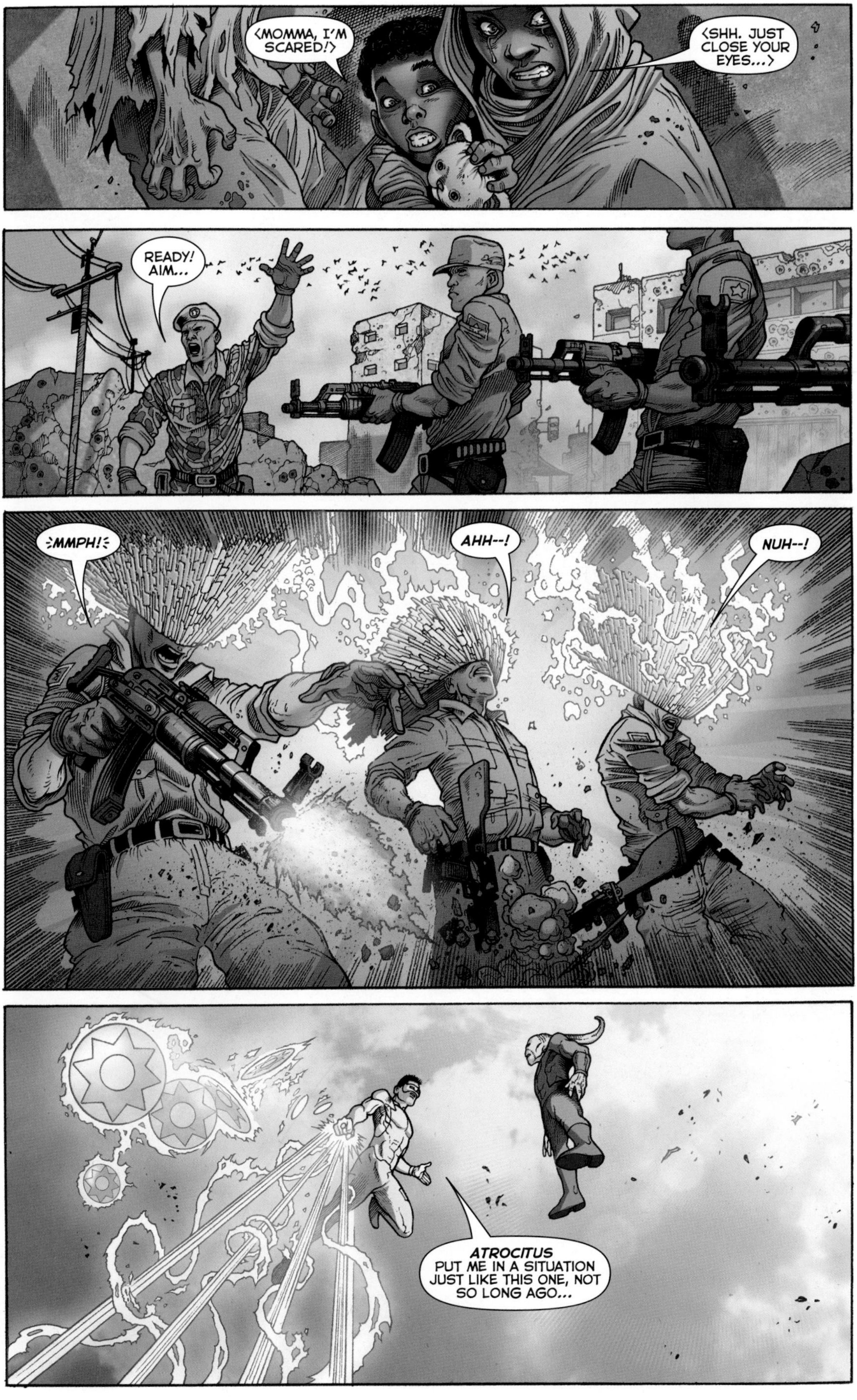
<MOMMA, I'M SCARED!>
<SHH. JUST CLOSE YOUR EYES...>
READY! AIM...
MMPH!
AHH--!
NUH--!
ATROCITUS PUT ME IN A SITUATION JUST LIKE THIS ONE, NOT SO LONG AGO...

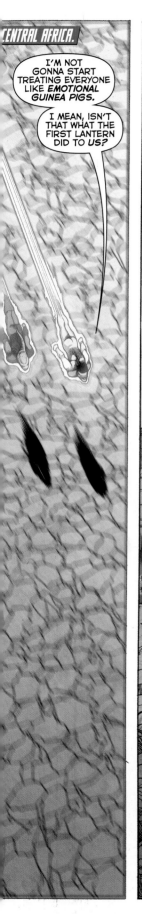

I'M NOT GONNA START TREATING EVERYONE LIKE *EMOTIONAL GUINEA PIGS.*

I MEAN, ISN'T THAT WHAT THE FIRST LANTERN DID TO *US?*

INDEED. HE *REUNITED* ME WITH MY LONG-DEAD FAMILY--

--BUT ONLY SO HE COULD PLUNGE ME INTO *DESPAIR* WHEN I *LOST* THEM ONCE AGAIN.

HE DID *ALL KINDS* OF STUFF TO ME--RESURRECTING MY DEAD GIRL-FRIEND...

...MAKING ME RESPONSIBLE FOR THE *END* OF THE GREEN LANTERN CORPS...

...BUT THE BIGGEST *CHEAP-SHOT* WAS REUNITING ME WITH MY *DAD.*

WHY WAS *THAT* THE WORST?

DAD *ABANDONED* ME WHEN I WAS SIX.

MY WHOLE LIFE I'VE WONDERED WHAT HE'D BE LIKE TODAY...

KYLE, MY FRIEND, YOU HAVE NEVER BEEN A FATHER *YOURSELF,* NEVER SEEN IT FROM THE OTHER SIDE.

I *HAVE.*

ONE OF THE HARDEST THINGS TO *REALIZE* IS THAT YOUR PARENTS ARE JUST *PEOPLE.*

THEY ARE NOT THE *MONOLITHIC FIGURES* OF CHILDHOOD.

THEY ARE SIMPLY PEOPLE-- AS *FALLIBLE* AS YOU, AND AS *CHALLENGED* BY THEIR LIVES.

DO YOU KNOW *WHY* YOUR FATHER LEFT?

I NEVER ASKED MOM. I KINDA DOUBT *SHE* KNEW.

THEN I SUBMIT TO YOU THAT THE FIRST LANTERN GAVE US A *GIFT* WHEN HE TOYED WITH OUR PASTS.

I SPENT PRECIOUS MOMENTS WITH MY *FAMILY.* YOU MET YOUR *FATHER* AGAIN.

AND YOU *SAW* HIM AS HE APPEARS TODAY...

OH, NO. I SEE WHERE YOU'RE *GOING* WITH THIS.

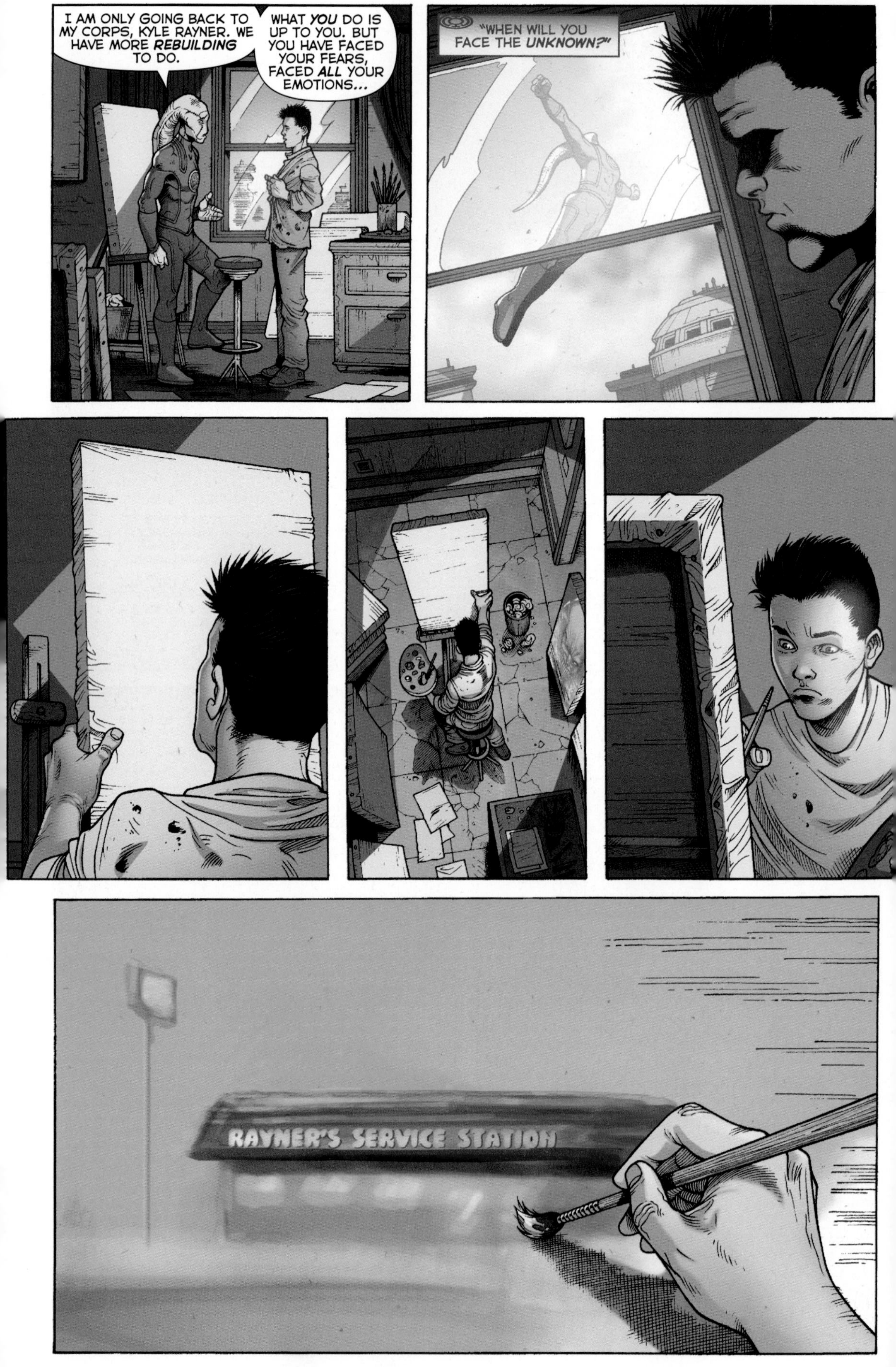
I AM ONLY GOING BACK TO MY CORPS, KYLE RAYNER. WE HAVE MORE *REBUILDING* TO DO.
WHAT *YOU* DO IS UP TO YOU. BUT YOU HAVE FACED YOUR FEARS, FACED *ALL* YOUR EMOTIONS...
"WHEN WILL YOU FACE THE *UNKNOWN?*"
RAYNER'S SERVICE STATION

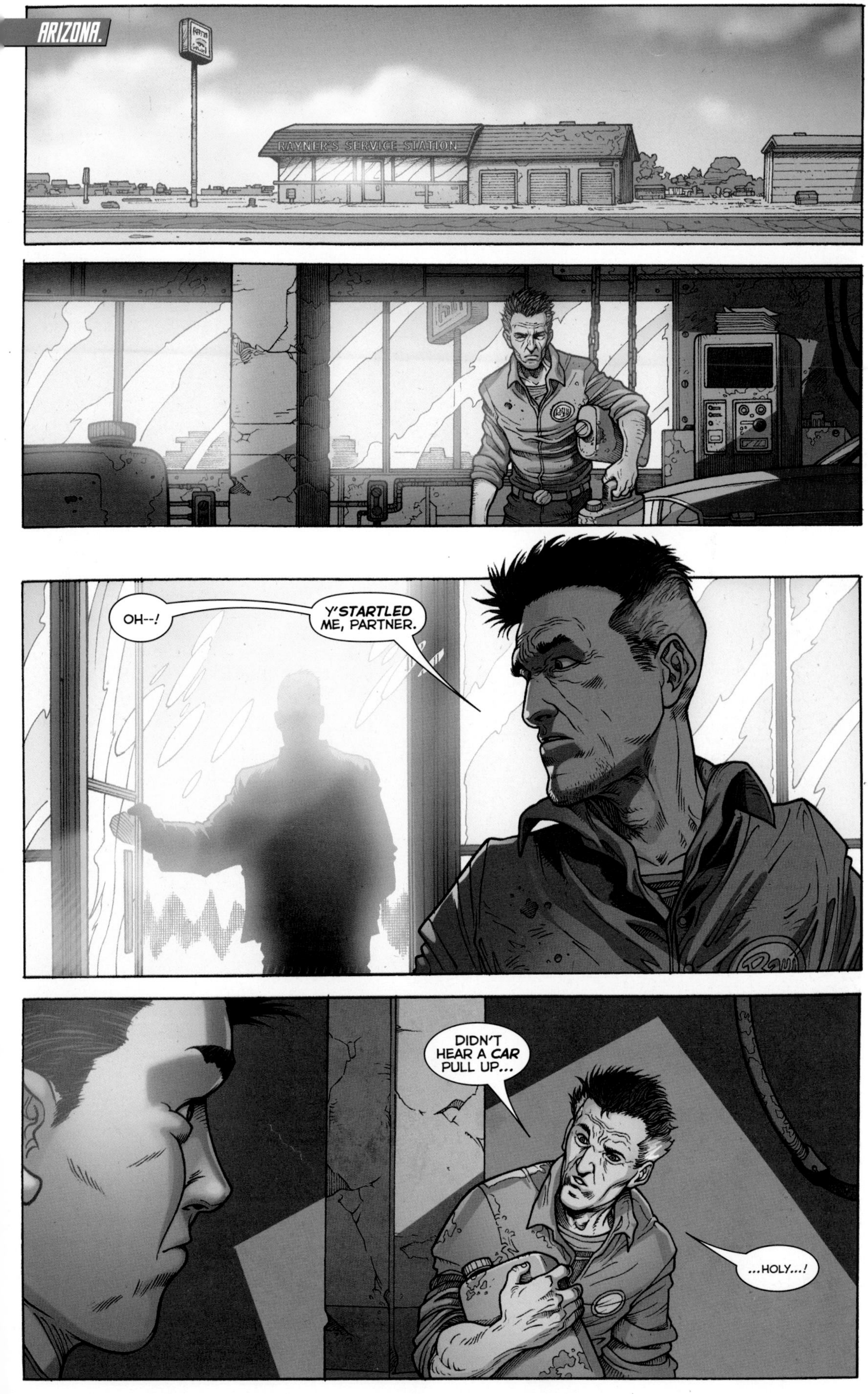
ARIZONA.
RAYNER'S SERVICE STATION
OH--!
Y'STARTLED ME, PARTNER.
DIDN'T HEAR A CAR PULL UP...
...HOLY...!

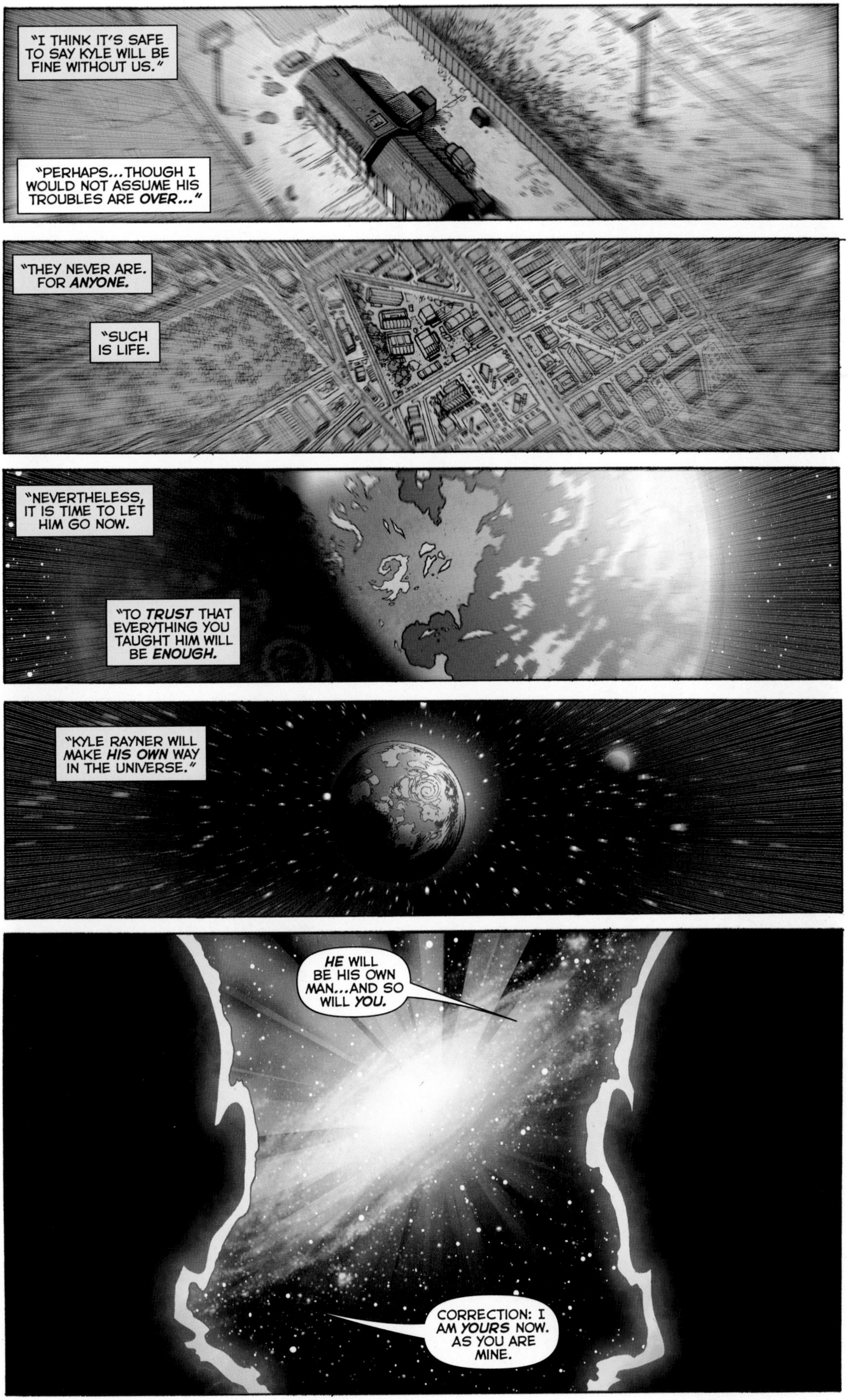
"I THINK IT'S SAFE TO SAY KYLE WILL BE FINE WITHOUT US."
"PERHAPS...THOUGH I WOULD NOT ASSUME HIS TROUBLES ARE OVER..."
"THEY NEVER ARE. FOR ANYONE.
"SUCH IS LIFE.
"NEVERTHELESS, IT IS TIME TO LET HIM GO NOW.
"TO TRUST THAT EVERYTHING YOU TAUGHT HIM WILL BE ENOUGH.
"KYLE RAYNER WILL MAKE HIS OWN WAY IN THE UNIVERSE."
HE WILL BE HIS OWN MAN...AND SO WILL YOU.
CORRECTION: I AM YOURS NOW. AS YOU ARE MINE.

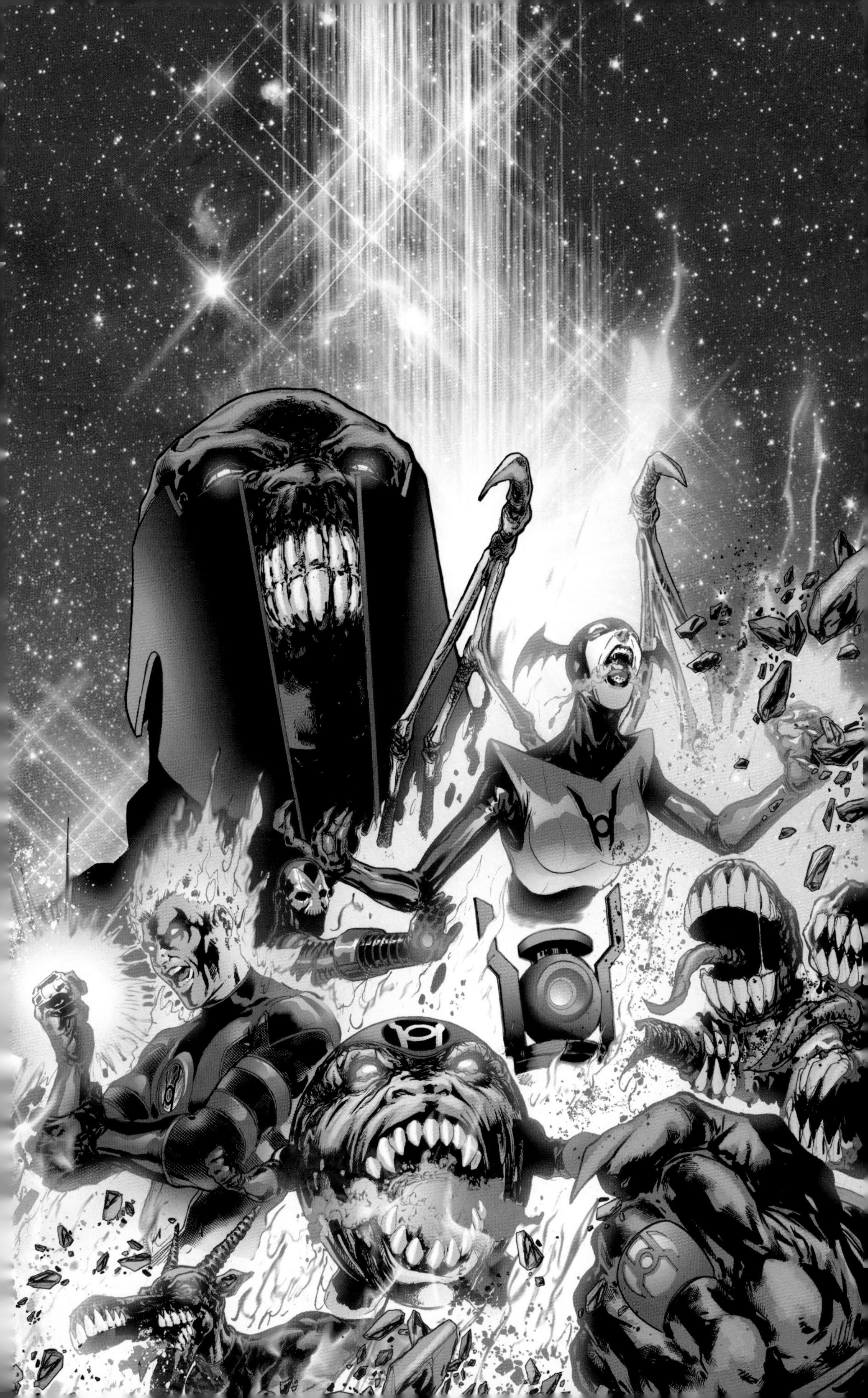

EPILOGUE: A DEATH LONG COMING...
PETER MILLIGAN writer WILL CONRAD artist
cover art by MIGUEL SEPULVEDA & RAIN BEREDO

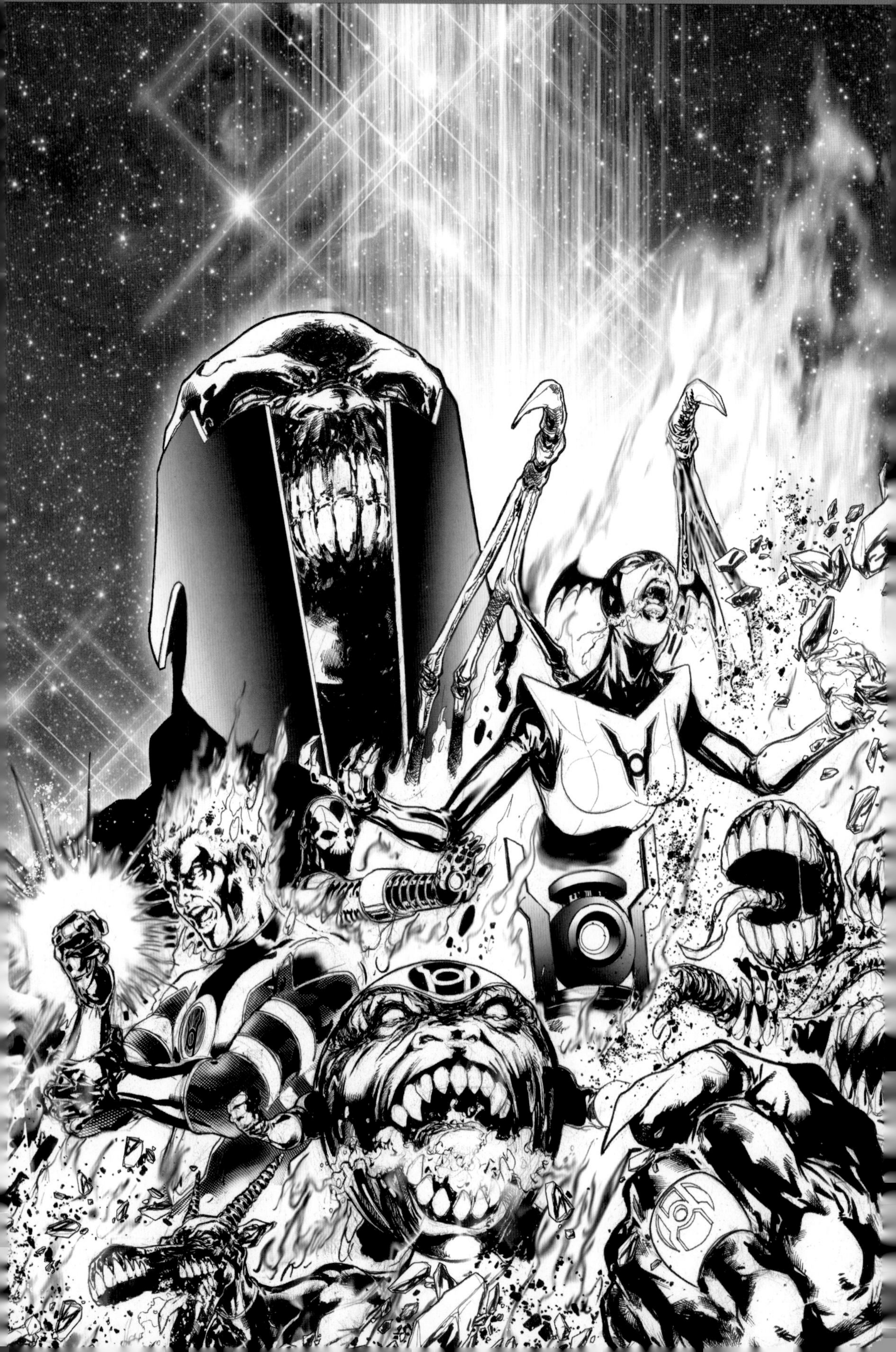

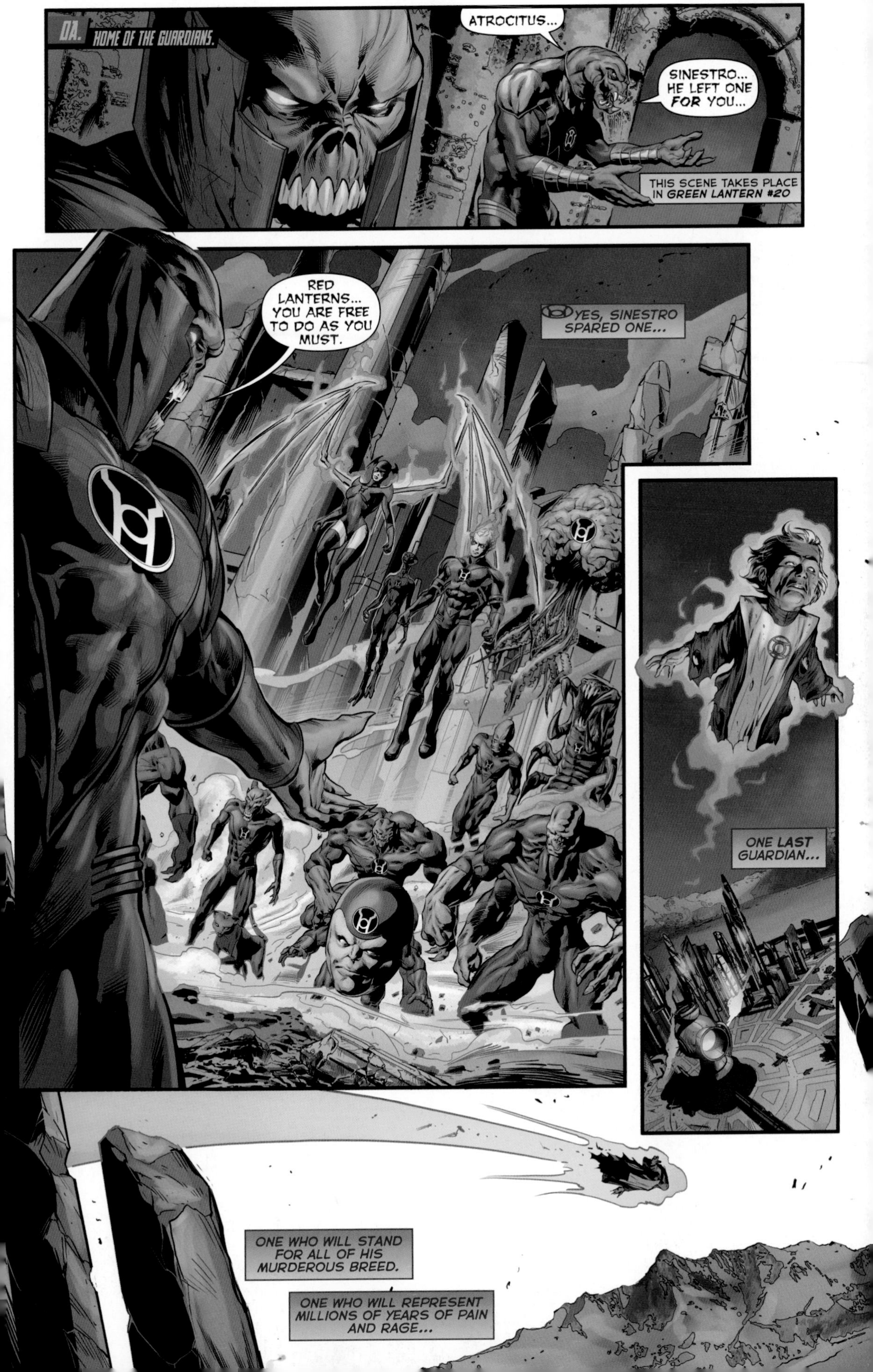
OA. HOME OF THE GUARDIANS.
ATROCITUS...
SINESTRO... HE LEFT ONE FOR YOU...
THIS SCENE TAKES PLACE IN GREEN LANTERN #20
RED LANTERNS... YOU ARE FREE TO DO AS YOU MUST.
YES, SINESTRO SPARED ONE...
ONE LAST GUARDIAN...
ONE WHO WILL STAND FOR ALL OF HIS MURDEROUS BREED.
ONE WHO WILL REPRESENT MILLIONS OF YEARS OF PAIN AND RAGE...

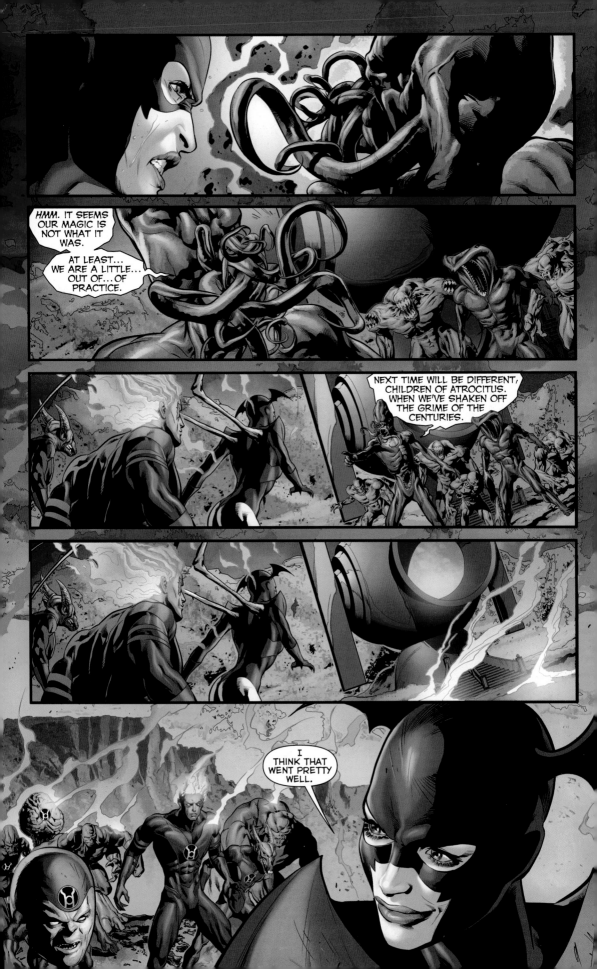

AAAH!

STILL ALIVE. GOOD.

UGHNN!

THDDDDD

AWKK!

WHAT HAS TAKEN SO LONG... SHOULD NOT BE FINISHED TOO QUICKLY.

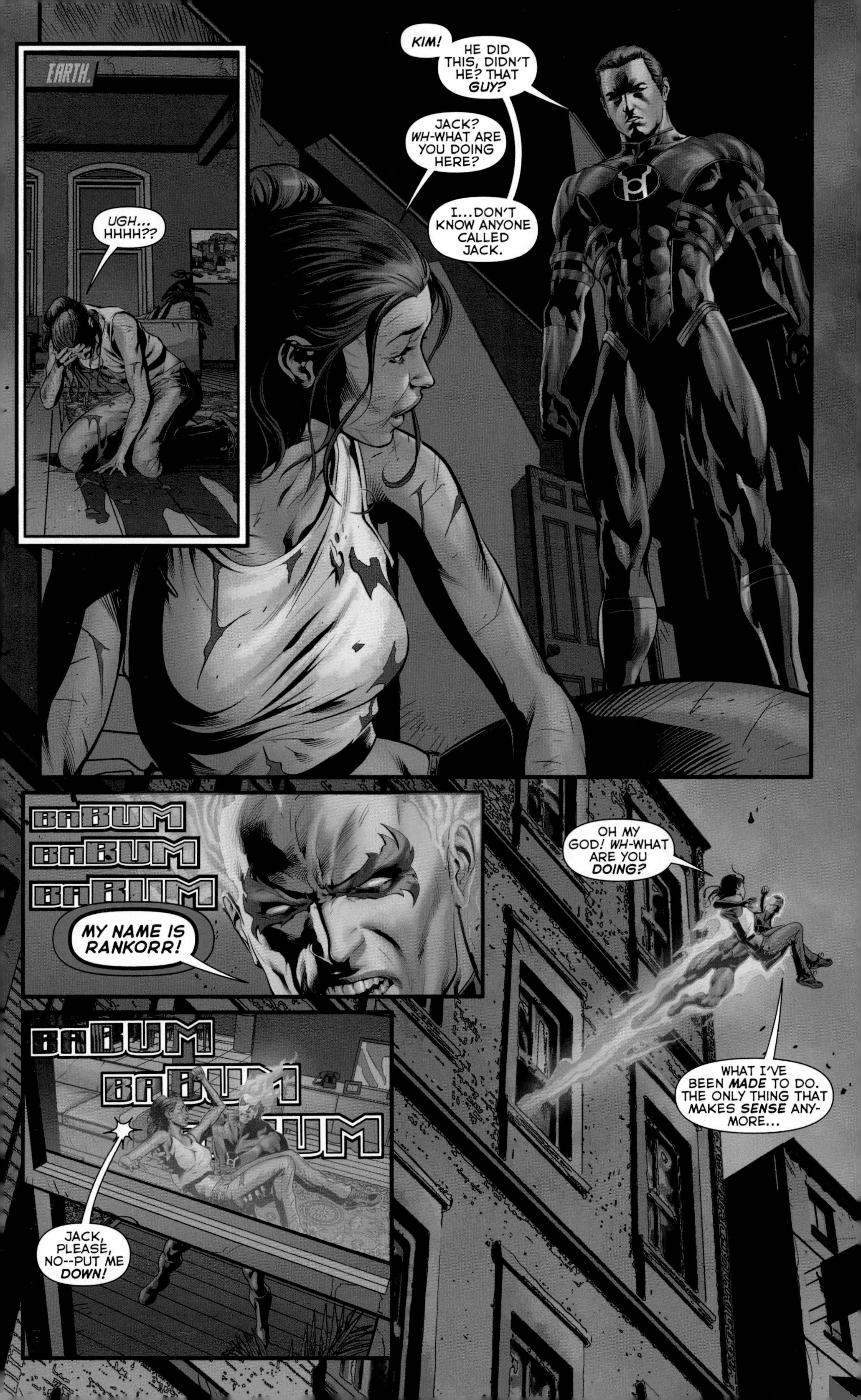
EARTH.
UGH... HHHH??
KIM!
HE DID THIS, DIDN'T HE? THAT GUY?
JACK? WH-WHAT ARE YOU DOING HERE?
I...DON'T KNOW ANYONE CALLED JACK.
BABUM
BABUM
BABUM
MY NAME IS RANKORR!
BABUM
BABUM
BABUM
JACK, PLEASE, NO--PUT ME DOWN!
OH MY GOD! WH-WHAT ARE YOU DOING?
WHAT I'VE BEEN MADE TO DO. THE ONLY THING THAT MAKES SENSE ANY-MORE...

WHY? HAVE YOU SEEN YOUR *FACE?* THIS IS WHERE ATROCITUS WENT WRONG.

A-ATROCITUS? WHO--

HIS *RAGE* WAS ALL FOR HIMSELF. BUT IT CAN BE A FORCE FOR GOOD, IF USED FOR *OTHERS.*

JUST TELL ME HOW YOU WANT ME TO KILL HIM.

STOP IT.

THIS ISN'T YOU, JACK. OR RANKORR. OR *WHATEVER* YOUR NAME IS. THIS ISN'T THE NICE SWEET PERSON I STARTED TO FALL IN LOVE WITH.

BUT--

SLAP

I THOUGHT... I COULD *USE* IT. I THOUGHT I... I COULD TURN THIS THING THAT'S HAPPENED TO ME TO SOME *GOOD.*

STEPHEN IS A *PIG.* HE'S STUPID, VIOLENT, AND DESERVES TO BE LOCKED UP. AND *WILL* BE. BUT *YOU.*

YOU'RE NOT EVEN HUMAN. NOT LIKE THIS.

RAGE, KIM. DON'T YOU FEEL *RAGE* AT WHAT HE DID TO YOU?

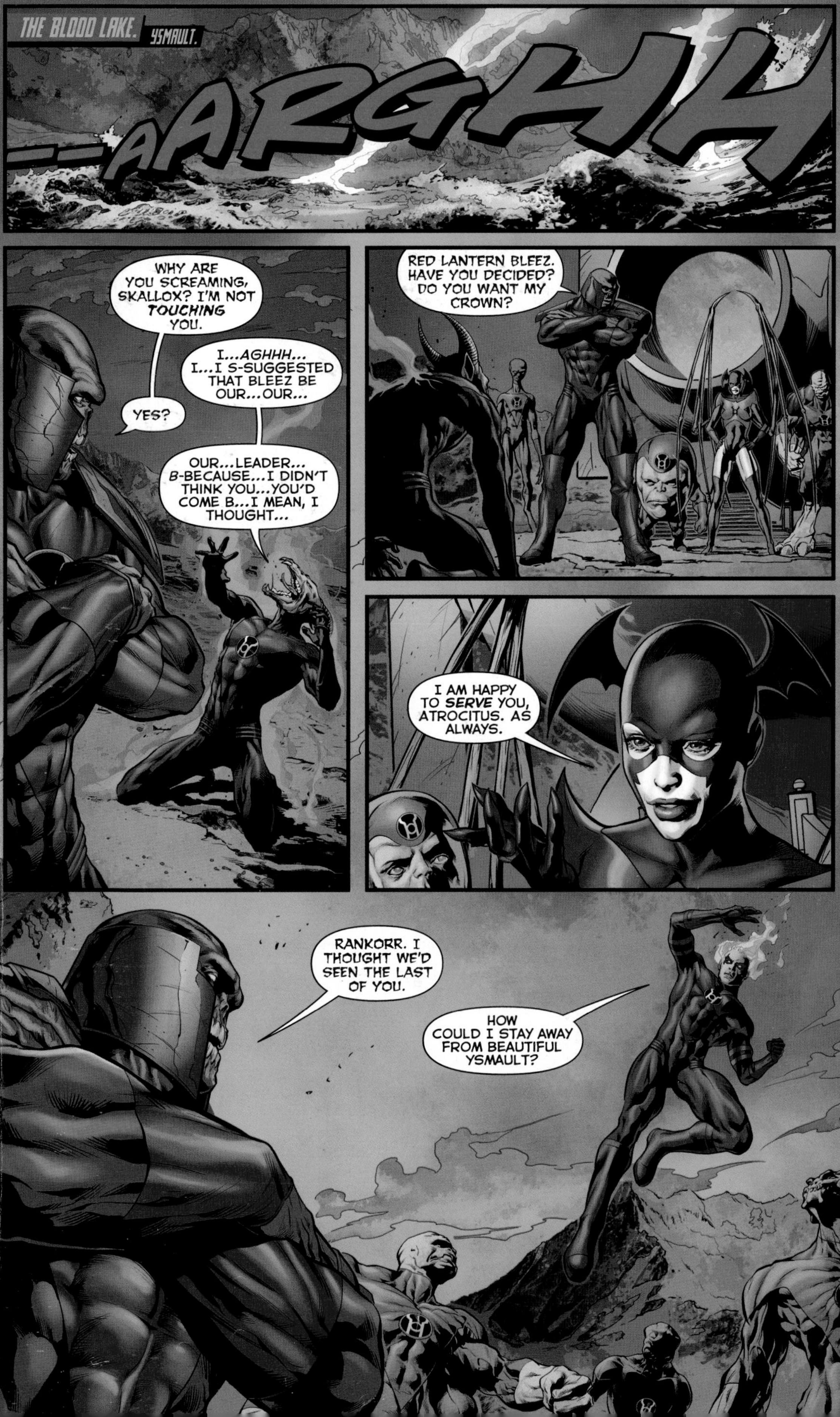

THE BLOOD LAKE. YSMAULT.
--AARGHHK
WHY ARE YOU SCREAMING, SKALLOX? I'M NOT TOUCHING YOU.
I...AGHHH... I...I S-SUGGESTED THAT BLEEZ BE OUR...OUR...
YES?
OUR...LEADER... B-BECAUSE...I DIDN'T THINK YOU...YOU'D COME B...I MEAN, I THOUGHT...
RED LANTERN BLEEZ. HAVE YOU DECIDED? DO YOU WANT MY CROWN?
I AM HAPPY TO SERVE YOU, ATROCITUS. AS ALWAYS.
RANKORR. I THOUGHT WE'D SEEN THE LAST OF YOU.
HOW COULD I STAY AWAY FROM BEAUTIFUL YSMAULT?

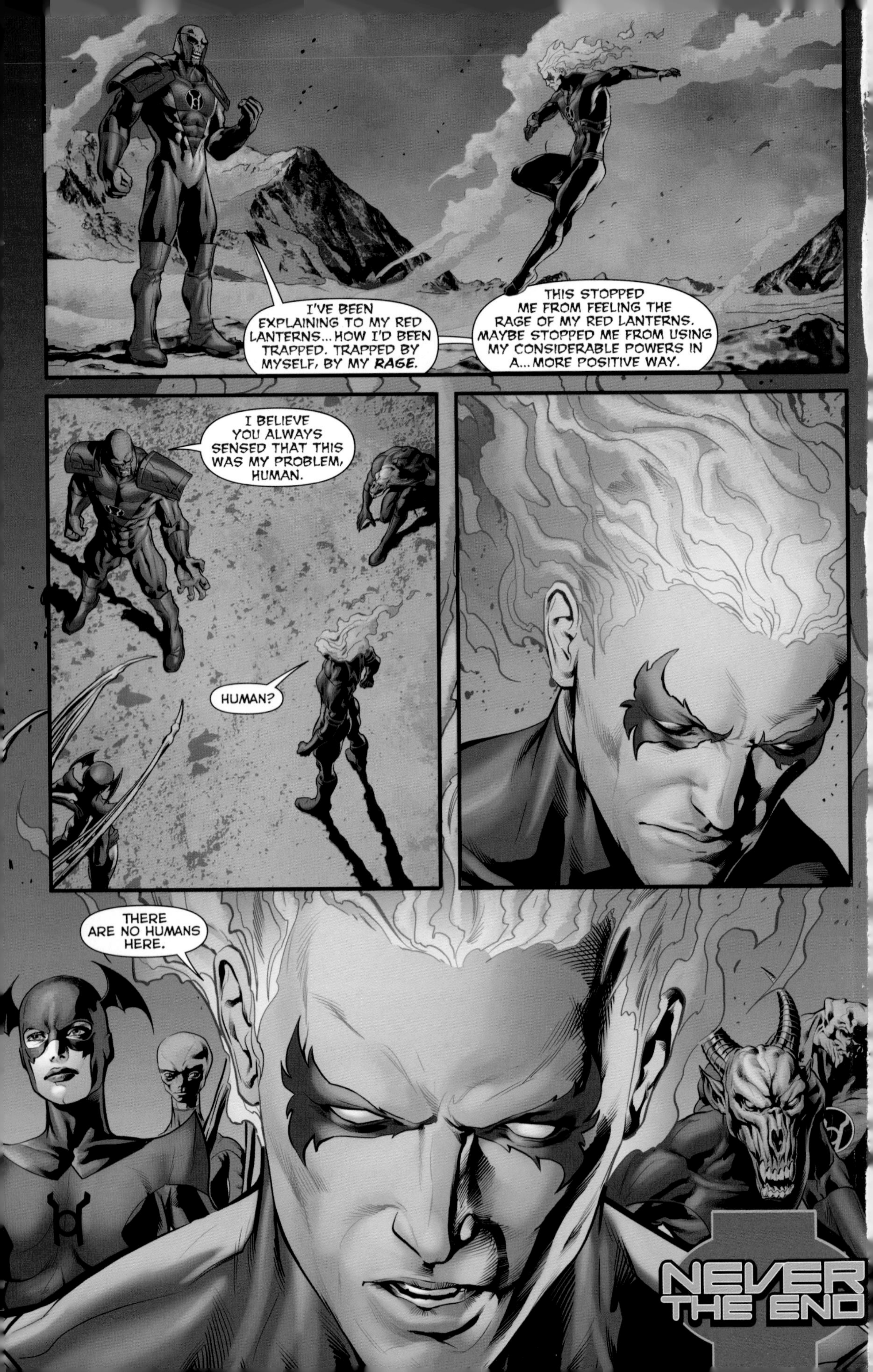
I'VE BEEN EXPLAINING TO MY RED LANTERNS... HOW I'D BEEN TRAPPED. TRAPPED BY MYSELF, BY MY RAGE.
THIS STOPPED ME FROM FEELING THE RAGE OF MY RED LANTERNS. MAYBE STOPPED ME FROM USING MY CONSIDERABLE POWERS IN A... MORE POSITIVE WAY.
I BELIEVE YOU ALWAYS SENSED THAT THIS WAS MY PROBLEM, HUMAN.
HUMAN?
THERE ARE NO HUMANS HERE.
NEVER THE END

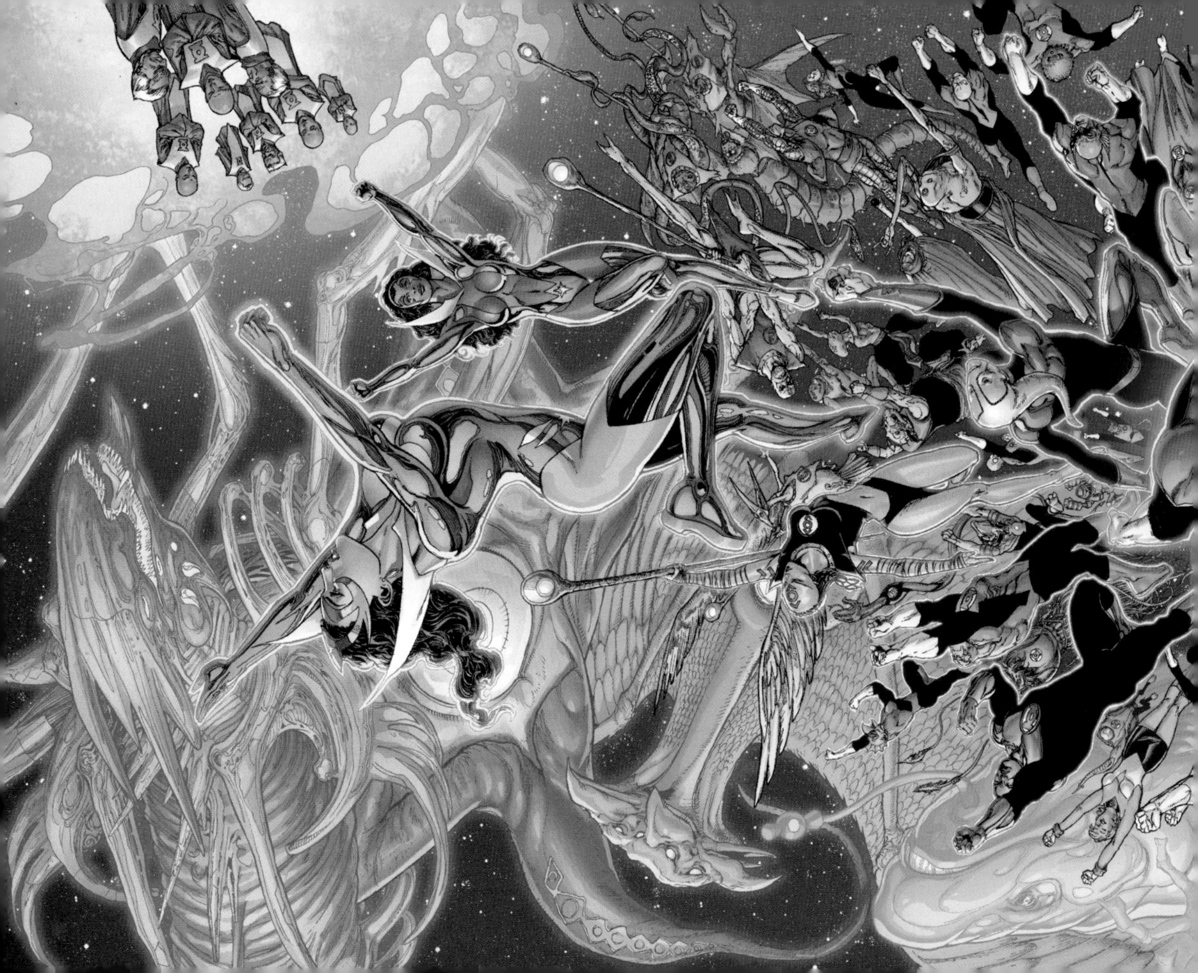